Great Britain
Northern Ireland
A-Z Road Atlas

Journey Route Planning maps

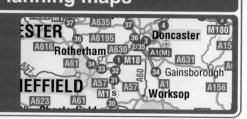

Sea Port & Channel Tunnel plans

Motorway Junctions

Junction	M67	
1	Eastbound	Access from A57 eastbound only
	Westbound	Exit to A57 westbound only
1a	Eastbound	No access, exit to A6017 only
	Westbound	No exit, access from A6017 only
2	Eastbound	No exit, access from A57 only
	Westbound	No access, exit to A57 only

Airport plans

Road map section

Over 32,000 Index References

A		Abingdon-on-Thames.
		Oxon ....
Abbas Combe. *Som*	..........3F 8	Abinger Common. *Surr* ....
Abberley. *Worc*	......5F 26	Abinger Hammer. *Surr*
Abberley Common.		Abington. *S Lan* ....
Worc	......5F 26	Abington Pigotts. *Cambs* ..
Abberton. *Essx*	......2G 23	Ab Kettleby. *Leics* ....
Abberton. *Worc*	......6H 27	Ab Lench. *Worc* ....
Abberwick. *Nmbd*	......8J 61	Ablington. *Glos* ....
Abbess Roding. *Essx*	......2B 22	Ablington. *Wilts* ....
Abbey. *Devn*	......4L 7	Abney. *Derbs* ....
		Aboyne. *Abers* ....

Detailed Main Route maps

Index to Places of Interest

L	Map Mark
Lacock Abbey (SN15 2LG) 7H 19	Mart
Lady Lever Art Gallery (CH62 5EQ) 1B 34	Mart
Lady of the North (NE23 8AU) 4F 54	Mar
Laing Art Gallery	Man
(NE1 8AG) ....Newcastle upon Tyne 111	Man
Lake District Nat. Pk. (LA9 7RL) 4B 46	Man
Lakeside & Haverthwaite Railway	Man
(LA12 8AL) 7B 46	Man

City and Town centre maps

Safety Camera Information

Details of Safety Camera symbols used on the maps, and the responsible use of Camera information ....Inside back cover

EDITION 34 2020

Copyright © Geographers' A-Z Map Company Ltd.

Contains OS data © Crown copyright and database rights 2019

Northern Ireland: This is Based upon Crown Copyright and is reproduced with the permission of Land & Property Services underdelegated authority from the Controller of Her Majesty's Stationery Office, © Crown copyright and database right 2019 PMLPA No 100508. The inclusion of parts or all of the Republic of Ireland is by permission of the Government of Ireland who retain copyright in the data used. © Ordnance Survey Ireland and Government of Ireland.

Land & Property Services Paper Map Licensed Partner

This is a registered Trade Mark of Department of Finance and Personnel.

Safety Camera & Fuel Station Databases copyright 2019, © PocketGPSWorld.com. PocketGPSWorld.com's CamerAlert is a self-contained speed and red light camera warning system for SatNavs and Android or Apple iOS smartphones/tablets. Visit www.cameralert.com to download.

Base Relief by Geo-Innovations, © www.geoinnovations.co.uk

The Shopmobility logo is a registered symbol of The National Federation of Shopmobility

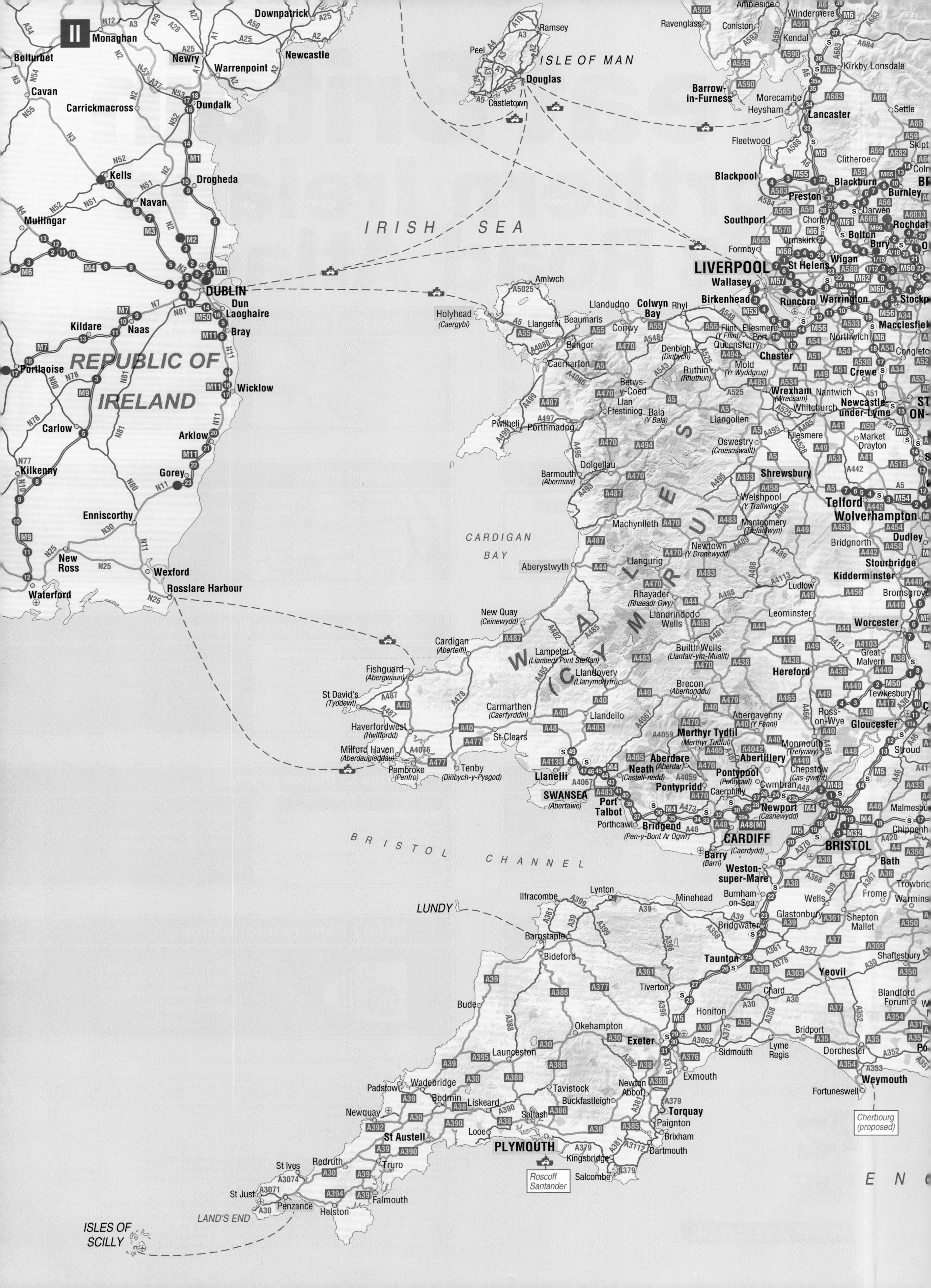
REPUBLIC OF IRELAND
IRISH SEA
ISLE OF MAN
CARDIGAN BAY
BRISTOL CHANNEL
WALES (CYMRU)
LUNDY
ISLES OF SCILLY
LAND'S END
EN
Belturbet
Monaghan
Downpatrick
Newry
Newcastle
Warrenpoint
Cavan
Carrickmacross
Dundalk
Kells
Drogheda
Navan
Mullingar
DUBLIN
Dun Laoghaire
Bray
Kildare
Naas
Portlaoise
Wicklow
Carlow
Arklow
Kilkenny
Gorey
Enniscorthy
New Ross
Wexford
Rosslare Harbour
Waterford
Ramsey
Peel
Douglas
Castletown
Amlwch
Holyhead
(Caergybi)
Llangefni
Beaumaris
Bangor
Caernarfon
Llandudno
Colwyn Bay
Conwy
Rhyl
Betws-y-Coed
Llan Ffestiniog
Pwllheli
Porthmadog
Bala
(Y Bala)
Denbigh
(Dinbych)
Ruthin
(Rhuthun)
Flint
(Y Fflint)
Mold
(Yr Wyddgrug)
Queensferry
Wrexham
(Wrecsam)
Llangollen
Oswestry
(Croesoswallt)
Dolgellau
Barmouth
(Abermaw)
Machynlleth
Aberystwyth
Newtown
(Y Drenewydd)
Montgomery
(Trefaldwyn)
Welshpool
(Y Trallwng)
Shrewsbury
Llangurig
Rhayader
(Rhaeadr Gwy)
Llandrindod Wells
New Quay
(Ceinewydd)
Cardigan
(Aberteifi)
Lampeter
(Llanbedr Pont Steffan)
Builth Wells
(Llanfair-ym-Muallt)
Llandovery
(Llanymddyfri)
Brecon
(Aberhonddu)
Fishguard
(Abergwaun)
St David's
(Tyddewi)
Haverfordwest
(Hwlffordd)
Milford Haven
(Aberdaugleddau)
Pembroke
(Penfro)
Tenby
(Dinbych-y-Pysgod)
Carmarthen
(Caerfyrddin)
St Clears
Llandeilo
Llanelli
SWANSEA
(Abertawe)
Neath
(Castell-nedd)
Port Talbot
Porthcawl
Bridgend
(Pen-y-Bont Ar Ogwr)
Aberdare
(Aberdar)
Merthyr Tydfil
(Merthyr Tudful)
Pontypridd
Pontypool
(Pontypwl)
Abertillery
Abergavenny
(Y Fenni)
Caerphilly
Cwmbran
Newport
(Casnewydd)
CARDIFF
(Caerdydd)
Barry
(Barri)
Monmouth
(Trefynwy)
Chepstow
(Cas-gwent)
Ambleside
Windermere
Ravenglass
Coniston
Kendal
Kirkby Lonsdale
Barrow-in-Furness
Morecambe
Heysham
Lancaster
Settle
Fleetwood
Clitheroe
Skipton
Colne
Blackpool
Blackburn
Burnley
Preston
Darwen
Southport
Chorley
Rochdale
Ormskirk
Bolton
Bury
Formby
Wigan
LIVERPOOL
St Helens
Wallasey
Birkenhead
Runcorn
Warrington
Stockport
Ellesmere Port
Macclesfield
Northwich
Chester
Congleton
Crewe
Nantwich
Newcastle-under-Lyme
Whitchurch
Ellesmere
Market Drayton
Telford
Wolverhampton
Bridgnorth
Dudley
Stourbridge
Kidderminster
Ludlow
Bromsgrove
Leominster
Worcester
Great Malvern
Hereford
Tewkesbury
Ross-on-Wye
Gloucester
Stroud
BRISTOL
Bath
Chippenham
Malmesbury
Weston-super-Mare
Trowbridge
Frome
Warminster
Wells
Shepton Mallet
Glastonbury
Burnham-on-Sea
Bridgwater
Minehead
Lynton
Ilfracombe
Barnstaple
Bideford
Taunton
Shaftesbury
Yeovil
Chard
Tiverton
Bude
Blandford Forum
Honiton
Okehampton
Exeter
Sidmouth
Lyme Regis
Bridport
Dorchester
Weymouth
Fortuneswell
Cherbourg
(proposed)
Exmouth
Launceston
Tavistock
Newton Abbot
Torquay
Paignton
Brixham
Dartmouth
Kingsbridge
Salcombe
Buckfastleigh
Wadebridge
Padstow
Bodmin
Liskeard
Saltash
Looe
PLYMOUTH
Roscoff
Santander
Newquay
St Austell
Truro
Redruth
St Ives
St Just
Penzance
Helston
Falmouth

REFERENCE

MOTORWAY WITH NUMBER — M4 (S) Service Area

MOTORWAY (Under Construction / Proposed)

MOTORWAY JUNCTIONS — 5 — 7 Limited

PRIMARY ROUTE — A5

A ROAD — A272

NATIONAL BOUNDARY

TOWNS SHOWN IN THE MILEAGE CHART — NORWICH

SCALE
0   10   20   30 Miles
0   10   20   30   40 Kilometres

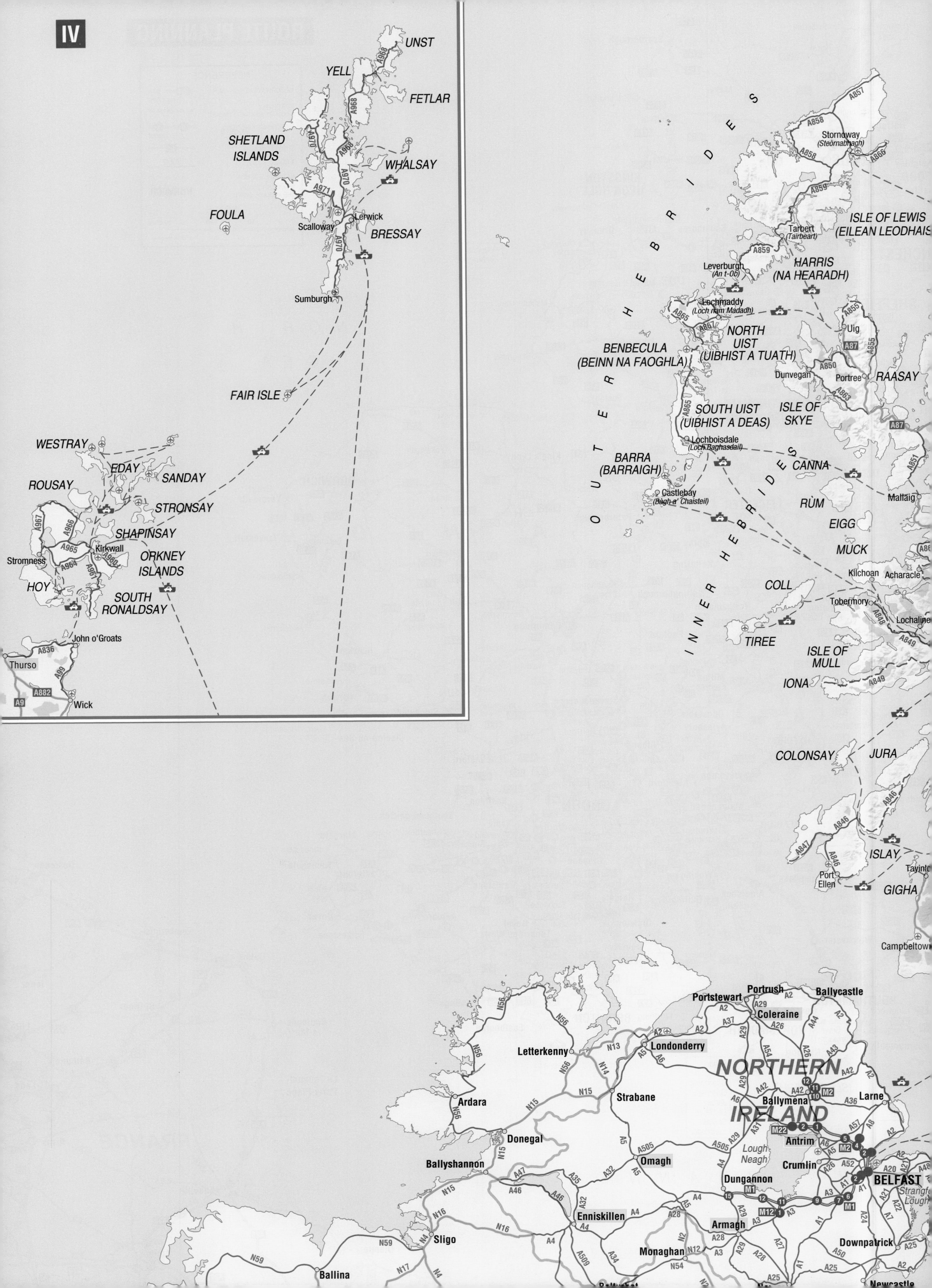
UNST
YELL
FETLAR
SHETLAND ISLANDS
WHALSAY
FOULA
Lerwick
Scalloway
BRESSAY
Sumburgh
FAIR ISLE
WESTRAY
EDAY
SANDAY
ROUSAY
STRONSAY
SHAPINSAY
Kirkwall
Stromness
ORKNEY ISLANDS
HOY
SOUTH RONALDSAY
John o'Groats
Thurso
Wick
OUTER HEBRIDES
Stornoway (Steòrnabhagh)
ISLE OF LEWIS (EILEAN LEODHAIS)
Tarbert (Tairbeart)
Leverburgh (An t-Ob)
HARRIS (NA HEARADH)
Lochmaddy (Loch nam Madadh)
NORTH UIST (UIBHIST A TUATH)
BENBECULA (BEINN NA FAOGHLA)
Uig
Dunvegan
Portree
RAASAY
SOUTH UIST (UIBHIST A DEAS)
ISLE OF SKYE
Lochboisdale (Loch Baghasdail)
BARRA (BARRAIGH)
Castlebay (Bàgh a' Chaisteil)
CANNA
Mallaig
RÙM
EIGG
MUCK
INNER HEBRIDES
Kilchoan
Acharacle
COLL
Tobermory
Lochaline
TIREE
ISLE OF MULL
IONA
COLONSAY
JURA
ISLAY
Port Ellen
GIGHA
Campbeltown
Portstewart
Portrush
Ballycastle
Coleraine
Londonderry
Letterkenny
NORTHERN IRELAND
Strabane
Ballymena
Larne
Ardara
Antrim
Donegal
Lough Neagh
Omagh
Ballyshannon
Crumlin
BELFAST
Dungannon
Enniskillen
Armagh
Sligo
Monaghan
Downpatrick
Ballina
Newcastle

V

Stromness
John o'Groats
Scrabster
Thurso
Wick
Tongue
Scourie
Lochinver
Helmsdale
NORTH SEA
Lairg
Ullapool
Bonar Bridge
Tain
Poolewe
Moray Firth
Lossiemouth
Fraserburgh
Kinlochewe
Cromarty
Banff
Dingwall
Achnasheen
Nairn
Elgin
Keith
Peterhead
Strathcarron
Inverness
Dufftown
Huntly
Kyle of Lochalsh
Caol Loch Ailse
Loch Ness
Grantown-on-Spey
Oldmeldrum
Inverurie
Invermoriston
Aviemore
ABERDEEN
Invergarry
Newtonmore
Peterculter
Ballater
Banchory
Braemar
Stonehaven
Spean Bridge
SCOTLAND
Fort William
Brechin
Montrose
Glencoe
Pitlochry
Blairgowrie
Forfar
Dunkeld
Arbroath
Dundee
Carnoustie
Oban
Perth
Crieff
Crianlarich
St Andrews
Inveraray
Kinross
Glenrothes
Pittenweem
Loch Lomond
Doune
Dunblane
Stirling
Kirkcaldy
Lochgilphead
Dunfermline
Cowdenbeath
Firth of Forth
North Berwick
Dunbar
Dunoon
Greenock
GLASGOW
Falkirk
EDINBURGH
Clydebank
Musselburgh
Rothesay
Paisley
Airdrie
Livingston
Dalkeith
Eyemouth
Largs
ISLE OF BUTE
Hamilton
Motherwell
Penicuik
Duns
Berwick-upon-Tweed
East Kilbride
Lauder
Ardrossan
Peebles
Galashiels
Coldstream
Irvine
Kilmarnock
Biggar
Kelso
Brodick
Troon
Prestwick
Selkirk
Wooler
ISLE OF ARRAN
Ayr
Cumnock
Hawick
Jedburgh
Alnwick
Sanquhar
Moffat
Amble
Girvan
Ashington
Langholm
Morpeth
Blyth
New Galloway
Lockerbie
NEWCASTLE UPON TYNE
Whitley Bay
Amsterdam
Tynemouth
Dumfries
South Shields
Newton Stewart
Castle Douglas
Annan
Brampton
Hexham
Corbridge
Dalbeattie
Gateshead
Washington
Stranraer
Carlisle
SUNDERLAND
Consett
Seaham
Kirkcudbright
Solway Firth
Alston
Durham
Peterlee
Whithorn
Cockermouth
Penrith
Workington
Bishop Auckland
HARTLEPOOL
STOCKTON-ON-TEES
Keswick
Whitehaven
Brough
MIDDLESBROUGH
Whitby
Barnard Castle
Egremont
Darlington
Ambleside
Richmond
Windermere
Catterick
Ramsey
Ravenglass
Coniston
Northallerton
Kendal
Leyburn
Scarborough
Peel
ISLE OF MAN
Thirsk

Mileage Chart and Journey Times

This chart shows the distance in miles and journey time between two cities or towns in Great Britain. Each route has been calculated using a combination of motorways, primary routes and other major roads. This is normally the quickest, though not always the shortest route.

Average journey times are calculated whilst driving at the maximum speed limit. These times are approximate and do not include traffic congestion or convenience breaks.

To find the distance and journey time between two cities or towns, follow a horizontal line and vertical column until they meet each other.

For example, the 285 mile journey from London to Penzance is approximately 4 hours and 59 minutes.

Northern Ireland

Journey times (upper right) / Distance in miles (lower left)

	Antrim	Armagh	Coleraine	Enniskillen	Londonderry	Newry	Omagh	Belfast
Antrim		1:01	0:53	1:41	1:14	1:07	1:13	0:30
Armagh	43		1:32	1:06	1:39	0:31	0:46	0:57
Coleraine	40	61		2:09	0:52	2:00	1:43	1:11
Enniskillen	86	49	94		1:29	1:37	0:39	1:38
Londonderry	55	69	31	60		2:09	0:54	1:33
Newry	53	19	92	69	88		1:15	0:51
Omagh	54	35	65	27	34	54		1:16
Belfast	22	41	56	84	72	37	68	

Distance in miles

Belfast to London = 440m / 9:46h (excluding ferry)
Belfast to Glasgow = 104m / 4:46h (excluding ferry)

Great Britain

Journey times (upper right) / Distance in miles (lower left)

	Aberdeen	Aberystwyth	Ayr	Birmingham	Bradford	Brighton	Bristol	Cambridge	Cardiff	Carlisle	Coventry	Derby	Doncaster	Dover	Edinburgh	Exeter	Fort William	Glasgow	Gloucester	Harwich	Holyhead	Inverness	Ipswich	Kendal	Kingston upon Hull	Leeds	Leicester	Lincoln	Liverpool	Manchester	Middlesbrough	Newcastle upon Tyne	Norwich	Nottingham	Oxford	Penzance	Perth	Plymouth	Portsmouth	Reading	Salisbury	Sheffield	Shrewsbury	Southampton	Southend-on-Sea	Stoke-on-Trent	Swansea	Thurso	Worcester	York	London
Aberdeen		8:21	3:31	7:13	6:28	9:56	8:26	8:15	8:55	4:08	7:27	7:09	6:25	10:16	2:39	9:38	3:38	2:50	7:55	9:32	7:41	2:30	9:08	4:55	6:51	6:16	7:40	7:07	6:13	6:01	5:16	4:39	9:18	7:14	8:18	11:22	1:48	10:16	9:33	8:57	9:21	6:42	7:07	9:25	9:22	6:28	9:31	4:52	7:35	6:07	9:03
Aberystwyth	471		6:34	2:34	3:27	5:21	2:44	4:00	2:29	4:24	2:52	2:56	3:45	5:41	6:20	3:51	8:13	5:53	2:34	5:17	2:29	8:39	4:53	3:40	4:20	3:29	3:18	4:11	2:39	2:54	4:34	5:07	5:03	3:17	3:43	5:35	6:41	4:29	4:27	3:50	4:01	3:41	1:47	4:18	4:56	2:48	1:48	11:00	2:19	4:00	4:28
Ayr	181	324		5:28	4:28	8:11	6:42	6:31	7:10	2:24	5:43	5:25	4:41	8:32	1:48	7:54	3:03	0:48	6:11	7:48	5:56	3:51	7:24	3:10	5:06	4:32	5:55	5:22	4:29	4:16	3:56	3:28	7:34	5:29	6:34	9:37	1:53	8:31	7:49	7:13	7:37	4:57	5:23	7:40	7:37	4:43	7:46	6:12	5:50	4:22	7:16
Birmingham	423	114	272		2:15	3:04	1:41	1:43	2:09	3:16	0:36	1:01	1:40	3:25	5:12	2:53	7:05	4:45	1:10	3:01	2:59	7:31	2:37	2:32	2:21	2:05	1:01	1:55	1:49	1:46	2:55	3:28	2:46	1:08	1:27	4:36	5:33	3:30	2:42	2:06	2:39	1:36	0:59	2:33	2:39	1:02	2:44	9:52	0:49	2:21	2:11
Bradford	377	159	196	124		4:30	3:34	2:43	4:03	2:17	2:19	1:34	0:53	4:37	4:17	4:46	6:06	3:46	3:03	4:01	2:49	6:31	3:37	1:32	1:18	0:28	2:02	1:35	1:22	0:57	1:32	2:06	3:46	1:37	3:05	6:29	4:33	5:24	4:20	3:44	4:18	1:00	2:15	4:12	3:50	1:36	4:38	8:52	2:42	0:59	3:32
Brighton	596	258	441	169	263		2:49	2:09	3:26	6:00	2:42	3:15	3:53	1:53	7:53	3:41	9:49	7:29	2:47	2:19	5:39	10:14	2:20	5:15	4:35	4:19	2:57	3:43	4:32	4:29	5:08	5:42	3:05	3:21	1:58	5:24	8:16	4:18	1:14	1:39	1:54	3:49	3:45	1:35	1:41	3:45	4:01	12:35	3:07	4:35	1:27
Bristol	505	122	375	88	215	129		3:02	0:56	4:31	1:44	2:21	2:59	3:18	6:27	1:37	8:20	6:00	0:47	3:27	4:13	8:45	3:28	3:46	3:41	3:25	2:17	3:11	3:03	3:01	4:15	4:48	3:58	2:28	1:30	3:20	6:48	2:14	2:03	1:26	1:37	2:56	2:14	1:54	2:58	2:17	1:30	11:07	1:07	3:41	2:07
Cambridge	487	198	366	102	156	117	167		3:28	4:20	1:30	1:52	2:03	2:06	6:04	4:11	8:09	5:49	2:29	1:28	4:20	8:35	1:04	3:56	2:37	2:34	1:25	1:47	3:12	3:10	3:19	3:52	1:13	1:41	1:55	5:54	6:37	4:49	2:34	1:51	2:47	2:15	2:26	2:35	1:19	2:26	4:03	10:56	2:08	2:45	1:17
Cardiff	525	106	377	106	233	168	42	201		4:58	2:15	2:48	3:27	3:54	6:54	2:02	8:47	6:27	1:16	4:03	4:23	9:13	4:03	4:14	4:09	3:53	2:46	3:39	3:31	3:28	4:42	5:16	4:31	2:55	2:05	3:46	7:15	2:40	2:38	2:01	2:12	3:23	2:24	2:29	3:33	2:44	0:53	11:34	1:35	4:09	2:43
Carlisle	229	232	89	183	107	345	286	256	288		3:30	3:12	2:28	6:19	2:08	5:41	4:01	1:41	3:58	5:35	3:44	4:27	5:11	0:58	2:54	2:19	3:43	3:10	2:16	2:04	1:44	1:15	5:21	3:17	4:21	7:25	2:29	6:19	5:36	5:00	5:24	2:45	3:10	5:28	5:25	2:31	5:34	6:48	3:38	2:10	5:07
Coventry	442	134	297	18	124	157	102	84	129	200		1:03	1:41	3:05	5:29	2:55	7:22	5:02	1:12	2:49	3:13	7:48	2:21	2:49	2:23	2:06	0:45	1:39	2:06	2:03	2:56	3:30	2:31	1:09	1:04	4:38	5:50	3:32	2:19	1:43	2:17	1:37	1:18	2:11	2:20	1:19	2:49	10:09	0:56	2:22	1:53
Derby	418	137	269	41	88	188	134	99	159	180	43		0:57	3:33	4:58	3:31	7:02	4:42	1:48	3:09	2:52	7:27	2:45	2:28	1:39	1:23	0:49	1:24	1:45	1:42	2:13	2:46	2:55	0:33	1:51	5:14	5:29	4:08	3:06	2:30	3:04	0:54	1:21	2:58	2:48	0:53	3:22	9:49	1:27	1:39	2:19
Doncaster	371	192	239	95	40	232	184	117	210	150	94	57		3:58	4:13	4:12	6:19	3:59	2:30	3:21	3:17	6:44	2:57	2:16	0:56	0:43	1:27	0:55	1:48	1:25	1:28	2:02	3:07	1:02	2:30	5:56	4:46	4:50	3:45	3:09	3:43	0:30	2:13	3:36	3:11	1:44	4:04	9:05	2:09	0:54	2:57
Dover	620	315	477	195	284	81	194	118	233	393	180	208	244		7:56	4:14	10:08	7:48	3:16	2:16	5:59	10:34	2:17	5:35	4:29	4:26	3:14	3:40	4:52	4:49	5:11	5:45	3:02	3:34	2:27	5:57	8:36	4:51	2:23	2:08	2:50	4:06	4:05	2:38	1:37	4:05	4:29	12:55	3:36	4:38	1:34
Edinburgh	126	340	75	284	198	466	377	326	379	91	303	266	212	444		7:38	3:01	1:05	5:55	7:20	5:41	3:02	6:56	2:55	4:38	4:04	5:26	4:54	4:13	4:00	3:00	2:23	7:06	5:01	6:18	9:21	1:02	8:16	7:33	6:57	7:21	4:29	5:07	7:25	7:09	4:28	7:30	5:24	5:34	3:54	6:57
Exeter	581	199	425	161	282	170	75	323	107	336	166	213	257	244	439		9:31	7:11	1:58	4:36	5:24	9:56	4:37	4:57	4:52	4:36	3:28	4:22	4:14	4:12	5:26	5:59	5:07	3:39	2:46	1:54	7:59	0:53	2:38	2:43	1:55	4:07	3:25	2:27	4:02	3:28	2:37	12:18	2:18	4:52	3:16
Fort William	159	430	136	391	305	568	478	456	486	198	415	387	345	591	131	549		2:26	7:49	9:26	7:35	1:32	9:02	4:49	6:44	6:10	7:34	7:00	6:07	5:54	5:34	5:06	9:12	7:07	8:12	11:15	2:09	10:10	9:27	8:51	9:15	6:35	7:01	9:19	9:16	6:22	9:24	4:04	7:28	6:01	8:56
Glasgow	146	322	36	291	203	468	378	355	384	96	313	282	245	491	46	449	100		5:28	7:05	5:13	3:08	6:41	2:28	4:23	3:49	5:12	4:39	3:46	3:33	3:13	2:45	6:51	4:46	5:51	8:54	1:10	7:48	7:06	6:30	6:54	4:14	4:40	6:57	6:55	4:01	7:03	5:29	5:07	3:40	6:36
Gloucester	473	109	317	53	171	152	35	132	53	228	59	93	149	189	331	107	435	324		3:25	3:42	8:14	3:22	3:15	3:10	2:54	1:46	2:39	2:32	2:29	3:43	4:17	3:31	1:56	1:11	3:39	6:16	2:33	2:00	1:24	1:42	2:24	1:42	1:52	2:56	1:45	1:49	10:35	0:36	3:10	2:05
Harwich	568	258	411	170	224	130	203	64	234	323	152	167	185	129	397	262	524	419	171		5:38	9:53	0:42	5:13	3:55	3:52	2:43	3:05	4:30	4:28	4:37	5:10	1:32	2:59	2:26	6:20	7:55	5:14	2:49	2:17	3:12	3:33	3:44	3:01	1:09	3:44	4:38	12:14	3:26	4:03	1:42
Holyhead	452	96	315	151	158	330	204	252	209	226	167	156	169	358	316	279	423	323	189	331		7:58	5:16	2:59	3:39	2:49	3:23	3:52	1:53	2:13	3:53	4:26	5:25	3:15	4:06	7:06	6:00	6:00	5:21	4:45	5:05	3:06	2:10	5:12	5:18	2:11	4:33	10:19	3:19	3:19	4:47
Inverness	105	492	198	449	353	620	536	490	558	260	458	421	369	601	157	607	63	162	496	554	481		9:27	5:14	7:10	6:35	7:59	7:26	6:32	6:20	5:41	5:04	9:37	7:33	8:37	11:41	2:10	10:35	9:52	9:16	9:40	7:01	7:26	9:44	9:41	6:47	9:50	2:31	7:54	6:26	9:21
Ipswich	538	268	420	156	210	125	206	54	240	311	138	155	171	127	381	264	510	409	177	21	307	538		4:50	3:31	3:28	2:20	2:41	4:06	4:04	4:13	4:46	1:08	2:35	2:27	6:21	7:31	5:15	2:50	2:18	3:13	3:09	3:20	3:02	1:10	3:20	4:39	11:50	3:02	3:39	1:43
Kendal	280	182	139	151	62	324	235	215	232	50	170	136	99	344	141	307	248	146	200	279	180	310	268		2:44	1:53	3:02	3:00	1:36	1:23	1:38	1:59	5:00	2:54	3:41	6:44	3:13	5:38	4:56	4:20	4:44	2:22	2:30	4:47	4:53	1:50	4:53	7:32	2:57	2:04	4:22
Kingston upon Hull	398	235	255	139	68	243	228	134	239	165	123	94	37	254	230	290	367	255	195	204	218	387	189	127		1:08	2:08	0:58	2:13	1:49	1:54	2:27	3:18	1:43	3:10	6:36	5:12	5:30	4:25	3:49	4:23	1:11	2:53	4:17	3:43	2:25	4:44	9:31	2:49	1:02	3:39
Leeds	359	171	198	119	9	256	209	144	226	111	117	74	32	275	190	279	309	208	167	217	162	345	197	72	60		1:53	1:25	1:23	0:58	1:20	1:53	3:37	1:27	2:55	6:21	4:38	5:15	4:10	3:34	4:08	0:50	2:16	4:02	3:40	1:37	4:29	8:57	2:34	0:46	3:23
Leicester	445	155	294	43	99	163	118	70	140	214	24	30	73	183	282	189	412	312	83	146	182	431	125	166	98	97		1:16	2:17	2:14	2:42	3:15	2:27	0:46	1:32	5:11	6:01	4:05	2:47	2:11	2:45	1:23	1:43	2:39	2:29	1:24	3:20	10:20	1:25	2:08	2:01
Lincoln	411	208	249	87	80	207	170	88	192	178	76	53	41	206	247	241	376	274	135	152	204	402	124	140	46	72	52		2:31	2:02	2:11	2:44	2:20	0:59	2:28	6:07	5:29	5:01	3:43	3:07	3:41	1:07	2:33	3:34	2:54	2:10	4:16	9:48	2:21	1:35	2:51
Liverpool	354	120	199	99	67	267	180	179	169	110	113	90	89	294	201	240	308	213	142	265	95	370	236	75	126	73	110	118		0:48	2:28	3:01	4:16	2:10	2:56	6:00	4:33	4:54	4:11	3:35	3:59	1:52	1:25	4:03	4:09	1:06	3:48	8:53	2:13	1:54	3:39
Manchester	349	128	204	87	37	252	167	159	188	117	99	58	51	273	208	239	315	215	132	230	120	363	211	72	96	42	95	87	34		2:03	2:36	4:12	1:51	2:52	5:55	4:22	4:49	4:07	3:30	3:55	1:14	1:41	3:58	4:04	1:01	4:04	8:41	2:08	1:29	3:37
Middlesbrough	289	233	181	174	69	316	265	196	287	92	175	130	84	316	147	337	279	192	230	266	226	306	253	77	88	64	154	127	134	106		0:55	4:20	2:15	3:43	7:09	3:40	6:03	4:58	4:22	4:56	1:43	3:20	4:50	4:24	2:40	5:17	8:02	3:22	1:05	4:12
Newcastle upon Tyne	252	266	146	209	98	345	300	232	312	58	209	165	115	350	104	369	237	153	263	297	257	263	287	88	130	96	188	153	167	136	40		4:54	2:49	4:17	7:43	3:03	6:37	5:32	4:56	5:30	2:17	3:54	5:24	4:58	3:14	5:51	7:25	3:56	1:43	4:46
Norwich	536	270	348	163	185	174	234	62	256	280	142	146	142	169	351	284	478	378	193	72	289	505	44	249	145	178	112	103	222	177	221	252		2:44	2:58	6:51	7:40	5:45	3:31	2:48	3:43	3:18	3:29	3:32	2:00	3:28	5:06	11:59	3:10	3:48	2:13
Nottingham	416	155	267	54	78	191	140	84	165	188	52	15	48	210	256	218	386	286	108	165	177	410	140	141	92	72	27	37	107	68	128	159	118		1:57	5:23	5:34	4:17	3:12	2:36	3:10	0:57	1:44	3:04	2:49	1:18	3:31	9:53	1:36	1:42	2:25
Oxford	497	151	335	68	167	106	73	92	106	267	57	101	138	142	358	151	465	365	47	134	208	515	128	223	175	162	76	123	168	157	218	253	159	104		4:30	6:40	3:24	1:28	0:45	1:25	2:25	2:08	1:19	1:56	2:09	2:40	10:59	1:31	3:10	1:15
Penzance	688	301	552	269	394	279	184	343	218	463	278	316	369	355	551	109	663	561	217	374	388	715	375	419	412	391	310	359	353	344	449	481	393	323	261		9:43	1:41	4:22	4:27	3:39	5:51	5:09	4:11	5:46	5:12	4:20	14:02	4:02	6:36	4:59
Perth	86	366	85	336	245	509	412	370	422	134	346	309	254	485	43	487	103	59	362	439	360	113	424	184	273	233	326	290	244	254	191	148	394	299	404	598		8:37	7:54	7:18	7:42	5:03	5:28	7:46	7:43	4:49	7:52	4:30	5:55	4:28	7:24
Plymouth	619	232	461	203	325	206	111	274	159	372	209	254	300	286	485	43	592	490	150	305	322	648	305	348	326	323	231	284	299	281	379	412	327	255	193	75	529		3:16	3:20	2:32	4:44	4:02	3:04	4:39	4:05	3:14	12:55	2:55	5:29	3:54
Portsmouth	579	231	440	147	274	50	95	132	138	357	132	184	231	137	448	127	555	455	114	161	303	603	158	308	268	245	166	209	254	237	315	360	200	191	83	235	486	170		1:18	0:52	3:39	3:23	0:32	2:11	3:23	3:13	12:13	2:20	4:25	1:39
Reading	538	180	399	103	213	79	77	90	112	309	90	138	184	115	402	141	506	406	75	129	264	554	126	263	209	207	113	168	193	197	264	295	152	129	25	251	445	184	60		1:22	3:01	2:45	1:09	1:46	2:45	2:37	11:35	1:44	3:47	0:56
Salisbury	538	178	383	121	245	82	53	140	101	312	113	159	207	158	400	91	510	408	73	177	262	569	177	265	251	230	132	187	213	208	287	318	200	162	65	201	443	132	43	57		3:37	3:09	0:40	2:37	3:12	2:47	12:02	2:02	4:22	1:52
Sheffield	390	173	235	79	40	225	163	121	193	154	75	35	21	268	230	245	352	250	139	185	164	387	176	102	66	33	68	46	74	40	102	133	144	37	137	361	273	293	228	160	203		2:08	3:32	3:22	1:40	3:59	9:22	2:04	1:11	2:53
Shrewsbury	419	73	260	47	100	216	116	140	107	171	64	67	114	249	262	175	369	267	77	215	104	424	195	125	163	102	79	123	59	67	166	203	196	86	105	286	309	218	195	147	150	85		3:16	3:22	1:04	2:45	9:46	1:23	2:46	2:53
Southampton	564	213	401	128	235	64	75	129	122	330	114	167	201	150	433	106	528	426	98	157	287	590	162	276	249	230	136	189	235	215	288	320	190	162	66	217	476	149	20	47	23	206	175		2:26	3:15	3:05	12:05	2:12	4:16	1:40
Southend-on-Sea	549	258	431	152	220	85	177	64	211	342	129	168	185	89	395	226	548	438	152	57	303	549	57	283	200	213	139	156	255	225	262	299	99	160	105	337	439	269	117	98	132	197	173	126		3:21	4:09	12:02	3:03	3:51	1:07
Stoke-on-Trent	381	108	243	47	75	217	127	137	140	150	64	36	74	236	241	202	348	248	95	201	122	410	179	121	117	78	55	87	56	36	142	173	171	55	118	311	287	241	201	147	168	50	35	183	199		3:18	9:08	1:23	2:09	2:53
Swansea	529	76	368	124	220	209	80	236	41	279	150	184	244	264	370	154	477	375	91	279	172	578	279	249	262	229	174	226	168	187	293	323	286	178	144	266	446	196	175	147	136	202	124	159	245	159		12:11	2:10	4:44	3:18
Thurso	212	584	304	557	461	728	644	589	640	352	552	529	475	706	262	715	169	268	604	657	589	108	654	402	492	453	544	510	463	471	410	367	613	519	621	823	220	758	709	662	664	506	523	682	659	502	631		10:15	8:47	11:43
Worcester	448	96	309	29	135	162	62	119	73	220	46	68	124	197	306	136	418	311	28	168	151	480	174	169	166	146	72	118	108	101	203	229	180	85	57	244	350	177	146	95	101	103	49	124	150	65	97	572		2:49	2:24
York	345	193	201	129	34	269	227	151	237	116	129	84	33	269	187	289	314	214	181	232	185	344	200	81	38	24	108	76	96	65	48	83	176	84	174	400	230	331	257	217	244	54	132	244	214	114	268	450	164		3:39
London	537	228	440	118	203	53	118	61	151	309	97	129	171	76	403	179	511	404	116	86	277	562	82	263	214	195	103	155	211	209	251	283	117	128	59	285	451	216	84	41	92	166	161	82	43	161	187	669	136	211	

Distance in miles

Scales to Map Pages

BRITAIN
1:221,760 = 3.5 miles to 1 inch (2.54 cm)
2.2 km to 1 cm

NORTHERN IRELAND
1:380,160 = 6 miles to 1 inch (2.54 cm)
3.8 km to 1 cm

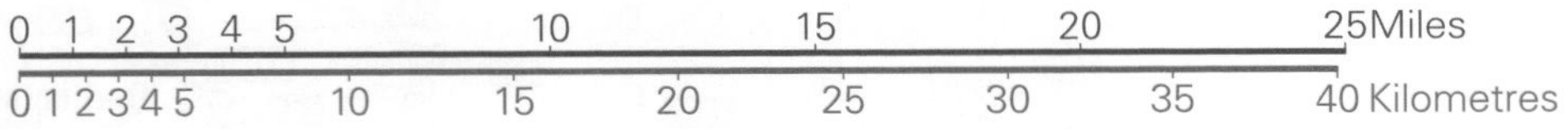

Limited Interchange Motorway Junctions are shown on the mapping pages by red junction indicators 2

M1

Junction		
2	Northbound	No exit, access from A1 only
	Southbound	No access, exit to A1 only
4	Northbound	No exit, access from A41 only
	Southbound	No access, exit to A41 only
6a	Northbound	No exit, access from M25 only
	Southbound	No access, exit to M25 only
17	Northbound	No access, exit to M45 only
	Southbound	No exit, access from M45 only
19	Northbound	Exit to M6 only, access from A14 only
	Southbound	Access from M6 only, exit to A14 only
21a	Northbound	No access, exit to A46 only
	Southbound	No exit, access from A46 only
24a	Northbound	No exit
	Southbound	Access from A50 only
35a	Northbound	No access, exit to A616 only
	Southbound	No exit, access from A616 only
43	Northbound	Exit to M621 only
	Southbound	Access from M621 only
48	Eastbound	Exit to A1(M) northbound only
	Westbound	Access from A1(M) southbound only

M2

Junction		
1	Eastbound	Access from A2 eastbound only
	Westbound	Exit to A2 westbound only

M3

Junction		
8	Eastbound	No exit, access from A303 only
	Westbound	No access, exit to A303 only
10	Northbound	No access from A31
	Southbound	No exit to A31
13	Southbound	No access from A335 to M3 leading to M27 Eastbound

M4

Junction		
1	Eastbound	Exit to A4 eastbound only
	Westbound	Access from A4 westbound only
21	Eastbound	No exit to M48
	Westbound	No access from M48
23	Eastbound	No access from M48
	Westbound	No exit to M48
25	Eastbound	No exit
	Westbound	No access
25a	Eastbound	No exit
	Westbound	No access
29	Eastbound	No exit, access from A48(M) only
	Westbound	No access, exit to A48(M) only
38	Westbound	No access, exit to A48 only
39	Eastbound	No access or exit
	Westbound	No exit, access from A48 only
42	Eastbound	No access from A48
	Westbound	No exit to A48

M5

Junction		
10	Northbound	No exit, access from A4019 only
	Southbound	No access, exit to A4019 only
11a	Southbound	No exit to A417 westbound
18a	Northbound	No access from M49
	Southbound	No exit to M49

M6

Junction		
3a	Eastbound	No exit to M6 Toll
	Westbound	No access from M6 Toll
4	Northbound	No exit to M42 northbound No access from M42 southbound
	Southbound	No exit to M42 No access from M42 southbound
4a	Northbound	No exit, access from M42 southbound only
	Southbound	No access, exit to M42 only
5	Northbound	No access, exit to A452 only
	Southbound	No exit, access from A452 only
10a	Northbound	No access, exit to M54 only
	Southbound	No exit, access from M54 only
11a	Northbound	No exit to M6 Toll
	Southbound	No access from M6 Toll
20	Northbound	No exit to M56 eastbound
	Southbound	No access from M56 westbound
24	Northbound	No exit, access from A58 only
	Southbound	No access, exit to A58 only
25	Northbound	No access, exit to A49 only
	Southbound	No exit, access from A49 only
30	Northbound	No exit, access from M61 northbound only
	Southbound	No access, exit to M61 southbound only
31a	Northbound	No access, exit to B6242 only
	Southbound	No exit, access from B6242 only
45	Northbound	No access onto A74(M)
	Southbound	No exit from A74(M)

M6 Toll

Junction		
T1	Northbound	No exit
	Southbound	No access
T2	Northbound	No access or exit
	Southbound	No access
T5	Northbound	No exit
	Southbound	No access
T7	Northbound	No access from A5
	Southbound	No exit
T8	Northbound	No exit to A460 northbound
	Southbound	No exit

M8

Junction		
6	Eastbound	No exit, access only
	Westbound	No access, exit only
6a	Eastbound	No access, exit only
	Westbound	No exit, access only
7	Eastbound	No Access, exit only
	Westbound	No exit, access only
7a	Eastbound	No exit, access from A725 Northbound only
	Westbound	No access, exit to A725 Southbound only
8	Eastbound	No exit to M73 northbound
	Westbound	No access from M73 southbound
9	Eastbound	No access, exit only
	Westbound	No exit, access only
13	Eastbound	No access from M80 southbound
	Westbound	No exit to M80 northbound
14	Eastbound	No access, exit only
	Westbound	No exit, access only
16	Eastbound	No exit, access only
	Westbound	No access, exit only
17	Eastbound	No exit, access from A82 only
	Westbound	No access, exit to A82 only
18	Westbound	No exit, access only
19	Eastbound	No exit to A814 eastbound
	Westbound	No access from A814 westbound
20	Eastbound	No exit, access only
	Westbound	No access, exit only
21	Eastbound	No access, exit only
	Westbound	No exit, access only
22	Eastbound	No exit, access from M77 only
	Westbound	No access, exit to M77 only
23	Eastbound	No exit, access from B768 only
	Westbound	No access, exit to B768 only
25	Eastbound & Westbound	Access from A739 southbound only Exit to A739 northbound only
25a	Eastbound	Access only
	Westbound	Exit only
28	Eastbound	No exit, access from airport only
	Westbound	No access, exit to airport only
29a	Eastbound	No exit, access only
	Westbound	No access, exit only

M9

Junction		
2	Northbound	No exit, access from B8046 only
	Southbound	No access, exit to B8046 only
3	Northbound	No access, exit to A803 only
	Southbound	No exit, access from A803 only
6	Northbound	No exit, access only
	Southbound	No access, exit to A905 only
8	Northbound	No access, exit to M876 only
	Southbound	No exit, access from M876 only

M11

Junction		
4	Northbound	No exit, access from A406 eastbound only
	Southbound	No access, exit to A406 westbound only
5	Northbound	No access, exit to A1168 only
	Southbound	No exit, access from A1168 only
8a	Northbound	No access, exit only
	Southbound	No exit, access only
9	Northbound	No access, exit only
	Southbound	No exit, access only
13	Northbound	No access, exit only
	Southbound	No exit, access only
14	Northbound	No access from A428 eastbound No exit to A428 westbound
	Southbound	No exit, access from A428 eastbound only

M20

Junction		
2	Eastbound	No access, exit to A20 only (access via M26 Junction 2a)
	Westbound	No exit, access only (exit via M26 Jun.2a)
3	Eastbound	No exit, access from M26 eastbound only
	Westbound	No access, exit to M26 westbound only
10	Eastbound	No access, exit only
	Westbound	No exit, access only
11a	Eastbound	No access from Channel Tunnel
	Westbound	No exit to Channel Tunnel

M23

Junction		
7	Northbound	No exit to A23 southbound
	Southbound	No access from A23 northbound

M25

Junction		
5	Clockwise	No exit to M26 eastbound
	Anti-clockwise	No access from M26 westbound
Spur to A21	Northbound	No exit to M26 eastbound
	Southbound	No access from M26 westbound
19	Clockwise	No access, exit only
	Anti-clockwise	No exit, access only
21	Clockwise & Anti-clockwise	No exit to M1 southbound No access from M1 northbound
31	Northbound	No access, exit only (access via Jun.30)
	Southbound	No exit, access only (exit via Jun.30)

M26

Junction with M25 (M25 Jun.5)

Eastbound	No access from M25 clockwise or spur from A21 northbound
Westbound	No exit to M25 anti-clockwise or spur to A21 southbound

Junction with M20 (M20 Jun.3)

Eastbound	No exit to M20 westbound
Westbound	No access from M20 eastbound

M27

Junction		
4	Eastbound & Westbound	No exit to A33 southbound (Southampton) No access from A33 northbound
10	Eastbound	No exit, access from A32 only
	Westbound	No access, exit to A32 only

M40

Junction		
3	North-Westbound	No access, exit to A40 only
	South-Eastbound	No exit, access from A40 only
7	N.W bound	No access, exit only
	S.E bound	No exit, access only
13	N.W bound	No access, exit only
	S.E bound	No exit, access only
14	N.W bound	No exit, access only
	S.E bound	No access, exit only
16	N.W bound	No exit, access only
	S.E bound	No access, exit only

M42

Junction		
1	Eastbound	No exit
	Westbound	No access
7	Northbound	No access, exit to M6 only
	Southbound	No exit, access from M6 northbound only
8	Northbound	No exit, access from M6 southbound only
	Southbound	Exit to M6 nothbound only Access from M6 southbound only

M45

Junction with M1 (M1 Jun.17)

Eastbound	No exit to M1 northbound
Westbound	No access from M1 southbound

Junction with A45 east of Dunchurch

Eastbound	No access, exit to A45 only
Westbound	No exit, access from A45 northbound only

M48

Junction with M4 (M4 Jun.21)

Eastbound	No exit to M4 westbound
Westbound	No access from M4 eastbound

Junction with M4 (M4 Jun.23)

Eastbound	No access from M4 westbound
Westbound	No exit to M4 eastbound

M53

Junction		
11	Northbound & Southbound	No access from M56 eastbound, no exit to M56 westbound

M56

Junction		
1	Eastbound	No exit to M60 N.W bound No exit to A34 southbound
	S.E bound	No access from A34 northbound
	Westbound	No access from M60
2	Eastbound	No exit, access from A560 only
	Westbound	No access, exit to A560 only
3	Eastbound	No access, exit only
	Westbound	No exit, access only
4	Eastbound	No exit, access only
	Westbound	No access, exit only
7	Westbound	No access, exit only
8	Eastbound	No access or exit
	Westbound	No exit, access from A556 only
9	Eastbound	No access from M6 northbound
	Westbound	No exit to M60 southbound
10a	Northbound	No exit, access only
	Southbound	No access, exit only
15	Eastbound	No exit to M53
	Westbound	No access from M53

M57

Junction		
3	Northbound	No exit, access only
	Southbound	No access, exit only
5	Northbound	No exit, access from A580 westbound only
	Southbound	No access, exit to A580 eastbound only

M60

Junction		
2	N.E bound	No access, exit to A560 only
	S.W bound	No exit, access from A560 only
3	Eastbound	No access from A34 southbound
	Westbound	No exit to A34 northbound
4	Eastbound	No exit to M56 S.W bound No exit to A34 northbound
	Westbound	No access from A34 southbound No access from M56 eastbound
5	N.W bound	No access from or exit to A5103 southbound
	S.E bound	No access from or exit to A5103 northbound
14	Eastbound	No exit to A580 No access from A580 westbound
	Westbound	No exit to A580 eastbound No access from A580
16	Eastbound	No exit, access from A666 only
	Westbound	No access, exit to A666 only
20	Eastbound	No access from A664
	Westbound	No exit to A664
22	Westbound	No access from A62
25	S.W bound	No access from A560 / A6017
26	N.E bound	No access or exit
27	N.E bound	No access, exit only
	S.W bound	No exit, access only

M61

Junction		
2&3	N.W bound	No access from A580 eastbound
	S.E bound	No exit to A580 westbound

Junction with M6 (M6 Jun.30)

N.W bound	No exit to M6 southbound
S.E bound	No access from M6 northbound

M62

Junction		
23	Eastbound	No access, exit to A640 only
	Westbound	No exit, access from A640 only

M65

Junction		
9	N.E bound	No access, exit to A679 only
	S.W bound	No exit, access from A679 only
11	N.E bound	No exit, access only
	S.W bound	No access, exit only

M66

Junction		
1	Northbound	No access, exit to A56 only
	Southbound	No exit, access from A56 only

M67

Junction		
1	Eastbound	Access from A57 eastbound only
	Westbound	Exit to A57 westbound only
1a	Eastbound	No access, exit to A6017 only
	Westbound	No exit, access from A6017 only
2	Eastbound	No exit, access from A57 only
	Westbound	No access, exit to A57 only

M69

Junction		
2	N.E bound	No exit, access from B4669 only
	S.W bound	No access, exit to B4669 only

M73

Junction		
1	Southbound	No exit to A721 eastbound
2	Northbound	No access from M8 eastbound No exit to A89 eastbound
	Southbound	No exit to M8 westbound No access from A89 westbound
3	Northbound	No exit to A80 S.W bound
	Southbound	No access from A80 N.E bound

M74

Junction		
1	Eastbound	No access from M8 Westbound
	Westbound	No exit to M8 Westbound
3	Eastbound	No exit
	Westbound	No access
7	Northbound	No exit, access from A72 only
	Southbound	No access, exit to A72 only
9	Northbound	No access or exit
	Southbound	No access, exit to B7078 only
10	Southbound	No exit, access from B7078 only
11	Northbound	No exit, access from B7078 only
	Southbound	No access, exit to B7078 only
12	Northbound	No access, exit to A70 only
	Southbound	No exit, access from A70 only

M77

Junction with M8 (M8 Jun.22)

Northbound	No exit to M8 westbound
Southbound	No access from M8 eastbound

Junction		
4	Northbound	No exit
	Southbound	No access
6	Northbound	No exit to A77
	Southbound	No access from A77
7	Northbound	No access from A77 No exit to A77

M80

Junction		
1	Northbound	No access from M8 westbound
	Southbound	No exit to M8 eastbound
4a	Northbound	No access
	Southbound	No exit
6a	Northbound	No exit
	Southbound	No access
8	Northbound	No access from M876
	Southbound	No exit to M876

M90

Junction		
1	Northbound	No exit
	Southbound	No Access from A90
2a	Northbound	No access, exit to A92 only
	Southbound	No exit, access from A92 only
7	Northbound	No exit, access from A91 only
	Southbound	No access, exit to A91 only
8	Northbound	No access, exit to A91 only
	Southbound	No exit, access from A91 only
10	Northbound	No access from A912 Exit to A912 northbound only
	Southbound	No exit to A912 Access from A912 southbound only

M180

Junction		
1	Eastbound	No access, exit only
	Westbound	No exit, access from A18 only

M606

Junction		
2	Northbound	No access, exit only

M621

Junction		
2a	Eastbound	No exit, access only
	Westbound	No access, exit only
4	Southbound	No exit
5	Northbound	No access, exit to A61 only
	Southbound	No exit, access from A61 only
6	Northbound	No exit, access only
	Southbound	No access, exit only
7	Eastbound	No access, exit only
	Westbound	No exit, access only
8	Northbound	No access, exit only
	Southbound	No exit, access only

M876

Junction with M80 (M80 Jun.5)

N.E bound	No access from M80 southbound
S.W bound	No exit to M80 northbound

Junction with M9 (M9 Jun.8)

N.E bound	No exit to M9 northbound
S.W bound	No access from M9 southbound

A1(M)

Junction		
	Hertfordshire Section	
2	Northbound	No access, exit only
	Southbound	No exit, access from A1001 only
3	Southbound	No access, exit only
5	Northbound	No exit, access only
	Southbound	No access or exit
	Cambridgeshire Section	
14	Northbound	No exit, access only
	Southbound	No access, exit only
	Leeds Section	
40	Southbound	Exit to A1 southbound only
43	Northbound	Access from M1 eastbound only
	Southbound	Exit to M1 westbound only
	Durham Section	
57	Northbound	No access, exit to A66(M) only
	Southbound	No exit, access from A66(M)
65	Northbound	Exit to A1 N.W bound and to A194(M) only
	Southbound	Access from A1 S.E bound and from A194(M) only

A3(M)

Junction		
4	Northbound	No access, exit only
	Southbound	No exit, access only

Aston Expressway A38(M)

Junction with Victoria Road, Aston

Northbound	No exit, access only
Southbound	No access, exit only

A48(M)

Junction with M4 (M4 Jun.29)

N.E bound	Exit to M4 eastbound only
S.W bound	Access from M4 westbound only

Junction		
29a	N.E bound	Access from A48 eastbound only
	S.W bound	Exit to A48 westbound only

Mancunian Way A57(M)

Junction with A34 Brook Street, Manchester

Eastbound	No access, exit to A34 Brook Street, southbound only
Westbound	No exit, access only

Leeds Inner Ring Road A58(M)

Junction with Park Lane / Westgate

Southbound	No access, exit only

Leeds Inner Ring Road A64(M) (continuation of A58(M))

Junction with A58 Clay Pit Lane

Eastbound	No access
Westbound	No exit

A66(M)

Junction with A1(M) (A1(M) Jun.57)

N.E bound	Access from A1(M) northbound only
S.W bound	Exit to A1(M) southbound only

A74(M)

Junction		
18	Northbound	No access
	Southbound	No exit

Newcastle Central Motorway A167(M)

Junction with Camden Street

Northbound	No exit, access only
Southbound	No access or exit

A194(M)

Junction with A1(M) (A1(M) Jun.65) **and A1 Gateshead Western By-Pass**

Northbound	Access from A1(M) only
Southbound	Exit to A1(M) only

Northern Ireland

M1

Junction		
3	Northbound	No exit, access only
	Southbound	No access, exit only
7	Westbound	No access, exit only

M2

Junction		
2	Eastbound	No access to M5 northbound
	Westbound	No exit to M5 southbound

M5

Junction		
2	Northbound	No access from M2 eastbound
	Southbound	No exit to M2 westbound

Reference

Motorway
Autoroute
Autobahn
M1

Motorway Under Construction
Autoroute en construction
Autobahn im Bau

Motorway Proposed
Autoroute prévue
Geplante Autobahn

Motorway Junctions with Numbers
Unlimited Interchange **4**
Limited Interchange **5**

Autoroute échangeur numéroté
Echangeur complet
Echangeur partiel

Autobahnanschlußstelle mit Nummer
Unbeschränkter Fahrtrichtungswechsel
Beschränkter Fahrtrichtungswechsel

Motorway Service Area (with fuel station)
S
with access from one carriageway only
S

Aire de services d'autoroute (avec station service)
accessible d'un seul côté
Rastplatz oder Raststätte (mit tankstelle)
Einbahn

Major Road Service Area (with fuel station) with 24 hour facilities
Primary Route **S** Class A Road **S**
Aire de services sur route prioritaire (avec station service) Ouverte 24h sur 24
Route à grande circulation Route de type A
Raststätte (mit tankstelle) Durchgehend geöffnet
Hauptverkehrsstraße A- Straße

Major Road Junctions
Jonctions grands routiers
Hauptverkehrsstraße Kreuzungen
Detailed **4**
Détaillé
Ausführlich
Other Autre Andere

Truckstop (selection of)
Sélection d'aire pour poids lourds
Auswahl von Fernfahrerrastplatz
T

Primary Route
Route à grande circulation
Hauptverkehrsstraße
A41

Primary Route Junction with Number
Echangeur numéroté
Hauptverkehrsstraßenkreuzung mit Nummer
5

Primary Route Destination
Route prioritaire, direction
Hauptverkehrsstraße Richtung
DOVER

Dual Carriageways (A & B roads)
Route à double chaussées séparées (route A & B)
Zweispurige Schnellstraße (A- und B- Straßen)

Class A Road
Route de type A
A-Straße
A129

Class B Road
Route de type B
B-Straße
B177

Narrow Major Road (passing places)
Route prioritaire étroite (possibilité de dépassement)
Schmale Hauptverkehrsstaße (mit Überholmöglichkeit)

Major Roads Under Construction
Route prioritaire en construction
Hauptverkehrsstaße im Bau

Major Roads Proposed
Route prioritaire prévue
Geplante Hauptverkehrsstaße

Safety Cameras with Speed Limits
Single Camera **30**
Multiple Cameras located along road **50**
Single & Multiple Variable Speed Cameras **V** **V**

Radars de contrôle de vitesse
Radar simple
Radars multiples situés le long de la route
Radars simples et multiples de contrôle de vitesse variable

Sicherheitskameras mit Tempolimit
Einzelne Kamera
Mehrere Kameras entlang der Straße
Einzelne und mehrere Kameras für variables Tempolimit

Fuel Station
Station service
Tankstelle

Gradient 1:7 (14%) **& steeper**
(descent in direction of arrow)
Pente égale ou supérieure à 14% (dans le sens de la descente)
14% Steigung und steiler (in Pfeilrichtung)

Toll
Barrière de péage
Gebührenpflichtig
Toll

Dart Charge
www.gov.uk/pay-dartford-crossing-charge
C

Park & Ride
Parking avec Service Navette
Parken und Reisen
P+R

Mileage between markers
Distence en miles entre les flèches
Strecke zwischen Markierungen in Meilen
8

Airport
Aéroport
Flughafen

Airfield
Terrain d'aviation
Flugplatz

Heliport
Héliport
Hubschrauberlandeplatz
H

Ferry
(vehicular, sea) Bac (auto, meer) Fähre
(vehicular, river) (véhicules, mer) (auto, fluß)
(foot only) (véhicules, rivière) (nur für Personen)
(piétons)

Railway and Station
Voie ferrée et gare
Eisenbahnlinie und Bahnhof

Level Crossing and Tunnel
Passage à niveau et tunnel
Bahnübergang und Tunnel

River or Canal
Rivière ou canal
Fluß oder Kanal

County or Unitary Authority Boundary
Limite de comté ou de division administrative
Grafschafts- oder Verwaltungsbezirksgrenze

National Boundary
Frontière nationale
Landesgrenze

Built-up Area
Agglomération
Geschloßene Ortschaft

Town, Village or Hamlet
Ville, Village ou hameau
Stadt, Dorf oder Weiler

Wooded Area
Zone boisée
Waldgebiet

Spot Height in Feet · *813*
Altitude (en pieds)
Höhe in Fuß

Relief above 400' (122m)
Relief par estompage au-dessus de 400' (122m)
Reliefschattierung über 400' (122m)

National Grid Reference (kilometres) ¹00
Coordonnées géographiques nationales (Kilomètres)
Nationale geographische Koordinaten (Kilometer)

Page Continuation
Suite à la page indiquée
Seitenfortsetzung
48

Area covered by Main Route map
Repartition des cartes des principaux axes routiers
Von Karten mit Hauptverkehrsstrecken
MAIN ROUTE 94

Area covered by Town Plan
Ville ayant un plan à la page indiquée
Von Karten mit Stadtplänen erfaßter Bereich
PAGE 109

Tourist Information

Abbey, Church, Friary, Priory †
Abbaye, église, monastère, prieuré
Abtei, Kirche, Mönchskloster, Kloster

Animal Collection
Ménagerie
Tiersammlung

Aquarium
Aquarium
Aquarium

Arboretum, Botanical Garden
Jardin Botanique
Botanischer Garten

Aviary, Bird Garden
Volière
Voliere

Battle Site and Date
Champ de bataille et date *1066*
Schlachtfeld und Datum

Blue Flag Beach
Plage Pavillon Bleu
Blaue Flagge Strand

Bridge
Pont
Brücke

Butterfly Farm
Ferme aux Papillons
Schmetterlingsfarm

Castle (open to public)
Château (ouvert au public)
Schloß / Burg (für die Öffentlichkeit zugänglich)

Castle with Garden (open to public)
Château avec parc (ouvert au public)
Schloß mit Garten (für die Öffentlichkeit zugänglich)

Cathedral ‡
Cathédrale
Kathedrale

Cidermaker
Cidrerie (fabrication)
Apfelwein Hersteller

Country Park
Parc régional
Landschaftspark

Distillery
Distillerie
Brennerei

Farm Park, Open Farm
Park Animalier
Bauernhof Park

Fortress, Hill Fort
Château Fort
Festung

Garden (open to public)
Jardin (ouvert au public)
Garten (für die Öffentlichkeit zugänglich)

Golf Course
Terrain de golf
Golfplatz

Historic Building (open to public)
Monument historique (ouvert au public)
Historisches Gebäude (für die Öffentlichkeit zugänglich)

Historic Building with Garden (open to public)
Monument historique avec jardin (ouvert au public)
Historisches Gebäude mit Garten (für die Öffentlichkeit zugänglich)

Horse Racecourse
Hippodrome
Pferderennbahn

Industrial Monument
Monument Industrielle
Industriedenkmal

Leisure Park, Leisure Pool
Parc d'Attraction, Loisirs Piscine
Freizeitpark, Freizeit pool

Lighthouse
Phare
Leuchtturm

Mine, Cave
Mine, Grotte
Bergwerk, Höhle

Monument
Monument
Denkmal

Motor Racing Circuit
Circuit Automobile
Automobilrennbahn

Museum, Art Gallery **M**
Musée
Museum, Galerie

National Park
Parc national
Nationalpark

National Trail
Sentier national
Nationaler Weg

National Trust Property
National Trust Property
National Trust- Eigentum

Natural Attraction ★
Attraction Naturelle
Natürliche Anziehung

Nature Reserve or Bird Sanctuary
Réserve naturelle botanique ou ornithologique
Natur- oder Vogelschutzgebiet

Nature Trail or Forest Walk
Chemin forestier, piste verte
Naturpfad oder Waldweg

Picnic Site
Lieu pour pique-nique
Picknickplatz

Place of Interest *Craft Centre* •
Site, curiosité
Sehenswürdigkeit

Prehistoric Monument
Monument Préhistorique
Prähistorische Denkmal

Railway, Steam or Narrow Gauge
Chemin de fer, à vapeur ou à voie étroite
Eisenbahn, Dampf- oder Schmalspurbahn

Roman Remains
Vestiges Romains
Römischen Ruinen

Theme Park
Centre de loisirs
Vergnügungspark

Tourist Information Centre **i**
Office de Tourisme
Touristeninformationen

Viewpoint (360 degrees) (180 degrees)
Vue panoramique (360 degrés) (180 degrés)
Aussichtspunkt (360 Grade) (180 Grade)

Vineyard
Vignoble
Weinberg

Visitor Information Centre **V**
Centre d'information touristique
Besucherzentrum

Wildlife Park
Réserve de faune
Wildpark

Windmill
Moulin à vent
Windmühle

Zoo or Safari Park
Parc ou réserve zoologique
Zoo oder Safari-Park

ISLES OF SCILLY
Round Island
St Helen's
White Island
BRYHER
Tean
Middle Town
Lower Town
Day Mark
Old Grimsby
ST MARTIN'S
Higher Town
Gweal
The Town
New Grimsby
TRESCO
Maiden Bower
Valhalla Ships' Figurehead Collection
Samson
EASTERN ISLES
Mincarlo
ISLES OF SCILLY
Maypole
Hugh Town
ST MARY'S
Porth Hellick Down Burial Chamber
ISLES OF SCILLY (St Mary's)
Old Town
Giant's Castle
Crim Rocks
Annet
Gugh
Hugh Town to Penzance 2hrs. 40mins. (Seasonal)
Western Rocks
Punch Bowl
ST AGNES
Bishop Rock
The Isles of Scilly lie 28 miles WSW of Land's End
ATLANTIC OCEAN
Gulland Rock
TREVOSE HEAD
Constantine Bay
Park Head
Berryl's Point
Watergate Bay
Towan Head
NEWQUAY
Fistral Bay
Kelsey Head
Holywell Bay
Penhale Point
Ligger or Perran Bay
Perranporth
Bawden Rocks
St Agnes Head
St Agnes
Portreath
Crane Islands
Navax Point
Godrevy Island
The Carracks
St Ives
St Ives Bay
Gurnard's Head
Pendeen Watch
Cape Cornwall
The Brisons
St Just
Whitesand Bay
Longships
Sennen
LAND'S END
Gwennap Head
Runnel Stone
Cribba Head
PENZANCE
Newlyn
St Clement's Isle
Penzance to Hugh Town 2hrs. 40mins. (Seasonal)
MOUNT'S BAY
Marazion
Cudden Point
Trewavas Head
Porthleven
Helston
CORNWALL
CAMBORNE
REDRUTH
Hayle
TRURO
FALMOUTH
Penryn
St Mawes
Falmouth Bay
Pendennis Point
Zone Point
Rosemullion Head
Nare Point
Manacle Point
The Manacles
Coverack
Black Head
Poldhu Point
Mullion
Mullion Island
Vellan Head
Kynance Cove
Lizard
Hot Point
LIZARD POINT
A30
A39
A390
A393
A394
A3071
A3074
A3075
A3076
A3078
A3083
A3058
A3059
A392

4
A
B
C
D
E
F
1
2
3
4
5
6
7
8
TREVOSE HEAD
Quies
Constantine Bay
Padstow Bay
Padstow
Wadebridge
Bodmin
St Columb Major
Newquay
Roche
St Austell
Lostwithiel
Fowey
Polruan
Polperro
Looe
East Looe
Liskeard
Callington
Launceston
Camelford
Boscastle
Tintagel
Tintagel Head
Bude
Bude Bay
Stratton
Holsworthy
Kilkhampton
Dizzard Point
Cambeak
Fire Beacon Point
Gull Rock
Port Isaac
Port Isaac Bay
Rumps Point
The Mouls
Pentire Point
Newland
Gulland Rock
Gunver Head
Park Head
Berryl's Point
Watergate Bay
Newquay Bay
Truro
Tresillian
Probus
Grampound
Mevagissey
Mevagissey Bay
Chapel Point
Gorran Haven
Dodman Point
Veryan
Veryan Bay
Gerrans Bay
Nare Head
Gull Rock
Portscatho
Gerrans
St Mawes
Falmouth
Falmouth Bay
Pendennis Point
Zone Point
Greeb Point
Rosemullion Head
St Austell Bay
Gribbin Head
Black Head
Pencarrow Head
Talland Bay
Looe Bay
St George's or Looe Island
Whitsand Bay
Eddystone Rocks
ENGLISH
C O R N W A L L
B O D M I N M O O R
Lanreath
Pelynt
Duloe
St Keyne
Menheniot
St Germans
Crafthole
Portwrinkle
Downderry
Seaton
Saltash
Pillaton
St Mellion
Kelly Bray
Linkinhorne
Upton Cross
Pensilva
St Cleer
Darite
Minions
Altarnun
Lewannick
Polyphant
South Petherwin
Lezant
North Hill
Bolventor
St Neot
Cardinham
St Breward
St Tudy
St Mabyn
St Kew
St Minver
Rock
Trebetherick
Polzeath
St Merryn
St Issey
St Eval
St Mawgan
St Wenn
Withiel
Lanivet
Bugle
Luxulyan
Lanlivery
St Blazey
Par
Tywardreath
Charlestown
Pentewan
St Ewe
Tregony
Ruan Lanihorne
Philleigh
St Just in Roseland
St Dennis
Indian Queens
Fraddon
Summercourt
Mitchell
Ladock
Grampound Road
Trewoon
Polgooth
Sticker
Warbstow
Otterham
North Petherwin
Egloskerry
Tresmeer
Week St Mary
Whitstone
Marhamchurch
Bridgerule
Pyworthy
Lifton
Milton Damerel
Sutcombe
A30
A39
A38
A389
A390
A391
A392
A395
A3058
A3059
A3075
A3076
A3078
A3082
A387
A388
A374
A3072
B3254
B3263
B3266
B3274
B3275
B3287
B3314
B3253
B3252
B3257
90
200
10
20
30
100
80
70
35mins. (Seasonal)

5
G
H
J
K
L
M
DARTMOOR
DARTMOOR FOREST
NATIONAL PARK
D E V O N
PLYMOUTH
EXETER
TAVISTOCK
TORQUAY
PAIGNTON
NEWTON ABBOT
Okehampton
Crediton
Moretonhampstead
Bovey Tracey
Kingsteignton
Teignmouth
Dawlish
Starcross
Exminster
Topsham
Ashburton
Buckfastleigh
South Brent
Ivybridge
Totnes
Dartmouth
Kingswear
Brixham
Kingsbridge
Salcombe
Modbury
Plympton
Plymstock
Torpoint
Saltash
Princetown
Chagford
Hatherleigh
Lydford
Yelverton
Berry Head
Sharkham Point
Hope's Nose
Babbacombe Bay
Tor Bay
TORBAY
Start Bay
Start Point
Prawle Point
Bolt Head
Bolt Tail
Bigbury Bay
Burgh Island
Mew Stone
Great Mew Stone
Stoke Point
Penlee Point
Rame Head
The Sound
Plymouth Breakwater
C H A N N E L
Plymouth to:
Roscoff 6hrs. (Seasonal)
Santander 20hrs. (Seasonal)
A30
A38
A380
A379
A381
A382
A383
A385
A386
A3072
A3122
M5
6
7
1
2
3
4
5
6
7
8
250
60
70
80
90
30
40
50
60
70

6
A
B
C
D
E
F
1
2
3
4
5
6
7
8
North West Point
LUNDY
Lundy Marine Conservation Zone
Rat Island
South West Point
Ilfracombe to Lundy 2hrs. (Seasonal)
Bideford to Lundy 2hrs. (Seasonal)
ILFRACOMBE
Bull Point
Rockham Bay
Morte Point
Mortehoe
Woolacombe
Morte Bay
Baggy Point
Croyde Bay
Croyde
Georgeham
Braunton
Ashford
Combe Martin Bay
Combe Martin
Woody Bay
Parracombe
Berrynarbor
West Down
BARNSTAPLE
Bishop's Tawton
Swimbridge
Instow
Appledore
Northam
Westward Ho!
BIDEFORD
East-the-Water
BARNSTAPLE OR BIDEFORD BAY
HARTLAND POINT
Windbury Point
Hartland
Hartland Quay
Clovelly
Higher Clovelly
Woolfardisworthy or Woolsery
Parkham
Buckland Brewer
Littleham
Abbotsham
Weare Giffard
Great Torrington
St Giles in the Wood
High Bickington
Chittlehampton
King's Nympton
Knaps Longpeak
Morwenstow
Higher Sharpnose Point
Lower Sharpnose Point
Kilkhampton
Bradworthy
Sutcombe
Bulkworthy
Milton Damerel
Shebbear
Langtree
Beaford
Merton
Dolton
Winkleigh
Wembworthy
Flexbury
Bude
Bude Bay
Stratton
Marhamchurch
Widemouth Bay
Holsworthy
Pyworthy
Bridgerule
Black Torrington
Sheepwash
Highampton
Hatherleigh
Exbourne
Sampford Courtenay
North Tawton
Dizzard Point
Halwill Junction
Northlew
Folly Gate
Okehampton
Week St Mary
Whitstone
Tetcott
Ashwater
Cambeak
Crackington Haven
Beacon Point
Boscastle
Warbstow
North Petherwin
Bratton Clovelly
Belstone
South Zeal
Throwleigh
Egloskerry
Launceston
Lifton
Stowford
Lydford
Camelford
Altarnun
Polyphant
Lewannick
South Petherwin
Milton Abbot
Mary Tavy
Peter Tavy
Lamerton
CORNWALL
BODMIN MOOR
DARTMOOR NATIONAL PARK
North Hill
Linkinhorne
Sydenham Damerel
TAVISTOCK
Princetown
Two Bridges
Gunnislake
Chilsworthy
Calstock
Buckland Monachorum
Horrabridge
Walkhampton
Yelverton
Dousland
Pensilva
Darite
Callington
Kelly Bray
Cardinham
St Cleer
St Neot
St Breward
Tremar
A39
A361
A377
A386
A388
A3072
A3079
A30
A395
A390
A3124
A399
A3123
A382
B3231
B3227
B3217
B3220
B3216
B3254
B3257
B3262
B3266
B3263
B3357
B3212

BRIDGWATER BAY
BURNHAM-ON-SEA
Foreland Point
Lynton
Lynmouth
Countisbury
Porlock Bay
Porlock
MINEHEAD
Blue Anchor Bay
Dunster
Watchet
Williton
EXMOOR
NATIONAL PARK
EXMOOR FOREST
Exford
Simonsbath
BRENDON HILLS
SOMERSET
QUANTOCK HILLS
Dulverton
Wiveliscombe
Bampton
South Molton
Bishop's Nympton
TAUNTON
PAGE 117
VALE OF TAUNTON DEANE
Wellington
Milverton
BLACKDOWN HILLS
TIVERTON
Cullompton
Uffculme
Hemyock
Crediton
Honiton
Yarcombe
Ottery St Mary
EXETER
PAGE 109
Topsham
Exmouth
Budleigh Salterton
SIDMOUTH
Seaton
Beer
Beer Head
Seaton Bay
Colyton
Axminster
Moretonhampstead
Bovey Tracey
Chudleigh
Dawlish
Teignmouth
Kingsteignton
NEWTON ABBOT
Ashburton
Babbacombe
A39
A396
A358
A38
A361
A30
A373
A375
A3052
A376
A379
A377
A3072
A380
A382
A383
A381
A35
M5
G
H
J
K
L
M
1
2
3
4
5
6
7
8

BURNHAM-ON-SEA
BRIDGWATER
TAUNTON
Glastonbury
Street
Wells
Shepton Mallet
FROME
Bruton
Wincanton
Castle Cary
Somerton
Langport
Ilchester
YEOVIL
Sherborne
Ilminster
Chard
Crewkerne
Axminster
Lyme Regis
Seaton
Bridport
DORCHESTER
WEYMOUTH
Fortuneswell
ISLE OF PORTLAND
BILL OF PORTLAND
LYME BAY
Weymouth Bay
Portland Harbour
Chesil Beach
DEVON
POLDEN HILLS
BLACKMOOR VALE
Weymouth to Cherbourg (Proposed)
M5
A39
A303
A37
A35
A30
A354
A352
A371
A358
A3088
A3066
A356
A372
A361
A359
A357
A3030
A353
A3052
A378
A362
A367
A365
PAGE 117

9
SALISBURY PLAIN
WILTSHIRE
HAMPSHIRE
NEW FOREST NATIONAL PARK
ENGLISH CHANNEL
POOLE BAY
Poole Harbour
Christchurch Bay
Brownsea Island
ISLE OF PURBECK
HENGISTBURY HEAD
DURLSTON HEAD
ST ALDHELM'S OR ST ALBAN'S HEAD
THE NEEDLES
The Foreland or Handfast Point
Westbury
Warminster
Andover
Salisbury
PAGE 115
Amesbury
Durrington
Tidworth
Ludgershall
Romsey
Totton
Shaftesbury
Gillingham
Blandford Forum
Wimborne Minster
Ringwood
Fordingbridge
Ferndown
Christchurch
Poole
Bournemouth
PAGE 106
Wareham
Swanage
Lymington
Lyndhurst
New Milton
Highcliffe
Yarmouth
Poole to:
Cherbourg 4hrs. 30mins.
Guernsey 3hrs.
(Fast Ferry, Seasonal)
Jersey 4hrs. 30mins.
(Fast Ferry, Seasonal)
St Malo 6hrs.
(Fast Ferry, Seasonal)
G H J K L M
90 400 10 20 30
80 70

10
A
B
C
D
E
F
BASINGSTOKE
ALDERSHOT
FARNHAM
NORTH
ANDOVER
Whitchurch
Overton
Oakley
Alton
WINCHESTER
PAGE 117
Stockbridge
Romsey
EASTLEIGH
Chandler's Ford
Bishop's Waltham
New Alresford
Petersfield
PETERSFIELD
HAMPSHIRE
SOUTH DOWNS
NATIONAL PARK
SOUTHAMPTON
PAGE 116
Totton
Hythe
Fareham
FAREHAM
Gosport
GOSPORT
PORTSMOUTH
PAGE 115
HAVANT
Waterlooville
WATERLOOVILLE
Horndean
HORNDEAN
Emsworth
CHICHESTER
Selsey
SELSEY BILL
Lymington
LYMINGTON
Beaulieu
Fawley
Lee-on-the-Solent
THE SOLENT
SPITHEAD
HAYLING ISLAND
PORTSEA ISLAND
SOUTH HAYLING
COWES
East Cowes
RYDE
NEWPORT
Yarmouth
Freshwater
SANDOWN
SHANKLIN
VENTNOR
DUNNOSE
ISLE OF WIGHT
ST CATHERINE'S POINT
FORELAND
Bembridge
Culver Cliff
Needs Ore Point
Gilkicker Point
Stokes Bay
Osborne Bay
Whitecliff Bay
Bracklesham Bay
Chale Bay
Compton Bay
Brighstone Bay
Atherfield Point
Portsmouth to:
Bilbao 24hrs.
Caen 6hrs.
(Seasonal)
Cherbourg 3hrs.
(Fast Ferry, Seasonal)
Guernsey 7hrs.
Jersey 8hrs.
Le Havre 5hrs. 30mins.
St Malo 9hrs.
Santander 24hrs.
M3
M27
M271
M275
A3(M)
A3
A27
A31
A32
A33
A34
A35
A36
A303
A339
A272
A3057
A3055
A3054
A3020
A3021
A3056
40
450
60
70
80
1
2
3
4
5
6
7
8

GUILDFORD
PAGE 109
DORKING
REIGATE
REDHILL
Oxted
GODALMING
HORLEY
LONDON GATWICK
CRAWLEY
EAST GRINSTEAD
KENT
Edenbridge
HIGH WEALD
HORSHAM
ST LEONARDS FOREST
ASHDOWN FOREST
Haslemere
Cranleigh
Billingshurst
Petworth
Pulborough
HAYWARDS HEATH
Cuckfield
BURGESS HILL
Uckfield
WEST SUSSEX
EAST SUSSEX
SURREY
SOUTH DOWNS
Arundel
Storrington
Steyning
Henfield
Hassocks
LEWES
Chichester
LITTLEHAMPTON
WORTHING
SHOREHAM-BY-SEA
Portslade-by-Sea
HOVE
BRIGHTON
PAGE 106
Rottingdean
Peacehaven
NEWHAVEN
SEAFORD
BOGNOR REGIS
Middleton-on-Sea
Newhaven to: Dieppe 4hrs.
ENGLISH CHANNEL
MAIN ROUTE 99
MAIN ROUTE 100
M23
A23
A24
A29
A264
A272
A27
A259
G
H
J
K
L
M
1
2
3
4
5
6
7
8
12
500
10
20
30
40
90
80
70

12
MAIN ROUTE 101
22
11
A
B
C
D
E
F
TONBRIDGE
ROYAL TUNBRIDGE WELLS
CROWBOROUGH
EAST GRINSTEAD
HIGH WEALD
ASHDOWN FOREST
Uckfield
Heathfield
EAST SUSSEX
KENT
LOW WEALD
ASHFORD
Tenterden
Cranbrook
Rye
Camber
Rye Bay
Winchelsea
Battle
HASTINGS
St Leonards
BEXHILL
Pevensey Bay
Pevensey
HAILSHAM
Polegate
EASTBOURNE
PAGE 108
BEACHY HEAD
SEAFORD
NEWHAVEN
Peacehaven
LEWES
SOUTH DOWNS
Newhaven to: Dieppe 4hrs.
ENGLISH CHANNEL
WALLAND

Molash
Challock
Godmersham
Chilham
Petham
Hardres
Pett Bottom
Kingston
Barham
Aylesham
Nonington
Tilmanstone
Eythorne
Betteshanger
Northbourne
Great Mongeham
DEAL
Timeball Tower
Lifeboat Station
Walmer
The Downs
Upper Hardres Court
Womenswold
Woolage Village
Woolage Green
Barfrestone
East Kent Railway
Shepherdswell or Sibertswold
East Studdal
Ashley
Sutton
Ripple
Kingsdown
DANGER AREA
Ringwould
West Langdon
Martin
Martin Mill
Dover Patrol Memorial
Whitfield
East Langdon
Guston
St Margaret's at Cliffe
St Margaret's Bay
West Cliffe
White Cliffs
Pines
SOUTH FORELAND
Buckland
River
Crabble Corn Mill
Temple Ewell
Kearsney
Maxton
DOVER
PAGE 108
Western Docks
Dover to: Calais 1hr. 30mins. Dunkirk 2hrs.
Sole Street
Waltham
Bossingham
Stelling Minnis
North Leigh
Bodsham
Maxted Street
Elmsted
Crundale
Bilting
Boughton Aluph
Boughton Lees
Wye
Wye Crown
Hassell Street
Kempe's Corner
Goat Lees
Hastingleigh
NORTH DOWNS
Kennington
Brook
Agricultural Museum
West Brabourne
Willesborough Lees
Hinxhill
Junc 10a due open mid 2020
Willesborough
Sevington
Brabourne
Brabourne Lees
Stowting
Rhodes Minnis
Lymbridge Green
Ottinge
Elham
Acrise
Swingfield Minnis
Swingfield Street
St John's Commandery
Wingmore
Denton
Wootton
Lydden
Lydden Hill
Selsted
Ewell Minnis
Alkham
Densole
Drellingore
Hawkinge
Paddlesworth
Land Army
West Hougham
Church Hougham
Capel-le-Ferne
Battle of Britain
Samphire Hoe
East Wear Bay
East Cliff & Warren
Channel Tunnel
Newington
Etchinghill
Lyminge
Broad Street
Smeeth
Mersham
Kingsnorth
Stone Hill
Sellindge
Stanford
Postling
North Downs Way
Peene Rly.
Cheeseman's Green
The Forstal
Clap Hill
Aldington
Aldington Frith
Bonnington
Court-at-Street
Westenhanger
STOP 24
Newingreen
Pedlinge
Saltwood
Cheriton
FOLKESTONE
PAGE 109
Metropole Galleries
CHANNEL TUNNEL Folkestone to Calais 35mins.
Bilsington
Royal Military Canal
Lympne
Port Lympne
West Hythe
HYTHE
Seabrook
Sandgate
Waterworld
Palmarsh
DANGER AREA
Monument
Ruckinge
Hamstreet
Lathe Barn
Donkey Street
Newchurch
Burmarsh
ROMNEY MARSH
Snave
Romney, Hythe & Dymchurch Railway
Dymchurch
Martello Tower
Ivychurch
St Mary in the Marsh
St Mary's Bay
Aeronautical
New Romney
Old Romney
Littlestone-on-Sea
Greatstone-on-Sea
East Road
LONDON ASHFORD (Lydd)
MARSH
Lydd
Town
Denge Marsh
Lydd-on-Sea
Lifeboat Station
DANGER AREA
Power Station
Dungeness
Old
DUNGENESS
West Road
STRAIT OF DOVER
A252
A251
A28
A2
A256
A258
A260
A20
M20
A261
A259
A2070
B2068
B2011
B2067
B2075
G
H
J
K
L
M
1
2
3
4
5
6
7
8
10
20
30
40
650
150
100
90
80
70

CHANNEL TUNNEL

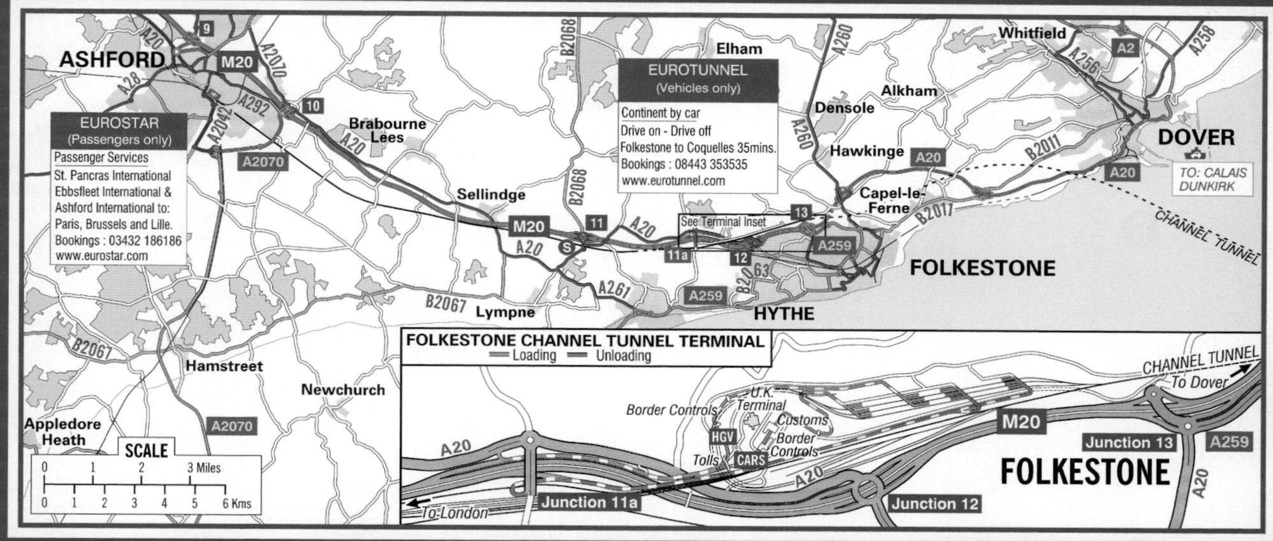

ASHFORD
EUROSTAR (Passengers only)
Passenger Services
St. Pancras International Ebbsfleet International & Ashford International to: Paris, Brussels and Lille.
Bookings : 03432 186186
www.eurostar.com
Brabourne Lees
Sellindge
EUROTUNNEL (Vehicles only)
Continent by car
Drive on - Drive off
Folkestone to Coquelles 35mins.
Bookings : 08443 353535
www.eurotunnel.com
Elham
Densole
Alkham
Hawkinge
Whitfield
DOVER
TO: CALAIS DUNKIRK
CHANNEL TUNNEL
Capel-le-Ferne
See Terminal Inset
FOLKESTONE
HYTHE
Lympne
Hamstreet
Newchurch
Appledore Heath
SCALE
0 1 2 3 Miles
0 1 2 3 4 5 6 Kms
FOLKESTONE CHANNEL TUNNEL TERMINAL
Loading
Unloading
Border Controls
U.K. Terminal
Customs
Border Controls
HGV
Tolls
CARS
To Dover
To London
Junction 11a
Junction 12
Junction 13
FOLKESTONE
M20
A20
A259
A261
A2070
A292
B2068
B2067
B2011

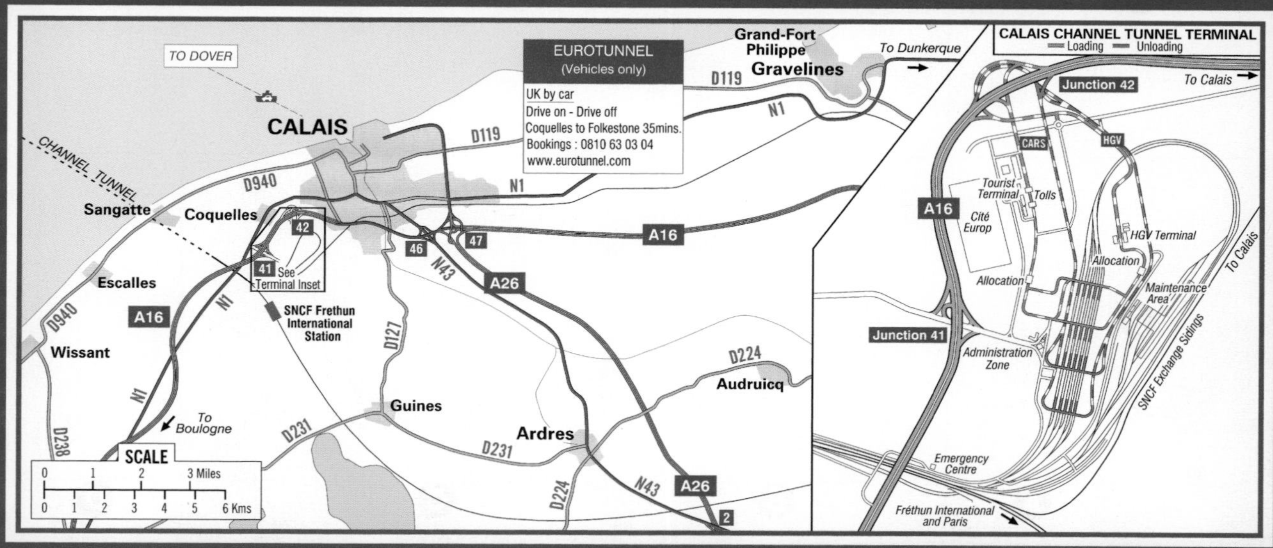

TO DOVER
EUROTUNNEL (Vehicles only)
UK by car
Drive on - Drive off
Coquelles to Folkestone 35mins.
Bookings : 0810 63 03 04
www.eurotunnel.com
Grand-Fort Philippe
Gravelines
To Dunkerque
CALAIS
CHANNEL TUNNEL
Sangatte
Coquelles
See Terminal Inset
Escalles
Wissant
SNCF Frethun International Station
Guines
Ardres
Audruicq
To Boulogne
SCALE
0 1 2 3 Miles
0 1 2 3 4 5 6 Kms
CALAIS CHANNEL TUNNEL TERMINAL
Loading
Unloading
Junction 42
To Calais
CARS
HGV
Tourist Terminal
Tolls
Cité Europ
HGV Terminal
Allocation
Maintenance Area
Junction 41
Administration Zone
SNCF Exchange Sidings
Emergency Centre
Fréthun International and Paris
A16
A26
N1
N43
D119
D940
D127
D224
D231
D238

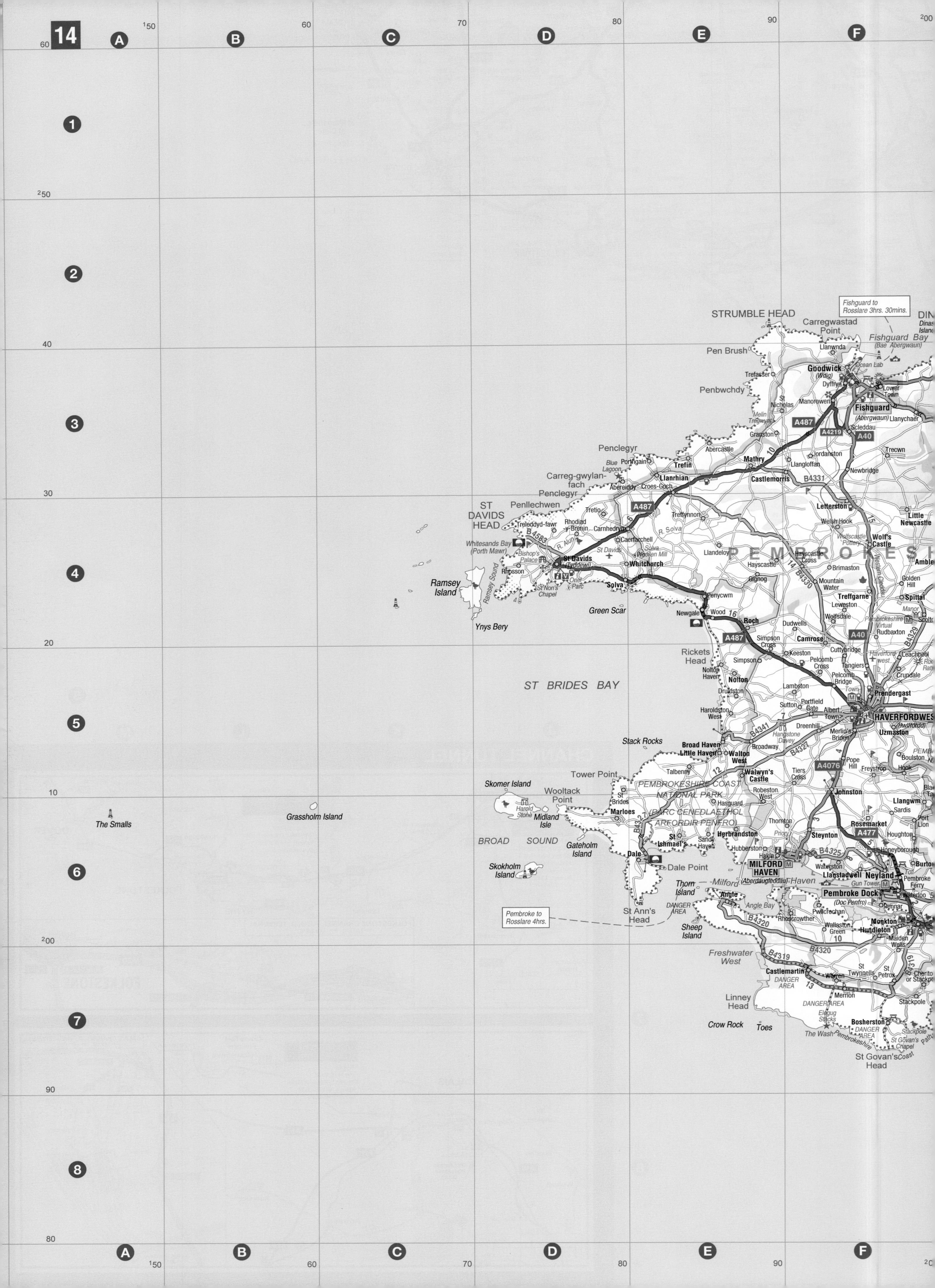

STRUMBLE HEAD
Carregwastad Point
Pen Brush
Penbwchdy
Penclegyr
Carreg-gwylan-fach
Penclegyr
ST DAVIDS HEAD
Penllechwen
Whitesands Bay (Porth Mawr)
Bishop's Palace
Ramsey Island
Ynys Bery

Fishguard to Rosslare 3hrs. 30mins.
Dinas Island
Fishguard Bay (Bae Abergwaun)
Llanwnda
Goodwick (Wdig)
Dyffryn
Ocean Lab
Lower Town
Fishguard (Abergwaun) Llanychaer
Trefasser
St Nicholas
Manorowen
Melin Tregwynt
Trefin
Abercastle
Mathry
Jordanston
Llangloffan
Trecwn
Porthgain
Blue Lagoon
Llanrhian
Castlemorris
Newbridge
Abereiddy
Croes-Goch
Letterston
Tretio
Treffynnon
Welsh Hook
Little Newcastle
Treleddyd-fawr
Rhodiad y-Brenin
Carnhedryn
Caerfforchell
R. Solva
Wolfscastle Pottery
Wolf's Castle
Amble
St Davids (Tyddewi)
Solva Woollen Mill
Hayscastle Cross
Brimaston
Whitchurch
Llandeloy
Mountain Water
Treffgarne
Spittal
Rhosson
St Non's Chapel
One y-Parc
Solva
Penycwm
Hayscastle
Bignog
Lewston
Wolfsdale
Golden Hill
Green Scar
Newgale
Wood
Roch
Dudwells
Camrose
A40
Pembrokeshire Virtual Rudbaxton
Manor
Scott
Simpson Cross
Keeston
Cuttybridge
Haverfordwest
Rickets Head
Simpson
Pelcomb Cross
Tangiers
Leachpool
Rox
Rail
Nolton Haven
Nolton
Pelcomb Bridge
Crundale
Druidston
Lambston
Town
Prendergast
ST BRIDES BAY
Sutton
Portfield Gate
Albert Town
HAVERFORDWEST (Hwlffordd)
Haroldston West
Broadway
Dreenhill
Merlin's Bridge
Uzmaston
Stack Rocks
Broad Haven
Walton West
Hangstone Davey
B4341
PEMB
Little Haven
Talbenny
Walwyn's Castle
B4327
Boulston
Tower Point
Pope Hill
Freystrop
Hook
Skomer Island
Wooltack Point
St Brides
Hasguard
Robeston West
A4076
Johnston
Llangwm
Grassholm Island
Harold Stone
Midland Isle
Marloes
PEMBROKESHIRE COAST NATIONAL PARK (PARC CENEDLAETHOL ARFORDIR PENFRO)
Thornton
Sardis
Port
The Smalls
Rosemarket
Houghton
BROAD SOUND
Gateholm Island
St Ishmael's
Sandy Haven
Herbrandston
Priory
Steynton
A477
Skokholm Island
Dale
Hubberston
Hakin
B4325
Honeyborough
Dale Point
MILFORD HAVEN (Aberdaugleddau) Haven
Waterston
Burto
Thorn Island
Milford
Llanstadwell Neyland
Pembroke Ferry
St Ann's Head
Angle
Angle Bay
DANGER AREA
Gun Tower
Toll
Pembroke to Rosslare 4hrs.
Pwllcrochan
Rhoscrowther
Pembroke Dock (Doc Penfro)
Pennar
Pembroke to Rosslare 4hrs.
Sheep Island
Wallaston Green
Monkton
Hundleton
Maiden Wells
Freshwater West
B4319
B4320
Castlemartin
St Twynnells
St Petrox
Cheriton or Stackpole
DANGER AREA
Warren
Linney Head
Merrion
Stackpole
DANGER AREA
Elegug Stacks
Bosherston
Crow Rock
Toes
The Wash
DANGER AREA
St Govan's Chapel
St Govan's Coast Head

STRUMBLE HEAD

CEREDIGION
CARMARTHENSHIRE
PEMBROKESHIRE COAST NATIONAL PARK
PARC CENEDLAETHOL ARFORDIR PENFRO
MYNYDD PRESELI
FOREST OF BRECHFA
GOWER
SWANSEA
CARMARTHEN BAY
(BAE CAERFYRDDIN)
New Quay
(Ceinewydd)
Cwmtudu
Ynys-Lochtyn
Llangranog
Penbryn
Aberporth
Cardigan Island
Cemaes Head
Pwllygranant
Cardigan
(Aberteifi)
St Dogmaels
(Llandudoch)
Moylgrove
(Trewyddel)
Trwyn-y-bwa
Pembrokeshire Coast Path
Dinas Cross
Newport
(Trefdraeth)
Nevern
(Nanhyfer)
Eglwyswrw
Boncath
Crymych
Cilgerran
Llechryd
Cenarth
Newcastle Emlyn
(Castell Newydd Emlyn)
Llandyfriog
Henllan
Llandysul
Llanarth
Mydroilyn
Talgarreg
Synod Inn
(Post-Mawr)
Llanwnnen
Lampeter
Llanybydder
Alltwalis
Brechfa
Llanpumsaint
Cynwyl Elfed
Pencader
Abernant
Bronwydd Arms
CARMARTHEN
(Caerfyrddin)
Nantgaredig
Llangunnor
Meidrim
St Clears
Whitland
Narberth
(Arberth)
Llanboidy
Efailwen
Maenclochog
Puncheston
(Cas-Mael)
Henry's Moat
(Castell Hendre)
Clarbeston Road
Llawhaden
Templeton
Kilgetty
Saundersfoot
Tenby
(Dinbych-y-Pysgod)
Penally
Manorbier
Lamphey
Carew
Caldey Island
St Margaret's Island
Old Castle Head
Giltar Point
Caldey Sound
Monkstone Point
Amroth
Pendine
(Pentywyn)
Laugharne
Llansteffan
Ferryside
Kidwelly
(Cydweli)
Pembrey
Burry Port
(Porth Tywyn)
LLANELLI
Trimsaran
Pontyates
Pontyberem
Cwmffrwd
Llanddarog
Cross Hands
Tumble
(Y Tymbl)
Gorslas
PONT ABRAHAM
GORSEINON
Loughor
Gowerton
Three Crosses
Dunvant
Upper Killay
Crofty
Pen-clawdd
Llanmadoc
Whiteford Point
Burry Holms
Rhossili
WORMS HEAD
(Penrhyn-gwyr)
Reynoldston
Port-Eynon
Port-Eynon Point
Oxwich Point
Pwlldu Head
Bishopston
Southgate
Ginst Point
A487
A482
A486
A475
A484
A485
A478
A40
A477
A4075
A4115
A4139
A4066
A48
A476
A4138
A4118
M4
24
16
G
H
J
K
L
M
1
2
3
4
5
6
7
8
10
20
30
40
250
60
80

PEMBROKESHIRE
PEMBROKESHIRE COAST NATIONAL PARK (PARC CENEDLAETHOL ARFORDIR PENFRO)
CARMARTHENSHIRE
FOREST OF BRECHFA
SWANSEA
GOWER
CARMARTHEN BAY (BAE CAERFYRDDIN)
B R I S T O L
Newcastle Emlyn (Castell Newydd Emlyn)
Llandysul
Crymych
Whitland
St Clears
CARMARTHEN (Caerfyrddin)
Llandeilo
Ammanford (Rhydaman)
Kidwelly (Cydweli)
Burry Port
Pembrey
LLANELLI
GORSEINON
Loughor
SWANSEA (Abertawe)
Mumbles (Mwmbwls)
Tenby (Dinbych-y-Pysgod)
Saundersfoot
Laugharne
Pendine (Pentywyn)
Caldey Island
Worms Head (Penrhyn-gwyr)
Port-Eynon Point
Oxwich Point
Pwlldu Head
Mumbles Head
Whiteford Point
Burry Holms
Rhossili Bay
Swansea Bay (Bae Abertawe)
Gilter Point
Caldey Sound
Monkstone Point
Ginst Point
DANGER AREA
A B C D E F
1 2 3 4 5 6 7 8
15
24

G
H
J
K
L
M
25
26
18
Hay-on-Wye
(Y Gelli Gandryll)
Llandovery
(Llanymddyfri)
Brecon
(Aberhonddu)
Crickhowell
(Crughywel)
Talgarth
Glasbury
Bronllys
Llyswen
Sennybridge
Trecastle
Llangadog
Llanwrda
Myddfai
Defynnog
Libanus
Llangorse
BLACK MOUNTAINS
Abergavenny
Gilwern
Govilon
Blaenavon
P O W Y S
PEN Y FAN
2906
BRECON BEACONS
BRECON BEACONS NATIONAL PARK
(PARC CENEDLAETHOL BANNAU BRYCHEINIOG)
BLACK MOUNTAIN
FFOREST FAWR
MERTHYR TYDFIL
(Merthyr Tudful)
TREDEGAR
RHYMNEY
(Rhymni)
EBBW VALE
(Glyn Ebwy)
BLAENAU GWENT
Brynmawr
Nantyglo
Blaina
ABERTILLERY
(Abertyleri)
Abersychan
CWMBRAN
Pontypool
Hirwaun
Penderyn
ABERDARE
(Aberdar)
RHONDDA
CYNON TAFF
MOUNTAIN ASH
(Aberpennar)
Treharris
Bedlinog
Abercynon
PONTYPRIDD
Porth
Tonypandy
Treorchy
(Treorci)
Treherbert
Ferndale
Maerdy
Llantrisant
Talbot Green
Pontyclun
CAERPHILLY
(Caerffili)
Bargoed
Blackwood
(Coed Duon)
Newbridge
(Cefn Bychan)
Risca
Rogerstone
Bedwas
Llanbradach
NEATH
(Castell-Nedd)
PORT TALBOT
Resolven
(Resolfen)
Glyn-neath
Ystradgynlais
Ystalyfera
Pontardawe
Skewen
Briton Ferry
(Llansawel)
Aberavon
(Aberafan)
Baglan
Cwmafan
MAESTEG
Margam
Pyle
Kenfig
Cornelly
PORTHCAWL
Porthcawl Point
Sker Point
Ogmore-by-Sea
Tusker Rock
BRIDGEND
(Pen-y-Bont Ar Ogwr)
Pencoed
Tondu
Sarn
Bettws
Pontycymer
Nantyffyllon
Ogmore Vale
Llanharan
Llanharry
Cowbridge
(Y Bont-Faen)
THE VALE OF GLAMORGAN
Llantwit Major
(Llanilltud Fawr)
St Athan
(Sain Tathan)
St Donat's
(Sain Dunwyd)
Nash Point
Wick
St Brides Major
Llanblethian
Breaksea Point
Rhoose
(Y Rhws)
BARRY
(Barri)
Barry Island
(Ynys y Barri)
Sully
Sully Island
Dinas Powys
Penarth
Lavernock Point
CARDIFF
(Caerdydd)
Radyr
Whitchurch
Llandaff
St Fagans
Tongwynlais
Rumney
St Mellons
Marshfield
Flat Holm
Steep Holm
WESTON-SUPER-MARE
C H A N N E L
A40
A470
A465
A4059
A4061
A4063
A4107
A4109
A4067
A4069
A4221
A4233
A4119
A4222
A4226
A4232
A4050
A4055
A4160
A4054
A4058
A473
A48
A48(M)
A472
A469
A4048
A4046
A4043
A4042
A4077
A479
A438
A4078
A4215
A483
A474
A4068
A4241
A4229
A4106
A4093
A4064
M4
80
90
300
10
20
70
60

BLACK MOUNTAINS
HEREFORDSHIRE
MONMOUTHSHIRE
TORFAEN
ENGLAND
WALES
FOREST OF DEAN
RIVER SEVERN
NEWPORT
SOUTH GLOUCESTERSHIRE
NORTH SOMERSET
BATH AND NORTH EAST SOMERSET
MENDIP HILLS
SOMERSET
BRIDGWATER BAY
MOUTH OF THE SEVERN
Abergavenny
Monmouth
Ross-on-Wye
Newent
Cinderford
Coleford
Lydney
Chepstow
Usk
Pontypool
Cwmbran
Abertillery
Blaenavon
Caerleon
Newport
Cardiff
Caldicot
Thornbury
Yate
Chipping Sodbury
Wotton-under-Edge
Dursley
Bristol
Portishead
Clevedon
Nailsea
Weston-super-Mare
Keynsham
Bath
Midsomer Norton
Radstock
Cheddar
Burnham-on-Sea
Wells
Frome
Severn Bridge
Second Severn Crossing
Severn Tunnel
Avonmouth
Flat Holm
Steep Holm
PAGE 107
PAGE 106
PAGE 113
M4
M5
M32
M48
M49
M50
A40
A48
A38
A4
A449
A466
A465
A37
A36
A368
A370
A371

19
Tewkesbury
Cheltenham
Gloucester
Bishop's Cleeve
Winchcombe
Stow-on-the-Wold
Chipping Norton
Bourton-on-the-Water
Charlton Kings
Northleach
Burford
Witney
Carterton
Charlbury
Stroud
Cirencester
Nailsworth
Tetbury
Malmesbury
Cricklade
Fairford
Lechlade on Thames
Faringdon
Highworth
Swindon
Stratton St Margaret
Royal Wootton Bassett
Wroughton
Chippenham
Calne
Corsham
Melksham
Devizes
Marlborough
Hungerford
Pewsey
Trowbridge
Westbury
Bradford-on-Avon
Ludgershall
Tidworth
Lambourn
Shrivenham
Stanford in the Vale
OXFORDSHIRE
WILTSHIRE
GLOUCESTERSHIRE
M4
M5
A419
A417
A429
A361
A338
A346
A4
A40
A420
A350
A342
G H J K L M
1 2 3 4 5 6 7 8

OXFORDSHIRE
BUCKINGHAMSHIRE
WEST BERKSHIRE
HAMPSHIRE
CHILTERN HILLS
VALE OF WHITE HORSE
VALE OF AYLESBURY
OXFORD
PAGE 114
READING
PAGE 115
AYLESBURY
HIGH WYCOMBE
MAIDENHEAD
BRACKNELL
WOKINGHAM
BASINGSTOKE
NEWBURY
CAMBERLEY
FARNBOROUGH
ALDERSHOT
FLEET
HENLEY-ON-THAMES
ABINGDON-ON-THAMES
WITNEY
Bicester
Banbury
Chipping Norton
Woodstock
Kidlington
Thame
Wantage
Didcot
Wallingford
Hungerford
Marlow
Princes Risborough
Chinnor
Watlington
Wheatley
Eynsham
Charlbury
Goring
Pangbourne
Thatcham
Kingsclere
Tadley
Hook
Odiham
Sandhurst
Yateley
Twyford
Wendover
Stokenchurch
Haddenham
Long Crendon
Brill
Grendon Underwood
Waddesdon
Winslow
Steeple Claydon
Faringdon
Lambourn
Kintbury
Burghclere
Highclere
Whitchurch
Overton
Oakley
Old Basing
Hartley Wintney
Crowthorne
Burghfield Common
Theale
Sonning Common
Shiplake
Caversham
Woodley
Benson
Dorchester on Thames
Stadhampton
Chalgrove
Sutton Courtenay
Drayton
Steventon
Harwell
Blewbury
Chilton
Cholsey
Streatley
Compton
Chieveley
Hermitage
Stanford Dingley
Bradfield
Mortimer
Silchester
Aldermaston
Woolhampton
Beenham
M40
M4
M3
A34
A40
A41
A44
A413
A418
A420
A4074
A4130
A329
A338
A339
A340
A343
A4
A33
A30
A327
A321
A404
A4155
A4010
A4129
A4260
A4095
A415
A417
A4185
A3095
A4421
28
19
A
B
C
D
E
F
1
2
3
4
5
6
7
8

21
22
HERTFORDSHIRE
NORTH DOWNS
LONDON
PAGE 112-113
LUTON
DUNSTABLE
HITCHIN
STEVENAGE
BISHOP'S STORTFORD
HARPENDEN
WELWYN GARDEN CITY
HERTFORD
WARE
HARLOW
TRING
BERKHAMSTED
HEMEL HEMPSTEAD
ST ALBANS
HATFIELD
HODDESDON
CHESHAM
AMERSHAM
WATFORD
BOREHAMWOOD
POTTERS BAR
CHESHUNT
ENFIELD
EPPING
BEACONSFIELD
CHORLEYWOOD
RICKMANSWORTH
BARNET
LOUGHTON
CHIGWELL
NORTHWOOD
STANMORE
EDGWARE
SOUTHGATE
EDMONTON
CHINGFORD
PINNER
HARROW
HENDON
TOTTENHAM
WOODFORD
WALTHAMSTOW
RUISLIP
UXBRIDGE
WEMBLEY
HAMPSTEAD
ISLINGTON
HACKNEY
LEYTON
ILFORD
SLOUGH
NORTHOLT
GREENFORD
EALING
ACTON
KENSINGTON
WESTMINSTER
CITY
STRATFORD
BARKING
DAGENHAM
WINDSOR
HAYES
SOUTHALL
BRENTFORD
HAMMERSMITH
CHELSEA
LAMBETH
BERMONDSEY
GREENWICH
WOOLWICH
HOUNSLOW
ISLEWORTH
RICHMOND
PUTNEY
WANDSWORTH
BATTERSEA
CLAPHAM
BRIXTON
LEWISHAM
ELTHAM
BEXLEY
EGHAM
STAINES-UPON-THAMES
FELTHAM
TWICKENHAM
ASHFORD
TEDDINGTON
WIMBLEDON
STREATHAM
CATFORD
SIDCUP
CHISLEHURST
BROMLEY
SUNBURY
KINGSTON UPON THAMES
MERTON
MITCHAM
BECKENHAM
CHERTSEY
WEYBRIDGE
WALTON-ON-THAMES
NEW MALDEN
MORDEN
SURBITON
CROYDON
ORPINGTON
ESHER
CARSHALTON
SUTTON
WALLINGTON
EWELL
EPSOM
PURLEY
WOKING
COBHAM
LEATHERHEAD
BANSTEAD
COULSDON
WARLINGHAM
CATERHAM
GUILDFORD
DORKING
REIGATE
REDHILL
OXTED
WESTERHAM
PAGE 109
PAGE 117
MAIN ROUTE 95
MAIN ROUTE 96
MAIN ROUTE 99
MAIN ROUTE 100
M1
M4
M11
M25
M40
A1(M)
M3
M23

BISHOP'S STORTFORD
Stansted Mountfitchet
Great Dunmow
BRAINTREE
Halstead
Coggeshall
Witham
Kelvedon
Tiptree
HARLOW
Sawbridgeworth
CHELMSFORD
MALDON
Danbury
Great Baddow
EPPING
Chipping Ongar
LOUGHTON
Theydon Bois
BRENTWOOD
BILLERICAY
Ingatestone
Wickford
South Woodham Ferrers
Burnham-on-Crouch
Hockley
RAYLEIGH
Rochford
Southminster
BASILDON
Laindon
Thundersley
Hadleigh
SOUTHEND-ON-SEA
Shoeburyness
SHOEBURY NESS
CANVEY ISLAND
Corringham
Stanford-le-Hope
ROMFORD
UPMINSTER
HORNCHURCH
DAGENHAM
ILFORD
BARKING
WANSTEAD
EAST HAM
Rainham
THURROCK
GRAYS
TILBURY
Chadwell St Mary
WOOLWICH
ERITH
Bexleyheath
DARTFORD
GRAVESEND
Northfleet
Swanscombe
ELTHAM
SIDCUP
CHISLEHURST
BROMLEY
ORPINGTON
Swanley
Farnborough
Biggin Hill
Westerham
SEVENOAKS
Otford
Kemsing
West Kingsdown
Wrotham
STROOD
ROCHESTER
CHATHAM
GILLINGHAM
Rainham
Walderslade
SHEERNESS
Minster
Queenborough
ISLE OF SHEPPEY
SITTINGBOURNE
MAIDSTONE
Aylesford
Snodland
West Malling
Hollingbourne
Harrietsham
Lenham
Charing
Hildenborough
Isle of Grain
Thamesport
River Thames
Osea Island
Northey Island
Wallasea Island
Potton Island
Elmley Island
NORTH DOWNS

Harwich to:
Hook of Holland 6hrs. 15mins.
Mistley
Manningtree
Parkeston
Harwich
Harwich Harbour
Dovercourt
Upper Dovercourt
Landguard Fort
Martello Tower
Langham
Lawford
Bradfield
Wrabness
Ramsey
Little Bromley
Bradfield Heath
Mistley Heath
Horsleycross Street
Horsley Cross
Great Oakley
Little Oakley
Wix
Stones Green
Ardleigh
Burnt Heath
Great Bromley
Tendring Green
Beaumont
Hamford Water
Horsey Island
The Naze
Kirby-le-Soken
Walton-on-the-Naze
Kirby Cross
Frinton-on-Sea
Great Holland
Holland Haven
Holland-on-Sea
COLCHESTER
Elmstead
Elmstead Market
Elmstead Heath
Little Bentley
Hare Green
Frating Green
Great Bentley
Tendring
Weeley
Thorpe Green
Thorpe-le-Soken
Weeley Heath
Aingers Green
Thorrington
Wivenhoe
Alresford
Rowhedge
Fingringhoe
Blackheath
Abberton
Langenhoe
South Green
South Heath
Row Heath
Little Clacton
St Osyth Heath
Great Clacton
Brightlingsea
St Osyth
Point Clear
Jaywick
Seawick
CLACTON-ON-SEA
MERSEA ISLAND
Blue Row
East Mersea
West Mersea
Colne Point
Virley Channel
Sales Point
St Peter's Chapel
Bradwell-on-Sea
NORTH SEA
Holliwell Point
Foulness Sands
Foulness Point
Courtsend
Churchend
Maplin Sands
Warden Point
Warden
Leysdown-on-Sea
SHEPPEY
Isle of Harty
Shell Ness
Whitstable Bay
WHITSTABLE
Tankerton
Swalecliffe
Herne Bay
HERNE BAY
Hampton
Eddington
Beltinge
Reculver
Reculver Towers
Hillborough
Regulbium Roman Fort
Minnis Bay
Birchington
South Channel
Turner Contemporary
Lifeboat Station
Walpole Bay Hotel
Foreness Point
Westgate on Sea
MARGATE
Westbrook
Cliftonville
Kingsgate
ISLE OF THANET
Westwood
Lydden
Northwood
St Peter's
NORTH FORELAND
BROADSTAIRS
Dickens House
RAMSGATE
Maritime
Manston
Spitfire & Hurricane
Acol
Minster
Monkton
St Nicholas at Wade
Sarre
Marshside
Greenhill
Hunters Forstal
Broomfield
Herne
West End
Herne Common
Maypole
Boyden Gate
Chislet
Hoath
Upstreet
Seasalter
South Street
Radfall
Calcott
Hersden
West Stourmouth
Plucks Gutter
East Stourmouth
Westmarsh
Cliffsend
Pegwell Bay
Richborough Port
Richborough Fort
Oare
FAVERSHAM
Graveney
Goodnestone
Yorkletts
Dargate
Denstroude
Honey Hill
Broad Oak
Tyler Hill
Blean
Sturry
Westbere
Fordwich
Stodmarsh
Grove
Preston
Elmstone
Paramour Street
Ware
Cooper Street
Goldstone
Hoaden
Nash
Great Stonar
Sandwich Bay
Sandwich
Hernhill
Mount Ephraim
Boughton under Blean
Dunkirk
Rough Common
CANTERBURY
PAGE 107
Wickhambreaux
Wingham
Ickham
Ash
Marshborough
Hogben's Hill
South Street
Selling
Oversland
Chartham Hatch
Harbledown
Littlebourne
Howletts
Staple
Woodnesborough
Bramling
Sheldwich
Sheldwich Lees
Perrywood
Old Wives Lees
Thanington Without
Bekesbourne
Patrixbourne
Bridge
Adisham
Goodnestone
Chillenden
Hammill
Eastry
Worth
The Small Downs
Sandown Castle
Badlesmere
Leaveland
Shottenden
Chilham
Chartham
Shalmsford Street
Bagham
Street End
Nackington
Bishopsbourne
Knowlton
Heronden
Ham
Finglesham
Betteshanger
Sholden
Timeball Tower
DEAL
The Downs
Molash
Mountain Street
Garlinge Green
Petham
Lower Hardres
Pett Bottom
Kingston
Aylesham
Nonington
Tilmanstone
Northbourne
Great Mongeham
Lifeboat Station
Walmer
Challock
Godmersham
Upper Hardres Court
Barham
Womenswold
Frogham
Elvington
Barfrestone
East Studdal
Ripple
Sole Street
Bilting
Crundale
Waltham
Derringstone
Woolage Village
Woolage Green
Eythorne
Ashley
Sutton
West Langdon
Ringwould
Kingsdown
Boughton Aluph
Wye
Hassell
North Leigh
Stelling Minnis
Denton
Shepherdswell or Sibertswold
Martin
DANGER

Bardsey Island (Ynys Enlli)
Trwyn Cilan
CARDIGAN BAY
(BAE CEREDIGION)
Barmouth (Abermaw)
Barmouth Bay (Bae Bermo)
The Bar
Fairbourne Steam Railway
Fairbourne
Friog
Llanaber
Cutiau
Caerdeon
Bontddu
Arthog
CADAIR
GWYNE
Llwyngwril
Llanfihangel-y-pennant
Castell y Bere
Abergynolwyn
Llangelynin
Rhoslefain
Peniarth
Llanegryn
Dolgoch
Talyllyn Railway
Llanfendigaid
Tonfanau
Bryncrug
Pandy
Rhyd-yr-onen
Aber Dysynni
Broad Water
Tywyn
Narrow Gauge Railway
Trum Gelli
Corlan-fraith
Penhelig
Aberdovey (Aberdyfi)
Snowdonia National Park
Glandyfi
Eglwys Fach
Dyfi Furnace
Ynyslas
Llancynfelyn
Tre'r-ddol
Tre Taliesin
Borth
Upper Borth
Animal Kingdom
Tal-y-bont
Dol-y-Bont
Rhyd-meirionydd
Llandre
Bow Street
Pen-y-garn
Bontgoch
Llangorwen
Camera Obscura
Cliff Railway
National Library
Penrhyn-coch
Cefn Llwyd
Penbont Rhydybeddau
Cwmsymlog
Salem
Garth
ABERYSTWYTH
Waun Fawr
Comins Coch
Capel Dewi
Blaen-geuffordd
Dollwen
Llanbadarn Fawr
Penparcau
Southgate
Capel Bangor
Aberffrwd
Vale of Rheidol
Moriah
Capel Seion
Rhydyfelin
Llanfarian
Gors
Chancery
New Cross
Llanfihangel-y-Creuddyn
Blaenplwyf
Llanilar
Cnwch Coch
Rhos-y-garth
Crosswood (Trawsgoed)
Llanafan
Wenallt
Llanddeiniol
Carreg Ti-pw
Llangwyryfon
Lledrod
Tynygraig
Llanrhystud
Trefenter
Rhyd-Rosser
Rhydfudr
Bronnant
Llansantffraed
Llan-non
Swyddffynnon
MYNYDD BACH
Bontnewydd
Rhos Haminiog
Nebo
Aberarth
Bethania
Blaenpennal
Aberaeron
Pennant
Cross Inn
Penuwch
Cors Caron
Ty'n-yr-eithin
Monachty
Ffos-y-ffin
Llanerchaeron
Cilcennin
Llangeitho
Tregaron
New Quay (Ceinewydd)
Marine Wildlife Centre
Llwyncelyn
Ciliau Aeron
Newbridge
Bwlch-Llan
Capel Betws Lleucu
Maen-y-groes
Gilfachreda
Llanarth
Oakford (Derwen Gam)
Trefilan
Cwmtudu
Cross Inn
Nanternis
Caerwedros
Pen-cae
Geneva
Ystrad Aeron
Abermeurig
Gartheli
Talsarn
Llundain-fach
Llwyn-y-groes
Olmarch
Llanddewi Brefi
Ynys-Lochtyn
Blaen Celyn
Llwyndafydd
Synod Inn (Post-Mawr)
Dihewyd
Felinfach
Mydroilyn
Llangranog
Morfa
Pontgarreg
Ffynnon-oer
Bettws Bledrws
Llangybi
Cardigan Island
Penbryn
Plwmp
Pentregat
Talgarreg
Gorsgoch
Cribyn
Silian
Llanfair Clydogau
Cemaes Head
Gwbert
Cardigan Island Coastal Farm Park
Parcllyn
Aberporth
Tresaith
Brynhoffnant
Sarnau
Felinwynt
Capel Cynon
Maestir
Cellan
Allt-y-goed
Y Ferwig
Blaenannerch
Tan-y-groes
Bwlch-y-fadfa
Lampeter (Llanbedr Pont Steffan)
Pentrefelin
Cippyn
Cardigan (Aberteifi)
Penparc
Tremain
Blaenporth
Glynarthen
Aber
Cwrtnewydd
Cwmann
St Dogmaels (Llandudoch)
Noyadd Trefawr
Bettws Ifan
Brithdir
Rhydlewis
Ffostrasol
Pont-Sian
Cwmsychpant
Llanwnnen
Pentre-bach
Moylgrove (Trewyddel)
Pantgwyn
Beulah
Hawen
Drefach
Alltyblacca
Llangoedmor
Ponthirwaun
Troedyraur
Penrhiw-pal
Maes Llyn
Rhydowen
Llanwenog
Pencarreg
Ffaldybrenin
Farmers
Monington
Pen-y-bryn
Llechryd
Llandygwydd
Brongest
Coed-y-bryn
Croes-lan
Tre-groes
Llanybydder
Glan Duar
Cwrt-y-Cadno
Glanrhyd
Bridell
Cwm Plysgog
Cilgerran
Cwncau
National Coracle Centre
Brongwyn
Cenarth
Horeb
Pren-gwyn
Capel Dewi
Rhuddlan
Llantood
Cwm-cou
Llandyfriog
Penrhiw-llan
Maesycrugiau
Aber-Giâr
Rhos-hill
Newchapel (Capel Newydd)
Abercych
Penrhiw
Adpar
Newcastle Emlyn (Castell Newydd Emlyn)
Llandysul
Pontweli
Llanfihangel-ar-Arth
Llanllwni
Pumsaint
Five Saints
Dolaucothi Gold Mines
Felindre Farchog
Eglwyswrw
Llanfair-Nant-Gwyn
Boncath
Cilwendeg Shell House
Penrherber
Llangeler
Drefach
National Wool Museum
Felindre
Pentre-cwrt
Rhydcymerau
Crugybar

Dolgellau
Llanelltyd
Llanfachreth
Brithdir
Cross Foxes
Dinas Mawddwy
Mallwyd
Llanymawddwy
Pennant
Llanwddyn
Lake Vyrnwy
Abertridwr
Llanfyllin
Llanfechain
Llansantffraid-ym-Mechain
Llanymynech
Llandysilio
Four Crosses
Llandrinio
Meifod
Guilsfield
Welshpool
Llangadfan
Llanerfyl
Llanfair Caereinion
Castle Caereinion
Heniarth
Berriew
Montgomery
Chirbury
Church Stoke
Newtown
Kerry
Llanbrynmair
Carno
Caersws
Llanidloes
Llangurig
Machynlleth
Penegoes
Corris
Aberangell
Cemmaes
Cemmaes Road
Staylittle
Trefeglwys
Llandinam
Ponterwyd
Devil's Bridge
Pont-rhyd-y-groes
Pontrhydfendigaid
Rhayader
Llansantffraed Cwmdeuddwr
Elan Valley
St Harmon
Nantmel
Llanbadarn Fynydd
Llanbister
Llanddewi Ystradenni
Crossgates
Llandrindod Wells
Penybont
Llandegley
Newbridge on Wye
Builth Wells
Llanwrtyd Wells
Garth
Beulah
Abergwesyn
Rhandirmwyn
Cilycwm
Cynghordy
Erwood
Gwenddwr
Crickadarn
Aberedw
Llandeilo Graban
Painscastle
Clyro
Hay-on-Wye
Clifford
Glasbury
Llyswen
Knighton
Knucklas
Beguildy
Felindre
Newcastle
Llanfair Waterdine
Bleddfa
Kinnerton
New Radnor
Old Radnor
Gladestry
Kington
Presteigne
Newchurch
Llanfihangel-Nant-Melan
Llansantffraed-in-Elwel
PLYNLIMON (PUMLUMON FAWR)
CAMBRIAN MOUNTAINS
POWYS
MYNYDD EPYNT
RADNOR FOREST
WALES
ENGLAND
DYFI FOREST
Clun Forest
A470
A458
A495
A490
A483
A489
A44
A4081
A481
A488
A438
A4079
G
H
J
K
L
M
33
17
34
26

26
A
B
C
D
E
F
1
2
3
4
5
6
7
8
PAGE 116
34
25
17
18
SHREWSBURY
TELFORD
Wellington
Hadley
Oakengates
Shifnal
Ironbridge
Madeley
Much Wenlock
Bridgnorth
Church Stretton
Bishop's Castle
Montgomery
Chirbury
Minsterley
Pontesbury
Clun
Knighton
Craven Arms
Ludlow
Cleobury Mortimer
Bewdley
Tenbury Wells
Leominster
Presteigne
Kington
Bromyard
Hereford
Ledbury
Hay-on-Wye
Malvern Wells
SHROPSHIRE
HEREFORDSHIRE
WALES
ENGLAND
THE LONG MYND
WYRE FOREST
MALVERN
BLACK
M54
M50
A5
A49
A488
A489
A490
A4113
A4117
A456
A44
A465
A438
A480
A417
A4103

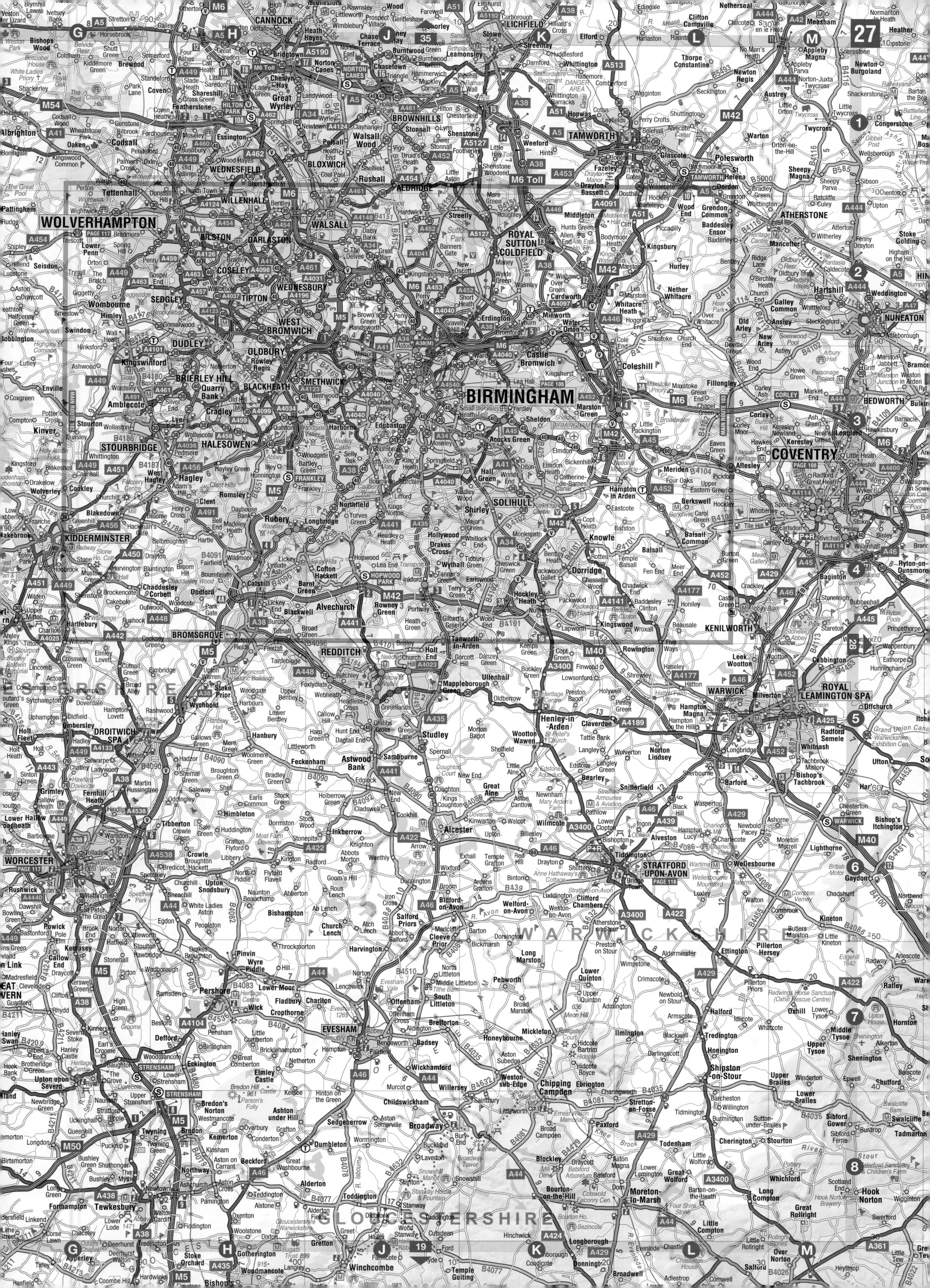
WOLVERHAMPTON
BIRMINGHAM
COVENTRY
WORCESTER
STRATFORD -UPON-AVON
ROYAL LEAMINGTON SPA
WARWICK
KENILWORTH
NUNEATON
BEDWORTH
ATHERSTONE
TAMWORTH
LICHFIELD
CANNOCK
WALSALL
WEST BROMWICH
DUDLEY
STOURBRIDGE
HALESOWEN
KIDDERMINSTER
BROMSGROVE
REDDITCH
DROITWICH SPA
EVESHAM
TEWKESBURY
SOLIHULL
ROYAL SUTTON COLDFIELD
WEDNESFIELD
WILLENHALL
DARLASTON
BILSTON
COSELEY
SEDGLEY
TIPTON
WEDNESBURY
OLDBURY
SMETHWICK
BRIERLEY HILL
BLACKHEATH
BROWNHILLS
ALDRIDGE
BLOXWICH
Alcester
Henley-in-Arden
Shipston-on-Stour
Chipping Campden
Moreton-in-Marsh
Pershore
Broadway
Studley
Coleshill
WARWICKSHIRE
GLOUCESTERSHIRE
WORCESTERSHIRE
PAGE 117
PAGE 106
PAGE 108
PAGE 116
35
28
19
M5
M6
M6 Toll
M40
M42
M50
M54
A5
A38
A46
A44
A45
A435
A3400
A429
A422

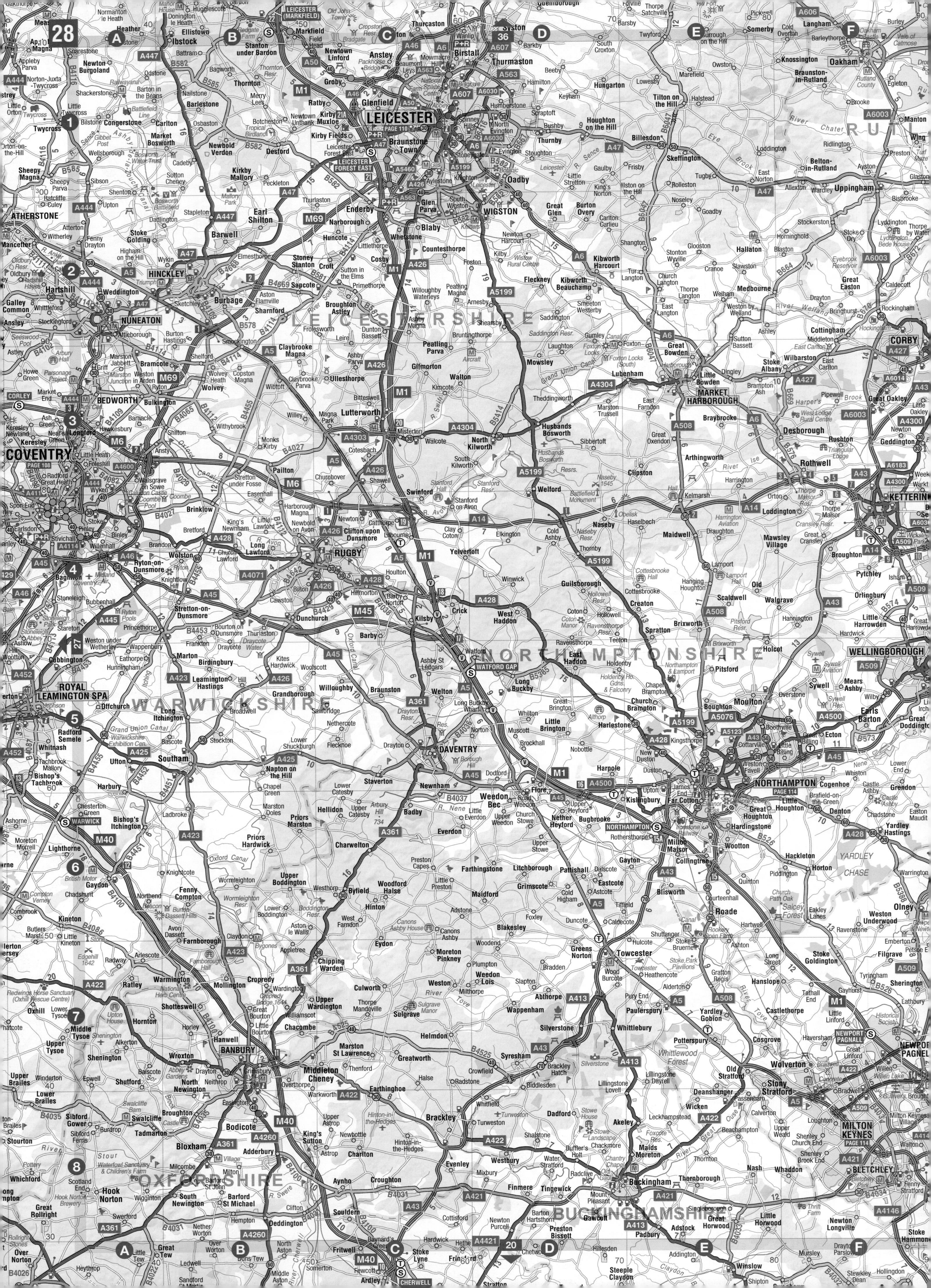
28
36
27
20
A
B
C
D
E
F
1
2
3
4
5
6
7
8
LEICESTER
LEICESTERSHIRE
NORTHAMPTONSHIRE
WARWICKSHIRE
OXFORDSHIRE
BUCKINGHAMSHIRE
COVENTRY
NUNEATON
HINCKLEY
RUGBY
DAVENTRY
NORTHAMPTON
BANBURY
MILTON KEYNES
BLETCHLEY
KETTERING
WELLINGBOROUGH
CORBY
MARKET HARBOROUGH
ROYAL LEAMINGTON SPA
WARWICK
WIGSTON
ATHERSTONE
Oakham
Uppingham
Lutterworth
Towcester
Brackley
Buckingham
Bedworth
WATFORD GAP
M1
M6
M40
M45
M69

29
G
H
J
K
L
M
1
2
3
4
5
6
7
8
30
STAMFORD
PETERBOROUGH
PAGE 115
WISBECH
March
Chatteris
Ramsey
Whittlesey
Oundle
Thrapston
Raunds
Rushden
Higham Ferrers
Irthlingborough
Finedon
HUNTINGDON
St Ives
Godmanchester
St Neots
BEDFORD
Kempston
Sandy
Biggleswade
Ampthill
Flitwick
Shefford
Stotfold
LETCHWORTH GARDEN CITY
BALDOCK
HITCHIN
Royston
CAMBRIDGE
PAGE 107
Cottenham
Histon
Sawston
Melbourn
Great Shelford
Potton
Gamlingay
Toddington
Harlington
Barton-le-Clay
Woburn Sands
Crowland
Thorney
Yaxley
Sawtry
Somersham
Buntingford
CAMBRIDGESHIRE
BEDFORD
CENTRAL BEDFORDSHIRE
HERTFORDSHIRE
BEDFORD (NORTH LEVEL)
BEDFORD (MIDDLE LEVEL)
ROCKINGHAM
FOREST
A1
A1(M)
A14
A47
A6
A428
A603
A505
A507
A10
A1198
A141
A142
A605
A15
A16
M1
M11
37
21
Scheme due to open late 2020

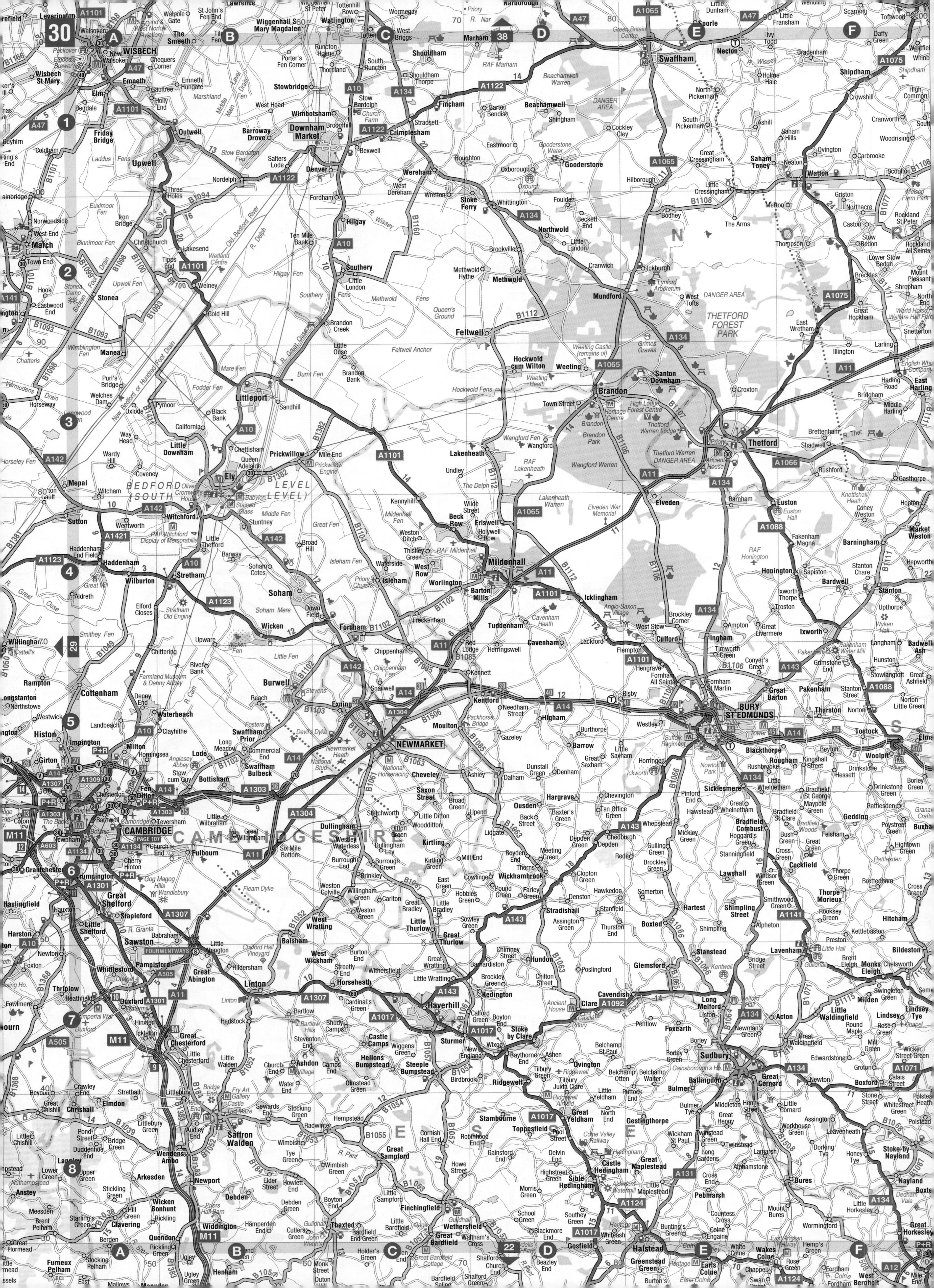
30
A
B
C
D
E
F
38
29
22
WISBECH
Swaffham
Downham Market
Upwell
March
Littleport
Ely
Brandon
Thetford
Mildenhall
Newmarket
BURY ST EDMUNDS
CAMBRIDGE
PAGE 107
CAMBRIDGESHIRE
NORFOLK
THETFORD FOREST PARK
BEDFORD LEVEL (SOUTH LEVEL)
Haverhill
Saffron Walden
Sudbury
Halstead
Great Shelford
Sawston
Linton
Soham
Burwell
Stradishall
Lavenham
Long Melford
Clare
Watton
Mundford
Methwold
Feltwell
Lakenheath
Elveden
Ixworth
Woolpit
Stowmarket
Chatteris
Cottenham
Histon
Thaxted
Finchingfield
Great Bardfield
Castle Hedingham
Sible Hedingham
A10
A11
A14
A47
A134
A142
A143
A1065
A1101
A1122
A1307
M11

NORWICH
PAGE 114
GREAT YARMOUTH
THE BROADS
LOWESTOFT
IPSWICH
PAGE 110
FELIXSTOWE
WOODBRIDGE
Harwich
Harwich to:
Hook of Holland 6hrs. 15mins.
NORTH SEA
Orford Ness
Hollesley Bay
Aldeburgh Bay
Southwold
Aldeburgh
Beccles
Bungay
Halesworth
Saxmundham
Leiston
Framlingham
Stowmarket
Diss
Eye
Attleborough
Wymondham
Hadleigh
Dereham
Caister-on-Sea
Gorleston-on-Sea
Kessingland
Dunwich
Thorpeness
Wickham Market
Needham Market
Manningtree
Mistley
Dedham
Debenham
Harleston
Loddon
Acle
G
H
J
K
L
M
39
23
1
2
3
4
5
6
7
8

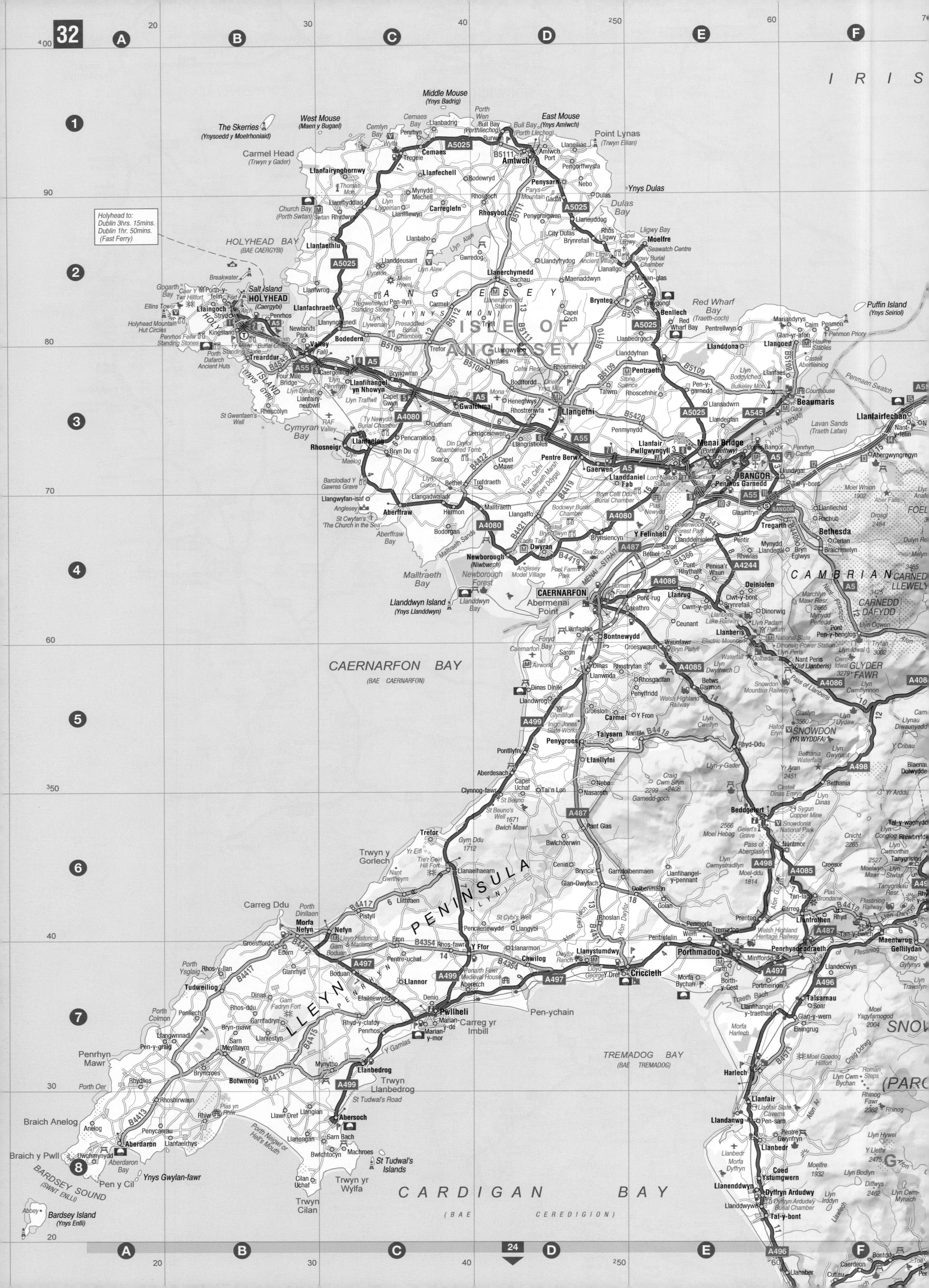
IRISH SEA
Middle Mouse (Ynys Badrig)
West Mouse (Maen y Bugael)
The Skerries (Ynysoedd y Moelrhoniaid)
East Mouse (Ynys Amlwch)
Point Lynas (Trwyn Eilian)
Carmel Head (Trwyn y Gader)
Cemaes
Amlwch
Llanfairynghornwy
Llanfechell
Penysarn
Ynys Dulas
Dulas Bay
Carreglefn
Rhosybol
Church Bay (Porth Swtan)
Holyhead to: Dublin 3hrs. 15mins. Dublin 1hr. 50mins. (Fast Ferry)
HOLYHEAD BAY (BAE CAERGYBI)
Llanfaethlu
Moelfre
Lligwy Bay
Llanerchymedd
Salt Island
HOLYHEAD (Caergybi)
Llanfachraeth
ANGLESEY (YNYS MÔN)
ISLE OF ANGLESEY
Brynteg
Benllech
Red Wharf Bay (Traeth-coch)
Puffin Island (Ynys Seiriol)
Bodedern
Valley
Trearddur
Llanfihangel yn Nhowyn
Pentraeth
Beaumaris
Gwalchmai
Llangefni
Rhosneigr
Cymyran Bay
Aberffraw
Menai Bridge (Porthaethwy)
BANGOR
Llanfairfechan
Llanfair Pwllgwyngyll
Gaerwen
Pentre Berw
Malltraeth Bay
Newborough (Niwbwrch)
Llanddwyn Island (Ynys Llanddwyn)
Y Felinheli
CAERNARFON
Bethesda
Tregarth
Deiniolen
Llanrug
Llanberis
CAMBRIAN
CARNEDD DAFYDD
GLYDER FAWR
SNOWDON (YR WYDDFA)
CAERNARFON BAY (BAE CAERNARFON)
Bontnewydd
Dinas Dinlle
Penygroes
Llanllyfni
Beddgelert
Clynnog-fawr
Trefor
Trwyn y Gorlech
Carreg Ddu
Morfa Nefyn
Nefyn
PENINSULA
LLEYN
Tudweiliog
Y Ffor
Llanystumdwy
Chwilog
Criccieth
Porthmadog
Penrhyndeudraeth
Pwllheli
Carreg yr Imbill
Pen-ychain
TREMADOG BAY (BAE TREMADOG)
Harlech
Llanbedrog
Trwyn Llanbedrog
Abersoch
Botwnnog
Penrhyn Mawr
Braich Anelog
Aberdaron
Braich y Pwll
BARDSEY SOUND (SWNT ENLLI)
Pen y Cil
Ynys Gwylan-fawr
Bardsey Island (Ynys Enlli)
St Tudwal's Islands
Trwyn yr Wylfa
Trwyn Cilan
CARDIGAN BAY (BAE CEREDIGION)
Llanbedr
Dyffryn Ardudwy
Tal-y-bont
A B C D E F
1 2 3 4 5 6 7 8

24

SEA
LIVERPOOL BAY
Liverpool to Dublin 8hrs.
Liverpool to Douglas 2hrs. 30mins. (Fast Ferry, Seasonal)
Birkenhead to: Belfast 8hrs. Douglas 4hrs. 15mins. (Seasonal)
Great Ormes Head (Pen-y-Gogarth)
Little Ormes Head
LLANDUDNO
CONWY BAY
Colwyn Bay
Abergele Roads
COLWYN BAY (Bae Colwyn)
Rhôs-on-Sea (Llandrillo-yn-Rhos)
Penrhyn Bay (Bae Penrhyn)
Deganwy
Llandudno Junction
Conwy
Penmaenmawr
Old Colwyn
Llanddulas
Abergele
RHYL
Kinmel Bay (Bae Cinmel)
Prestatyn
Point of Ayr
Talacre
Rhuddlan
Bodelwyddan
St Asaph (Llan-Elwy)
Dyserth
Meliden (Gallt Melyd)
Holywell (Treffynnon)
Flint (Y Fflint)
Bagillt
Greenfield (Maes-glas)
Mostyn
Whitford (Chwitffordd)
Caerwys
Trefnant
Bodfari
Denbigh (Dinbych)
Henllan
Llannefydd
Llanfair Talhaiarn
Llansannan
Llangernyw
Bylchau
Nantglyn
Llanrhaeadr
Ruthin (Rhuthun)
Mold (Yr Wyddgrug)
BUCKLEY
CONNAH'S QUAY
Northop
Rhydymwyn
Cilcain
Gwernaffield
Gwernymynydd
Llanarmon-yn-Ial
Llandegla
Bwlchgwyn
Brymbo
Coedpoeth
Minera
Rhosllanerchrugog
Penycae
Acrefair
Cefn-mawr
Llangollen
Froncysyllte
Chirk
Glyn Ceiriog
Pontfadog
Weston Rhyn
Selattyn
Llansilin
Llanarmon Dyffryn Ceiriog
Llanrhaeadr-ym-Mochnant
Llangedwyn
Llanyblodwel
Llanymynech
Llansantffraid-ym-Mechain
Llanfechain
Llanfyllin
Llanwddyn
Lake Vyrnwy
Llangynog
Penybontfawr
Llandrillo
Corwen
Cynwyd
Carrog
Gwyddelwern
Bryneglwys
Derwen
Clocaenog
CLOCAENOG FOREST
Efenechtyd
Cyffylliog
Llanelidan
Pentrefoelas
Cerrigydrudion
Betws-y-Coed
Llanrwst
Trefriw
Dolgarrog
Llanddoged
Eglwysbach
Tal-y-Bont
Dolwyddelan
Blaenau Ffestiniog
Llan Ffestiniog
Trawsfynydd
Bala (Y Bala)
Llanuwchllyn
Llanycil
Llandderfel
Frongoch
Glan-yr-afon
Betws Gwerfil Goch
Llanfihangel Glyn Myfyr
Dolgellau
Llanelltyd
Llanfachreth
Dinas Mawddwy
Llanymawddwy
HOYLAKE
West Kirby
HESWALL
NESTON
Parkgate
WALLASEY
Hilbre Islands
RIVER DEE
ENGLAND
WALES
C O N W Y
FLINTSHIRE
DENBIGHSHIRE
G W Y N E D D
P O W Y S
ONIA NATIONAL PARK
CENEDLAETHOL ERYRI
CAMBRIAN MOUNTAINS
B E R W Y N
GWYDYR FOREST PARK
COED Y BRENIN FOREST PARK
Penllyn Forest
Cynwyd Forest
Llyn Brenig
Llyn Celyn
Bala Lake (Llyn Tegid)
Llyn Alwen
A55
A548
A547
A525
A541
A543
A544
A470
A5
A494
A4212
A5104
A542
A539
A483
A495
A490
M53

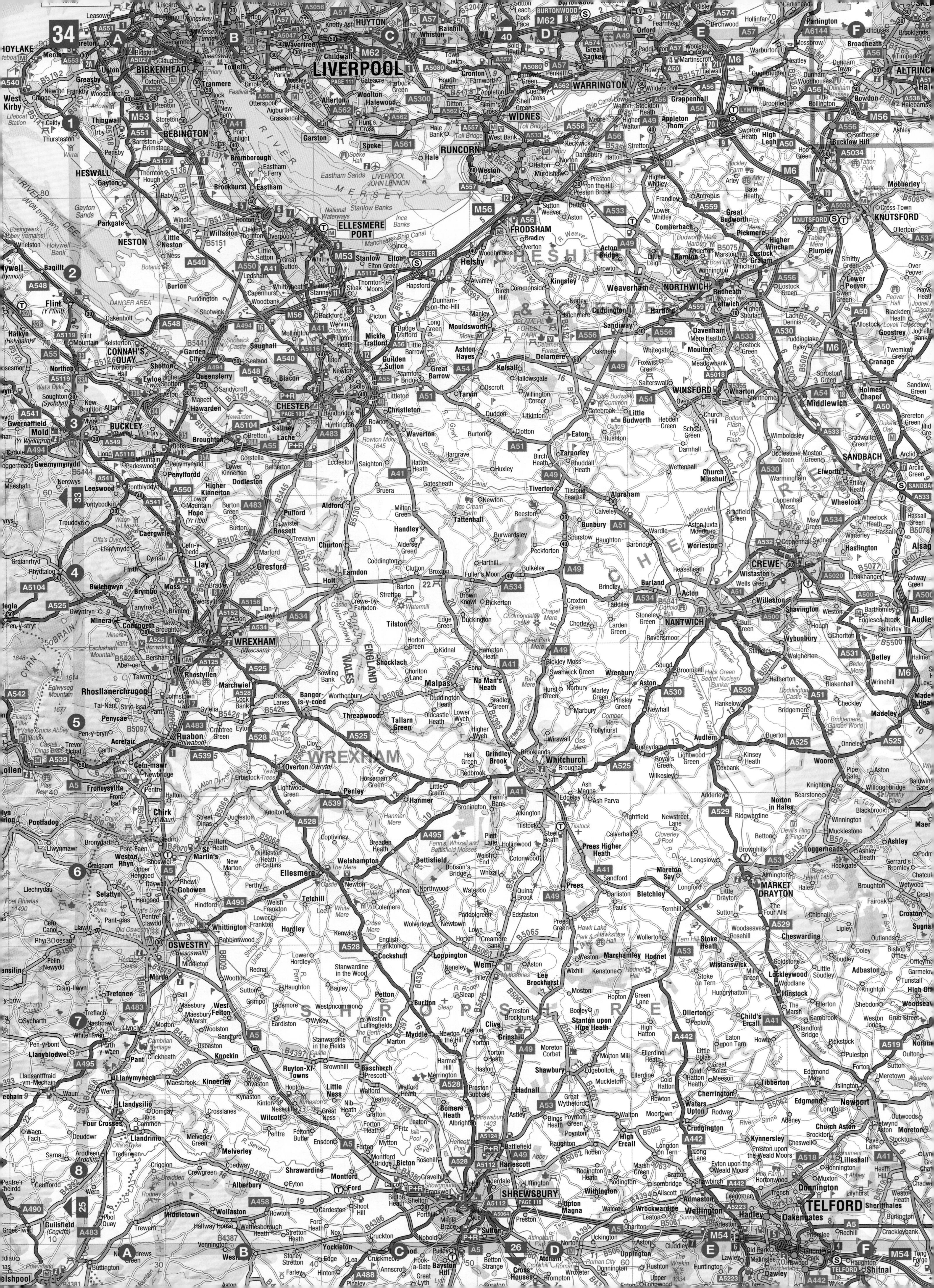
LIVERPOOL
BIRKENHEAD
HUYTON
WARRINGTON
WIDNES
RUNCORN
ELLESMERE PORT
FRODSHAM
NORTHWICH
KNUTSFORD
ALTRINCHAM
CHESTER
CONNAH'S QUAY
BUCKLEY
Mold
Flint
WINSFORD
Middlewich
SANDBACH
CREWE
NANTWICH
WREXHAM
Ruabon
Chirk
OSWESTRY
Ellesmere
Whitchurch
Malpas
Wem
MARKET DRAYTON
Newport
TELFORD
SHREWSBURY
Wellington
Hadley
Oakengates
SHROPSHIRE
CHESHIRE WEST & CHESTER
WREXHAM
WALES
ENGLAND
RIVER MERSEY
LIVERPOOL JOHN LENNON
Manchester Ship Canal
HESWALL
NESTON
BEBINGTON
West Kirby
HOYLAKE
Gresford
Holt
Farndon
Tarporley
Audlem
Hodnet
Shawbury
M62
M56
M53
M6
M54
A41
A49
A5
A483
A525
A534
A51
A54
A556
A55
A550
A541
A495
A528
A53
A442
A529
A530
A500
A5112
A458

33
25
26
PAGE 111
PAGE 108
PAGE 116

PEAK DISTRICT
PEAK DISTRICT NATIONAL PARK
HIGH PEAK
Kinder Scout 2088
SHEFFIELD
STOCKPORT
CHEADLE
Cheadle Hulme
Hazel Grove
Marple
Bramhall
WILMSLOW
Alderley Edge
Prestbury
BOLLINGTON
MACCLESFIELD
New Mills
Whaley Bridge
Chapel-en-le-Frith
Hayfield
Castleton
Hathersage
BUXTON
Tideswell
DRONFIELD
CHESTERFIELD
Bakewell
Ashford in the Water
Rowsley
Darley Dale
MATLOCK
Matlock Bath
Wirksworth
Cromford
Youlgreave
Hartington
CONGLETON
BIDDULPH
KIDSGROVE
LEEK
Tunstall
Burslem
Hanley
STOKE-ON-TRENT
NEWCASTLE-UNDER-LYME
Longton
Cheadle
Ashbourne
DERBYSHIRE
Belper
Duffield
DERBY
Uttoxeter
Rocester
STONE
Sudbury
Tutbury
STAFFORD
STAFFORDSHIRE
Rugeley
CANNOCK CHASE
NEEDWOOD FOREST
BURTON UPON TRENT
SWADLINCOTE
Ashby-de-la-Zouch
Penkridge
CANNOCK
LICHFIELD
Alrewas
PAGE 116
PAGE 108

36
A
B
C
D
E
F
1
2
3
4
5
6
7
8
35
42
28
SHEFFIELD
PAGE 116
DRONFIELD
CHESTERFIELD
MATLOCK
ALFRETON
BELPER
HEANOR
ILKESTON
DERBY
PAGE 108
MALTBY
WORKSOP
RETFORD
GAINSBOROUGH
MANSFIELD
SUTTON IN ASHFIELD
KIRKBY-IN-ASHFIELD
MANSFIELD WOODHOUSE
HUCKNALL
EASTWOOD
ARNOLD
CARLTON
PAGE 114
NOTTINGHAM
WEST BRIDGFORD
STAPLEFORD
BEESTON
LONG EATON
NEWARK-ON-TRENT
LOUGHBOROUGH
MELTON MOWBRAY
COALVILLE
SWADLINCOTE
NOTTINGHAMSHIRE
LEICESTERSHIRE
THE DUKERIES
SHERWOOD PINES FOREST PARK
THE NATIONAL FOREST
CHARNWOOD FOREST
EAST MIDLANDS
LEICESTER (MARKFIELD)
DONINGTON PARK
TROWELL
WOODALL
TIBSHELF
SWANWICK
MARKHAM MOOR
SHARDLOW
GRANTHAM NORTH
BLYTH

LINCOLN
LOUTH
Market Rasen
Horncastle
Woodhall Spa
Coningsby
Sleaford
BOSTON
GRANTHAM
Bourne
SPALDING
Holbeach
Long Sutton
WISBECH
Market Deeping
Crowland
Spilsby
Alford
Wragby
Skegness
L I N C O L N S H I R E
THE WASH
LOUTH
Wrangle
Leverton
Kirton
Donington
Swineshead
Billinghay
Tattershall
Navenby
Leadenham
Waddington
North Hykeham
Welbourn
Ancaster
Caythorpe
Colsterworth
Deeping St Nicholas
Deeping St James
Sutton Bridge
Gosberton
Pinchbeck
Surfleet
Fosdyke
Sutterton
Wigtoft
Sibsey
Stickney
Friskney
Old Leake
Frithville
Tetford
Legbourne
Manby
Saltfleetby St Peter
Kelstern
Ludford
Caistor
Welton
Dunholme
Nettleham
Sudbrooke
Langworth
Washingborough
Heighington
Branston
Metheringham
Martin
Digby
Ruskington
Heckington
Helpringham
Horbling
Billingborough
Rippingale
Dowsby
Thurlby
Baston
Langtoft
Corby Glen
Castle Bytham
Ropsley
Old Somerby
Great Ponton
North Witham
Swinstead
Edenham
Ryhall
Great Casterton
Empingham
Uffington
Tallington
Market Deeping
Moulton
Whaplode
Weston
Cowbit
Moulton Chapel
Holbeach St Johns
Gedney
Fleet Hargate
Lutton
Tydd St Mary
Tydd Gote
Leverington
Newton
Walsoken
THE WOLDS
A15
A16
A17
A46
A52
A57
A151
A153
A155
A157
A158
A631
A1104
A1121
A1175
A6121
A607
A1
38
43
29

38
A
B
C
D
E
F
50
60
70
80
90
600
1
2
3
4
5
6
7
8
Skidbrooke
Saltfleetby St Peter
Saltfleetby All Saints
Theddlethorpe St Helen
Theddlethorpe All Saints
Seal Sanctuary & Wildlife Centre
Three Bridges
A1031
Manby
Great Carlton
Meers Bridge
Lifeboat Station
Mablethorpe
Ye Olde Curiosity
Gayton le Marsh
South Reston
A1104
Trusthorpe
Withern
Strubby
Thorpe
Sutton on Sea
A157
Tothill
Maltby le Marsh
Sandilands
Beesby
A1111
Claythorpe
Claythorpe Watermill & Wildfowl Gardens
Hannah
A52
Saleby
Markby
Aby
South Thoresby
Manor House
Bilsby
Thurlby
Huttoft
Anderby Creek
Alford
B1449
Anderby
Drainage
Haugh
Rigsby
Mumby
On Your Marques
Well
Farlesthorpe
Cumberworth
Authorpe Row
Ulceby
Mawthorpe
B1196
Bonthorpe
Helsey
Chapel St Leonards
Skendleby Psalter
Claxby
Willoughby
Hogsthorpe
A16
Fordington
Slootby
Ashley's Field
A52
Hardys Animal Farm
A1028
Hasthorpe
Slackholme End
Skendleby
Grebby
Addlethorpe
Ingoldmells
Ingoldmells Point
Partney
Scremby
Welton le Marsh
Skegness (Ingoldmells)
Butlin's
A158
Ashby by Partney
Candlesby
Orby
Orby Marsh
Water Leisure Park
Spilsby
Gunby Hall
Halton Holegate
Monksthorpe
A158
Seathorne
Bratoft
Winthorpe
Great Steeping
Northcotes Heavy Horse Centre
Irby in the Marsh
Burgh le Marsh
Natureland Seal Sanctuary
B1195
Church Farm
Bottons Pleasure Beach
Halton Fenside
Little Steeping
Firsby
SKEGNESS
Model Village
Croft
A52
Thorpe St Peter
Seacroft
Croft Marsh
Thorpe Fendike
Batemans Brewery
Magdalen
Wainfleet Bank
Wainfleet St Mary
Wainfleet All Saints
Gibraltar
Key's Toft
Gibraltar Point
Friskney Eaudyke
Eastville
East Fen
DANGER AREA
Friskney
Lade Bank
Deeps
Wrangle Lowgate
Boston
Old Leake
Wrangle
Leake Hurn's End
37
A52
Leverton Outgate
Leverton Lucasgate
Benington Sea End
Freiston Shore
THE WASH
Holbeach St Matthew
Scolt Head Island
Holme Dunes
Brancaster Bay
Holkham Bay
Lifeboat Station
Titchwell Marsh
Marsh Side
Burnham Deepdale
Burnham Norton
Burnham Overy Staithe
Wells Harbour Railway
Salt Marshes
Holme next the Sea
A149
Titchwell
Brancaster
Brancaster Staithe
Friary
B1105
A149
Stiffkey
Cockthorpe
Lifeboat Station
Thornham
Burnham Market
Burnham Overy Town
Holkham
Wells-next-the-Sea
Warham
Warham Camp Hillfort
Cliffs
Old Hunstanton
Norfolk Coast Path
Burnham Thorpe
Wells and Walsingham Light Railway
Wighton
Binham
Sea Life Sanctuary
Hunstanton
Ringstead
B1153
New Holkham
Westgate
Wayside Cross
B1161
B1155
Muckleton
Creake Abbey
Copy's Green
Lower
Heacham
Norfolk Lavender
Peddars Way
B1454
Docking
Stanhoe
North Creake
Forge
Ruined Church
Egmere
Little Walsingham
Great Walsingham
Eaton
Sedgeford
Burntstalk
South Creake
Abbey
Shrine
Shirehall
Hindringham
B1355
North Barsham
Slipper Chapel
Great Snoring
Shepherd's Port
Shettisham
Fring
Bircham Newton
Southgate
West Barsham
Houghton St Giles
Thursford Green
Thursford
Snettisham Park
Barmer
East Barsham
Ingoldisthorpe
Shernborne
Bircham
Great Bircham
Bircham Tofts
Syderstone
Wicken Green Village
Little Snoring
Barney
A148
Bagthorpe
Sculthorpe
Kettlestone
Croxton
Dersingham
Dunton Patch
Fakenham
Fulmodeston
Doddshill
Anmer
Tattersett
Coxford
Dunton
Pensthorpe
Houghton Hall
East Rudham
Shereford
Hempton
The Heath
Fakenham
Wolferton
Sandringham
New Houghton
Priory
Gas & Local History
Little Ryburgh
Stibbard
Babingley
B1439
West Newton
B1440
Tatterford
Toftrees
Great Ryburgh
A148
West Rudham
Helhoughton
A1065
Babingley River
Flitcham
Colkirk
Guist
Hillington
Harpley
Oxwick
A149
Little Massingham
East Raynham
West Raynham
Broom Green
North Wootton
Castle Rising
Great Massingham
Hamrow
Horningtoft
Congham
Raynham South
Whissonsett
B1146
A148
Congham Hall Herbs
South Wootton
Roydon
Grimston
Great Massingham
Weasenham St Peter
Wellingham
Godwick Deserted Village
Gateley
A1078
Potthorpe
Pott Row
Massingham Heath
Weasenham All Saints
Tittleshall
Brisley
A148
Gaywood
A149
Stanfield
A1076
Bawsey
Rougham
B1145
North Elmham
Fairstead
Ashwicken
Mileham
East Bilney
KING'S LYNN
Leziate
B1145
Gayton
Gayton Thorpe
Castle
Beetley
West Lexham
Litcham
B1145
Fair Green
Tower End
East Winch
East Lexham
Bittering
Farm & Workhouse
Gressenhall
East Walton
Beeston
West Winch
North Runcton
Middleton
A47
Castle Acre
Newton
Great Dunham
Longham
West Acre
Blackborough End
Blackborough
West Bilney
Priory
Sparrow Green
Drury Square
Bishop Bonner's Cottage
Setchey
Pentney
South Acre
Great Fransham
Crane's Corner
Bushy Common
Narborough
Little Dunham
Wendling
DEREHAM
Tottenhill Row
A1065
Wormegay
Priory
Scarning
Toftwood
R. Nar
Little Fransham
Watlington
Tottenhill
West Briggs
Sporle
A47
Green Britain Centre
Daffy Green
Marham
Ivy Todd
Runcton Holme
Shouldham
30
RAF Marham
Swaffham
Necton
Bradenham
Shipdham
A1075
A10
South Runcton
A134
Shouldham Thorpe
A1122
Beachamwell Warren
Holme Hale
Stowbridge
Porter's Fen Corner
Thorpland
14
Dawsmere
Gedney Marsh
Gedney Drove End
Black Barn
B1359
Gedney Dyke
Lutton
Sutton Corner
Guy's Head
Ongar Hill
Chapelgate
Terrington Marsh
Gedney
Little London
Long Sutton
Little Sutton
Sutton Bridge
Garnsgate
Bellmount
Terrington St Clement
Clenchwarton
True's Yard Fisherfolk
Walpole Cross Keys
West Lynn
Sutton Crosses
Tydd St Mary
Tydd Gote
Walpole Marsh
Walpole St Andrew
A17
Hay Green
Shepherd's Gate
Tilney All Saints
Foul Anchor
Tilney High End
Great Ouse
Saddle Bow
Tydd St Giles
Four Gotes
A1101
Walpole St Peter
Church End
Eau Brink
Walpole Water
B1165
R. Nene
Ingleborough
A47
Terrington St John
Wiggenhall St Mary the Virgin
Wiggenhall St Germans
A10
Newton
Fitton End
West Walton
Walton Highway
Walpole Highway
Tilney St Lawrence
Wiggenhall St Peter
Gorefield
Leverington
Walpole Gate
St John's Fen End
Wiggenhall St Mary Magdalen
Fenland & West Norfolk Aviation
The Smeeth
Tilney Fen End
Walsoken
Peckover House
Elgood's Brewery
WISBECH
B1166
Chequers Corner
Wisbech St Mary
Emneth
Emneth Hungate
Bunker's Hill
Gaultree
Level Drain

G
H
J
K
L
M
NORTH SEA
Blakeney Point
Cley next the Sea
Blakeney
Salthouse
Wiveton
Glandford
Weybourne
Kelling
Sheringham
West Runton
East Runton
CROMER
Overstrand
Sidestrand
Trimingham
Holt
Letheringsett
Bodham
Upper Sheringham
Beeston Regis
Aylmerton
Felbrigg
Roughton
Northrepps
Gresham
Baconsthorpe
Hempstead
Southrepps
Gimingham
Mundesley
Trunch
Paston
Bacton
Walcott
Happisburgh
Aldborough
Erpingham
Itteringham
Saxthorpe
Corpusty
Melton Constable
Briston
Hindolveston
Banningham
North Walsham
Eccles on Sea
Lessingham
Sea Palling
Waxham
Aylsham
Blickling
Cawston
Reepham
Foxley
Bawdeswell
Hevingham
Buxton
Coltishall
Stalham
Hickling
Horsey
Ludham
Catfield
Winterton-on-Sea
Martham
Hemsby
Scratby
California
Ormesby St Margaret
Caister-on-Sea
Rollesby
Fleggburgh
Filby
Hemsby Hole
Wroxham
Hoveton
Horning
Horsford
Felthorpe
Taverham
Drayton
Hellesdon
Costessey
Ringland
Easton
NORWICH
Sprowston
Old Catton
Spixworth
Salhouse
Blofield
Brundall
Acle
Upton
South Walsham
Lingwood
Halvergate
THE BROADS
GREAT YARMOUTH
Welborne
Barford
Bawburgh
Mattishall
A149
A148
A1082
A140
A1067
A1151
A1062
A1270
A1064
A47
A1074
PAGE 114

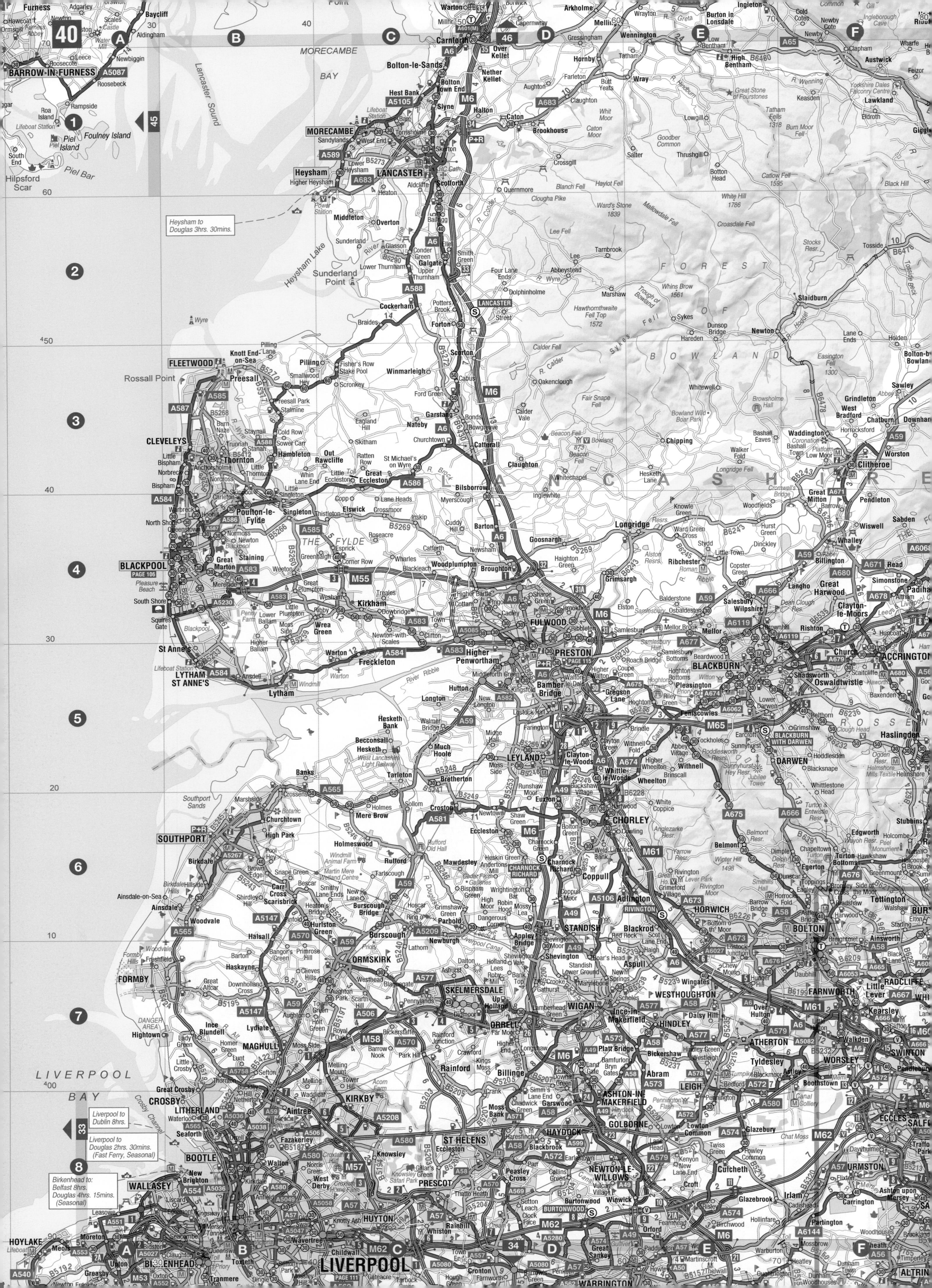
40
46
45
33
MORECAMBE
BAY
Lancaster Sound
LIVERPOOL
BAY
Heysham to
Douglas 3hrs. 30mins.
Liverpool to
Dublin 8hrs.
Liverpool to
Douglas 2hrs. 30mins.
(Fast Ferry, Seasonal)
Birkenhead to:
Belfast 8hrs.
Douglas 4hrs. 15mins.
(Seasonal)
BARROW-IN-FURNESS
Foulney Island
Piel Island
Hilpsford Scar
MORECAMBE
Heysham
LANCASTER
Carnforth
Bolton-le-Sands
Sunderland Point
Heysham Lake
FLEETWOOD
Rossall Point
CLEVELEYS
BLACKPOOL
PAGE 106
THE FYLDE
LYTHAM
ST ANNE'S
Lytham
Kirkham
Garstang
FOREST
OF
BOWLAND
LANCASHIRE
PRESTON
PAGE 115
BLACKBURN
ACCRINGTON
Clitheroe
DARWEN
LEYLAND
CHORLEY
BOLTON
SOUTHPORT
FORMBY
ORMSKIRK
SKELMERSDALE
WIGAN
CROSBY
BOOTLE
WALLASEY
HOYLAKE
BIRKENHEAD
LIVERPOOL
PAGE 111
ST HELENS
HUYTON
PRESCOT
KIRKBY
MAGHULL
NEWTON-LE-WILLOWS
ASHTON-IN-MAKERFIELD
LEIGH
FARNWORTH
WORSLEY
SWINTON
ECCLES
URMSTON
WARRINGTON
ALTRINCHAM
M6
M55
M65
M61
M58
M57
M62
LANCASTER
CHARNOCK RICHARD
RIVINGTON
BLACKBURN WITH DARWEN
BURTONWOOD

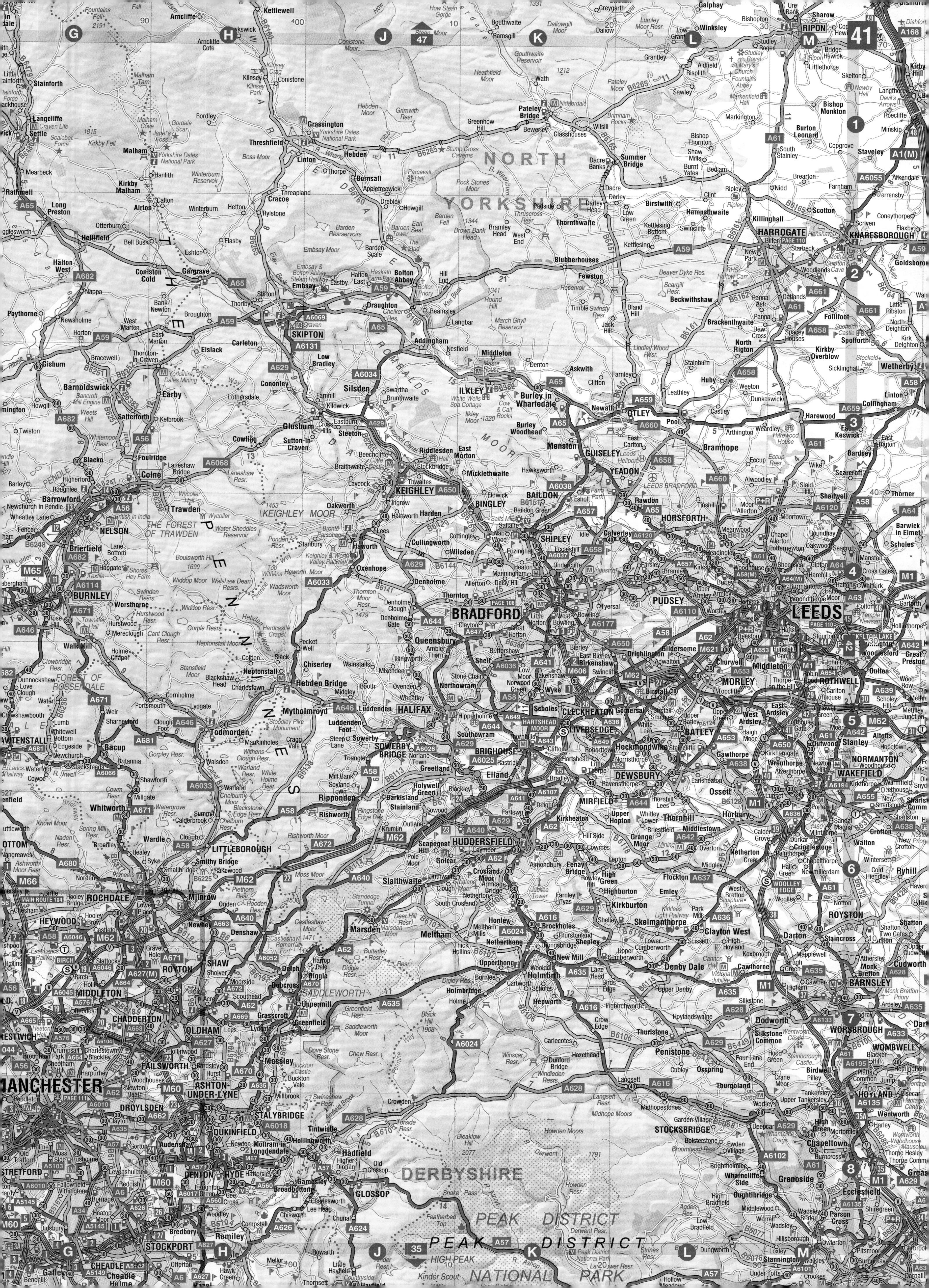
NORTH
YORKSHIRE
THE PENNINES
DERBYSHIRE
PEAK DISTRICT
PEAK DISTRICT NATIONAL PARK
47
35
G
H
J
K
L
M
RIPON
HARROGATE
KNARESBOROUGH
SKIPTON
ILKLEY
OTLEY
KEIGHLEY
BRADFORD
LEEDS
HALIFAX
HUDDERSFIELD
DEWSBURY
WAKEFIELD
BARNSLEY
ROCHDALE
OLDHAM
MANCHESTER
STOCKPORT
BURNLEY
NELSON
COLNE
TODMORDEN
HEBDEN BRIDGE
GLOSSOP
PUDSEY
MORLEY
BATLEY
CLECKHEATON
BRIGHOUSE
HEYWOOD
MIDDLETON
ROYTON
SHAW
CHADDERTON
ASHTON-UNDER-LYNE
STALYBRIDGE
DUKINFIELD
DENTON
HYDE
DROYLSDEN
FAILSWORTH
STOCKSBRIDGE
ROTHWELL
NORMANTON
WOMBWELL
ROYSTON
RAWTENSTALL
LITTLEBOROUGH
PATELEY BRIDGE
WETHERBY
PAGE 110
PAGE 106
PAGE 111

HOWARDIAN HILLS
NORTH
YORKSHIRE
EAST
YORK
OF
NOTTINGHAMSHIRE
48
36
Malton
Norton-on-Derwent
Easingwold
Boroughbridge
Knaresborough
Harrogate
Wetherby
York
Pocklington
Market Weighton
Tadcaster
Selby
Leeds
Garforth
Castleford
Pontefract
Knottingley
Wakefield
Normanton
Featherstone
Rothwell
Howden
Goole
Thorne
Crowle
Doncaster
Bentley
Armthorpe
Barnsley
Wombwell
Hoyland
Mexborough
Conisbrough
Rotherham
Maltby
Tickhill
Bawtry
Gainsborough
Hemsworth
Askern
Epworth
Isle of Axholme
Stanley
Royston
Worsbrough
Swinton
Rawmarsh
Wath upon Dearne
Haxey
Misterton

43
FLAMBOROUGH HEAD
Flamborough
BRIDLINGTON
Bridlington Bay
DRIFFIELD
RIDING
YORKSHIRE
NORTH SEA
Hornsea
BEVERLEY
COTTINGHAM
KINGSTON UPON HULL
PAGE 110
HESSLE
Humber Bridge
RIVER HUMBER
Withernsea
Patrington
Easington
SPURN HEAD
Hull to:
Rotterdam (Europoort) 10hrs.
Zeebrugge 12hrs. 30mins.
Barton-upon-Humber
NORTH LINCOLNSHIRE
SCUNTHORPE
Immingham
GRIMSBY
CLEETHORPES
Brigg
NORTH EAST LINCOLNSHIRE
Mouth of the Humber
Caistor
LINCOLNSHIRE
THE WOLDS
Market Rasen
LOUTH
Saltfleet
Theddlethorpe St Helen
49
37

44
Point
Port Logan
A716
Kilstay Bay
Drummore
Kirkmaiden
B7065
B7041
Cailiness Point
Maryport Bay
Scares
Port Kemin
MULL OF GALLOWAY
Barsalloch Point
Monreith
Gavin Maxwell Memorial
Monreith Animal World
A747
Craiglemine
Point of Cairndoon
Glasserton
480 Fell of Carleton
St Ninian's Cave
Port Castle Bay
BURROW HEAD
Bishopton
Priory
Rispain Camp
A746
Whithorn
Whithorn Story
B7004
B7063
Isle of Whithorn
Chapel
Port Allen
Portyerrock Bay
Cairn Head
51
I R I S H
S E A
POINT OF AYRE
Rue Point
The Ayres
A16
Cranstal
The Lhen
A10
B6
Dhowin
A17
Bride
A19
B2
B3
Andreas
Shellag Point
Jurby Head
Jurby West
Jurby
Jurby East
B4
A9
B5
Ballasalla
Sandygate
Civil War Fort
B7
Regaby
A13
Dhoor
Grove
Ramsey Bay
The Cronk
B9
A14
A17
St Judes
Curraghs
Sulby
A3
Ramsey
Lhergy Frissel
Churchtown
Glen Auldyn
Elfin Glen
Manx Electric Railway
Port e Vullen
Orrisdale
Orrisdale Head
Ballaugh
A15
Crosses
Maughold
Maughold Head
Lewaigue
Ravensdale
Bishopscourt Glen
Glen Wyllin
Kirk Michael
A14
Tholt-y-Will Glen
1854 North Barrule
Ballajora
Port Mooar
A18
Corrany
Cornaa
Glen Mooar
Ballaleigh
Slieau Dhoo 1601
SNAEFELL 2036
Clagh Ouyr
Glen Mona
A2
Ballacarnane Beg
Barregarrow
Sulby Resr.
Port Cornaa
Gob y Deigan
A4
B10
Dhoon
Dhoon Glen
Snaefell Mountain
Great Laxey Mine
Bulgham Bay
Knocksharry
A3
Cronk-y-Voddy
Laxey Wheel
Laxey Glen
St Patrick's Isle
Leece
Ballagyr
Lambfell Moar
Rhenass Waterfall
Glen Helen
Colden 1599
Minorca
Old Laxey
Laxey Head
House of Manannan
A20
I S L E   O F   M A N
A18
Laxey
Peel
A1
Ballacannell
Contrary Head
Patrick
Tynwald Hill
Ballig
St John's
Slieau Ruy 1570
Injebreck Resr.
B22
B12
Ballalheannagh
Laxey Bay
A30
Greeba Castle
Baldwin
Glen Maye
A1
A23
B21
T. T. Course
Baldrine
A2
Clay Head
Hillberry
Onchan
Lower Foxdale
Crosby
Glen Vine
A22
Groudle Glen Railway
Dalby Point
A27
A3
Strang
Willaston
Groudle Glen
Port Groudle
Dalby
Niarbyl
Foxdale
Eairy
A24
B35
A1
Union Mills
A6
A11
Onchan Head
A36
South Barrule 1586
B36
B32
Spring Valley
DOUGLAS
Manx Museum
Douglas Bay
Niarbyl Bay
Hill Fort
B39
Braaid
A24
Cooil
Kewaigue
A36
Close Clark
B35
A5
B37
Douglas Head
Stroin Vuigh
Ballamodha
St Mark's
Quine's Hill
B80
A27
B41
B30
Home for Old Horses
Newtown
A25
Keristal
Little Ness
Fleshwick Bay
Lingague
Ronague
Grenaby
B42
A3
B29
A26
Port Soderick
Isle of Man Steam
B40
B25
Santon Head
Bradda Head
Bradda
Surby
B44
Ballabeg
Rushen Abbey
Bradda Glen
Colby
A7
Ballasalla
A5
Port Erin
Railway
Chambered Cairn
Four Roads
A5
Ship Bonaf
ISLE OF MAN
The Sound
Cregneash
The Howe
Port St Mary
Castletown
A12
Derby Fort
St Michael's Island
Kitterland
A31
B18
National Folk
Nautical
Scarlett
Rushen Keys
Derbyhaven
SPANISH HEAD
Calf of Man
Dreswick Point
Douglas to:
Belfast 2hrs.45mins. (Fast Ferry, Seasonal)
Birkenhead 4hrs. 15mins. (Seasonal)
Heysham 3hrs. 30mins.
Dublin 2hrs. 45mins. (Fast Ferry, Seasonal)
Liverpool 2hrs. 30mins. (Fast Ferry, Seasonal)
A
B
C
D
E
F
1
2
3
4
5
6
7
8
20
30
40
250
60
70
10
500
90
80

45
G
H
J
K
L
M
52
53
46
40
80
90
300
10
20
30
40
50
60
70
SOLWAY FIRTH
IRISH SEA
CUMBRIA
CUMBRIAN MOUNTAINS
LAKE DISTRICT NATIONAL PARK
FURNESS
Allonby Bay
Aspatria
Hayton
Blennerhasset
Mealsgate
Prospect
Harriston
Kirkland Guards
Salt Pans
Milefortlet 21
Oughterside
Allerby
Westmoor End
Threapland
Torpenhow
Ireby
Crosscanonby
Crosby Villa
Bullgill
Parsonby
Plumbland
Bothel
Whitrigg
Senhouse Roman Museum
Alauna Roman Fort
Crosby
Birkby
Gilcrux
Aughertree
Maryport
Dearham
Greengill
Moota Hill
Uldale
Maritime Museum
Netherton
Ellenborough
Townhead
Tallentire
Sunderland
Longlands
Binsey 1467
Bewaldeth
Fothergill
Blindcrake
Over Water
Orthwaite
Flimby
Bridekirk
Redmain
Isel Hall
Dovenby
Broughton Moor
Little Broughton
St Helens
River Derwent
Lake District Visitor Centre
North Row
Bassenthwaite
Siddick
Seaton
Camerton
Great Broughton
Papcastle
Wordsworth House
Elva Plain Stone Circle
Kilnhill
Chapel
Knott 2329
Embleton
North Side
Great Clifton
Broughton Cross
Brigham
Cockermouth
Wythop Mill
Whitewater Great Calva
Stainburn
SKIDDAW FOREST
SKIDDAW 3054
WORKINGTON
Helena Thompson
Greysouthen
Bridgefoot
Little Clifton
Eaglesfield
WHINLATTER FOREST PARK
Jane Pit
Westfield
Mirehouse
Little Crosthwaite
Moss Bay
Winscales
Deanscales
Spout Force
Lord's Seat 1811
Whinlatter Forest
High Harrington
Harrington
Low Lorton
High Lorton
Lorton Yew
Millbeck
Applethwaite
Ormathwaite
Thornthwaite
Grayson Green
Branthwaite
Dean
Whinlatter Pass
Distington
Ullock
Pardshaw
Keswick
Braithwaite
Portinscale
Common End
Gilgarran
Mockerkin
Loweswater
Grisedale Pike 2593
Lowca
Pica
Kidburngill
Castlerigg
Parton
Asby
Lamplugh
Loweswater
Causey Pike
Centenary Stone
Derwent Water
Grasmoor 2795
Moresby Parks
R. Keekle
Loweswater Fell
Brandelhow Memorial
Barrow Falls
Bransty
Rum Story
Arlecdon
Rowrah
Little Town
Legburthwaite
The Beacon
Murton Fell
1880
Crummock Water
WHITEHAVEN
High Leys
Kirkland
Moss Force
Lodore Falls
Grange
High Seat 1996
Saltom Pit
Kells
Frizington
Scale Force
Derwent Fells
Bowder Stone
Saltom Bay
Hensingham
Cleator Moor
Ennerdale Bridge
Great Borne 2021
Buttermere
Hassness
Jaws of Borrowdale
Watendlath
Mirehouse
Keekle
R. Ehen
Sour Milk Gill
Dale Head 2470
St Bees Head
Sandwith
Moor Row
Wath Brow
Ennerdale Water
Red Pike
Buttermere Fell
Rosthwaite
Lourdes Grotto
Blakeley Raise (Kinniside) Stone Circle
High Stile
Gatesgarth
Seatoller
Bigrigg
Cleator
Ennerdale Fell
Hay Stacks
Honister Pass
Stonethwaite
Borrowdale Fells
Rottington
Priory
Lifeboat Station
Egremont
Kinniside Common
Pillar 2927
Scoat Fell
Black Sail Pass
Honister Slate Mine
Borrowdale Yews
Galleny Force
Ullscarf 2382
St Bees
Lowes Court Gallery
Wilton
Caw Fell
Haycock
Seathwaite
Taylorgill Force
Glaramara 2569
Carleton
Thornhill
Monks Bridge
Wasdale Head
Great Gable
Seathwaite Fell
High Raise 2500
Coulderton
Middletown
Haile
Seatallan 2270
Packhorse Bridge
St Olaf's Church
Lingmell
Great End
Langdale Pikes 2415
Nethertown
Beckermet
Calder Bridge
Calder Abbey
R. Calder
COPELAND FOREST
SCAFELL PIKE 3209
SCAFELL 3162
Bow Fell 2960
Dungeon Ghyll Force
Braystones
Wasl Water
The Screes 1998
Burnmoor Tarn
Nether Wasdale
Wellington
Cross
Gosforth
Lingcove Packhorse Bridge
Eskdale Moor Stone Circles
Whillan Beck
Three Shire Stone
Wrynose Pass
Grey Croft Stone Circle
Seascale
Santon
Santon Bridge
Hallsenna Moor
Giggle Alley Japanese Garden
Eskdale Mill
Boot
Hardknott Roman Fort
Hardknott Pass
Cockley Beck
Irton Cross
Eskdale Green
Beckfoot
Eskdale
Harter Fell 2142
FURNESS FELLS
Levers Water
Stubble Green
Holmrook
Stanley Ghyll Force
Birker Force
Birks Bridge Rapids
THE OLD MAN OF CONISTON 2635
Drigg
R. Mite
Ravenglass & Eskdale Railway
R. Esk
Devoke Water
Seathwaite Tarn
DANGER AREA
Saltcoats
Ravenglass
Roman Bath House
Muncaster Castle
Woodend
Bowmanstead
Hall Waberthwaite
Ulpha Fell
Hall Dunnerdale
Seathwaite
Broad Oak
Stainton Fell
Caw 1735
Torver
Newbiggin
Waberthwaite
Whitfell 1880
Ulpha
R. Duddon
1231 Stickle Pike
Corney Fell
Corney
Ulpha Park
Broughton Mills
Sunny Bank
Beacon 836
Woodland Fell
Bridge End
Hycemoor
Selker Bay
Stoneside Hill
Swinside Stone Circle
Bootle Fell
Beckfoot
Duddon Bridge
Lower Hawthwaite
Broughton in Furness
Blawith
Hyton
Bootle
Duddon Ironworks
Broadgate
Lady Hall
Foxfield
Lowick
Annaside
Black Combe 1969
Hallthwaites
The Green
Grizebeck
Gawthwaite
Whitbeck
Dunningwell
Chapels
Broughton Beck
The Hill
Wall End
Kirkby-in-Furness
Netherhouses
Silecroft
Glant's Grave
Whicham
Lacra Stone Circles
Soutergate
Beck Side
1088 Shooting House Hill
Kirksanton
Millom
Millom Discovery Centre
Mansriggs
Laurel & Hardy Museum
Haverigg
ULVERSTON
Pennington
Askam in Furness
Ireleth
Marton
Lindal in Furness
Swarthmoor
South Lakes Wild Animal Park
Great Urswick
Bardsea
Dalton-in-Furness
Stainton with Adgarley
Little Urswick
Barrow (Walney) Airfield
Hawcoat
Newton
Scales
Baycliff
Ormsgill
Furness Abbey
Gleaston Castle
Walney
Dendron
Aldingham
North Scale
North Walney
Dock Museum
Leece
Newbiggin
Roosecote
Vickerstown
BARROW-IN-FURNESS
Roosebeck
Walney Island
Biggar
Rampside
Roa Island
Lifeboat Station
Foulney Island
Piel Island
South End
Piel Bar
Hilpsford Scar
A596
A594
A595
A66
A5086
A597
A591
B5299
B5301
B5292
B5289
B5306
B5295
B5294
B5345
B5344
A593
A5092
A5093
A590
A5087
A5084
B5278

46
53
45
40
A
B
C
D
E
F
1
2
3
4
5
6
7
8
NOR
Wigton
Thursby
Dalston
Carleton
Cotehill
Armathwaite
Alston
Nenthead
GILDERDALE FOREST
INGLEWOOD FOREST
Kirkoswald
Lazonby
Caldbeck
Sebergham
Ireby
Plumpton
Skelton
Catterlen
Greystoke
Greystoke Forest
PENRITH
Langwathby
Culgaith
Temple Sowerby
Kirkby Thore
Long Marton
Dufton
Appleby-in-Westmorland
MILBURN FOREST
Cross Fell 2930
Bassenthwaite
SKIDDAW FOREST
SKIDDAW 3054
Mungrisdale
Threlkeld
Keswick
Portinscale
Braithwaite
Penruddock
Stainton
Clifton
Eamont Bridge
Askham
Shap
Bampton
Glenridding
Patterdale
HELVELLYN 3117
LAKE DISTRICT NATIONAL PARK
CUMBRIAN MOUNTAINS
CUMBRIA
Grasmere
Ambleside
Clappersgate
Troutbeck
Windermere
Bowness-on-Windermere
Coniston
THE OLD MAN OF CONISTON 2635
FURNESS FELLS
GRIZEDALE FOREST
Hawkshead
SCAFELL PIKE 3209
Staveley
Kendal
Orton
Tebay
TEBAY (EAST)
TEBAY (WEST)
Ravenstonedale
Kirkby Stephen
Warcop
Brough
Great Asby
Crosby Ravensworth
HOWGILL FELLS
Sedbergh
Dent
Grayrigg
Burneside
Oxenholme
Natland
Levens
Milnthorpe
Heversham
Beetham
Arnside
Grange-over-Sands
Cartmel
Lindale
Newby Bridge
Haverthwaite
ULVERSTON
Broughton in Furness
Kirkby-in-Furness
Dalton-in-Furness
Askam in Furness
Bardsea
Flookburgh
Humphrey Head Point
MORECAMBE BAY
Silverdale
Carnforth
Bolton-le-Sands
Burton-in-Kendal
Kirkby Lonsdale
Casterton
Ingleton
Bentham
Austwick
Whernside 2414
Ingleborough 2376
Over Kellet
Nether Kellet
Hornby
Wray
Wennington
KILLINGTON LAKE
BURTON-IN-KENDAL
SOUTHWAITE
M6
A6
A66
A591
A592
A590
A595
A683
A684
A685
A686
A65
A5074
A5092
A5084
A593
A6070
A687
A689
A5087
BARROW-IN-FURNESS

47
48
54
55
41
THUMBERLAND
DURHAM
NORTH YORKSHIRE
YORKSHIRE DALES
NATIONAL PARK
THE PENNINES
SWALEDALE
WENSLEYDALE
LUNE FOREST
HAMSTERLEY FOREST
LANGSTROTHDALE CHASE
CONSETT
CHESTER-LE-STREET
DURHAM
BISHOP AUCKLAND
NEWTON AYCLIFFE
DARLINGTON
BARNARD CASTLE
Stanhope
Wolsingham
Crook
Willington
Spennymoor
Ferryhill
Sedgefield
Shildon
Middleton-in-Teesdale
Staindrop
Richmond
Catterick Garrison
Catterick
Leyburn
Bedale
Masham
Hawes
Askrigg
Aysgarth
Middleham
RIPON
Scotch Corner
Allenheads
Westgate
Eastgate
St John's Chapel
Cowshill
Rookhope
Lanchester
Sacriston
Brandon
Tow Law
Evenwood
Cockfield
Gainford
Piercebridge
Bowes
Reeth
Muker
Keld
Gunnerside
Kettlewell
Buckden
Arncliffe
Pateley Bridge
A1(M)
A66
A67
A68
A689
A684
A6108
A167
A688
A690
A691
A692
A693
A6055
A61
A1150
A177
A181
A182
G
H
J
K
L
M
1
2
3
4
5
6
7
8

48
55
47
42
A
B
C
D
E
F
1
2
3
4
5
6
7
8
Ryhope
Seaton
SEAHAM
Murton
Hetton-le-Hole
Dalton-le-Dale
Beacon Point
Easington Colliery
Easington
Horden Point
Horden
PETERLEE
Dene Mouth
Blackhall Colliery
Blackhall Rocks
Haswell
Shotton Colliery
Sherburn
Thornley
Wheatley Hill
Wingate
Station Town
Trimdon Grange
Trimdon Colliery
Trimdon
Hart
Hart Station
West View
HARTLEPOOL
Hartlepool Bay
Maritime Experience
Elwick
DURHAM
Fishburn
Bishop Middleham
Sedgefield
Butterwick
Embleton
Seaton Carew
Tees Bay
Greatham
Wolviston
BILLINGHAM
TEESSIDE
Coatham
REDCAR
Marske-by-the-Sea
Saltburn-by-the-Sea
Teesport
Dormanstown
Grangetown
Eston
South Bank
Normanby
Ormesby
MIDDLESBROUGH
STOCKTON-ON-TEES
Thornaby-on-Tees
Yarm
Eaglescliffe
Stainton
Nunthorpe
Marton
GUISBOROUGH
Brotton
Skelton
Skinningrove
Loftus
Easington
Staithes
Boulby Cliffs
Runswick Bay
Runswick
Hinderwell
Lythe
Sandsend
REDCAR & CLEVELAND
Moorsholm
Lingdale
Boosbeck
Scaling Dam
Great Ayton
Captain Cook's Monument
Roseberry Topping
Stokesley
Kildale
Commondale
Castleton
Danby
Lealholm
Glaisdale
Egton
Grosmont
Goathland
Sleights
Ruswarp
Aislaby
Westerdale
Battersby
Ingleby Greenhow
Great Broughton
Kirkby
Carlton in Cleveland
Swainby
Osmotherley
NORTH YORK MOORS NATIONAL PARK
Church Houses
Rosedale Abbey
Lastingham
Hutton-le-Hole
Gillamoor
Kirkbymoorside
Sinnington
Pickering
Thornton-le-Dale
Levisham
Lockton
Newton-on-Rawcliffe
Dalby Forest
Helmsley
Rievaulx
Hawnby
Chop Gate
Cleveland Way
HAMBLETON HILLS
NORTH YORKSHIRE
DARLINGTON
Middleton St George
DURHAM TEES VALLEY
Kirklevington
Crathorne
Hutton Rudby
Appleton Wiske
Great Smeaton
Welbury
Brompton
NORTHALLERTON
Romanby
Thornton-le-Beans
South Otterington
Knayton
Borrowby
Thirsk
Sowerby
Sutton Bank
Kilburn White Horse
Ampleforth
Ampleforth College
Coxwold
Husthwaite
Easingwold
Crayke
Brandsby
Gilling East
Oswaldkirk
Hovingham
Slingsby
Nunnington
HOWARDIAN HILLS
Terrington
Malton
Old Malton
Norton-on-Derwent
Rillington
Settrington
Topcliffe
Dishforth
RIPON
Sharow
Baldersby
Pickhill
Sandhutton
Carlton Miniott
Dalton
Raskelf
Stillington
Farlington
Bulmer
Welburn
Whitwell Corner
Sedgefield
Bishopton
Great Stainton
Long Newton
Sadberge
Great Burdon
Low Worsall
Picton
Entercommon
Danby Wiske
Yafforth
Morton-on-Swale
Ainderby Steeple
Maunby
Kirby Wiske
Newby Wiske
A1(M)
A19
A66
A67
A167
A168
A170
A171
A172
A173
A174
A177
A178
A179
A181
A182
A184
A185
A689
A1086
A1185
A169
A64
B1257
B1248

G
H
J
K
L
M
1
2
3
4
5
6
7
8
N O R T H S E A
WHITBY
Saltwick Bay
Long Lease
High Hawsker
Stainsacre
Low Hawsker
Ness Point or North Cheek
Cleveland Way
B1447
A171
Raw
Fylingthorpe
Robin Hood's Bay
Old Coastguard Station
Boggle Hole
Robin Hood's Bay & Fylingdales
Old Peak or South Cheek
Coastal Centre
Peak Alum Works
Ravenscar
Stainsondale
Staintondale Shire Horse Farm
Crowdon
Harwood Dale Forest
Harwood Dale
Cloughton Newlands
Cloughton
Burniston
A165
A171
Scalby Mills
Sea Life
North Bay Railway
Bickley
Broxa
Silpho
Suffield
Langdale End
Hackness
Scalby
Everley
Throxenby
Newby
Rotunda
Art Gallery
Barrowcliff
Falsgrave
SCARBOROUGH
Wykeham Forest
North Moor
Trouts Dale
Forge Valley Woods
East Ayton
A170
Betton Farm
P+R
Osgodby
Cayton Bay
Sawdon
Hutton Buscel
West Ayton
B1267
Irton
Crossgates
Eastfield
A165
Seamer
Cayton
The Wyke
Ruston
Wykeham
Snainton
Brompton
B1261
A64
Lebberston
Gristhorpe
A1039
Newbiggin
Lifeboat Station
Filey
THE CARRS
Flixton
Folkton
Willerby
Staxton
A1039
Muston
Primrose Valley
Royal Oak
Hunmanby Sands
East Heslerton
Ganton
Yorkshire Wolds Way
Hunmanby
Sherburn
Potter Brompton
West Heslerton
B1249
Reighton
Speeton
Fordon
Wold Newton
Foxholes
A165
B1229
Buckton
Bempton
FLAMBOROUGH HEAD
Burton Fleming
Danes Dyke
B1255
Grindale
Butterwick
Helperthorpe
Weaverthorpe
Thwing
Flamborough
B1259
Octon
Marton
Sewerby
Bondville Model Village
Lifeboat Station
West Lutton
Kirby Grindalythe
B1253
Boynton
Rudston
Gypsey Race
BRIDLINGTON
43

Rubha' a' Mharaiche
Remuil Hill
Glen Breackerie
Tod Hill
A' Chruach
56
57
93
Polliwilline Bay
Beinn na Lice
Lephenstrath
Glemanuilt Hill
Cnoc Mór
Southend
Macharioch
Carskiey
High Keil
Feorlan
Port Mean
Brunerican Bay
Cove Point
MULL OF KINTYRE
Rubha Chlachan
Sheep Island
Black Point
Sanda Island
Ailsa Craig
Bennane Head
Ballantrae Bay
Ballantrae
Garleffin
Downan Point
Cairnryan (Loch Ryan Port) to Belfast 2hrs. 15mins. (Fast Ferry, Seasonal)
Cairnryan to Larne 2hrs.
Currarie Port
Low Ballochdowan
Carlock Hill
Penderry Hill
Water of App
Glen App
Mid Moile
Milleur Point
Corsewall Point
Portencalzie
Finnarts Bay
Barnhills
Cairnryan
Knockcoid
Kirkcolm
Dounan Bay
Loch Connell
The Wig
Airies
Ervie
Portobello
Loch Ryan
Innermessan
Leswalt
Slouchnawen Bay
Galdenoch Castle
Glenstockadale
Stranraer
Aird
St John
Soulseat Loch
Broadsea Bay
Craigenlee Fell
Lochans
Black Head
Dunskey Estate
Cairn Pat
Portpatrick
Lifeboat Station
Bean Hill
Stoneykirk
Dunskey Castle
Kildonan
Port of Spittal Bay
Kirklauchline
Sandhead
Cairngarroch Bay
Cairngarroch
Kirkmadrine Stones
Money Head
Low Ardwell
Float Bay
Ardwell Point
Logan Botanic Garden
Mull of Logan
Logan Fish Pond
Port Logan Bay
Cairnywellan Head
Clanyard Bay
Laggantalluch Head
Crammag Head
THE RHINNS
NORTH CHANNEL
Ballygally
Carncastle
Carnfunnock Country Park
Drains Bay
Larne to: Cairnryan 2hrs.
Killyglen
LARNE
Island Magee
Ballylumford Dolmen
Portmuck
Millbrook
Mullaghboy
Glynn
Swan Island
Millbay
Glenoe
Larne Lough
Beltoy
Ballycarry
Lough Mourne
Ballystrudder
Black Head
Woodburn Forest
Reservoir
Whitehead
County Antrim War Memorial
Eden
CARRICKFERGUS
Carrickfergus
Greenisland
Belfast to: Birkenhead 8hrs. Douglas 2hrs. 45mins. (Fast Ferry, Seasonal) Cairnryan (Loch Ryan Port) 2hrs. 15mins. (Fast Ferry, Seasonal)
BELFAST LOUGH
Light House Island
Mew Island
Grey Point
Helen's Bay
Crawfordsburn
BANGOR
Groomsport
Copeland Island
Ulster Folk & Transport Mus.
Reservoir
HOLYWOOD
Foreland Point
Cairn Wood
Reservoirs
Six Road Ends
DONAGHADEE
Redburn
Conlig
Whitespots
DUNDONALD
Stormont
Ballycopeland
MILLISLE
NEWTOWNARDS
Scrabo Tower
Barkley Rock

51
EAST AYRSHIRE
SOUTH AYRSHIRE
DUMFRIES & GALLOWAY
THE GLENKENS
THE MACHARS
RHINNS OF KELLS
CAIRNSMORE OF FLEET
GALLOWAY FOREST PARK MERRICK
CARRICK FOREST
GLENTROOL FOREST
KIRROUGHTREE FOREST
PENNINGHAME FOREST
DUNDEUGH FOREST
CHANGUE FOREST
LAURIESTON FOREST
CAIRN EDWARD
GLENGAP FOREST
Culzean Bay
Maidenhead Bay
Turnberry Bay
Matthew's Port
Woodland Bay
Maybole
Kirkmichael
Maidens
Kirkoswald
Turnberry
Crosshill
Straiton
Dipple
Dailly
Girvan
Glendoune
Barr
Pinmore
Lendalfoot
Pinwherry
Colmonell
Barrhill
Patna
Waterside
Dalmellington
Bellsbank
Carsphairn
Knowehead
Kyle Forest
High Bridge of Ken
St John's Town of Dalry
New Galloway
Balmaclellan
Mossdale
Laurieston
Glentrool Village
Bargrennan
Newton Stewart
Minnigaff
Creebridge
Palnure
Creetown
Kirkcowan
Shennanton
New Luce
Glenluce
Dunragit
Castle Kennedy
Wigtown
Bladnoch
Kirkinner
Sorbie
Garlieston
Whithorn
Isle of Whithorn
Port William
Monreith
Glasserton
Gatehouse of Fleet
Twynholm
Borgue
Kirkandrews
LUCE BAY
Auchenmalg Bay
Garheugh Port
Milton Point
Barsalloch Point
Monreith Bay
Point of Cairndoon
Port Castle Bay
BURROW HEAD
Cairn Head
Portyerrock Bay
Port Allen
Eggerness Point
Innerwell Port
Wigtown Bay
Ravenshall Point
Fleet Bay
Islands of Fleet
Borness Point
Little Ross
Scares
MULL OF GALLOWAY
Port Kemin
Maryport Bay
Drummore
Cailiness Point
Kilstay Bay
Terally Point
Balgowan Point
Chapel Rossan Bay
Ardwell
A77
A713
A714
A712
A75
A747
A746
A762
A702
A716
B7004
B7005
B7052
B7085
B741
B734
B729
G
H
J
K
L
M
1
2
3
4
5
6
7
8
58
44
52

A
B
C
D
E
F
58
59
51
44
45
Kirkconnel
Sanquhar
Crawick
Mennock
Wanlockhead
Leadhills
Moffat
Beattock
Thornhill
Penpont
Moniaive
Tynron
Kirkland
Closeburn
Durisdeer
Enterkinfoot
Carronbridge
Auldgirth
Dunscore
Lochmaben
Lockerbie
Torthorwald
Dumfries
PAGE 108
Maxwelltown
Locharbriggs
Heathhall
Holywood
Crocketford or Ninemile Bar
Springholm
Kirkpatrick Durham
Corsock
Balmaclellan
New Galloway
St John's Town of Dalry
Mossdale
Parton
Crossmichael
Laurieston
Castle Douglas
Bridge of Dee
Dalbeattie
Haugh of Urr
Kirkgunzeon
New Abbey
Kirkbean
Carsethorn
Southerness
Southerness Point
Kippford or Scaur
Rockcliffe
Colvend
Sandyhills
Auchencairn
Kirkcudbright
Tongland
Twynholm
Borgue
Dundrennan
Gatehouse of Fleet
Ringford
Gelston
Palnackie
Caerlaverock
Glencaple
Bankend
Ruthwell
Cummertrees
Annan
Ecclefechan
Dalton
Mouswald
Carrutherstown
Silloth
Abbeytown
Allonby
Aspatria
Maryport
Flimby
Seaton
Workington
Cockermouth
Dearham
Crosby
NITHSDALE
LOWTHER HILLS
DUMFRIES & GALLOWAY
SOLWAY FIRTH
FOREST OF AE
LAURIESTON FOREST
DALBEATTIE FOREST
GLENGAP FOREST
Abbey Head
Balcary Point
Port Mary
Little Ross
Borness Point
Dubmill Point
Allonby Bay
Auchencairn Bay
Rascarrel Bay
Hestan Island
Rough Island
A76
A702
A701
A708
A74(M)
A709
A75
A712
A713
A762
A711
A710
A745
A755
A780
A596
A594
A595
A66
A5086
B729
B7076
B725
B724

TEVIOTDALE
SCOTTISH BORDERS
ESKDALE
LIDDESDALE
NORTHUMBERLAND
CUMBRIA
CUMBRIAN MOUNTAINS
CRAIK FOREST
ESKDALEMUIR FOREST
WAUCHOPE FOREST
REDESDALE FOREST
KIELDER FOREST
KIELDER WATER & FOREST PARK
KERSHOPE FOREST
WARK FOREST
GILDERDALE FOREST
MILBURN FOREST
INGLEWOOD FOREST
King's Forest of Geltsdale
Newcastleton Forest
Bonchester Bridge
Hawick
Carter Bar
Teviothead
Mosspaul
Eskdalemuir
Langholm
Canonbie
Newcastleton or Copshaw Holm
Kielder
Saughtree
Deadwater
Hermitage
Bentpath
Falstone
Bewcastle
Gretna
Gretna Green
Longtown
Eaglesfield
Annan
Eastriggs
Gilsland
Greenhead
Haltwhistle
Brampton
Carlisle
Dalston
Wigton
Thursby
Caldbeck
Penrith
Alston
Nenthead
Kirkoswald
Lazonby
Armathwaite
Langwathby
Greystoke
Hadrian's Wall
Solway Moss
Skiddaw
SOUTHWAITE
TODHILLS
A7
A74(M)
A6071
A69
A689
A595
A596
A6
M6
A686
A66
A591
A6088
A68
B6357
B6318
B6413
B6412
B709
B7068
B5299
B5305
54
60
46
G
H
J
K
L
M
1
2
3
4
5
6
7
8

NORTHUMBERLAND
NATIONAL PARK
N O R T H U M B E R L A N D
D U R H A M
SCOTLAND
ENGLAND
REDESDALE FOREST
WARK FOREST
Kidland Forest
HARWOOD FOREST
Slaley Forest
HAMSTERLEY FOREST
MILBURN FOREST
Alnmouth Bay
Druridge Bay
Carter Bar
Catcleugh
Byrness
Redesdale Camp
Rochester
Otterburn Camp
Elsdon
Otterburn
Alwinton
Harbottle
Holystone
Netherton
Thropton
Rothbury
Snitter
Whittingham
Edlingham
Shilbottle
Alnmouth
Warkworth
Amble
Acklington
Felton
Longframlington
Longhorsley
Widdrington
Ulgham
Ellington
ASHINGTON
MORPETH
Pegswood
Stakeford
BEDLINGTON
Cramlington
Seghill
Ponteland
Darras Hall
Stannington
Mitford
Hartburn
Cambo
Kirkwhelpington
Bellingham
West Woodburn
Ridsdale
Great Bavington
Capheaton
Belsay
Wark
Barrasford
Colwell
Gunnerton
Humshaugh
Chollerton
Matfen
Great Whittington
Stamfordham
Chollerford
Wall
Acomb
Haydon Bridge
Haltwhistle
Bardon Mill
Corbridge
HEXHAM
Riding Mill
Broomhaugh
Ovington
Ovingham
Prudhoe
Wylam
Crawcrook
Ryton
Heddon-on-the-Wall
Throckley
NEWBURN
GOSFORTH
NEWCASTLE UPON TYNE
GATESHEAD
FELLING
BLAYDON
WHICKHAM
Winlaton
Rowlands Gill
Sunniside
Birtley
Chopwell
Ebchester
Medomsley
Dipton
Tantobie
Burnopfield
STANLEY
Annfield Plain
CONSETT
Leadgate
Delves
Lanchester
Burnhope
Sacriston
Chester-le-Street
DURHAM
Brandon
Esh Winning
Willington
Crook
Tow Law
Wolsingham
Frosterley
Stanhope
Eastgate
Westgate
St John's Chapel
Cowshill
Allenheads
Nenthead
Alston
Allendale Town
Blanchland
Edmundbyers
Hamsterley
BISHOP AUCKLAND
Spennymoor
Middlestone Moor
Newbiggin
Rookhope
Slaley
Whitfield
Langley
A68
A69
A696
A697
A1
A1068
A189
A19
A192
A6079
A695
A686
A689
A691
A692
A693
A694
A690
A688
A167
53
60
61
46
47

NORTH SEA
Beacon Point
Newbiggin-by-the-Sea
Cambois
North Blyth
BLYTH
Seaton Sluice
Hartley
St Mary's Lighthouse
St Mary's or Bait Island
Holywell
WHITLEY BAY
Monkseaton
Shiremoor
New York
Cullercoats
Blue Reef Aquarium
TYNEMOUTH
Newcastle to: Amsterdam (IJmuiden) 15hrs.
North Shields
Arbeia Roman Fort
SOUTH SHIELDS
Tyne Tunnel
Marsden Bay
Marsden
JARROW
Harton
Souter Lizard Point
Whitburn Colliery
Whitburn
Boldon Colliery
Boldon
Cleadon
South Bents
Seaburn
Southwick
Roker
National Glass Centre
Castletown
WASHINGTON
Monkwearmouth
SUNDERLAND
PAGE 116
Hendon
Pennywell
Offerton
Ryhope Colliery
Penshaw
New Herrington
Herrington
Tunstall
Ryhope
Philadelphia
Silksworth
Newbottle
HOUGHTON-LE-SPRING
Fence Houses
Seaton
SEAHAM
Deneside
Dawdon
Great Eppleton
East Rainton
West Rainton
Hetton-le-Hole
Murton
Dalton-le-Dale
Cold Hesledon
Middle Rainton
Low Moorsley
Easington Lane
South Hetton
Beacon Point
Hawthorn
Easington Colliery
Easington
Pittington
High Haswell
Carrville
Hallgarth
Littletown
Sherburn
Sherburn Hill
Haswell
Haswell Plough
Horden Point
Shotton Colliery
PETERLEE
Horden
Ludworth
Shadforth
Dene Mouth
Thornley
Wheatley Hill
Castle Eden Dene
Blackhall Colliery
Shotton
Castle Eden
Blackhall Rocks
Old Cassop
Quarrington Hill
Cassop
Wingate
Hesleden
High Hesleden
Crimdon Park
Deaf Hill
Eden Vale
Station Town
Monk Hesleden
Hart Station
Kelloe
Town Kelloe
Trimdon Grange
Hutton Henry
Coxhoe
Trimdon Colliery
Sheraton
Hart
West View
Garmondsway
Trimdon
High Throston
Middleton
Maritime Experience
Fishburn
Elwick
West Park
Dalton Piercy
Rift House
HARTLEPOOL
Hartlepool Bay
Bishop Middleham
Summerhill
Brierton
Butterwick
Embleton
Owton Manor
Seaton Carew
Sedgefield
Tees Bay
Bradbury
Greatham
Graythorp
North Gare
Newton Rewley
A1(M)
A19
A1018
A183
A184
A1290
A1300
A690
A182
A181
A688
A177
A179
A1086
A1049
A178
A689
A193
A1148
A186
A191
A185
A187
A194
A195
A1231
A1052
A190
A192
B1325
B1329
B1404
B1285
B1283
B1280
B1278
B1279
B1281
B1432
B1287
B1405
B1299

Colonsay
Garvard
B8085
Rubha Dubh
Corpach Bay
na Beinne
Cruach Ionnastail 967
Laogh
Eilean Leathann
63
Beinn Bhreac 1532
1106 Cruach an Uillt Fhearna
Lussa River
Lealt
Dubh Eilean
Priory
Oronsay
ORONSAY
Eilean Ghaoideamal
Eilean nan Ron
Ceann Riobha
Colonsay to Port Askaig 1hr. 10mins. (Seasonal)
Shian Bay
Allt an Tairbh
Rainberg Mòr 1487
Dubh Bheinn
Maol nam Damh 887
Loch Cathar nan Eun
Fishing Loch
Ardlussa
Ardlussa Bay
Inverlussa
Lussagiven
Lussa Point
Eilean Coir
Gob Dubh
Caves
Loch an Tuim Uaine
Shian River
Loch Fad'a Chruib
Loch Righ Mor
Loch Righ Beag
Cruib 1036
Loch Lùbanach
622 Beinn Sgaillinish
Tarbert
Loch Tarbert
JURA
Keills Chapel
Keillmore
Rubh'an t-Sailein
Rubh' a' chrois-aoinidh
Cnoc an Ime 927
A846
Post Rocks
RUBHA A'MHAIL
Lochan Maol an t-somaich
Glen Batrick
JURA
Allt na Gile
Loch an Aircill
1439 Beinn Bhreac
Loch Lesgamail
Lagg
Loch Sween
Rubha Bholsa
Sgarbh Breac 1195
Bachlaig
Loch an Oir
Beinn an Oir 2576
2477
Loch na Fudarlaich
Port Doir' a' Chrorain
Nave Island
Sgarbh Dubh 965
Loch Smigeadail
Eilean Beag
ARGYLL
Loch a' Chnuic Bhric
PAPS OF JURA
Eilean Mor
Chapel
Ardnave Point
Sgarrail
Gortantaoid
Loch Giur-bheinn
Distillery
Bunnahabhain
JURA FOREST
Lochan Gleann Astaile
Loch an t-Siob
Corran
Knockrome
An Dùnan
Ardnave Loch
1037 Giur-bheinn
Ardnahoe Distillery
Sound
Gleann Astaile
Leargybreck
Jura
Ardfernal
Skervuile
Tòn Mhòr
Beinn Bhreac 940
Loch Staoisha
Ardnahoe Loch
Caol Ila
Glas Bheinn 1839
Loch na Mile
Point of Knap
Loch Laingeadail
Kilnave
Gruinart
Distillery
Gleann Iubharnadeal
B8018
Sanaigmore
Loch Còrr
Loch an Fhir Mhòir
Leckgruinart
Braigo
Loch
Loch Leathan
Keills
Feolin Ferry
Port Askaig (Port Asgaig)
Keills
Small Isles
Craighouse to Tayvallich 1hr. (Seasonal)
SOUND OF JURA
Rubha Lamanais
Grulinbeg
Finlaggan
Loch Finlaggan
A846
Loch Allan
Loch a' Bhaile-Mhargaidh
Craighouse
Isle of Jura Distillery
Saligo Bay
B8017
Gruinart
Abhainn Ghlas
Loch Drolsay
Ballygrant
Loch Ballygrant
Gleann Ullibh
1123 Brat Bheinn
Saligo
Loch Gorm
Castle
ISLAY
Loch Cam
Loch Sibhinn
R. Drolsay
Skerrols
Esknish
Kilmeny
Loch Lossit
A846
Port na Birlinne
Na Cùiltean
Kilberry Head
Coul Point
B8018
Islay Ales Brewery
Ballabus
Islay Woolen Mill
Loch Bharradail
Beinn Dubh 875
Cabrach
Glas Eilean
Ardfin
Rubha na Tràille
Machir Bay
Distillery
Kilchoman
Blackrock
Carnain
A847
Redhouses
Bridgend (Beul an Atha)
Am Fraoch Eilean
Brosdale Island
Cnoc Dubh
Conisby
Carraigo Dhubh
Sound of Islay
Port
Distillery
Bruichladdich
Indaal
Dun Nosebridge Hillfort
Kilchiaran Bay
Kilchiaran
Loch Gearach
Distillery
Bowmore
Church
B8016
McArthur's Head
Islay Life
Octomore
Natural History Centre
Mulindry
Glas Bheinn 1544
Kennacraig to Port Askaig 2hrs.
Cultoon Stone Circle
Port Charlotte
Beinn Tart a' Mhill 760
Laggan Bri.
Kilennan River
Loch Allallaidh
Lossit
Loch
Laggan River
Beinn Bhàn 1544
1612
Loch nan Breac
Beinn Bheigeir
Carraig Mhòr
An Dubh-sgeir
Gamhr Gigha
Lossit Bay
Neribus
RHINNS OF ISLAY
Laggan
Torra
1490 Beinn Uraraidh
Claggain River
Ardtalla
Claggain Bay
Eilean Garbh
West Tarbert Bay
Laggan Point
Duich
River
Gleann Leora
354 Cnoc Mòr na Claigin
Octofad
A846
East Tarbert Bay
Kennacraig to Port Ellen 2hrs. 20mins.
Portnahaven
A847
Port Gleann na Gaoidh
Loch Beinn Uraraidh
Aros Bay
Laggan
Glenegedale Lots
Loch Leathann an Sgorra
Kintour
Orsay
Port Wemyss
RHINNS POINT
Glenegedale
ISLAY
Bay
Ardmore Point
Beinn Sholum 1138
Loch Uigeadail
Loch Cam a' Mhaoil
Kildalton Cross
ISLE OF GIGHA
Creag Bhan
Druimyeon Bay
Eilean Craobhach
Mill Loch
Eilean a' Chuirn
Port Alsaig
Kintra
Leorin Lochs
Loch Iarnan
Lochan Sholum
Ardminish
Ardminish Bay
Loch nan Gabhar
Eilean Bhride
Craro Island
Achamore
Slugaide Glas
Loch Muchairt
Maol Buidhe 541
A846
Lagavulin
Ardbeg
Loch a' Chnuic
Rubha na Gainmhich
Gigalum Island
Tayinloan
Glenastle Loch
Cragabus
Port Ellen
Laphroaig
Distillery
Dunyvaig Castle
Eilean Imersay
Killean
Dùn Mòr Ghil
THE OA
Texa
Cara Island
Risabus
Mull of Cara
Sound of Gigha
A83
Lower Killeyan
Loch Kinnabus
American Monument
A' Chleit
MULL OF OA
Rubha na Meise Bàine
Beinn Mhòr 661
Muasdale
Rubha nan Leacan
Port Ellen to Ballycastle 1hr. (Seasonal)
Glenacardoch Point
Glenbarr
Port a' Bhorrain
Glenbarr Abbey
Bellochantuy Bay
Bellochantuy
Cnoc Buidhe 1023
Port Corbert
Tangy Loch
Ranachan Hill 696
Kilchenzie
A83
Machrihanish Bay
CAMPBELTOWN
Machrihanish
Springbank
B843
Drumlemble
Stewart
Killypole Loch
Tirfergus Hill 854
Earadale Point
The Slate 1263
Cnoc Moy 1465
Killellan
B842
Rubha Dùin Bhàin
Dalsmirren
Cnoc Odhar 908
Conie Glen
Rubha' a' Mharaiche
Remuil Hill
Glen Breackerie
A' Chruach
Rathlin Island
Doonmore
93
Bull Point
Bruce's
Beinn na Lice 1404
Glenamuilt Hill
Lephenstrath
High Keil
Southend
Carskiey
Cnoc Mòr

KNAPDALE
FOREST
Lochgilphead
Ardrishaig
Tayvallich
Eilean Loain
Achnamara
Kilmichael of Inverlussa
LOCH FYNE
Lephinchapel
Largiemore
Port Ann
Castleton
Otter Ferry
Eilean Mór
Liath Eilean
Bàgh an Tailleir
Inverneill House
Kilfinan
Kilfinan Bay
Port Leathan
Auchalick Bay
Ardmarnock Bay
Barmore Island
Tighnabruaich
Kames
Portavadie
Millhouse
Tarbert
East Loch Tarbert
West Tarbert
Eilean Aoidhe
Asgog Bay
Fionn Phort
Kilbride Bay
Ardlamont Bay
Ardlamont Point
Camas na Ceardaich
Rubha Leathan
Glendaruel Forest
Clachan of Glendaruel
Auchenbreck
Colintraive
Kyles of Bute
Strone Point
Port Lamont
ISLE OF BUTE
Port Bannatyne
Kames Bay
Rothesay Bay
Bogany Point
Ettrick Bay
ROTHESAY
Craigmore
Montford
Ascog
Kerrycroy
Straad
Inchmarnock
Scoulag Point
Mount Stuart
Kilchattan Bay
Kingarth
Stravanan Bay
Dunagoil Bay
Garroch Head
Ardscalpsie Point
SOUND OF BUTE
Toward
Toward Point
Innellan
DUNOON
Hunter's Quay
Kirn
Sandbank
Holy Loch
Strone
Blairmore
Ardentinny
Benmore Forest
Glenmassan
Garvie
Conchra
Gourock
Greenock
Kilcreggan
Cove
Rosneath
Rhu
HELENSBURGH
Clynder
Shandon
Gare Loch
Inverkip
Wemyss Bay
Skelmorlie
Largs
GREAT CUMBRAE ISLAND
Millport
Little Cumbrae Island
FIRTH OF CLYDE
Fairlie
Hunterston
Portencross
Farland Head
Ardneil Bay
Seamill
West Kilbride
Ardrossan
Saltcoats
Stevenston
Horse Isle
NORTH AYRSHIRE
Ardrossan to Brodick 55mins.
Campbeltown to Brodick 2hrs. 20mins. (Seasonal)
Ardrossan to Campbeltown 2hrs. 40mins. (Seasonal)
Tarbert to Lochranza 1hr. 25mins. (Seasonal)
Claonaig to Lochranza 30mins. (Seasonal)
Lady Isle
Heads of Ayr
Dunure
Culzean Bay
Maidenhead Bay
Maidens
Turnberry
Kirkoswald
Skipness
Skipness Point
Claonaig
Claonaig Bay
Eascairt Point
Kennacraig
Whitehouse
Clachan
Ronachan Point
Ardpatrick Point
Kilberry
Crossaig
Cour Bay
Grogport
Carradale
Port Righ
Carradale Point
Rubha nan Sgarbh
Saddell
Saddell Bay
Ugadale Point
Black Bay
Ardnacross Bay
Campbeltown
Island Davaar
Campbeltown to Ballycastle 1hr. 30 mins. (Seasonal)
Achinhoan Head
Johnston's Point
Polliwilline Bay
Cove Point
KILBRANNAN SOUND
ISLE OF ARRAN
NORTH
Lochranza
Cock of Arran
Millstone Point
Rubha Creagan Dubha
Rubha Airigh Bheirg
North Sannox
Sannox Bay
Corrie
GOATFELL 2866
Merkland Point
Brodick
Brodick Bay
Whitefarland Point
Dougarie Point
Machrie Bay
Drumadoon Point
Drumadoon Bay
Brown Head
Lamlash
Lamlash Bay
Holy Island
Clauchlands Point
Kingscross Point
Whiting Bay
Largybeg Point
Dippin Head
Sound of Pladda
Pladda
Bennan Head
Kildonan
Blackwaterfoot
Kilmory
A83
A886
A815
A78
A841
A844
A8003
A8015
B842
B8001
B8024

58
65
51
57
ARGYLL & BUTE
WEST DUNBARTONSHIRE
EAST DUNBARTONSHIRE
STIRLING
INVERCLYDE
RENFREWSHIRE
EAST RENFREWSHIRE
NORTH AYRSHIRE
SOUTH AYRSHIRE
EAST AYRSHIRE
SOUTH LANARK
DUMFRIES & GALLOWAY
GLASGOW
PAGE 109
PAGE 110
Helensburgh
Greenock
Port Glasgow
Gourock
Dumbarton
Alexandria
Clydebank
Bearsden
Milngavie
Kirkintilloch
Cumbernauld
Paisley
Renfrew
Johnstone
Rutherglen
Coatbridge
Airdrie
Motherwell
Hamilton
East Kilbride
Wishaw
Barrhead
Newton Mearns
Largs
Kilbirnie
Beith
Dalry
Kilwinning
Ardrossan
Saltcoats
Stevenston
Irvine
Kilmarnock
Stewarton
Troon
Prestwick
Ayr
Galston
Darvel
Strathaven
Mauchline
Cumnock
New Cumnock
Maybole
Muirkirk
Sanquhar
Kilsyth

G
H
J
K
L
M
66
67
59
FIRTH OF FORTH
EDINBURGH
PAGE 109
DUNFERMLINE
KIRKCALDY
GRANGEMOUTH
FALKIRK
LIVINGSTON
MUSSELBURGH
DALKEITH
FALKIRK
WEST LOTHIAN
MIDLOTHIAN
PENTLAND
SCOTTISH BORDERS
LANARKSHIRE
MOORFOOT
SOUTHERN UPLANDS
ETTRICK FOREST
DUMFRIES & GALLOWAY
LOWTHER HILLS
Queensferry Crossing
Forth Road Bridge
Forth Bridge
Kincardine Bridge
Clackmannanshire Bridge
Inchkeith
Inchcolm
Inchmickery
Cramond Island
Linlithgow
Bathgate
Armadale
Whitburn
Broxburn
Penicuik
Peebles
Innerleithen
Walkerburn
Biggar
Carnwath
Carluke
Lanark
Douglas
Abington
Crawford
Leadhills
Wanlockhead
Tweedsmuir
West Linton
Prestonpans
Gorebridge
Bonnyrigg
Newtongrange
Roslin
Lasswade
Loanhead
Kirkliston
South Queensferry
North Queensferry
Inverkeithing
Rosyth
Burntisland
Kinghorn
Aberdour
Bo'ness
Stenhousemuir
Larbert
Denny
Shotts
Stane
Newmains
Forth
Carstairs
Carstairs Junction
Symington
Coulter
Lamington
Broughton
Drumelzier
Skirling
Elsrickle
Dolphinton
Blyth Bridge
Romannobridge
Eddleston
Leadburn
Howgate
Carlops
Traquair
Yarrow
Ettrick
Mountbenger
Cappercleuch
CRAIK FOREST
Craik
A70
A71
A72
A73
A74(M)
A701
A702
A703
A708
A720
M8
M9
M74
M90
52
53
60
1
2
3
4
5
6
7
8
300
90
80
70
60
50
40
30
20
10

FIRTH OF FORTH
EDINBURGH
PAGE 109
EAST LOTHIAN
MIDLOTHIAN
LAMMERMUIR HILLS
MOORFOOT HILLS
SOUTHERN UPLANDS
LAUDERDALE
SCOTTISH BORDERS
MERSE
TEVIOTDALE
ETTRICK FOREST
CRAIK FOREST
SCOTLAND
ENGLAND
CHEVIOT
Bass Rock
Fidra
Lamb
Craigleith
Eyebroughy
North Berwick
Scottish Seabird Centre
Tantallon
Dirleton
Gullane Bay
Gullane
North Berwick Law
Kingston
Whitekirk
Aberlady Bay
Aberlady
Saltcoats Castle
Fenton Barns
Drem
Myreton Motor Museum
Tyninghame
Dunbar
Dunbar Castle
Town House
Barns Ness
Craigielaw
Gosford Bay
Ballencrieff
East Fortune
Preston
Knowes
West Barns
Belhaven
Spittal
Camptoun
Athelstaneford
East Linton
Broxburn
East Barns
Pinkerton
Skateraw
Power Station
Thorntonloch
Cockenzie and Port Seton
Longniddry
Prestonpans
Portobello
Joppa
MUSSELBURGH
Fisherrow
Inveresk
Newcraighall
Wallyford
Tranent
Macmerry
Haddington
Elvingston
Huntington
Meadowmill
Gladsmuir
Penston
Stenton
Pitcox
Spott
Innerwick
Luggate Burn
Papple
Garvald
Morham
Samuelston
Colstoun House
Bolton
Elphinstone
Whitecraig
Crossgatehall
Ormiston
Pencaitland
Cousland
DALKEITH
Eskbank
Bonnyrigg
Easthouses
Mayfield
Newtongrange
Dewartown
Edgehead
Newlandrig
Gorebridge
Arniston
Hunterfield
Crichton
Carrington
Borthwick
North Middleton
Middleton
Temple
Rosebery Reservoir
Gifford
Yester Castle
East Saltoun
West Saltoun
Peastonbank
Peaston
Pathhead
Gilchriston
Longyester
Humbie
Fala
Fala Dam
Fala Moor
Tynehead
Soutra Aisle
Gilston
Heriot
Reed Point
Cove
Cockburnspath
Oldhamstocks
Siccar Point
Fast Castle Head
Lumsdaine
Coldingham Moor
Grantshouse
Houndwood
Abbey St Bathans
Reston
Auchencrow
Cranshaws
Ellemford
Whitchester
Longformacus
Preston
Chirnside
Chirnsidebridge
Edrom
Allanton
Duns
Gavinton
Nisbet Hill
Whitsome
Polwarth
Fogo
Fogorig
Horndean
Ladykirk
Swinton
Simprim
Upsettlington
Greenlaw
Westruther
Halliburton
Houndslow
Bassendean
Lauder
Thirlestane
Carfrae
Oxton
Addinston
Cleekhimin Bridge
Edgarhope Wood
Fountainhall
Killochyett
Stow
Legerwood
Huntlywood
Gordon
Hume
Leitholm
Lambden
Eccles
Coldstream
Lennel
Cornhill-on-Tweed
Melkington
Birgham
Carham
Wark
Nenthorn
Stichill
Ednam
Kelso
Earlston
Smailholm
Innerleithen
Walkerburn
Traquair
Clovenfords
GALASHIELS
Gattonside
Caddonfoot
Peel
Tweedbank
Melrose
Newstead
Leaderfoot
Darnick
Boleside
Abbotsford
Bemersyde
Dryburgh
Newtown St Boswells
Clintmains
Makerstoun
Maxwellheugh
Sprouston
Hadden
Lindean
Bowden
St Boswells
Maxton
Roxburgh
Heiton
Yarrow Ford
Yarrow
Yarrow Feus
Philiphaugh
Selkirk
Midlem
Longnewton
Sandystones
Lilliesleaf
Ancrum
Crailing
Eckford
Nisbet
Morebattle
Cessford
Town Yetholm
Kirk Yetholm
Linton
Ettrickbridge
Ashkirk
Bloomfield
Jedburgh
Lanton
Bonjedward
Crailinghall
Newton
Minto
Spittal-on-Rule
Hassendean
Horsleyhill
Denholm
Bedrule
Clarilaw
Appletreehall
Burnfoot
Cauldmill
Wilton
HAWICK
Kirkton
Bonchester Bridge
Hobkirk
Chesters
Southdean
Camptown
Oxnam
Mossburnford
Swinside Hall
Hownam
Mowhaugh
Buccleuch
Robertson
Burnfoot
Branxholme
Deanburnhaugh
Newmill
Tushielaw
Redfordgreen
Gilmanscleuch
Craik
Stobs Castle
Carter Bar
Blindburn
Barrowburn
A1
A68
A7
A72
A697
A698
A699
A6105
A6112
A6089
A6088
A6091
A6093
A6106
A6124
A6137
A198
A199
A707
A708
A1107
B6355
B6456
B6362
B6397
B6400
B6352
53
59
67

G
H
J
K
L
M
400
10
20
30
40
90
80
70
60
50
40
30
20
10
1
2
3
4
5
6
7
8
N O R T H
S E A
ST ABB'S HEAD
St Abbs
Lifeboat Station
Coldingham Bay
Lifeboat Station
Priory
Coldingham
Gunsgreen House
Eyemouth
Gunsgreenhill
A1107
B6355
Ayton
Burnmouth
Ross
A1
Lamberton
Marshall Meadows
Tithe Barn
Clappers
Foulden
Halidon Hill
1333
A6105
Hutton
Bell Tower
Cell Block
Paxton
B6461
B6460
Castle
BERWICK-UPON-TWEED
Tweedmouth
Lifeboat Station
Spittal
Loanend
Union Bridge
Chain Bridge Honey Farm
Fishwick
East Ord
A1167
A698
Horncliffe
Redshin Cove
Scremerston
Murton
Thornton
B6470
B6354
B6525
West Allerdean
Shoreswood
Shoresdean
Cheswick
Goswick
Grindon
Felkington
Ancroft
Berrington Law
Haggerston
Duddo Stone Circle
Berrington
LINDISFARNE
HOLY ISLAND
Keel Head
Holy Island
Lindisfarne Centre
Lindisfarne Castle
Lindisfarne Priory
Castle Point
Beal
Castle Heaton
Duddo
Bowsden
Fenham
A1
Burrows Hole
Barmoor
B6353
Lowick
West Kyloe
East Kyloe
Fenwick
Kyloe Hills
Buckton
Longstone
Etal
Lady Waterford Hall
B6353
Ford
B6354
Elwick
Ross
Budle Bay
Staple Sound
FARNE ISLANDS
Chapel
Inner Sound
Holburn
St Cuthbert's Cave
Detchant
Bamburgh
Flodden
Kimmerston
Hetton Steads
North Hazelrigg
Middleton
Easington
Waren Mill
Budle
Grace Darling
B1340
Lifeboat Station
Milfield
Maelmin Heritage Trail
Fenton
Fenton Centre
Nesbit
B6525
Belford
New Shoreston
Seahouses
Heritage
Carr End
Spindlestone
Bradford
Burton
River Till
Doddington
South Hazelrigg
Lanton
Coupland
West Horton
East Horton
Lyham
ADDERSTONE
Elford
North Sunderland
Kirknewton
Yeavering
Homildon Hill 1402
Warenton
Bellshill
Adderstone
Lucker
B1341
Beadnell
Yeavering 1415
Weetwood Hall
B6349
Lime Kilns
Yeavering Bell
Akeld
Humbleton
Wooler
Greendykes
B6348
Warenford
Newham
Swinhoe
West Fleetham
Beadnell Bay
B6348
Chatton
A697
1761 Newton Tors
Fredden Hill
Earle
Haugh Head
Chillingham
Ros Castle
Chathill
Ellingham
Tughall
Snook Point
Wild Cattle
Newtown
A1
High Newton-by-the-Sea
Low Newton-by-the-Sea
North Middleton
South Middleton
Preston Hill
Cold Law 1485
Lilburn Tower
Hepburn
East Lilburn
876 Cateran Hill
Middle Moor
North Charlton
Preston
Tower
Brunton
B1340
B1339
Embleton Bay
N O R T H U M B E R L A N D
THE CHEVIOT 2674
Langleeford
Langlee Crags
Ilderton
Roseden
Old Bewick
Doxford
Christon Bank
Embleton
Dunstanburgh
Armstrong's Household & Farming
B6347
Harehope
Hedgehope Hill
Roddam
Wooperton
Hedgeley Moor 1464
New Bewick
Percy's Cross
Eglingham
South Charlton
Rock
Dunstan
Craster
Harthope Burn
Comb Fell
Dunmoor Hill 1860
Beanley
B6346
B6341
Rennington
Stamford
Littlemill
Howick
Howick Hall
R. Breamish
Brandon
Ingram
Branton
Northumberland National Park
Powburn
East Bolton
Shipley
Heiferlaw Tower
B6341
B1340
Greensidehill
Shill Moor
Glanton Pyke
Titlington
Hulne Priory
Hulne Park
Littlehoughton
Longhoughton
Boulmer
Cushat Law 2020
Woodybush Edge
Glanton
R. Aln
B6346
Abbey
Bailiffgate
ALNWICK
Denwick
B1339
Great Ryle
High Knowes
Bolton
Abberwick
1093
Kidland Forest
Prendwick
Eslington Hall
Whittingham
House of Hardy
B6341
Lesbury
Hipsburn
B1338
Weather Cairn
Little Ryle
Thrunton
A697
Bilton
Alnmouth
Alnham
Yetlington
54
Callaly
A1
Scrainwood
Biddlestone
Edlingham
Shilbottle
Shilbottle Grange
High Buston
Alnmouth Bay
55
Netherton
Clennell
A1068

Tiree to
Barra 2hrs. 45mins.
(Seasonal)

Gunna

Gunna Sound

Miodaro

*Vaul
Bay*

Carnan

*Hough
Skerries*

Sraid
Ruadh

Cornaigmore

*Balephetrish
Bay*

*Loch
Riaghain*

Vaul

Salum

Caolas

Ruaig

Balevullin

Kilmoluaig

Cornaigbeg

Balephetrish

B8069

Gott

Kirkapol

Hough

Kenovay

Gott Bay

Kilkenneth

TIREE
(Port Adhair Thiriodh)

*An
Iodhlann*

Scarinish

Sandaig

Moss

*Loch an
Eilein*

B8065

Baugh

*Rubha Tràigh
an Duin*

Middleton

B8065

Crossapol

Heanish

Port Mor

Barrapol

Heylipol

*Hynish
Bay*

TIREE

*Port
Bharrapool*

Island Life

*Loch a
Phuill*

Balephuil

Balemartine

B8067

Mannal

*Balephuil
Bay*

West
Hynish

Hynish

Port Snog

*Skerryvore
Lighthouse*

I N N E R

N O R T H   A T L A N T I C

O C E A N

G
H
68
J
K
L
69
M
Oban to Castlebay 5hrs.
Oban to Lochboisdale 5hrs. 20mins. (Seasonal)
Sanna Point
Ockle Point
Farquhar's Point
Port Bàn
Fascadale
Kilmory
Achateny
Branault
Ockle
Sanna
Sanna Bay
Portuairk
Achnaha
Point of Ardnamurchan
Ardnamurchan Lighthouse
Achosnich
A R D N A M U R C H A N
Meall nan Con 1433
Beinn Bhraec 1171
Gortenfern
Kentra Bay
Kentra
Arivegaig
Acharacle (Ath-Tharracail)
Gorteneorn
Blain
Mingarrypark
Moss
Shiel Br.
B8044
A861
Loch Mudle
Beinn nan Losgann 1026
Leac Shoilleir
Lochan Sligneach
Meall nan Each 1607
Salen (An Sailean)
Loch Caorach
Beinn Na Seilg 1123
B8007
Kilchoan
Ormsaigmore
Ormsaigbeg
Mingary
Mingary Castle
Kilchoan Bay
Ben Hiant 1731
Lochan nam Fiann
Loch Laga
Ben Laga 1679
Glenmore
Glenbeg
Ardnamurchan Natural History Centre
Glenborrodale
Laga
Cladh Chiaran Burial Ground
Ardslignish
Maclean's Nose
An Acairseid
Cairns of Coll
Eag na Maoile
Eilean Mór
Rubha Mór
Rubh'a' Bhinnein
Bousd
Sorisdale
Cornaigmore
B8072
COLL
Loch Fada
Cliad Bay
Grishipoll
Rubha Hogh
Clabhach
B8071
Hogh Bay
Ben Nogh 340
Loch Cliad
Bagh Feisdlum
Arinagour
Stables
Loch nan Cinneachan
Loch Anlaimh
Loch Eathama
Totronald
Coll
Acha
B8070
Eilean Ornsay
Feall Bay
Calgary Point
Uig
Friesland Bay
Port na h-Eathar
Crossapol Bay
Loch Breachacha
Port a' Mhurain
Soa
Rubha Dubh
Coll to Tiree 55mins.
Coll to Oban 2hrs. 45mins.
Oban to Tiree 3hrs. 20mins. (Seasonal)
H E B R I D E S
35mins.
Oronsay
Risga
Carna
Loch Sunart
Glencripesdale
Ardmore Bay
Ardmore Point
Rubha nan Gall
Auliston Point
HIGHLAND
Quinish Point
Glengorm Castle
Meall an Inbhire 865
An Tobar
Mull
Tobermory
Hebridean Whale and Dolphin Trust
Tobermory Distillery
Isle of Mull Cheese
Calve Island
Drimnin
Beinn Bhuidhe 1481
Loch Doire nam Mart
Beinn na h-Uamha
Beinn Iadain 1873
Caliach Point
Croig
Loch a' Chumhainn
Loch an Torr
Dervaig
'S Airde Beinn 959
B8073
Loch Peallach
M O R V E R N
Sithean na Raplaich 1806
An t-Aoineadh Mor Deserted Village
Claggan
Calgary
Calgary Bay
Old Byre Heritage Centre
Cruachan Druim na Croise 866
A R O S
Sound of Mull
Rhemore
Killundine
Caisteal nan Con
Fiunary Forest
Larachbeg
A884
Treshnish Point
Ensay
Carn Mor 1122
Speinne Mór 1458
Lettermore
Salen Forest
Ardnacross
A848
Haunn
Kengharair
Loch Frisa
River Bellart
Tenga
Aros
Aros Mains
Aros Castle
Fiunary
B849
Lochaline
Loch Aline
Cairn na Burgh Beg
Rubh a' Chaoil
Burg
Kilninian
Achleck
Fanmore
Cnoc an da Chinn 1280
Crannich
Rubha Mór
Treshnish Isles
Fladda
Loch Tuath
Ballygown
Eas Fors Waterfall
Beinn na Drise 1392
Salen
Fishnish Bay
Fishnish
Ardtornish Castle
Eilean Dioghlum
Lunga
Gometra House
Gometra
Beinn Chreagach 1026
Isle of Ulva Heritage Centre
ULVA
Ulva House
Laggan Bay
Lagganulva
Oskamull
B8073
Kellan
Killiechronan
Gruline
A R G Y L L
Loch na Dairidh
Macquarie Mausoleum
Beinn Bhuidhe 1352
Beinn Chreagach Mhór 1903
A849
Bailemeonach
Garmony
Scallastle Bay
Bac Mor or Dutchman's Cap
Bac Beag
Màisgeir
Eilean na Creiche
Sound of Ulva
Eorsa
Knock
Loch na Keal
& ISLE
Samalan Island
Beinn a' Ghràig 1939
Tomsléibhe
Dùn da Ghaoithe 2512
Staffa
Fingal's Cave
Little Colonsay
Inch Kenneth
Chapel
B8035
Derryguaig
B U T E O F
Glen Clachaig
Beinn Talaidh 2502
Sgurr Dearg 2429
Gribun
BEN MORE 3171
Coirc Bheinn 1837
M U L L
Glen Cannel
Corra-bheinn 2311
Erisgeir
Lussa River
Strathcoil
Loch Beamach
Bein na Sreine 1704
Glen Seilisdeir
B8035
Coladoir River
Glen More
Loch Sguabain
Loch Airdeglais
Creach Beinn 2290
Creach Bheinn 1613
ARDMEANACH
Rubha na h Uamha
MacCulloch's Fossil Tree
Tiroran
Kilfinichen Bay
Ben Buie 2354
Kinlochspelve
Loch Spelve
Tavool House
Port na Croise
Loch Scridain
Pennyghael
Loch Fuaran
Beinn na Croise 1649
Lochbuie
Moy Castle
Loch Uisg
Standing Stone Circle
Loch an t-sithein
Réidh Eilean
Eilean Annraidh
Rubha nan Cearc
Garbh Phort
IONA
Iona Heritage
Maclean's Cross
Abbey & Nunnery
Kintra
Creich
Columba Centre
Baile Mór
10mins.
Ardhglas
Fionnphort
Bun an Leoib
Ardchrishnish
Torrans
Stac an Aoineidh
Loch Poit na h-I
Eorabus
Knockan
Loch na Làthaich
A849
B R O L A S S
Carsaig
Loch Buie
Druim Fada 1329
Eilean nah-Aon Chaorach
Bunessan
Beinn a' Ghlinne Mhóir 369
Ross of Mull Historical Centre
Beinn Chreagach 1235
Greave
Sound of Iona
Fidden
Loch Assopol
ROSS OF MULL
Cruachan Min 1232
Beach River
Erraid
Knockvologan
Ardalanish
Uisken
Aoineadh Mór
Carsaig Bay
Soa Island
Eilean nam Muc
Beinn a' Chaol-Airigh 411
Ardchiavaig
Carsaig Arches
Frank Lockwood's Island
Eilean a' Chalmain
Ardalanish Bay
Rubha nam Bràithrean
Malcolm's Point
Rubh' Ardalanish
FIRTH OF LORN
Torran Rocks
West Reef
Sgeir Dhoirbh
Dubh-fheith
Garbh Eileach
Eilean Dubh Mór
Garvellachs
Eileach an Naoimh
Lunga
Guirasdeal
Rubha nam Faoilean
Cruach Scarba 1474
Gulf of Corryvreckan
Corryvreckan Whirlpool
Oban to Colonsay 2hrs 20mins.
Glengarrisdale Bay
An Cruachan
Port na Cuilce
Balnahard
Kiloran Bay
Port Ceann a' Gharraidh
Uragaig
Carnan Eoin 469
Loch an Sgoltaire
Kiloran
B8086
COLONSAY
Colonsay House
Port a' Bhàta
Sgreadan
Kilchattan
Glas Aird
Scalasaig
Eilean a' Chladaich
Colonsay
Loch Staosnaig
Garvard
B8085
Rubha Dubh
Colonsay to Port Askaig 1hr. 10mins. (Seasonal)
Eilean Leathann
Cruach na Seilcheig 971
Loch na Conaire
Loch Doire na h-Achlaise
Loch a' Bhurra
Glendebadel Bay
Ben Garrisdale 1198
Loch Gheoidh
Lochanan Tana
Loch Fada Cul na Beinne
Cruach Ionnastail 967
Port nan Laogh
Corpach Bay
Cruach an Uillt Fheàrna 1106
Lussa River
Lealt Burn
Lealt
Beinn Bhreac
Dubh Bheinn
Fishing Loch
Ardlussa
Ardlussa Bay
Loch Cathar nan Eun
Beinn an Tairbh
Rainberg Mór 1487
Shian Bay
Dubh Eilean
ORONSAY
Oronsay
56

69
BEN NEVIS
4411
SUNART
ARDGOUR
HIGHLAND
MORVERN
Salen
Acharacle
Strontian
Scotstown
Glenborrodale
Lochaline
Kingairloch
Inversanda
Onich
North Ballachulish
Ballachulish
Glencoe
Kinlochleven
Kentallen
Duror
Portnacroish
Port Appin
LISMORE
Eriska
Barcaldine
Benderloch
Connel
Dunbeg
OBAN
PAGE 115
KERRERA
Taynuilt
BEN CRUACHAN
Dalmally
Lochawe
Kilchrenan
ISLE OF MULL
Craignure
Lochdon
Lochbuie
63
FIRTH OF LORN
SEIL
Easdale
SLATE ISLANDS
LUING
SCARBA
Gulf of Corryvreckan
ARGYLL & BUTE
Kilmelford
Arduaine
Kilmartin
Lochgilphead
Inveraray
Furnace
Clachan Strachur
ARGYLL FOREST PARK
LOCH FYNE
LOCH ETIVE
LOCH LINNHE
LOCH AWE
KNAPDALE FOREST
KILMICHAEL FOREST
Oban to Colonsay 2hrs. 20 mins.
Oban to Craignure 45mins.
Oban to Lismore 50mins.
A82
A861
A884
A849
A828
A85
A816
A819
A83
A815
A886
B8043
B8045
B844
B840
B841
56
57

P E R T H
&
K I N R O S S
G R A M P I A N
M O U N T A I N S
R A N N O C H
M O O R
B R E A D A L B A N E
LOCH LOMOND & THE TROSSACHS
NATIONAL PARK
S T I R L I N G
PERTH & KINROSS
TAY FOREST PARK
QUEEN ELIZABETH FOREST PARK
Loch Rannoch
Kinloch Rannoch
Rannoch Station
Bridge of Gaur
Bridge of Ericht
Killichonan
Camghouran
Dall House
Carie
Tempar
Dunalastair
Tummel Bridge
Trinafour
Dalnacardoch Lodge
Schiehallion 3554
White Bridge
Kingshouse
Altnafeadh
Black Corries
White Corries
A' CHRUACH
BLACK MOUNT
Achallader
Bridge of Orchy
Victoria Bri.
Tyndrum
Clifton
Crianlarich
BEN MORE 3852
Stob Binnein 3821
Ben Lui 3708
Glen Lyon
Bridge of Balgie
Innerwick
Camusvrachan
Invervar
Fortingall
Bridge of Lyon
Kenmore
Fearnan
Lawers
BEN LAWERS 3984
Loch Tay
Killin
Morenish
Ardtalnaig
Ardeonaig
Glen Dochart
Luib
Ardchyle
Lochearnhead
St Fillans
Loch Earn
Comrie
Balquhidder
Strathyre
Kingshouse
BEN VORLICH 3231
FOREST OF GLENARTNEY
Ardchullarie
BEN LEDI 2882
Callander
Kilmahog
Loch Katrine
Stronachlachar
BEN VENUE 2386
Brig o' Turk
Loch Venachar
ACHRAY FOREST
Aberfoyle
Port of Menteith
Thornhill
Doune
Deanston
Dunblane
Bridge of Allan
Kippen
Gargunnock
Buchlyvie
Arnprior
Balfron
Drymen
Balmaha
Inchcailloch
Rowardennan
BEN LOMOND 3194
Inversnaid
Inveruglas
Tarbet
Arrochar
Succoth
LOCH LOMOND
Ardlui
BEN VORLICH 3093
BEINN IME 3318
Luss
Garelochhead
Cambusbarron
STIRLING
A9
A82
A85
A827
A84
A81
A821
A873
A811
A83
A814
A817
A875
B846
B847
M9

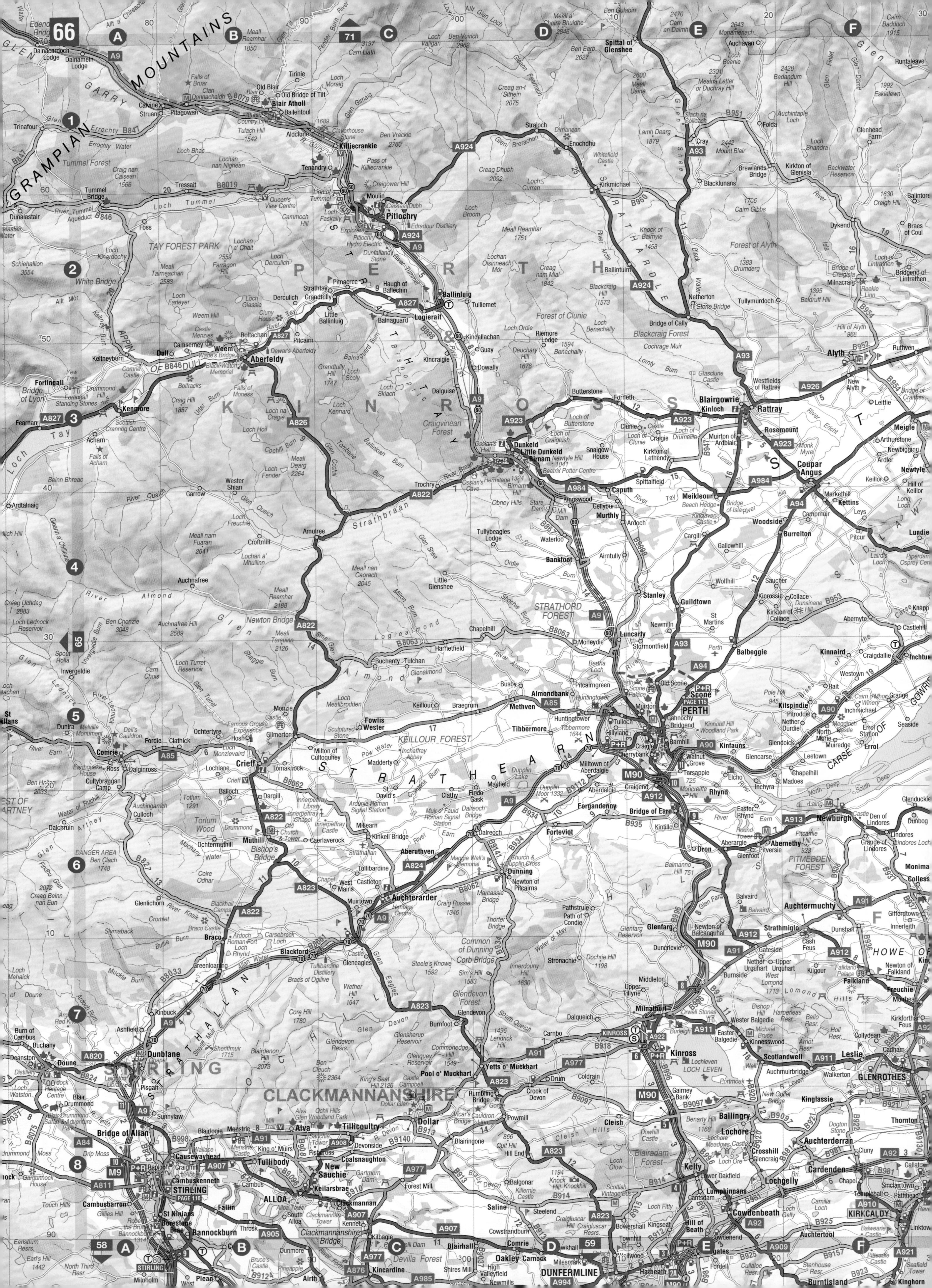
66
GRAMPIAN MOUNTAINS
71
58
59
65
PAGE 115
PAGE 116
A
B
C
D
E
F
1
2
3
4
5
6
7
8
Spittal of Glenshee
Glen Shee
Blair Atholl
Killiecrankie
Pass of Killiecrankie
Pitlochry
Loch Tummel
Tummel Bridge
Queen's View Centre
Kinloch Rannoch
Schiehallion 3554
TAY FOREST PARK
Ballinluig
Logierait
Aberfeldy
Weem
Dull
Fortingall
Kenmore
Loch Tay
P E R T H
&
K I N R O S S
Dunkeld
Birnam
Blairgowrie
Rattray
Alyth
Coupar Angus
Meigle
Kirkmichael
Bridge of Cally
Forest of Alyth
Forest of Clunie
STRATHARDLE
Amulree
Strathbraan
Glen Almond
Newton Bridge
Sma' Glen
Stanley
Luncarty
Bankfoot
Methven
Almondbank
Scone
PERTH
Kinfauns
CARSE OF GOWRIE
Errol
Newburgh
Abernethy
Bridge of Earn
Crieff
Comrie
S T R A T H E A R N
Muthill
Auchterarder
Gleneagles
Blackford
Dunning
Forteviot
Glenfarg
Milnathort
Kinross
LOCH LEVEN
Auchtermuchty
Falkland
HOWE OF FIFE
Leslie
GLENROTHES
Kirkcaldy
Lochgelly
Cowdenbeath
Kelty
Dunfermline
STIRLING
CLACKMANNANSHIRE
Dunblane
Doune
Bridge of Allan
Alloa
Alva
Tillicoultry
Dollar
Clackmannan
Kincardine
Bannockburn
Yetts o' Muckhart
Pool o' Muckhart
Glendevon
Braco
Greenloaning
OCHIL HILLS
A9
A93
A94
A822
A823
A827
A924
A923
A984
A85
A91
A977
A907
M9
M90

ABERDEENSHIRE
NORTH SEA
FIRTH OF TAY
FIRTH OF FORTH
ANGUS
FIFE
MONTROSE
BRECHIN
FORFAR
ARBROATH
DUNDEE
PAGE 108
St Andrews
Inverbervie
Laurencekirk
Edzell
Marykirk
St Cyrus
Johnshaven
Kirriemuir
Glamis
Letham
Friockheim
Carnoustie
Monifieth
Broughty Ferry
Tayport
Newport-on-Tay
Wormit
Tay Bridge
Tay Road Bridge
Leuchars
Guardbridge
Cupar
Kingsbarns
Crail
Anstruther
Pittenweem
St Monans
Elie
Earlsferry
Colinsburgh
Kilconquhar
Largo Bay
Lower Largo
Leven
Methil
Buckhaven
East Wemyss
West Wemyss
Dysart
Kennoway
Windygates
Markinch
Ladybank
Springfield
Pitlessie
Ceres
Lunan Bay
Boddin Point
Red Head
Auchmithie
Inverkeilor
Buddon Ness
Tentsmuir Forest
St Andrews Bay
Eden Mouth
Buddo Ness
Fife Ness
Isle of May
Bell Rock
Chapel Ness
Ruddons Point
Sauchar Point
Montrose Basin
Ferryden
Usan
Hillside
Tannadice
Finavon
Aberlemno
Guthrie
Carmyllie
Greystone
Colliston
Leysmill
Monikie
Muirdrum
Panbride
East Haven
Barry
Tealing
Kingoodie
Invergowrie
Longforgan
Muirhead
Balmerino
Kilmany
Balmullo
Dairsie
Strathkinness
Boarhills
Kilrenny
Cellardyke
A90
A92
A94
A935
A933
A934
A937
A926
A928
A932
A930
A914
A919
A91
A913
A915
A916
A917
A911
A955
A923
A85

SEA OF THE HEBRIDES
INNER HEBRIDES
ISLE OF SKYE
MINGINISH
CUILLIN HILLS
SOUND OF RÙM
Sound of Canna
Sound of Eigg
An Ceannaich
Oisgill Bay
Lower Milovaig
Upper Milovaig
Waterstein
Borrodale
Loch Mòr
Loch Pooltiel
Feriniquarrie
Glendale
Lephin
Colbost
Holmisdale
Colbost Croft
Skinidin
Dunvegan
Kilmuir
Lonmore
Giant Angus Macaskill
Dun Osdale Broch
Moonen Bay
Ben Corkeval
HEALABHAL MHOR
1538
HEALABHAL BHEAG
1600
Ramasaig
Hoe Rape
The Hoe
759
Loch Glen Ionadal
Ben Connan
799
Hoe Point
Beinn na Boineid
1207
Harlosh Point
Harlosh Island
Colbost Point
Tarner Island
Am Bi-bogha Mór
An Dubh-sgeir
Ben Idrigill
Macleod's Maidens
IDRIGILL POINT
Wiay
Loch Bracadale
Oronsay
Roskhill
Roag
Orbost
Ardroag
Vatten
Harlosh
Balmore
Loch Bharcasaig
Ose
Ullinish
Struan
Struanmore
Bracadale
Coillore
Totardor
Dun Beag
Dun Mor
Gnoc Ullinish Chambered Cairn
Cam Liath Chambered Cairn
Dun Ardtreck
Portnalong
Fernilea
Fiskavaig
Rubha nan Clach
Dun Ard an t-Sàbhail
Arnaval
1210
Gleann Oraid
Carbost
Talisker Distillery
Merkadale
Drynoch
Talisker
Talisker Bay
Loch Harport
Beinn nan Cuithean
Loch Sleadale
Eynort River
Beinn Bhreac
1468
Eynort
Glen Brittle Forest
Loch Eynort
An Dubh-sgeir
Stac an Tuill
River Brittle
Glen Brittle
Bualintur
Glenbrittle
Sgurr Alasdair
3257
Sgurr a' Ghreadaidh
3197
Sgurr nan Gillean
3167
Harta Corrie
Loch Coruisk
3037
Sgurr nan Eag
Ceann na Beinne
736
Loch Brittle
Rubh' an Dunain Chambered Cairn
Soay Sound
464
Beinn Bhreac
Mol-chlach
SOAY
Loch Scavaig
Sligachan
Glen Sligachan
River Drynoch
A863
A850
A87
A855
B884
B885
B8009
Fairy Bridge
Edinbane
Blackhill
Bernisdale
Glen Bernisdale
St Columba's Isle
Skeabost
Carbost
Borve
Kensaleyre
Rhenetra
Tote
Crepkill
Uigshader
Drumuie
Achachork
Glengrasco
Shulishadermor (Sulaisiadar Mòr)
Portree
Beinn na Greine
1376
Heatherfield
Glenmore
Mugeary
Tungadal Souterrain
Ben Duagrich
Roineval
1442
Meall an Fhuarain
Varragill River
Loch Ravag
Loch Connan
Beinn a' Ghlinne Bhig
682
Cruachan Beinn a' Chearcaill
Uig
Totaig
Suardal Hut Circle
Dun Fiadhairt
CANNA
Garrisdale Point
Ceann Creag-airighe
426
Carn a' Ghaill
693
A' Chill
An Coroghon
Castle
Canna Harbour
Sanday
Rùm to Canna 55mins.
Mallaig to Canna 2hrs. (Seasonal)
Rubha Shamhnan Insir
Kilmory
Guirdil Bay
Camas Pliasgaig
Mullach Mòr
997
Sgorr Mhòr
1273
Kinloch Castle
Kinloch
Loch Scresort
Orval
1874
Long Loch
Loch Gainmhich
Schooner Point
Sgorr Reidh
Glen Harris
Loch Fiachanis
Hallival
Askival
2663
Ainshval
2552
Ruinsival
Sgurr nan Gillean
Loch Papadil
RÙM
NATIONAL NATURE RESERVE
Rubha nam Meirleach
Mallaig to Rùm 1hr. 20mins.
Muck to Canna 1hr. 35mins. (Seasonal)
Rùm to Muck 1hr. 10mins. (Seasonal)
Oigh-sgeir
Cleadale
Bay of Laig
Rubha an Fhasaidh
Loch Beinn Tighe
EIGG
An Sgurr
1292
Sandavore
Kildonnan
Galmisdale
Sgeir Eskernish
Eilean nan Each
Godag
Port Mor
MUCK
Dubh Sgeir
Egg to Muck 35mins.
Mallaig to Muck
Sanna Point
Sanna Bay
Portuairk
Ardnamurchan Lighthouse
Point of Ardnamurchan
Achnaha
Achosnich
Fascadale
A B C D E F
1 2 3 4 5 6 7 8
850 40 30 20 10 800 90 80 70
100 10 20 30 40
76
74
62
63

77
70
64
G
H
J
K
L
M
1
2
3
4
5
6
7
8
Holm Island
Eilean Fladday
Manish Point
Torran
Loch Arnish
Arnish
SOUND OF RAASAY
INNER SOUND
Brochel
Brochel Castle
RAASAY
Glame
Balachuirn
Dun Caan
1455
Holoman Bay
Oskaig
Clachan
Inverarish
Suisnish
North Fearns
Eyre
Eyre Point
Rubha na Leac
Camastianavaig
Conordan
Lower Ollach
Upper Ollach
Gedintailor
Balmeanach
Peinchorran
Sconser
Loch Sligachan
GLAMAIG
2542
Moll
Loch Ainort
Luib
SKYE
Dunan
(An Dùnan)
Caolas Scalpay
SCALPAY
Scalpay House
Guillamon Island
Pabay
Mullach na Càrn
1298
Loch an Leòid
Sgeir Dhearg
Longay
CROWLIN ISLANDS
Eilean Beag
Eilean Mòr
Caolas Mòr
Eilean na Bà
Marsco
2414
Glas Bheinn Mhòr
1852
Beinn na Cro
Garbh-bheinn
2649
BLA BHEINN
3046
Loch na Creitheach
Broadford
(An t Ath Leathann)
Broadford Bay
Corry
Waterloo
(Achadh a' Chuirn)
Harrapool
(Harrapul)
Skulamus
(Sgulamus)
Lower Breakish
(Brecais Iosal)
Breakish
(Brecais Àrd)
Isle of Skye
Beinn na Caillich
2403
Strath Suardal
Loch Cill Chriosd
Suardal Chambered Cairn
Lochain Dubha
Torrin
Kilbride
Clach na h'Annait
Loch Slapin
Camasunary
Na Clachan Bhreige Stone Circle
Kirkibost
Kilmarie
Dun Ringill Fort
Elgol
Glasnakille
Prince Charlie's Cave
Dun Grugaig
Rubha na h-Easgainne
Eilean na h-Airde
Rubha Suisnish
Loch Eishort
Eilean Heast
Heaste
Loch Lonachan
Beinn nan Càrn
983
Eyre Kearstack Hillfort
Ord
(An t-Òrd)
Sgòrach Breac
981
Lochan Fada
Dunscaith Castle
Tokavaig
(Tocabhaig)
Tarskavaig
(Tarscabhaig)
Tarskavaig Point
Achnacloich
(Ach na Cloiche)
Loch Dhùghaill
Inver Dalavil
Teangue
(An Teanga)
Saasaig
Knock Bay
Ferindonald
(Fearann Dhomhnaill)
Kilmore
Kilbeg
Armadale Castle
Armadale Bay
Armadale
(Armadal)
Ardvasar
(Àird a Bhasair)
Calligarry
Tormore
Aird
(An Aird)
Rubha Charn nan Cearc
Sgurr nan Caorach
920
Geur Rubha
Ard Thurinish
Point of Sleat
SOUND OF SLEAT
An Fhaochag
Drumfearn
(Druim Fhearna)
Duisdalemore
(Duisdeil Mòr)
Gallery an Talla Dearg
Ornsay
Isleornsay
(Eilean Iarmain)
Camuscross
(Camus Croise)
Camas Baravaig
Camas Garbh
Sandaig Islands
A851
A87
A890
A896
A830
A861
A82
B883
B8083
Applecross
Applecross Bay
Applecross Forest
Milton
Camusteel
Camusterrach
Ard-dhubh
Culduie
Toscaig
Uags
River Applecross
Loch nan Eun
Loch Lundie
Loch Coire Attadale
Beinn Bhan
2938
Sgurr a' Chaorachain
2539
Bealach na Bà
Meall Gorm
Loch Coire nan Arr
Loch Gaineamhach
Loch Coultrie
Rassal Ashwood
Kishorn
Loch Kishorn
Kishorn Island
Ardarroch
Achintraid
Bad a' Chreamha
1296
Ardaneaskan
Stromemore
Strome Castle
Loch Carron
Plockton
Highland Farm
Craig
Duirinish
Drumbuie
Port Cam
Erbusaig
Badicaul
Black Islands
Kyle of Lochalsh
(Caol Loch Aillse)
Plock of Kyle
Bright Water
Kyleakin
Caisteal Maol
Kyle Akin
Donald Murchison's Monument
Lochalsh Woodland
Balmacara Square
Balmacara
Loch Alsh
Ardintoul Point
Auchtertyre
Kirkton
Nostie
Ardelve
Dornie
Conchra
Bundalloch
Carndu
Glas Eilean
Eilean Donan
Caisteal Grugaig Broch
Keppoch
Letterfearn
Loch Duich
Inverinate
Ratagan Forest
Ratagan
Invershiel
Shiel Bridge
Ault a' chruinn
Morvich
Ruarach
Lienassie
Countryside Centre
Stromeferry
Achmore
Ardnarff
Lochcarron
Attadale
Strathcarron
Achintee
New Kelso
Tullich
Kirkton
Coulags
Balnacra
Achnashellach
Achnashellach Forest
Craig
Glenshieldaig Forest
Beinn Damh
2957
Maol Chean-dearg
3060
Loch Coire an Ruadh-stic
An Gorm-loch
Sgurr a' Gharaidh
2396
Glas Bheinn
2332
Smithy Heritage Centre
Carn nan Iomairean
Carn Geuradainn
1950
Bendronaig Lodge
Attadale Forest
West Monar Forest
Killilan Forest
Killilan
Sallachy
Camas-luinie
Glen Elchaig
Inverinate Forest
Falls of Glomach
A' Ghlas-bheinn
3006
Sgurr a' Bhealaich Dheirg
BEINN FHADA OR BEN ATTOW
3385
Kintail Forest
FIVE SISTERS
Sgurr Fhuaran
3505
NORTH WEST HIGHLANDS
West Benula Forest
Glenshiel Forest
The Saddle
3319
GLEN SHIEL
Cluanie Inn
Cluanie Lodge
Cluanie Forest
Aonach air Chrith
3342
Maol Chinn-dearg
Sgurr a' Mhaoraich
3365
Glenquoich Forest
Kinloch Hourn
Loch Hourn
Gleouraich
3394
East Glenquoich Forest
Loch Quoich
Buidhe Bheinn
2884
Glenelg
Glenelg Bay
Galltair
Bernera
Kylerhea
(Caol Reatha)
Kyle Rhea
Ben Aslak
1984
Beinn na Seamraig
Eilanreach
Dun Troddan Broch
Dun Telve Broch
Balvraid
Chambered Cairn
Beinn a' Chapuill
2434
Dun Grugaig Broch
Upper Sandaig
Màm an Staing
BEINN SGRITHEALL
3194
Beinn nan Caorach
2539
Eilean Ràrsaidh
Arnisdale
Corran
Glen Arnisdale
Druim Fada
Barrisdale Bay
Inverguseran
Airor
KNOYDART
Ladhar Bheinn
3343
Sandaig
Sandaig Bay
Scottas
Inverie
Inverie Bay
Luinne Bheinn
3083
Meall Buidhe
3107
Kilchoan
Mallaig
(Malaig)
Mallaig Bheag
Mallaig to Lochboisdale 3hrs. 30mins. (Seasonal)
Mallaig to Armadale 25mins.
Mallaig to Eigg 1hr. 10mins.
Eigg to Rùm 1hr. (Seasonal)
Courteachan
Glasnacardoch
(Glas na Cardaich)
Heritage Centre
Loch Nevis
Beoraidbeg
Morar
Bracara
Stoul
Tarbet
Kylesmorar
NORTH MORAR
Ardnamurach
Finiskaig
Sgurr na Ciche
3412
Sgurr Mòr
3290
LOCHABER
Glen Dessarry
Strathan
Loch Arkaig
Murlaggan
Glenancross
Camusdarach
(An Camus Darach)
Lòn Liath
The Jacobite
Loch Morar
SOUTH MORAR
Portnaluchaig
Bunacaimb
Back of Keppoch
(Cul na Caepaich)
Kinloid
(Ceann an Leothaid)
ARISAIG
Arisaig
(Arasaig)
Luinga Bheag
Luinga Mhor
Rubh' Arisaig
Land, Sea and Islands Centre
Glen Cottage
Drumindarroch
Borrodale
Glen Beasdale
Prince's Cairn
Polnish
Loch nan Uamh
Lochailort
(Ceann Loch Ailleart)
Inverailort
Ranochan
Loch Eilt
Glenfinnan
Glenfinnan Monument
Viaduct
Station
Rubha nan Tri Chlach
Chathastail
Eilean a' Ghaill
Eilean an t-Snidhe
Sound of Arisaig
Eilean nan Gobhar
Samalaman Island
Glenuig Bay
Samalaman
Smirisary
Glenuig
(Gleann Uige)
Roshven
ROIS-BHEINN
2895
Druim Fiaclach
2852
Rubh' Aird an Fheidh
Eilean Shona
Rubha Aird Druimnich
Baramore
Arean
Ockle Point
Farquhar's Point
Port Bàn
Kilmory
Ockle
Kinlochmoidart
(Ceann Loch Muideirt)
Ardmolich
Brunery
MOIDART
Newton of Ardtoe
Ardtoe
Shielfoot
Blain
Dalnabreck
Langal
Dalelia
Mingarrypark
Moss
Acharacle
(Ath-Tharracail)
Arivegaig
Gorteneorn
Kentra Bay
Ardshealach
Achateny
Branault
Gortenfern
Beinn Bhreac
1171
Polloch
Glenhurich
Loch Doilet
Loch Shiel
Scamodale
Gaskan
Sgorr an Tarmachain
2474
Beinn Odhar Bheag
2895
Kinlocheil
Corribeg
Fassfern
Achdalieu
Loch Eil
South Garvan
Duisky
Blaich
Corpach
Achaphubuil
Camusnagaul
Trislaig
Stronchreggan
Achnanellan
Loch Arkaig
Locheil Forest
Glen Mallie
Meall Blàir
2154
Gleann Suileag
Druim Fada
Stob Coire a' Chearcaill
2528
Inverscaddle Bay
Druimarbin
Blarmachfoldach
ARDGOUR
NAMURCHAN

NORTH WEST HIGHLANDS
STRATHCONON
FOREST
Glen Carron
Glencarron Lodge
Craig
A890
Achnashellach Forest
Loch Sgamhain
Loch Cnoc na Mointeich
Carn Gorm
Moruisg 3026
Glencarron & Glenuig Forest
Gleann Fhiodhaig
River Meig
Creag na h-Iolaire
Maoile Lunndaidh 3304
Sgurr a' Chaorachain 3455
Beinn Tharsuinn
West Monar Forest
Loch Mhuilich
East Monar Forest
Loch Monar
Monar Lodge
Lurg Mhór 3234
Bendronaig Lodge
Beinn Dronaig
Loch Calavie
Lochan Gobhlach
Loch an Tachdaich
Meallan Buidhe
An Gead Loch
An Cruachan 2312
Carn na Sean-lùibe
Loch Cruoshie
Sgurr na Lapaich 3775
An Riabhachan 3696
Aonach Buidhe 2949
Killilan Forest
Loch Mhoicean
Loch Mullardoch
Glen Cannich
Glencannich Forest
Liatrie
Muchrachd
Loch Sealbhanach
Carnach
Loch na Leitreach
West Benula Forest
Coire Lochan
Toll Creagach 3457
Tom a' Chòinich 3646
Carn Eighe 3880
Gleann nam Fiadh
Falls of Glomach
Sgurr na Lapaich 3401
Sgurr nan Ceathreamhnan 3771
Ghlas-bheinn 3006
Loch a' Bhealaich
Affric Lodge
Loch Affric
Glen Affric
River Affric
Glenaffric Forest
Guisachan Forest
Loch Beinn a' Mheadhoin
Loch nan Sean-each
Fasnakyle Forest
Doire Tana
Tomich
Cannich
Kerrow
Gleann Gniomhaidh
Ciste Dhubh 3218
Mullach Fraoch-choire 3614
A' Chràlaig 3673
Sgurr nan Conbhairean 3634
Aonach Shasuinn 2913
Carn a' Chaochain 2314
Loch na Beinne Bàine
Ceannacroc Forest
River Doe
Cluanie Inn
GLEN SHIEL
A87
Cluanie Lodge
Loch Cluanie
Ceannacroc Lodge
A887
Ceannacroc Bridge
Beinneun Forest
Meall Dubh 2581
Beinn Loinne
Bunloinn Forest
Cluanie Forest
Aonach air Chrith 3342
Maol Chinn-dearg
Glenquoich Forest
Loch Loyne
River Loyne
East Glenquoich Forest
Loch Fearna
Loch Quoich
Kingie
Tomdoun
Inchlaggan
Ardochy House
Loch Garry
Glen Garry
Gairich 3015
Beinn Bheag
Lochan nan Sgùd
Glas Bheinn 1825
River Kingie
Glen Kingie
Lochan Dubh
Meall Blàir 2154
Loch Blàir
Sgurr Mhurlagain 2885
Murlaggan
Loch Arkaig
Ardechive
Locheil Forest
Inver Mallie
Achnacarry
Clan Cameron
Bunarkaig
Clunes
Chia-aig Falls
Glen Mallie
Meall a' Phubuill 2533
Druim Gleann Laoigh
Achnanellan
Glen Loy
Gairlochy
Gleann Suileag
Druim Fada
Stob a' Ghrianain
Muirshearlich
Fassfern
Achdalieu
Loch Eil
The Jacobite
A830
Duisky
Blaich
A861
Corpach
Caol
Banavie
Neptune's Staircase
FORT WILLIAM
Treasures of the Earth
Lochyside
Inverlochy
Victoria Bridge
Ben Nevis Distillery
Claggan
Bridge of Nevis
Achaphubuil
Camusnagaul
Trislaig
Stronchreggan
Stob Coire a' Chearcaill 2528
Achintee
Druimarbin
A82
Conaglen
Inverscaddle Bay
Blarmachfoldach
Nevis Forest
Glen Nevis
BEN NEVIS 4411
AONACH BEAG 4048
Lochan Meall an t-Suidhe
Killiechonate Forest
Stob Choire Claurigh 3858
Stob Coire Easain
Stob Coire Easain 3658
Torlundy
Nevis Range Gondola
Leanachan Forest
Spean Bridge
Commando Memorial
Highbridge
Brackletter
Stronenaba
Glenfintaig Lodge
Upper Glenfintaig
New Bridge
Altrua
Loch Lochy
Clunes Forest
South Laggan Forest
Kilfinnan
Laggan
Laggan Swing Bridge
Glengarry Forest
Ben Tee 2957
Sròn a' Choire Ghairbh 3066
Geal Charn
Invergarry
Invergarry Castle
Wester Mandally
Well of Seven Heads
Munerigie
Faichem
Bridge of Oich
Aberchalder
Loch Oich
Newtown
Culachy Falls
Fort Augustus
Jenkins Park
Auchteraw
Inchnacardoch Forest
Caledonian Canal
Glendoebeg
Loch Lundie
Allt Lundie
Invermoriston
Glen Moriston
Dundreggan
Dundreggan Forest
Dundreggan Reservoir
Dalchreichart
Torgyle
Portclair Forest
Inverwick Forest
Burach 1986
Levishie
Levishie Forest
Achnaconeran
Alltsigh
Loch nan Eun
Loch ma Stac
Loch a' Chràthaich
Meall a' Chràthaich 2226
Loch a' Mhuilinn
Loch na Ruighe Duibhe
River Enrick
Suidhe Ghuirmain 1896
Balmacaan Forest
Corrimony
Corrimony Chambered Cairn
Buntait
Braefield
A831
Balnain
Loch Meiklie
Glen Urquhart
Drumnadrochit
Lewiston
Strone
Urquhart Bay
Borlum
Divach
Falls of Divach
Lower Lenie
Upper Lenie
John Cobb Memorial
Bunloit
Balbeg
Loch Aslaich
Loch nam Breac Dearga
Inverfarigaig
Foyers
Falls of Foyers
Lyne of Gorthleck
Farigaig Forest
Errogie
Dunmaglass Lodge
Farraline
Loch Conagleann
Wester Aberchalder
Lochgarthside
Bunkegivie
Whitebridge
Loch Knockie
Knockie Lodge
Upper Knockchoilum
Garrogie Lodge
Glenbrein Lodge
Loch Tarff
Loch nan Eun
B862
LOCH NESS
GLEN MOR
Strath Errick
Killin Lodge
Loch Killin
Glen Markie
Burrach Mhor 2686
Carn na Saobhaidhe 2658
Carn na Làraiche Maoile 2658
Glendoe Forest
Carn a' Chuilinn 2677
Lochan na Stàirne
Carn Easgann Bàna 2554
Culachy Forest
Corrieyairack Pass
Gairbeinn 2929
Loch an Aonaich Odhair
Meall na h-Aisre 2828
Geal Charn 3036
Creag Mhòr 2498
Carn Leac 2889
Corrieyairack Forest
Melgarve
Garva Bridge
Garvamore
Carn Dearg 2677
River Spey
Loch Spey
Loch a' Bhànain
Drummin
Crathie
Glenshero Lodge
Strathmashie House
A86
Feagour
Cromra
Kinloch Laggan
Carn Liath 3298
Coillie Coire Chrannaig
Lochan a' Choire
Lochan Coire Choille-rais
Creag Meagaidh 3700
Beinn Teallach 2994
Beinn a' Chaorainn 3437
Moy Forest
Moy Lodge
Loch Laggan
Lochan na h-Earba
Binnein Shuas
Ardverikie Forest
Beinn Eilde 2207
Brae Roy Lodge
Glen Roy
Carn Dearg 2736
Beinn Iaruinn 2636
Parallel Roads
Coire Ceirsle Hill
Glen Gloy
Bohenie
Creag Dhubh 2160
Roybridge
Achluachrach
GLEN SPEAN
Monessie Falls
Tulloch
Inverlair Falls
Braes o' Lochaber
Bunroy
Inverroy
Beinn Chlianaig 2343
Fersit
Loch Treig
Meall Luidh Mòr
Loch Laggan Resr.
Lochan an Tuirc
Geal Charn 3443
Loch a' Bhealaich Leamhain
Beinn a' Chlachair 3569
An Lairig 3391
Càrn Dearg
Loch Pattack
Ben Alder Lodge
Meall Cruaidh 2941
Loch Ghuilbinn
Aonach Beag 3647
Chno Dearg 3433
Loch An Sgoir
Ben Alder 3765
Ben Alder Forest
Loch Ericht
Corrievarkie Lodge
Beinn Udlamain 3306
Loch na Lap
Beinn na Lap
Uisge Labhair
Corrour Shooting Lodge
Corrour Forest
Sgor Gaibhre 3124
Stob an Aonaich Mhoir
Talla Bheith Forest
Creaguaineach Lodge
MAMORE FOREST
Water of Nevis
Steall Falls
Glen Nevis Lower Falls
Achriabhach
Abhainn Rath
Glen Orrin
River Orrin
Orrin Reservoir
Corriehallie Forest
Loch na Caoidhe
Am Fiar-loch
An Gorm-loch
Meallan Buidhe 2505
Sgurr a' Choire Ghlais 3554
Sgurr na Ruaidhe 3254
Beinn a' Bha'ach Ard 2827
Carn Bàn
Erchless Forest
Erchless Castle
Struy
Leishmore
Culligran Falls
River Farrar
Glen Strathfarrar
Loch a' Mhuillidh
Sgorr na Diollaid 2676
Braulen Lodge
Uisge Misgeach
Loch Beannacharan
Inverchoran
Scardroy
Cabaan Forest
Loch an Spàrdain
Carn Gorm 2218
Balmore Forest
River Cannich
Glassburn
Strathglass
River Glass
Struy Forest
Loch Neaty
Boblainy Forest
Loch Bruicheach
Loch Garbh Iolachan
Carn Mòr 1497
Lochan an Tairt
Loch Gorm
Meall nan Caorach 1401
Glen Convinth
A833
Abriachan
Meall na h-Eilrig 1526
Dores
Tom Bailgeann 1522
Loch Ceo Glais
Torness
Lochend
Carn a' Bhodaich 1642
Cragganvallie
Ardendrain
Kiltarlity
Belladrum
THE AIRD
An Leacainn 1358
South Clunes
Culburnie
Camault Muir
Glaichbea
Eskadale
Craigdhu
Craobhnaclag
Crask of Aigas
Hughton
Fanellan
Kilmorack
Breakachy
Balblair
Beauly
Kirkhill
Lentran
Drumchardine
Newtonhill
Balchraggan
A862
A831
Farley
Broallan
Drumindorsair
Ruisaurie
Ruilick
Dunmore
Rheindown
Windhill
Milton
Muir of Ord
Ardnagrask
Corry of Ardnagrask
A832
Chapelton
Redcastle
Kilcoy
Urray Forest
Glen Ord Distillery
Allt Goibhre
Gleann Goibhre
Loch nam Bonnach
Cnoc Eille Mòr
Loch nan Eun
Lochan Fada
Balnagrantach
Balbeg
Balnaglaic
Rychraggan
Polmaily
Milton
Achmony
Drum Farm Centre
Loch Ness Centre
A82
B852
B862
Fort Augustus
Bunoich
Caledonian Canal
Clansman Centre
Fairburn
Cloiche Mòire
Loch Aradaidh
Carn na Gabhar
Loch Coire a' Bhuic
78
69
64
65
A B C D E F
1 2 3 4 5 6 7 8

MORAY FIRTH
Alturlie Point
Inverness
North Kessock
South Kessock
Charlestown
Craigton
Kilmuir
Bunchrew
Clachnaharry
Leachkin
Culcabock
Lochardil
PAGE 110
Milton of Leys
Culloden
Smithton
Balloch
Westhill
Newton
Tornagrain
Dalcross
Croy
Cantraywood
Cantray
Easter Galcantray
Wester Galcantray
Newlands
Cantraybruich
Clephanton
Cawdor
Culcharry
Urchany
Littlemill
Redburn
Lochardil
Dochgarroch
Scaniport
Essich
Daviot
Craggiemore
Drumashie Moor
Loch Ashie
Inverarnie
Farr
Dunlichity Lodge
Moy
Tomatin
Raigbeg
Corrybrough
Findhorn Bridge
East Croachy
Aberarder
Slochd
Clune
Corrievorrie
Glenmazeran Lodge
Dalmigavie
Coignafearn Lodge
Coignafearn Forest
MONADHLIATH MOUNTAINS
Strathnairn Forest
Carrbridge
Ellan
Sluggan
Duthil
Dulnain Bridge
Skye of Curr
Broomhill
Nethy Bridge
Boat of Garten
Drumuillie
Chapelton
Kinveachy
Avielochan
Granish
Aviemore
Coylumbridge
Inverdruie
Lynwilg
Doune
Alvie
Delfour
Kincraig
Speybank
Feshiebridge
Lagganlia
Insh
Kingussie
Lynchat
Strone
Ruthven
Newtonmore
Balla
Drumguish
Glentromie Lodge
Lynaberack Lodge
Glenfeshie Lodge
GLENFESHIE FOREST
Laggan
Balgowan
Drumgask
Catlodge
Etteridge
Crubenbeg
Crubenmore Lodge
Cuaich
Dalwhinnie
Gaick Lodge
Gaick Forest
Sronphadruig Lodge
Dalnamein Forest
FOREST OF ATHOLL
Dalnaspidal Lodge
Dalnacardoch Lodge
Edendon Bridge
GLEN GARRY
Bruar Lodge
BEINN DEARG
Forest Lodge
Old Blair
Tirinie
GRAMPIAN
PERTH & KINROSS
Glenlochsie Lodge
Spittal of Glenshee
GLAS MAOL
Devil's Elbow
The Cairnwell
AN SOCACH
Baddoch
Braemar
Castleton
Keiloch
Inverey
Mar Lodge
FOREST OF MAR
ABERDEENSHIRE
CAIRNGORMS NATIONAL PARK
CAIRN GORM
CAIRNGORM MOUNTAINS
BRAERIACH
BEN MACDUI
CAIRN TOUL
BEINN A' BHUIRD
BEN AVON
BRAEMAR
GLENMORE FOREST PARK
Glenmore
Abernethy Forest
Tulloch
West Croftmore
Clachaig
Dorback Lodge
Braes of Abernethy
Tomintoul
Bridge of Brown
Tomachlaggan
Tomnavoulin
Glenlivet
Grantown-on-Spey
Speybridge
Craggan
Achnahannet
Cromdale
HILLS OF CROMDALE
Dalvey
Advie
Cragganmore
Bridge of Avon
Dellefure
Cottartown
Balliewood
Glaschoil
Upper Derraid
Auchnagallin
Dava
Lochindorb
Lochindorb Lodge
Ferness
Glenferness Mains
Relugas
Dunphail
Carnach
Glenernie
Logie
Drumine Forest
Newtyle Forest
Dallas
Upper Knockando
Knockando
Birchview
Drynachan Lodge
Ruthven
Balvraid Lodge
M O R A Y
A N D
B A D E N O C H

72
A
B
C
D
E
F
1
2
3
4
5
6
7
8
Dallas
Rothes
Orton
Mulben
Keith
80
Drumnagorrach
Ramsburn
Aberchirder
Glen Grant Distillery
Ben Aigan 1546
Elchies Forest
Archiestown
Craigellachie
Maggieknockater
Keith & Dufftown Railway (Whisky Line)
Towiemore
Drummuir
Cairnie
Ruthven
Milltown of Rothiemay
Inverkeithny
Forgue
Fortrie
Upper Knockando
Knockando
Charlestown of Aberlour
Dufftown
Balvenie
Glenfiddich Distillery
Milltown of Auchindoun
Huntly
STRATHBOGIE
Drumblade
Largue
Corse
Aucharnie
Ythanwells
Badenscott
Milltown of Edinvillie
Kirktown of Mortlach
Invermarkie
Haugh of Glass
Blairmore
Bridgeswell
Birchview
Marypark
Inveravon Stones
Belleheiglash
Ballindalloch Castle
Cragganmore Distillery
Bridge of Avon
Advie
BEN RINNES 2759
Auchindoun
The Scalp
Laggan
Bailiesward
Succoth
Tillathrowie
Bridgend
Coynachie
Clashindarroch Forest
Clashindarroch
Kirkney
Gartly
Cults
Wardhouse
Hillhead
Bainshole
Glens of Foudland
Hill of Foudland
Lenchie
Largie
Upper Boddam
Kirkton of Culsalmond
Colpy
Cairnhill
Tochel
M O R A Y
Glenfiddich Lodge
Bridgend
Inverharroch
Ardwell
Dalvey
Drumin Castle
Drumin
Glenlivet
Packhorse Bridge
Shenval
Glenlivet 1594
Corryhabbie Hill 2561
Glenfiddich Forest
Cabrach
Mount of Haddoch 1708
Milton of Lesmore
Tap o' Noth 1848
Kennethmont
Leith Hall
Knockenbaird
Insch
Pitmachie
Old Rayne
Kirkton of Rayne
HILLS OF CROMDALE
Knock Earth House
Glenlivet Distillery
Castleton
Auchbreck
Carn Liath 1795
Cairn Muldonich 1857
Carn an t-Suidhe 2401
Round Hill
Belhinnie
Rhynie
Duncanston
Clatt
Leslie
Kirkton
Oyne
Kirkton of Oyne
Old Westhall
Tomnavoulin
Carn Daimh 1866
Knockandhu
Blackwater Forest
Cairnbrallan
Elrick
Craw Stane
St Mary's Kirk
Auchleven
Tomachlaggan
Clashnoir
Braes of Glenlivet
Chapeltown
Hill of Three Stones 2073
The Buck 2366
Clova
CORREEN HILLS 1599
Coldwells Croft
Whitehaugh Forest
GARI
Bennachie 1733
Bridge of Brown
Tomintoul
Milton
College of Scalan
Lumsden
Lord Arthur's Cairn 1699
Glenton
Millstone Hill 1340
Donview
Tom an t-Suidhe Mhoir
Carn Meadhonach
LADDER HILLS
Glenbuchat Lodge
Creag an Eunan
Mossatt
Tullynessle
Keig
Carn Mor 2639
Moss Hill 2159
Ladylea Hill
Rinmore
Kildrummy
Milltown
Bridge of Alford
Montgarrie
Alford Valley Railway
Rorandle
Ramstone
Carn Liath 2598
Lecht Mine
Belnacraig
Kirkton of Glenbuchat
HOWE OF ALFORD
Muir of Alford
Alford
Whitehouse
PITFICHIE FOREST
Pitfichie
Cairn William
Monymusk
Carn an Farraidh
Well of the Lecht
The Socach
Glenkindie
Towie
Sinnahard
Milltown of Towie
Kirkton
Tillyfourie
Ordhead
Sauchen
Whitehill Stone Circle
Black Hill 608
Breagach Hill
Bellabeg
Forbestown
Strathdon
Doune of Invernochty
Heugh-head
Tomashean Forest
Craig of Bunzeach
Milton of Cushnie
Frosty Hill
Muir of Fowlis
Mill of Craigievar
Leochel Cushnie
Craigievar
Correnie Forest
Correnie Moor
Benaquhallie
Cairn Ealasaid 2600
Craig Veann
A B E R D E E N S H
Cock Bridge
Milltown
Corgarff
Allt Tuileach
Pressendye 2031
Bankhead
Corners
Tillybirloch
Carn na Fainnaige
Big Garvoun
The Bruach
Forest of Glenavon
CAIRNGORMS NATIONAL PARK
Carn Leac Saighaeir
Cairn Mona Gowan 2456
Migvie
Coynach
Logie Coldstone
Tarland
Culsh Earth-house
Craiglich 1562
Corse Castle
Tornaveen
Drumlasie
Lumphanan
HILL OF FARE
Milton of Auchinhove
Peel Ring of Lumphanan
Milton
Auchlossan
Torphins
Brown Cow Hill 2721
Loch Builg
Morven 2861
MOUNTAINS
Stob an t-Sluichd
BEN AVON 3843
Tomnaverie Stone Circle
Coull Castle
Mortlich
Loch of Aboyne
Ordie
Scar Hill 984
Loch Davan
Loch Kinord
New Kinord Settlement
Gairnshiel Lodge
Lary
Peter's Hill 1863
Culblean Hill 1983
Cambus o' May
Dinnet
Aboyne
Kincardine O'Neil
Mid Beltie
Milltown of Campfield
Cluny Crichton Castle
Brathens
GRAMPIAN
Culardoch
Geallaig Hill
McEwan Gallery
Milton of Tullich
Pannanich Wells
Muir of Dinnet
Oakwood
Belwade Farm
Birsemore
Birse
Potarch
Bridge of Canny
Banchory
Creag an Dail Bheag
Crathie
Bridge of Gairn
Ballater
Littlemill
Millfield
Glen Tanar
Glen Tanar House
Braeloine
Marywell
Blackhall Forest
Scolty Woodland Park
Auchattie
Belts of Collonach
Meall Gorm 2029
Balmoral Castle
Inver
Easter Balmoral
Royal Lochnagar Distillery
Balnacroft
Birkhall
Knock Castle
Pannanich Hill
Black Craig 1742
Carnferg 1724
Glencat
Finzean
Whitestone
Strachan
Waulkmill
B R A E M A R
Braemar
Castleton
Keiloch
Linn of Quoich
Creag nan Gall
The Coyles of Muick
Aucholzie
Cairn Leuchan
Clachan Yell 2054
Forest of Birse
Lamahip
Ballochan
Craigmahandle
Invercauld Bridge
Gelder Shiel
Ballochbuie Forest
Balmoral Forest
Morrone or Morven
The Colonel's Bed
Cock Cairn 2387
White Hill
Cock Hill
Peter Hill 2025
Mount Shade
Craig of Dalfro
Sandy Beag
Cac Carn Beag 3789
Lochnagar
Conachcraig 2827
Fasheilach
Spittal of Glenmuick
Mount Keen 3080
Hill of Cat
Hill of Saughs
Mudlee Bracks 2259
Hill of Cammie
Mount Battock 2552
Hill of Edendocher
Bridge of Dye
Tipperwe
Loch Phadruig
Loch nan Eun
LOCHNAGAR
White Mounth
Dubh Loch
Glas-allt Shiel
Loch Callater
Glen Callater
Baddoch
Sgor Mor
Creag nan Gabhar
Cairn Bannoch
Broad Cairn
Glen Mark
Water of Mark
Glen Lee
Hill of Fingray 1593
Meluncart
Goyle Hill
Drumtochty Castle
Carn an Tuirc
Tolmount
Loch Esk
Black Hill of Mark
Easter Balloch 2731
Monawee 2276
Kirkton
Invermark Castle
Tarfside
Cairncross
Millden Lodge
Colmeallie Stone Circle
Glenesk Folk
Cairn o' Mount
Glensaugh
Loch Vrotachan
GLAS MAOL
The Cairnwell
Devil's Elbow
Caenlochan Forest
Creag Leacach
Lair of Aldararie
Carlochy
Glen Esk
Sturdy Hill
Deer Dyke
Strathfinnel Hill
A N G U S
Glendoll Forest
Acharn
Loch Brandy
Loch Wharral
Muckle Cairn
Ben Tirran
Cruys
West Knock
Bulg 1986
Finalty Hill
Mayar
Driesh
Clova
White Hill
Hill of Wirren
Auchmull
HOWE OF THE
Fettercairn
Bent
Gulabin
Carn Damh
Monamenach
Auchavan
Cairn Inks
Cairn of Barns
Cairn Baddoch
FINbracks
Hill of Glansie
Hunthill Lodge
Hill of Berran
Burn of Calletar
Gannochy
Edzell
Bridgend
Balfield
Dalhousie Memorial Arch
Dunlappie
Luthermuir
Spittal of Glenshee
Loch Beanie
Badandum Hill
Runtaleave
Rottal
Glen Prosen
Balnaboth
Hill of Garbet
66
67

ABERDEEN
PAGE 106
NORTH SEA
BUCHAN
FORMARTINE
Aberdeen to:
Kirkwall (Hatston) 6hrs.
Lerwick (Holmsgarth) 12hrs. 30mins.
Peterhead
Buchanhaven
Keith Inch
Burnhaven
Boddam
Stirling
Sandfordhill
Coldwells
Long Haven
Bullers of Buchan
North Haven
Cruden Bay
Port Erroll
Slains Castle
Bay of Cruden
Whinnyfold
Hatton
Bridgend
Chapel Hill
Longside
Mintlaw
Rora
St Fergus
Inverugie
Flushing
Cocklaw
Nether Kinmundy
Blackhill
Little Dens
Old Deer
Stuartfield
Maud
New Deer
Turriff
Cuminestown
Fyvie
Methlick
Auchnagatt
Kinknockie
Muirtack
Arthrath
Ellon
Collieston
Kirktown of Slains
Old Slains Castle
Hackley Head or Forvie Ness
Newburgh
Newburgh Bar
Foveran
Drums
Balmedie
Belhelvie
Potterton
Blackdog
DANGER AREA
Bridge of Don
Dyce
Stoneywood
Bankhead
Bucksburn
Oldmeldrum
Pitmedden
Udny Green
Udny Station
Tarves
Inverurie
Port Elphinstone
Kintore
Kemnay
Newmachar
Blackburn
Westhill
Kirkton of Skene
Lyne of Skene
Dunecht
Echt
Cults
Bieldside
Milltimber
Peterculter
Old Aberdeen
Footdee
Torry
Nigg Bay
Cove Bay
Souter Head
Charlestown
Findon
Portlethen
Portlethen Village
Cammachmore Bay
Newtonhill
Muchalls
Doonie Point
Bridge of Muchalls
Garron Point
Cowie
Stonehaven
Castle Haven
Dunnottar
Thornyhive Bay
Crawton
Crawton Bay
Catterline
Braidon Bay
Todhead Point
Kinneff
Little John's Haven
Inverbervie
Bervie Bay
Gourdon
Laurencekirk
Drumlithie
Durris Forest
Crathes
Banchory-Devenick
Kirkton of Durris
Kirkton of Maryculter
Drumoak
A90
A92
A93
A944
A947
A948
A950
A952
A956
A957
A96
A975
A981
A982
A920
A937
P+R
G
H
J
K
L
M
1
2
3
4
5
6
7
8
850
800
40
30
20
10
90
80
70
400

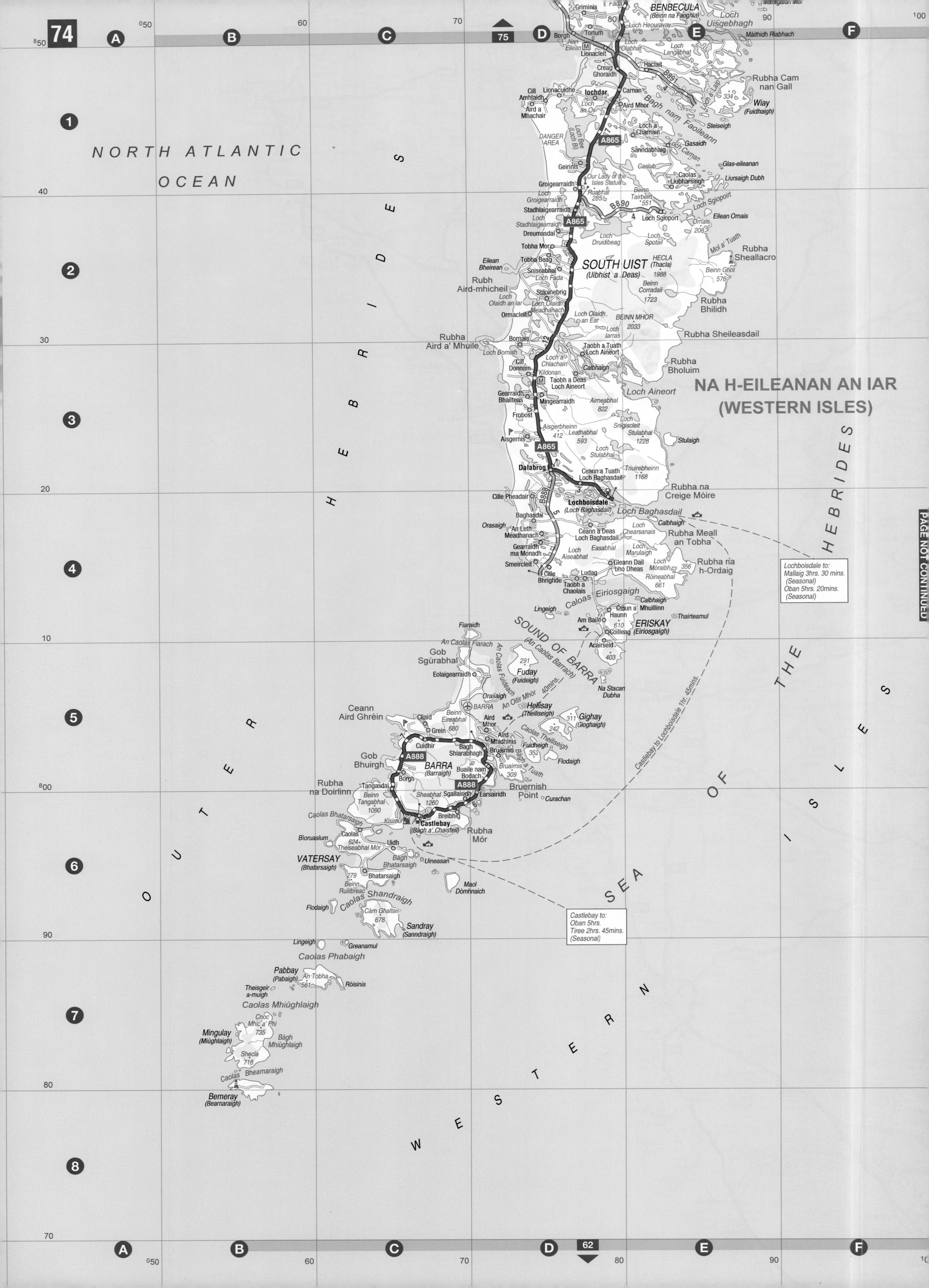
NORTH ATLANTIC
OCEAN
OUTER HEBRIDES
SEA OF THE HEBRIDES
WESTERN ISLES
NA H-EILEANAN AN IAR
(WESTERN ISLES)
BENBECULA
(Beinn na Faoghla)
SOUTH UIST
(Uibhist a Deas)
HECLA
(Thacla)
1988
BEINN MHOR
2033
Lochboisdale
(Loch Baghasdail)
Loch Baghasdail
ERISKAY
(Eiriosgaigh)
SOUND OF BARRA
(An Caolas Barrach)
Fuday
(Fuideigh)
Hellisay
(Theiliseigh)
Gighay
(Gioghaigh)
BARRA
(Barraigh)
Castlebay
(Bàgh a' Chaisteil)
VATERSAY
(Bhatarsaigh)
Sandray
(Sanndraigh)
Pabbay
(Pabaigh)
Mingulay
(Miùghlaigh)
Berneray
(Bearnaraigh)
Wiay
(Fuidhaigh)
Iochdar
Dalabrog
A865
A888
B890
B888
Lochboisdale to:
Mallaig 3hrs. 30 mins.
(Seasonal)
Oban 5hrs. 20mins.
(Seasonal)
Castlebay to:
Oban 5hrs.
Tiree 2hrs. 45mins.
(Seasonal)
Castlebay to Lochboisdale 1hr. 45mins.
40mins.
Rubha Aird-mhicheil
Rubha Aird a' Mhuile
Rubha Shellacro
Rubha Bhilidh
Rubha Sheileasdail
Rubha Bholuim
Rubha na Creige Mòire
Rubha Meall an Tobha
Rubha na h-Ordaig
Loch Aineort
Loch Sgioport
Loch Uisgebhagh
Bagh nam Faoileann
Caolas Eiriosgaigh
Caolas Shandraigh
Caolas Phabaigh
Caolas Mhiùghlaigh
Caolas Bhatarsaigh
Bruernish Point
Rubha Mór
Ceann Aird Ghrèin
Gob Sgùrabhal
Gob Bhuirgh
Rubha na Doirlinn
Maol Dòmhnaich
Flodaigh
Curachan
Stulaigh
Lingeigh
Greanamul
Na Stacan Dubha
Uineasan
Eolaigearraidh
Eilean Bheirean
Eilean Ornais
Glas-eileanan
Liursaigh Dubh
Rubha Cam nan Gall
Steiseigh
Gasaidh
Thairteamul
75
62
A B C D E F
1 2 3 4 5 6 7 8
PAGE NOT CONTINUED

75
82
74
76
G
H
J
K
L
M
60
70
80
90
100
PAGE NOT CONTINUED
NORTH ATLANTIC
OCEAN
OUTER HEBRIDES
NA H-EILEANAN AN IAR
(WESTERN ISLES)
SOUND OF HARRIS
(Caolas Na Hearadh)
SOUND OF MONACH
(Caolas Mhonach)
THE LITTLE MINCH
WESTERN ISLES
NORTH UIST
(Uibhist a Tuath)
BENBECULA
(Beinn na Faoghla)
SOUTH HARRIS
(Ceann a Deas na Hearadh)
TARANSAY
(Tarasaigh)
SCARP
PABBAY
(Pabaigh)
BERNERAY
(Bearnaraigh)
Boreray
(Boraraigh)
Killegray
(Ceileagraigh)
Ensay
(Easaigh)
TOE HEAD
(Gob an Tobha)
RENNISH POINT
(Rubha Reinis)
Leverburgh
(An t-Ob)
Lochmaddy
(Loch nam Madadh)
Lochmaddy to Uig 1hr. 40mins.
Heisker or Monach Islands
(Theisgeir no na H-Eileanan Monach)
Haskeir Island
(Eilean Hasgeir)
Haskeir Eagach
Kirkibost Island
(Eilean Chircebost)
Baleshare
(Baile Sear)
Grimsay
(Griomasaigh)
Ronay
(Ronaigh)
EAVAL (Eabhal)
Gàisgeir
Causamul
Deasker
Huskeiran
Stòcaidh
Ceann Iar
Ceann Ear
Eilean Mhealasta
Forest of Harris
Loch a Siar
Sound of Taransay
(Caolas Tharasaigh)
Caolas Shiolaigh
Caolas Phabaigh
Caolas Spuir
Rubha Huisinis
Huisinis
Rubha Leacach
Horsanais
Rubha Sgeirigin
Rubha Màs a' Chnuic
Rubh' an Teampaill
Rubha Bhreinis
Rubha Bhoisnis
Rubha Bheilis
Rubha Ghriminis
Rubha Mhànais
Rubha Port Scolpaig
Rubh' Arnal
Aird an Rùnair
Aird a' Mhòrain
Rubha an Dùine
Rubha an Fhigheadair
Rubha nam Plèac
An t-Aigeach
Eigneig Mhòr
Eigneig Bheag
Rubha Cam
Aird Feinis
Aird Bhreinis
Aird Nisabost
A865
A867
A859
B887
B893
B894
B892
B891
Barpa Langass Chambered Cairn
Pobull Fhinn Stone Circle
Hebridean Smokehouse
MacGillivray Centre
Beul an Toim BENBECULA
(Port Adhair Bheinn na Faoghla)

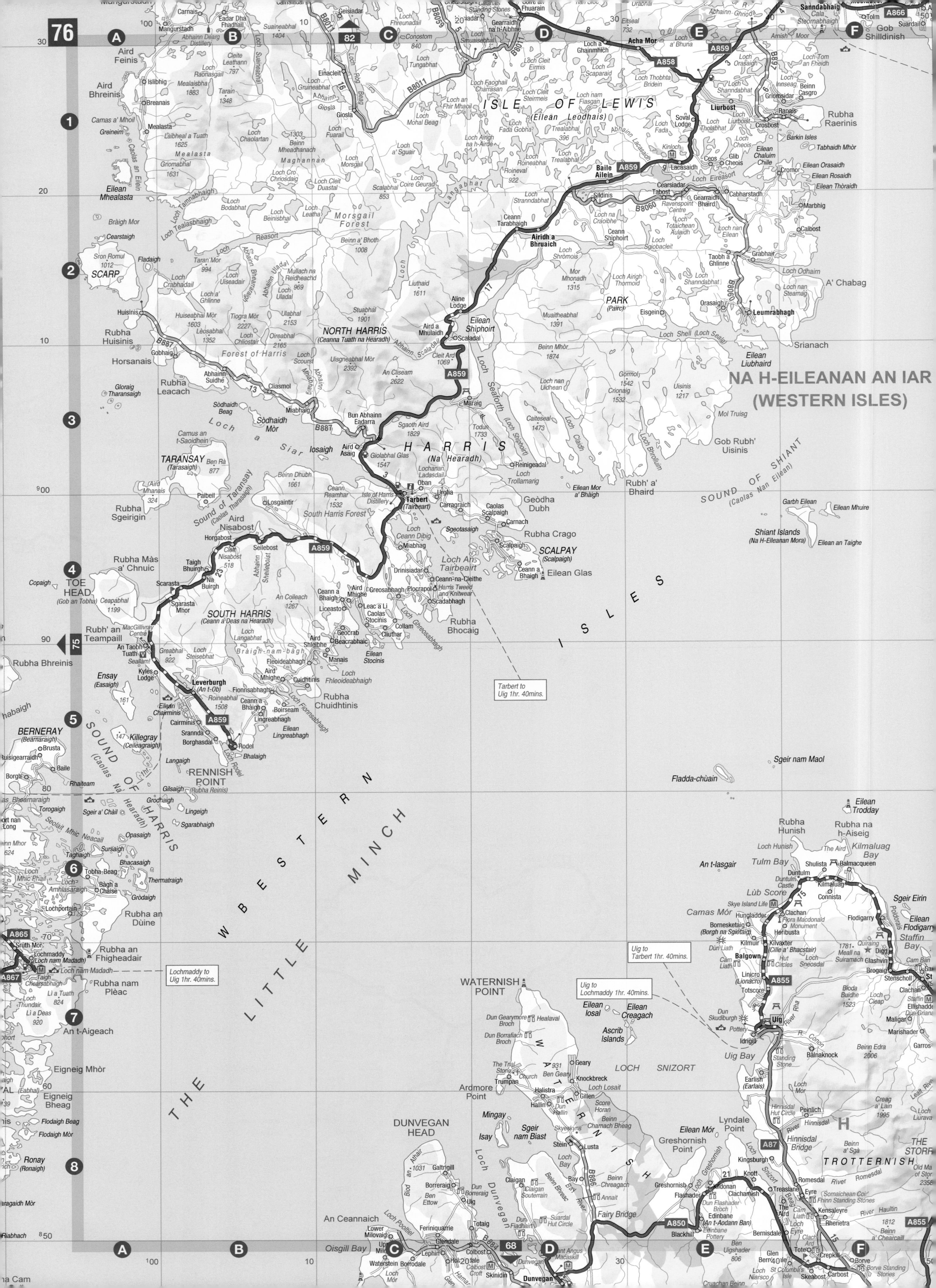
ISLE OF LEWIS
(Eilean Leodhais)
NA H-EILEANAN AN IAR
(WESTERN ISLES)
NORTH HARRIS
(Ceanna Tuath na Hearadh)
HARRIS
(Na Hearadh)
SOUTH HARRIS
(Ceann a Deas na Hearadh)
PARK
(Pairc)
SCARP
TARANSAY
(Tarasaigh)
SCALPAY
(Scalpaigh)
BERNERAY
(Bearnaraigh)
SOUND OF HARRIS
(Caolas Na Hearadh)
SOUND OF SHIANT
(Caolas Nan Eilean)
Sound of Taransay
(Caolas Tharasaigh)
Loch a Siar
THE LITTLE MINCH
THE WESTERN ISLES
Shiant Islands
(Na H-Eileanan Mora)
TOE HEAD
(Gob an Tobha)
RENNISH POINT
(Rubha Reinis)
WATERNISH POINT
WATERNISH
DUNVEGAN HEAD
TROTTERNISH
LOCH SNIZORT
Tarbert
(Tairbeart)
Leverburgh
(An t-Ob)
Rodel
Uig
Dunvegan
Lochmaddy
(Loch nam Madadh)
Balgown
Liurbost
Baile Ailein
Acha Mor
Tarbert to Uig 1hr. 40mins.
Uig to Tarbert 1hr. 40mins.
Uig to Lochmaddy 1hr. 40mins.
Lochmaddy to Uig 1hr. 40mins.
A859
A858
A855
A850
A87
A865
A867
A866
B887
B8060
B8011
B884
B886
82
75
68
A B C D E F
1 2 3 4 5 6 7 8

Pabail Uarach
Pabail Iarach
Bagh Phabail Iarach
Stornoway to Ullapool 2hrs. 40mins.
Ullapool to Stornoway 2hrs. 40mins.
83
84
69
78
Rhubha Stoer
Achnacarnin
Clashnessie Bay
Clashmore
Balchladich
Loch nan Lub
Stoer
Bay of Stoer
Clachtoll Broch
Clachtoll
B869
Achmelvich Bay
Achmelvich
Rhicarn
Rubha Rodha
Baddidarach
Lochinver
Soyea Island
Loch Inver
Kirkaig Point
A' Chleit
Badnaban
Inverkirkaig
Loch Kirkaig
Rubha Coigeach
Loch na Totaig
Camas Coille
Eilean Mór
Enard Bay
Camas Eilean Ghlais
Rubha Mór
Reiff
Brae of Achnahaird
Inverpolly Lodge
Altandhu
Loch Raa
Loch Vatachan
Eilean Mullagrach
Isle Ristol
Polbain
Badentarbat
Glas-leac Mór
Badentarbat Bay
Achiltibuie
Polglass
Tanera Beg
Tanera Mór
Badenscallie
Summer Isles
Horse Sound
COIGACH
Glas-leac Beag
Horse Island
Culnacraig
Achduart
Ben More Coigach
Eilean Dubh
Priest Island
Bottle Island
Carn nan Sgeir
Isle Martin
Greenstone Point
Cailleach Head
Leac Dhonn
Rubha Beag
Loch na Doire Duinne
Opinan
Mellon Udrigle
Static Point
Scoraig
Achmore
Annat Bay
Loch nan Clachan Geala
Gruinard Island
Carnach
Rireavach
Little Loch Broom
Loch a' Choire
Slaggan Bay
Badluarach
Eilean Furadh Mór
Loch an t-Slagain
Beinn Dearg Nhór 513
Achgarve
Gruinard Bay
Mungasdale
Durnamuck
Badcaul
Badrallach
Rubha Reidh
Camas Mór
Rubha nan Sasan
Mellon Charles
Laide
Gruinard House
Second Coast
First Coast
Sand
Ormiscaig
Loch an Draing
Cove
A832
Ardessie
Camusnagaul
Ardessie Falls
An Cuaidh 972
Loch Airigh an Eilein
Mellangaun
Aultbea
Drumchork
Isle of Ewe
Beinn Dearg Bad Chailleach 897
Dundonnell
Melvaig
Aultgrishan
B8021
Loch Sguod
B8057
Midtown
Brae
Loch Ewe
Seana Chamas
Cnoc Breac 962
Peterburn
Naast
Inverewe
Loch Fada
Loch Mhic' ille Riabhaich
Loch na Mòine Buige
Aird Dubh
AN TEALLACH 3484
Loch Toll an Lochain
Fisherfield Forest
Strathnasheallag Forest
Port Erradale
North Erradale
Big Sand
Caolas Beag
Longa Island
Loch nan Liagh
Loch Bad a' Chreamh
Poolewe
Londubh
River Ewe
Loch na Curra
Lonemore
Mial
Strath
Heritage
Smithstown
Gairloch
Tollie Farm
Loch Kernsary
Loch Tollaidh
Loch Gairloch
Eilean Horrisdale
Charlestown
Loch Airigh a' Phuill
Meall an Doirein 1381
Port Henderson
Aird
Badachro
B8056
Opinan
Loch nan Eun
Loch Shieldaig
Shieldaig
South Erradale
River Kerry
Eilean Subhainn
Loch Maree Islands
Letterewe
Letterewe Forest
Victoria Falls
Talladale
Redpoint
River Erradale
Loch Bad an Sgalaig
Loch Gaineamhach
WESTER ROSS
SLIOCH 3215
Flowerdale Forest
Bridge of Grudie
Sgeir Ghlas
Sgeir na Trian
Shieldaig Forest
Baosbheinn 2869
Beinn an Eòin
Kinlochewe Forest
Heights of Kinlochewe
Craig
Beinn Bhreac 2031
Lochan Sgeireach
Beinn Eighe
Incheril
Kinlochewe
Rubha na Fearn
Loch Torridon
Fearnmore
Fearnbeg
Lower Diabaig
Upper Diabaig
Beinn Alligin 3232
BEINN EIGHE
Ruadh-stac Mor 3313
Rubha Chuaig
Arinacrinachd
Kenmore
Alligin Shuas
Inveralligin
Torridon Forest
LIATHACH 3456
A896
Cuaig
Torridon
Fasag
Countryside Centre
Glen Torridon
Coulin Lodge
Loch Clair
Sgurr Dubh 2566
Coulin Forest
Callakille
Shieldaig Island
Shieldaig
Balgy
Falls of Balgy
Annat
Ben-damph Forest
Lonbain
Croic-bheinn 1619
Lochan Uaine
Carn Breac 2223
A890
Glencarron Lodge
Glen Carron
An Dubh-loch
Glenshieldaig Forest
Beinn Damph 2957
Maol Chean-dearg 3060
Sgorr Ruadh 3142
Achnashellach
Achnashellach Forest
Applecross
Loch Lundie
Kilt Rock
Mealt Falls
Valtos
Rubha nam Brathairean
A855
Culnacnoc
Lealt Falls
Leac Tressirnish
Bearreraig Bay
Holm Island
SOUND OF RAASAY
INNER SOUND
Loch a' Bhràige
Port an Fhearainn
RONA
Eilean Garbh
Eilean Tigh
Garbh Eilean
Eilean Fladday
Loch a' Sguirr
Manish Point
Torran
Loch Arnish
Arnish
HIGHLAND
G
H
J
K
L
M
60
70
80
90
200

78
84
77
70
A
B
C
D
E
F
1
2
3
4
5
6
7
8
Rhubha Stoer
Clashnessie Bay
Clashmore
Balchladich
Clashnessie
Drumbeg
Nedd
Glenleraig
Unapool
Newton
Loch Glencoul
Beinn Aird da Loch 1722
Loch Merkland
An Glas-loch
Meall an Fhuarain 1549
Meall nan Con 3157
Loch nan Lub
Gorm Loch Mór
Loch an Leothaid
QUINAG 2651
Loch na Gainmhich
Glen Coul
Beinn Leoid 2599
Merkland Lodge
Loch Fiag
Fiag Lodge
Cnoc an Alaskie 1024
Loch nan Uan
Loch Poll
Bay of Stoer
Stoer
Clachtoll
Clachtoll Broch
Loch nan Loinne
Loch Beannach
Lochassynt Lodge
Glas Bheinn 2541
Eas a' Chual Aluinn (Waterfall)
Loch an Eircill
Loch nan Caorach
Dubh a' Chuail
Loch a' Ghriama
Cnoc a' Ghriama 1221
River Fiag
Loch an Bhealaich
Achmelvich Bay
Rhicarn
Achmelvich
Loch Crócach
Loch Assynt
Ardvreck Castle
Beinn Uidhe 2410
Gorm Loch Mór
Corriekinloch
Abhainn a' Choire
Crask
Cnoc a' Ghiubhais 1135
Loch Gaineamhach
Rubha Rodha
Baddidarach
Lochinver
Assynt
Brackloch
Soyea Island
Loch Inver
Kirkaig Point
A' Chleit
Badnaban
Strathan
Loch Culag
Loch Fèith an Leòthaid
Glencanisp Forest
Beinn Gharbh 1769
Inchnadamph
Inchnadamph Forest
Gleann Dubh
River Traligill
BEN MORE ASSYNT 3273
Fionn Loch Mór
Overscaig
Loch an Ulbhaidh
Maovally 1673
Fiag Bridge
Loch Kirkaig
Inverkirkaig
CANISP 2779
Loch na Gainimh
SUILVEN 2399
Fionn Loch
Falls of Kirkaig
Loch a' Ghille
Lochan Fada
Inchnadamph Bone Caves
Breabag
2338
2670
Loch Carn nan Conbhairean
Meall an Aonaich 2344
Benmore Forest
Duchally
Strath an Lòin
Strath Tirry
River Tirry
Rhian
Rhian Bridge
Eilean Mór
Camas Coille
Enard Bay
Inverpolly Lodge
Loch Buine Mòire
Loch Awe
Cam Loch
Loch Veyatie
Ledbeg River
Beinn Sgreamhaidh 1428
Arscaig
Shinness
Achnairn
Achfrish
Tirryside
Brae of Achnahaird
Loch Raa
Loch Doire na h-Airbhe
Loch Sionascaig
Inverpolly Forest
CUL MOR 2787
Elphin
Ledmore
Altnacealgach
Loch Borralan
Benmore Lodge
Loch Ailsh
Loch Meall a' Bhuirich
River Cassley
Beinn Sgeireach 1561
Loch Sgeireach
Dalchork
Colaboll
Loch Vatachan
Badentarbat
Aird of Coigach
Stac Pollaidh 2009
Loch an Doire Dhuibh
Drumrunie Forest
Knockan
Knockan Crag
Loch Urigill
An Stùc 1195
Beinn an Eòin 1786
Glen Cassley
Loch an Ràsail
Loch na Caillich
Sallachy
Lairg Muir
Loch Bad a' Ghaill
Linneraineach
Cùl Beag 2523
Lochan an Ais
Cnoc na Glas Choille 1006
Glen Oykel
River Oykel
Glencassley Castle
Loch na Faic
Lairg
Achiltibuie
Polglass
Badenscallie
Lochan Dearg
Lochan Tuath
Clar Loch Mór
1692
CROMALT HILLS
Crom Allt
Allt a' Chaoruinn
Loch Craggie
Fionn Bheinn Mhór 1084
Loch na Claise Móire
Loch na Fuaralaich
Cnoc a' Choire 1318
Ferrycroft
The Ord
Balloan
Horse Sound
Horse Island
COIGACH
2438
Culnacraig
Ben More Coigach (Beinn Mhòr na Còigich)
Lochanan Dubha
Drumrunie
Strath Canaird
Loch Eadar dha Bheinn
Loch a' Chroisg
Meall an Fhuarain 1895
Coire a' Chonachair
Lubcroy
Oykel Bridge
Strath Oykel
Achness Waterfall
Invercassley
Rosehall
Chambered Cairn
Achany
Achany Glen
Cnoc Ceann nam Bad 881
Torroble
Achduart
Carn nan Sgeir
River Runie
Strathcanaird
River Canaird
Na Dromannan 1337
Strath nan Lòn
Rappach
Oape
Doune
Altass
Linsidemore
Shin Forest
Achinduich
Falls of Shin
Camas Mór
Isle Martin
Loch Kanaird
Loch Dubh
Loch na Maoile
Lochanan nan Sàilean Mòra
Beinn Donuill
Rappach Water
River Einig
Glen Einig
Meòir Langwell
Kyle of Sutherland
Achnahanat
Torroy
Inveran
Invershin
Leac Dhonn
Ullapool to Stornoway 2hrs. 40mins.
Ardmair
947
Creag na h-Iolaire
Loch ob an Lochain
Loch a' Choire Bhuig
Rhidorroch Forest
Beinn Ulbhaidh 1616
Loch nam Buidheag
Loch a' Choire
Scoraig
Achmore
Annat Bay
Rireavach
Carnach
Rhue
Morefield
Ullapool River
Rhidorroch
Meall Liath Choire 1798
Glen Achall
Clar Lochan
Loch an Daimh
Creag Loisgte 1353
Abhainn an t-Sratha Chuileannaich
Strath Cuileannach
Meall Dheirgidh 1659
Loch Meall Dheirgidh
Balblair
Culrain
Carbisdale
1650
Little Loch Broom
Beinn Ghobhlach 2082
Village Clock
Ullapool
Loch Achall
Rhidorroch River
East Rhidorroch Lodge
Corriemulzie River
Dundonnell
Loch na h-Uidhe
Allt na h-Airbhe
Loch Broom
Beinn Eilideach 1830
Glen Douchary
Lochan Badan Glasliath
Strath Mulzie
Sidhean Raireag 1769
Glasha Burn
Carn a' Choin Deirg 2301
Loch an Tuill Riabhaich
Croich
The Craigs
Amatnatua
Strathcarron
Wester Gruinards
Culeave
Soyal
Cornhill
Lower Gledfield
Dounie
Oldtown
Durnamuck
Badcaul
Badrallach
Dun an Ruigh Ruadh
Blarnalearoch
Dun Lagaidh
Loggie
Rhiroy
Leckmelm
Meall Dubh 2105
Meall nam Bràdham 2221
Amat Forest
Glencalvie Lodge
River Carron
Ardessie
Camusnagaul
Ardessie Falls
Sàil Mhòr 2508
Strath Beag
Ardindrean
Ardcharnich
Loch Lagaidh
Loch Reidh Creagain
Seana Bhraigh 3040
Loch a' Choire Mhóir
Freevater Forest
Alladale River
Alladale Lodge
Glencalvie Forest
Carn Bhrain 2117
Carn nam Buailtean 1283
Lochan Gaineamhaich
Loch an Eich Dhuibh
Letters
Loch a' Chaim Mor
Carn Mór 2122
River Douchary
Càrn Bàn 2772
AN TEALLACH 3484
Strathnasheallag Forest
Loch na Sealga
Loch Ghiubsachain
Fisherfield Forest
Inverlael
Inverlael Forest
River Lael
Eididh nan Clach Geala 3039
Loch Sruban Móra
Lochan Sgeireach
Gleann Mór
Loch Chuinneag
Lochan a' Chairn
Diebidale Forest
Meall Bhenneit 1744
Carn a' Bhiorain 1665
Loch Coire Chaorachain
Loch Toll an Lochain
Loch Allt Eigin
Loch an Airceil
Auchlunachan
Lael Forest
BEINN DEARG 3547
Gleann Beag
Abhainn a' Ghlinne Bhig
Loch Prille
Deanich Lodge
Beinn Tharsuinn 2330
Carn Chuinneag 2750
Diebidale River
Glen Diebidale
Dundonnell Forest
Lochan Fraoich
Lochan Fada
Loch an t-Sidhein
Beinn Dearg Mór 2974
River Broom
Beinn Enaiglair 2915
Loch Fèith nan Cleireach
Allt Mhucarnaich
Loch a' Choire Ghrànda
Tollomuick Forest
Crom Loch
Beinn a' Chaisteil 2404
EASTER ROSS
Carn Cas nan Gabhar 1976
Black Water
Carn Breac Beag 1270
Braemore
Corrieshalloch Gorge
Falls of Measach
Meall Leacachain 2028
Loch Coire Làir
Gorm Loch
Abhainn na Glasa
Loch a' Chaorainn
Kildermorie Lodge
Loch Bad a' Bhathaich
Braeantra
Kildermorie Forest
Strath Rusdale
Loch Beinn Dearg
Beinn a' Chlaidheimh
Meall an t-Sithe 1971
Loch a' Bhraoin
Braemore Forest
Meall a' Ghrianain 2531
Loch Magharaidh
Loch nan Amhaichean
Beinn nan Eun 2436
Loch Morie
Lochan Fèith Mhic'illean
Fuar Loch Mór
Loch a' Bhrisidh
Mullach Coire Mhic Fhearchair
Gorm Loch Mór
Allt a' Mhadaidh
Meall a' Chrasgaidh 3062
Loch a' Mhadaidh
Loch Sgeireach
Loch Droma
Loch a' Gharbhrain
Strathvaich Forest
Inchbae Forest
Strathrannoch
Carn nan Con Ruadha 2206
Abhainn Beinn nan Eun
Wyvis Lodge
Meall Mór 2421
Boath
Loch Toll an Lochain
A' Chailleach 3276
Sgurr Mór 3637
Abhainn a' Ghiubhais Li
Beinn Liath Mhór a' Ghiubhais Li 2464
Loch Glascarnoch
Strathvaich Lodge
Strath Vaich
Strath Rannoch
Loch Bealach Cùlaidh
Queen's Cairn 2109
Culzie Lodge
Bendeallt 1850
Cnoc Céislein 1716
Groban 2424
Allt a' Choire Mhóir
Aultguish Inn
Carn Mór 2095
Carn Gorm
Loch an Sgeireach
Fannich Forest
Meall Gorm
Loch Gorm
Kinlochluichart Forest
Meall Mhic Iomhair 1984
Inchbae Lodge
Garbat Forest
BEN WYVIS 3433
Loch a' Choire Mhóir
Meall na Drochaide
Eileanach Lodge
Glen Glass
SLIOCH 3215
WESTER ROSS
Abhainn a' Chadh' Bhuidhe
Gleann Tanagaidh
Beinn a' Mhùinidh 2231
Kinlochewe Forest
Fannich Lodge
An Coileachan 3015
Beinn Dearg 2230
Corriemoillie Forest
1571
Carn na Dubh Choille
Black Water
Black Rock Gorge
Meall nan Caorach
Meall na Speireig
River Glass
Heights of Kinlochewe
Abhainn Bruachaig
Beinn nan Ramh 2333
Loch Fannich
Aultdearg
River Grudie
Loch Bad Leabhraidh
Achnaclerach
Strathgarve Forest
Little Wyvis 2497
Swordale
Sgitheach
Storehouse of Foulis
NORTH WEST HIGHLANDS
An Cabar 1832
Loch na Moine Mór
Loch na Curra
Lochrosque Forest
Corriemoillie
Gorstan
Cam Gorm
Cloch Mhór 1580
Strath Sgitheach
Clach Liath
Ardullie
Beinn Eighe
Kinlochewe
Incheril
Carn a' Ghlinne 1769
Fionn Bheinn 3062
Loch na Moine Beag
Achanalt
Grudie
Lochluichart
Loch Luichart
Heights of Fodderty
Heights of Brae
Upper Dochcarty
Mountgerald
Glen Docherty
2313 Meall a' Chaorainn
Strath Bran
Loch Achanalt
Loch a' Chuilinn
Garve
Loch Garve
Bottacks
Castle Leod
Auchterneed
Fodderty
Castle Doocot
DANGER AREA
Dingwall
Badavanich
Loch a' Chroisg
Achnasheen
River Bran
Sgurr Marcasaidh 1904
Rogie Falls
Eagle Stone
Strathpeffer
Tarvie
Craigdarroch
Hill Fort
Knockfarrel
Highland Childhood
Abhainn Dubh
Loch Clair
Loch Coulin
Loch an Fhiarlaid
Loch Bhad Ghaineamhaich
Glenmarksie
Little Scatwell
Loch Ussie
Lochussie
Jamestown
Tollie
Alcaig
Duncanston
Carn Beag 1804
Ledgowan
Ledgowan Forest
Loch Gowan
Sgurr a' Ghlas Leathaid
2883 Sgurr a' Mhuilinn
Milton
Achlorachan
Porin
Bridgend
Loch Meig
Scatwell
Loch Achilty
Contin
Torrachilty Wood
Maryburgh
Conon Bridge
Corntown
Easter Kinkell
River Coulin
Carn Breac 2223
1765 Carn Martuin
Gleann Meinich
STRATHCONON
Strathconon
River Conon
Loch Achonachie
Marybank
Arcan
Newmore
Rootfield
Loch Sgamhain
Loch Cnoc na Mointeich
Loch Coire a' Bhuic
Loch Beannacharain
River Meig
1936 Carn na Cloiche Mòire
Loch Aradaidh
Muir of Fairburn
Urray
Balvraid
Drynie Park
Kilcoy
Glen Carron
Glencarron Lodge
Craig
Moruisg 3026
Carn Gorm
Creag na h-Iolaire
Scardroy
FOREST
Inverchoran
Carn na Coinnich 2209
Cabaan Forest
Urray Forest
River Orrin
Muir of Ord
Chapelton
Milton of Tarradale
Redcastle
Glen Orrin
Orrin Reservoir
Corry of Ardnagrask
Ardnagrask
Glencarron & Glenuig Forest
Gleann Fhiodhaig
Loch an Spàrdain
Corriehallie Forest
Loch nan Eun
Windhill
Rheindown
Achnashellach Forest
Gleann Gowrie
Allt Goibhre
Cnoc Eille Mor
Loch nam Bonnach
Dunmore
Beauly
A835
A837
A838
A836
A839
A832
A834
A862
A890
A896
A894
A9
B869
B864
B9163
B9169

BEN KLIBRECK
3152
Loch Choire
Loch Choire Forest
85
86
80
NORTH SEA
Kinbrace
Gobernuisgeach
Braemore
Dunbeath
Heritage Centre
Ramscraigs
Borgue
Newport
Berriedale
Berriedale Castle
Langwell Forest
Aultibea
Morven
2313
Maiden Pap
1587
Scaraben
2055
Borrobol Forest
Borrobol Lodge
Altanduin
Ben Armine Forest
Ben Armine Lodge
Kildonan
Craggie
Torrish
A897
Strath of Kildonan
Marrel
Navidale
Helmsdale
West Helmsdale
East Helmsdale
Gartymore
Timespan
Portgower
Ord Point
Badbea Clearance Village
Boch-ailean
Ousdale
Ousdale Broch
Lothmore
Kilmote
Lothbeg
Crackaig
Lothbeg Point
Gordonbush
Balnacoil
River Brora
Strath Brora
Dalreavoch
Rhilochan
Knockarthur
East Langwell
West Langwell
Achvoan
Achrimsdale
East Clyne
West Clyne
Clynelish
Distillery
Dalchalm
Badnellan
Heritage Centre
Brora
Doll
Uppat
Backies
Dunrobin
Carn Liath
Orcadian Stone Company
Duke of Sutherland Monument
Golspie
Mound Rock
Kirkton
A839
Tomich
Muie
Tressady
Ardachu
Little Rogart
Rogart
Dalmore
Pittentrail
Morvich
River Fleet
Loch Fleet
Little Torboll
Skelbo
Skelbo Street
Littleferry
Embo
Embo Street
Poles
Achvaich
Badninish
Lednabirichen
Birichen
Rearquhar
Astle
Fleuchary
Evelix
Pitgrudy
Clashmore Wood
Clashmore
Cuthill
Camore
Littletown
Dornoch
Carnegie Courthouse
Historylinks
Lonemore
Whiteface
Ospisdale
Spinningdale
Bardnabeinne
A949
Bonar Bridge
Airdens
Tulloch
Migdale
Ardgay
Kincardine
Little Creich
Ardchronie
Easter Fearn
Wester Fearn
A836
Dounie
Ardmore
Struie
Edderton
Cambuscurrie Bay
DORNOCH FIRTH
Glenmorangie Distillery
Morangie
Tarlogie
B9174
Tain
Tain Through Time
Hilton
Morangie Forest
Aultnamain Inn
TARBAT NESS
Wilkhaven
Bindal
Portmahomack
Tarbat Discovery Centre
Seafield
Rockfield
DANGER AREA
Inver
Lochslin
Lower Arboll
Toulvaddie
Tarrel
Lower Pitkerrie
Loch Eye
Geanies
B9165
Hill of Fearn
Fearn
Hilton of Cadboll
Balintore
Shandwick
Tullich
Arabella
Hartmount Holdings
Lamington
Brenachie
Scotsburn
Marybank
Pitmaduthy
Kildary
Milton
Kinrive
Strathy
Loanreoch
Ardross
Easter Ardross
Stittenham
Dalnavie
Ardross Forest
Tullich Muir
Delny
Kilmuir
Badachonacher
Coillemore
Rhicullen
Newmore
Nonikiln
Achandunie
Polio
Barbaraville
Broomhill
Balintraid
Achnagarron
Tomich
Bosskeen
Saltburn
Invergordon
Contullich
Crosshills
Obsdale
Alness
Distillery
Dalmore
A9
Nigg Bay
Ankerville
Wester Rarichie
Pitcalnie
Nigg
Hill of Nigg
Port an Righ
Balnabruaich
Balnapaling
Nigg Ferry
Castlecraig
Cromarty
Hugh Miller
Courthouse
Blue Head
Sutors of Cromarty
McFarquhar's Cave
Newton
CROMARTY FIRTH
Cromarty Bay
Udale Bay
A832
Balblair
Ferryton
Alness Bay
Evanton
Drummond
Alnessferry
Resolis
Newmills
Jemimaville
Davidston
B9163
Cullicudden
Springfield
Easter Brae
Wester Brae
Mount High
Mulrton
Millbuie Forest
B9160
Whitebog
Kinbeachie
Culbo
Braefindon
Culbokie
Mount Eagle
BLACK ISLE
Findon Forest
Killen
Rosemarkie
Rosemarkie Bay
Fortrose
Groam House
Chanonry Point
Fort George
Avoch
Easter Suddie
Knockbain
Belmaduthy
Munlochy
Munlochy Bay
Avoch Bay
Tore
Arpafeelie
Bogallan
Artafallie
Kilmuir
Charlestown
Craigton
North Kessock
Lifeboat Station
MORAY FIRTH
Whiteness Head
Ardersier
Connage Highland Dairy
B9092
B9006
B9039
Gollanfield
Muir of Gollanfield
Fisherton
Highland Aviation
Alturlie Point
Newton
A96
Tornagrain
Croy
Dalcross
Cantraywood
Balloch
Lochside
Loch Flemington
Muir of the Clans
Clephanton
Cawdor
Brackla
Piperhill
Culcharry
Geddes
Regoul
Foynesfield
NAIRN
Tradespark
Househill
Moss-side
Kingsteps
Auldearn
Boath Doocot
Blackhills
Lakten Forest
A939
Littlemill
Druim
Loch Loy
Cran Loch
Culbin Forest
Cloddymoss
Kintessack
Dyke
Brodie
Broom of Moy
Benromach Distillery
FORRES
Sueno's Stone
Nelson Tower
Falconer
Dallas Dhu Historic Distillery
Balnageith
Whiterow
Lochaber
Rafford
Califer
Moor of Granary
Damhead
Loch of Blairs
Altyre Woods
A940
MORAY
Whitemire
Conicaval
Darnaway Forest
Logie
Logie Steading
Drumine Forest
Romach Loch
Newtyle Forest
Branchill
Dallas
Hill of Tomechole
Mill Buie
Meikle Hill
Carnach
Dunphail
Relugas
Randolph's Leap
Findhorn
Heritage Centre
Findhorn Foundation
Findhorn Bay
Kinloss
Kinloss Abbey
Burghead
Burghead Bay
Cummingstown
Hopeman
Covesea
Duffus
Roseisle
Roseisle Forest
College of Roseisle
B9089
Coltfield
Alves
Newton
Quarrywood
Elgin
Quarrel Wood Woodland Park
Glen Moray Distillery
Miltonduff
Muir of Miltonduff
Monaughty Forest
Heldon Hill
Pluscarden Abbey
Barnhill
Foresterseat
Hill of the Wangie
Dallas Forest
Kellas
Cairn Uish
B9012
B9013
B9040

86
79
72
A
B
C
D
E
F
1
2
3
4
5
6
7
8
N O R T H
Smerral
Latheronwheel
Knockinnon
Dunbeath
Laidhay Croft
Balnabruich
Portormin
Knockally
Heritage Centre
Ramscraigs
A9
Borgue
Newport
Berriedale
Berriedale Castle
Boch-ailean
Caves
Covesea
Fisheries & Community
Branderburgh
Stotfield
Seatown
Lossiemouth
Hopeman
B9040
Burghead
Cummingstown
Duffus
St Peter's Kirk
Roseisle
Loch Spynie
Lossie Forest
A941
B9135
B9012
College of Roseisle
Quarrywood
Spynie Palace
Moray Motor
Elgin
Bishopmill
Newton
Coltfield
Alves
Quarrel Wood Woodland Park
Glen Moray Distillery
Ashgrove
A96
New Elgin
Glassgreen
Linkwood
Moss of Barmuckity
Miltonduff
Muir of Miltonduff
Monaughty Forest
Heldon Hill
Pluscarden Abbey
Foresterseat
Barnhill
Thornhill
Longmorn
Whitewreath
Millbuies
Clackmarras
Upper Bogside
Coleburn
Kellas
Dallas Forest
Dallas
Meikle Hill
Cairn Uish
Glenlatterach Reservoir
Pikey Hill
Glen of Rothes
Rothes
Glen Grant Distillery
Ben Aigan
Carn na Cailliche
Cairn Cattoch
Urquhart Stone Circle
Urquhart
Lhanbryde
Sheriffston
Scotsburn
Cranloch
Teindland
Teindland Forest
M O R A Y
Spey Bay
Tugnet Ice House
Scottish Dolphin Centre
Spey Bay
DANGER AREA
Kingston
Garmouth
Lochhill
Spey Viaduct
Nether Dallachy
Lower Auchenreath
Porttannachy
Bogmoor
Upper Dallachy
Auchenhalrig
Newlands of Tynet
Cowfords
Mosstodloch
Baxters
Crofts of Dipple
Fochabers
Folk
Whiteash Hill Wood
Speymouth Forest
Ordiquish
Inchberry
Wood of Ordiequish
A98
B9015
B9013
B9104
B9016
Forgie
Aultmore
Broadrashes
Millstone Hill
Auchroisk Distillery
Malcolmburn
Orton
Hill of Mulderie
Mulben
A95
Mount Pleasant
Buckpool
A990
Buckie
Portgordon
Portessie
Ianstown
Rathven
A942
Findochty
Findochty Castle
Bauds of Cullen
B9020
B9021
Portknockie
Cullen Bay
Logie Head
Bin of Cullen
Slackhead
Drybridge
Broadley
Clochan
Shiel Muir
Deerhill
Grange Crossroads
Newmill
B9017
Keith
Strathisla Distillery
Mains of Auchindachy
Upper Cuttlehill
Seatown
Cullen
Mercat Cross
Lintmill
Milton
Kirktown of Deskford
Deskford Church
Berryhillock
Aultmore
Lurg Hill
Mains of Edingight
Knock Hill
Crannoch
Sillyearn
Bracobrae
Knock
Drumnagorrach
Farmtown
Nethermills
B9018
B9022
B9117
Milltown of Rothiemay
Findlater Castle
Sandend
Sandend Bay
Redhythe Point
Portsoy
Salmon Bothy
Joiner's Workshop
Durn Hill
Fordyce
Brodiesord
Drums of Park
Gordonstown
Ramsburn
B9023
B9025
Cornhill
Boyne Bay
Boyne Castle
Knock Head
Whitehills
B9139
Boyndie
Inverboyndie
Boyndie Bay
Banff
A97
Wester Culbeuchly
Kirktown of Alvah
Itlaw
Finnygaud
Knowes of Elrick
Aberchirder
Newton of Mountblairy
Bogton
Marnoch
Turtory
Dubiton
Hillbrae
B9121

SEA
Troup Head
Pennan Head
Quarry Head
Head of Garness
Gamrie Bay
Rosehearty
Sandhaven
Pittulie
Scottish Lighthouses
Kinnaird Head
Heritage Centre
Broadsea
Fraserburgh
Fraserburgh Bay
Cairnbulg Point
Cairnbulg
Inverallochy
Charlestown
St Combs
Inzie Head
Macduff Marine Aquarium
Newtown
Macduff
Silverhillocks
Gardenstown
Crovie
Fort Fiddes
Pennan
Dubford
Longmanhill
New Aberdour
Upper Boyndlie
Tyrie
Mid Ardlaw
Peathill
Pitsligo Castle
Percyhorner
Cardno
Kirktown
Memsie
Memsie Cairn
Rathen
Cairness
Gowanhill
Moss-side of Cairness
Inverallochy Castle
Loch of Strathbeg
Woodhead
Blackhills
Ladysford
Corsehill
Hillhead of Auchentumb
Craigmaud
Netherbrae
Hill of Overbrae
Windyheads Hill
Hill of Fishrie
Clochforbie
King Edward
Crudie
Cauldwells
Plaidy
Craigston
Fintry
Litterty
New Byth
Garmond
Muiryfold
Delgatie
Turriff
Cuminestown
Balthangie
Whitestones
Oldwhat
Hill of Corsegight
Bonnykelly
New Pitsligo
Balnamoon
Middlemuir
Willows Animal Sanctuary
Strichen
Strichen Stone Circle
Waughton Hill
White Horse
White Stag
Cockmuir
New Leeds
Belfatton
Adziel
North Ugie Water
Denhead
Hythie
Forest of Deer
Fetterangus
Brucklay
Crimonmogate
Dartfield
Crimond
Rattray Head
Rattray
Keyhead
Longhill
Rowanhill
Balearn
St Fergus Moss
Middle Essie
Backfolds
Rora Moss
Shielhill
Gallowhills
Kirktown
St Fergus
Cuttyhill
Rora
North Commonty
Fedderate Castle
Cuilsh Monument
Aikey Brae
Old Deer
Deer Abbey
Mintlaw
Aberdeenshire Farming Museum
Longside
Peterhead
Inverugie
Ravenscraig Castle
Buchanhaven
New Deer
Maud
Howe of Teuchar
Darra
Slacks of
Auchnagatt
A98
A947
A950
A981
A90
A952
B9031
B9032
B9033
B9093
B9105
B9107
B9027
B9029
B9170
B9024
B9110
G
H
J
K
L
M
87
73
1
2
3
4
5
6
7
8
80
90
400
10
20
30
900
850

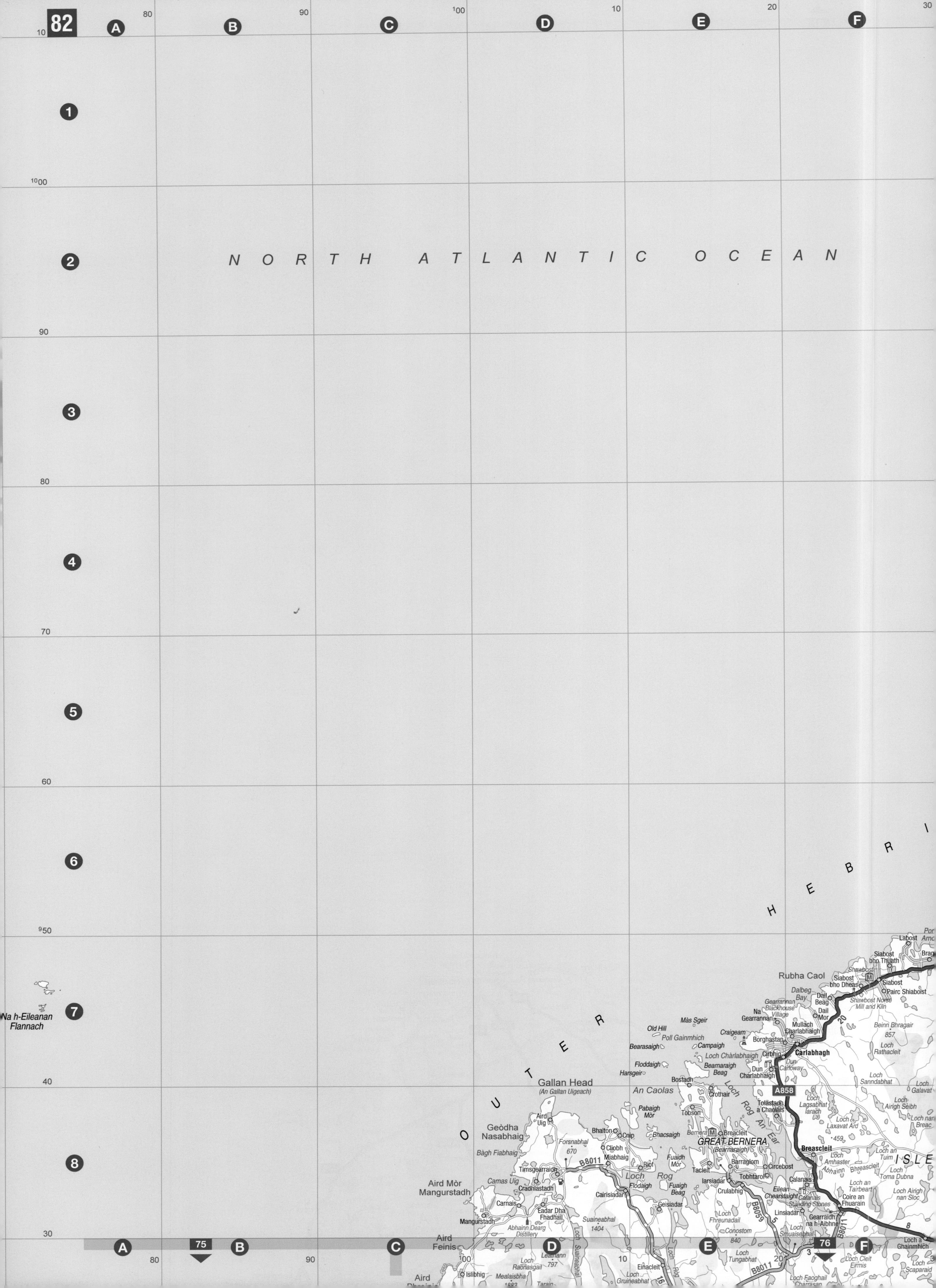

NORTH ATLANTIC OCEAN

Na h-Eileanan Flannach

OUTER HEBRIDES

ISLE

Rubha Caol

Labost
Brag
Siabost bho Thuath
Siabost bho Dheas
Pairc Shiabost
Shawbost Norse Mill and Kiln
Dalbeg Bay.
Gearrannan Blackhouse Village
Dail Beag
Dail Mòr
Na Gearrannan
Mullach Charlabhaigh
Beinn Bhragair 857
Loch Rathacleit
Craigeam
Borghastan
Carlabhagh
Loch Chàrlabhaigh
Dun Carloway
Loch Sanndabhat
Loch Galavat
Loch Airigh Seibh

Old Hill
Poll Gainmhich
Màs Sgeir
Campaigh
Bearasaigh
Floddaigh
Harsgeir

Carlabhagh

Loch Beàrnaraigh Beag
Bostadh
Dun Chàrlabhaigh
A858
Loch Lagsabhat Iarach
Loch Laxavat Ard
Loch nan Breac

Gallan Head
(An Gallan Uigeach)
An Caolas
Grothair
Tolastadh à Chaolais
Aird Uig
Pabaigh Mòr
Tobson
Loch Rog An Ear

Geòdha Nasabhaig
Bhalton
Cnip
Bhacsaigh
Bernera M
Breascleit
Breascleit
Loch an Tuim
Loch Amhaster
Abhainn Bhreascleit
Loch Toma Dubna

Bàgh Fiabhaig
Forsnabhal 670
Cliobh
Miabhaig
Bjòf
Fuaidh Mòr
GREAT BERNERA (Bearnaraigh)
459
Aird Mòr Mangurstadh
B8011
Loch Rog
Tacleit
Barraglom
Circebost
Loch an Tairbeart
Coire an Fhuarain
Loch Airigh nan Sloc

Camas Uig
Timsgearraidh
Flòdaigh
Fuaigh Beag
Iarsiadar
Calanais
Eilean Chearstaigh
Cradhlastadh
Cairisiadar
Tobhtarol
Crulabhig
Calanais Standing Stones
Linsiadar
Gearraidh na h-Aibhne

Carnais
Eadar Dha Fhadhail
Suaineabhal 1404
Geisiadar
B8059
Loch Faoghail Charrasan

Mangurstadh
Abhainn Dearg Distillery
Loch Frèunadail
Conostom
Loch Smuaisebhat

Aird Feinis
Leanann 797
Loch Tungabhat
Loch a' Ghainmhich

Aird
Loch Raónasgail
Mealaisbha 1632
Tarain
Einacleit
Loch Cléit Eirmis
Loch Sgaparaigh

75
76

BUTT OF LEWIS
(Rubha Robhanais)
Europaidh
Coig Peighinnean
B8014
An Cnoc Ard
Port Nis
Lional
Adabroc
Ness Heritage Centre
Suainebost
Tabost
B8013
B8015
Port Skigersta
Sgiogarstaigh
Meall Geal
Aird Dhail
Dail bho Dheas
Cros
NIS
Toa Galson
Gabhsann bho Thuath
Gabhsann bho Dheas
Mealabost
A857
Roinn a' Bhuic
Coig Peighinnean Bhuirgh
Borgh
Rubha Bhlanisgaidh
Siadar
Siadar Uarach
Steinacleit Cairn & Stone Circle
Aird Barvas
Baile an Truiseil
DANGER AREA
Cuidhsiadar
Ben Dell
Loch Langabhat
Cellar Head
Diaval 520
Loch Ceartabhat
Loch Mòr Shanndabhat
NA H-EILEANAN AN IAR
(WESTERN ISLES)
Rinn
Druim Tallig
Barabhas Iarach
Barabhas Uarach
Barabhas
Brù
Blackhouse
A858
Loch Casgro
Loch Urghag
Loch Breabhat
Loch Ghriais
Muirneag 813
Leac Dubh
Gob Hais
Bail' Ur Tholastaidh
Tolstadh bho Thuath
TOLSTA HEAD
(Ceann or Rubha Tholastaidh)
Port Beag
Loch Sgeireach Mòr
Loch an Tobair
B895
Gleann Tholastaidh
Port Bun a' Ghlinne
Loch Ullabhat a' Cli
Loch an Tuim
Loch Ullabhat a' Deas
Griais
Loch Gunna
Lacastal
Bac
Sgeir Leathann
Col
Col Uarach
Vatisker Point
Breibhig
Coll Sands
Loch Suainagadail
Beinn Mholach 955
Loch Scarabhat Mhòr
Glen Bragar
Loch Mòr an Starr
Loch nan Steamag
Tunga
Aird Thunga
Broad Bay
(Loch a'Tuath)
TIUMPAN HEAD
(Rubha an T-Siumpain)
Port Nan Giuran
Cnoc Amhlaigh
Port Mholair
Fleisirin
Bagh Phort Bholair
Aird
A866
Grianan
Newmarket
Lacasdail
Tràigh Mhealaboist
Sulaisiadar
Seisiadar
OF LEWIS
(Eilean Leodhais)
An Gleann Ur
STORNOWAY
(Steòrnabhagh)
Bruach Mairi
Nan Eilean
STORNOWAY
Garrabost
EYE PENINSULA
(An Rubha)
Creed
Greeta River
Sanndabhaig
Mealabost
Aiginis
Pabail Uarach
Abhainn Ghrioda
A859
Cala Steòrnabhaigh
Tolm
An Cnoc
Pabail Iarach
Suardail
Loch Thobhta Bridein
Loch a' Bhuna
Amish
Moor
Gob Shilldinish
288 Beinn Phabail
Bagh Phabail Iarach
Loch Orasaigh
B897
Loch Tom an Fheidh
Stornoway to Ullapool 2hrs. 40mins.
Loch Innseag
Bràigh
G
H
J
K
L
M
1
2
3
4
5
6
7
8
84
77
40
150
60
70
80
10
1000
90
80
70
60
950
40
30

THE MINCH
CAPE WRATH
Duslic
Stack Clò Kearvaig
Kearvaig
Clo Mor Cliffs
A' Ghoil
Faraid Head
Sgribhis-bheinn 1216
DANGER AREA
Inshore
Loch Inshore
Balnakeil Bay
Balnakeil
Craft Village
Cnoc a' Ghiubhais 976
Bay of Keisgaig
Loch Keisgaig
Kearvaig River
Achiemore
Loch Borralie
Fashven 1498
Loch Airigh na Beinne
Keoldale
Beinn an Amair 911
Loch Caladail
Loch a' Gheodha Ruaidh
Beinn Dearg 1390
Loch na Gainmhich
Kyle of Durness
Loch Meadaidh
Sandwood Loch
Creag Riabhach 1592
Strath Shinary
An Grianan 1527
Grudie River
Loch na Gainimh
Ghlas-bheinn 1085
Abhainn an t-Strathain
Sheigra
Blairmore
Balchrick
Droman
Loch Aisir Mor
Oldshore Beg
Oldshoremore
Farmheall 1709
A838
Eilean an Ròin Mór
An Socach 1165
Beinn Spionnaidh 2534
Loch Innis na Ba Buidhe
Gualin House
Loch na Gainimh
Loch Clash
Kinlochbervie
B801
Badcall
Cranstackie 2630
Polla
Inshegra
Bàgh Loch an Ròin
Achriesgill
Rhuvoult
Lochan Sgeireach
Loch Inchard
River Dionard
Strath Dionard
Strath Beag
Loch Crocach
Achlyness
Loch na Claise Carnaich
Loch Dughaill
Rhiconich
Ardmore Point
Ardmore
Skerricha
Loch na Thull
Ganu Mór 2980
Mathair a' Gharbh Uilt
FOINAVEN
Fanagmore
Loch Dionard
Tarbet
Foindle
Sound of Handa
Loch a' Gharbh-bhaid Mór
Loch Staonsaid
Laxford Bridge
Loch na Tuadh
Handa Island
Badnabay
Loch a' Bhadaidh Daraich
River Laxford
Arkle 2580
Loch an Easain Uaine
Lochan Sgèireach
Scourie Bay
Scourie
A894
Scourie More
Loch an Nighe Leathaid
Loch na Seilge
Gorm Loch
Lochstack Lodge
Rubh' Aird an t-Sionnaich
Upper Badcall
Lower Badcall
Loch Stack
Lone
Sàbhal Beag 2393
Loch a' Mhuilinn
Ben Stack 2356
Clàr Loch
Cnoc Thormaid
Abhainn an Loin
Badcall Bay
Reay Forest
Ben Auskaird 1265
Achfary
Meallan Liath Coire Mhic Dhughaill 2627
Coire Loch
Eilean a Bhreitheimh
Loch Crocach
Loch na Mucnaich
Meall Mór
Duartmore Bridge
Allt nan Ramh
Loch na Creige Duibhe
Loch More
Loch Ulbhach Coire
Calbha Beag
Calbha Mór
Sgeir nan Gall
Eddrachillis Bay
Ben Strome 1374
Loch an Leathiad Bhuain
Beinn a' Bhuta 1777
Point of Stoer
Old Man of Stoer
Oldany Island
Loch a' Chàirn Bhàin
Kylestrome
Glendhu Forest
Kinloch
Loch Cùl Fraioch
Eilean Chrona
Culkein Drumbeg
Kylesku
Loch Glendhu
Gleann Dubh
A838
Cluas Deas
Culkein
Rhubha Stoer
Loch Nedd
Unapool
Oldany
B869
Beinn Aird da Loch 1722
Achnacarnin
Clashnessie Bay
Drumbeg
Nedd
Loch Glencoul
Loch Merkland
Clashmore
Glenleraig
Newton
Balchladich
Clashnessie
Loch Poll
Loch an Leothaid
A894
Glen Coul
Stoer
Loch nan Lub
Loch na Loinne
Gorm Loch Mór
QUINAG 2651
Gleann Leireag
Loch na Gainmhich
Dubh a' Chuail
Merklan Lodge
Bay of Stoer
Clachtoll
Loch Beannach
Lochassynt Lodge
Eas a' Chual
Loch an Eircill
Clachtoll Broch
77
78
83

G
H
J
K
L
M
NORTH SEA
STRATHY POINT
Totegan
Whiten Head or An Ceann Geal
Eilean Hoan
Eilean Clùimhrig
Smoo Cave
Sangobeg
Rispond
Beinn Ceannabeinne 1257
Loch Eriboll
Portnancon
Eilean Choraidh
Eriboll
Hope
Ben Arnaboll
Ben Hutig 1338
Port Vasgo
Achininver
Midfield
Lubinvullin
Strathan
West Strathan
Achinahuagh
Talmine
Skinnet
Midtown
Rabbit Islands
Loch a' Mhuillinn
Loch Maovally
A838
Achuvoldrach
Tongue
Rhitongue
Coldbackie
Kyle of Tongue
Braetongue
Loch Fhionnaich
Caisteal Bharraich
Ribigill
Beinn Bhreac 1018
Kinloch Lodge
Lochan Hakel
Loch na Seilg
Meallan Liath 1962
Eilean nan Ron
Tongue Bay
Caol Raineach
Strathan Skerray
Skerray
Clashbuidh
Achtoty
Modsarie
Torrisdale
Torrisdale Bay
Neave or Coombe Island
Skullomie
Blandy
A836
Dalcharn
Loch Cormaic
Borgie
River Borgie
Borgie Forest
Farr Point
Farr Bay
Farr
Clerkhill
Swordly
Kirtomy
Bay of Swordly
Kirtomy Point
Crask
Clachan
Bettyhill
Achina
Invernaver
Strathnaver
Leckfurin
Coille na Borgie Chambered Tomb
Skelpick
Archargary
River Naver
Na Caol Lochan
Loch Stephan
Lochan nan Carn
Loch nan Ealachan
Carnachy
Rhifail
Rough Haugh
Beinn Rifa-gil 963
B871
Skail Chambered Cairn
Skail
Ardmore Point
Armadale Bay
Armadale
Port Allt a' Mhuilinn
Aultivullin
Brawl
Aultiphurst
Strathy
Strathy Bay
Baligill
Portskerra
Melvich
Melvich Bay
Lednagullin
Strathy Forest
Loch Gaineimh
Loch Meadie
Loch Buidhe Beag
Beinn nam Bò 751
Loch Buidhe Mòr
Loch Meala
Loch Mòr na Caorach
Loch nan Clach
Dunviden Lochs
Skelpick Burn
River Strathy
Bowside Lodge
Loch Baligill
Loch nan Gall
Caol-loch
Cnoc Badaireach na Gaoithe 698
Red Point
Bighouse
Upper Bighouse
Drum Hollistan 608
A897
Achiemore
Halladale
Smigel Burn
Craigtown
Dalhalvaig
Croick
Trantlemore
Trantlebeg
Fresgoe
Sandside Bay
Reay
Isauld
Lower Dounreay
Upper Dounreay
Beinn Ratha 795
Loch Akran
Loch na Seilge
Cnoc an Fhuarain Bhain
Loch Sàinn
Loch Saird
Loch Tuim Ghlais
Lochan Ealach Beag
Cnoc Preas a' Mhadaidh 665
Forsinain Burn
Loch Sletill
Sletill Hill 918
Loch Leir
Loch nan Cloiche
Forsinard
Forsinard Flows
Loch Rumsdale
Rumsdale Water
Ben Hope 3040
Cashel Dhu
Loch Crocach
An Lean-charm 1705
Loch Hope
Strathmore River
Fèinne-bheinn Mhòr 1519
Alltnacaillich
Dun Domaigil
Glen Golly River
Gobernuisgach Lodge
Ben Loyal 2509
Loch an Dherue
Loch Haluim
Loch Loyal Lodge
Cnoc nan Cuilean 1828
Loch nan Ealachan
Loch Coulside
Cnoc Craggie 1043
Loch Craggie
Beinn Stumanadh 1728
Loch nam Breac
Loch Meleag
Loch Syre
Loch Bad na Gallaig
Pole Hill 965
Loch Eileanach
Grumbeg Settlement
Grummore
Syre
Rosal Clearance Village
Navar Forest
Rhifail Loch
Loch Meadie
Mudale
River Mudale
Altnaharra
B873
Loch Naver
Loch Coire na Saidhe Duibhe
Loch an t-Seilg
Ben Hee 2863
Loch a' Ghorm-choire
Loch Ben Harrald
Meall an Fhuarain 1549
An Glas-loch
BEN KLIBRECK 3152
Meall nan Con 3157
Loch Choire Lodge
Loch Choire Forest
Creag na h-Iolaire 2278
Loch nan Uan
Fiag Lodge
Loch Fiag
Rimsdale
Garvault
Ben Griam Mòr 1938
Ben Griam Beg
Loch Druim a' Chliabhain 1902
Caol-loch Mòr
Cnoc nan Tri-chlach 1133
Loch Crocach
Loch Strathy
Loch na Saobhaidhe
The Cross Lochs
Badanloch Forest
Loch nan Clàr
Loch Badanloch
Badanloch Lodge
Loch Rimsdale
Loch Truderscaig
Loch an Alltan Fhèarna
Loch Achnamoine
River Helmsdale
Kinbrace
Achentoul
Achentoul Forest
Loch an Ruathair
Lochside
Loch Arichlinie
Knockfin Heights 1437
Cnoc an Liath-bhaid Mhòir 1423
Loch na Gaineimh
Gobernuisgach
Cnoc Coire na Fèarna 1434
Glutt Lodge
79
86

ORKNEY ISLANDS
MAINLAND
Kirkwall
Stromness
Scapa Flow
HOY
South Walls
Flotta
Burray
SOUTH RONALDSAY
St Margaret's Hope
Swona
Island of Stroma
Pentland Skerries
PENTLAND FIRTH
Stromness to Scrabster 1hr. 30mins.
Stromness 1hr. 30mins.
Gills Bay to St Margaret's Hope, Orkney 1hr.
40mins. (Seasonal)
DUNNET HEAD
DUNCANSBY HEAD
John o' Groats
Thurso
Scrabster
Castletown
Dunnet
Halkirk
Reay
Watten
Wick
Lybster
Dunbeath
Latheron
H I G H L A N D
Sinclair's Bay
Freswick Bay
Noss Head
South Head
Helman Head
Sarclet Head
Halberry Head
Old Man of Hoy
Rora Head
Brims Ness
Holborn Head
Dunnet Bay
Tang Head
St John's Point
A9
A99
A836
A882
A897
A961
A964
A965
B870
B874
B876
B855
B9047
85
88
79
80

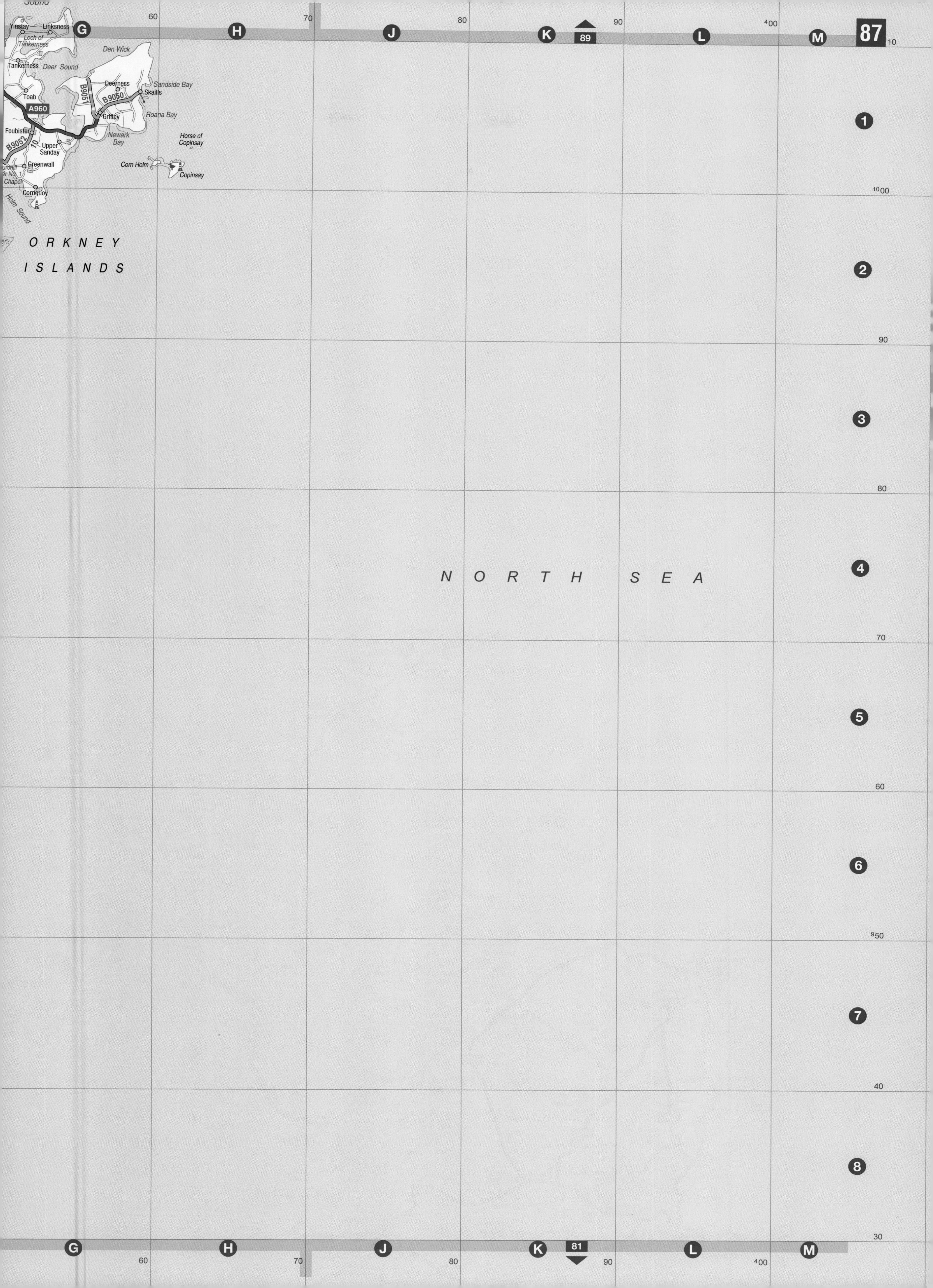

Sound

Yinstay Linksness
Loch of
Tankerness
Tankerness Deer Sound
Den Wick
Deerness
Toab Deerness Sandside Bay
B9051 B9050 Skaills
A960 Gritley
Foubister Roana Bay
Newark
Upper Bay Horse of
Sanday Copinsay
Greenwall Corn Holm
Cletch Copinsay
air No.1
Chapel
Cornquoy

O R K N E Y

I S L A N D S

N O R T H   S E A

NORTH SEA
ORKNEY ISLANDS
Papa Westray
Mull Head
The Bore
Holm of Papa
Holm of Papa Westray Chambered Cairn
Knap of Howar
Holland
Backaskaill
Loch of St Tredwell
Gayfield
Papa Sound
Papa Westray to North Ronaldsay 1hr. 10mins. (Seasonal)
Noup Head
Bay of Noup
Rack Wick
Bay of Skail
Rackwick
Noltland
Pierowall
Broughton
Braehead
Westray Heritage Centre
Monivey
20mins. (Seasonal)
Bay of Cleat
Bay of Swartmill
Cleat
WESTRAY
THE NORTH SOUND
Fitty Hill 555
Midbea
Skelwick
Skel Wick
Bay of Tuquoy
Westside Church
Rack Wick
Rapness
Skea Skerries
WESTRAY FIRTH
Wart Holm
Rapness Sound
Sound of Faray
Kirkwall to Westray 1hr. 25mins.
Rusk Holm
Faray
Kirkwall to North Ronaldsay 2hrs. 40mins.
Calf of Eday
Carrick Ho
Calf Sound
Calfsound
Benstonhall
Mill Bay
Millbounds
Lashy Sound
Fersness Bay
Bay of London
EDAY
Eday Sound
Bay of Backaland
Backaland
Southside
Veness
Holmes of Ire
Whitemill Bay
Scar
Burness
North Bay
Bay of Brough
Broughtown
SANDAY
Lady
Overbister
Kettletoft
Kettletoft Bay
Backaskaill Bay
Laminess
Braeswick
Sty Wick
Quoyness Chambered Cairn
Stove
Sanday Sound
The Keld
Bay of Stove
35mins. (Seasonal)
Spurnness Sound
Holm of Huip
Papa Stronsay
Huip Sound
Odie
STRONSAY
Whitehall
Linga Holm
Linga Sound
Mill Bay
St Catherine's Bay
Samsonslane
Everbay
Bay of Bomasty
Grobister
Odin Bay
Kirbuster
Dishes
Rothiesholm
Cott
Bay of Holland
Holland
Bay of Houseby
Ingale Skerry
Auskerry Sound
Auskerry
STRONSAY FIRTH
Kirkwall to Papa Westray 1hr. 50mins.
Kirkwall to Eday, Sanday & Stronsay
Kili Holm
Saviskaill Bay
Wasbister
Kierfea Hill 771
Midhowe Broch
Midhowe Chambered Cairn
ROUSAY
Muckle Water
Sourin
Westside
Eynhallow
Eynhallow Church
Westness
Blotchnie Fold
Cairns 821
Brinian
Frotoft
Rousay Sound
St Magnus Kirk
Egilsay
Muckle Green Holm
Cubbie Row's Castle
Wyre
Wyre Sound
St Mary's Chapel
Eynhallow Sound
Broch of Gurness
Gairsay Sound
Sweyn Holm
Wood Wick
Tingwall
Wass Wick
Gairsay
Hackland
Gorseness
Isbister
Bay of Isbister
Pulldrite Skerry
Wide Firth
Bay of Furrowend
Veantrow Bay
Burroughston
Edmonstone
Bay of Linton
Crossgate
SHAPINSAY
Balfour
Helliar Holm
Newlot
The String
Shapinsay Sound
Thieves Holm
Damsay
Work
Bay of Meil
Kirkwall (Hatston) to:
Aberdeen 7hrs. 15mins.
Lerwick (Holmsgarth) 7hrs. 45mins.
Brough Head
Earl's Palace
The Barony
Brough of Birsay
Birsay Bay
Abune-the-Hill
Loch of Boardhouse
Loch Swannay
Costa
Kirbuster Museum
Loch of Hundland
Stenso
Georth
Redland
Mar Wick
Marwick
Twatt
Burn of Hillside
Hillside
Beaquoy
Click Mill
Woodwick
Northdyke
Quoyloo
Skeabrae
Dounby
Milldoe 726
Mirbister
Corrigall Farm
Corrigall
Bay of Skaill
Skara Brae Prehistoric Village
Skaill
Skaill House
Sandwick
Loch of Skaill
Brough
Russland
Settiscarth
Yesnaby
Ness of Tenston
Hestwall
Netherbrough
Bimbister
Loch of Harray
Stones of Stenness Circle & Henge
Grimeston
Finstown
Bay of Firth
Rennibister Earth House
Voy
Kirbister
Ring of Brodgar Stone Circle & Henge
Loch of Stenness
Cuween Hill Chambered Cairn
Heddle
Grimbister
Wideford Hill Chambered Cairn
Bay of Kirkwall
Grain Earth-house
Quholm
Cairn
Tormiston Mill
Keelylang Hill 721
Orkney Wireless
Kirkwall
Bishop's Palace
Outertown
Cairston
Clouston
MAINLAND
Bay of Ireland
Stromness
Pier Arts Centre
Hoy Sound
Ward Hill 883
Kirbister
Loch of Kirbister
Greenigoe
Scapa
Highland Park Distillery
Tradespark
Borrowstonehill
KIRKWALL
Inganess Bay
Yinstay
Loch of Tankerness
Linksness
Tankerness
Deer Sound
Den Wick
Deerness
Sandside Bay
A966
A967
A986
A965
A964
A960
B9064
B9057
B9055
B9056
B9066
B9067
B9068
B9069
B9070
B9063
B9058
B9059
B9062
B9060
B9061
86
A
B
C
D
E
F
1
2
3
4
5
6
7
8

1

80

Fair Isle to
Grutness / Sumburgh
2hrs. 30mins

2

**SHETLAND
ISLANDS**

Skroo○ North Haven——— Fair Isle to
Lerwick 5hrs.
(Seasonal)

FAIR ISLE

Stonybreck○ Fair Isle
Leogh○

70

South Harbour

3

60

*Seal
Skerry*

Garso
Wick

North
Ronaldsay

NORTH
RONALDSAY Linklet
Bay

Hollandstoun

*South
Bay*

4

1050

NORTH RONALDSAY FIRTH

North
Loch

Bay of
Sandquoy

Northwall Lettan

Scuthvie Bay

Bay of
Lopeness

Start
Point

B9069 Newark

SANDAY

Bay of
Newark

40

*Tres
Ness*

5

6

N   O   R   T   H   S   E   A

30

7

20

8

10

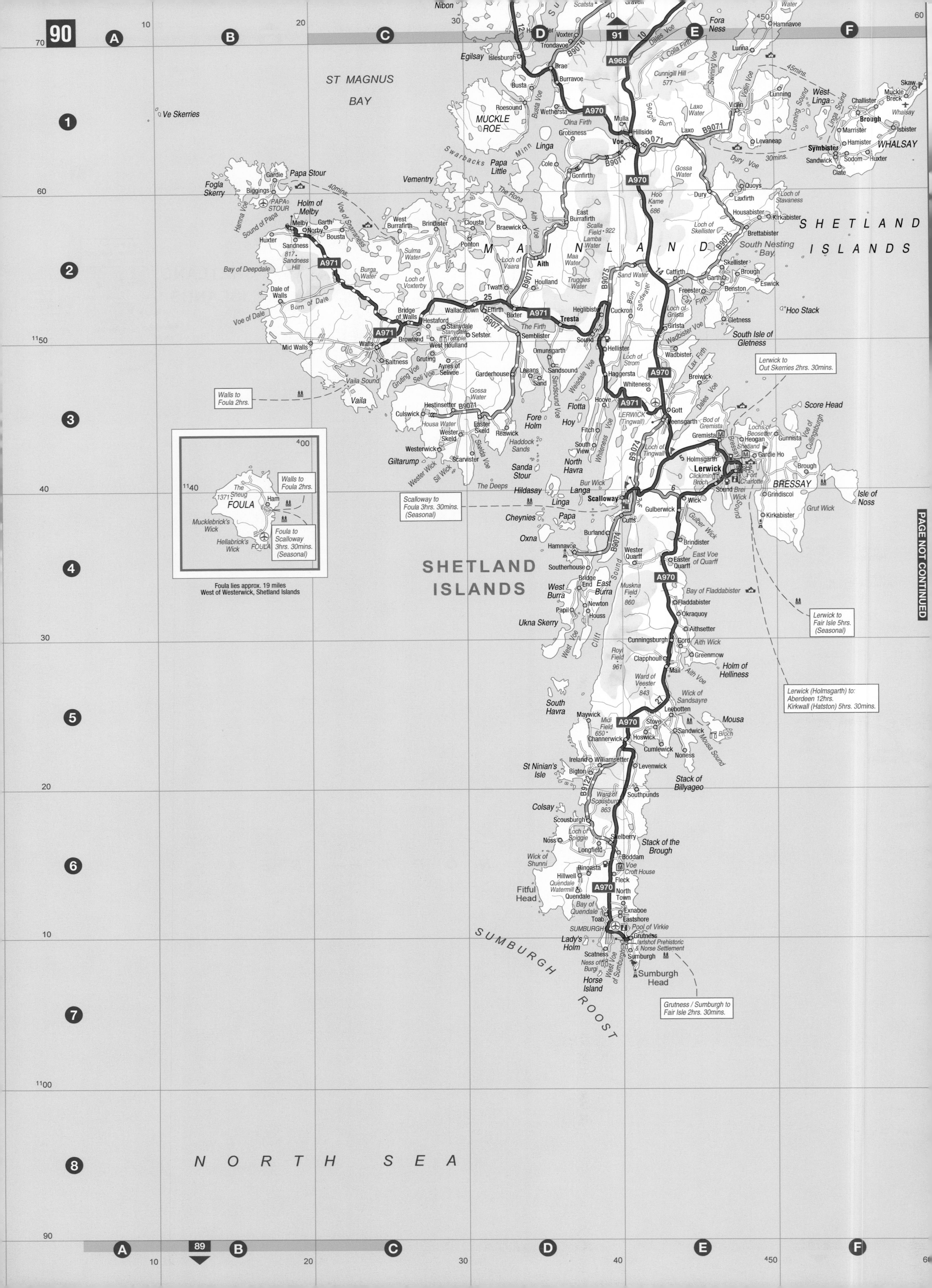

ST MAGNUS
BAY

Ve Skerries

Fogla
Skerry

Papa Stour
Gardie Biggings
Holm of Melby
PAPA STOUR
Melby Garth
Huxter Norby Bousta
Sandness
817 Sandness Hill
Bay of Deepdale

West
Burrafirth
Brindister
Clousta
Braewick

Vementry
Papa
Little
Linga
Cole
Gonfirth

MUCKLE
ROE
Roesound
Busta
Wethersta
Grobsness
Olna Firth
Mulla
Hillside
Voe

Nibon
Scatsta
Graven
Hamnavoe
Water

Egilsay Islesburgh
Voxter
Trondavoe
B9076
91
A968
Dales Voe
Colla Firth
Lunna
Fora
Ness

Brae
Busta Voe
Burravoe
A970
Swarbacks Minn
Aith Voe

Segeg Burn
Laxo
Burn
Laxo
B9071
A970

Cunningill Hill
577
Swining Voe

West
Linga
Muckle
Breck
Whalsay
Brough
Marrister
Hamister
WHALSAY
Symbister
Sandwick Sodom Huxter
Clate

Skaw
Isbister
Challister

Lunning
Lunning Sound
Linga Sound

Vidlin
Vidlin Voe
Levaneap

Dury Voe
30mins.
Quoys
Loch of
Stavaness
Kirkabister
Brettabister
SHETLAND
ISLANDS

MAINLAND

Sound of Papa
Vaila Voe
Hanna Voe

Burga
Water
Loch of
Voxterby

Aith
Twatt
Houlland
25

Sulma
Water
Loch of
Vaara

East
Burrafirth
Scalla
Field 922
Lamba
Water
Maa Water
Truggles
Water

Hoo Kame
686
Dury
Laxfirth

Gossa
Water
Laxo

Housabister
Loch of
Skellister

Catfirth
Freester
Girlsta
Loch of
Grista
Wadbister Voe

South Nesting
Bay
Skellister
Brough
Garth
Eswick
Gletness

Benston

South Isle of
Gletness
Hoo Stack

40mins.
Voe of Snarraness
A971
Dale of
Walls
Burn of Dale
Voe of Dale

Bridge
of Walls
Wallacetown
Effirth
Bixter
A971
Tresta
Heglibister
Cuckron
Sound
Hellister
A971

Hestaford
Stanydale
Stanydale
Temple
Sefster
The Firth
Semblister

Burn of
Sandwater
Sand Water

Wadbister

Breiwick
Dales Voe

Lerwick to
Out Skerries 2hrs. 30mins.

Mid Walls
Walls
Browland
West Houlland
Saltness
Gruting
Ayres of
Selivoe
Garderhouse
Leeans
Sand

Omunsgarth
Sandsound

Loch of
Strom
Haggersta
Whiteness
Hoove
A970
Wadbister
Lax Firth

Score Head

Vaila
Gruting Voe
Seli Voe
Gossa
Water
Hestinsetter
B9071
Sandsound Voe
Westside Voe

Loch of
Grista

Lerwick
(Tingwall)
Gott
M
Gremista

Lochs of
Beosetter
Heogan
Voe of
Cullingsburgh
Gunnista
Gardie Ho

Culswick
Easter
Skeld
Wester
Skeld
Reawick
Fore
Holm
Hoy
Fitch
Flotta

Whiteness Voe
South
View
North
Havra
Haddock
Sands
Skelda Voe

B9074
Loch of
Tingwall
Greensgarth
Holmgarth
M
Lochs of
Shetland

Lerwick
Clickimin
Broch
Fort
Charlotte

Brough
BRESSAY

Walls to
Foula 2hrs.
Westerwick
Scarvister
Sil Wick

Sanda
Stour

Hildasay
The Deeps
Langa
Linga
Scalloway
Cutts

6
Gulberwick
Wick

Sound Brei
Wick Sound

Kirkabister
Grut Wick

Isle of
Noss

Giltarump
Wester Wick
Housa Water

Walls to
Foula 2hrs.

The
Sneug
1371
FOULA
Ham

Scalloway to Foula 3hrs. 30mins.
(Seasonal)

Cheynies
Oxna
Papa

Burland
Hamnavoe
Southerhouse

Brindister
Wester
Quarff
East Voe
of Quarff
Easter
Quarff
Bay of Fladdabister

Lerwick to
Fair Isle 5hrs.
(Seasonal)

Mucklebrick's
Wick

Hellabrick's
Wick
FOULA

Foula to
Scalloway
3hrs. 30mins.
(Seasonal)

SHETLAND
ISLANDS

West
Burra
Bridge
End
East
Burra
Newton
Papil
Houss
Houss

A970
Muskna
Field
860
Fladdabister
Okraquoy
Aithsetter

Holm of
Helliness

Foula lies approx. 19 miles
West of Westerwick, Shetland Islands

Ukna Skerry
West Voe
Clift Sound

Cunningsburgh
Gord Aith Wick
Greenmow
Mail
Clapphoull
Royl
Field
961
Ward of
Veester
843

Lerwick (Holmsgarth) to:
Aberdeen 12hrs.
Kirkwall (Hatston) 5hrs. 30mins.

South
Havra
Maywick
Midi
Field
650
Channerwick
A970
Stove
Hoswick
Sandwick
Cumlewick
Noness

Wick of
Sandsayre
Leebotten
21
Mousa
Birch
Mousa Sound

St Ninian's
Isle
Ireland
Williamsetter
Bigton
Levenwick
Stack of
Billyageo

Colsay
Ward of
Scousburgh
863
Southpunds

Noss
Scousburgh
Loch of
Spiggie
Selberry

Wick of
Shunni
Longfield
Hillwell
Hingasta
Boddam

Stack of
the Brough

Quendale
Watermill
Quendale
Fleck
Voe
Croft House
North
Town
A970

Fitful
Head
Bay of
Quendale
Toab
SUMBURGH
Exnaboe
Eastshore
Pool of Virkie
Grutness

Lady's
Holm
Scatness
Ness of
Burgi
Jarlshof Prehistoric
& Norse Settlement
Sumburgh

Horse
Island
West Voe
of Sumburgh
Sumburgh
Head

Grutness / Sumburgh to
Fair Isle 2hrs. 30mins.

SUMBURGH
ROOST

NORTH   SEA

PAGE NOT CONTINUED

NORTH SEA
Out Stack
Tipta Skerry
Muckle Flugga
Herma Ness
Saxa Vord
936
Wick of Skaw
Hermaness
Burra Firth
Nor Wick
Norwick
Burrafirth
Valsgarth
Heimar Water
Quoys
Clibberswick
Haroldswick
Loch of Cliff
Gardie
Harold's Wick
North Holms
South Holms
UNST
Baliasta
Buness
Baltasound
Balta Sound
Balta
Caldback
Ordale
Westing
Huney
Gloup Holm
Loch of Watlee
Lunda Wick
Underhoull
Haa of Houlland
Gloup
Greenbank
Moarfield
Cullivoe
Stronganess
Bluemull Sound
Wick
Burragarth
Sand Wick
Ham of Muness
Belmont
Uyeasound
Clivocast
Muness
Ramnageo
Gossa Water
Uyea Sound
Skuda Sound
Haaf Gruney
Gutcher
Linga
Uyea
Lochs of Lumbister
Sellafirth
Bayanne House
Colvister
Cunnister
Mid Ho
Sound Gruney
Urie Lingey
Wedder Holm
Daaey
Ramna Stacks
Gruney
Basta
Basta Voe
Hamars Ness
Oddsta
Vord Hill 518
YELL
Efstigarth
Grimister
Camb
Brough Lodge
FETLAR
Wick of Gruting
Ler Wick
Hascosay Sound
Hascosay
Herra
Fetlar
Houbie
Mid Yell Voe
Mid Yell
South Sound
Colgrave Sound
Tresta
Funzie
Aith
Funzie Bay
Wick of Tresta
Uyea
Barrier Wick
Sandvoe
Isbister
South Wick
North Roe
Burravoe
Burra Voe
Harkland
Vatsetter
Loch of Vatsetter
West Sandwick
Lang Clodie Wick
Gruna Stack
Burn of Sandvoe
Yell Sound
Muckle Holm
Moorbrae
Laxa Burn
Skelberry
Ay Wick
Aywick
Roer Water
Little Holm
Hill of Arisdale 673
Otterswick
Otters Wick
Muckle Ossa
Housetter
Fladda
Ronas Voe
Ronas Hill 1476
Man o'Scord 740
North Collafirth
Colla Firth
Swarister
Burn of Arisdale
SHETLAND ISLANDS
Lamba
Brother Isle
West Yell
Newtown
Gossabrough
Setter
Hamna Voe
Gluss Water
White Grunafirth 568
Quey Firth
Hamnavoe
Voe
Ollaberry
Uynarey
Ulsta
Hamnavoe
Upper Neepaback
Littlester
Ure
Braehoulland
Swinister
Eela Water
Hogaland
Eastwick
Gluss Voe
Houlland
Burravoe
West Heogaland
Tangwick
Brae Wick
Burnside
Urafirth
Little Roe
Orka Voe
Bigga
Copister
Vats Wick
Haa
Hillswick
Ura Firth
North Gluss
Bardister
20mins.
Orfasay
Isle of Stenness
South Gluss
Brough
Skerry of Eshaness
Dore Holm
Booth of Toft
Tofts Voe
Samphrey
The Drongs
Mossbank
Lunna Holm
Sand Water
Isle of Nibon
Sullom
Garths Voe
Voe of Scatsta
Firths Voe
Fish Holm
Linga
Muckle Skerry
Sullom Voe
Scatsta
Graven
Firth
Fugla Water
Little Skerry
Skerries
Housay
Grunay
Haggrister
Fora Ness
Hamnavoe
Out Skerries
Voxter
Trondavoe
Dales Voe
1hr. 30mins.
Mio Ness
Egilsay
Isleburgh
Lunna
Filla
ST MAGNUS BAY
Brae
Colla Firth
Cunnigill Hill 577
Swining Voe
45mins.
The Guens
Out Skerries to Lerwick 2hrs. 30mins.
Busta
Burravoe
Vidlin Voe
Skaw
Roesound
Busta Voe
Lunning
West Linga
Challister
Muckle Breck
Whalsay
MUCKLE ROE
Wethersta
Olna Firth
Mulla
Laxo Water
Lunning Sound
Linga Sound
Brough
Marrister
Isbister
East Linga
Grobsness
Hillside
Segge Burn
Laxo
Vidlin
Swarbacks Minn
Linga
Voe
Levaneap
Hamister
Symbister
WHALSAY
Papa Little
Cole
Dury Voe
30mins.
Sandwick
Sodom
Huxter
Grif Skerry
Vementry
Gonfirth
Gossa Water
Clate
West Burrafirth to Papa Stour 40mins.
The Rona
Rumble
Voe of Snarraness
Hoo Kame 686
Quoys
Dury
Laxfirth
Loch of Stavaness
Garth
West Burrafirth
Brindister
Clousta
East Burrafirth
Housabister
Kirkabister
Bousta
Aith Voe
Scalla Field 922
Loch of Skellister
Brettabister
SHETLAND ISLANDS
Braewick
Lamba Water
Sulma Water
Ponton
South Nesting Bay
MAINLAND
Burga Water
Loch of Vaara
Maa Water
Aith
Skellister
Loch of Voxterby
Sand Water
Catfirth
Brough
Houlland
Truggles Water
Burn of Sandwater
Garth
Eswick
Twatt
Freester
Benston
Wallacetown
Effirth
Cat Firth
Bridge of Walls
Heglibister
Bixter
Cuckron
Hoo Stack
Hestaford
Tresta
Loch of Grista
Stanydale Temple
The Firth
Gletness
Browland
Sefster
Semblister
Girlsta
Walls
West Houlland
Sound
Wadbister Voe
South Isle of Gletness
Saltness
Gruting
Garth
Wadbister
Ayres
Selivoe
Loch of Strom
Vaila Sound
Gruting Voe
Sell Voe
Garderhouse
Leeans
Sandsound
Haggersta
Whiteness
Lax
Breiwick
Sand
PAGE NOT CONTINUED

NORTHERN IRELAND
Scale: 6 miles to 1 inch 1:380,160
0 1 2 3 4 5 10 Miles
0 1 2 3 4 5 10 15 Kilometres
A
B
C
D
E
1
2
3
4
5
6
7
Tory Sound
GLENVEAGH NATIONAL PARK
Muckish Mountain 2198
Errigal Mountain 2467
Slieve Snaght 2241
Slieve Snaght 2017
Carndonagh
Moville
Buncrana
LOUGH FOYLE
Letterkenny
LONDONDERRY (DERRY)
CITY OF DERRY
BALLYKELLY
GREYSTEEL
EGLINTON
LIMAVADY
NEW BUILDINGS
CLAUDY
DUNGIVEN
STRABANE
Stranorlar
Ballybofey
Gaugin Mountain 1863
SION MILLS
DERRY & STRABANE
DRAPERSTOWN
Croaghnageer 1794
NEWTOWNSTEWART
CASTLEDERG
Donegal
Inver Bay
OMAGH
Drumnakilly
DONEGAL BAY
Ballyshannon
Bundoran
LOWER LOUGH ERNE
FERMANAGH & OMAGH
IRVINESTOWN
FINTONA
DUNGANNON
BALLINAMALLARD
ENNISKILLEN
FIVEMILETOWN
Manorhamilton
Lisbellaw
LISNASKEA
Monaghan
Cuilcagh 2184
The Playbank 1781
Benbrack 1637
LOUGH ALLEN
Slieve Anierin 1919
Belturbet
Cootehill
Newtownbutler (An Baile Nua)

Ballycastle to
Campbeltown 1hr. 30mins.
(Seasonal)
Port Ellen 1hr. (Seasonal)
Larne to:
Cairnryan 2hrs.
Belfast to:
Birkenhead 8hrs.
Douglas 2hrs. 45mins.
(Fast Ferry, Seasonal)
Cairnryan (Loch Ryan Port)
2hrs. 15mins.
(Fast Ferry, Seasonal)
NORTH CHANNEL
IRISH SEA
LOUGH NEAGH
RATHLIN SOUND
Rathlin Island
MULL OF KINTYRE
CAUSEWAY COAST & GLENS
MID & EAST ANTRIM
ANTRIM & NEWTOWNABBEY
LISBURN & CASTLEREAGH
ARDS & NORTH DOWN
ARMAGH, BANBRIDGE & CRAIGAVON
NEWRY, MOURNE & DOWN
PORTRUSH
PORTBALLINTRAE
BUSHMILLS
BALLYCASTLE
COLERAINE
BALLYMONEY
CUSHENDALL
CARNLOUGH
LARNE
BALLYMENA
ANTRIM
CARRICKFERGUS
NEWTOWNABBEY
BANGOR
BELFAST
HOLYWOOD
DUNDONALD
NEWTOWNARDS
DONAGHADEE
LISBURN
LURGAN
CRAIGAVON
PORTADOWN
ARMAGH
BANBRIDGE
NEWRY
DOWNPATRICK
NEWCASTLE
KILKEEL
WARRENPOINT
ROSTREVOR
CASTLEWELLAN
BALLYNAHINCH
PORTAFERRY
Castleblayney
CROSSMAGLEN
KEADY
MAGHERAFELT
COOKSTOWN
MONEYMORE
DUNDRUM BAY
CARLINGFORD LOUGH

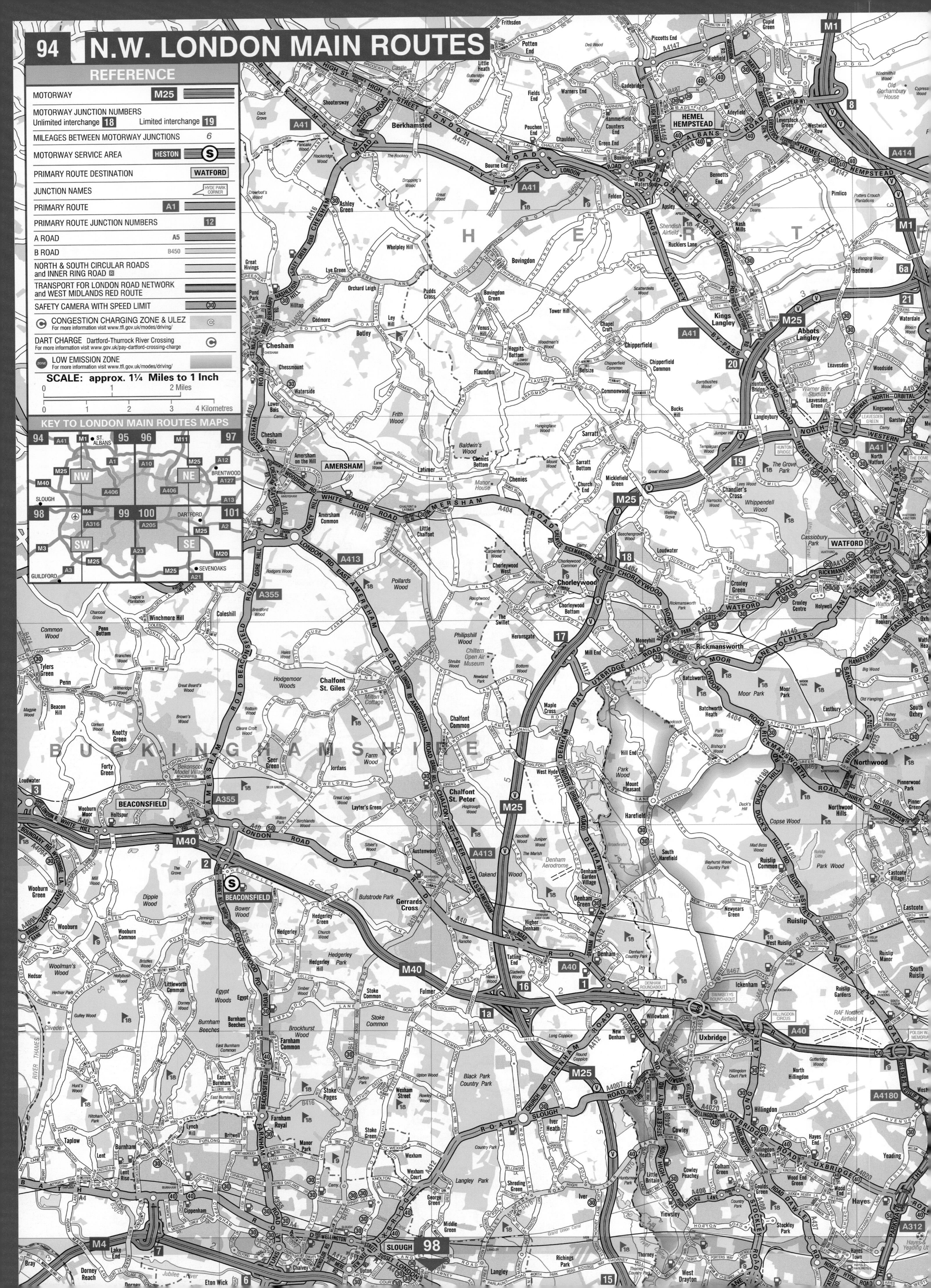
REFERENCE
MOTORWAY M25
MOTORWAY JUNCTION NUMBERS
Unlimited interchange 18
Limited interchange 19
MILEAGES BETWEEN MOTORWAY JUNCTIONS 6
MOTORWAY SERVICE AREA HESTON S
PRIMARY ROUTE DESTINATION WATFORD
JUNCTION NAMES HYDE PARK CORNER
PRIMARY ROUTE A1
PRIMARY ROUTE JUNCTION NUMBERS 12
A ROAD A5
B ROAD B450
NORTH & SOUTH CIRCULAR ROADS and INNER RING ROAD R
TRANSPORT FOR LONDON ROAD NETWORK and WEST MIDLANDS RED ROUTE
SAFETY CAMERA WITH SPEED LIMIT 30
CONGESTION CHARGING ZONE & ULEZ
For more information visit www.tfl.gov.uk/modes/driving/
DART CHARGE Dartford-Thurrock River Crossing
For more information visit www.gov.uk/pay-dartford-crossing-charge
LOW EMISSION ZONE
For more information visit www.tfl.gov.uk/modes/driving/
SCALE: approx. 1¼ Miles to 1 Inch
0 1 2 Miles
0 1 2 3 4 Kilometres
KEY TO LONDON MAIN ROUTES MAPS
94 95 96 97 98 99 100 101
NW NE SW SE
ST. ALBANS
BRENTWOOD
SLOUGH
DARTFORD
GUILDFORD
SEVENOAKS
HERTS
BUCKINGHAMSHIRE
Berkhamsted
HEMEL HEMPSTEAD
Kings Langley
Abbots Langley
Chesham
AMERSHAM
Chorleywood
Rickmansworth
WATFORD
Northwood
Ruislip
BEACONSFIELD
Chalfont St. Giles
Chalfont St. Peter
Gerrards Cross
Denham
Uxbridge
Hillingdon
Hayes
SLOUGH
98

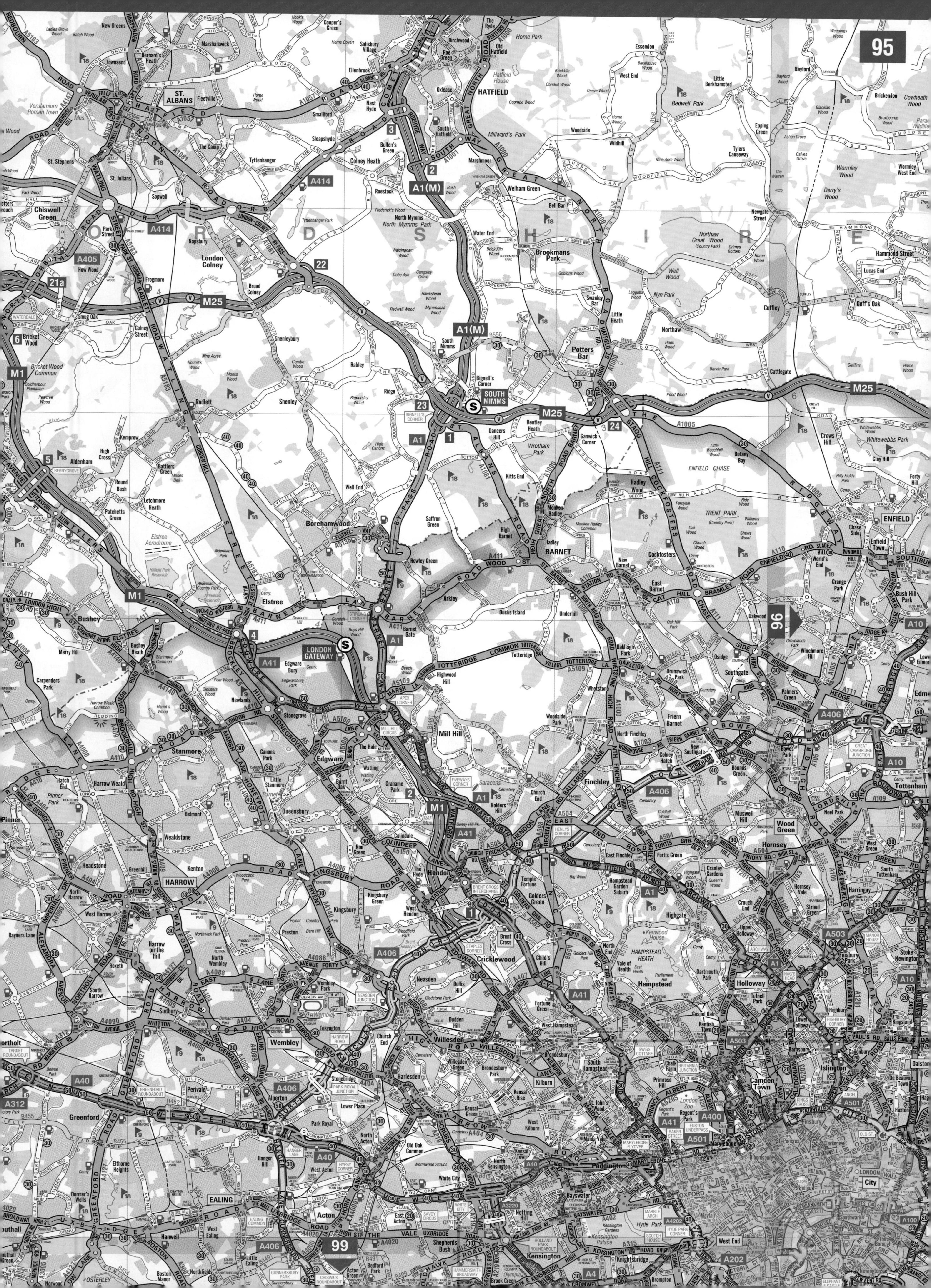
ST. ALBANS
HATFIELD
London Colney
Colney Heath
Welham Green
Brookmans Park
South Mimms
Potters Bar
Cuffley
Northaw
Shenley
Radlett
Aldenham
Borehamwood
Elstree
Bushey
BARNET
New Barnet
East Barnet
Cockfosters
Southgate
ENFIELD
Mill Hill
Edgware
Stanmore
Harrow Weald
HARROW
Kenton
Queensbury
Kingsbury
Hendon
Finchley
Muswell Hill
Wood Green
Hornsey
Tottenham
Highgate
Hampstead
Cricklewood
Willesden
Wembley
Harlesden
Kilburn
Holloway
Camden Town
Islington
Greenford
EALING
Acton
Paddington
Kensington
Notting Hill
Hanwell
City
M1
M25
A1(M)
A41
A406
A40
A10
A1
99
96
SOUTH MIMMS
LONDON GATEWAY

HERTFORDSHIRE
Hoddesdon
Broxbourne
Cheshunt
Waltham Cross
Waltham Abbey
Enfield
Edmonton
Tottenham
Chingford
Walthamstow
Woodford
Loughton
Epping
Harlow
Chigwell
Ilford
Barking
Stratford
Hackney
Islington
Camden Town
Holloway
Hampstead
Hornsey
Wood Green
Southgate
Cockfosters
Cuffley
Northaw
Goff's Oak
Nazeing
Theydon Bois
Leyton
Leytonstone
Wanstead
West Ham
East Ham
Canning Town
Docklands
Woolwich
Thamesmead
Stepney
Whitechapel
Shoreditch
City
Marylebone
Knightsbridge
Bermondsey
Rotherhithe
Wapping
Poplar
Bow
LONDON CITY AIRPORT
Dalston
Stoke Newington
Highbury
Walthamstow
Redbridge
Gants Hill
Hainault
Fairlop
Barkingside
Goodmayes
Seven Kings
Becontree
Beckton
Silvertown
North Woolwich
M25
M11
A10
A12
A13
A406
A503
A1
100
95

Threshers Bush
Little Laver
Blackcat
Foster Street
Tilegate Green
High Laver
Norwood End
Magdalen Laver
Moreton Mill
Newhouse
Roxwell
Hastingwood
Moreton
Miller's Green
Shellow Bowells
Willingale
Fyfield
Clatterford End
Pedlars End
Wall's Green
Newney Green
Great Oxney Green
Writtle
Tyler's Green
Bobbingworth
Cannon's Green
Pigstye Green
Cooksmill Green
Radley Green
Little Oxney Green
Bovinger
Lower Bobbingworth Green
Shelley
Norton Mandeville
Widford
North Weald Airfield
North Weald Bassett
Norton Heath
Highwood
Edney Common
Hylands House
Hylands Park
Loves Green
Greensted Green
Chipping Ongar
High Ongar
King Street
Greensted
Toot Hill
High Woods
Marden Ash
Nine Ashes
Colliers Hatch
Clatterford End
Paslow Wood Common
Blackmore
Elkins Green
Handley Green
Tawney Common
Beggar Hill
Crondon
Mill Green
Margaretting
Margaretting Tye
Mount End
Stanford Rivers
Littlebury
Stondon Massey
Clapgate
Fryerning
Little End
Hay Green
Green Street
Hare Street
Tip's Cross
Hook End
Ingatestone
Tye Green
Theydon Mount
Wyatt's Green
Stapleford Tawney
Doddinghurst
Swallows Cross
Beacon Hill
Kelvedon Hatch
Peartree Green
Ingatestone Hall
Buttsbury
Stock
Fox Hatch
Kelvedon Common
Heybridge
Mountnessing
Passingford Bridge
Navestock
Padhams Green
Stapleford Tawney Airfield
Navestock Side
Bentley
Curtismill Green
Crow Green
Sabine's Green
Horseman Side
Coxtie Green
Queen's Park
Stapleford Abbotts
Pilgrims Hatch
Hutton
Gooseberry Green
Waterhales
Watton's Green
Shenfield
Weald Country Park
Nuper's Hatch
Hutton Mount
Havering's Grove
Billericay
Bournebridge
St. Vincent's Hamlet
South Weald
Brentwood
Tye Common
Noak Hill
Havering-atte-Bower
Dagnam Park
Brook Street
Ingrave Common
South Green
Chase Cross
Bedfords Park
Harold Hill
Warley
Laindon Common
Great Burstead
Ingrave
Little Burstead
Collier Row
Harold Park
Thorndon Country Park
Noak Hill
Rise Park
Harold Wood
Herongate
Great Warley
Steeple View
Marks Gate
Little Warley
Noak Bridge
Mawney
Gidea Park
Squirrel's Heath
Southfields
Laindon
Romford
Ardleigh Green
Childerditch
West Horndon
Lee Chapel North
Crowlands
Heath Park
Emerson Park
Great Berry
Langdon Hills
Hornchurch
Cranham
Lee Chapel South
Beacontree Heath
Rush Green
St. Leonards Hamlet
Central Park
Harrow Lodge Park
Upminster
Dry Street
Elm Park
Bulphan
Dagenham
Corbets Tey
Hacton
North Ockendon
Hornchurch Country Park
Horndon on the Hill
Basildon
South Hornchurch
Belhus Woods Country Park
Orsett Fen
Orsett
Rainham
Baker Street
Stanford-le-Hope
South Ockendon
Hornchurch Marshes
Belhus Park
Mucking
Wennington
North Stifford
Southfields
Rainham Marshes
Aveley
Mucking Marshes
Thamesmead East
Wennington Marshes
Thurrock
Orsett Heath
Linford
Aveley Marshes
Chafford Hundred
Thurrock Lakeside
Grays
Chadwell St. Mary
Muckingford
PROPOSED
M25
A12
A13
A127
A128
A414
A1060
A113
A129
A1306
A1013
A1089
101

94

SLOUGH
BUCKS.
M4
M25
M3
A4
A30
A308
A322
A3
Windsor
Eton
Datchet
Colnbrook
Langley
West Drayton
Harmondsworth
Harlington
HESTON
LONDON HEATHROW AIRPORT
Stanwell
Ashford
Feltham
STAINES-UPON-THAMES
Egham
Englefield Green
Virginia Water
WINDSOR GREAT PARK
Windsor Forest
Ascot
Sunningdale
Sunninghill
Windlesham
Bagshot
Lightwater
Chertsey
Addlestone
Weybridge
Walton-on-Thames
Shepperton
Sunbury
Laleham
Thorpe
Ottershaw
Chobham
West End
Bisley
Byfleet
West Byfleet
Pyrford
WOKING
Knaphill
Brookwood
Pirbright
Worplesdon
Send
Ripley
Ockham
Cobham
Wisley
Burpham
GUILDFORD
West Clandon
East Clandon
West Horsley
East Horsley
Effingham

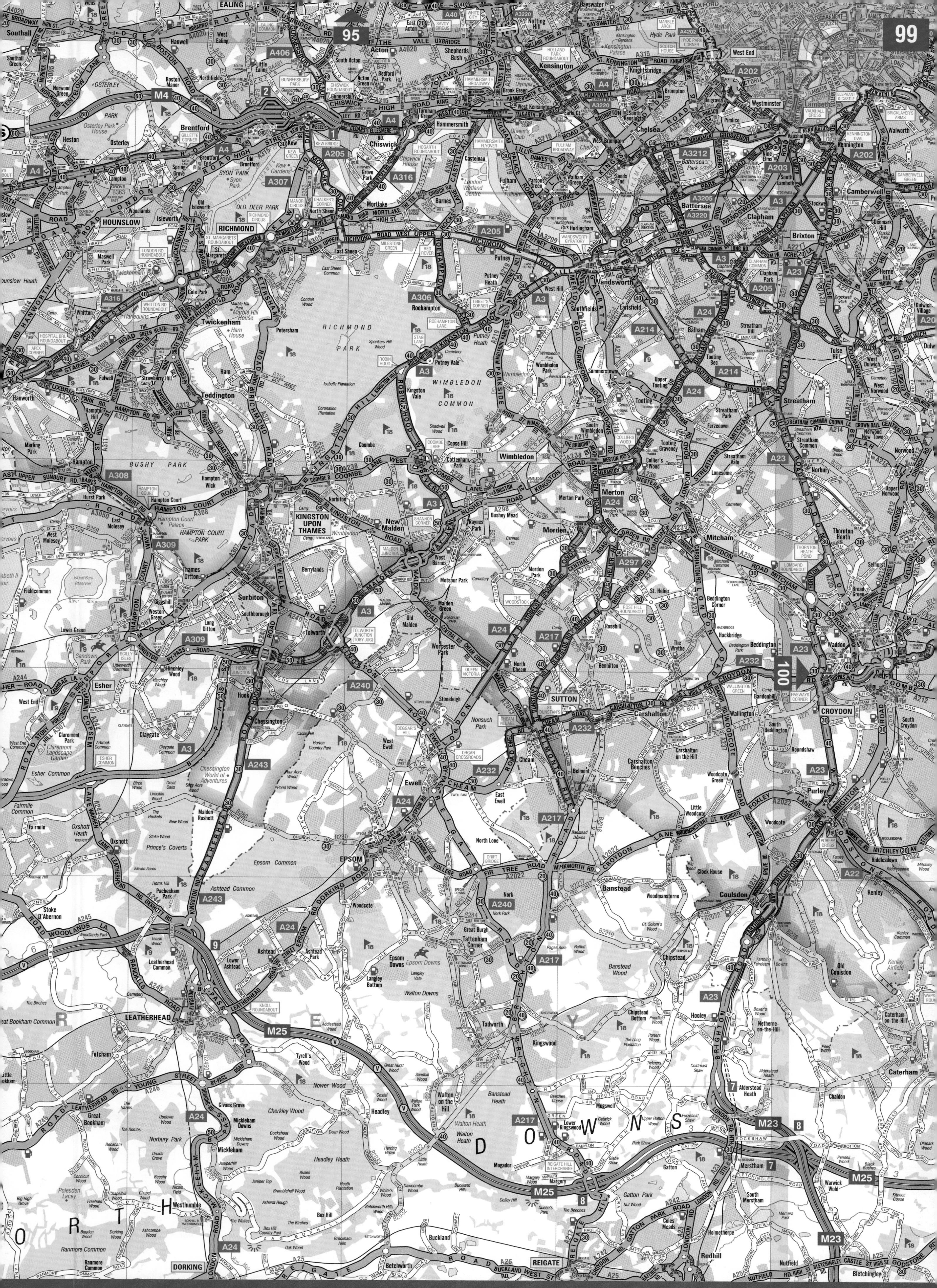
95
100
EALING
Southall
Hanwell
Acton
Shepherds Bush
Notting Hill
Bayswater
Kensington
Knightsbridge
Hyde Park
West End
Brentford
Chiswick
Hammersmith
Fulham
Chelsea
Westminster
Lambeth
Pimlico
Vauxhall
Kennington
Walworth
Camberwell
Heston
Osterley
Isleworth
HOUNSLOW
RICHMOND
Kew
Mortlake
Barnes
Putney
Battersea
Clapham
Brixton
Stockwell
Wandsworth
Roehampton
Twickenham
Whitton
RICHMOND PARK
Earlsfield
Balham
Streatham Hill
Teddington
Hampton
WIMBLEDON COMMON
Wimbledon
Tooting
Streatham
Hanworth
BUSHY PARK
Coombe
Merton
Mitcham
Norbury
KINGSTON UPON THAMES
New Malden
Morden
East Molesey
Thames Ditton
Surbiton
Tolworth
Worcester Park
Thornton Heath
Esher
Hook
Chessington
Stoneleigh
SUTTON
Carshalton
Waddon
CROYDON
Claygate
Ewell
Cheam
Wallington
Purley
Oxshott
EPSOM
Banstead
Coulsdon
Kenley
Ashtead
Chipstead
Caterham
LEATHERHEAD
Tadworth
Kingswood
Fetcham
Great Bookham
Headley
Mickleham
Merstham
Westhumble
Box Hill
Redhill
DORKING
REIGATE
Bletchingley
NORTH DOWNS
M4
M25
M23
A3
A4
A23
A24
A217

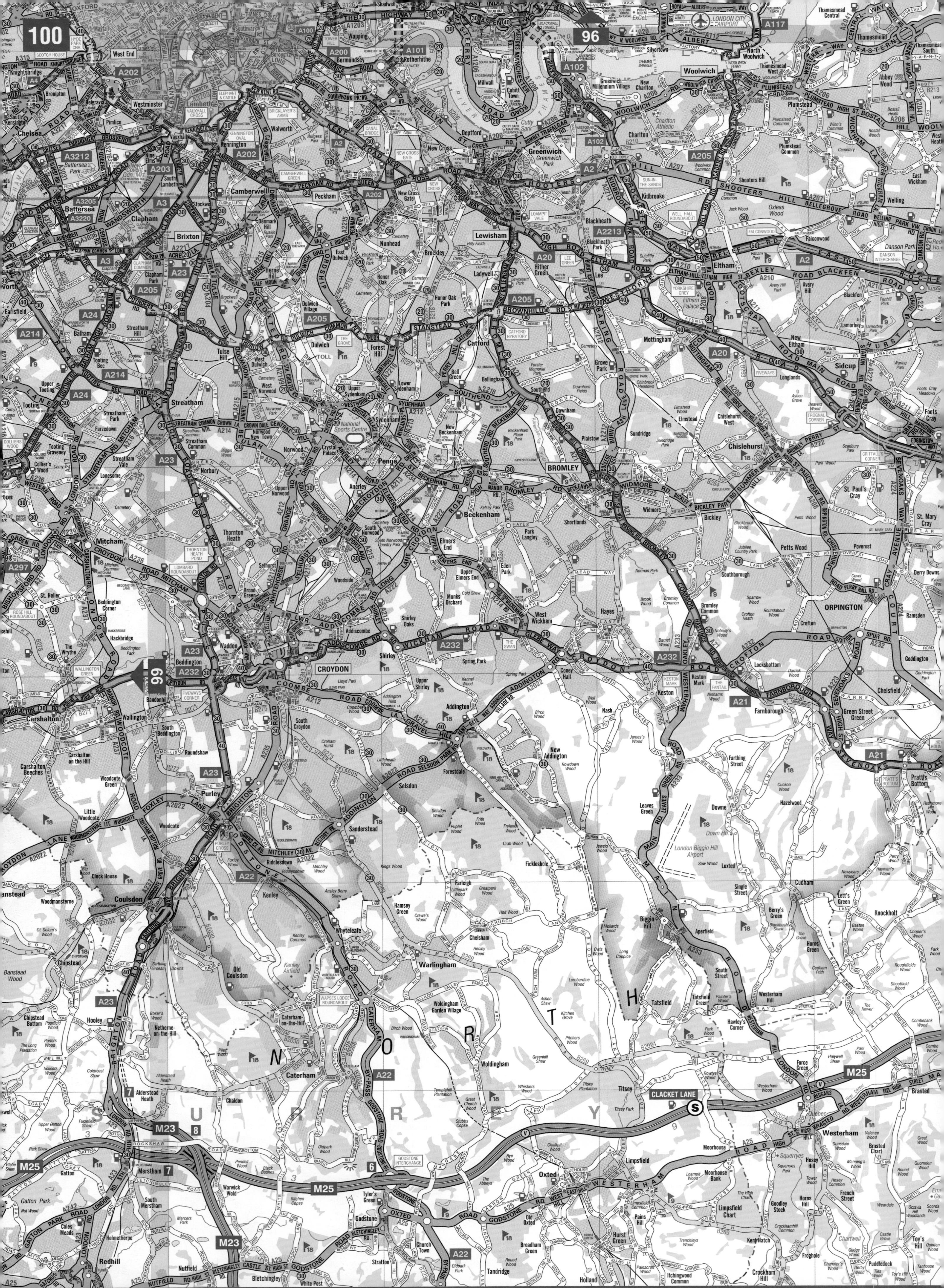
96
99
LONDON CITY AIRPORT
West End
Westminster
Chelsea
Battersea
Clapham
Brixton
Camberwell
Peckham
Bermondsey
Rotherhithe
Deptford
Greenwich
Woolwich
Charlton
Plumstead
Thamesmead
Lewisham
Blackheath
Eltham
Welling
Sidcup
Catford
Dulwich
Forest Hill
Sydenham
Streatham
Norwood
Penge
Beckenham
BROMLEY
Chislehurst
Mitcham
Croydon
CROYDON
Carshalton
Wallington
Purley
Coulsdon
Sanderstead
Selsdon
Addington
New Addington
West Wickham
Hayes
Keston
ORPINGTON
Farnborough
Biggin Hill
London Biggin Hill Airport
Tatsfield
Westerham
Warlingham
Whyteleafe
Caterham
Oxted
Limpsfield
Godstone
Redhill
Merstham
Chipstead
Kenley
CLACKET LANE
M25
M23
A23
A22
A21
A20
A2
A232
A233
N O R T H
S U R R E Y

97
M25
Thurrock
Rainham Marshes
Wennington Marshes
Aveley Marshes
Erith Marshes
Thamesmead East
Belvedere
Erith
Lessness Heath
Northumberland Heath
North End
Slade Green
Dartford Marshes
Crayford Marshes
Barnehurst
Barnes Cray
Bexleyheath
Bexley
Crayford
Dartford
Hall Place
Old Bexley
Joydens Wood
North Cray
Ruxley
Wilmington
Hextable
Swanley
Swanley Village
Crockenhill
Kevington
Farningham
Eynsford
Lullingstone Roman Villa
Eagle Heights
Chelsfield Village
Maypole
Well Hill
Badgers Mount
Shoreham
Halstead
Twitton
Otford
Chevening
Dunton Green
Chipstead
Riverhead
Bessels Green
Sundridge
Sevenoaks
Knole
Knole Park
Kippington
Dibden
Cross Keys
Sevenoaks Common
Ide Hill
Goathurst Common
Bayley's Hill
Sevenoaks Weald
Underriver
Oakhurst
Kemsing
Heaverham
Crowdleham
Seal
Noah's Ark
Greatness
Wildernesse
Godden Green
Seal Chart
Fawke Common
Bitchet Green
Stone Street
Ightham Common
Ightham
Ightham Mote
Shipbourne
Budds
Plaxtol
Dunk's Green
Claygate
Oldbury
Styants Bottom
Ivy Hatch
Wrotham
Wrotham Heath
Borough Green
St. Marys Platt
Basted
Crouch
Yopps Green
Roughway
West Peckham
Mereworth
Mereworth Woods
Swanton
Kent Street
Herne Pound
Kings Hill
Wateringbury
Nettlestead
Nettlestead Green
Kenward
Pizien Well
Offham
Addington
West Malling
Leybourne
Ryarsh
Birling
Trottiscliffe
Vigo Village
Fairseat
Stansted
Hodsall Street
Culverstone Green
Harvel
Ridley
Pettings
New Ash Green
Hartley
Hartley Green
Fawkham
Fawkham Green
West Yoke
Ash
West Kingsdown
Maplescombe
Brands Hatch
East Hill
Knatts Valley
Romney Street
Knockmill
Woodlands
Cotman's Ash
Horton Kirby
South Darenth
Darenth
Sutton at Hone
Hawley
Green Street Green
Betsham
Southfleet
Longfield
New Barn
Pinden
Grubb Street
Dean Bottom
Mile End Green
Hook Green
Northfleet Green
Istead Rise
Nash Street
Nurstead
Longfield Hill
Meopham Station
Meopham
Meopham Green
Hook Green
Sole Street
Camer
Henley Street
Cobham
Cobham Park
Lower Luddesdown
Luddesdown
Foxendown
Priestwood
David Street
South Street
Priestwood Green
Great Buckland
Upper Halling
Rochester Forest
Holly Hill
Paddlesworth
Bean
Bluewater
Stone
Greenhithe
Swanscombe
Swanscombe Marshes
Ebbsfleet
Northfleet
Rosherville
Gravesend
Perry Street
New House
Kings Farm
Singlewell
Riverview Park
Westcourt
Chalk
Denton
Milton
Thong
Shorne
Shorne Ridgeway
Lower Shorne
Shorne Marshes
Tilbury
Tilbury Fort
West Tilbury
West Tilbury Marshes
East Tilbury
East Tilbury Marshes
Coalhouse Fort
Linford
Mucking
Muckingford
Chadwell St. Mary
Orsett Heath
Grays
Little Thurrock
South Stifford
West Thurrock
Purfleet
Chafford Hundred
Thurrock Lakeside
Aveley
Wennington
Stanford
Dartford-Thurrock River Crossing
Dart Charge
Princes
Temple Hill
Joyce Green
Horns Cross
New Town
Fleet Downs
M20
M26
A2
A20
A21
A25
A26
A228
A1089
A282
River Thames
Essex
Kent
Downs
Proposed

WOLVERHAMPTON
WALSALL
Willenhall
Bilston
Darlaston
Wednesbury
Coseley
Sedgley
Tipton
DUDLEY
WEST BROMWICH
OLDBURY
Smethwick
Brierley Hill
STOURBRIDGE
HALESOWEN
Kingswinford
Wombourne
Kinver
Harborne
Edgbaston
Northfield
Bournville
Selly Oak
Rubery
Longbridge
BROMSGROVE
Catshill
Alvechurch
Hagley
FRANKLEY
HOPWOOD PARK
STAFFORDSHIRE
WORCESTERSHIRE
M5
M6
M42
A449
A491
A456
A38
A41
A454
A461
A4123
A448
A441

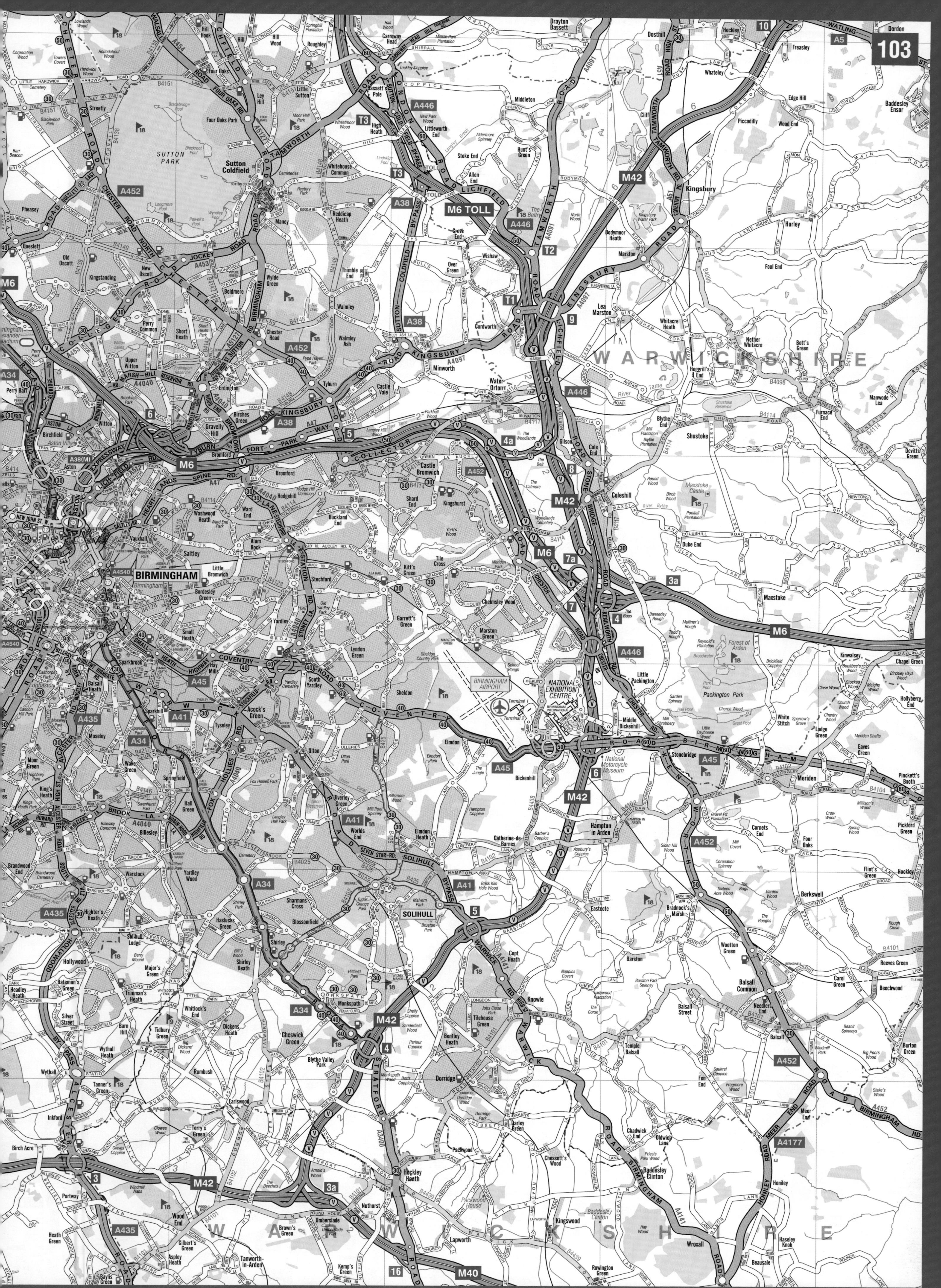
BIRMINGHAM
Sutton Coldfield
SUTTON PARK
Four Oaks
Four Oaks Park
Streetly
Walmley
Erdington
Castle Bromwich
Kingshurst
Coleshill
Water Orton
Minworth
Curdworth
Wishaw
Middleton
Kingsbury
Hurley
Marston
Lea Marston
Whitacre Heath
Shustoke
Maxstoke
Fillongley
WARWICKSHIRE
Meriden
Berkswell
Balsall Common
Hampton in Arden
Catherine-de-Barnes
Bickenhill
Elmdon
BIRMINGHAM AIRPORT
NATIONAL EXHIBITION CENTRE
National Motorcycle Museum
Packington Park
Forest of Arden
SOLIHULL
Shirley
Knowle
Dorridge
Hockley Heath
Lapworth
Kingswood
Baddesley Clinton
Wroxall
Honiley
Haseley Knob
Beausale
Rowington Green
Tanworth-in-Arden
Earlswood
Wythall
Hollywood
Yardley
Acock's Green
Tyseley
Sparkhill
Moseley
Kings Heath
Hall Green
Olton
Sheldon
Stechford
Saltley
Aston
Witton
Perry Barr
Kingstanding
Great Barr
Drayton Bassett
Dosthill
Dordon
Freasley
Baddesley Ensor
M6
M6 TOLL
M42
M40
A38
A45
A452
A446
A34
A435
A41
A4177
A5
10
103

MANCHESTER MAIN ROUTES

MANCHESTER
SALFORD
BURY
ROCHDALE
OLDHAM
ASHTON-UNDER-LYNE
STOCKPORT
ALTRINCHAM
BIRCH
MANCHESTER AIRPORT
M60
M62
M61
M66
M602
M67
M56
A627(M)
A57(M)
Tottington
Brandlesholme
Birtle
Bamford
Heywood
Middleton
Radcliffe
Whitefield
Prestwich
Farnworth
Kearsley
Walkden
Worsley
Swinton
Pendlebury
Eccles
Urmston
Stretford
Sale
Chorlton-cum-Hardy
Didsbury
Withington
Fallowfield
Rusholme
Moss Side
Hulme
Ardwick
Levenshulme
Gorton
Openshaw
Droylsden
Denton
Reddish
Failsworth
Chadderton
Royton
Shaw
Heaton Park
Cheetham Hill
Crumpsall
Blackley
Moston
Harpurhey
Newton Heath
Clayton
Wythenshawe
Northenden
Gatley
Cheadle
Cheadle Hulme
Bramhall
Hazel Grove
Timperley
Hale
Bowdon
Carrington
Partington
Ringway
Handforth
Styal
Woodford
Poynton

Reference Légende Zeichenerklärung

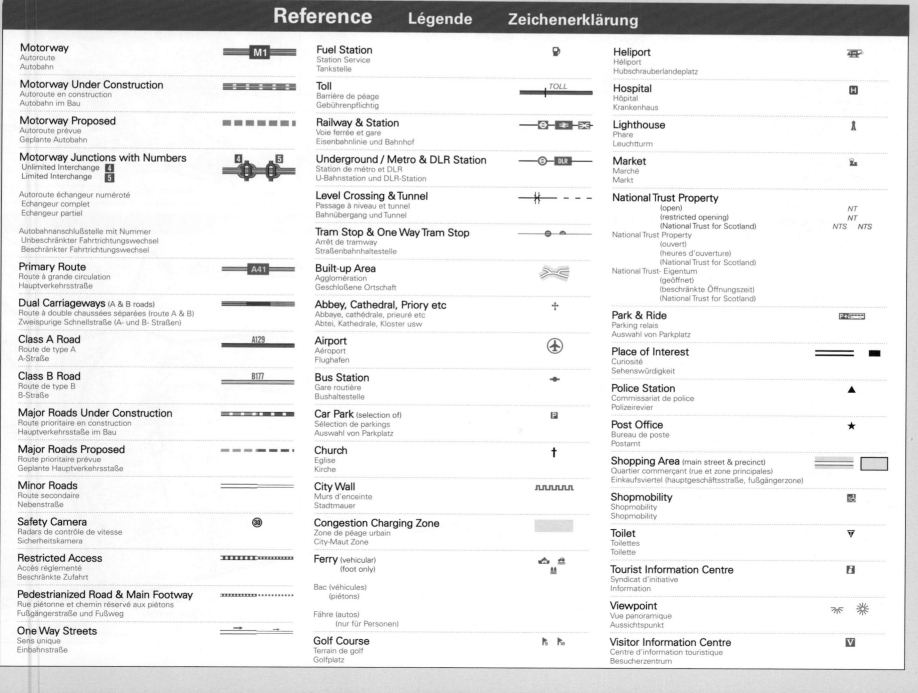

Motorway Autoroute Autobahn	M1	
Motorway Under Construction Autoroute en construction Autobahn im Bau		
Motorway Proposed Autoroute prévue Geplante Autobahn		
Motorway Junctions with Numbers Unlimited Interchange Limited Interchange Autoroute échangeur numéroté Echangeur complet Echangeur partiel Autobahnanschlußstelle mit Nummer Unbeschränkter Fahrtrichtungswechsel Beschränkter Fahrtrichtungswechsel		
Primary Route Route à grande circulation Hauptverkehrsstraße	A41	
Dual Carriageways (A & B roads) Route à double chaussées séparées (route A & B) Zweispurige Schnellstraße (A- und B- Straßen)		
Class A Road Route de type A A-Straße	A129	
Class B Road Route de type B B-Straße	B177	
Major Roads Under Construction Route prioritaire en construction Hauptverkehrsstaße im Bau		
Major Roads Proposed Route prioritaire prévue Geplante Hauptverkehrsstaße		
Minor Roads Route secondaire Nebenstraße		
Safety Camera Radars de contrôle de vitesse Sicherheitskamera	30	
Restricted Access Accès réglementé Beschränkte Zufahrt		
Pedestrianized Road & Main Footway Rue piétonne et chemin réservé aux piétons Fußgängerstraße und Fußweg		
One Way Streets Sens unique Einbahnstraße		

Fuel Station Station Service Tankstelle	
Toll Barrière de péage Gebührenpflichtig	TOLL
Railway & Station Voie ferrée et gare Eisenbahnlinie und Bahnhof	
Underground / Metro & DLR Station Station de métro et DLR U-Bahnstation und DLR-Station	DLR
Level Crossing & Tunnel Passage à niveau et tunnel Bahnübergang und Tunnel	
Tram Stop & One Way Tram Stop Arrêt de tramway Straßenbahnhaltestelle	
Built-up Area Agglomération Geschloßene Ortschaft	
Abbey, Cathedral, Priory etc Abbaye, cathédrale, prieuré etc Abtei, Kathedrale, Kloster usw	†
Airport Aéroport Flughafen	✈
Bus Station Gare routière Bushaltestelle	
Car Park (selection of) Sélection de parkings Auswahl von Parkplatz	P
Church Eglise Kirche	†
City Wall Murs d'enceinte Stadtmauer	
Congestion Charging Zone Zone de péage urbain City-Maut Zone	
Ferry (vehicular) (foot only) Bac (véhicules) (piétons) Fähre (autos) (nur für Personen)	
Golf Course Terrain de golf Golfplatz	

Heliport Héliport Hubschrauberlandeplatz	
Hospital Hôpital Krankenhaus	H
Lighthouse Phare Leuchtturm	
Market Marché Markt	
National Trust Property (open) (restricted opening) (National Trust for Scotland) National Trust Property (ouvert) (heures d'ouverture) (National Trust for Scotland) National Trust- Eigentum (geöffnet) (beschränkte Öffnungszeit) (National Trust for Scotland)	NT NTS NTS
Park & Ride Parking relais Auswahl von Parkplatz	P
Place of Interest Curiosité Sehenswürdigkeit	
Police Station Commissariat de police Polizeirevier	▲
Post Office Bureau de poste Postamt	★
Shopping Area (main street & precinct) Quartier commerçant (rue et zone principales) Einkaufsviertel (hauptgeschäftsstraße, fußgängerzone)	
Shopmobility Shopmobility Shopmobility	
Toilet Toilettes Toilette	▽
Tourist Information Centre Syndicat d'initiative Information	i
Viewpoint Vue panoramique Aussichtspunkt	
Visitor Information Centre Centre d'information touristique Besucherzentrum	V

ABERDEEN

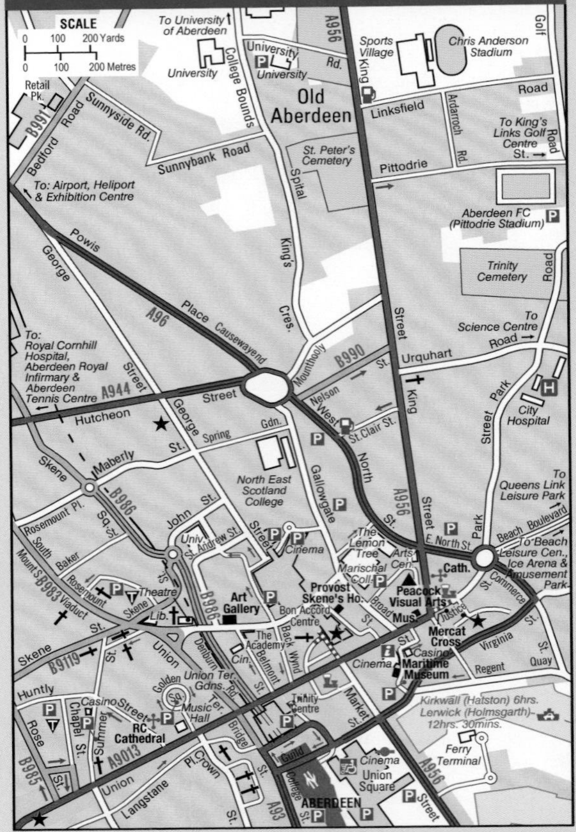

BATH

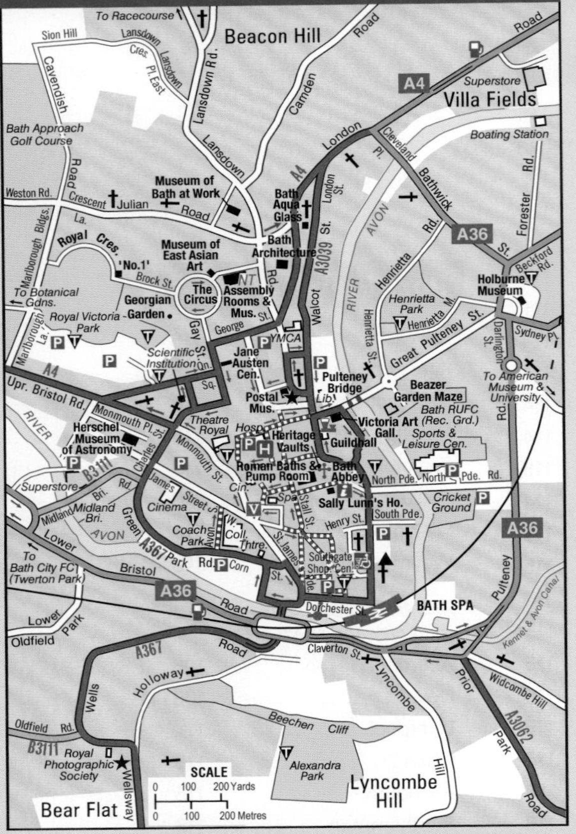

BLACKPOOL

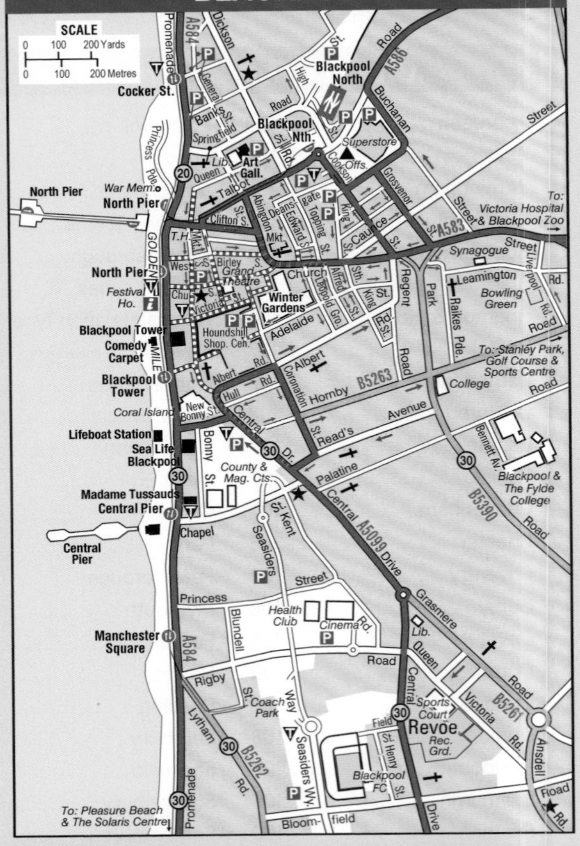

BIRMINGHAM (CITY CENTRE)

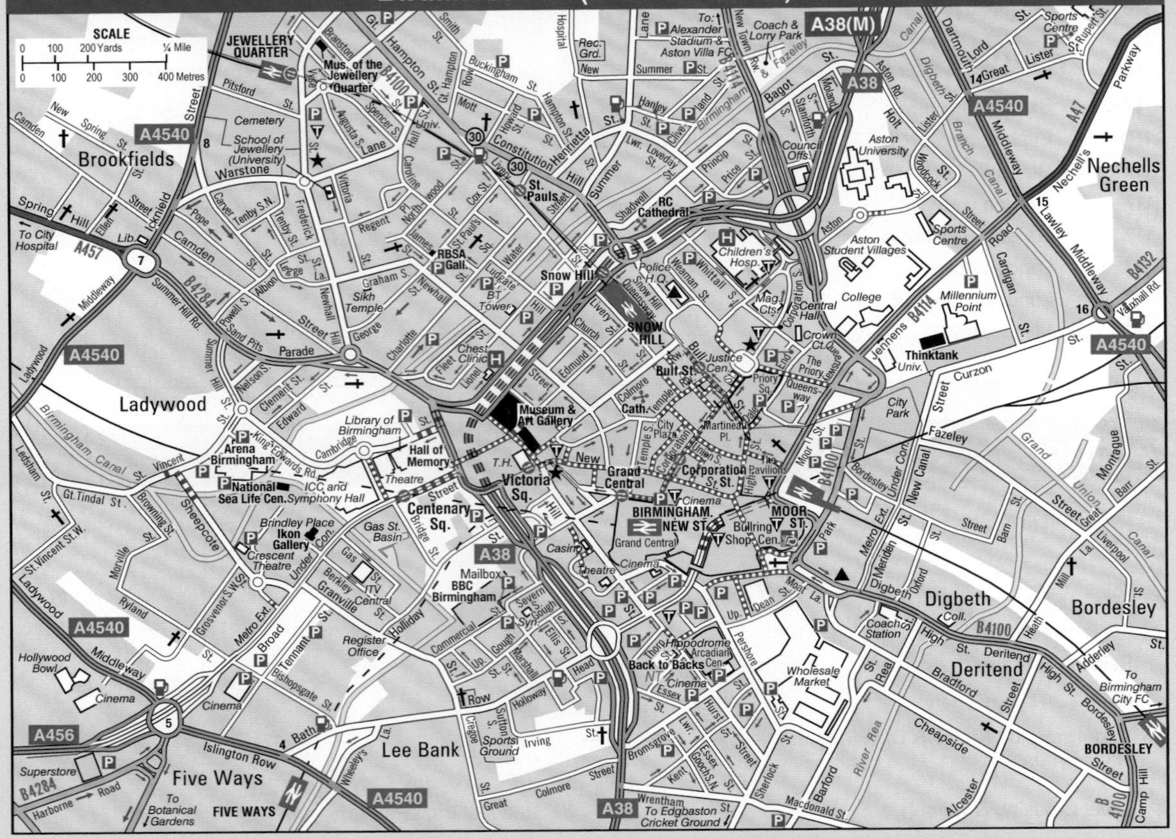

BOURNEMOUTH

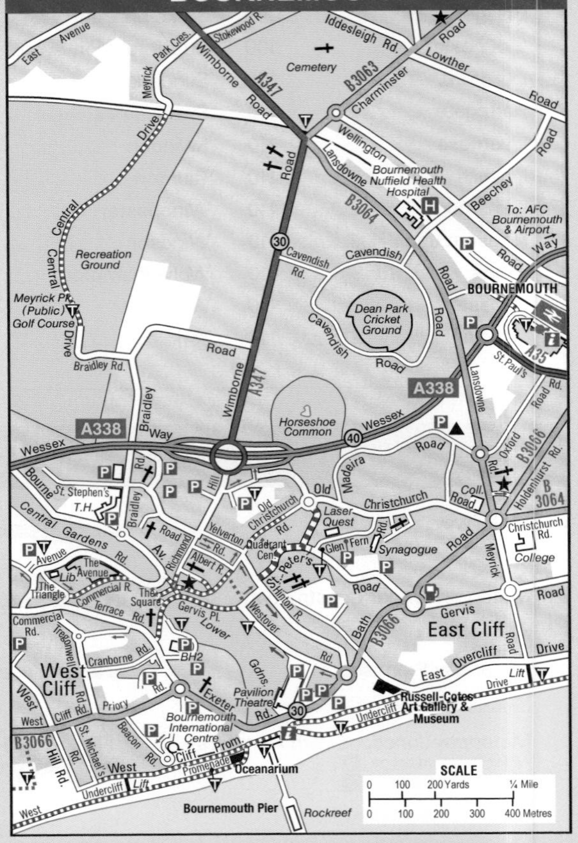

BRADFORD

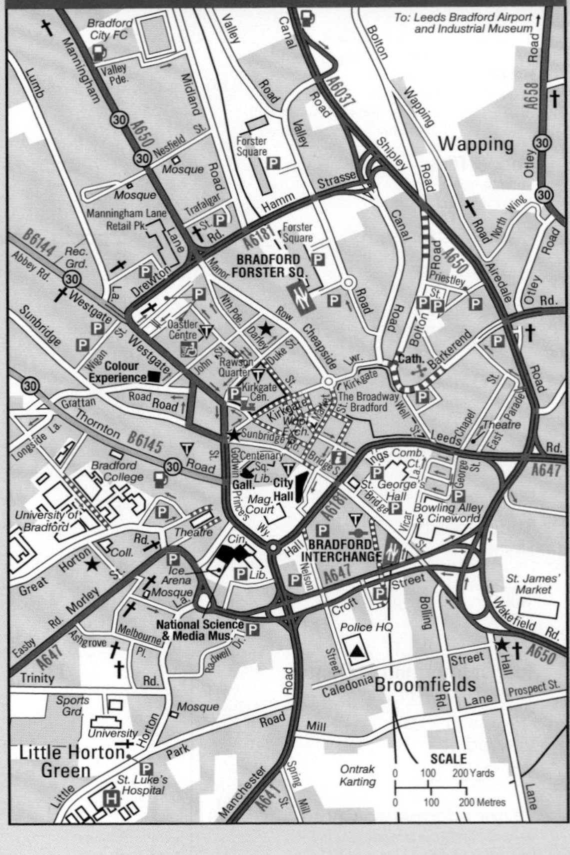

BRIGHTON and HOVE

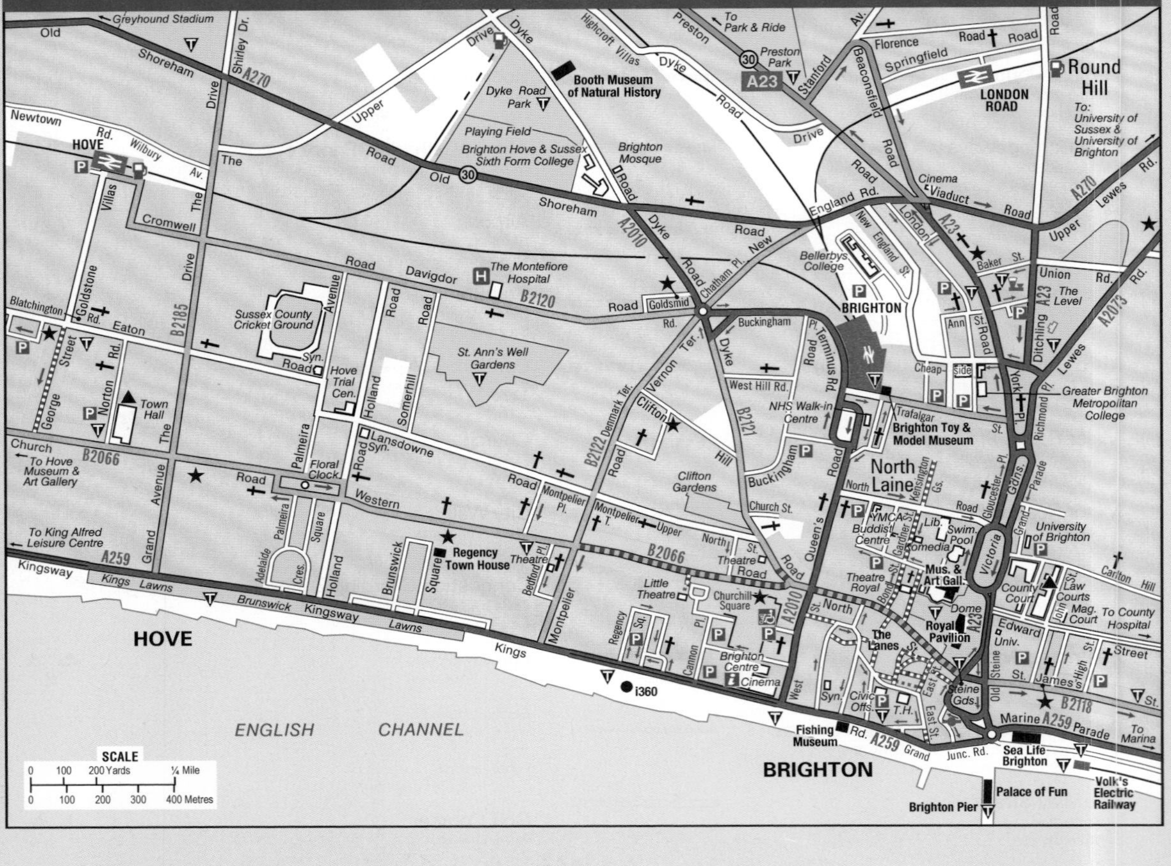

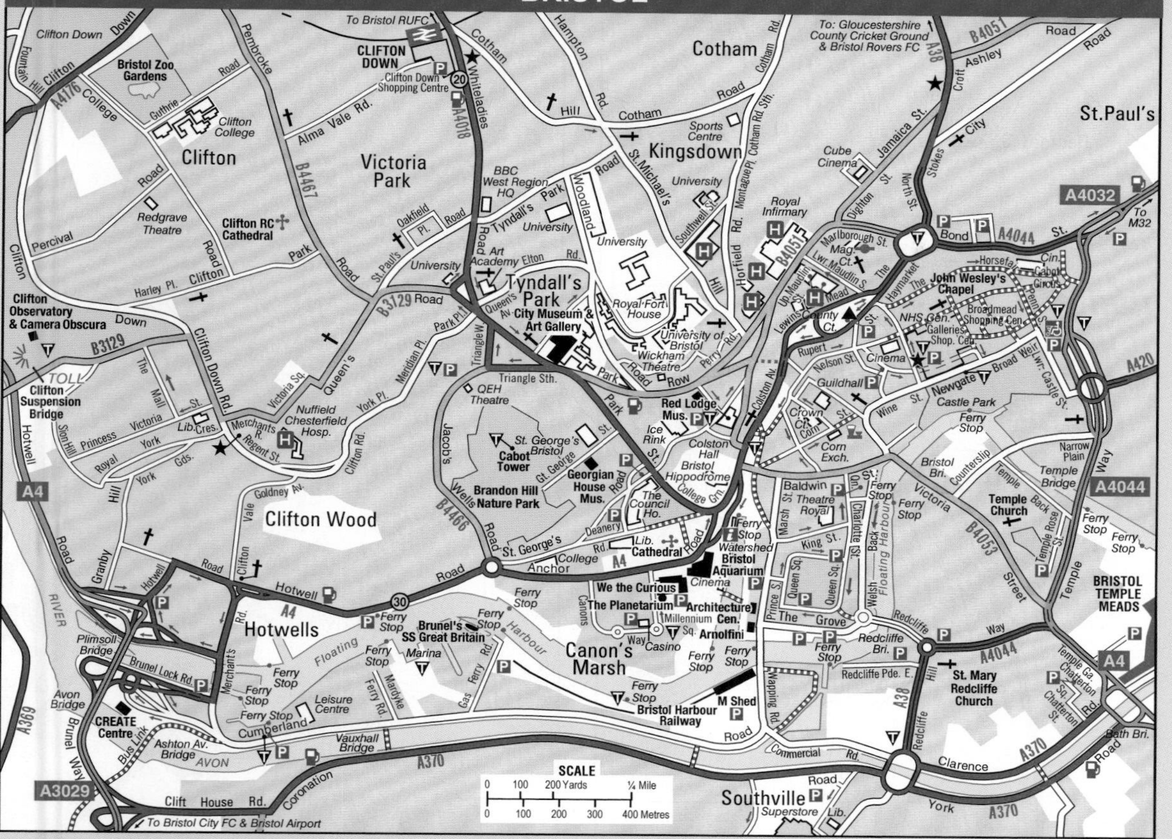

BRISTOL

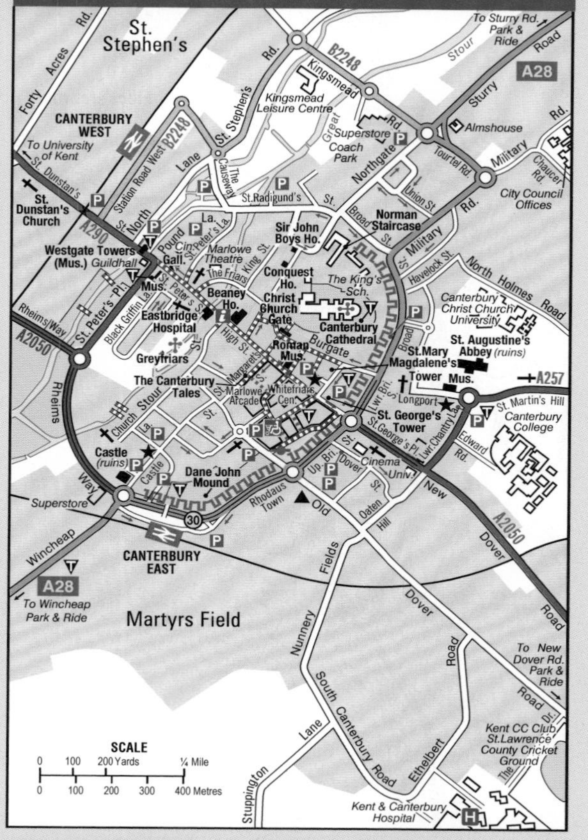

CANTERBURY

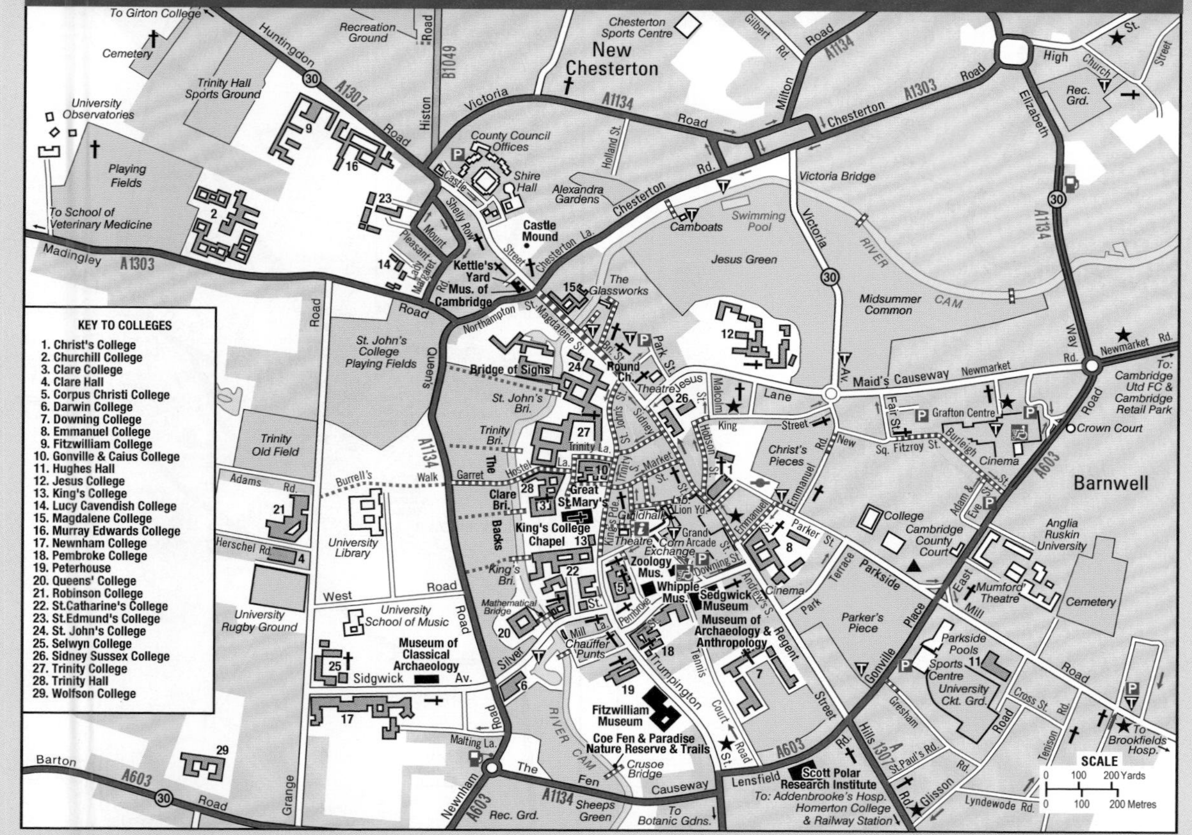

CAMBRIDGE

KEY TO COLLEGES
1. Christ's College
2. Churchill College
3. Clare College
4. Clare Hall
5. Corpus Christi College
6. Darwin College
7. Downing College
8. Emmanuel College
9. Fitzwilliam College
10. Gonville & Caius College
11. Hughes Hall
12. Jesus College
13. King's College
14. Lucy Cavendish College
15. Magdalene College
16. Murray Edwards College
17. Newnham College
18. Pembroke College
19. Peterhouse
20. Queens' College
21. Robinson College
22. St.Catharine's College
23. St.Edmund's College
24. St. John's College
25. Selwyn College
26. Sidney Sussex College
27. Trinity College
28. Trinity Hall
29. Wolfson College

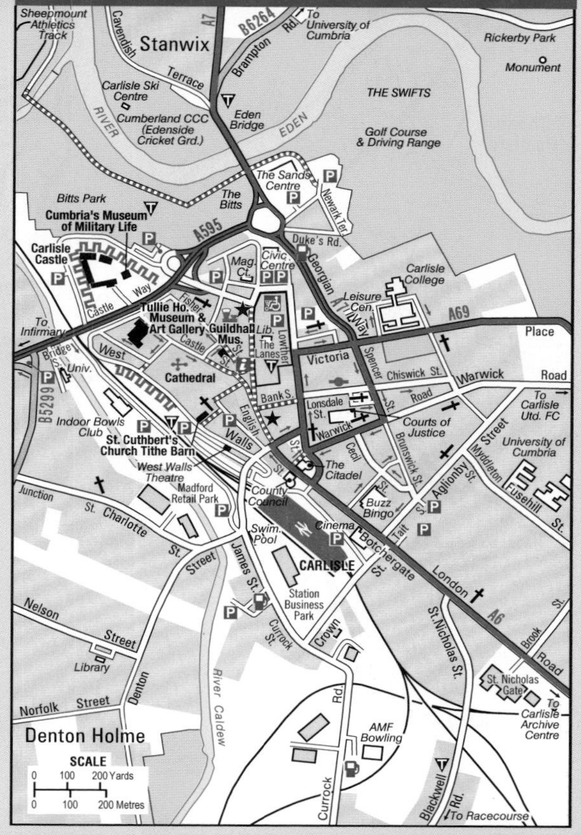

CARLISLE

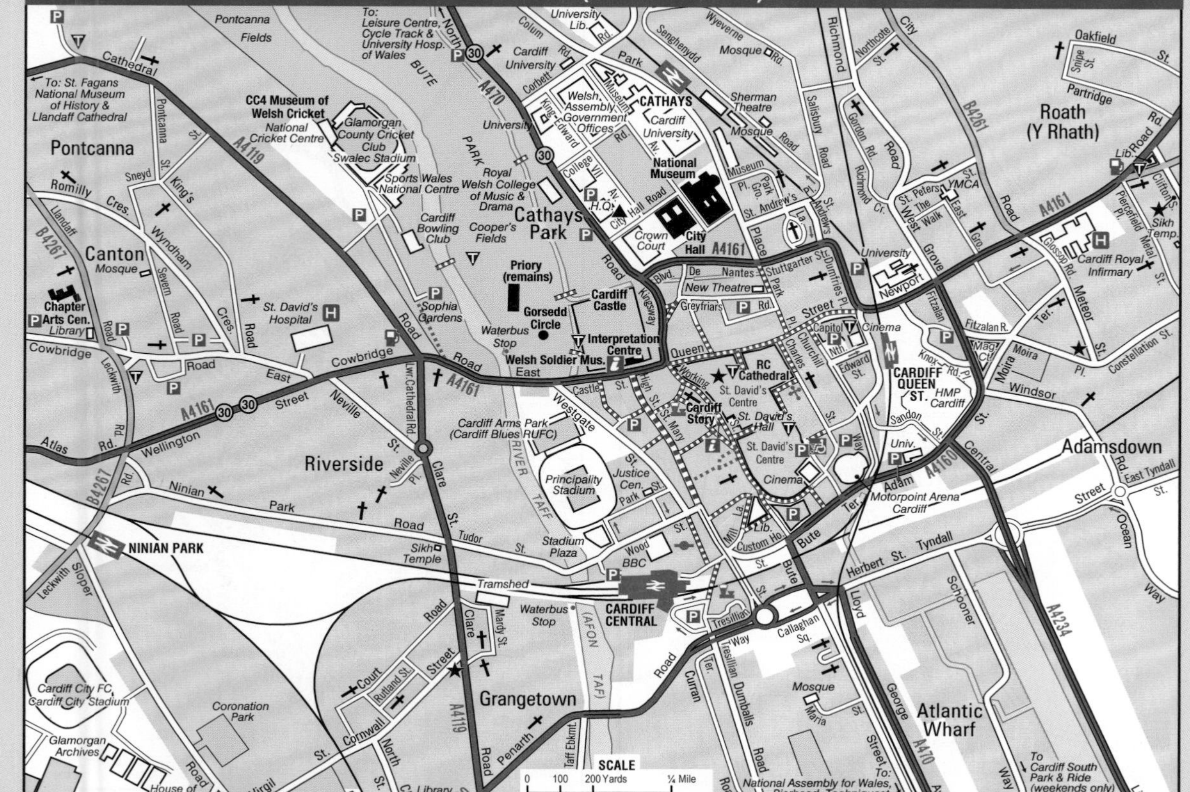

CARDIFF (CAERDYDD)

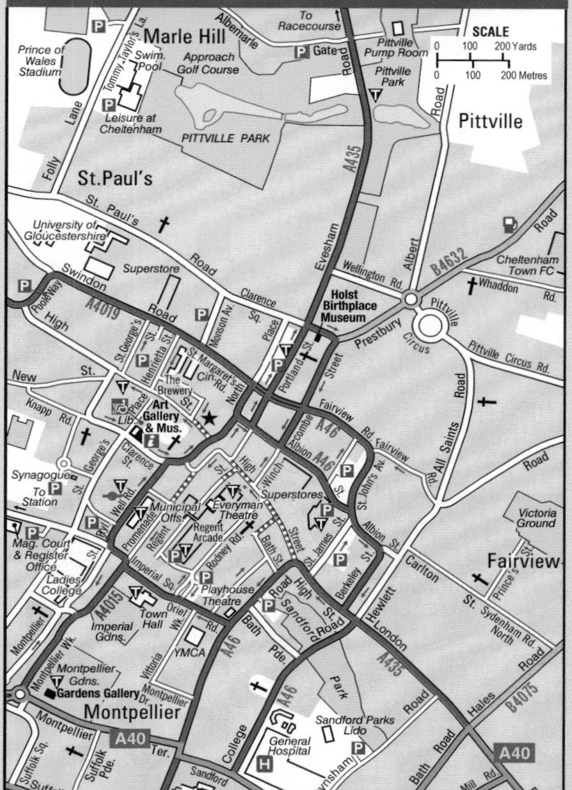

CHELTENHAM

CHESTER
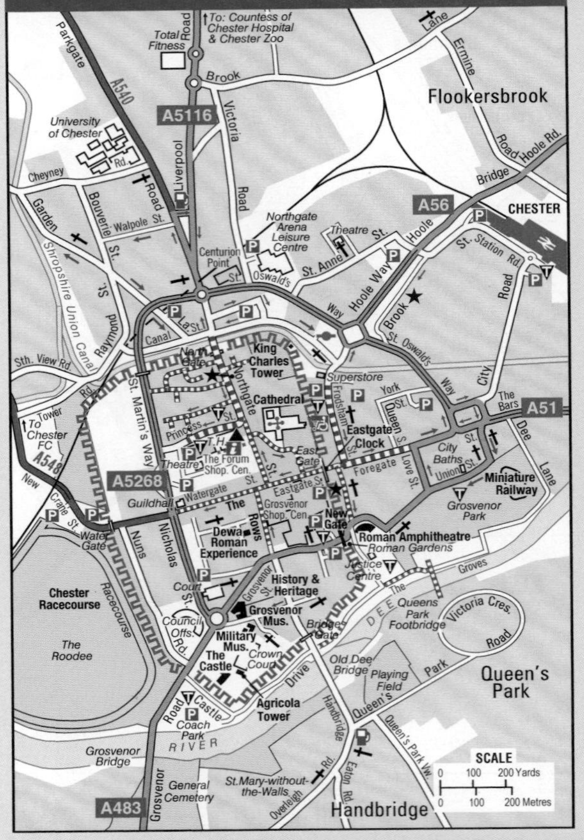

COVENTRY
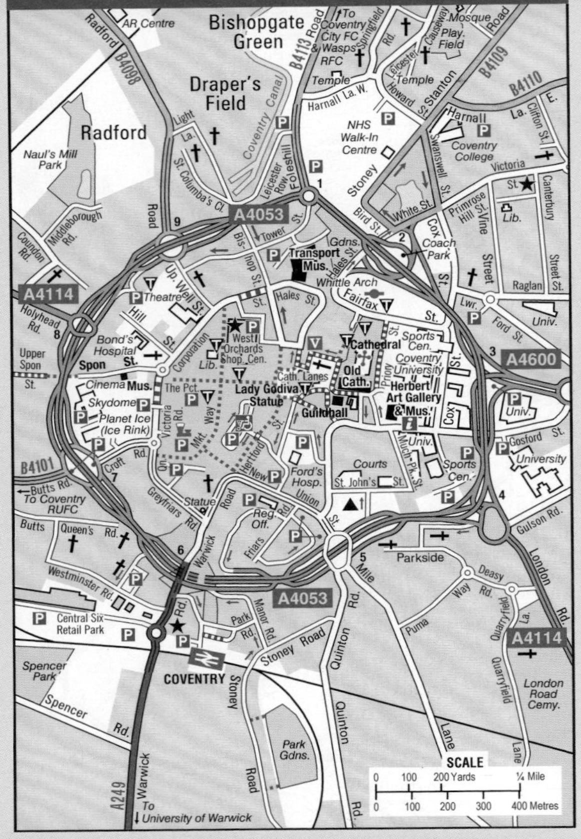

DERBY
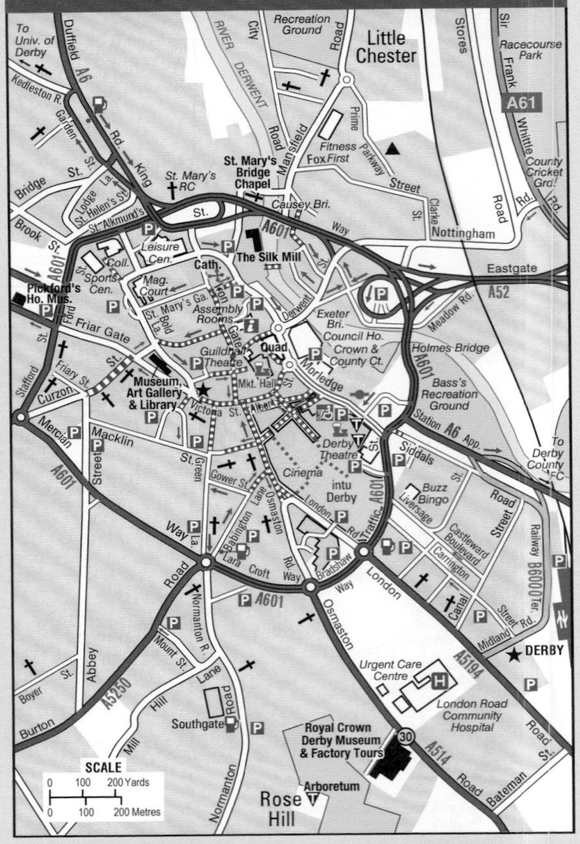

DOVER
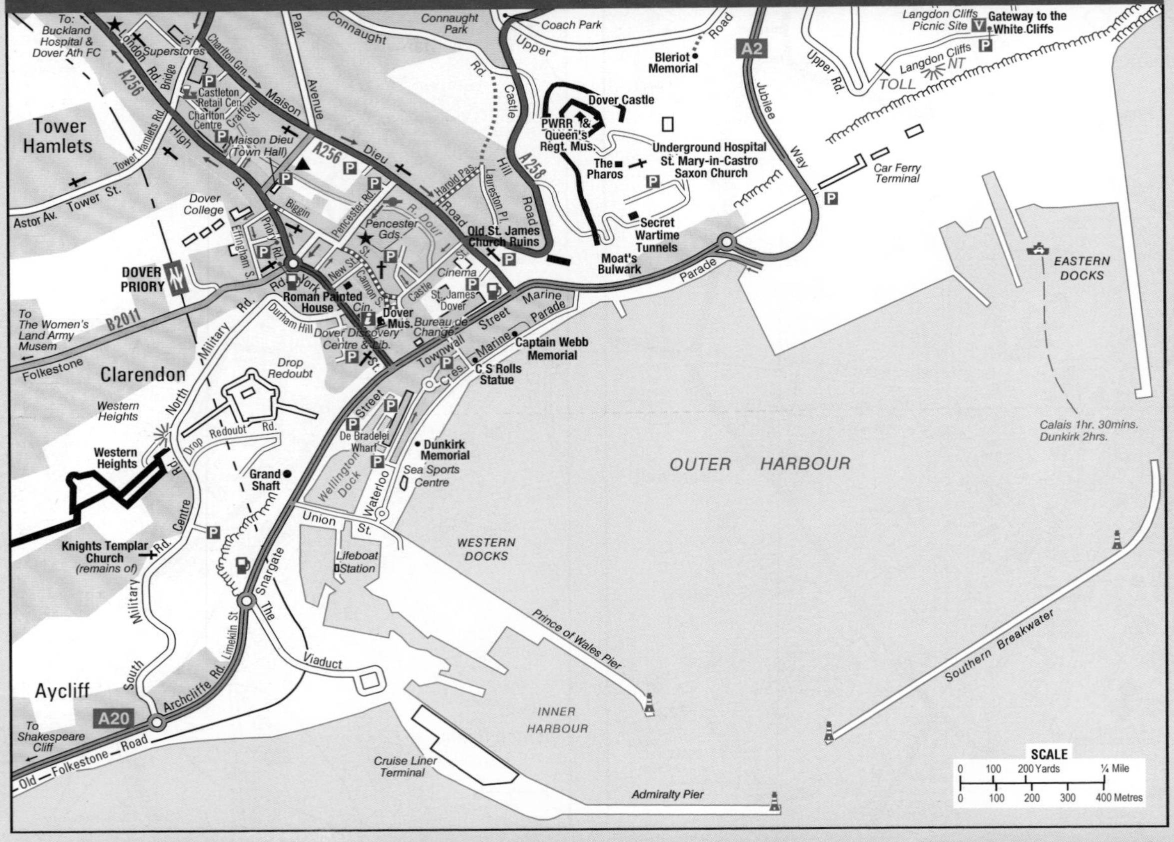

DUMFRIES
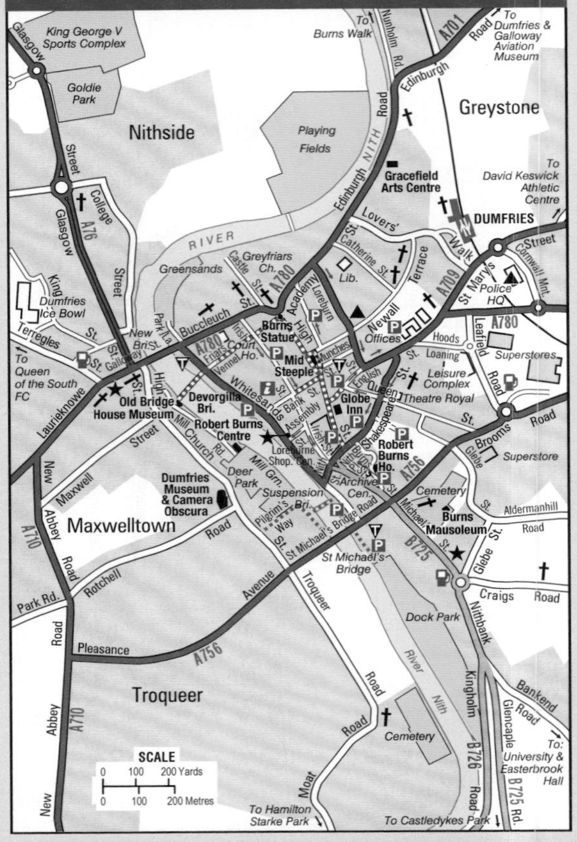

DUNDEE
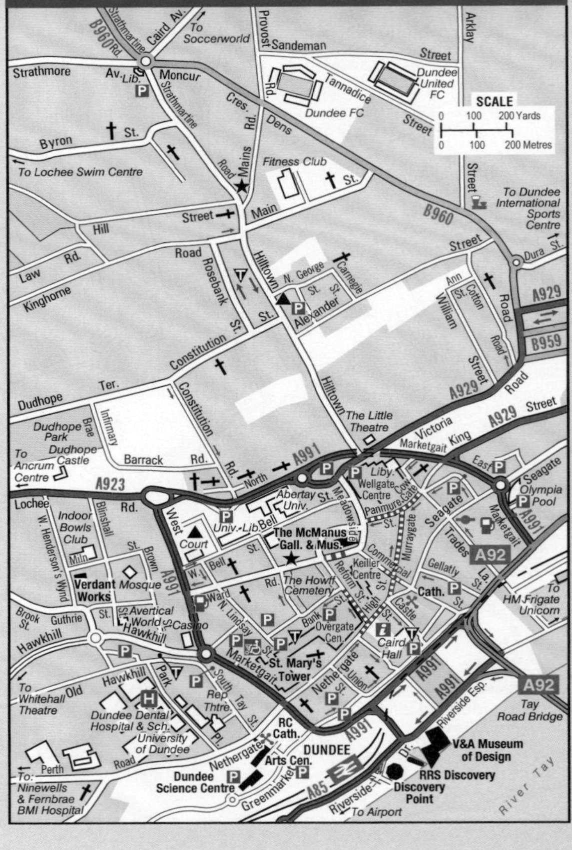

DURHAM
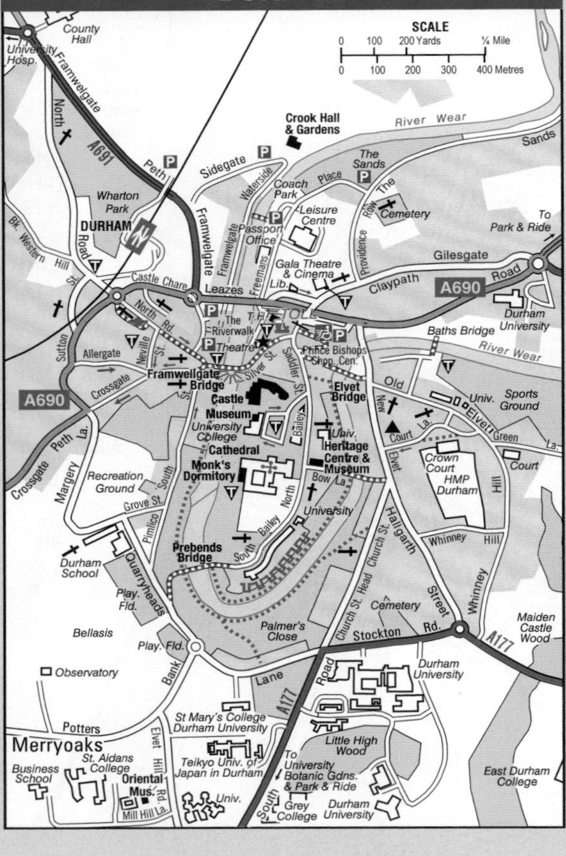

EASTBOURNE
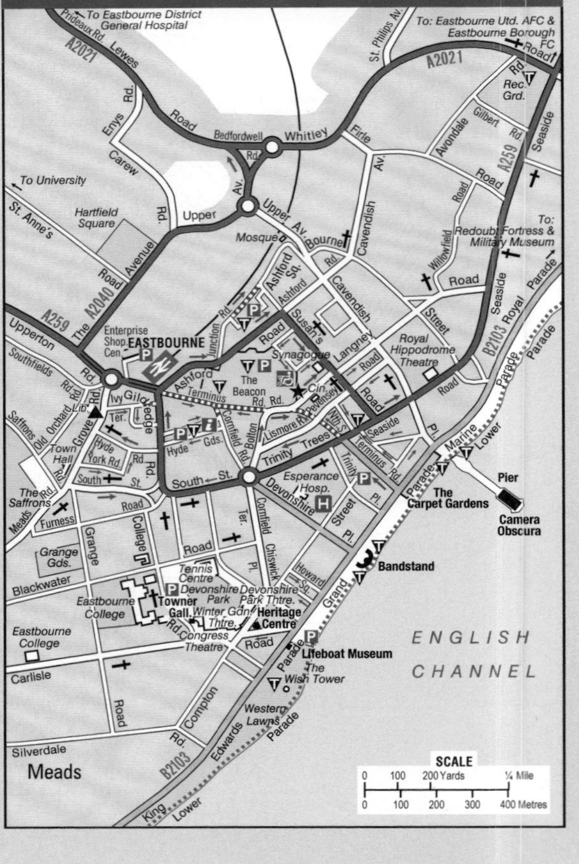

EDINBURGH

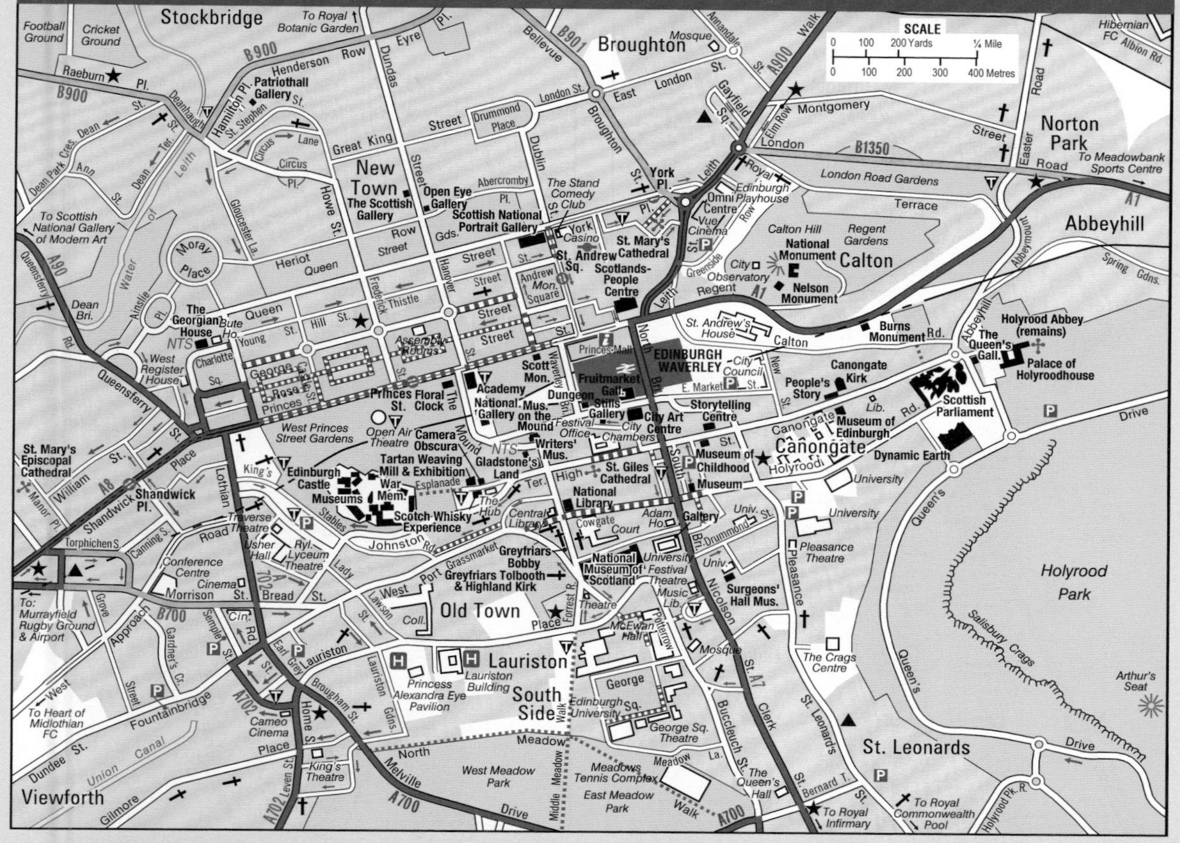

FOLKESTONE

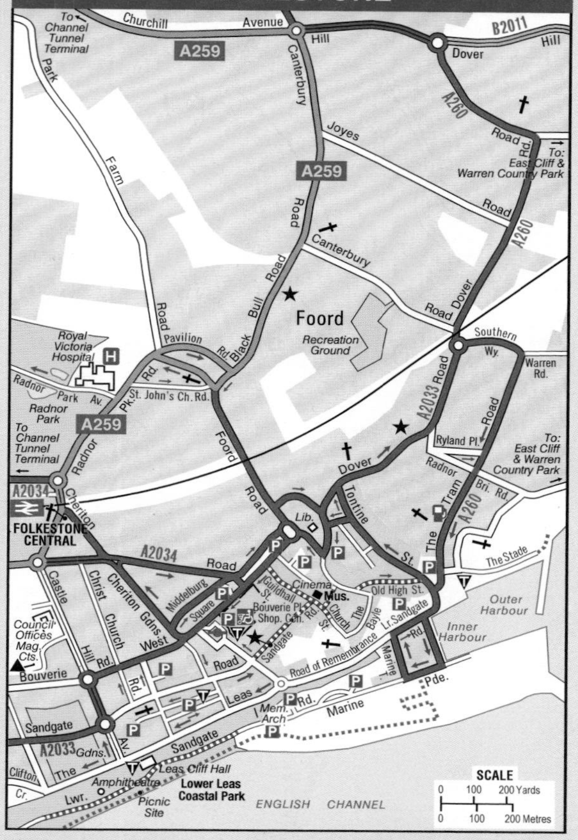

EXETER

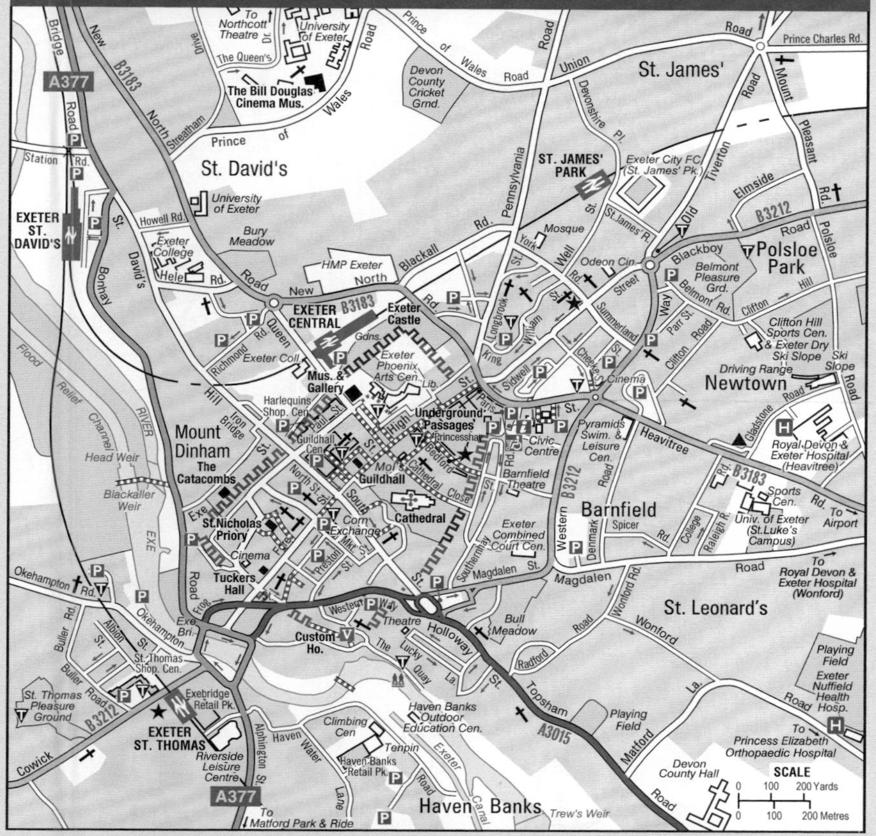

GUILDFORD

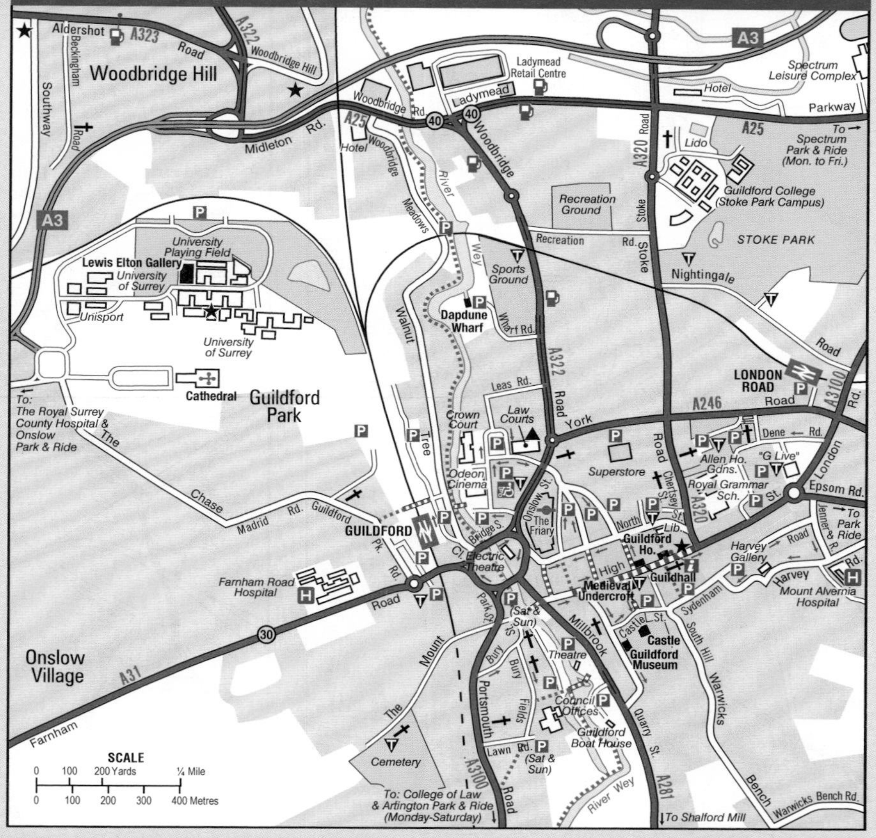

GLASGOW

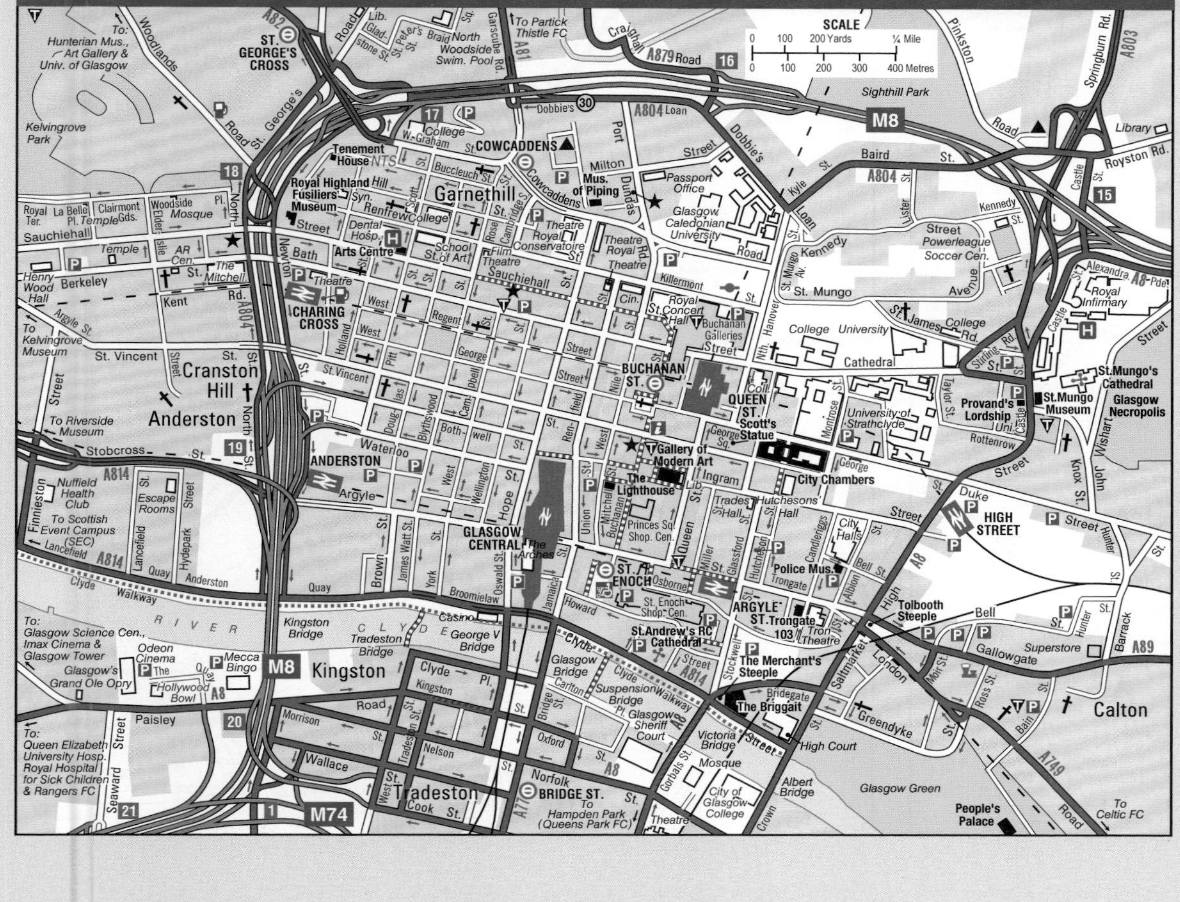

GLOUCESTER

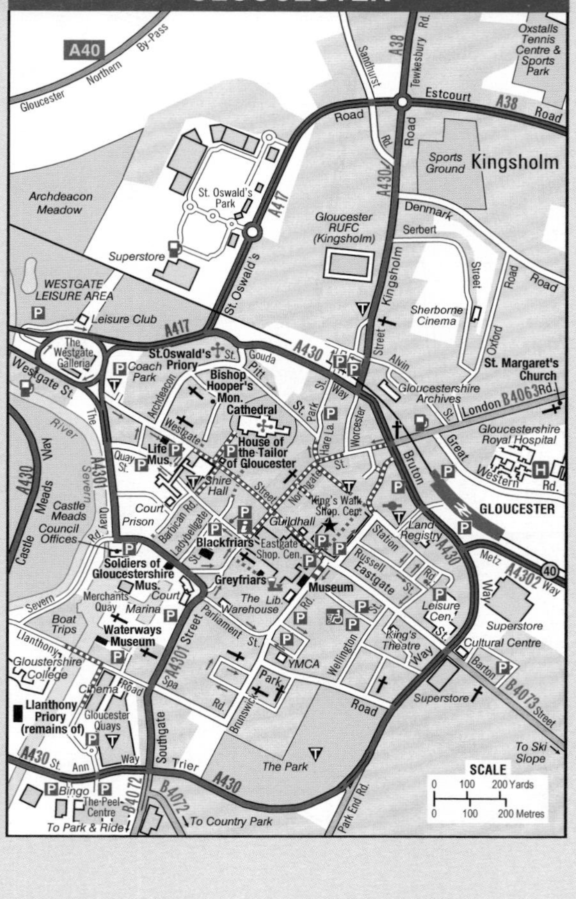

HARROGATE

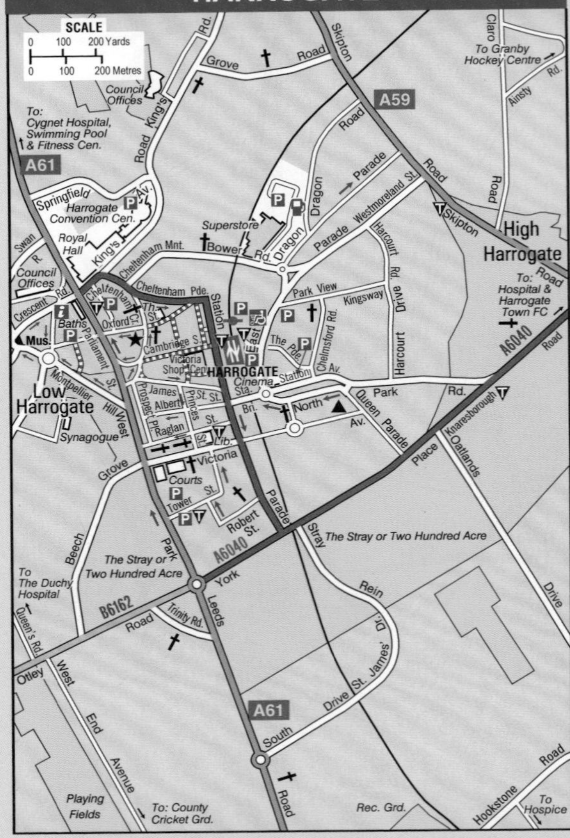

INVERNESS

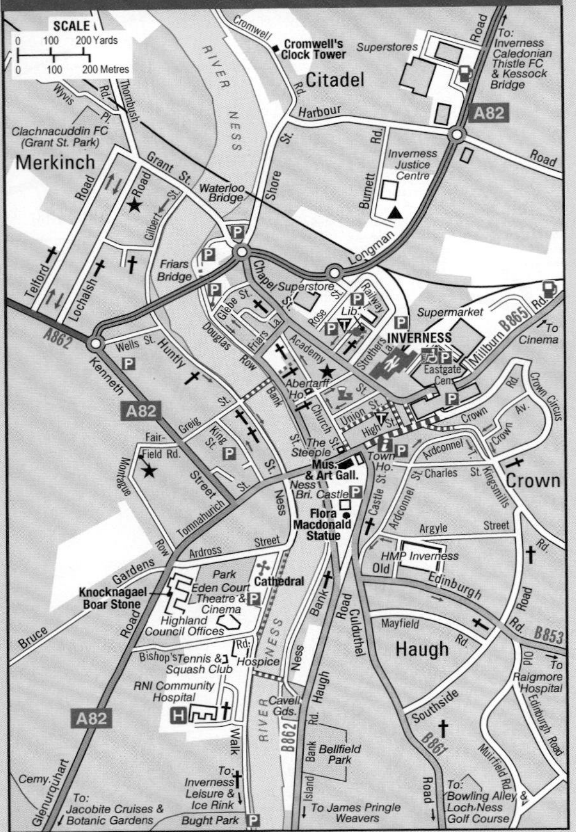

IPSWICH

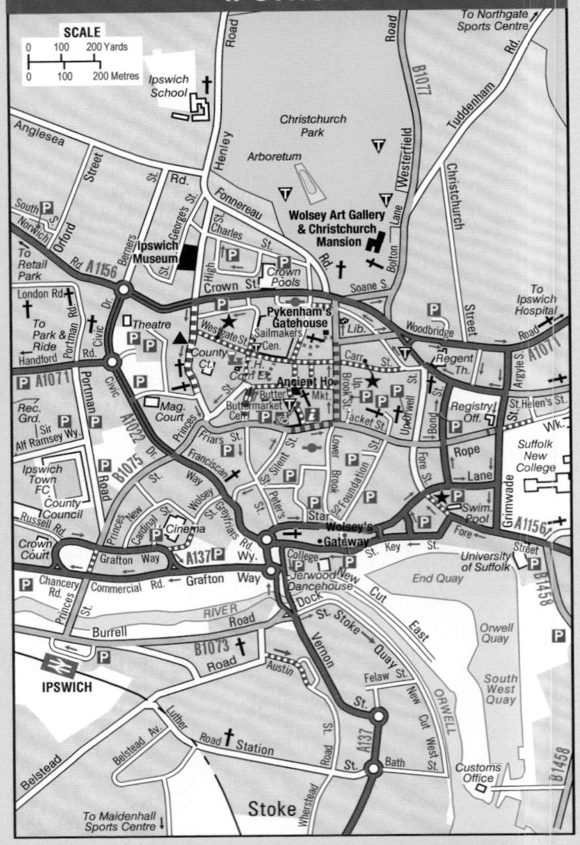

KILMARNOCK

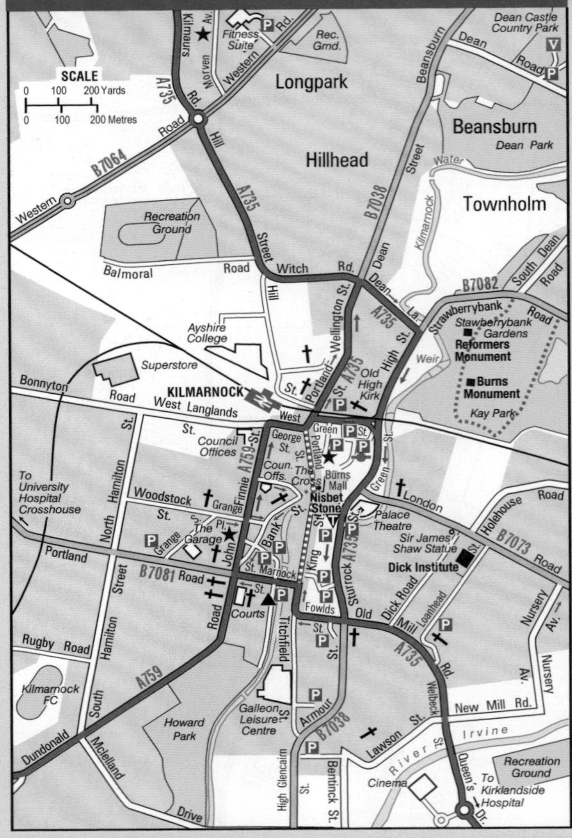

LEEDS

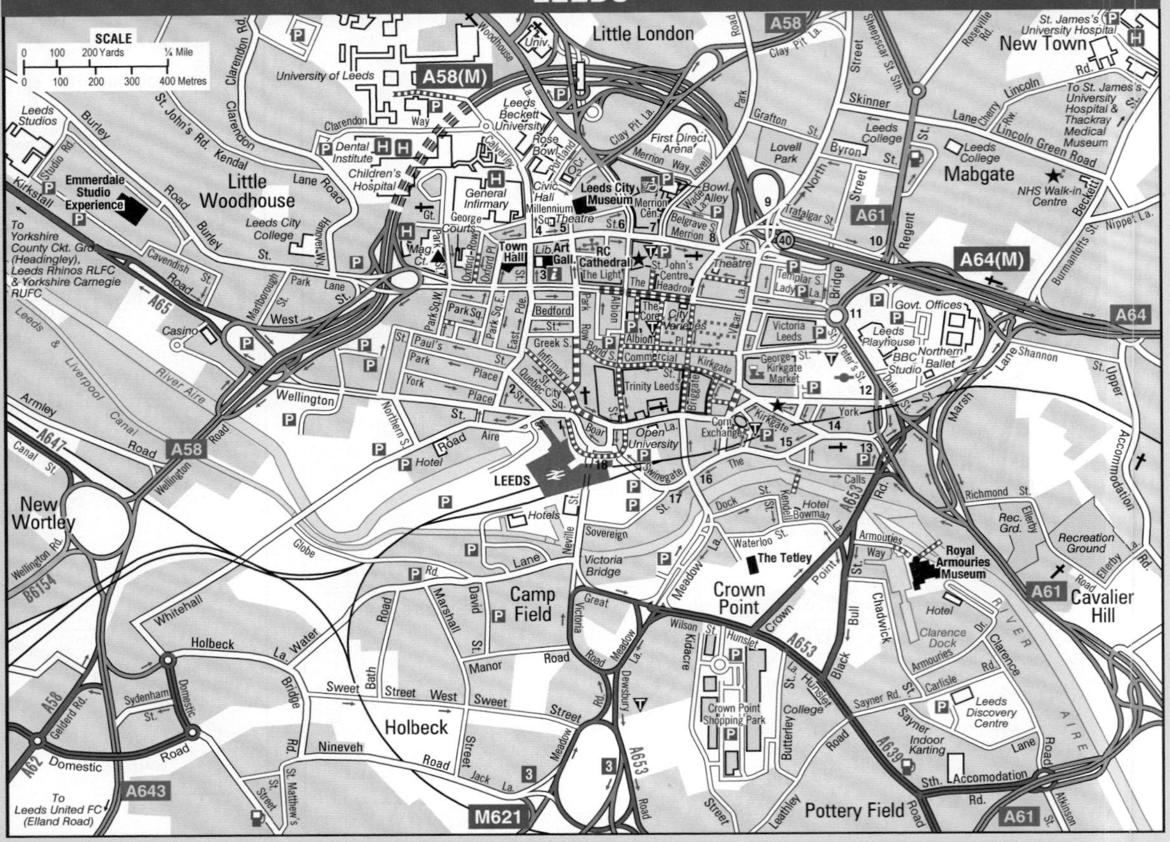

KINGSTON upon HULL

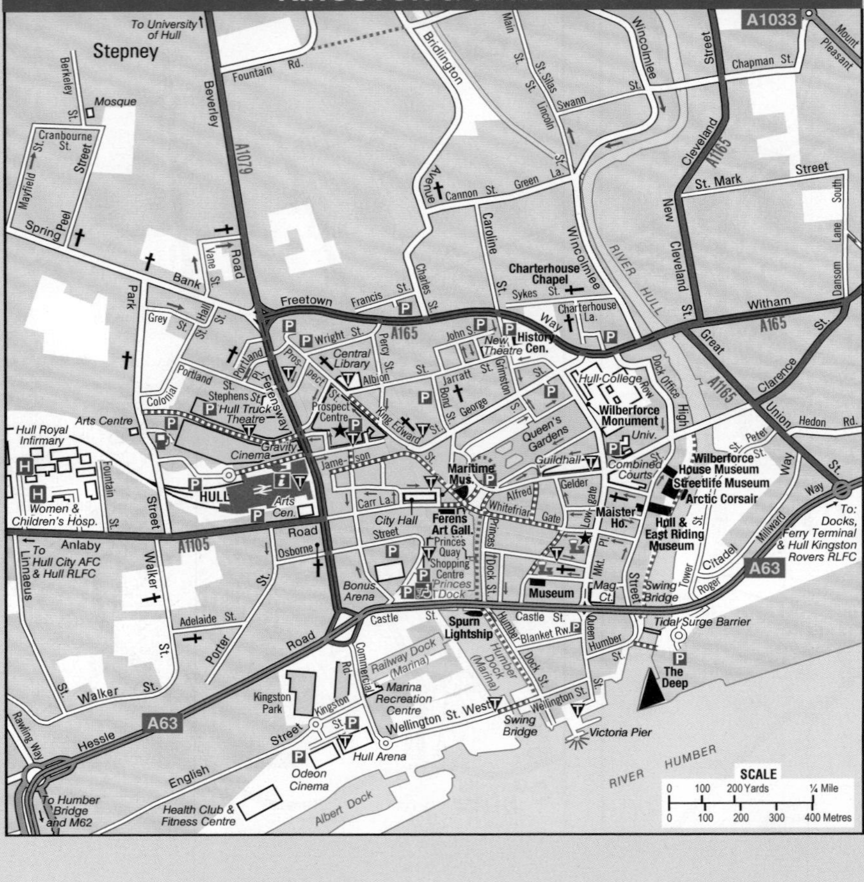

LEICESTER

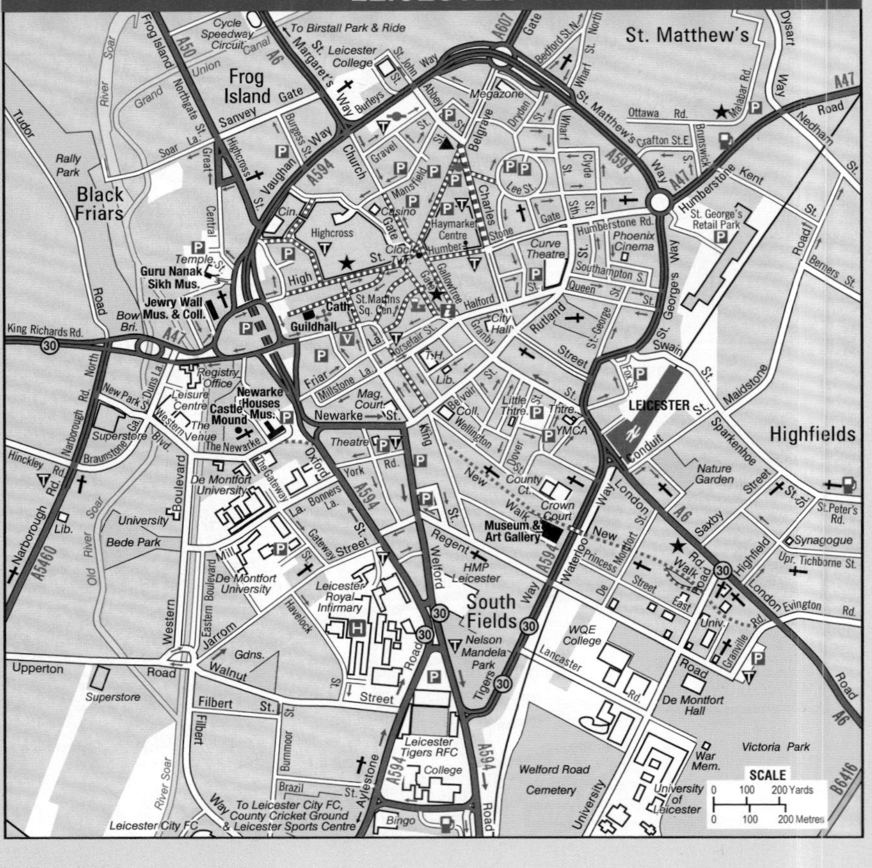

LINCOLN

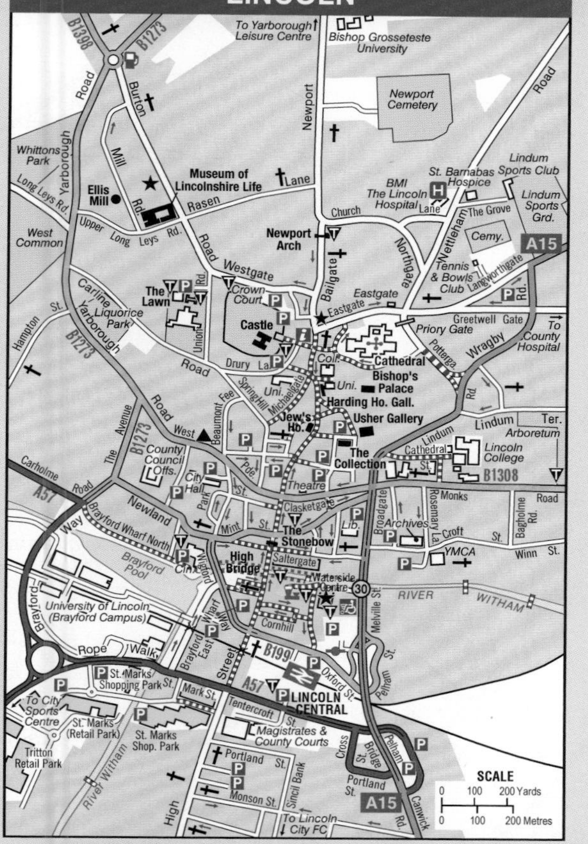

LIVERPOOL

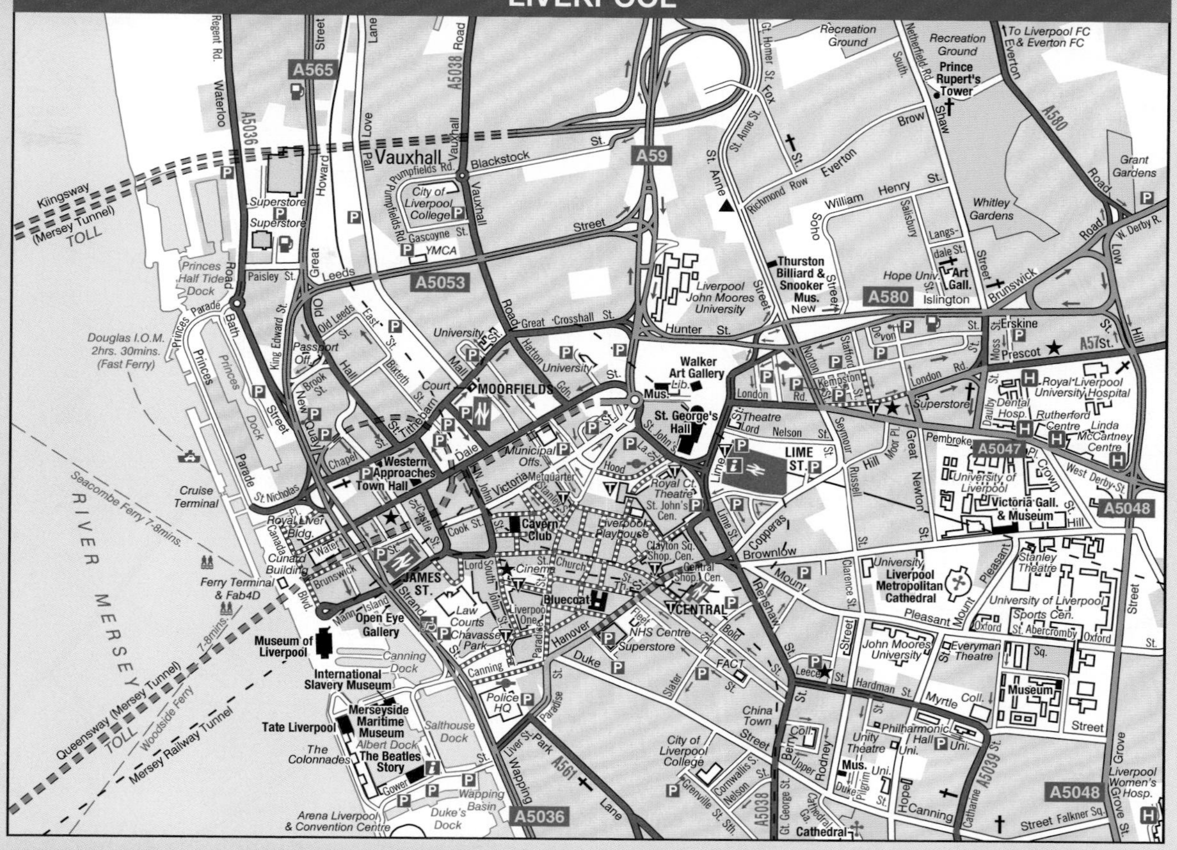

MANCHESTER (CITY CENTRE)

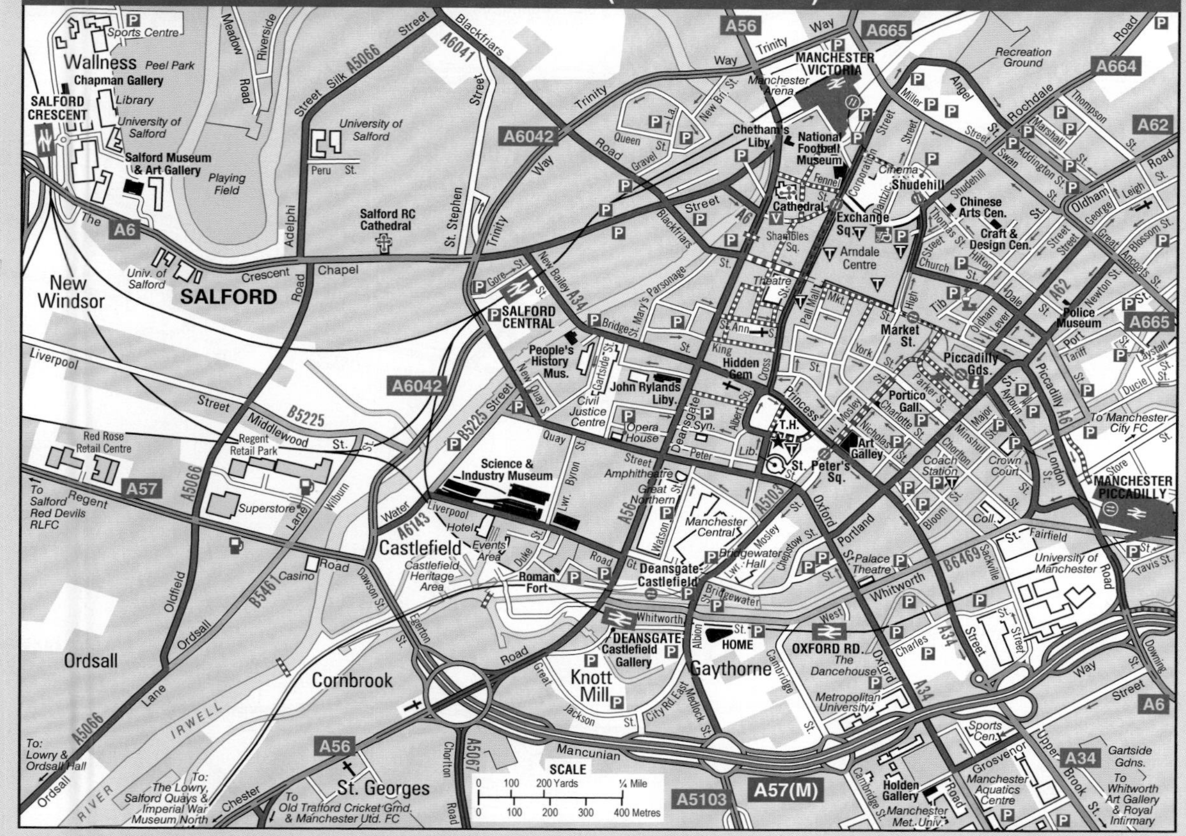

MIDDLESBROUGH

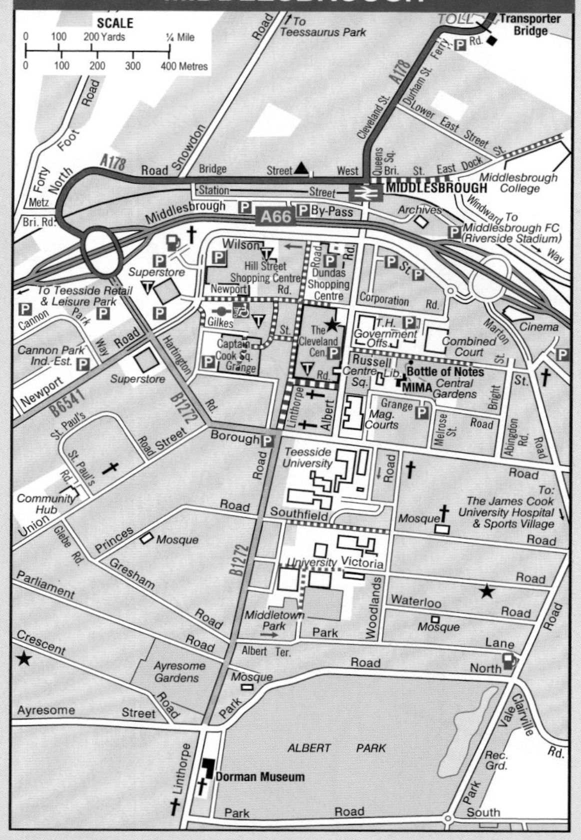

MEDWAY TOWNS

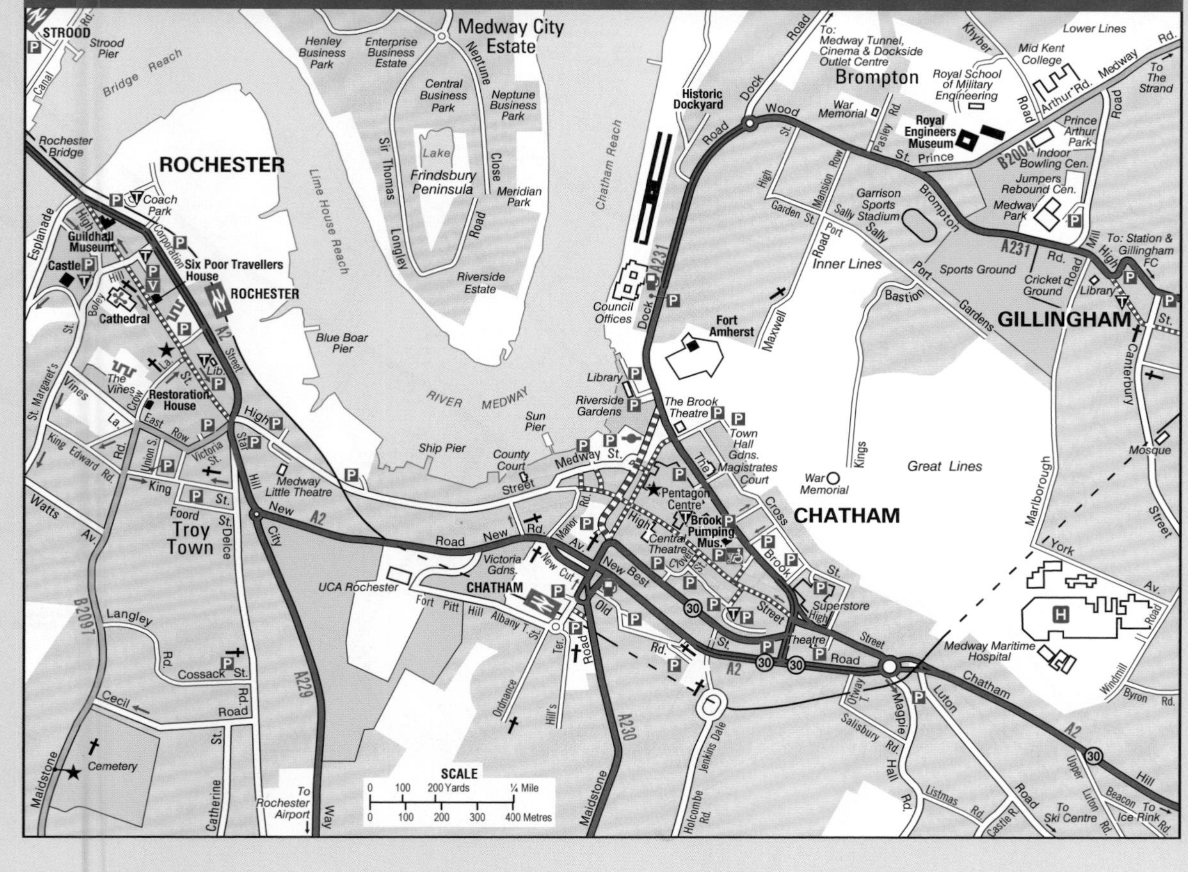

NEWCASTLE UPON TYNE

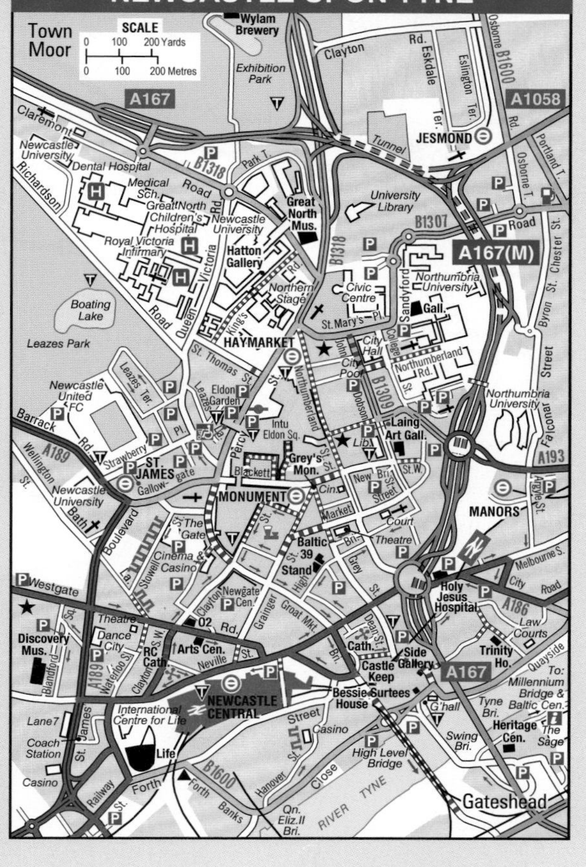

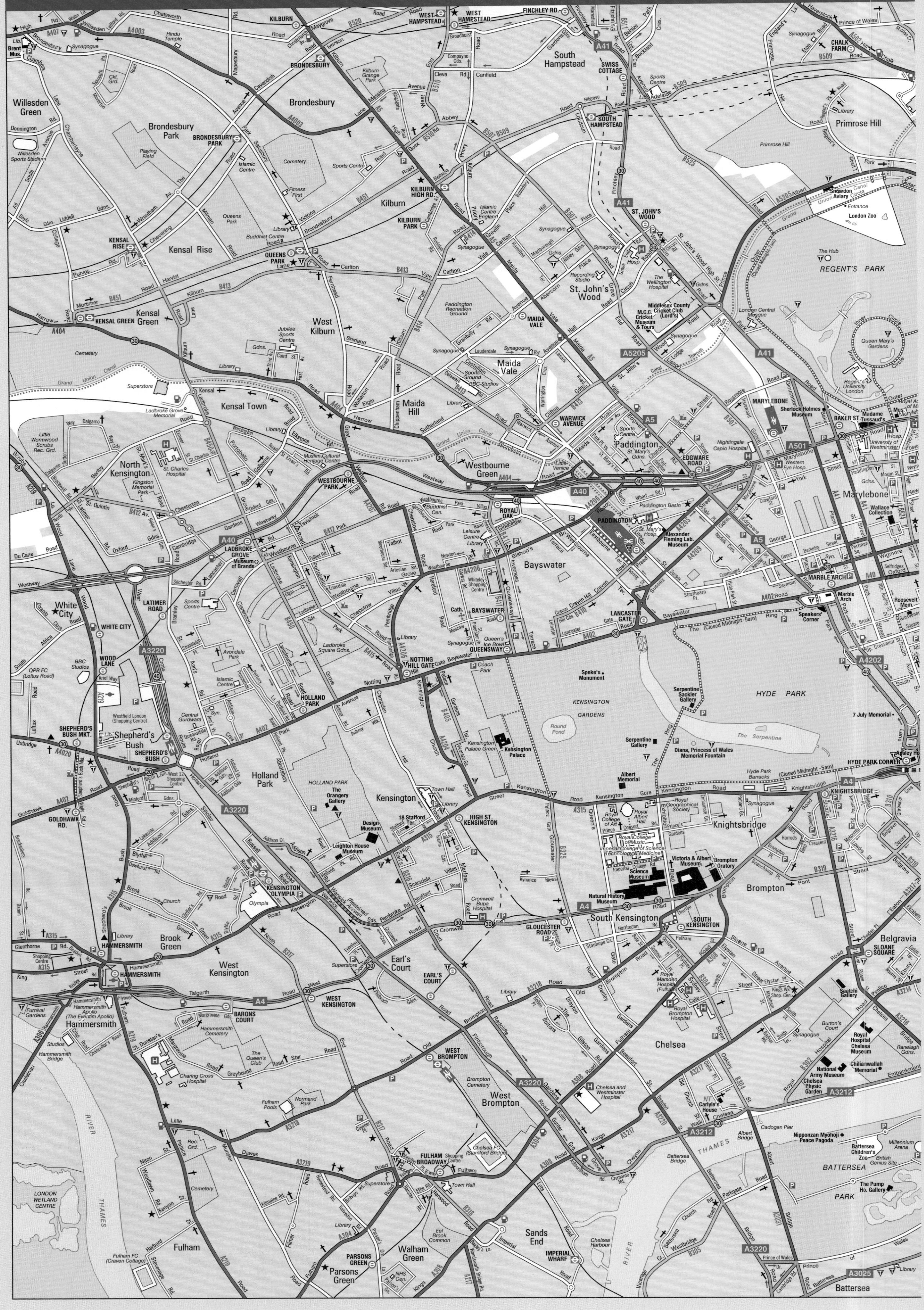
Willesden Green
Brondesbury
Brondesbury Park
Kilburn
South Hampstead
SWISS COTTAGE
SOUTH HAMPSTEAD
CHALK FARM
Primrose Hill
Kensal Rise
Kensal Green
West Kilburn
St. John's Wood
ST. JOHN'S WOOD
REGENT'S PARK
London Zoo
Maida Vale
MAIDA VALE
Maida Hill
Kensal Town
North Kensington
Westbourne Green
WARWICK AVENUE
Paddington
PADDINGTON
MARYLEBONE
BAKER ST.
Marylebone
Madame Tussaud's
Sherlock Holmes Museum
EDGWARE ROAD
ROYAL OAK
WESTBOURNE PARK
LADBROKE GROVE
Bayswater
BAYSWATER
QUEENSWAY
LANCASTER GATE
MARBLE ARCH
Speakers' Corner
White City
WHITE CITY
LATIMER ROAD
WOOD LANE
NOTTING HILL GATE
HOLLAND PARK
KENSINGTON GARDENS
HYDE PARK
The Serpentine
Serpentine Gallery
Kensington Palace
Diana, Princess of Wales Memorial Fountain
Albert Memorial
HYDE PARK CORNER
KNIGHTSBRIDGE
Knightsbridge
SHEPHERD'S BUSH
SHEPHERD'S BUSH MKT.
Shepherd's Bush
Holland Park
Kensington
HIGH ST. KENSINGTON
Royal Albert Hall
Victoria & Albert Museum
Science Museum
Natural History Museum
Brompton Oratory
Brompton
GOLDHAWK RD.
KENSINGTON OLYMPIA
Olympia
HAMMERSMITH
Hammersmith
Brook Green
West Kensington
WEST KENSINGTON
Earl's Court
EARL'S COURT
GLOUCESTER ROAD
SOUTH KENSINGTON
South Kensington
SLOANE SQUARE
Belgravia
Saatchi Gallery
BARONS COURT
WEST BROMPTON
West Brompton
Brompton Cemetery
Chelsea
Royal Hospital Chelsea Museum
National Army Museum
Chelsea Physic Garden
Chelsea and Westminster Hospital
Carlyle's House
Chelsea FC Stamford Bridge
FULHAM BROADWAY
Fulham
Walham Green
PARSONS GREEN
Parsons Green
Sands End
IMPERIAL WHARF
LONDON WETLAND CENTRE
THAMES
RIVER
Battersea Bridge
Albert Bridge
Nipponzan Myohoji Peace Pagoda
BATTERSEA PARK
Battersea
Fulham FC (Craven Cottage)
Hammersmith Bridge
Cemetery
Grand Union Canal

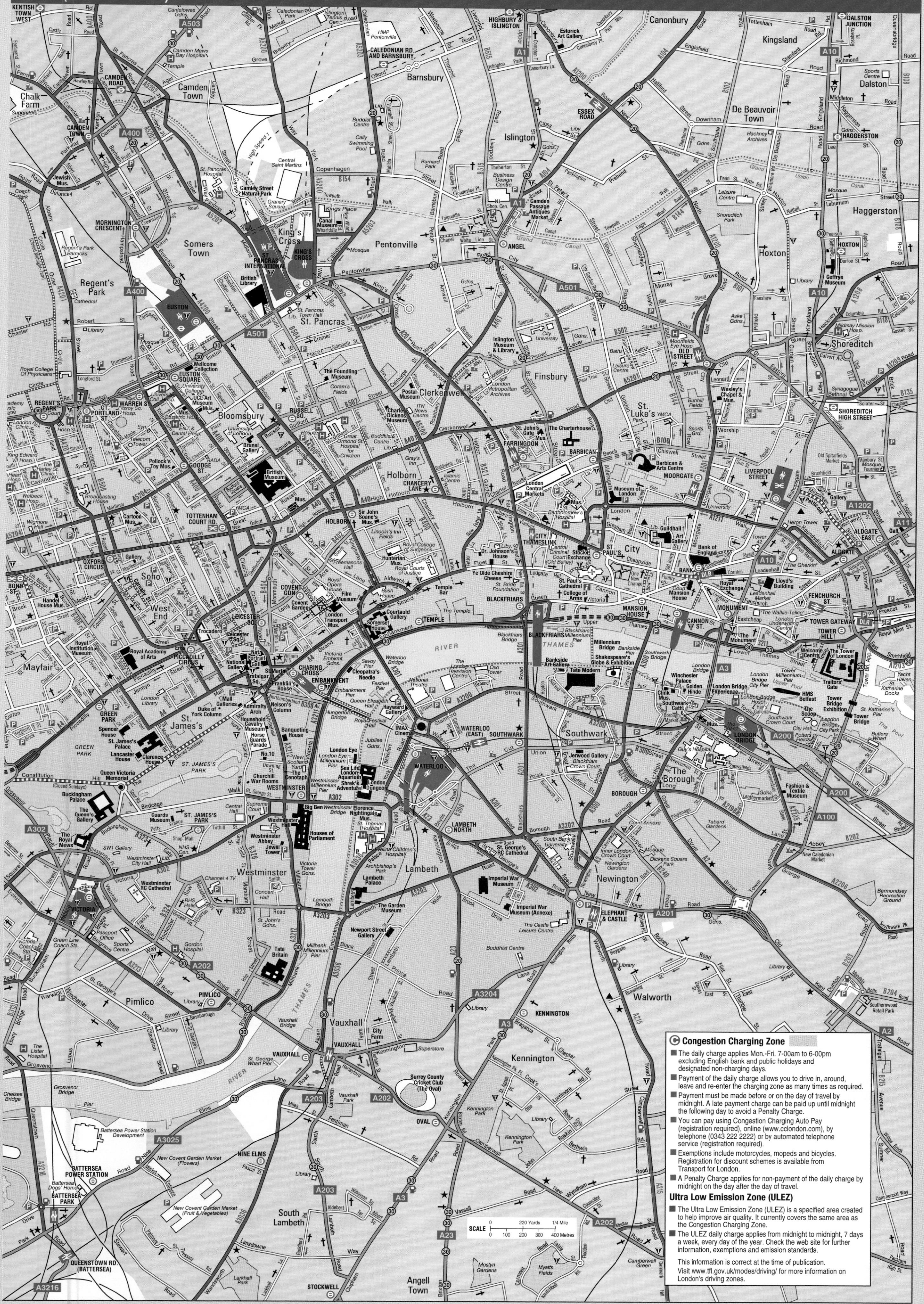
SCALE
0 220 Yards 1/4 Mile
0 100 200 300 400 Metres

Congestion Charging Zone

- The daily charge applies Mon.-Fri. 7-00am to 6-00pm excluding English bank and public holidays and designated non-charging days.
- Payment of the daily charge allows you to drive in, around, leave and re-enter the charging zone as many times as required.
- Payment must be made before or on the day of travel by midnight. A late payment charge can be paid up until midnight the following day to avoid a Penalty Charge.
- You can pay using Congestion Charging Auto Pay (registration required), online (www.cclondon.com), by telephone (0343 222 2222) or by automated telephone service (registration required).
- Exemptions include motorcycles, mopeds and bicycles. Registration for discount schemes is available from Transport for London.
- A Penalty Charge applies for non-payment of the daily charge by midnight on the day after the day of travel.

Ultra Low Emission Zone (ULEZ)

- The Ultra Low Emission Zone (ULEZ) is a specified area created to help improve air quality. It currently covers the same area as the Congestion Charging Zone.
- The ULEZ daily charge applies from midnight to midnight, 7 days a week, every day of the year. Check the web site for further information, exemptions and emission standards.

This information is correct at the time of publication.
Visit www.tfl.gov.uk/modes/driving/ for more information on London's driving zones.

MILTON KEYNES

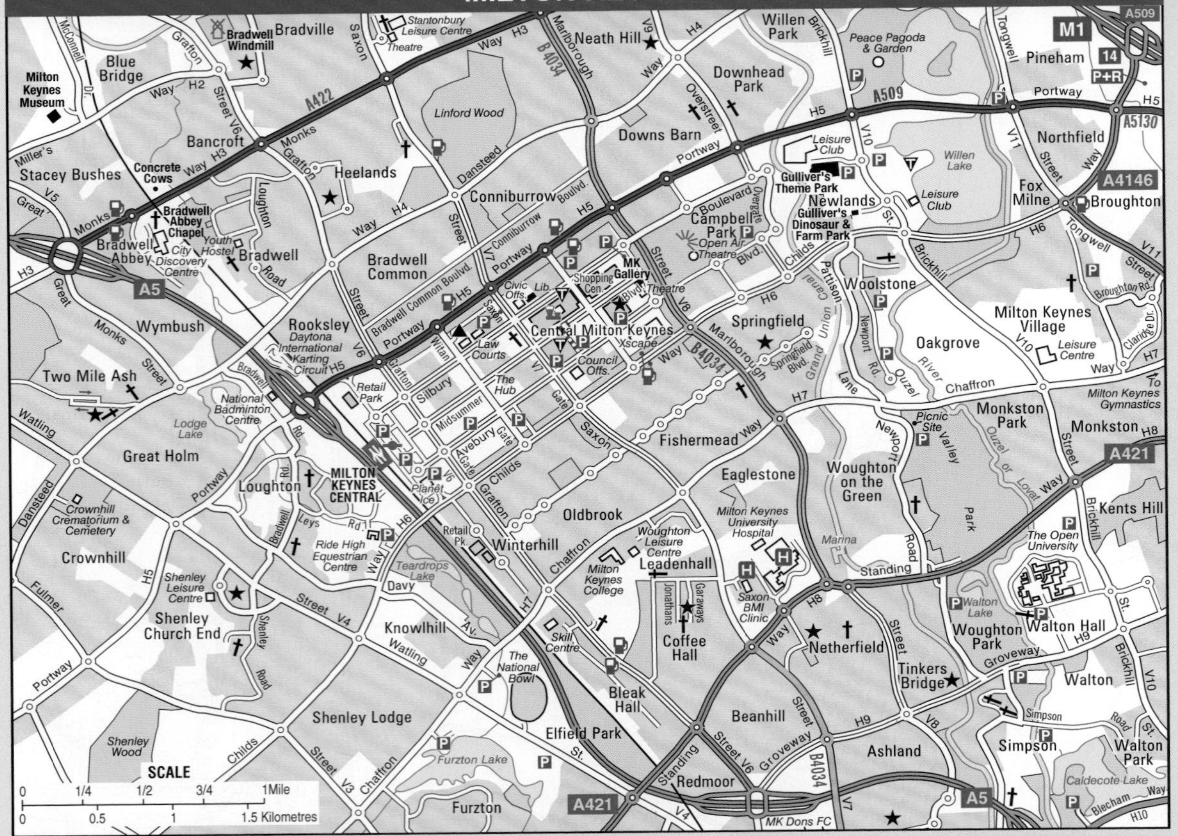

NEWPORT (CASNEWYDD)

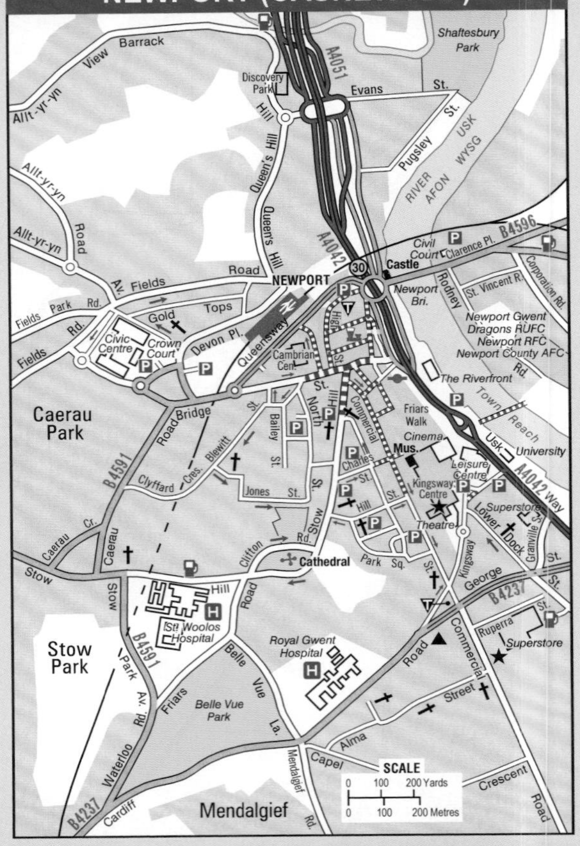

NORWICH

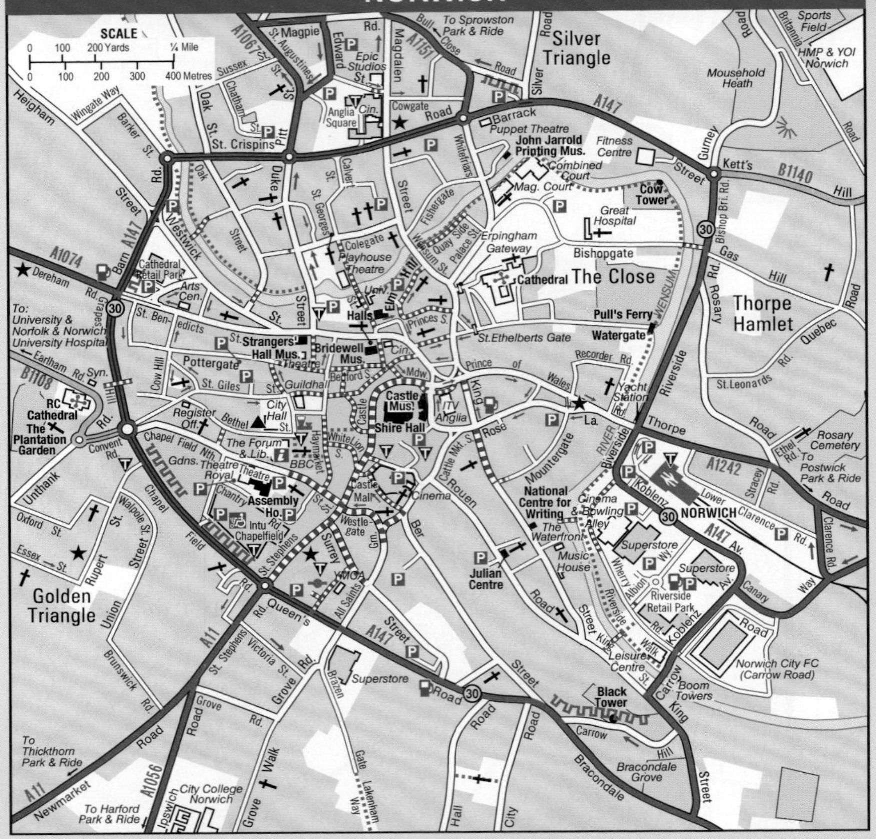

NOTTINGHAM

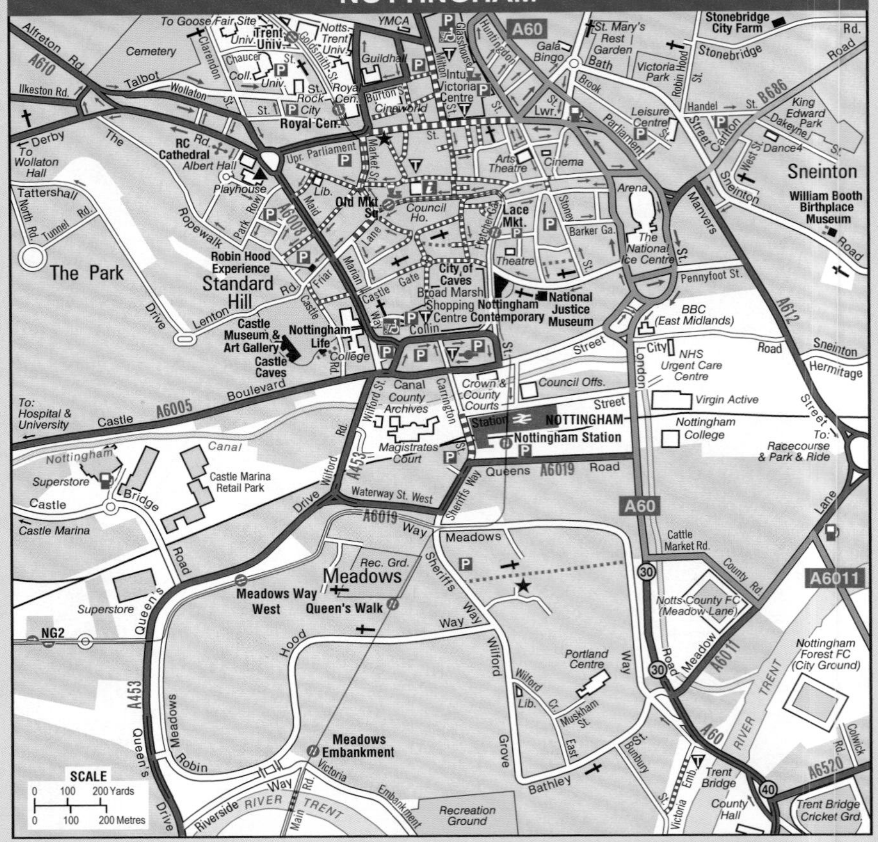

NORTHAMPTON

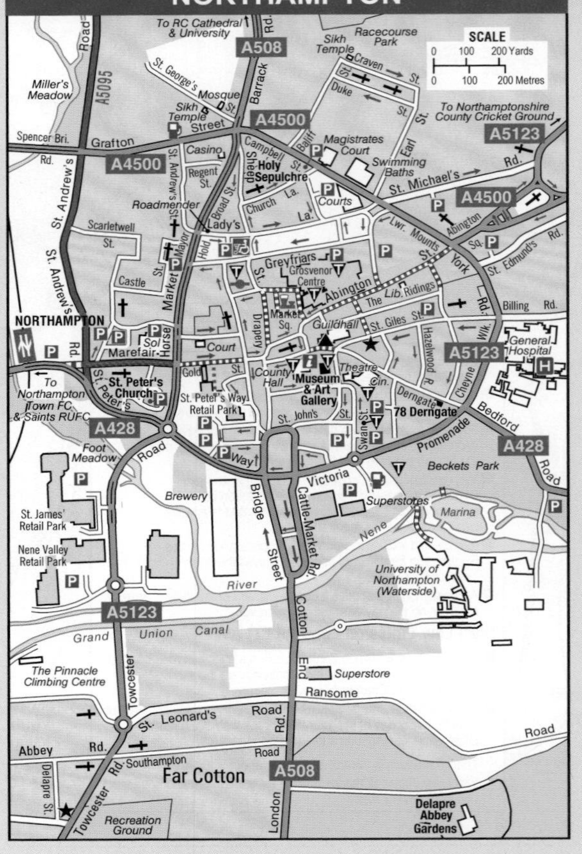

OXFORD

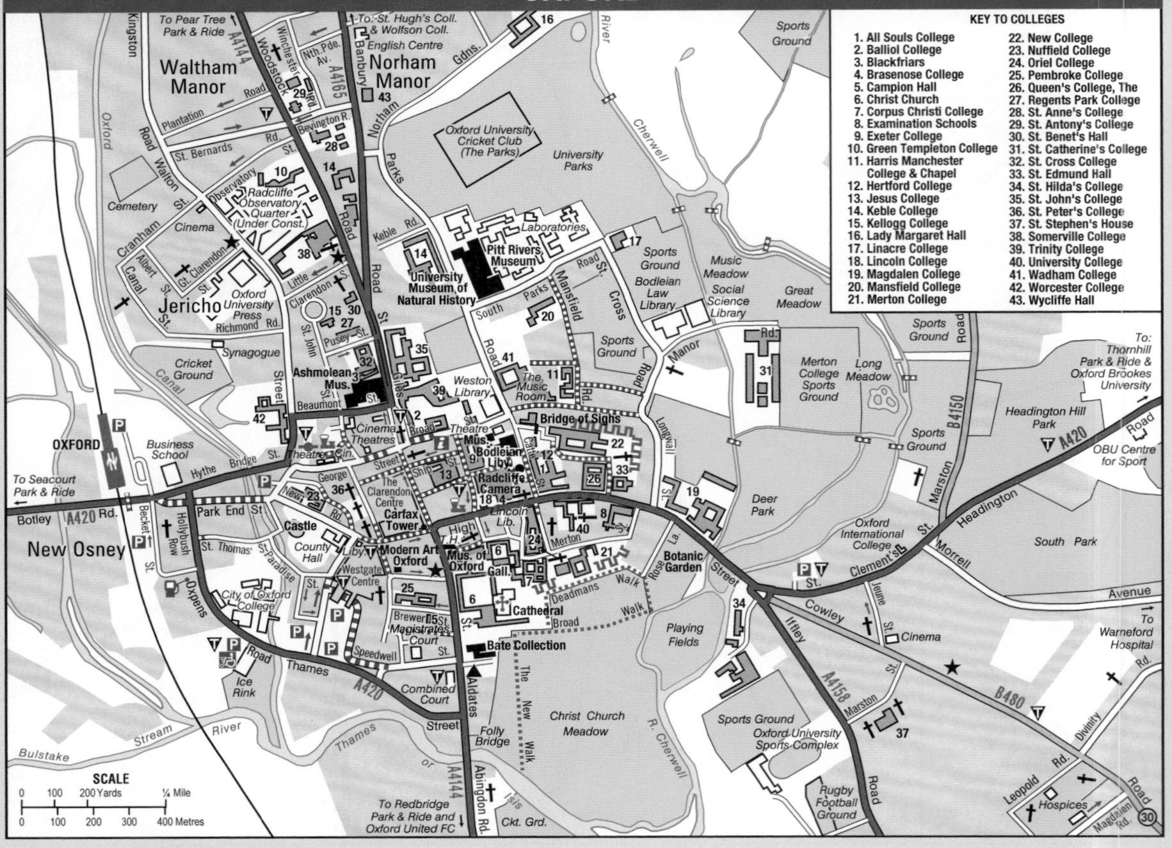

KEY TO COLLEGES

1. All Souls College
2. Balliol College
3. Blackfriars
4. Brasenose College
5. Campion Hall
6. Christ Church
7. Corpus Christi College
8. Examination Schools
9. Exeter College
10. Green Templeton College
11. Harris Manchester College & Chapel
12. Hertford College
13. Jesus College
14. Keble College
15. Kellogg College
16. Lady Margaret Hall
17. Linacre College
18. Lincoln College
19. Magdalen College
20. Mansfield College
21. Merton College
22. New College
23. Nuffield College
24. Oriel College
25. Pembroke College
26. Queen's College, The
27. Regents Park College
28. St. Anne's College
29. St. Antony's College
30. St. Benet's Hall
31. St. Catherine's College
32. St. Cross College
33. St. Edmund Hall
34. St. Hilda's College
35. St. John's College
36. St. Peter's College
37. St. Stephen's House
38. Somerville College
39. Trinity College
40. University College
41. Wadham College
42. Worcester College
43. Wycliffe Hall

OBAN

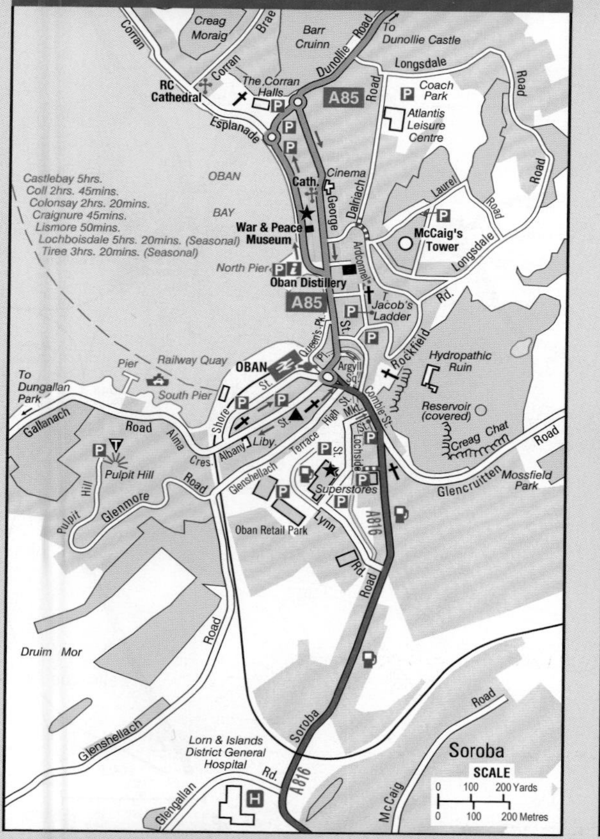

PERTH

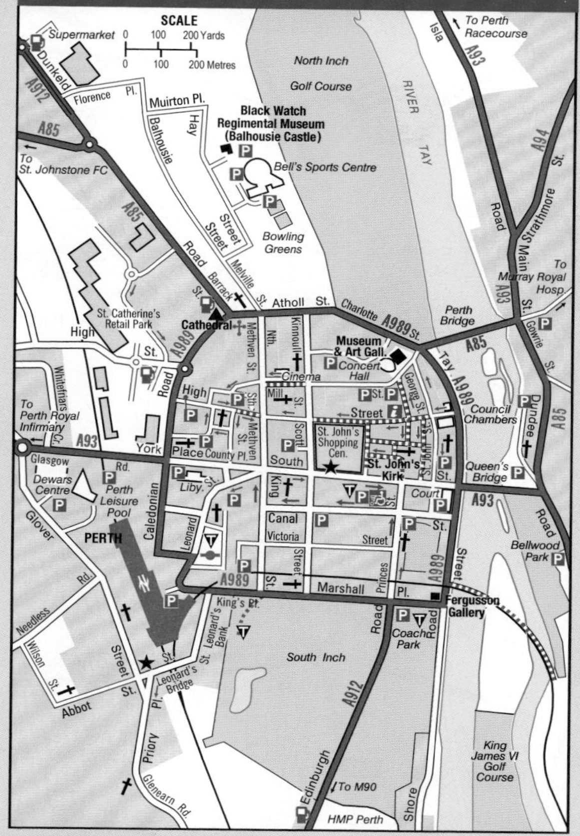

PETERBOROUGH

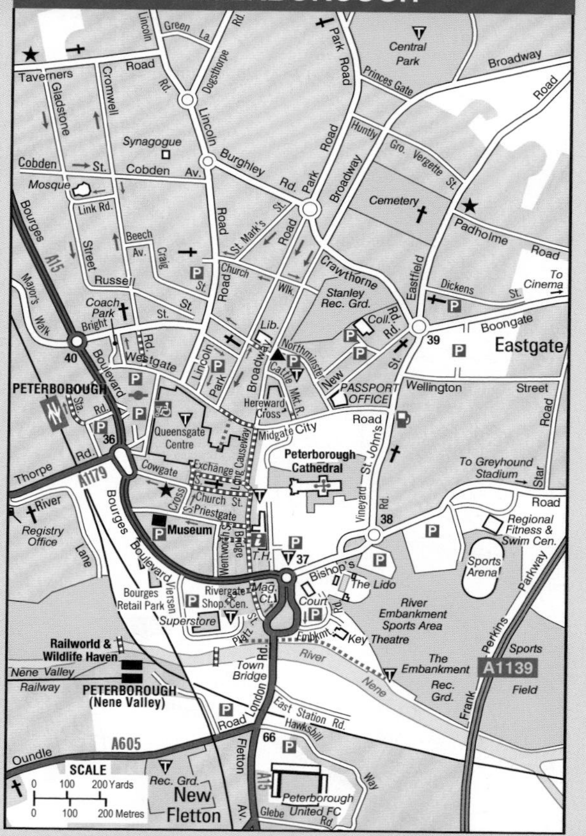

PLYMOUTH

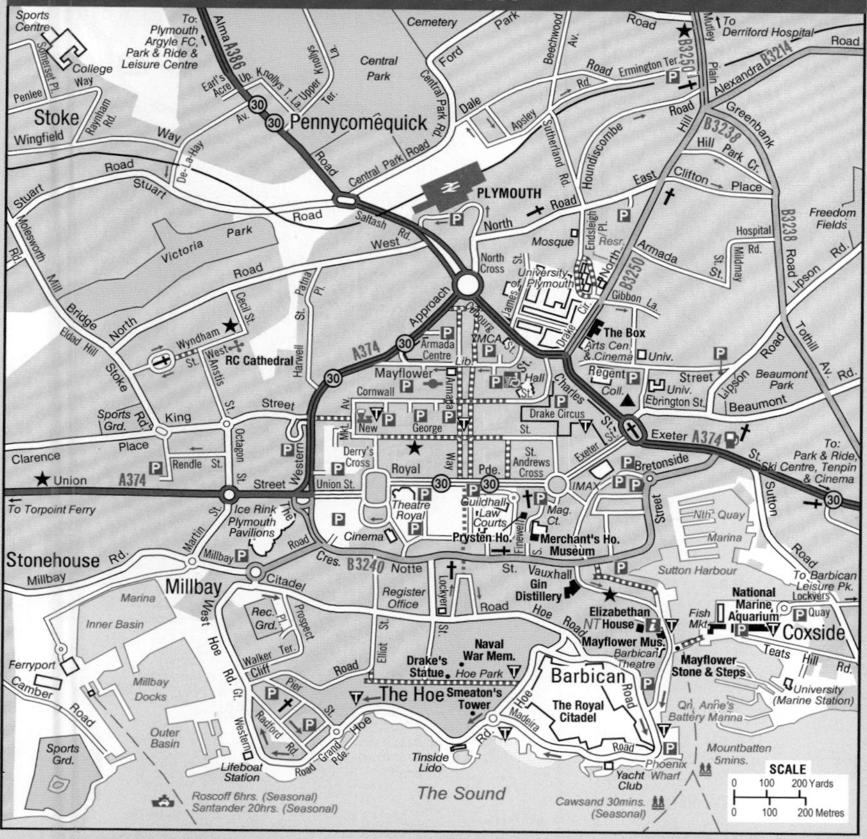

PORTSMOUTH

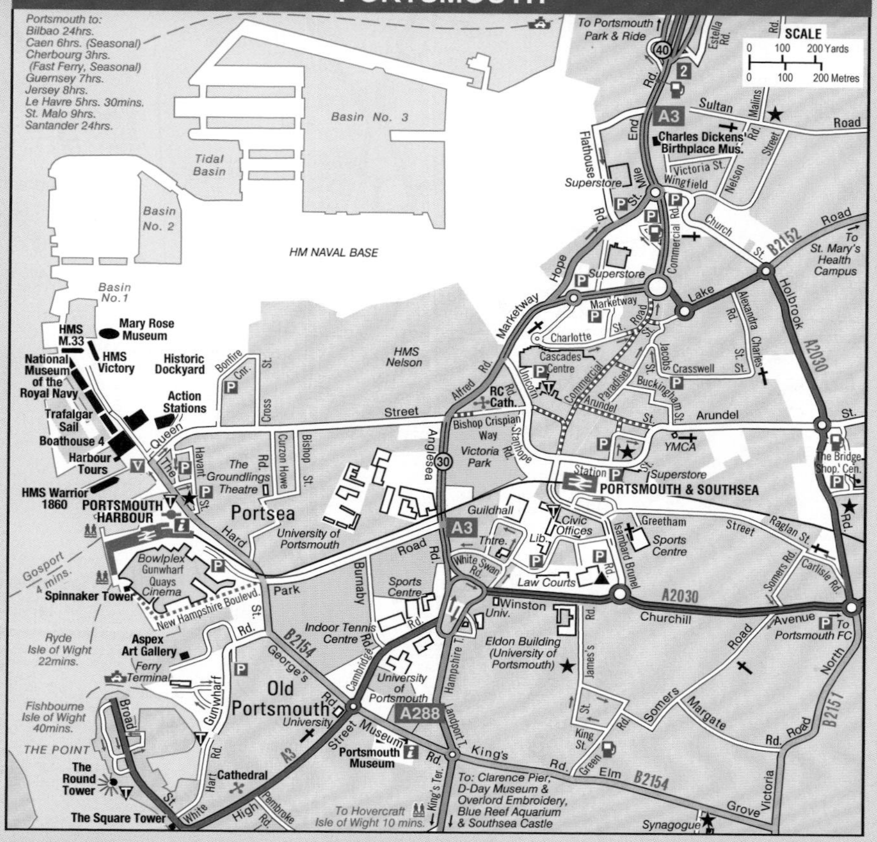

PRESTON

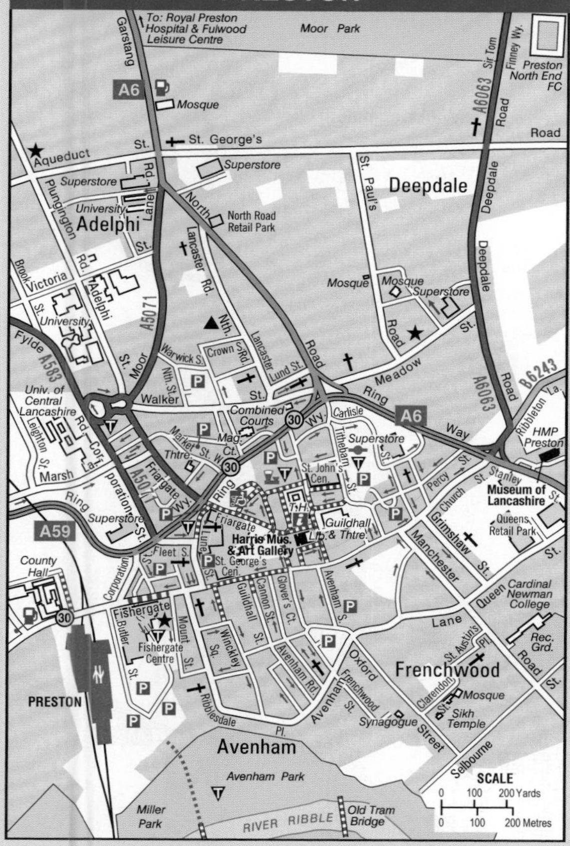

READING

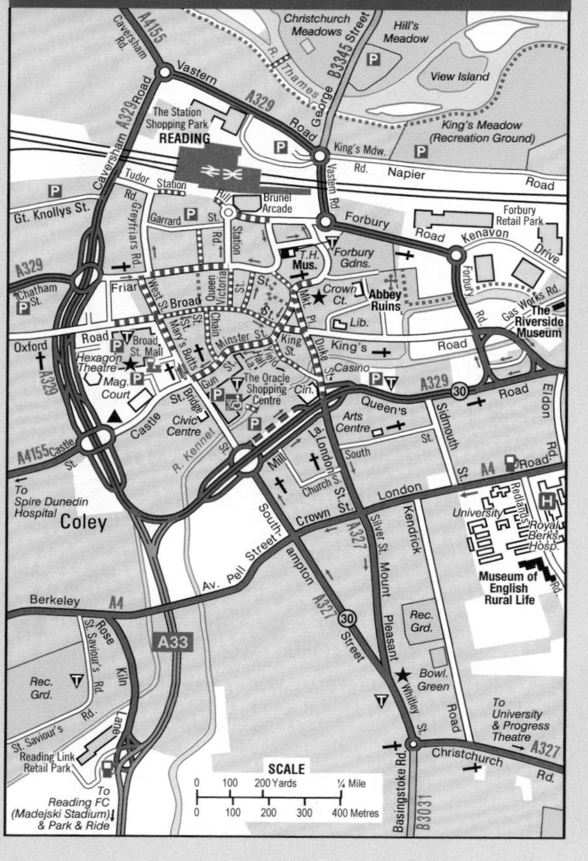

SALISBURY

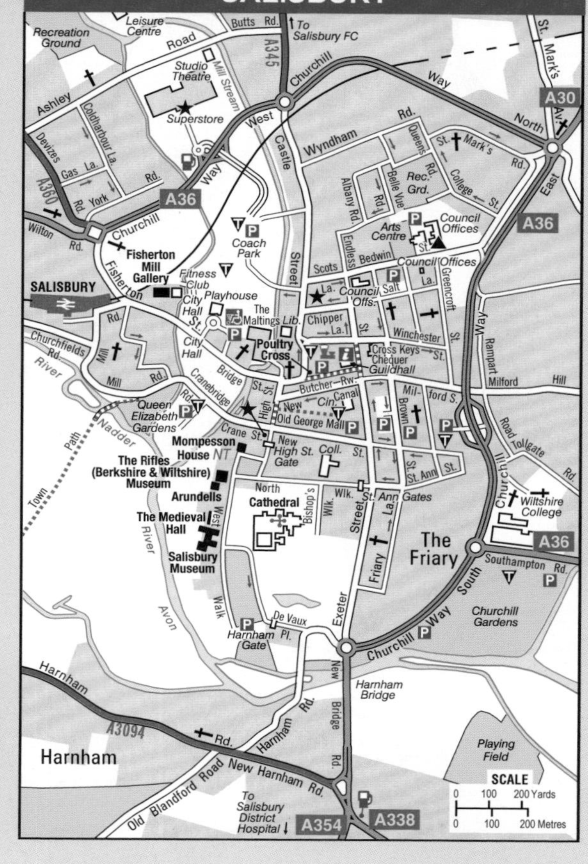

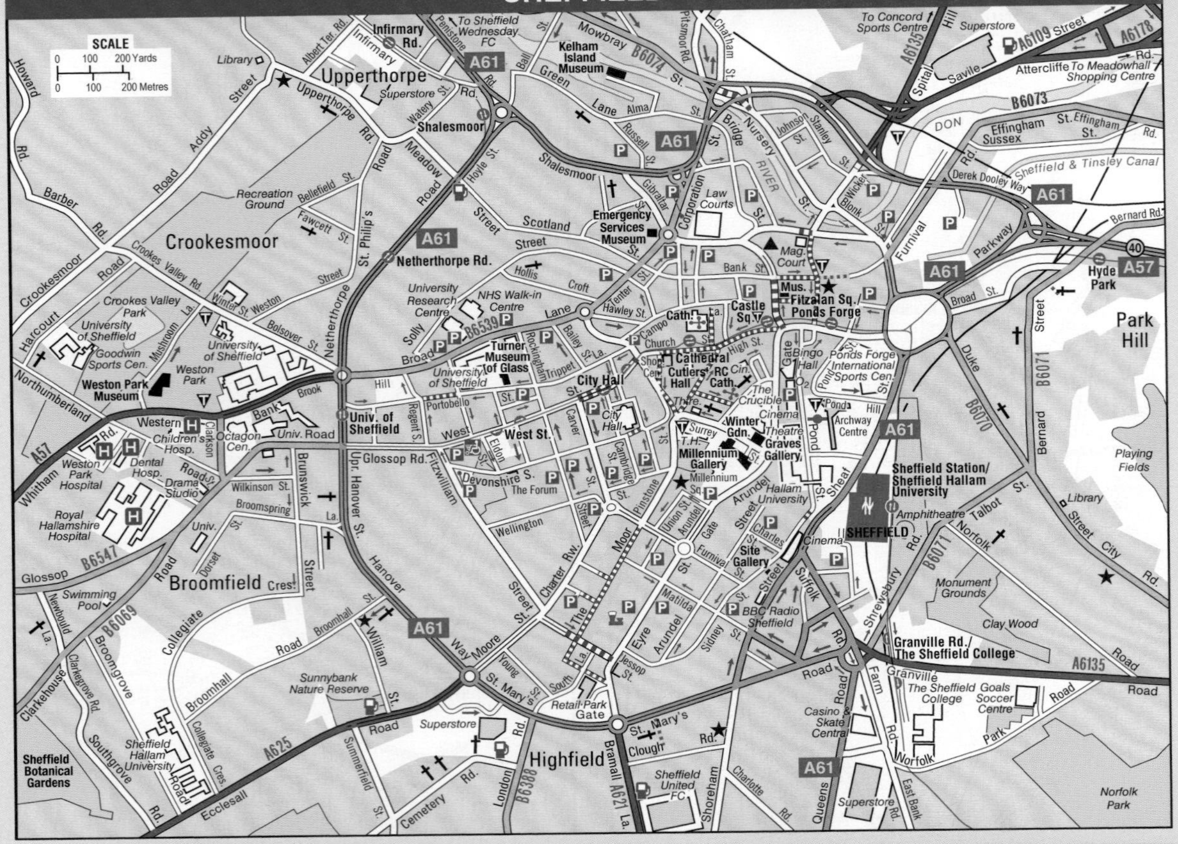

SHEFFIELD

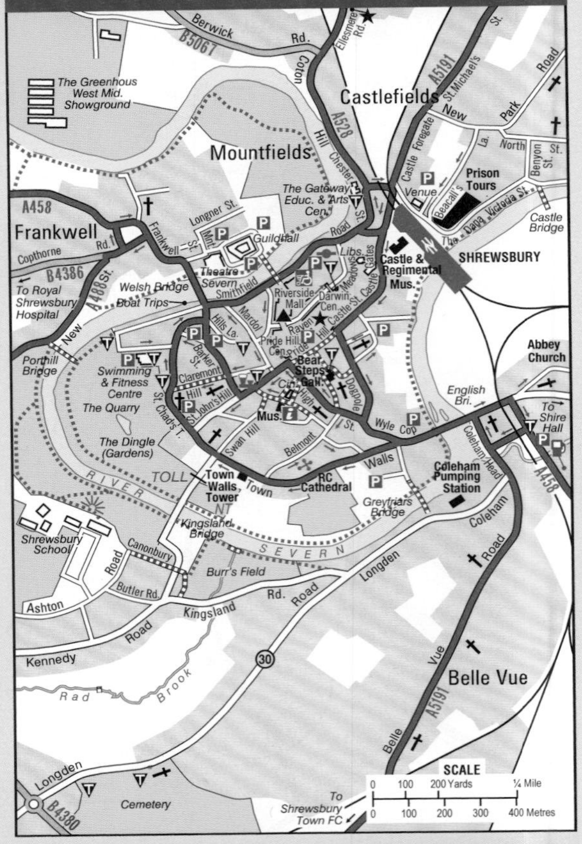

SHREWSBURY

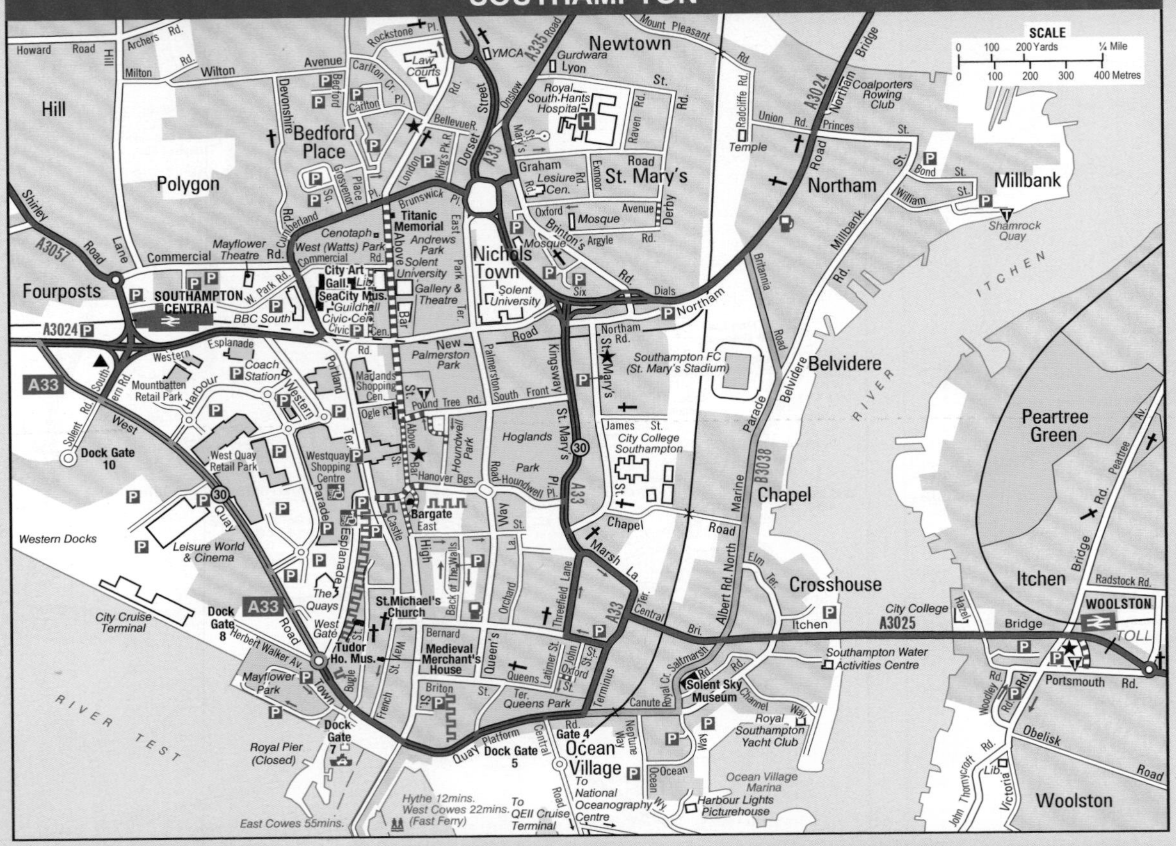

SOUTHAMPTON

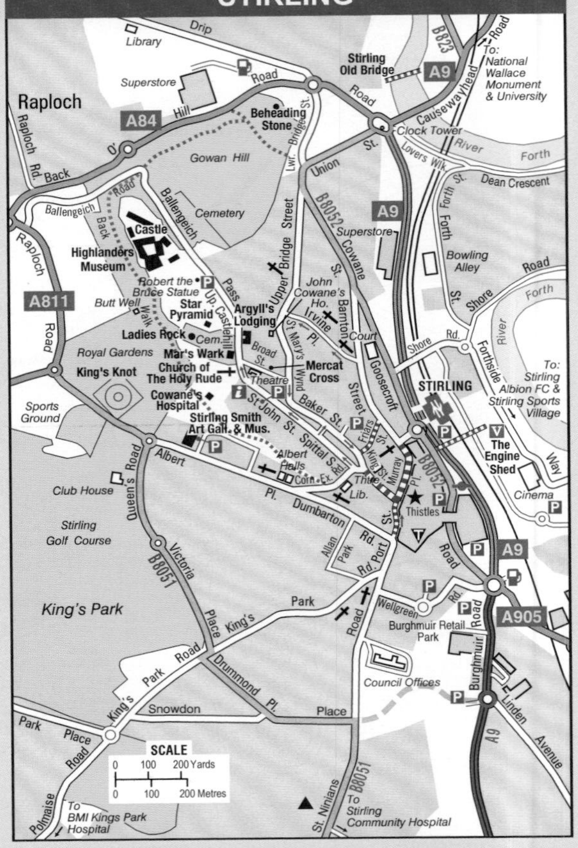

STIRLING

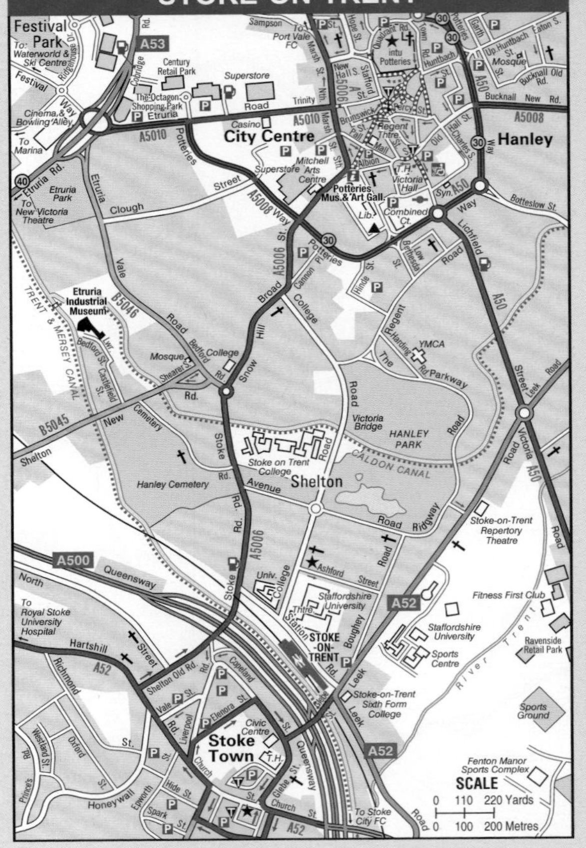

STOKE-ON-TRENT

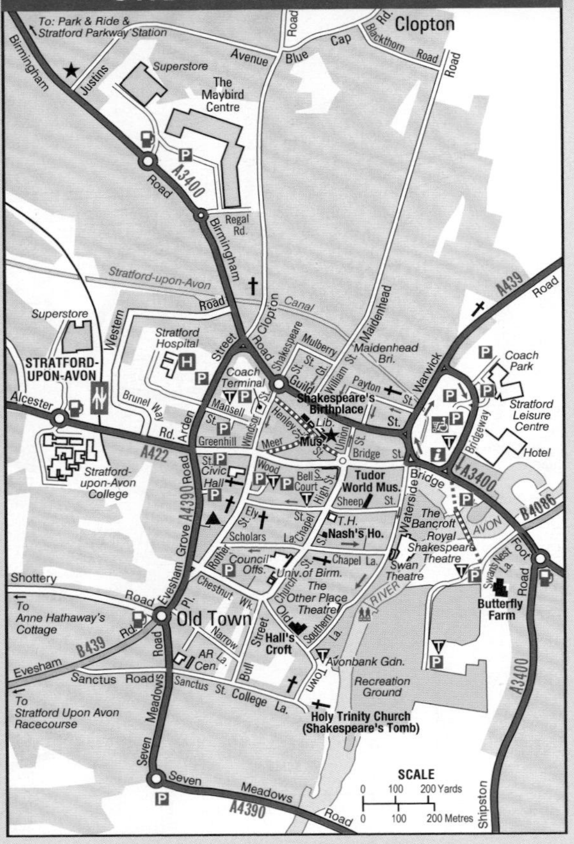

STRATFORD UPON AVON

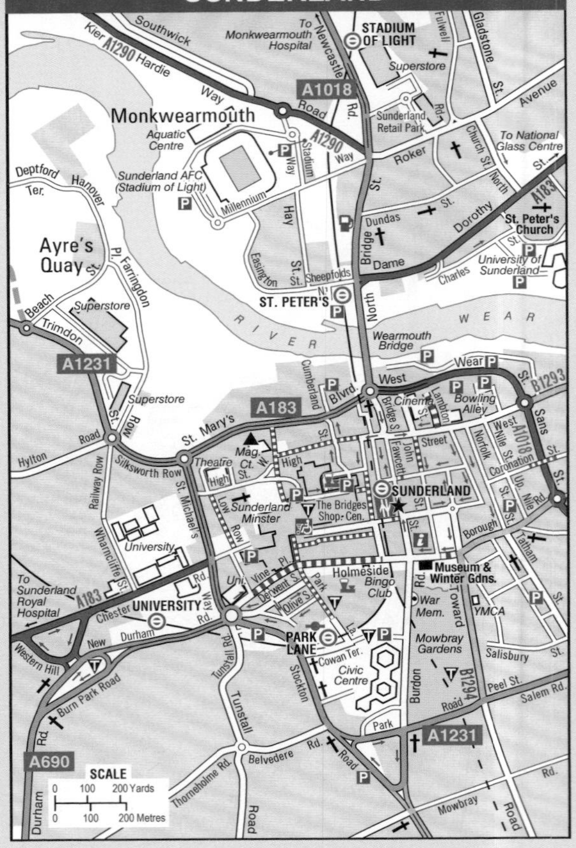

SUNDERLAND

SWANSEA (ABERTAWE)

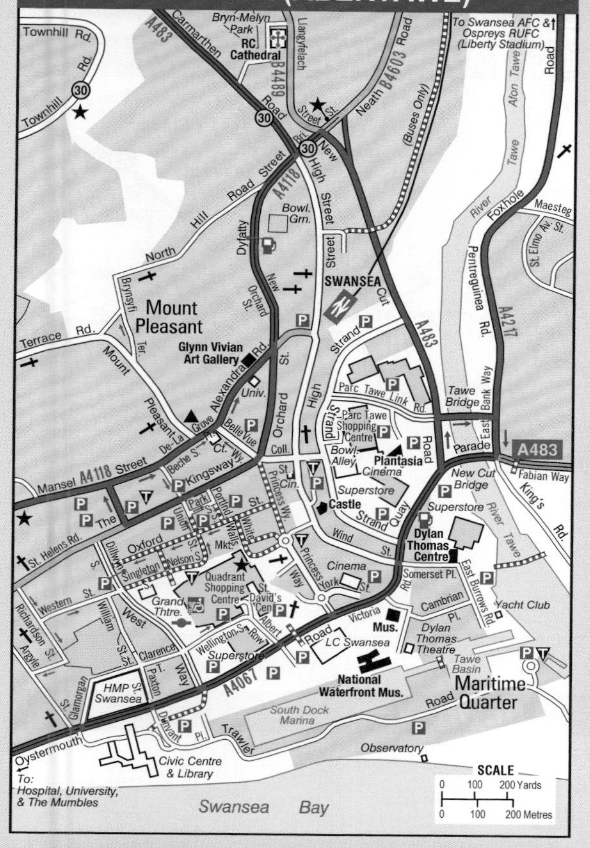

SWINDON

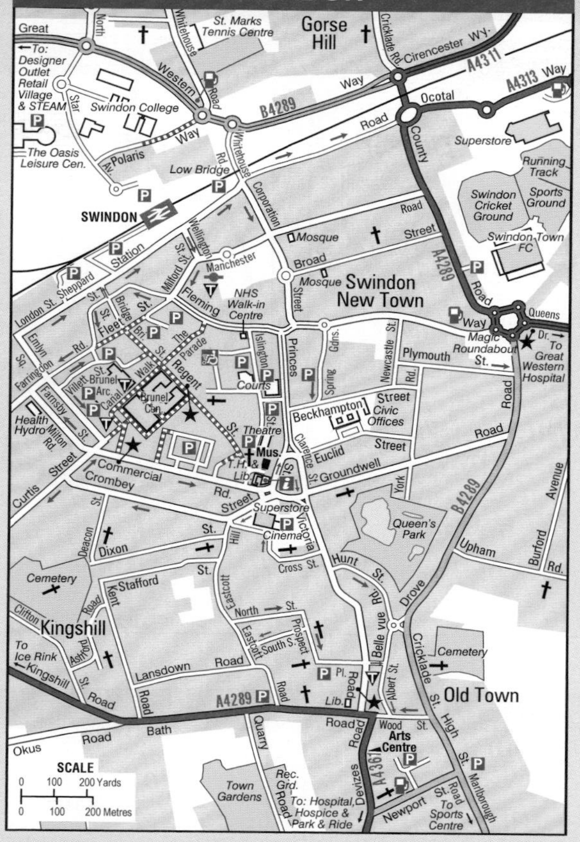

TAUNTON

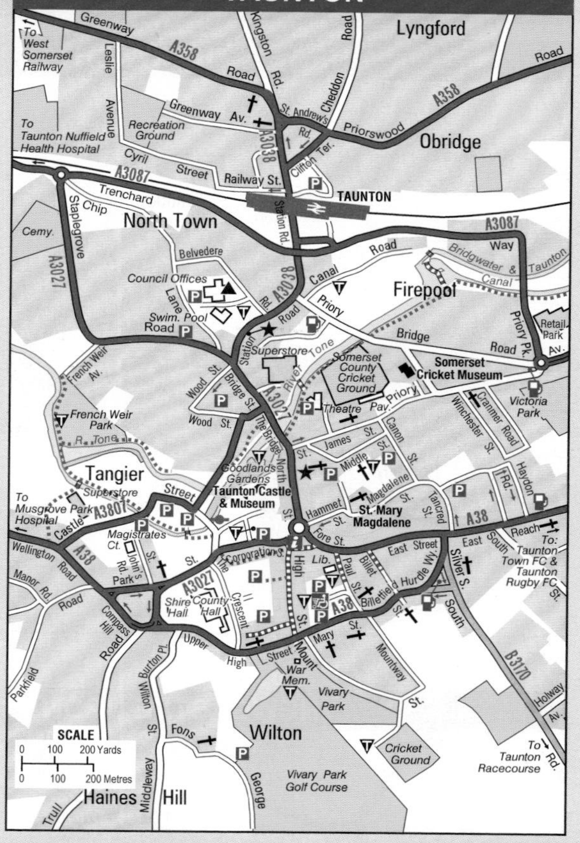

WINCHESTER

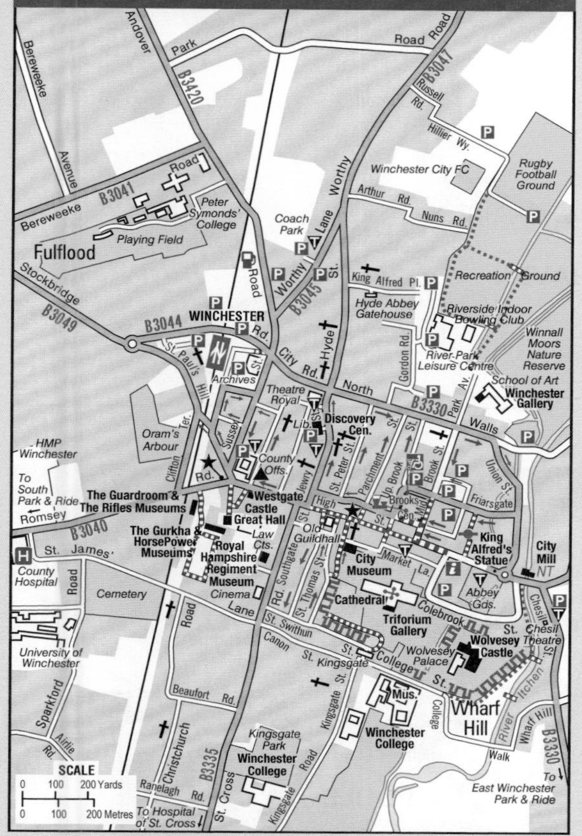

WINDSOR

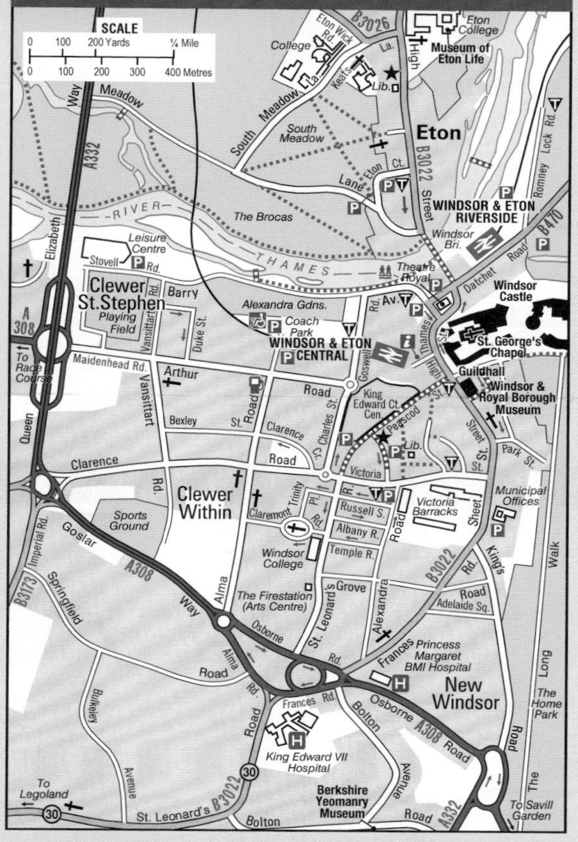

WOLVERHAMPTON

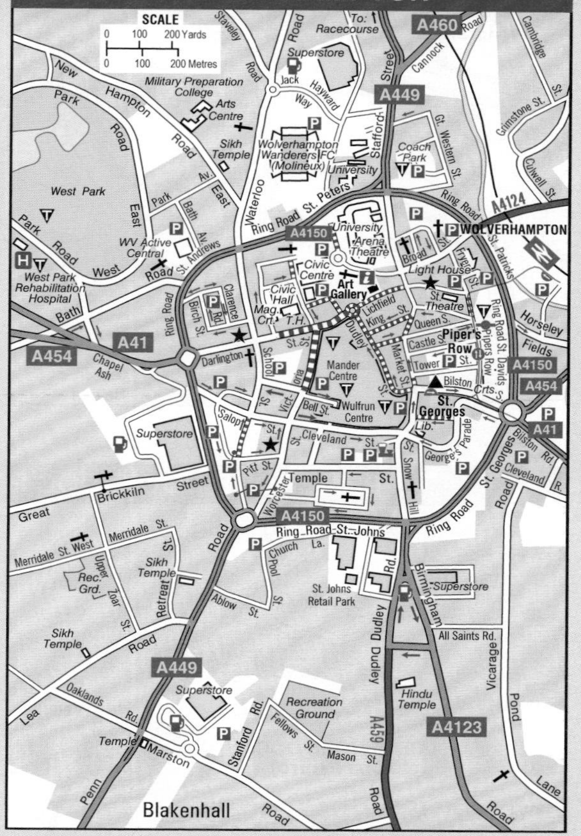

WORCESTER

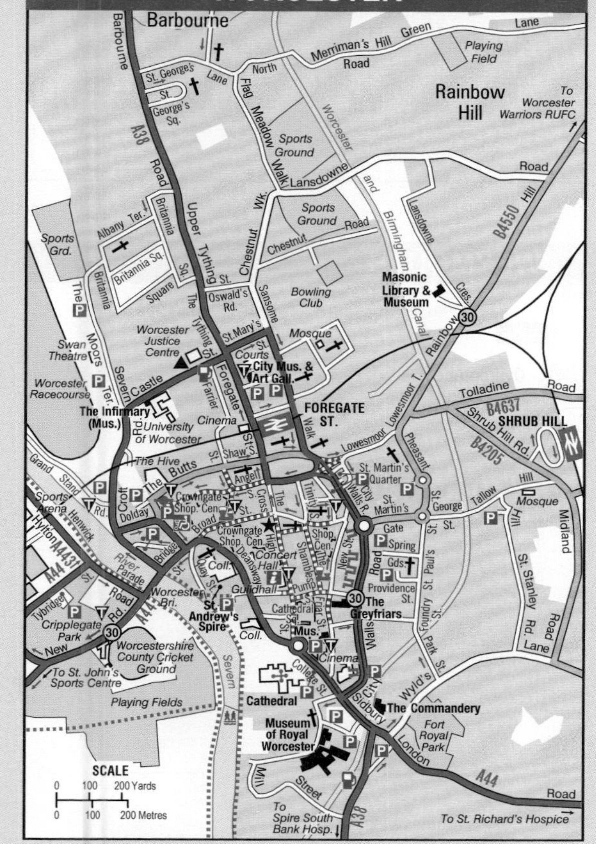

YORK

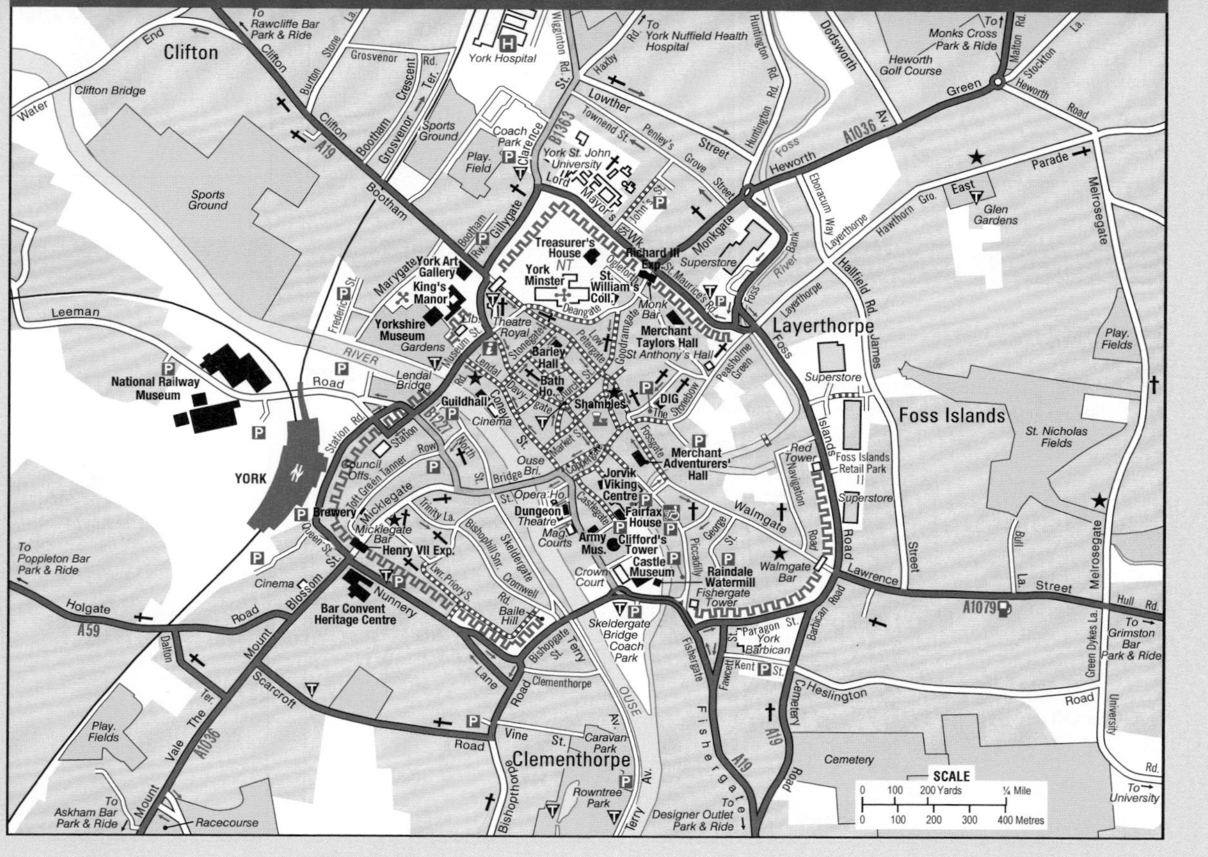

PORT PLANS

For detailed Plans of DOVER, PLYMOUTH and SOUTHAMPTON refer to Town Plans

HARWICH

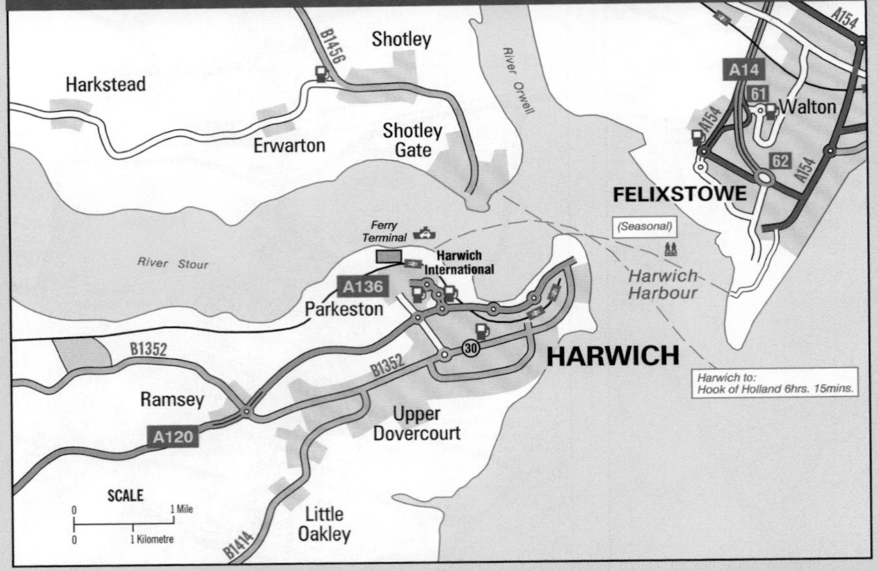

KINGSTON UPON HULL

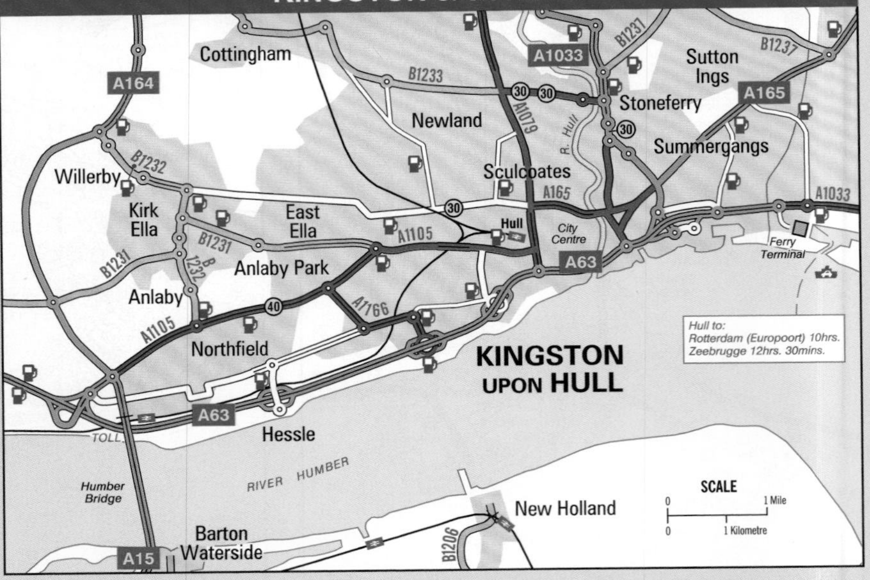

NEWCASTLE UPON TYNE

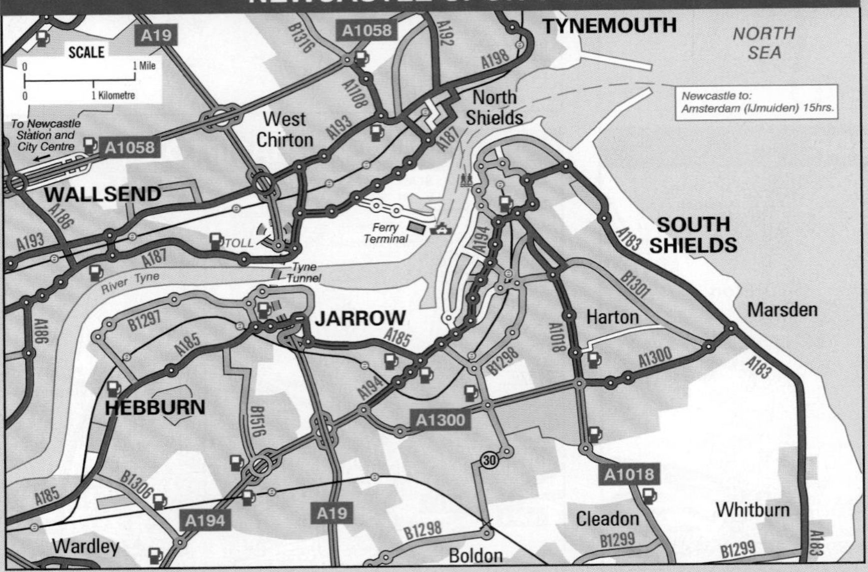

NEWHAVEN

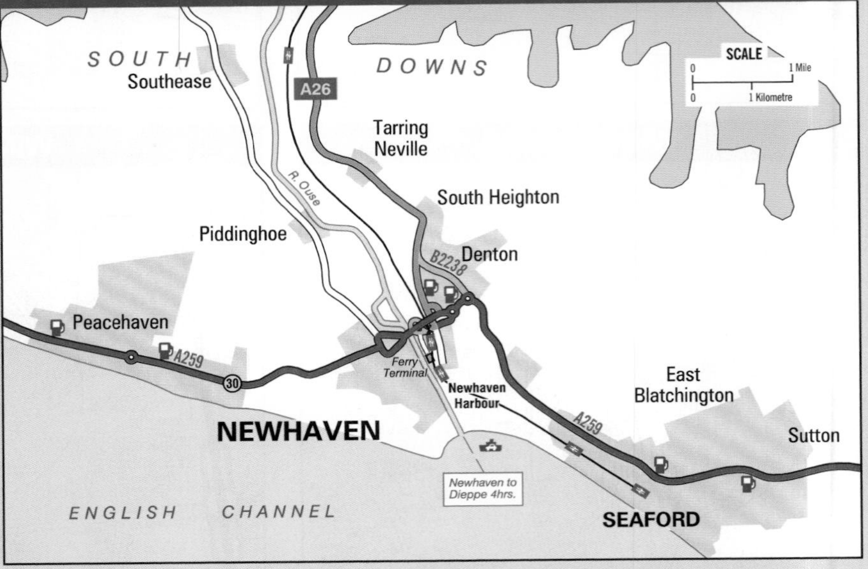

PEMBROKE DOCK (DOC PENFRO)

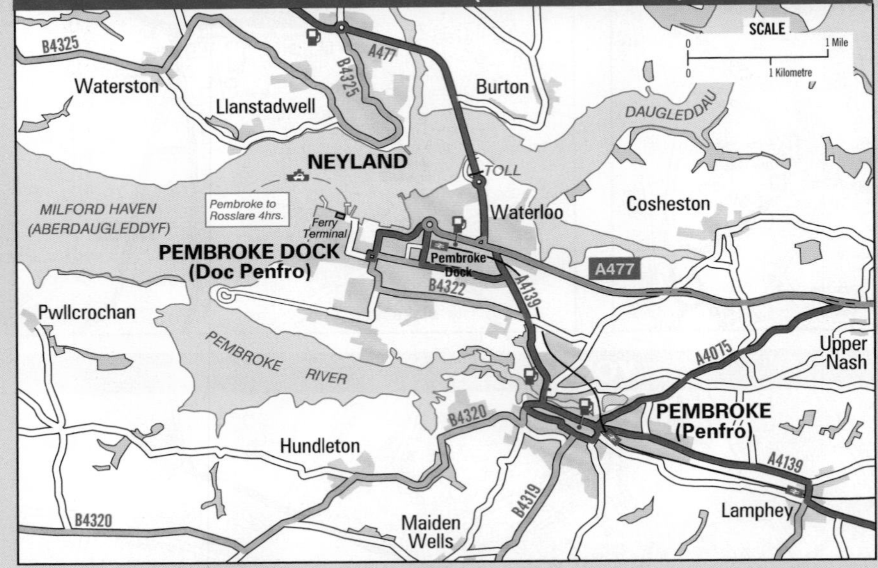

POOLE

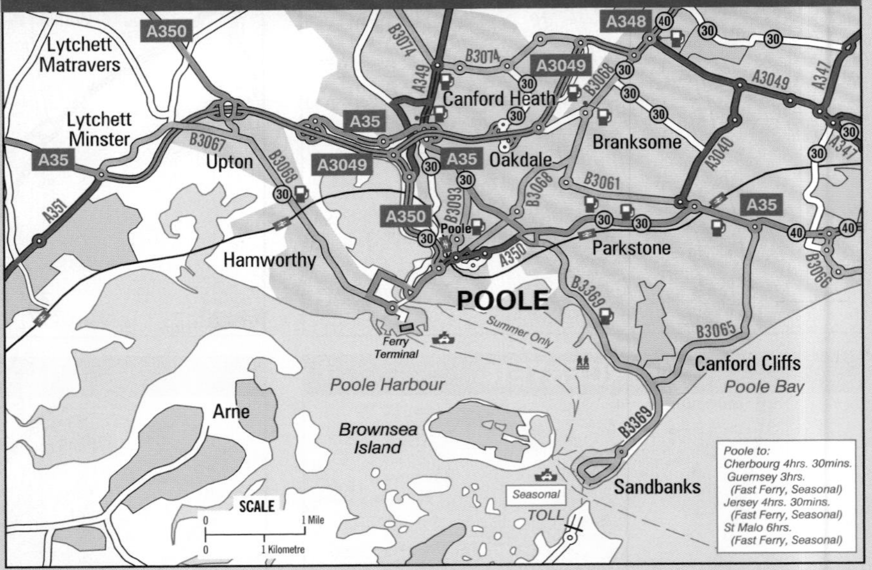

PORTSMOUTH

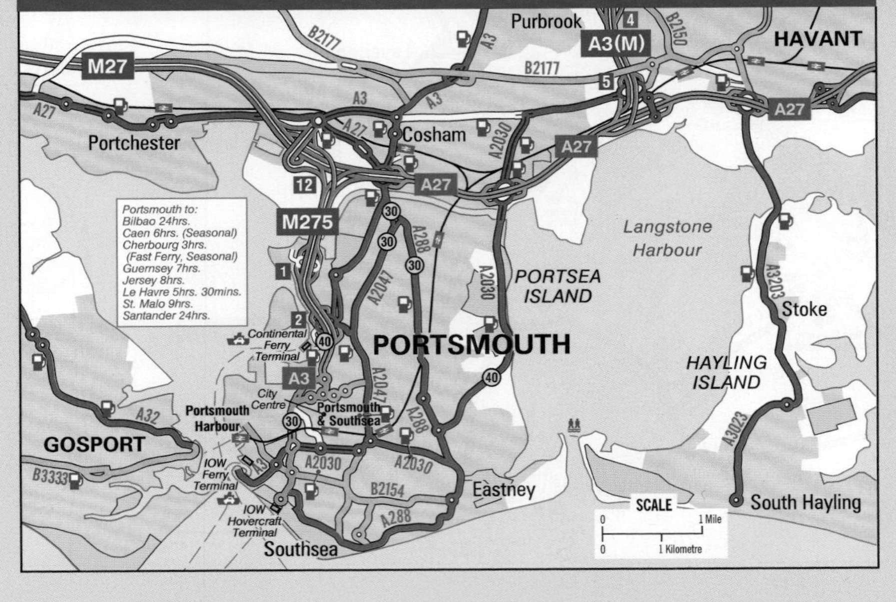

WEYMOUTH

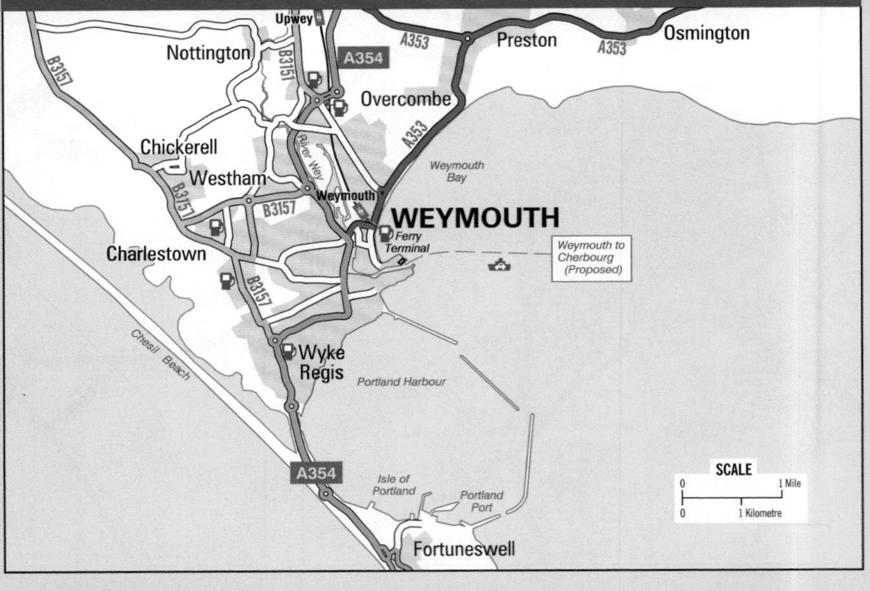

BIRMINGHAM

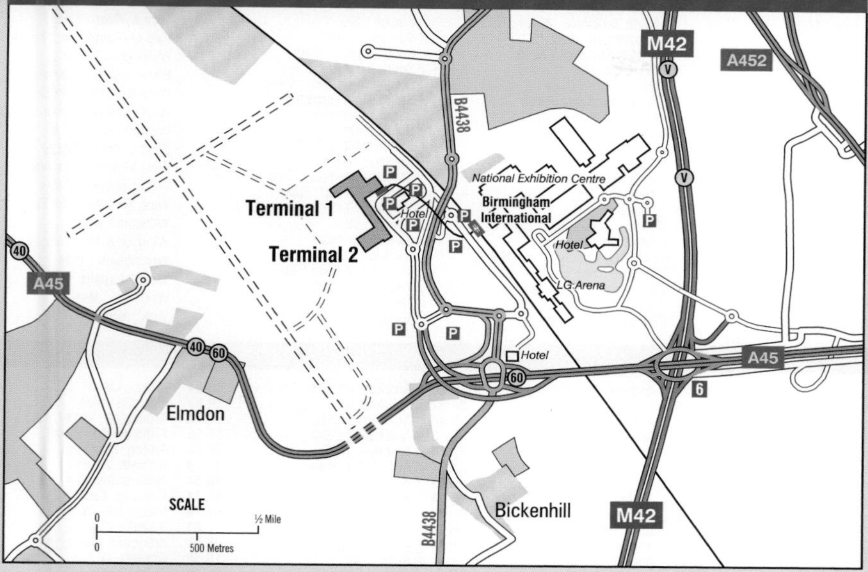

EAST MIDLANDS

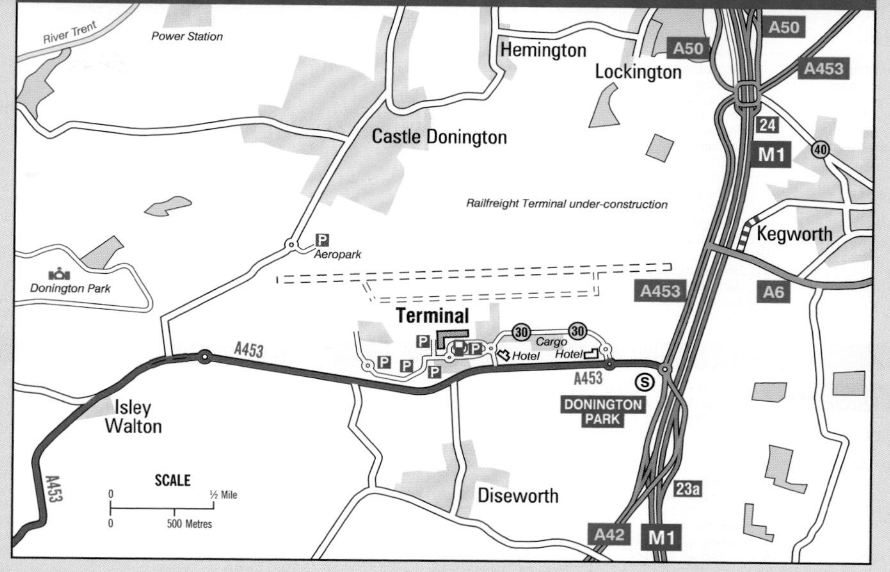

GLASGOW

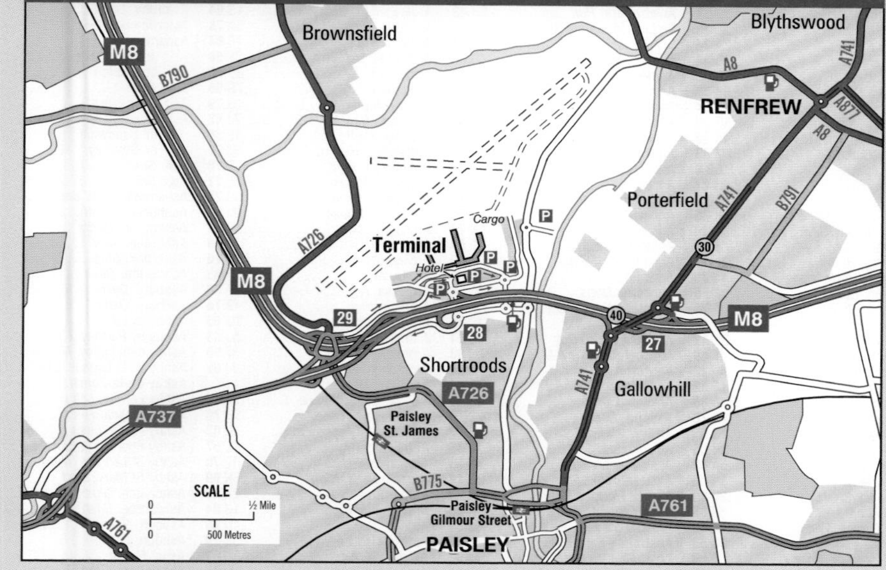

LONDON GATWICK

LONDON HEATHROW

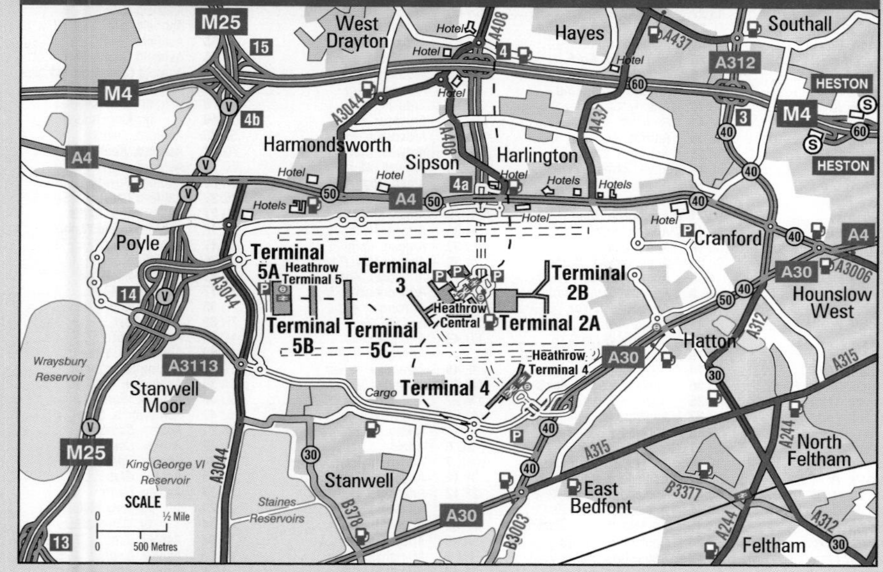

LONDON LUTON

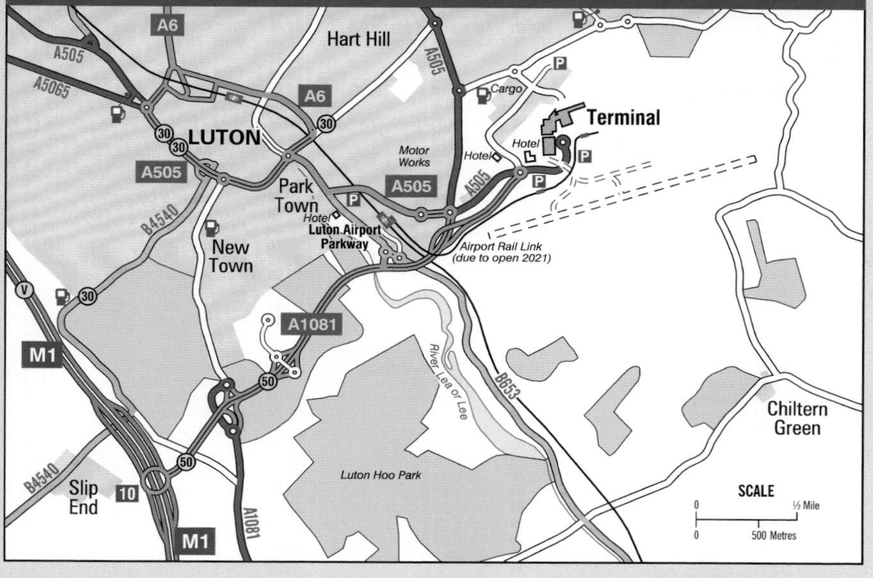

LONDON STANSTED

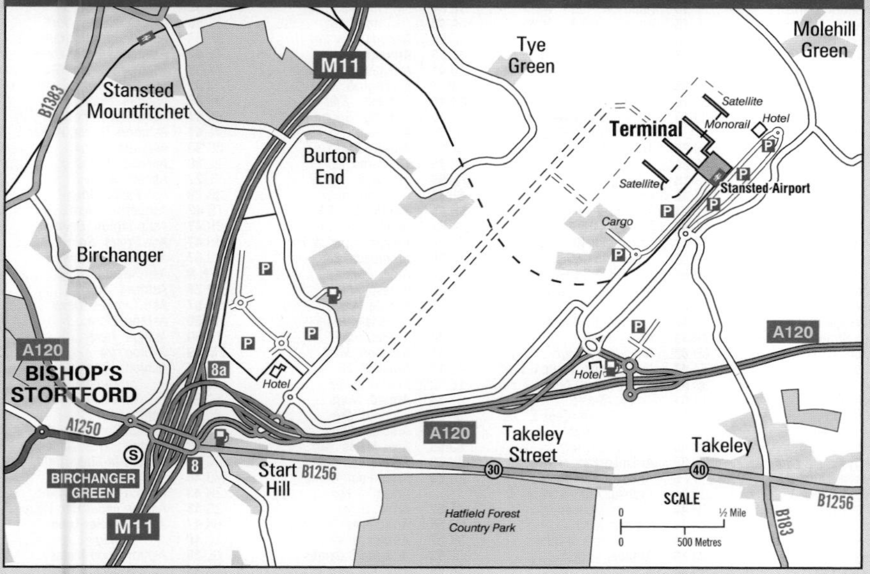

MANCHESTER

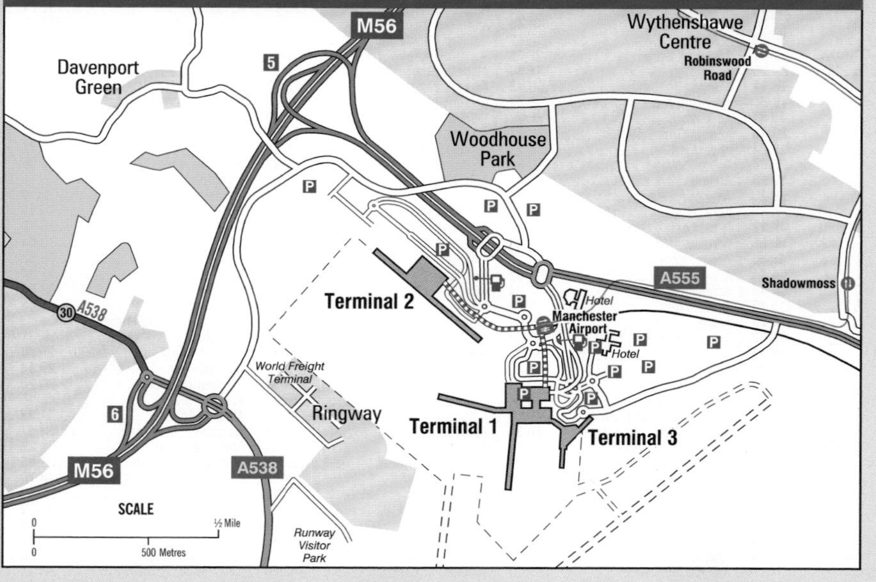

(1) A strict alphabetical order is used e.g. An Dùnan follows Andreas but precedes Andwell.

(2) The map reference given refers to the actual map square in which the town spot or built-up area is located and not to the place name.

(3) Major towns and destinations are shown in bold, i.e. **Aberdeen**. *Aber* **106** (5J **73**)
Page references for Town Plan entries are shown first.

(4) Where two or more places of the same name occur in the same County or Unitary Authority, the nearest large town is also given; e.g. Achiemore. *High* nr. *Durness* . . . .5F **84** indicates that Achiemore is located in square 5F on page **84** and is situated near Durness in the Unitary Authority of Highland.

(5) Only one reference is given although due to page overlaps the place may appear on more than one page.

INDEX

A

Ashurst. Kent 2B 12
Ashurst. Lanc 7C 40
Ashurst. W Sus 4J 11
Ashurst Wood. W Sus 2M 11
Ash Vale. Surr 8F 20
Ashwater. Devn 6C 6
Ashwell. Herts 8K 29
Ashwell. Rut 8F 36
Ashwellthorpe. Norf 2H 31
Ashwick. Som 1E 8
Ashwicken. Norf 8D 38
Ashwood. Staf 3G 27
Askam in Furness. Cumb 7M 45
Askern. S Yor 6C 42
Askerswell. Dors 6D 8
Askett. Buck 3F 20
Askham. Cumb 3D 46
Askham. Notts 2E 36
Askham Bryan. York 3C 42
Askham Richard. York 3C 42
Askrigg. N Yor 6H 47
Askwith. N Yor 3K 41
Aslackby. Linc 6H 37
Aslacton. Norf 2H 31
Aslockton. Notts 5E 36
Aspatria. Cumb 7F 52
Aspenden. Herts 1L 21
Asperton. Linc 6K 37
Aspley Guise. C Beds 8G 29
Aspley Heath. C Beds 8G 29
Aspull. G Man 7E 40
Asselby. E Yor 5E 42
Assington. Suff 8F 30
Assington Green. Suff 6D 30
Astbury. Ches E 3G 35
Astcote. Nptn 6D 28
Asterby. Linc 2K 37
Asterley. Shrp 1B 26
Asterton. Shrp 2B 26
Asthall. Oxon 2L 19
Asthall Leigh. Oxon 2M 19
Astle. High 4H 79
Astley. G Man 7F 40
Astley. Shrp 8D 34
Astley. Warw 3M 27
Astley. Worc 5F 26
Astley Abbotts. Shrp 2F 26
Astley Bridge. G Man 6F 40
Astley Cross. Worc 5G 27
Aston. Ches E 5E 34
Aston. Ches W 2D 34
Aston. Derbs
nr. Hope 1K 35
nr. Sudbury 6K 35
Aston. Flin 3B 34
Aston. Here 5C 26
Aston. Herts 1K 21
Aston. Oxon 3M 19
Aston. Shrp
nr. Bridgnorth 2G 27
nr. Wem 7D 34
Aston. S Yor 1B 36
Aston. Staf 5F 34
Aston. Telf 1E 26
Aston. W Mid 2J 27
Aston. Wok 5E 20
Aston Abbotts. Buck 1F 20
Aston Botterell. Shrp 3E 26
Aston-by-Stone. Staf 6H 35
Aston Cantlow. Warw 6K 27
Aston Clinton. Buck 2F 20
Aston Crews. Here 1E 18
Aston Cross. Glos 8H 27
Aston End. Herts 1K 21
Aston Eyre. Shrp 2E 26
Aston Fields. Worc 5H 27
Aston Flamville. Leics 2B 28
Aston Ingham. Here 1E 18
Aston juxta Mondrum. Ches E 4E 34
Astonlane. Shrp 2E 26
Aston le Walls. Nptn 6B 28
Aston Magna. Glos 8K 27
Aston Munslow. Shrp 3D 26
Aston on Carrant. Glos 8H 27
Aston on Clun. Shrp 3B 26
Aston-on-Trent. Derbs 7B 36
Aston Pigott. Shrp 1B 26
Aston Rogers. Shrp 1B 26
Aston Rowant. Oxon 4E 20
Aston Sandford. Buck 3E 20
Aston Somerville. Worc 8J 27
Aston Subedge. Glos 7K 27
Aston Tirrold. Oxon 5C 20
Aston Upthorpe. Oxon 5C 20
Astrop. Nptn 8C 28
Astwick. C Beds 8K 29
Astwood. Mil 7G 29
Astwood Bank. Worc 5J 27
Aswarby. Linc 6H 37
Aswardby. Linc 2L 37
Atcham. Shrp 1D 26
Atch Lench. Worc 6J 27
Athelhampton. Dors 6F 8
Athelington. Suff 4J 31
Athelney. Som 3B 8
Athelstaneford. E Lot 2C 60
Atherfield Green. IOW 8B 10
Atherington. Devn 3E 6
Atherington. W Sus 5H 11
Athersley. S Yor 7A 42
Atherstone. Warw 2M 27
Atherstone on Stour. Warw 6L 27
Atherton. G Man 7E 40
Ath-Tharracail. High 1A 64
Atlow. Derbs 5L 35
Attadale. High 2L 69
Attenborough. Notts 6C 36
Atterby. Linc 8G 43
Atterley. Shrp 2E 26
Atterton. Leics 2A 28
Attical. New M 7H 93
Attleborough. Norf 2G 31
Attleborough. Warw 2A 28
Attlebridge. Norf 8H 39
Atwick. E Yor 2J 43
Atworth. Wilts 7G 19
Auberrow. Here 7C 26
Aubourn. Linc 3G 37
Aucharnie. Abers 1F 72
Auchattie. Abers 6F 72
Auchavan. Ang 1E 66
Auchbreck. Mor 3B 72
Auchenback. E Ren 4D 58
Auchenblae. Abers 8G 73
Auchenbrack. Dum 2B 52
Auchenbreck. Arg 1K 57
Auchencairn. Dum
nr. Dalbeattie 6B 52
nr. Dumfries 3D 52
Auchencarroch. W Dun 1C 58
Auchencrow. Bord 3F 60
Auchendennan. Arg 1B 58
Auchendinny. Midl 3L 59
Auchengray. S Lan 4H 59
Auchenhalrig. Mor 7C 80
Auchenheath. S Lan 5G 59
Auchenlochan. Arg 2J 57
Auchenmade. N Ayr 5B 58
Auchenmalg. Dum 6H 51
Auchentiber. N Ayr 5B 58
Auchenvennel. Arg 1A 58
Auchindrain. Arg 7E 64
Auchininna. Abers 1F 72
Auchinleck. Dum 4K 51
Auchinleck. E Ayr 7D 58
Auchinloch. N Lan 2E 58
Auchinstarry. N Lan 2F 58
Auchleven. Abers 3F 72
Auchlochan. S Lan 6G 59
Auchlunachan. High 5B 78
Auchmillan. E Ayr 7D 58
Auchmithie. Ang 3K 67
Auchmuirbridge. Fife 7F 66
Auchmull. Ang 8E 72
Auchnacree. Ang 1H 67
Auchnafree. Per 4B 66
Auchnagallin. High 2L 71
Auchnagatt. Abers 1J 73
Aucholzie. Abers 6C 72
Auchreddie. Abers 1H 73
Auchterarder. Per 6C 66
Auchteraw. High 5D 70
Auchterderran. Fife 8F 66
Auchterhouse. Ang 4G 67
Auchtermuchty. Fife 6F 66
Auchterneed. High 8E 78
Auchtertool. Fife 8F 66
Auchtertyre. High 3K 69
Auchtubh. Stir 5K 65
Auckengill. High 5E 86
Auckley. S Yor 7D 42
Audenshaw. G Man 8H 41
Audlem. Ches E 5E 34
Audley. Staf 4F 34
Audley End. Essx 8B 30
Audmore. Staf 7G 35
Auds. Abers 7F 80
Augher. M Ulst 6D 92
Aughertree. Cumb 8G 53
Aughnacloy. M Ulst 6E 92
Aughton. E Yor 4E 42
Aughton. Lanc
nr. Lancaster 1D 40
nr. Ormskirk 7B 40
Aughton. S Yor 1B 36
Aughton. Wilts 8L 19
Aughton Park. Lanc 7C 40
Auldearn. High 8K 79
Aulden. Here 6C 26
Auldgirth. Dum 3D 52
Auldhouse. S Lan 4E 58
Ault a' chruinn. High 3L 69
Aultbea. High 5K 77
Aultdearg. High 7C 78
Aultgrishan. High 5J 77
Aultguish Inn. High 6D 78
Ault Hucknall. Derbs 3B 36
Aultibea. High 1L 79
Aultiphurst. High 5L 85
Aultivullin. High 5L 85
Aultmore. Mor 8D 80
Aultnamain Inn. High 5G 79
Aunby. Linc 8H 37
Aunsby. Linc 6H 37
Aust. S Glo 5D 18
Austerfield. S Yor 8D 42
Austin Fen. Linc 8L 43
Austrey. Warw 1L 27
Austwick. N Yor 1F 40
Authorpe. Linc 1M 37
Authorpe Row. Linc 2B 38
Avebury. Wilts 7K 19
Avebury Trusloe. Wilts 7J 19
Aveley. Thur 5B 22
Avening. Glos 4G 19
Averham. Notts 4E 36
Aveton Gifford. Devn 7J 5
Avielochan. High 4K 71
Aviemore. High 4J 71
Avington. Hants 2C 10
Avoch. High 8H 79
Avon. Hants 6K 9
Avonbridge. Falk 2H 59
Avon Dassett. Warw 6B 28
Avonmouth. Bris 6D 18
Avonwick. Devn 6K 5
Awbridge. Hants 3M 9
Awliscombe. Devn 5L 7
Awre. Glos 3F 18
Awsworth. Notts 5B 36
Axbridge. Som 8C 18
Axford. Hants 1D 10
Axford. Wilts 7L 19
Axminster. Devn 6B 8
Axmouth. Devn 6A 8
Aycliffe Village. Dur 3L 47
Aydon. Nmbd 5D 54
Aykley Heads. Dur 7F 54
Aylburton. Glos 3E 18
Aylburton Common. Glos 3E 18
Ayle. Nmbd 7M 53
Aylesbeare. Devn 6K 7
Aylesbury. Buck 2F 20
Aylesby. NE Lin 7K 43
Aylescott. Devn 4F 6
Aylesford. Kent 8D 22
Aylesham. Kent 8J 23
Aylestone. Leic 1C 28
Aylmerton. Norf 6H 39
Aylsham. Norf 7H 39
Aylton. Here 8E 26
Aylworth. Glos 1K 19
Aymestrey. Here 5C 26
Aynho. Nptn 8C 28
Ayot Green. Herts 2K 21
Ayot St Lawrence. Herts 2J 21
Ayot St Peter. Herts 2K 21
Ayr. S Ayr 7B 58
Ayres of Selivoe. Shet 3C 90
Ayreville. Torb 5L 5
Aysgarth. N Yor 7J 47
Ayshford. Devn 4K 7
Ayside. Cumb 7B 46
Ayston. Rut 1F 28
Ayton. Bord 3G 61
Aywick. Shet 5K 91
Azerley. N Yor 8L 47

B

Babbacombe. Torb 5M 5
Babbinswood. Shrp 6B 34
Babbs Green. Herts 2L 21
Babcary. Som 3D 8
Babel. Carm 1H 17
Babell. Flin 3L 33
Babingley. Norf 7C 38
Bablock Hythe. Oxon 3B 20
Babraham. Cambs 6B 30
Babworth. Notts 1D 36
Bac. W Isl 7H 83
Bachau. IOA 2D 32
Bacheldre. Powy 3M 25
Bachymbyd Fawr. Den 4K 33
Backaland. Orkn 6E 88
Backaskaill. Orkn 4D 88
Backbarrow. Cumb 7B 46
Backe. Carm 5J 15
Backfolds. Abers 8K 81
Backford. Ches W 2C 34
Backhill. Abers 2G 73
Backhill of Clackriach. Abers 1J 73
Backies. High 3J 79
Backmuir of New Gilston. Fife 7H 67
Back of Keppoch. High 7H 69
Back Street. Suff 6D 30
Backwell. N Som 7C 18
Backworth. Tyne 4G 55
Bacon End. Essx 2C 22
Baconsthorpe. Norf 6H 39
Bacton. Here 8B 26
Bacton. Norf 6K 39
Bacton. Suff 5G 31
Bacton Green. Norf 6K 39
Bacup. Lanc 5G 41
Badachonacher. High 6G 79
Badachro. High 6J 77
Badanloch Lodge. High 8K 85
Badavanich. High 8B 78
Badbury. Swin 5K 19
Badby. Nptn 6C 28
Badcall. High 6E 84
Badcaul. High 4M 77
Baddeley Green. Stoke 4H 35
Baddesley Clinton. W Mid 4L 27
Baddesley Ensor. Warw 2L 27
Baddidarach. High 1A 78
Baddoch. Abers 7M 71
Badenscallie. High 3M 77
Badenscoth. Abers 2G 73
Badentarbat. High 2M 77
Badgall. Corn 7B 6
Badgers Mount. Kent 7A 22
Badgeworth. Glos 2H 19
Badgworth. Som 8B 18
Badicaul. High 3J 69
Badingham. Suff 5K 31
Badlesmere. Kent 8G 23
Badlipster. High 7D 86
Badluarach. High 4L 77
Badminton. S Glo 5G 19
Badnaban. High 1A 78
Badnabay. High 7E 84
Badnagie. High 8C 86
Badnellan. High 3J 79
Badninish. High 4H 79
Badrallach. High 4A 78
Badsey. Worc 7J 27
Badshot Lea. Surr 1F 10
Badsworth. W Yor 6B 42
Badwell Ash. Suff 5F 30
Bae Cinmel. Cnwy 2J 33
Bae Colwyn. Cnwy 3H 33
Bae Penrhyn. Cnwy 2H 33
Bagby. N Yor 7B 48
Bag Enderby. Linc 2L 37
Bagendon. Glos 3J 19
Bagginswood. Shrp 3E 26
Bàgh a Chàise. W Isl 6A 76
Bàgh a' Chaisteil. W Isl 6C 74
Bagham. Kent 8G 23
Baghasdal. W Isl 4D 74
Bagh Mor. W Isl 8K 75
Bagh Shiarabhagh. W Isl 5D 74
Bagillt. Flin 3M 33
Baginton. Warw 4M 27
Baglan. Neat 5G 17
Bagley. Shrp 7C 34
Bagley. Som 1C 8
Bagnall. Staf 4H 35
Bagnor. W Ber 7B 20
Bagshot. Surr 7G 21
Bagshot. Wilts 7M 19
Bagstone. S Glo 5E 18
Bagthorpe. Norf 6D 38
Bagthorpe. Notts 4B 36
Bagworth. Leics 1B 28
Bagwy Llydiart. Here 1C 18
Baildon. W Yor 4K 41
Baildon Green. W Yor 4K 41
Baile. W Isl 5L 75
Baile Ailein. W Isl 1D 76
Baile an Truiseil. W Isl 6G 83
Baile Boidheach. Arg 2G 57
Baile Glas. W Isl 8K 75
Bailemeonach. Arg 3A 64
Baile Mhanaich. W Isl 8J 75
Baile Mhartainn. W Isl 6J 75
Baile MhicPhail. W Isl 6K 75
Baile Mor. W Isl 7J 75
Baile Mór. Arg 5H 63
Baile nan Cailleach. W Isl 8J 75
Baile Raghaill. W Isl 7J 75
Bailey Green. Hants 3D 10
Baileyhead. Cumb 3K 53
Baileysmill. Lis 6H 93
Bailiesward. Abers 2D 72
Bail' Iochdrach. W Isl 8K 75
Baillieston. Glas 3E 58
Bailrigg. Lanc 2C 40
Bail Uachdraich. W Isl 7K 75
Bail' Ur Tholastaidh. W Isl 7J 83
Bainbridge. N Yor 6H 47
Bainsford. Falk 1G 59
Bainshole. Abers 2F 72
Bainton. E Yor 2G 43
Bainton. Oxon 1C 20
Bainton. Pet 1H 29
Baintown. Fife 7G 67
Baker Street. Thur 5C 22
Bakewell. Derbs 3L 35
Bala. Gwyn 7J 33
Y Bala. Gwyn 7J 33
Balachuirn. High 1G 69
Balbeg. High
nr. Cannich 2E 70
nr. Loch Ness 3E 70
Balbeggie. Per 5E 66
Balblair. High
nr. Bonar Bridge 4F 78
nr. Invergordon 7H 79
nr. Inverness 1F 70
Balby. S Yor 7C 42
Balcathie. Ang 4K 67
Balchladich. High 8C 84
Balchraggan. High 1F 70
Balchrick. High 6D 84
Balcombe. W Sus 2L 11
Balcombe Lane. W Sus 2L 11
Balcurvie. Fife 7G 67
Baldersby. N Yor 8A 48
Baldersby St James. N Yor 8A 48
Balderstone. Lanc 4E 40
Balderton. Ches W 3B 34
Balderton. Notts 4F 36
Baldinnie. Fife 6H 67
Baldock. Herts 8K 29
Baldrine. IOM 6D 44
Baldslow. E Sus 4E 12
Baldwin. IOM 6C 44
Baldwinholme. Cumb 6H 53
Baldwin's Gate. Staf 6F 34
Bale. Norf 6G 39
Balearn. Abers 8K 81
Balemartine. Arg 3E 62
Balephetrish. Arg 3F 62
Balephuil. Arg 3E 62
Balerno. Edin 3K 59
Balevullin. Arg 3E 62
Balfield. Ang 1J 67
Balfour. Orkn 8D 88
Balfron. Stir 1D 58
Balgaveny. Abers 1F 72
Balgonar. Fife 8D 66
Balgowan. High 6G 71
Balgown. High 7E 76
Balgrochan. E Dun 2E 58
Balgy. High 8K 77
Balhalgardy. Abers 3G 73
Baliasta. Shet 3L 91
Baligill. High 5L 85
Balintore. Ang 2F 66
Balintore. High 6J 79
Balintraid. High 6H 79
Balk. N Yor 7B 48
Balkeerie. Ang 3G 67
Balkholme. E Yor 5E 42
Ball. Shrp 7B 34
Ballabeg. IOM 7B 44
Ballacannell. IOM 6D 44
Ballacarnane Beg. IOM 6C 44
Ballachulish. High 2E 64
Ballagyr. IOM 6B 44
Ballajora. IOM 5D 44
Ballaleigh. IOM 6C 44
Ballamodha. IOM 7B 44
Ballantrae. S Ayr 3F 50
Ballards Gore. Essx 4F 22
Ballasalla. IOM
nr. Castletown 7B 44
nr. Kirk Michael 5C 44
Ballater. Abers 6C 72
Ballaugh. IOM 5C 44
Ballencrieff. E Lot 2B 60
Ballencrieff Toll. W Lot 2H 59
Ballentoul. Per 1B 66
Ball Hill. Hants 7B 20
Ballidon. Derbs 4L 35
Balliemore. Arg
nr. Dunoon 1K 57
nr. Oban 5C 64
Ballieward. High 2L 71
Ballig. IOM 6B 44
Ballimore. Stir 6K 65
Ballinamallard. Ferm 6C 92
Ballindarragh. Ferm 7C 92
Ballingdon. Suff 7E 30
Ballinger Common. Buck 3G 21
Ballingham. Here 8D 26
Ballingry. Fife 8E 66
Ballinluig. Per 2C 66
Ballintoy. Caus 1G 93
Ballintuim. Per 2E 66
Balliveolan. Arg 3C 64
Balloan. High 3F 78
Balloch. High 1H 71
Balloch. N Lan 2F 58
Balloch. Per 6B 66
Balloch. W Dun 1B 58
Ballochan. Abers 6E 72
Ballochgoy. Arg 3K 57
Ballochmyle. E Ayr 7D 58
Ballochroy. Arg 4G 57
Balloo. Ards 5J 93
Balls Cross. W Sus 3G 11
Ball's Green. E Sus 2A 12
Ballsmill. New M 7F 93
Ballyalton. New M 6J 93
Ballybogy. Caus 2F 93
Ballycarry. ME Ant 4J 93
Ballycassidy. Ferm 6C 92
Ballycastle. Caus 1G 93
Ballyclare. Ant 4H 93
Ballyeaston. Ant 4H 93
Ballygally. ME Ant 3H 93
Ballygawley. M Ulst 6E 92
Ballygowan. Ards 5J 93
Ballygown. Arg 3K 63
Ballygrant. Arg 3C 56
Ballyhalbert. Ards 5K 93
Ballyholland. New M 7G 93
Ballyhornan. New M 6J 93
Ballykelly. Caus 2E 92
Ballykinler. New M 7J 93
Ballylesson. Lis 5H 93
Ballymagorry. Derr 3C 92
Ballymartin. New M 7H 93
Ballymena. ME Ant 3G 93
Ballymichael. N Ayr 6J 57
Ballymoney. Caus 2F 93
Ballynagard. Derr 2D 92
Ballynahinch. New M 6H 93
Ballynakilly. M Ulst 5F 93
Ballynoe. New M 6J 93
Ballynure. Ant 4H 93
Ballyrashane. Caus 2F 93
Ballyrobert. Ant 4H 93
Ballyronan. M Ulst 4F 93
Ballyroney. Arm 7H 93
Ballyscullion. Caus 2E 92
Ballystrudder. ME Ant 4J 93
Ballyvoy. Caus 1G 93
Ballyward. New M 7H 93
Ballywater. Ards 5K 93
Ballywonard. Ant 4H 93
Balmacara. High 3K 69
Balmaclellan. Dum 4A 52
Balmacqueen. High 6F 76
Balmaha. Stir 8J 65
Balmalcolm. Fife 7G 67
Balmalloch. N Lan 2F 58
Balmeanach. High 2G 69
Balmedie. Abers 4J 73
Balmerino. Fife 5G 67
Balmerlawn. Hants 5M 9
Balmore. E Dun 2E 58
Balmore. High 1D 68
Balmullo. Fife 5H 67
Balmurrie. Dum 5H 51
Balnaboth. Ang 1G 67
Balnabruaich. High 6H 79
Balnabruich. High 1A 80
Balnacoil. High 2J 79
Balnacra. High 1L 69
Balnacroft. Abers 6B 72
Balnageith. Mor 8L 79
Balnaglaic. High 2E 70
Balnagrantach. High 2E 70
Balnaguard. Per 2C 66
Balnahard. Arg 8K 63
Balnain. High 2E 70
Balnakeil. High 5F 84
Balnaknock. High 7F 76
Balnamoon. Abers 8J 81
Balnamoon. Ang 1J 67
Balnamore. Caus 2F 93
Balnapaling. High 7H 79
Balornock. Glas 3E 58
Balquhidder. Stir 5K 65
Balsall. W Mid 4L 27
Balsall Common. W Mid 4L 27
Balscote. Oxon 7A 28
Balsham. Cambs 6B 30
Balstonia. Thur 5C 22
Baltasound. Shet 3L 91
Balterley. Staf 4F 34
Baltersan. Dum 5K 51
Balthangie. Abers 8H 81
Baltonsborough. Som 2D 8
Balvaird. High 8F 78
Balvaird. Per 6E 66
Balvenie. Mor 1C 72
Balvicar. Arg 6B 64
Balvraid. High 4K 69
Balvraid Lodge. High 2J 71
Bamber Bridge. Lanc 5D 40
Bamber's Green. Essx 1B 22
Bamburgh. Nmbd 6J 61
Bamford. Derbs 1L 35
Bamfurlong. G Man 7D 40
Bampton. Cumb 4D 46
Bampton. Devn 3J 7
Bampton. Oxon 3M 19
Bampton Grange. Cumb 4D 46
Banavie. High 8B 70
Banbridge. Arm 6G 93
Banbury. Oxon 7B 28
Bancffosfelen. Carm 5L 15
Banchory. Abers 6F 72
Banchory-Devenick. Abers 5J 73
Bancycapel. Carm 5L 15
Bancyfelin. Carm 5K 15
Banc-y-ffordd. Carm 3L 15
Banff. Abers 7F 80
Bangor. Ards 4J 93
Bangor. Gwyn 3E 32
Bangor-is-y-coed. Wrex 5B 34
Bangors. Corn 6B 6
Bangor's Green. Lanc 7B 40
Banham. Norf 3G 31
Bank. Hants 5L 9
The Bank. Ches E 4G 35
The Bank. Shrp 2E 26
Bankend. Dum 5E 52
Bankfoot. Per 4D 66
Bankglen. E Ayr 8E 58
Bankhead. Aber 4H 73
Bankhead. Abers 5F 72
Bankhead. S Lan 5G 59
Bankland. Som 3B 8
Bank Newton. N Yor 2H 41
Banknock. Falk 2F 58
Banks. Cumb 5K 53
Banks. Lanc 5B 40
Bankshill. Dum 3F 52
Bank Street. Worc 5E 26
Bank Top. Lanc 7D 40
Banners Gate. W Mid 2J 27
Banningham. Norf 7J 39
Banniskirk. High 6C 86
Bannister Green. Essx 1C 22
Bannockburn. Stir 8B 66
Banstead. Surr 8K 21
Bantham. Devn 7J 5
Banton. N Lan 2F 58
Banwell. N Som 8B 18
Banyard's Green. Suff 4K 31
Bapchild. Kent 7F 22
Bapton. Wilts 2H 9
Barabhas. W Isl 6G 83
Barabhas Iarach. W Isl 7G 83
Baramore. High 8H 69
Barassie. S Ayr 6B 58
Baravullin. Arg 3D 64
Barbaraville. High 6H 79
Barber Booth. Derbs 1K 35
Barber Green. Cumb 7B 46
Barbhas Uarach. W Isl 6G 83
Barbieston. S Ayr 8C 58
Barbon. Cumb 7E 46
Barbourne. Worc 6G 27
Barbridge. Ches E 4E 34
Barbrook. Devn 1G 7
Barby. Nptn 4C 28
Barby Nortoft. Nptn 4C 28
Barcaldine. Arg 3D 64
Barcheston. Warw 8L 27
Barclose. Cumb 5J 53
Barcombe. E Sus 4M 11
Barcombe Cross. E Sus 4M 11
Barden. N Yor 6K 47
Barden Scale. N Yor 2J 41
Bardfield End Green. Essx 8C 30
Bardfield Saling. Essx 1C 22
Bardister. Shet 6H 91
Bardnabeinne. High 4H 79
Bardney. Linc 3J 37
Bardon. Leics 8B 36
Bardon Mill. Nmbd 5A 54
Bardowie. E Dun 2D 58
Bardrainney. Inv 2B 58
Bardsea. Cumb 8B 46
Bardsey. W Yor 3A 42
Bardsley. G Man 7H 41
Bardwell. Suff 4F 30
Bare. Lanc 1C 40
Barelees. Nmbd 6F 60
Barewood. Here 6B 26
Barford. Hants 2F 10
Barford. Norf 1H 31
Barford. Warw 5L 27
Barford St John. Oxon 8B 28
Barford St Martin. Wilts 2J 9
Barford St Michael. Oxon 8B 28
Barfrestone. Kent 8J 23
Bargeddie. N Lan 3E 58
Bargod. Cphy 5L 17
Bargoed. Cphy 5L 17
Bargrennan. Dum 4J 51
Barham. Cambs 4J 29
Barham. Kent 8J 23
Barham. Suff 6H 31
Barharrow. Dum 6M 51
Bar Hill. Cambs 5L 29
Barholm. Linc 8H 37
Barkby. Leics 1D 28
Barkestone-le-Vale. Leics 6E 36
Barkham. Wok 7E 20
Barking. G Lon 5M 21
Barking. Suff 6G 31
Barkingside. G Lon 5A 22
Barking Tye. Suff 6G 31
Barkisland. W Yor 6J 41
Barkston. Linc 5G 37
Barkston Ash. N Yor 4B 42
Barkway. Herts 8L 29
Barlanark. Glas 3E 58
Barlaston. Staf 6G 35
Barlavington. W Sus 4G 11
Barlborough. Derbs 2B 36
Barlby. N Yor 4D 42
Barlestone. Leics 1B 28
Barley. Herts 8L 29
Barley. Lanc 3G 41
Barley Mow. Tyne 6F 54
Barleythorpe. Rut 1F 28
Barling. Essx 5F 22
Barlings. Linc 2H 37
Barlow. Derbs 2M 35
Barlow. N Yor 5D 42
Barlow. Tyne 5E 54
Barmby Moor. E Yor 3E 42
Barmby on the Marsh. E Yor 5D 42
Barmer. Norf 6E 38
Barming. Kent 8D 22
Barming Heath. Kent 8D 22
Barmoor. Nmbd 6H 61
Barmouth. Gwyn 1F 24
Barmpton. Darl 4M 47
Barmston. E Yor 2J 43
Barmulloch. Glas 3E 58
Barnack. Pet 1H 29
Barnacle. Warw 3A 28
Barnard Castle. Dur 4J 47
Barnard Gate. Oxon 2B 20
Barnardiston. Suff 7D 30
Barnbarroch. Dum 6C 52
Barnburgh. S Yor 7B 42
Barnby. Suff 3L 31
Barnby Dun. S Yor 7D 42
Barnby in the Willows. Notts 4F 36
Barnby Moor. Notts 1D 36
Barnes. G Lon 6K 21
Barnes Street. Kent 1C 12
Barnet. G Lon 4K 21
Barnetby le Wold. N Lin 7H 43
Barney. Norf 6F 38
Barnham. Suff 4E 30
Barnham. W Sus 5G 11
Barnham Broom. Norf 1G 31
Barnhead. Ang 2K 67
Barnhill. D'dee 4H 67
Barnhill. Mor 8M 79
Barnhill. Per 5E 66
Barnhills. Dum 4E 50
Barningham. Dur 4J 47
Barningham. Suff 4F 30
Barnoldby le Beck. NE Lin 7K 43
Barnoldswick. Lanc 3G 41
Barns Green. W Sus 3J 11
Barnsley. Glos 3J 19
Barnsley. Shrp 2F 26
Barnsley. S Yor 7M 41
Barnstaple. Devn 2E 6
Barnston. Essx 2C 22
Barnston. Mers 1A 34
Barnstone. Notts 6E 36
Barnt Green. Worc 4J 27
Barnton. Ches W 2E 34
Barnwell. Cambs 6A 30
Barnwell. Nptn 3H 29
Barnwood. Glos 2G 19
Barons Cross. Here 6C 26
The Barony. Orkn 7B 88
Barr. Dum 1B 52
Barr. S Ayr 2H 51
Barra Airport. W Isl 5C 74
Barrachan. Dum 7J 51
Barraglom. W Isl 8E 82
Barrahormid. Arg 1G 57
Barrapol. Arg 3E 62
Barrasford. Nmbd 4C 54
Barravullin. Arg 7C 64
Barregarrow. IOM 6C 44
Barrhead. E Ren 4D 58
Barrhill. S Ayr 3H 51
Barri. V Glam 8L 17
Barrington. Cambs 7L 29
Barrington. Som 4B 8
Barripper. Corn 5K 3
Barrmill. N Ayr 4B 58
Barrock. High 4D 86
Barrow. Lanc 4F 40
Barrow. Rut 8F 36
Barrow. Shrp 1E 26
Barrow. Som 2F 8
Barrow. Suff 5D 30
Barroway Drove. Norf 1B 30
Barrow Bridge. G Man 6E 40
Barrowburn. Nmbd 8F 60
Barrowby. Linc 6F 36
Barrowcliff. N Yor 7H 49
Barrow Common. N Som 7D 18
Barrowden. Rut 1G 29
Barrowford. Lanc 4G 41
Barrow Gurney. N Som 7D 18
Barrow Haven. N Lin 5H 43
Barrow Hill. Derbs 2B 36
Barrow-in-Furness. Cumb 8M 45
Barrow Nook. Lanc 7C 40
Barrow's Green. Hal 1D 34
Barrows Green. Cumb 7D 46
Barrow Street. Wilts 2G 9
Barrow upon Humber. N Lin 5H 43
Barrow upon Soar. Leics 8C 36
Barrow upon Trent. Derbs 7A 36
Barry. Ang 4J 67
Barry. V Glam 8L 17
Barry Island. V Glam 8L 17
Barsby. Leics 8D 36
Barsham. Suff 3K 31
Barston. W Mid 4L 27
Bartestree. Here 7D 26
Barthol Chapel. Abers 2H 73
Bartholomew Green. Essx 1D 22
Barthomley. Ches E 4F 34
Bartley. Hants 4M 9
Bartley Green. W Mid 3J 27
Bartlow. Cambs 7B 30
Barton. Cambs 6M 29
Barton. Ches W 4C 34
Barton. Cumb 3C 46
Barton. Glos 1K 19
Barton. IOW 7C 10
Barton. Lanc
nr. Ormskirk 7B 40
nr. Preston 4D 40
Barton. N Som 8B 18
Barton. N Yor 5L 47
Barton. Oxon 3C 20
Barton. Torb 5M 5
Barton. Warw 6K 27
Barton Bendish. Norf 1D 30
Barton Gate. Staf 8K 35
Barton Green. Staf 8K 35
Barton Hartsthorn. Buck 8D 28
Barton Hill. N Yor 1E 42
Barton in Fabis. Notts 6C 36
Barton in the Beans. Leics 1A 28
Barton-le-Clay. C Beds 8H 29
Barton-le-Street. N Yor 8E 48
Barton-le-Willows. N Yor 1E 42
Barton Mills. Suff 4D 30
Barton on Sea. Hants 6L 9
Barton-on-the-Heath. Warw 8L 27
Barton St David. Som 2D 8
Barton Seagrave. Nptn 4F 28
Barton Stacey. Hants 1B 10
Barton Town. Devn 1F 6
Barton Turf. Norf 7K 39
Barton-Under-Needwood. Staf 8K 35
Barton-upon-Humber. N Lin 5H 43
Barton Waterside. N Lin 5H 43
Barugh Green. S Yor 7M 41
Barway. Cambs 4B 30
Barwell. Leics 2B 28
Barwick. Herts 2L 21
Barwick. Som 4D 8
Barwick in Elmet. W Yor 4A 42
Baschurch. Shrp 7C 34
Bascote. Warw 5B 28
Basford Green. Staf 4H 35
Bashall Eaves. Lanc 3E 40
Bashall Town. Lanc 3F 40
Bashley. Hants 6L 9
Basildon. Essx 5D 22
Basingstoke. Hants 8D 20
Baslow. Derbs 2L 35
Bason Bridge. Som 1B 8
Bassaleg. Newp 5A 18
Bassendean. Bord 5D 60
Bassenthwaite. Cumb 8G 53
Bassett. Sotn 4B 10
Bassingbourn. Cambs 7L 29
Bassingfield. Notts 6D 36
Bassingham. Linc 3G 37
Bassingthorpe. Linc 7G 37
Bassus Green. Herts 1L 21
Basta. Shet 4K 91
Baston. Linc 8J 37
Bastonford. Worc 6G 27
Bastwick. Norf 8L 39
Batchley. Worc 5J 27
Batchworth. Herts 4H 21
Batcombe. Dors 5E 8
Batcombe. Som 2E 8
Bate Heath. Ches E 2E 34
Bath. Bath 106 (7F 18)
Bathampton. Bath 7F 18
Bathealton. Som 3K 7
Batheaston. Bath 7F 18
Bathford. Bath 7F 18
Bathgate. W Lot 3H 59
Bathley. Notts 4E 36
Bathpool. Corn 8B 6
Bathpool. Som 3A 8
Bathville. W Lot 3H 59
Bathway. Som 8D 18
Batley. W Yor 5L 41
Batsford. Glos 8K 27
Batson. Devn 8K 5
Battersby. N Yor 5C 48
Battersea. G Lon 6K 21
Battisborough Cross. Devn 7J 5
Battisford. Suff 6G 31
Battisford Tye. Suff 6G 31
Battle. E Sus 4D 12
Battle. Powy 1K 17
Battleborough. Som 8B 18
Battledown. Glos 1H 19
Battlefield. Shrp 8D 34
Battlesbridge. Essx 4D 22
Battlesden. C Beds 1G 21
Battlesea Green. Suff 4J 31
Battleton. Som 3J 7
Battram. Leics 1B 28
Battramsley. Hants 6M 9
Batt's Corner. Surr 1F 10
Bauds of Cullen. Mor 7D 80
Baugh. Arg 3F 62
Baughton. Worc 7G 27
Baughurst. Hants 7C 20
Baulking. Oxon 4M 19
Baumber. Linc 2K 37
Baunton. Glos 3J 19
Baverstock. Wilts 2J 9
Bawburgh. Norf 1H 31
Bawdeswell. Norf 7G 39
Bawdrip. Som 2B 8
Bawdsey. Suff 7K 31
Bawsey. Norf 8C 38
Bawtry. S Yor 8D 42
Baxenden. Lanc 5F 40
Baxterley. Warw 2L 27
Baxter's Green. Suff 6D 30
Bay. High 8D 76
Baybridge. Hants 3C 10
Baybridge. Nmbd 6C 54
Baycliff. Cumb 8A 46
Baydon. Wilts 6L 19
Bayford. Herts 3L 21
Bayford. Som 3F 8
Bayles. Cumb 7M 53
Baylham. Suff 6H 31
Baynard's Green. Oxon 1C 20
Bayston Hill. Shrp 1C 26
Baythorne End. Essx 7D 30
Baythorpe. Linc 5K 37
Bayton. Worc 4E 26
Bayton Common. Worc 4F 26
Bayworth. Oxon 3C 20
Beach. S Glo 6F 18
Beachampton. Buck 8E 28
Beachamwell. Norf 1D 30
Beachley. Glos 4D 18
Beacon. Devn 5L 7
Beacon End. Essx 1F 22
Beacon Hill. Surr 2F 10
Beacon's Bottom. Buck 4E 20
Beaconsfield. Buck 4G 21
Beacrabhaic. W Isl 4C 76
Beadlam. N Yor 7D 48
Beadnell. Nmbd 7K 61
Beaford. Devn 4E 6
Beal. Nmbd 5H 61
Beal. N Yor 5C 42
Bealsmill. Corn 8C 6
Beam Hill. Staf 7L 35
Beamhurst. Staf 6J 35
Beaminster. Dors 5C 8
Beamish. Dur 6F 54
Beamond End. Buck 4G 21
Beamsley. N Yor 2J 41
Bean. Kent 6B 22
Beanacre. Wilts 7H 19
Beanley. Nmbd 8H 61
Beaquoy. Orkn 7C 88
Beardwood. Bkbn 5E 40
Beare Green. Surr 1J 11
Bearley. Warw 5K 27
Bearpark. Dur 7F 54
Bearsbridge. Nmbd 6A 54
Bearsden. E Dun 2D 58
Bearsted. Kent 8D 22
Bearstone. Shrp 6F 34
Bearwood. Pool 6J 9
Bearwood. W Mid 3J 27
Beattock. Dum 1E 52
Beauchamp Roding. Essx 2B 22
Beauchief. S Yor 1M 35
Beaufort. Blae 3L 17
Beaulieu. Hants 5A 10
Beauly. High 1F 70
Beaumaris. IOA 3F 32
Beaumont. Cumb 6H 53
Beaumont. Essx 1H 23
Beaumont Hill. Darl 4L 47
Beaumont Leys. Leic 1C 28
Beausale. Warw 4L 27
Beauvale. Notts 5B 36
Beauworth. Hants 3C 10
Beaworthy. Devn 6D 6
Beazley End. Essx 1D 22
Bebington. Mers 1B 34
Bebside. Nmbd 3F 54
Beccles. Suff 3L 31
Becconsall. Lanc 5C 40
Beckbury. Shrp 1F 26
Beckenham. G Lon 7L 21
Beckermet. Cumb 4K 45
Beckett End. Norf 2D 30
Beck Foot. Cumb 6E 46
Beckfoot. Cumb
nr. Broughton in Furness 6L 45
nr. Seascale 4L 45
nr. Silloth 7E 52
Beckford. Worc 8H 27
Beckhampton. Wilts 7J 19
Beck Hole. N Yor 5F 48
Beckingham. Linc 4F 36
Beckingham. Notts 8E 42
Beckington. Som 8G 19
Beckley. E Sus 3E 12
Beckley. Hants 6L 9
Beckley. Oxon 2C 20
Beck Row. Suff 4C 30
Beck Side. Cumb
nr. Cartmel 7B 46
nr. Ulverston 6M 45
Beckside. Cumb 7E 46
Beckton. G Lon 5M 21
Beckwithshaw. N Yor 2L 41
Becontree. G Lon 5A 22
Bedale. N Yor 7L 47
Bedburn. Dur 8E 54
Bedchester. Dors 4G 9
Beddau. Rhon 6K 17
Beddgelert. Gwyn 6E 32
Beddingham. E Sus 5M 11
Beddington. G Lon 7L 21
Bedfield. Suff 5J 31
Bedford. Bed 7H 29
Bedford. G Man 8E 40
Bedham. W Sus 3H 11
Bedhampton. Hants 5E 10
Bedingfield. Suff 5H 31
Bedingham Green. Norf 2J 31
Bedlam. N Yor 1L 41
Bedlar's Green. Essx 1B 22
Bedlington. Nmbd 3F 54
Bedlinog. Mer T 4K 17
Bedminster. Bris 6D 18
Bedmond. Herts 3H 21
Bednall. Staf 8H 35
Bedrule. Bord 8D 60
Bedstone. Shrp 4B 26
Bedwas. Cphy 6L 17
Bedwellty. Cphy 4L 17
Bedworth. Warw 3A 28
Beeby. Leics 1D 28
Beech. Hants 2D 10
Beech. Staf 6G 35
Beechcliffe. W Yor 3J 41
Beech Hill. W Ber 7D 20
Beechingstoke. Wilts 8J 19
Beedon. W Ber 6B 20
Beeford. E Yor 2J 43
Beeley. Derbs 3L 35
Beelsby. NE Lin 7K 43
Beenham. W Ber 7C 20
Beeny. Corn 2D 4
Beer. Devn 7M 7
Beer. Som 2C 8
Beercrocombe. Som 3B 8
Beer Hackett. Dors 4E 8
Beesands. Devn 7L 5
Beesby. Linc 1A 38
Beeson. Devn 7L 5
Beeston. C Beds 7J 29
Beeston. Ches W 4D 34
Beeston. Norf 8F 38
Beeston. Notts 6C 36
Beeston. W Yor 4L 41
Beeston Regis. Norf 5H 39
Beeswing. Dum 5C 52
Beetham. Cumb 8C 46
Beetham. Som 4A 8
Beetley. Norf 8F 38
Beffcote. Staf 8G 35
Began. Card 6M 17
Begbroke. Oxon 2B 20
Begdale. Cambs 1A 30
Begelly. Pemb 6H 15
Beggar Hill. Essx 3C 22
Beggar's Bush. Powy 5A 26
Beggearn Huish. Som 2K 7
Beguildy. Powy 5L 25
Beighton. Norf 1K 31
Beighton. S Yor 1B 36
Beighton Hill. Derbs 4L 35
Beinn Casgro. W Isl 1F 76
Beith. N Ayr 4B 58
Bekesbourne. Kent 8H 23
Belaugh. Norf 8J 39
Belbroughton. Worc 4H 27
Belchalwell. Dors 5F 8
Belchalwell Street. Dors 5F 8
Belchamp Otten. Essx 7E 30
Belchamp St Paul. Essx 7D 30
Belchamp Walter. Essx 7E 30
Belchford. Linc 2K 37
Belcoo. Ferm 7B 92
Belfast. Bel 5H 93
Belfast City George Best Airport. Bel 5H 93
Belfast International Airport. Ant 4G 93
Belfatton. Abers 8K 81
Belford. Nmbd 6J 61
Belgrano. Cnwy 3J 33
Belhaven. E Lot 2D 60
Belhelvie. Abers 4J 73
Belhinnie. Abers 3D 72
Bellabeg. Abers 4C 72
Belladrum. High 1F 70
Bellaghy. M Ulst 4F 93
Bellamore. S Ayr 3H 51
Bellanaleck. Ferm 7C 92
Bellanoch. Arg 8C 64
Bell Busk. N Yor 2H 41
Belleau. Linc 2M 37
Belleek. Ferm 6A 92
Belleek. New M 7F 93
Belleheiglash. Mor 2A 72
Bell End. Worc 4H 27
Bellerby. N Yor 6K 47
Bellerby Camp. N Yor 6J 47
Bellever. Devn 8F 6
Belle Vue. Cumb 8F 52
Belle Vue. Shrp 8C 34
Bellfield. S Lan 6G 59
Belliehill. Ang 1J 67
Bellingdon. Buck 3G 21
Bellingham. Nmbd 3B 54
Bellmount. Norf 7B 38
Bellochantuy. Arg 6F 56
Bellsbank. E Ayr 1K 51
Bell's Cross. Suff 6H 31
Bellshill. N Lan 4F 58
Bellshill. Nmbd 6J 61
Bellside. N Lan 4G 59
Bellspool. Bord 6K 59
Bellsquarry. W Lot 3J 59
Bells Yew Green. E Sus 2C 12
Belmaduthy. High 8G 79
Belmesthorpe. Rut 8H 37
Belmont. Bkbn 6E 40
Belmont. Shet 3K 91
Belmont. S Ayr 7B 58
Belnacraig. Abers 4C 72
Belnie. Linc 6K 37
Belowda. Corn 5B 4
Belper. Derbs 5A 36
Belper Lane End. Derbs 5M 35
Belph. Derbs 2C 36
Belsay. Nmbd 4E 54
Belsford. Devn 6K 5
Belsize. Herts 3H 21
Belstead. Suff 7H 31
Belston. S Ayr 7B 58
Belstone. Devn 6F 6
Belstone Corner. Devn 6F 6
Belthorn. Lanc 5F 40
Beltinge. Kent 7H 23
Beltoft. N Lin 7F 42
Belton. Leics 7B 36
Belton. Linc 6G 37
Belton. Norf 1L 31
Belton. N Lin 7E 42
Belton-in-Rutland. Rut 1F 28
Beltring. Kent 1C 12
Belts of Collonach. Abers 6F 72
Belvedere. G Lon 6A 22
Belvoir. Leics 6F 36
Bembridge. IOW 7D 10
Bemersyde. Bord 6C 60
Bemerton. Wilts 2K 9
Bempton. E Yor 8J 49
Benacre. Suff 3M 31
Ben Alder Lodge. High 8F 70
Ben Armine Lodge. High 2H 79
Benbecula Airport. W Isl 8J 75
Benbuie. Dum 2B 52
Benburb. M Ulst 6F 93
Benchill. G Man 1G 35
Benderloch. Arg 4D 64
Bendish. Herts 1J 21
Bendooragh. Caus 2F 93
Bendronaig Lodge. High 2M 69
Benenden. Kent 2E 12
Benfieldside. Dur 6D 54
Bengate. Norf 7K 39
Bengeworth. Worc 7J 27
Benhall Green. Suff 5K 31
Benholm. Abers 1M 67
Beningbrough. N Yor 2C 42
Benington. Herts 1K 21
Benington. Linc 5L 37
Benington Sea End. Linc 5M 37
Benllech. IOA 2E 32
Benmore Lodge. High 2D 78
Bennacott. Corn 6B 6
Bennah. Devn 7H 7
Bennecarrigan. N Ayr 7J 57
Bennethead. Cumb 3C 46
Benniworth. Linc 1K 37
Benover. Kent 1D 12
Benson. Oxon 4D 20
Benston. Shet 2E 90
Benstonhall. Orkn 6E 88
Bent. Abers 8F 72
Benthall. Shrp 1E 26
Bentham. Glos 2H 19
Bentlawnt. Shrp 1B 26
Bentley. E Yor 4H 43
Bentley. Hants 1E 10
Bentley. S Yor 7C 42
Bentley. Suff 8H 31
Bentley. Warw 2L 27
Bentley. W Mid 2H 27
Bentley Heath. Herts 4K 21
Bentley Heath. W Mid 4K 27
Bentpath. Dum 2H 53
Bents. W Lot 3H 59
Bentworth. Hants 1D 10
Benvie. D'dee 4G 67
Benville. Dors 5D 8
Benwell. Tyne 5F 54
Benwick. Cambs 2L 29
Beoley. Worc 5J 27
Beoraidbeg. High 6H 69
Bepton. W Sus 4F 10
Beragh. Ferm 5D 92
Berden. Essx 1A 22
Bere Alston. Devn 5G 5
Bere Ferrers. Devn 5G 5
Berepper. Corn 6K 3
Bere Regis. Dors 6G 9
Bergh Apton. Norf 1K 31
Berinsfield. Oxon 4C 20
Berkeley. Glos 4E 18
Berkhamsted. Herts 3G 21
Berkley. Som 1G 9
Berkswell. W Mid 4L 27
Bermondsey. G Lon 6L 21
Bernera. High 3K 69
Bernice. Arg 8F 64
Bernisdale. High 8F 76
Berrick Salome. Oxon 4D 20
Berriedale. High 1M 79
Berrier. Cumb 3B 46
Berriew. Powy 2L 25
Berrington. Nmbd 5H 61
Berrington. Shrp 1D 26
Berrington. Worc 5D 26
Berrington Green. Worc 5D 26
Berrington Law. Nmbd 5G 61
Berrow. Som 8B 18
Berrow Green. Worc 6F 26
Berry Cross. Devn 4D 6
Berry Down Cross. Devn 1E 6
Berry Hill. Glos 2D 18
Berry Hill. Pemb 2G 15
Berryhillock. Mor 7E 80
Berrynarbor. Devn 1E 6
Berry Pomeroy. Devn 5L 5
Berryscaur. Dum 2F 52
Berry's Green. G Lon 8M 21
Bersham. Wrex 5B 34
Berthengam. Flin 3L 33
Berwick. E Sus 5B 12
Berwick Bassett. Wilts 6K 19
Berwick Hill. Nmbd 4E 54
Berwick St James. Wilts 2J 9
Berwick St John. Wilts 3H 9
Berwick St Leonard. Wilts 2H 9
Berwick-upon-Tweed. Nmbd 4G 61
Berwyn. Den 6L 33
Bescaby. Leics 7F 36
Bescar. Lanc 6B 40
Besford. Worc 7H 27
Bessacarr. S Yor 7D 42
Bessbrook. New M 7G 93
Bessels Leigh. Oxon 3B 20
Bessingby. E Yor 1J 43
Bessingham. Norf 6H 39
Best Beech Hill. E Sus 2C 12
Besthorpe. Norf 2G 31
Besthorpe. Notts 3F 36
Bestwood Village. Notts 5C 36
Beswick. E Yor 3H 43
Betchworth. Surr 8K 21
Bethania. Cdgn 6E 24
Bethania. Gwyn
nr. Blaenau Ffestiniog 6G 33
nr. Caernarfon 5F 32
Bethel. Gwyn
nr. Bala 7J 33
nr. Caernarfon 4E 32
Bethel. IOA 3C 32
Bethersden. Kent 1F 12
Bethesda. Gwyn 4F 32
Bethesda. Pemb 5G 15
Bethlehem. Carm 2F 16
Bethnal Green. G Lon 5L 21
Betley. Staf 5F 34
Betsham. Kent 6C 22
Betteshanger. Kent 8K 23
Bettiscombe. Dors 6C 8
Bettisfield. Wrex 6C 34
Betton. Shrp 6E 34
Betton Strange. Shrp 1D 26
Bettws. B'end 6J 17
Bettws. Newp 4A 18
Bettws Bledrws. Cdgn 7E 24
Bettws Cedewain. Powy 3L 25
Bettws Gwerfil Goch. Den 6K 33
Bettws Ifan. Cdgn 2K 15
Bettws Newydd. Mon 3B 18
Bettyhill. High 5K 85
Betws. Carm 3F 16
Betws Garmon. Gwyn 5E 32
Betws-y-Coed. Cnwy 5G 33
Betws-yn-Rhos. Cnwy 3J 33
Beulah. Cdgn 2J 15
Beulah. Powy 7J 25
Beul an Atha. Arg 3C 56
Bevendean. Brig 5L 11
Bevercotes. Notts 2E 36
Beverley. E Yor 4H 43
Beverston. Glos 4G 19
Bevington. Glos 4E 18
Bewaldeth. Cumb 8G 53

Bewcastle—Bridlington

Bewcastle. *Cumb* 4K **53**
Bewdley. *Worc* 4F **26**
Bewerley. *N Yor* 1K **41**
Bewholme. *E Yor* 2J **43**
Bexfield. *Norf* 7G **39**
Bexhill. *E Sus* 5D **12**
Bexley. *G Lon* 6A **22**
Bexleyheath. *G Lon* 6A **22**
Bexleyhill. *W Sus* 3G **11**
Bexwell. *Norf* 1C **30**
Beyton. *Suff* 5F **30**
Bhalton. *W Isl* 8D **82**
Bhatarsaigh. *W Isl* 6C **74**
Bibbington. *Derbs* 2J **35**
Bibury. *Glos* 3K **19**
Bicester. *Oxon* 1C **20**
Bickenhall. *Som* 4A **8**
Bickenhill. *W Mid* 3K **27**
Bicker. *Linc* 6K **37**
Bicker Bar. *Linc* 6K **37**
Bicker Gauntlet. *Linc* 6K **37**
Bickershaw. *G Man* 7E **40**
Bickerstaffe. *Lanc* 7C **40**
Bickerton. *Ches E* 4D **34**
Bickerton. *Nmbd* 1C **54**
Bickerton. *N Yor* 2B **42**
Bickford. *Staf* 8G **35**
Bickington. *Devn*
nr. Barnstaple 2E **6**
nr. Newton Abbot 8G **7**
Bickleigh. *Devn*
nr. Plymouth 5H **5**
nr. Tiverton 5J **7**
Bickleton. *Devn* 2E **6**
Bickley. *N Yor* 6G **49**
Bickley Moss. *Ches W* 5D **34**
Bickmarsh. *Worc* 7K **27**
Bicknacre. *Essx* 3D **22**
Bicknoller. *Som* 2L **7**
Bicknor. *Kent* 8E **22**
Bickton. *Hants* 4K **9**
Bicton. *Here* 5C **26**
Bicton. *Shrp*
nr. Bishop's Castle 3A **26**
nr. Shrewsbury 8C **34**
Bicton Heath. *Shrp* 8C **34**
Bidborough. *Kent* 1B **12**
Biddenden. *Kent* 2E **12**
Biddenden Green. *Kent* 1E **12**
Biddenham. *Bed* 6H **29**
Biddestone. *Wilts* 6G **19**
Biddisham. *Som* 8B **18**
Biddlesden. *Buck* 7D **28**
Biddlestone. *Nmbd* 1C **54**
Biddulph. *Staf* 4G **35**
Biddulph Moor. *Staf* 4H **35**
Bideford. *Devn* 3D **6**
Bidford-on-Avon. *Warw* 6J **27**
Bidlake. *Devn* 7E **6**
Bidston. *Mers* 1A **34**
Bielby. *E Yor* 3E **42**
Bieldside. *Aber* 5H **73**
Bierley. *IOW* 8C **10**
Bierley. *W Yor* 4K **41**
Bierton. *Buck* 2F **20**
Bigbury. *Devn* 7J **5**
Bigbury-on-Sea. *Devn* 7J **5**
Bigby. *Linc* 7H **43**
Biggar. *Cumb* 8L **45**
Biggar. *S Lan* 6J **59**
Biggin. *Derbs*
nr. Hartington 4K **35**
nr. Hulland 5L **35**
Biggin. *N Yor* 4C **42**
Biggings. *Shet* 1B **90**
Biggin Hill. *G Lon* 8M **21**
Biggleswade. *C Beds* 7J **29**
Bighouse. *High* 5L **85**
Bighton. *Hants* 2D **10**
Biglands. *Cumb* 6G **53**
Bignall End. *Staf* 4G **35**
Bignor. *W Sus* 4G **11**
Bigrigg. *Cumb* 3K **45**
Big Sand. *High* 6J **77**
Bigton. *Shet* 5D **90**
Bilberry. *Corn* 6C **4**
Bilborough. *Nott* 5C **36**
Bilbrook. *Som* 1K **7**
Bilbrook. *Staf* 1G **27**
Bilbrough. *N Yor* 3C **42**
Bilbster. *High* 6D **86**
Bilby. *Notts* 1D **36**
Bildershaw. *Dur* 3L **47**
Bildeston. *Suff* 7F **30**
Billericay. *Essx* 4C **22**
Billesdon. *Leics* 1E **28**
Billesley. *Warw* 6K **27**
Billingborough. *Linc* 6J **37**
Billinge. *Mers* 7D **40**
Billingford. *Norf*
nr. Dereham 7G **39**
nr. Diss 4H **31**
Billingham. *Stoc T* 3B **48**
Billinghay. *Linc* 4J **37**
Billingley. *S Yor* 7B **42**
Billingshurst. *W Sus* 3H **11**
Billingsley. *Shrp* 3F **26**
Billington. *C Beds* 1G **21**
Billington. *Lanc* 4F **40**
Billington. *Staf* 7G **35**
Billockby. *Norf* 8L **39**
Billy Row. *Dur* 8E **54**
Bilsborrow. *Lanc* 3D **40**
Bilsby. *Linc* 2A **38**
Bilsham. *W Sus* 5G **11**
Bilsington. *Kent* 2G **13**
Bilson Green. *Glos* 2E **18**
Bilsthorpe. *Notts* 3D **36**
Bilston. *Midl* 3L **59**
Bilston. *W Mid* 2H **27**
Bilstone. *Leics* 1A **28**
Bilting. *Kent* 1G **13**
Bilton. *E Yor* 4J **43**
Bilton. *Nmbd* 8K **61**
Bilton. *N Yor* 2M **41**
Bilton. *Warw* 4B **28**
Bilton in Ainsty. *N Yor* 3B **42**
Bimbister. *Orkn* 8C **88**
Binbrook. *Linc* 8K **43**
Binchester. *Dur* 8F **54**
Bincombe. *Dors* 7E **8**
Bindal. *High* 5K **79**
Binegar. *Som* 1E **8**
Bines Green. *W Sus* 4J **11**
Binfield. *Brac* 6F **20**
Binfield Heath. *Oxon* 6E **20**
Bingfield. *Nmbd* 4C **54**
Bingham. *Notts* 6E **36**
Bingham's Melcombe. *Dors* 5F **8**
Bingley. *W Yor* 4K **41**
Bings Heath. *Shrp* 8D **34**
Binham. *Norf* 6F **38**
Binley. *Hants* 8B **20**
Binley. *W Mid* 4A **28**
Binnegar. *Dors* 7G **9**
Binniehill. *Falk* 2G **59**
Binsoe. *N Yor* 8L **47**
Binstead. *IOW* 6C **10**
Binsted. *Hants* 1E **10**
Binsted. *W Sus* 5G **11**
Binton. *Warw* 6K **27**
Bintree. *Norf* 7G **39**
Binweston. *Shrp* 1B **26**
Birch. *Essx* 2F **22**
Birch. *G Man* 7G **41**
Birchall. *Staf* 4H **35**
Bircham Newton. *Norf* 6D **38**
Bircham Tofts. *Norf* 6D **38**
Birchanger. *Essx* 1B **22**
Birchburn. *N Ayr* 7J **57**
Birch Cross. *Staf* 6K **35**
Bircher. *Here* 5C **26**
Birch Green. *Essx* 2F **22**
Birchgrove. *Card* 6L **17**
Birchgrove. *Swan* 5G **17**
Birch Heath. *Ches W* 3D **34**
Birch Hill. *Ches W* 2D **34**
Birchill. *Devn* 5B **8**
Birchington. *Kent* 7J **23**
Birchley Heath. *Warw* 2L **27**
Birchmoor. *Warw* 1L **27**
Birchmoor Green. *C Beds* 8G **29**
Birchover. *Derbs* 3L **35**
Birch Vale. *Derbs* 1J **35**
Birchview. *Mor* 2A **72**
Birchwood. *Linc* 3G **37**
Birchwood. *Som* 4M **7**
Birchwood. *Warr* 8E **40**
Bircotes. *Notts* 8D **42**
Birdbrook. *Essx* 7D **30**
Birdham. *W Sus* 5F **10**
Birdholme. *Derbs* 3A **36**
Birdingbury. *Warw* 5B **28**
Birdlip. *Glos* 2H **19**
Birdsall. *N Yor* 1F **42**
Birds Edge. *W Yor* 7L **41**
Birds Green. *Essx* 3B **22**
Birdsgreen. *Shrp* 3F **26**
Birdsmoorgate. *Dors* 5B **8**
Birdston. *E Dun* 2E **58**
Birdwell. *S Yor* 7M **41**
Birdwood. *Glos* 2F **18**
Birgham. *Bord* 6E **60**
Birichen. *High* 4H **79**
Birkby. *Cumb* 8E **52**
Birkby. *N Yor* 5M **47**
Birkdale. *Mers* 6B **40**
Birkenhead. *Mers* 1B **34**
Birkenhills. *Abers* 1G **73**
Birkenshaw. *N Lan* 3E **58**
Birkenshaw. *W Yor* 5L **41**
Birkhall. *Abers* 6C **72**
Birkhill. *Ang* 4G **67**
Birkholme. *Linc* 7G **37**
Birkin. *N Yor* 5C **42**
Birley. *Here* 6C **26**
Birling. *Kent* 7C **22**
Birling. *Nmbd* 1F **54**
Birling Gap. *E Sus* 6B **12**
Birlingham. *Worc* 7H **27**
Birmingham. *W Mid* **106** (3J **27**)
Birmingham Airport.
W Mid **119** (3K **27**)
Birnam. *Per* 3D **66**
Birse. *Abers* 6E **72**
Birsemore. *Abers* 6E **72**
Birstall. *Leics* 1C **28**
Birstall. *W Yor* 5L **41**
Birstall Smithies. *W Yor* 5L **41**
Birstwith. *N Yor* 2L **41**
Birthorpe. *Linc* 6J **37**
Birtle. *G Man* 6G **41**
Birtley. *Here* 5B **26**
Birtley. *Nmbd* 4B **54**
Birtley. *Tyne* 6F **54**
Birtsmorton. *Worc* 8G **27**
Birts Street. *Worc* 8F **26**
Bisbrooke. *Rut* 2F **28**
Bisham. *Wind* 5F **20**
Bishampton. *Worc* 6H **27**
Bish Mill. *Devn* 3G **7**
Bishop Auckland. *Dur* 3L **47**
Bishopbridge. *Linc* 8H **43**
Bishopbriggs. *E Dun* 2E **58**
Bishop Burton. *E Yor* 4G **43**
Bishopdown. *Wilts* 2K **9**
Bishop Middleham. *Dur* 8G **55**
Bishopmill. *Mor* 7B **80**
Bishop Monkton. *N Yor* 1M **41**
Bishop Norton. *Linc* 8G **43**
Bishopsbourne. *Kent* 8H **23**
Bishops Cannings. *Wilts* 7J **19**
Bishop's Castle. *Shrp* 3B **26**
Bishop's Caundle. *Dors* 4E **8**
Bishop's Cleeve. *Glos* 1H **19**
Bishops Court. *New M* 6J **93**
Bishop's Down. *Dors* 4E **8**
Bishop's Frome. *Here* 7E **26**
Bishop's Green. *Essx* 2C **22**
Bishop's Green. *Hants* 7C **20**
Bishop's Hull. *Som* 3M **7**
Bishop's Itchington. *Warw* 6A **28**
Bishops Lydeard. *Som* 3L **7**
Bishop's Norton. *Glos* 1G **19**
Bishop's Nympton. *Devn* 3G **7**
Bishop's Offley. *Staf* 7F **34**
Bishop's Stortford. *Herts* 1A **22**
Bishop's Sutton. *Hants* 2D **10**
Bishop's Tachbrook. *Warw* 5M **27**
Bishop's Tawton. *Devn* 2E **6**
Bishopsteignton. *Devn* 8J **7**
Bishopstoke. *Hants* 4B **10**
Bishopston. *Swan* 6E **16**
Bishopstone. *Buck* 2F **20**
Bishopstone. *E Sus* 5A **12**
Bishopstone. *Here* 7C **26**
Bishopstone. *Swin* 5L **19**
Bishopstone. *Wilts* 3J **9**
Bishopstrow. *Wilts* 1G **9**
Bishop Sutton. *Bath* 8D **18**
Bishop's Waltham. *Hants* 4C **10**
Bishops Wood. *Staf* 1G **27**
Bishopswood. *Som* 4A **8**
Bishopsworth. *Bris* 7D **18**
Bishop Thornton. *N Yor* 1L **41**
Bishopthorpe. *York* 3C **42**
Bishopton. *Darl* 3A **48**
Bishopton. *Dum* 7K **51**
Bishopton. *N Yor* 8L **47**
Bishopton. *Ren* 2C **58**
Bishopton. *Warw* 6K **27**
Bishop Wilton. *E Yor* 2E **42**
Bishton. *Newp* 5B **18**
Bishton. *Staf* 7J **35**
Bisley. *Glos* 3H **19**
Bisley. *Surr* 8G **21**
Bispham. *Bkpl* 3B **40**
Bispham Green. *Lanc* 6C **40**
Bissoe. *Corn* 4L **3**
Bisterne. *Hants* 5K **9**
Bisterne Close. *Hants* 5L **9**
Bitchfield. *Linc* 7G **37**
Bittadon. *Devn* 1E **6**
Bittaford. *Devn* 6J **5**
Bittering. *Norf* 8F **38**
Bitterley. *Shrp* 4D **26**
Bitterne. *Sotn* 4B **10**
Bitteswell. *Leics* 3C **28**
Bitton. *S Glo* 7E **18**
Bix. *Oxon* 5E **20**
Bixter. *Shet* 2D **90**
Blaby. *Leics* 2C **28**
Blackawton. *Devn* 6L **5**
Black Bank. *Cambs* 3B **30**
Black Barn. *Linc* 7M **37**
Blackborough. *Devn* 5K **7**
Blackborough. *Norf* 8C **38**
Blackborough End. *Norf* 8C **38**
Black Bourton. *Oxon* 3L **19**
Blackboys. *E Sus* 3B **12**
Blackbrook. *Derbs* 5M **35**
Blackbrook. *Mers* 8D **40**
Blackbrook. *Staf* 6F **34**
Blackbrook. *Surr* 1J **11**
Blackburn. *Abers* 4H **73**
Blackburn. *Bkbn* 5E **40**
Blackburn. *W Lot* 3H **59**
Black Callerton. *Tyne* 5E **54**
Black Carr. *Norf* 2G **31**
Black Clauchrie. *S Ayr* 3H **51**
Black Corries. *High* 2G **65**
Black Crofts. *Arg* 4D **64**
Black Cross. *Corn* 5B **4**
Blackden Heath. *Ches E* 2F **34**
Blackditch. *Oxon* 3B **20**
Black Dog. *Devn* 5H **7**
Blackdog. *Abers* 4J **73**
Blackdown. *Dors* 5B **8**
Blackdyke. *Cumb* 6F **52**
Blacker Hill. *S Yor* 7A **42**
Blackfen. *G Lon* 6A **22**
Blackfield. *Hants* 5B **10**
Blackford. *Cumb* 5H **53**
Blackford. *Per* 7B **66**
Blackford. *Shrp* 3D **26**
Blackford. *Som*
nr. Burnham-on-Sea 1C **8**
nr. Wincanton 3E **8**
Blackfordby. *Leics* 8M **35**
Blackgang. *IOW* 8B **10**
Blackhall. *Edin* 2L **59**
Blackhall. *Ren* 3C **58**
Blackhall Colliery. *Dur* 8H **55**
Blackhall Mill. *Tyne* 6E **54**
Blackhall Rocks. *Dur* 8H **55**
Blackham. *E Sus* 2A **12**
Blackheath. *Essx* 1G **23**
Blackheath. *G Lon* 6L **21**
Blackheath. *Suff* 4L **31**
Blackheath. *Surr* 1H **11**
Blackheath. *W Mid* 3H **27**
Black Heddon. *Nmbd* 4D **54**
Black Hill. *Warw* 6L **27**
Blackhill. *Abers* 1K **73**
Blackhill. *High* 8E **76**
Blackhills. *Abers* 7J **81**
Blackhills. *High* 8K **79**
Blackjack. *Linc* 6K **37**
Blackland. *Wilts* 7J **19**
Black Lane. *G Man* 7F **40**
Blackleach. *Lanc* 4C **40**
Blackley. *G Man* 7G **41**
Blackley. *W Yor* 6K **41**
Blacklunans. *Per* 1E **66**
Blackmill. *B'end* 6J **17**
Blackmoor. *G Man* 7E **40**
Blackmoor. *Hants* 2E **10**
Blackmoor Gate. *Devn* 1F **6**
Blackmore. *Essx* 3C **22**
Blackmore End. *Essx* 8D **30**
Blackmore End. *Herts* 2J **21**
Black Mount. *Arg* 3G **65**
Blackness. *Falk* 2J **59**
Blacknest. *Hants* 1E **10**
Blackney. *Dors* 6C **8**
Blacknoll. *Dors* 7G **9**
Black Notley. *Essx* 1D **22**
Blacko. *Lanc* 3G **41**
Black Pill. *Swan* 5F **16**
Blackpool. *Bkpl* **106** (4B **40**)
Blackpool. *Devn* 7L **5**
Blackpool Corner. *Dors* 6B **8**
Blackpool Gate. *Cumb* 4K **53**
Blackridge. *W Lot* 3G **59**
Blackrock. *Arg* 3C **56**
Blackrock. *Mon* 3M **17**
Blackrod. *G Man* 6E **40**
Blackshaw. *Dum* 5E **52**
Blackshaw Head. *W Yor* 5H **41**
Blackshaw Moor. *Staf* 4J **35**
Blackskull. *Arm* 6G **93**
Blacksmith's Green. *Suff* 5H **31**
Blacksnape. *Bkbn* 5F **40**
Blackstone. *W Sus* 4K **11**
Black Street. *Suff* 3M **31**
Black Tar. *Pemb* 6F **14**
Blackthorn. *Oxon* 2D **20**
Blackthorpe. *Suff* 5F **30**
Blacktoft. *E Yor* 5F **42**
Blacktop. *Aber* 5H **73**
Black Torrington. *Devn* 5D **6**
Blacktown. *Newp* 5A **18**
Blackwall Tunnel. *G Lon* 5L **21**
Blackwater. *Corn* 4L **3**
Blackwater. *Hants* 8F **20**
Blackwater. *IOW* 7C **10**
Blackwater. *Som* 4A **8**
Blackwaterfoot. *N Ayr* 7H **57**
Blackwatertown. *Arm* 6F **93**
Blackwell. *Darl* 4L **47**
Blackwell. *Derbs*
nr. Alfreton 4B **36**
nr. Buxton 2K **35**
Blackwell. *Som* 3K **7**
Blackwell. *Warw* 7L **27**
Blackwell. *Worc* 4H **27**
Blackwood. *Cphy* 5L **17**
Blackwood. *Dum* 3D **52**
Blackwood. *S Lan* 5F **58**
Blackwood Hill. *Staf* 4H **35**
Blacon. *Ches W* 3B **34**
Bladnoch. *Dum* 6K **51**
Bladon. *Oxon* 2B **20**
Blaenannerch. *Cdgn* 2J **15**
Blaenau Dolwyddelan.
Cnwy 5F **32**
Blaenau Ffestiniog. *Gwyn* 6G **33**
Blaenavon. *Torf* 3A **18**
Blaenawey. *Mon* 2A **18**
Blaen Celyn. *Cdgn* 1K **15**
Blaen Clydach. *Rhon* 5J **17**
Blaencwm. *Rhon* 5J **17**
Blaendulais. *Neat* 4H **17**
Blaenffos. *Pemb* 3H **15**
Blaengarw. *B'end* 5J **17**
Blaen-geufford. *Cdgn* 4F **24**
Blaengwrach. *Neat* 4H **17**
Blaengwynfi. *Neat* 5H **17**
Blaenllechau. *Rhon* 5J **17**
Blaenpennal. *Cdgn* 6F **24**
Blaenplwyf. *Cdgn* 5E **24**
Blaenporth. *Cdgn* 2J **15**
Blaenrhondda. *Rhon* 4J **17**
Blaenwaun. *Carm* 4J **15**
Blaen-y-coed. *Carm* 4K **15**
Blagdon. *N Som* 8D **18**
Blagdon. *Torb* 5L **5**
Blagdon Hill. *Som* 4M **7**
Blagill. *Cumb* 7M **53**
Blaguegate. *Lanc* 7C **40**
Blaich. *High* 8M **69**
Blain. *High* 1A **64**
Blaina. *Blae* 4M **17**
Blair Atholl. *Per* 1B **66**
Blair Drummond. *Stir* 8M **65**
Blairgowrie. *Per* 3E **66**
Blairhall. *Fife* 1J **59**
Blairingone. *Per* 8C **66**
Blairlogie. *Stir* 8B **66**
Blairmore. *Abers* 2D **72**
Blairmore. *Arg* 1L **57**
Blairmore. *High* 6D **84**
Blairquhanan. *W Dun* 1C **58**
Blaisdon. *Glos* 2F **18**
Blakebrook. *Worc* 4G **27**
Blakedown. *Worc* 4G **27**
Blake End. *Essx* 1D **22**
Blakemere. *Here* 7B **26**
Blakeney. *Glos* 3E **18**
Blakeney. *Norf* 5G **39**
Blakenhall. *Ches E* 5F **34**
Blakeshall. *Worc* 3G **27**
Blakesley. *Nptn* 6D **28**
Blanchland. *Nmbd* 6C **54**
Blandford Camp. *Dors* 5H **9**
Blandford Forum. *Dors* 5G **9**
Blandford St Mary. *Dors* 5G **9**
Bland Hill. *N Yor* 2L **41**
Blandy. *High* 5J **85**
Blanefield. *Stir* 2D **58**
Blaney. *Ferm* 6B **92**
Blankney. *Linc* 3H **37**
Blantyre. *S Lan* 4E **58**
Blarmachfoldach. *High* 1E **64**
Blarnalearoch. *High* 4B **78**
Blashford. *Hants* 5K **9**
Blaston. *Leics* 2F **28**
Blatchbridge. *Som* 1F **8**
Blathaisbhal. *W Isl* 6K **75**
Blatherwycke. *Nptn* 2G **29**
Blawith. *Cumb* 7A **46**
Blaxhall. *Suff* 6K **31**
Blaxton. *S Yor* 7D **42**
Blaydon. *Tyne* 5E **54**
Bleadney. *Som* 1C **8**
Bleadon. *N Som* 8B **18**
Blean. *Kent* 7H **23**
Bleary. *Arm* 6G **93**
Bleasby. *Linc* 1J **37**
Bleasby. *Notts* 5E **36**
Bleasby Moor. *Linc* 1J **37**
Blebocraigs. *Fife* 6H **67**
Bleddfa. *Powy* 6M **25**
Bledington. *Glos* 1L **19**
Bledlow. *Buck* 3E **20**
Bledlow Ridge. *Buck* 4E **20**
Blencarn. *Cumb* 8L **53**
Blencogo. *Cumb* 7F **52**
Blendworth. *Hants* 4E **10**
Blennerhasset. *Cumb* 7F **52**
Bletchingdon. *Oxon* 2C **20**
Bletchingley. *Surr* 8L **21**
Bletchley. *Mil* 8F **28**
Bletchley. *Shrp* 6E **34**
Bletherston. *Pemb* 4G **15**
Bletsoe. *Bed* 6H **29**
Blewbury. *Oxon* 5C **20**
Blickling. *Norf* 7H **39**
Blidworth. *Notts* 4C **36**
Blindburn. *Nmbd* 8F **60**
Blindcrake. *Cumb* 8F **52**
Blindley Heath. *Surr* 1L **11**
Blindmoor. *Som* 4A **8**
Blisland. *Corn* 4D **4**
Blissford. *Hants* 4K **9**
Bliss Gate. *Worc* 4F **26**
Blists Hill. *Telf* 1E **26**
Blisworth. *Nptn* 6E **28**
Blithbury. *Staf* 7J **35**
Blitterlees. *Cumb* 6F **52**
Blockley. *Glos* 8K **27**
Blofield. *Norf* 1K **31**
Blofield Heath. *Norf* 8K **39**
Blo' Norton. *Norf* 4G **31**
Bloomfield. *Bord* 7C **60**
Blore. *Staf* 5K **35**
Blount's Green. *Staf* 6J **35**
Bloxham. *Oxon* 8B **28**
Bloxholm. *Linc* 4H **37**
Bloxwich. *W Mid* 1H **27**
Bloxworth. *Dors* 6G **9**
Blubberhouses. *N Yor* 2K **41**
Blue Anchor. *Som* 1K **7**
Blue Anchor. *Swan* 5E **16**
Blue Bell Hill. *Kent* 7D **22**
Blue Row. *Essx* 2G **23**
Bluetown. *Kent* 8F **22**
Blundeston. *Suff* 2M **31**
Blunham. *C Beds* 6J **29**
Blunsdon St Andrew. *Swin* 5K **19**
Bluntington. *Worc* 4G **27**
Bluntisham. *Cambs* 4L **29**
Blunts. *Corn* 5F **4**
Blurton. *Stoke* 5G **35**
Blyborough. *Linc* 8G **43**
Blyford. *Suff* 4L **31**
Blymhill. *Staf* 8G **35**
Blymhill Lawns. *Staf* 8G **35**
Blyth. *Nmbd* 3G **55**
Blyth. *Notts* 1D **36**
Blyth. *Bord* 5K **59**
Blyth Bank. *Bord* 5K **59**
Blyth Bridge. *Bord* 5K **59**
Blythburgh. *Suff* 4L **31**
The Blythe. *Staf* 7J **35**
Blythe Bridge. *Staf* 5H **35**
Blythe Marsh. *Staf* 5H **35**
Blyton. *Linc* 8F **42**
Boardmills. *Lis* 6H **93**
Boarhills. *Fife* 6J **67**
Boarhunt. *Hants* 5D **10**
Boar's Head. *G Man* 7D **40**
Boarshead. *E Sus* 2B **12**
Boars Hill. *Oxon* 3B **20**
Boarstall. *Buck* 2D **20**
Boasley Cross. *Devn* 6E **6**
Boath. *High* 6F **78**
Boat of Garten. *High* 4K **71**
Bobbing. *Kent* 7E **22**
Bobbington. *Staf* 2G **27**
Bobbingworth. *Essx* 3B **22**
Bocaddon. *Corn* 6D **4**
Bocking. *Essx* 1D **22**
Bocking Churchstreet. *Essx* 1D **22**
Boddam. *Abers* 1L **73**
Boddam. *Shet* 6D **90**
Boddington. *Glos* 1G **19**
Bodedern. *IOA* 2C **32**
Bodelwyddan. *Den* 3K **33**
Bodenham. *Here* 6D **26**
Bodenham. *Wilts* 3K **9**
Bodewryd. *IOA* 1C **32**
Bodfari. *Den* 3K **33**
Bodffordd. *IOA* 3D **32**
Bodham. *Norf* 5H **39**
Bodiam. *E Sus* 3D **12**
Bodicote. *Oxon* 8B **28**
Bodieve. *Corn* 4B **4**
Bodinnick. *Corn* 6D **4**
Bodle Street Green. *E Sus* 4C **12**
Bodmin. *Corn* 5C **4**
Bodnant. *Cnwy* 3H **33**
Bodney. *Norf* 2E **30**
Bodorgan. *IOA* 4C **32**
Bodrane. *Corn* 5E **4**
Bodsham. *Kent* 1H **13**
Boduan. *Gwyn* 7C **32**
Bodymoor Heath. *Warw* 2K **27**
The Bog. *Shrp* 2B **26**
Bogallan. *High* 8G **79**
Bogbrae Croft. *Abers* 2K **73**
Bogend. *S Ayr* 6B **58**
Boghall. *Midl* 3L **59**
Boghall. *W Lot* 3H **59**
Boghead. *S Lan* 5F **58**
Bogindollo. *Ang* 2H **67**
Bogmoor. *Mor* 7C **80**
Bogniebrae. *Abers* 1E **72**
Bognor Regis. *W Sus* 6G **11**
Bograxie. *Abers* 4G **73**
Bogside. *N Lan* 4G **59**
Bogton. *Abers* 8F **80**
Bogue. *Dum* 3M **51**
Bohenie. *High* 7C **70**
Bohortha. *Corn* 8A **4**
Boirseam. *W Isl* 5B **76**
Bokiddick. *Corn* 5C **4**
Bolam. *Dur* 3K **47**
Bolam. *Nmbd* 3D **54**
Bolberry. *Devn* 8J **5**
Bold Heath. *Mers* 1D **34**
Boldon. *Tyne* 5G **55**
Boldon Colliery. *Tyne* 5G **55**
Boldre. *Hants* 6M **9**
Boldron. *Dur* 4J **47**
Bole. *Notts* 1E **36**
Bolehall. *Staf* 1L **27**
Bolehill. *Derbs* 4L **35**
Bolenowe. *Corn* 5K **3**
Boleside. *Bord* 6B **60**
Bolham. *Devn* 4J **7**
Bolham Water. *Devn* 4L **7**
Bolingey. *Corn* 3L **3**
Bollington. *Ches E* 2H **35**
Bolney. *W Sus* 3K **11**
Bolnhurst. *Bed* 6H **29**
Bolshan. *Ang* 2K **67**
Bolsover. *Derbs* 2B **36**
Bolsterstone. *S Yor* 8L **41**
Bolstone. *Here* 8D **26**
Boltachan. *Per* 2B **66**
Boltby. *N Yor* 7B **48**
Bolton. *Cumb* 3E **46**
Bolton. *E Lot* 2C **60**
Bolton. *E Yor* 2E **42**
Bolton. *G Man* 7F **40**
Bolton. *Nmbd* 8J **61**
Bolton Abbey. *N Yor* 2J **41**
Bolton-by-Bowland. *Lanc* 3F **40**
Boltonfellend. *Cumb* 5J **53**
Boltongate. *Cumb* 7G **53**
Bolton Green. *Lanc* 6D **40**
Bolton-le-Sands. *Lanc* 1C **40**
Bolton Low Houses. *Cumb* 7G **53**
Bolton New Houses. *Cumb* 7G **53**
Bolton-on-Swale. *N Yor* 6L **47**
Bolton Percy. *N Yor* 3C **42**
Bolton Town End. *Lanc* 1C **40**
Bolton upon Dearne. *S Yor* 7B **42**
Bolton Wood Lane. *Cumb* 7G **53**
Bolventor. *Corn* 8A **6**
Bomarsund. *Nmbd* 3F **54**
Bomere Heath. *Shrp* 8C **34**
Bonar Bridge. *High* 4G **79**
Bonawe. *Arg* 4E **64**
Bonby. *N Lin* 6H **43**
Boncath. *Pemb* 3J **15**
Bonchester Bridge. *Bord* 8C **60**
Bonchurch. *IOW* 8C **10**
Bond End. *Staf* 8K **35**
Bondleigh. *Devn* 5F **6**
Bonds. *Lanc* 3C **40**
Bonehill. *Devn* 8G **7**
Bonehill. *Staf* 1K **27**
Bo'ness. *Falk* 1H **59**
Boney Hay. *Staf* 8J **35**
Bonham. *Wilts* 2F **8**
Bonhill. *W Dun* 2B **58**
Boningale. *Shrp* 1G **27**
Bonjedward. *Bord* 7D **60**
Bonkle. *N Lan* 4G **59**
Bonnanaboigh. *Caus* 3E **92**
Bonnington. *Ang* 4J **67**
Bonnington. *Edin* 3K **59**
Bonnington. *Kent* 2G **13**
Bonnybank. *Fife* 7G **67**
Bonnybridge. *Falk* 1G **59**
Bonnykelly. *Abers* 8H **81**
Bonnyrigg. *Midl* 3M **59**
Bonnyton. *Ang* 4G **67**
Bonnytown. *Fife* 6J **67**
Bonsall. *Derbs* 4L **35**
Bont. *Mon* 2B **18**
Bontddu. *Gwyn* 1F **24**
Bont Dolgadfan. *Powy* 2H **25**
Y Bont-Faen. *V Glam* 7J **17**
Bontgoch. *Cdgn* 4F **24**
Bonthorpe. *Linc* 2A **38**
Bont Newydd. *Gwyn* 6G **33**
Bont-newydd. *Cnwy* 3K **33**
Bontnewydd. *Cdgn* 6F **24**
Bontnewydd. *Gwyn* 4D **32**
Bontuchel. *Den* 5K **33**
Bonvilston. *V Glam* 7K **17**
Bon-y-maen. *Swan* 5F **16**
Booker. *Buck* 4F **20**
Booley. *Shrp* 7D **34**
Boorley Green. *Hants* 4C **10**
Boosbeck. *Red C* 4D **48**
Boot. *Cumb* 4L **45**
Booth. *W Yor* 5J **41**
Boothby Graffoe. *Linc* 4G **37**
Boothby Pagnell. *Linc* 6G **37**
Booth Green. *Ches E* 1H **35**
Booth of Toft. *Shet* 6J **91**
Boothstown. *G Man* 7F **40**
Boothville. *Nptn* 5E **28**
Bootle. *Cumb* 6L **45**
Bootle. *Mers* 8B **40**
Booton. *Norf* 7H **39**
Booze. *N Yor* 5J **47**
Boquhan. *Stir* 1D **58**
Boraston. *Shrp* 4E **26**
Borden. *Kent* 7E **22**
Borden. *W Sus* 3F **10**
Bordlands. *Bord* 5K **59**
Bordley. *N Yor* 1H **41**
Bordon. *Hants* 2E **10**
Boreham. *Essx* 3D **22**
Boreham. *Wilts* 1G **9**
Boreham Street. *E Sus* 4C **12**
Borehamwood. *Herts* 4J **21**
Boreland. *Dum* 2F **52**
Boreston. *Devn* 6K **5**
Borestone Brae. *Stir* 8A **66**
Boreton. *Shrp* 1D **26**
Borgh. *W Isl*
on Barra 5C **74**
on Benbecula 8J **75**
on Berneray 5L **75**
on Isle of Lewis 6H **83**
Borghasdal. *W Isl* 5B **76**
Borghastan. *W Isl* 7E **82**
Borgh na Sgiotaig. *High* 6E **76**
Borgie. *High* 6J **85**
Borgue. *Dum* 7M **51**
Borgue. *High* 1M **79**
Borley. *Essx* 7E **30**
Borley Green. *Essx* 7E **30**
Borley Green. *Suff* 5F **30**
Borlum. *High* 3F **70**
Bornais. *W Isl* 3D **74**
Bornesketaig. *High* 6E **76**
Boroughbridge. *N Yor* 1A **42**
Borough Green. *Kent* 8C **22**
Borreraig. *High* 8C **76**
Borrobol Lodge. *High* 1J **79**
Borrodale. *High* 1C **68**
Borrowash. *Derbs* 6B **36**
Borrowby. *N Yor*
nr. Northallerton 7B **48**
nr. Whitby 4E **48**
Borrowston. *High* 7E **86**
Borrowstonehill. *Orkn* 1F **86**
Borrowstoun. *Falk* 1H **59**
Borstal. *Medw* 7D **22**
Borth. *Cdgn* 4F **24**
Borthwick. *Midl* 4A **60**
Borth-y-Gest. *Gwyn* 7E **32**
Borve. *High* 1F **68**
Borwick. *Lanc* 8D **46**
Bosbury. *Here* 7E **26**
Boscastle. *Corn* 2C **4**
Boscombe. *Bour* 6K **9**
Boscombe. *Wilts* 2L **9**
Boscoppa. *Corn* 6C **4**
Bosham. *W Sus* 5F **10**
Bosherston. *Pemb* 7F **14**
Bosley. *Ches E* 3H **35**
Bossall. *N Yor* 1E **42**
Bossiney. *Corn* 3C **4**
Bossingham. *Kent* 1H **13**
Bossington. *Som* 1H **7**
Bostadh. *W Isl* 7E **82**
Bostock Green. *Ches W* 3E **34**
Boston. *Linc* 5L **37**
Boston Spa. *W Yor* 3B **42**
Boswarthen. *Corn* 5H **3**
Boswinger. *Corn* 7B **4**
Botallack. *Corn* 5G **3**
Botany Bay. *G Lon* 4K **21**
Botcheston. *Leics* 1B **28**
Botesdale. *Suff* 4G **31**
Bothal. *Nmbd* 3F **54**
Bothampstead. *W Ber* 6C **20**
Bothamsall. *Notts* 2D **36**
Bothel. *Cumb* 8F **52**
Bothenhampton. *Dors* 6C **8**
Bothwell. *S Lan* 4F **58**
Botley. *Buck* 3G **21**
Botley. *Hants* 4C **10**
Botley. *Oxon* 3B **20**
Botloe's Green. *Glos* 1F **18**
Botolph Claydon. *Buck* 1E **20**
Botolphs. *W Sus* 5J **11**
Bottacks. *High* 7E **78**
Bottesford. *Leics* 6F **36**
Bottesford. *N Lin* 7F **42**
Bottisham. *Cambs* 5B **30**
Bottlesford. *Wilts* 8K **19**
Bottomcraig. *Fife* 5G **67**
Bottom o' th' Moor. *G Man* 6E **40**
Botton. *N Yor* 5D **48**
Botton Head. *Lanc* 1E **40**
Bottreaux Mill. *Devn* 3H **7**
Botus Fleming. *Corn* 5G **5**
Botwnnog. *Gwyn* 7B **32**
Bough Beech. *Kent* 1A **12**
Boughrood. *Powy* 1L **17**
Boughspring. *Glos* 4D **18**
Boughton. *Norf* 1C **30**
Boughton. *Nptn* 5E **28**
Boughton. *Notts* 3D **36**
Boughton Aluph. *Kent* 1G **13**
Boughton Green. *Kent* 8D **22**
Boughton Lees. *Kent* 1G **13**
Boughton Malherbe. *Kent* 1E **12**
Boughton Monchelsea.
Kent 8D **22**
Boughton under Blean.
Kent 8G **23**
Boulby. *Red C* 4E **48**
Bouldnor. *IOW* 7A **10**
Bouldon. *Shrp* 3D **26**
Boulmer. *Nmbd* 8K **61**
Boulston. *Pemb* 5F **14**
Boultham. *Linc* 3G **37**
Boulton. *Derb* 6A **36**
Boundary. *Staf* 5H **35**
Bounds. *Here* 8E **26**
Bourn. *Cambs* 6L **29**
Bournbrook. *W Mid* 3J **27**
Bourne. *Linc* 7H **37**
The Bourne. *Surr* 1F **10**
Bourne End. *Bed* 5H **29**
Bourne End. *Buck* 5F **20**
Bourne End. *C Beds* 7G **29**
Bourne End. *Herts* 3H **21**
Bournemouth. *Bour* **106** (6J **9**)
Bournemouth Airport. *Dors* 6K **9**
Bournes Green. *Glos* 3H **19**
Bournes Green. *S'end* 5F **22**
Bournheath. *Worc* 4H **27**
Bournmoor. *Dur* 6G **55**
Bournville. *W Mid* 3J **27**
Bourton. *Dors* 2F **8**
Bourton. *N Som* 7B **18**
Bourton. *Oxon* 5L **19**
Bourton. *Shrp* 2D **26**
Bourton. *Wilts* 7J **19**
Bourton on Dunsmore.
Warw 4B **28**
Bourton-on-the-Hill. *Glos* 8K **27**
Bourton-on-the-Water. *Glos* 1K **19**
Bousd. *Arg* 1H **63**
Bousta. *Shet* 2C **90**
Boustead Hill. *Cumb* 6G **53**
Bouth. *Cumb* 7B **46**
Bouthwaite. *N Yor* 8K **47**
Boveney. *Buck* 6G **21**
Boveridge. *Dors* 4J **9**
Boverton. *V Glam* 8J **17**
Bovey Tracey. *Devn* 8H **7**
Bovingdon. *Herts* 3H **21**
Bovingdon Green. *Buck* 5F **20**
Bovinger. *Essx* 3B **22**
Bovington Camp. *Dors* 7G **9**
Bow. *Devn* 5G **7**
Bowbank. *Dur* 3H **47**
Bow Brickhill. *Mil* 8G **29**
Bowbridge. *Glos* 3G **19**
Bowburn. *Dur* 8G **55**
Bowcombe. *IOW* 7B **10**
Bowd. *Devn* 7L **7**
Bowden. *Devn* 7L **5**
Bowden. *Bord* 6C **60**
Bowden Hill. *Wilts* 7H **19**
Bowdens. *Som* 3C **8**
Bowderdale. *Cumb* 5E **46**
Bowdon. *G Man* 1F **34**
Bower. *Nmbd* 3A **54**
Bowerchalke. *Wilts* 3J **9**
Bowerhill. *Wilts* 7H **19**
Bower Hinton. *Som* 4C **8**
Bowermadden. *High* 5D **86**
Bowers. *Staf* 6G **35**
Bowers Gifford. *Essx* 5D **22**
Bowershall. *Fife* 8D **66**
Bowertower. *High* 5D **86**
Bowes. *Dur* 4H **47**
Bowgreave. *Lanc* 3C **40**
Bowhousebog. *N Lan* 4G **59**
Bowithick. *Corn* 7A **6**
Bowland Bridge. *Cumb* 7C **46**
Bowlees. *Dur* 3H **47**
Bowley. *Here* 6D **26**
Bowlhead Green. *Surr* 2G **11**
Bowling. *W Dun* 2C **58**
Bowling. *W Yor* 4K **41**
Bowling Bank. *Wrex* 5B **34**
Bowling Green. *Worc* 6G **27**
Bowlish. *Som* 1E **8**
Bowmanstead. *Cumb* 6B **46**
Bowmore. *Arg* 4C **56**
Bowness-on-Solway.
Cumb 5G **53**
Bowness-on-Windermere.
Cumb 6C **46**
Bow of Fife. *Fife* 6G **67**
Bowriefauld. *Ang* 3J **67**
Bowscale. *Cumb* 8H **53**
Bowsden. *Nmbd* 5G **61**
Bowside Lodge. *High* 5L **85**
Bowston. *Cumb* 6C **46**
Bow Street. *Cdgn* 4F **24**
Bowthorpe. *Norf* 1H **31**
Box. *Glos* 3G **19**
Box. *Wilts* 7G **19**
Boxbush. *Glos* 1E **18**
Box End. *Bed* 7H **29**
Boxford. *Suff* 7F **30**
Boxford. *W Ber* 6B **20**
Boxgrove. *W Sus* 5G **11**
Box Hill. *Wilts* 7G **19**
Boxley. *Kent* 8D **22**
Boxmoor. *Herts* 3H **21**
Box's Shop. *Corn* 5B **6**
Boxted. *Essx* 8F **30**
Boxted. *Suff* 6E **30**
Boxted Cross. *Essx* 8G **31**
Boxworth. *Cambs* 5L **29**
Boxworth End. *Cambs* 5L **29**
Boyden End. *Suff* 6D **30**
Boyden Gate. *Kent* 7J **23**
Boylestone. *Derbs* 6K **35**
Boylestonfield. *Derbs* 6K **35**
Boyndie. *Abers* 7F **80**
Boynton. *E Yor* 1J **43**
Boys Hill. *Dors* 4E **8**
Boythorpe. *Derbs* 3A **36**
Boyton. *Corn* 6C **6**
Boyton. *Suff* 7K **31**
Boyton. *Wilts* 2H **9**
Boyton Cross. *Essx* 3C **22**
Boyton End. *Essx* 8C **30**
Boyton End. *Suff* 7D **30**
Bozeat. *Nptn* 6G **29**
Braaid. *IOM* 7C **44**
Braal Castle. *High* 6C **86**
Brabling Green. *Suff* 5J **31**
Brabourne. *Kent* 1H **13**
Brabourne Lees. *Kent* 1G **13**
Brabster. *High* 5E **86**
Bracadale. *High* 2E **68**
Bracara. *High* 6J **69**
Braceborough. *Linc* 8H **37**
Bracebridge. *Linc* 3G **37**
Bracebridge Heath. *Linc* 3G **37**
Braceby. *Linc* 6H **37**
Bracewell. *Lanc* 3G **41**
Brackenber. *Cumb* 4F **46**
Brackenfield. *Derbs* 4A **36**
Brackenlands. *Cumb* 7G **53**
Brackenthwaite. *Cumb* 7G **53**
Brackenthwaite. *N Yor* 2L **41**
Brackla. *B'end* 7J **17**
Brackla. *High* 8J **79**
Bracklesham. *W Sus* 6F **10**
Brackletter. *High* 7B **70**
Brackley. *Nptn* 8C **28**
Brackley Hatch. *Nptn* 7D **28**
Brackloch. *High* 1B **78**
Bracknell. *Brac* 7F **20**
Braco. *Per* 7B **66**
Bracobrae. *Mor* 8E **80**
Bracon. *N Lin* 7E **42**
Bracon Ash. *Norf* 2H **31**
Bradbourne. *Derbs* 4L **35**
Bradbury. *Dur* 3M **47**
Bradda. *IOM* 7A **44**
Bradden. *Nptn* 7D **28**
Bradenham. *Buck* 4F **20**
Bradenham. *Norf* 1F **30**
Bradenstoke. *Wilts* 6J **19**
Bradfield. *Essx* 8H **31**
Bradfield. *Norf* 6J **39**
Bradfield. *W Ber* 6D **20**
Bradfield Combust. *Suff* 6E **30**
Bradfield Green. *Ches E* 4E **34**
Bradfield Heath. *Essx* 1H **23**
Bradfield St Clare. *Suff* 6F **30**
Bradfield St George. *Suff* 5F **30**
Bradford. *Derbs* 3L **35**
Bradford. *Devn* 5D **6**
Bradford. *Nmbd* 6J **61**
Bradford. *W Yor* **106** (4K **41**)
Bradford Abbas. *Dors* 4D **8**
Bradford Barton. *Devn* 4H **7**
Bradford Leigh. *Wilts* 7G **19**
Bradford-on-Avon. *Wilts* 7G **19**
Bradford-on-Tone. *Som* 3L **7**
Bradford Peverell. *Dors* 6E **8**
Bradiford. *Devn* 2E **6**
Brading. *IOW* 7D **10**
Bradley. *Ches W* 2D **34**
Bradley. *Derbs* 5L **35**
Bradley. *Glos* 4F **18**
Bradley. *Hants* 1D **10**
Bradley. *NE Lin* 7K **43**
Bradley. *N Yor* 7J **47**
Bradley. *Staf* 8G **35**
Bradley. *W Mid* 2H **27**
Bradley. *W Yor* 5K **41**
Bradley. *Wrex* 4B **34**
Bradley Cross. *Som* 8C **18**
Bradley Green. *Ches W* 5D **34**
Bradley Green. *Som* 2A **8**
Bradley Green. *Warw* 1L **27**
Bradley Green. *Worc* 5H **27**
Bradley in the Moors. *Staf* 5J **35**
Bradley Mount. *Ches E* 2H **35**
Bradley Stoke. *S Glo* 5E **18**
Bradlow. *Here* 8F **26**
Bradmore. *Notts* 6C **36**
Bradmore. *W Mid* 2G **27**
Bradninch. *Devn* 5K **7**
Bradnop. *Staf* 4J **35**
Bradpole. *Dors* 6C **8**
Bradshaw. *G Man* 6F **40**
Bradstone. *Devn* 7C **6**
Bradwall Green. *Ches E* 3F **34**
Bradway. *S Yor* 1M **35**
Bradwell. *Derbs* 1K **35**
Bradwell. *Essx* 1E **22**
Bradwell. *Mil* 8F **28**
Bradwell. *Norf* 1M **31**
Bradwell-on-Sea. *Essx* 3G **23**
Bradwell Waterside. *Essx* 3F **22**
Bradworthy. *Devn* 4C **6**
Brae. *High* 5K **77**
Brae. *Shet* 1D **90**
Braeantra. *High* 6F **78**
Braefield. *High* 2E **70**
Braefindon. *High* 8G **79**
Braegrum. *Per* 5D **66**
Braehead. *Ang* 2K **67**
Braehead. *Dum* 6K **51**
Braehead. *Mor* 1B **72**
Braehead. *Orkn* 5D **88**
Braehead. *S Lan*
nr. Coalburn 6G **59**
nr. Forth 4H **59**
Braehoulland. *Shet* 6G **91**
Braemar. *Abers* 6A **72**
Braemore. *High*
nr. Dunbeath 8B **86**
nr. Ullapool 6B **78**
Brae of Achnahaird. *High* 2M **77**
Brae Roy Lodge. *High* 6D **70**
Braeside. *Abers* 2J **73**
Braeside. *Inv* 2M **57**
Braes of Coul. *Ang* 2F **66**
Braeswick. *Orkn* 6F **88**
Braetongue. *High* 6H **85**
Braeval. *Stir* 7K **65**
Braevallich. *Arg* 7D **64**
Braewick. *Shet* 2D **90**
Brafferton. *Darl* 3L **47**
Brafferton. *N Yor* 8B **48**
Brafield-on-the-Green. *Nptn* 6F **28**
Bragar. *W Isl* 7F **82**
Bragbury End. *Herts* 1K **21**
Bragleenbeg. *Arg* 5D **64**
Braichmelyn. *Gwyn* 4F **32**
Braides. *Lanc* 2C **40**
Braidwood. *S Lan* 5G **59**
Braigo. *Arg* 3B **56**
Brailsford. *Derbs* 5L **35**
Braintree. *Essx* 1D **22**
Braiseworth. *Suff* 4H **31**
Braishfield. *Hants* 3A **10**
Braithwaite. *Cumb* 2M **45**
Braithwaite. *S Yor* 6D **42**
Braithwaite. *W Yor* 3J **41**
Braithwell. *S Yor* 8C **42**
Brakefield Green. *Norf* 1G **31**
Bramber. *W Sus* 4J **11**
Brambridge. *Hants* 3B **10**
Bramcote. *Notts* 6C **36**
Bramcote. *Warw* 3B **28**
Bramdean. *Hants* 3D **10**
Bramerton. *Norf* 1J **31**
Bramfield. *Herts* 2K **21**
Bramfield. *Suff* 4K **31**
Bramford. *Suff* 7H **31**
Bramhall. *G Man* 1G **35**
Bramham. *W Yor* 3B **42**
Bramhope. *W Yor* 3L **41**
Bramley. *Hants* 8D **20**
Bramley. *S Yor* 8B **42**
Bramley. *Surr* 1H **11**
Bramley. *W Yor* 4L **41**
Bramley Green. *Hants* 8D **20**
Bramley Head. *N Yor* 2K **41**
Bramley Vale. *Derbs* 3B **36**
Bramling. *Kent* 8J **23**
Brampford Speke. *Devn* 6J **7**
Brampton. *Cambs* 4K **29**
Brampton. *Cumb*
nr. Appleby-in-Westmorland 3E **46**
nr. Carlisle 5K **53**
Brampton. *Linc* 2F **36**
Brampton. *Norf* 7J **39**
Brampton. *S Yor* 7B **42**
Brampton. *Suff* 3L **31**
Brampton Abbotts. *Here* 1E **18**
Brampton Ash. *Nptn* 3E **28**
Brampton Bryan. *Here* 4B **26**
Brampton en le Morthen.
S Yor 1B **36**
Bramshall. *Staf* 6J **35**
Bramshaw. *Hants* 4L **9**
Bramshill. *Hants* 7E **20**
Bramshott. *Hants* 2F **10**
Branault. *High* 1L **63**
Brancaster. *Norf* 5D **38**
Brancaster Staithe. *Norf* 5D **38**
Brancepeth. *Dur* 8F **54**
Branch End. *Nmbd* 5D **54**
Branchill. *Mor* 8L **79**
Brand End. *Linc* 5L **37**
Branderburgh. *Mor* 6B **80**
Brandesburton. *E Yor* 3J **43**
Brandeston. *Suff* 5J **31**
Brand Green. *Glos* 1F **18**
Brandhill. *Shrp* 4C **26**
Brandis Corner. *Devn* 5D **6**
Brandish Street. *Som* 1J **7**
Brandiston. *Norf* 7H **39**
Brandon. *Dur* 8F **54**
Brandon. *Linc* 5G **37**
Brandon. *Nmbd* 8H **61**
Brandon. *Suff* 3D **30**
Brandon. *Warw* 4B **28**
Brandon Bank. *Cambs* 3C **30**
Brandon Creek. *Norf* 2C **30**
Brandon Parva. *Norf* 1G **31**
Brandsby. *N Yor* 8C **48**
Brandy Wharf. *Linc* 8H **43**
Brane. *Corn* 6H **3**
Bran End. *Essx* 1C **22**
Branksome. *Pool* 6J **9**
Bransbury. *Hants* 1B **10**
Bransby. *Linc* 2F **36**
Branscombe. *Devn* 7L **7**
Bransford. *Worc* 6F **26**
Bransgore. *Hants* 6K **9**
Bransholme. *Hull* 4J **43**
Bransley. *Shrp* 4E **26**
Branston. *Leics* 7F **36**
Branston. *Linc* 3H **37**
Branston. *Staf* 7L **35**
Branston Booths. *Linc* 3H **37**
Branstone. *IOW* 7C **10**
Bransty. *Cumb* 3J **45**
Brant Broughton. *Linc* 4G **37**
Brantham. *Suff* 8H **31**
Branthwaite. *Cumb*
nr. Caldbeck 8G **53**
nr. Workington 2K **45**
Brantingham. *E Yor* 5G **43**
Branton. *Nmbd* 8H **61**
Branton. *S Yor* 7D **42**
Branton Green. *N Yor* 1B **42**
Branxholme. *Bord* 8B **60**
Branxton. *Nmbd* 6F **60**
Brassington. *Derbs* 4L **35**
Brasted. *Kent* 8A **22**
Brasted Chart. *Kent* 8A **22**
The Bratch. *Staf* 2G **27**
Brathens. *Abers* 6F **72**
Bratoft. *Linc* 3A **38**
Brattleby. *Linc* 1G **37**
Bratton. *Som* 1J **7**
Bratton. *Telf* 8E **34**
Bratton. *Wilts* 8H **19**
Bratton Clovelly. *Devn* 6D **6**
Bratton Fleming. *Devn* 2F **6**
Bratton Seymour. *Som* 3E **8**
Braughing. *Herts* 1L **21**
Braulen Lodge. *High* 2C **70**
Braunston. *Nptn* 5C **28**
Braunstone Town. *Leics* 1C **28**
Braunston-in-Rutland. *Rut* 1F **28**
Braunton. *Devn* 2D **6**
Brawby. *N Yor* 8E **48**
Brawl. *High* 5L **85**
Brawlbin. *High* 6B **86**
Bray. *Wind* 6G **21**
Braybrooke. *Nptn* 3E **28**
Brayford. *Devn* 2F **6**
Bray Shop. *Corn* 8C **6**
Braystones. *Cumb* 4K **45**
Brayton. *N Yor* 4D **42**
Bray Wick. *Wind* 6F **20**
Brazacott. *Corn* 6B **6**
Brea. *Corn* 4K **3**
Breach. *W Sus* 5E **10**
Breachwood Green. *Herts* 1J **21**
Breacleit. *W Isl* 8E **82**
Breaden Heath. *Shrp* 6C **34**
Breadsall. *Derbs* 5A **36**
Breadstone. *Glos* 3F **18**
Breage. *Corn* 6K **3**
Breakachy. *High* 1E **70**
Breakish. *High* 3H **69**
Bream. *Glos* 3E **18**
Breamore. *Hants* 4K **9**
Bream's Meend. *Glos* 3E **18**
Brean. *Som* 8A **18**
Breanais. *W Isl* 1A **76**
Brearton. *N Yor* 1M **41**
Breascleit. *W Isl* 8F **82**
Breaston. *Derbs* 6B **36**
Brecais Àrd. *High* 3H **69**
Brecais Iosal. *High* 3H **69**
Brechfa. *Carm* 3M **15**
Brechin. *Ang* 2K **67**
Breckles. *Norf* 2F **30**
Brecon. *Powy* 2K **17**
Bredbury. *G Man* 8H **41**
Brede. *E Sus* 4E **12**
Bredenbury. *Here* 6E **26**
Bredfield. *Suff* 6J **31**
Bredgar. *Kent* 7E **22**
Bredhurst. *Kent* 7D **22**
Bredicot. *Worc* 6H **27**
Bredon. *Worc* 8H **27**
Bredon's Norton. *Worc* 8H **27**
Bredwardine. *Here* 7B **26**
Breedon on the Hill. *Leics* 7B **36**
Breibhig. *W Isl*
on Barra 6C **74**
on Isle of Lewis 8H **83**
Breich. *W Lot* 3H **59**
Breightmet. *G Man* 7F **40**
Breighton. *E Yor* 4E **42**
Breinton. *Here* 8C **26**
Breinton Common. *Here* 8C **26**
Breiwick. *Shet* 3E **90**
Brelston Green. *Here* 1D **18**
Bremhill. *Wilts* 6H **19**
Brenachie. *High* 6H **79**
Brenchley. *Kent* 1C **12**
Brendon. *Devn* 1G **7**
Brent Cross. *G Lon* 5K **21**
Brent Eleigh. *Suff* 7F **30**
Brentford. *G Lon* 6J **21**
Brentingby. *Leics* 8E **36**
Brent Knoll. *Som* 8B **18**
Brent Pelham. *Herts* 8M **29**
Brentwood. *Essx* 4B **22**
Brenzett. *Kent* 3G **13**
Brereton. *Staf* 8J **35**
Brereton Cross. *Staf* 8J **35**
Brereton Green. *Ches E* 3F **34**
Brereton Heath. *Ches E* 3G **35**
Bressingham. *Norf* 3G **31**
Bretby. *Derbs* 7L **35**
Bretford. *Warw* 4B **28**
Bretforton. *Worc* 7J **27**
Bretherdale Head. *Cumb* 5D **46**
Bretherton. *Lanc* 5C **40**
Brettabister. *Shet* 2E **90**
Brettenham. *Norf* 3F **30**
Brettenham. *Suff* 6F **30**
Bretton. *Flin* 3B **34**
Bretton. *Pet* 1J **29**
Brewlands Bridge. *Ang* 1E **66**
Brewood. *Staf* 1G **27**
Briantspuddle. *Dors* 6G **9**
Bricket Wood. *Herts* 3J **21**
Bricklehampton. *Worc* 7H **27**
Bride. *IOM* 4D **44**
Bridekirk. *Cumb* 8F **52**
Bridell. *Pemb* 2H **15**
Bridestowe. *Devn* 7E **6**
Brideswell. *Abers* 2E **72**
Bridford. *Devn* 7H **7**
Bridge. *Corn* 4K **3**
Bridge. *Kent* 8H **23**
Bridge. *Som* 5B **8**
Bridge End. *Bed* 6H **29**
Bridge End. *Cumb*
nr. Broughton in Furness 5M **45**
nr. Dalston 7H **53**
Bridge End. *Linc* 6J **37**
Bridge End. *Shet* 4D **90**
Bridgefoot. *Ang* 4G **67**
Bridgefoot. *Cumb* 2K **45**
Bridge Green. *Essx* 8A **30**
Bridgehampton. *Som* 3D **8**
Bridge Hewick. *N Yor* 8M **47**
Bridgehill. *Dur* 6D **54**
Bridgemary. *Hants* 5C **10**
Bridgemere. *Ches E* 5F **34**
Bridgemont. *Derbs* 1J **35**
Bridgend. *Abers*
nr. Huntly 2E **72**
nr. Peterhead 2K **73**
Bridgend. *Ang*
nr. Brechin 1J **67**
nr. Kirriemuir 3G **67**
Bridgend. *Arg*
nr. Lochgilphead 8C **64**
on Islay 3C **56**
Bridgend. *B'end* 6J **17**
Bridgend. *Cumb* 4B **46**
Bridgend. *Devn* 7H **5**
Bridgend. *Fife* 6G **67**
Bridgend. *High* 8D **78**
Bridgend. *Mor* 2C **72**
Bridgend. *Per* 5E **66**
Bridgend. *W Lot* 2J **59**
Bridgend of Lintrathen. *Ang* 2F **66**
Bridgeness. *Falk* 1J **59**
Bridge of Alford. *Abers* 4E **72**
Bridge of Allan. *Stir* 8A **66**
Bridge of Avon. *Mor* 2A **72**
Bridge of Awe. *Arg* 5E **64**
Bridge of Balgie. *Per* 3K **65**
Bridge of Brown. *High* 3M **71**
Bridge of Cally. *Per* 2E **66**
Bridge of Canny. *Abers* 6F **72**
Bridge of Dee. *Dum* 5B **52**
Bridge of Don. *Aber* 4J **73**
Bridge of Dun. *Ang* 2K **67**
Bridge of Dye. *Abers* 7F **72**
Bridge of Earn. *Per* 6E **66**
Bridge of Ericht. *Per* 2K **65**
Bridge of Feugh. *Abers* 6G **73**
Bridge of Gairn. *Abers* 6C **72**
Bridge of Gaur. *Per* 2K **65**
Bridge of Muchalls. *Abers* 6H **73**
Bridge of Oich. *High* 5D **70**
Bridge of Orchy. *Arg* 4H **65**
Bridge of Walls. *Shet* 2C **90**
Bridge of Weir. *Ren* 3B **58**
Bridge Reeve. *Devn* 4F **6**
Bridgerule. *Devn* 5B **6**
Bridge Sollers. *Here* 7C **26**
Bridge Street. *Suff* 7E **30**
Bridge Town. *Warw* 6L **27**
Bridgetown. *Devn* 5L **5**
Bridgetown. *Som* 2J **7**
Bridge Trafford. *Ches W* 2C **34**
Bridgeyate. *S Glo* 6E **18**
Bridgham. *Norf* 3F **30**
Bridgnorth. *Shrp* 2F **26**
Bridgtown. *Staf* 1H **27**
Bridgwater. *Som* 2B **8**
Bridlington. *E Yor* 1J **43**

Bridport—Carlton-on-Trent

Bridport. Dors 6C 8
Bridstow. Here 1D 18
Brierfield. Lanc 4G 41
Brierley. Glos 2E 18
Brierley. Here 6C 26
Brierley. S Yor 6B 42
Brierley Hill. W Mid 3H 27
Brierton. Hart 8H 55
Briestfield. W Yor 6L 41
Brigg. N Lin 7H 43
Briggate. Norf 7K 39
Briggswath. N Yor 5F 48
Brigham. Cumb 8E 52
Brigham. E Yor 2H 43
Brighouse. W Yor 5K 41
Brighstone. IOW 7B 10
Brightgate. Derbs 4L 35
Brighthampton. Oxon 3A 20
Brightholmlee. S Yor 8L 41
Brightley. Devn 6F 6
Brightling. E Sus 3C 12
Brightlingsea. Essx 2G 23
Brighton. Brig 106 (5L 11)
Brighton. Corn 6B 4
Brighton Hill. Hants 1D 10
Brightons. Falk 2H 59
Brightwalton. W Ber 6B 20
Brightwalton Green. W Ber 6B 20
Brightwell. Suff 7J 31
Brightwell Baldwin. Oxon 4D 20
Brightwell-cum-Sotwell. Oxon 4C 20
Brigmerston. Wilts 1K 9
Brignall. Dur 4J 47
Brig o' Turk. Stir 7K 65
Brigsley. NE Lin 7K 43
Brigsteer. Cumb 7C 46
Brigstock. Nptn 3G 29
Brill. Buck 2D 20
Brill. Corn 6L 3
Brilley. Here 7A 26
Brimaston. Pemb 4F 14
Brimfield. Here 5D 26
Brimington. Derbs 2B 36
Brimley. Devn 8H 7
Brimpsfield. Glos 2H 19
Brimpton. W Ber 7C 20
Brims. Orkn 3D 86
Brimscombe. Glos 3G 19
Brimstage. Mers 1B 34
Brincliffe. S Yor 1M 35
Brind. E Yor 4E 42
Brindister. Shet
nr. West Burrafirth 2C 90
nr. West Lerwick 4E 90
Brindle. Lanc 5D 40
Brindley. Ches E 4D 34
Brindley Ford. Stoke 4G 35
Brineton. Staf 8G 35
Bringhurst. Leics 2F 28
Bringsty Common. Here 6E 26
Brington. Cambs 4H 29
Brinian. Orkn 7D 88
Briningham. Norf 6G 39
Brinkhill. Linc 2L 37
Brinkley. Cambs 6C 30
Brinklow. Warw 4B 28
Brinkworth. Wilts 5J 19
Brinscall. Lanc 5E 40
Brinscombe. Som 8C 18
Brinsley. Notts 5B 36
Brinsworth. S Yor 1B 36
Brinton. Norf 6G 39
Brisco. Cumb 6J 53
Brisley. Norf 7F 38
Brislington. Bris 6E 18
Brissenden Green. Kent 2F 12
Bristol. Bris 107 (6D 18)
Bristol Airport. N Som 7D 18
Briston. Norf 6G 39
Britannia. Lanc 5G 41
Britford. Wilts 3K 9
Brithdir. Cphy 4L 17
Brithdir. Cdgn 2K 15
Brithdir. Gwyn 1G 25
Briton Ferry. Neat 5G 17
Britwell Salome. Oxon 4D 20
Brixham. Torb 6M 5
Brixton. Devn 6H 5
Brixton. G Lon 6L 21
Brixton Deverill. Wilts 2G 9
Brixworth. Nptn 4E 28
Brize Norton. Oxon 3M 19
The Broad. Here 5C 26
Broad Alley. Worc 5G 27
Broad Blunsdon. Swin 4K 19
Broadbottom. G Man 8H 41
Broadbridge. W Sus 5F 10
Broadbridge Heath. W Sus 2J 11
Broad Campden. Glos 8K 27
Broad Chalke. Wilts 3J 9
Broadclyst. Devn 6J 7
Broadfield. Inv 2B 58
Broadfield. Pemb 6H 15
Broadfield. W Sus 2K 11
Broadford. High 3H 69
Broadford Bridge. W Sus 3H 11
Broadgate. Cumb 6L 45
Broad Green. Cambs 6C 30
Broad Green. C Beds 7G 29
Broad Green. Worc
nr. Bromsgrove 4H 27
nr. Worcester 6F 26
Broad Haven. Pemb 5E 14
Broadhaven. High 6E 86
Broad Heath. Staf 7G 35
Broadheath. G Man 1F 34
Broadheath. Worc 5E 26
Broadheath Common. Worc 6G 27
Broadhembury. Devn 5L 7
Broadhempston. Devn 5L 5
Broad Hill. Cambs 4B 30
Broad Hinton. Wilts 6K 19
Broadholme. Derbs 5A 36
Broadholme. Linc 2F 36
Broadlay. Carm 6K 15
Broad Laying. Hants 7B 20
Broadley. Lanc 6G 41
Broadley. Mor 7C 80
Broadley Common. Essx 3M 21
Broad Marston. Worc 7K 27
Broadmayne. Dors 7F 8
Broadmere. Hants 1D 10
Broadmoor. Pemb 6G 15
Broad Oak. Carm 2E 16
Broad Oak. Cumb 5L 45
Broad Oak. Devn 6K 7
Broad Oak. Dors 4F 8
Broad Oak. E Sus
nr. Hastings 4E 12
nr. Heathfield 3C 12
Broad Oak. Here 1C 18
Broad Oak. Kent 7H 23
Broadoak. Dors 6C 8
Broadoak. Glos 2E 18
Broadoak. Hants 4C 10
Broadrashes. Mor 8D 80
Broadsea. Abers 7J 81
Broad's Green. Essx 2C 22
Broadshard. Som 4C 8
Broadstairs. Kent 7K 23
Broadstone. Pool 6J 9
Broadstone. Shrp 3D 26
Broad Street. E Sus 4E 12
Broad Street. Kent
nr. Ashford 1H 13
nr. Maidstone 8E 22
Broad Street Green. Essx 3E 22
Broad Town. Wilts 6J 19
Broadwas. Worc 6F 26
Broadwath. Cumb 6J 53
Broadway. Carm
nr. Kidwelly 6K 15
nr. Laugharne 6J 15
Broadway. Pemb 5E 14
Broadway. Som 4B 8
Broadway. Suff 4K 31
Broadway. Worc 8J 27
Broadwell. Glos
nr. Cinderford 2D 18
nr. Stow-on-the-Wold 1L 19
Broadwell. Oxon 3L 19
Broadwell. Warw 5B 28
Broadwell House. Nmbd 6C 54
Broadwey. Dors 7E 8
Broadwindsor. Dors 5C 8
Broadwoodkelly. Devn 5F 6
Broadwoodwidger. Devn 7D 6
Broallan. High 1E 70
Brobury. Here 7B 26
Brochel. High 1G 69
Brockaghboy. Caus 3F 93
Brockamin. Worc 6F 26
Brockbridge. Hants 4D 10
Brockdish. Norf 4J 31
Brockencote. Worc 4G 27
Brockenhurst. Hants 5L 9
Brocketsbrae. S Lan 6G 59
Brockford Street. Suff 5H 31
Brockhall. Nptn 5D 28
Brockham. Surr 1J 11
Brockhampton. Glos
nr. Bishop's Cleeve 1H 19
nr. Sevenhampton 1J 19
Brockhampton. Here 8D 26
Brockhill. Bord 7A 60
Brockholes. W Yor 6K 41
Brockhurst. Hants 5C 10
Brocklesby. Linc 6J 43
Brockley. N Som 7C 18
Brockley Corner. Suff 4E 30
Brockley Green. Suff
nr. Bury St Edmunds 7D 30
nr. Haverhill 6E 30
Brockleymoor. Cumb 8J 53
Brockmoor. W Mid 3H 27
Brockton. Shrp
nr. Bishop's Castle 3B 26
nr. Madeley 1F 26
nr. Much Wenlock 2D 26
nr. Pontesbury 1B 26
Brockton. Staf 6G 35
Brockton. Telf 8F 34
Brockweir. Glos 3D 18
Brockworth. Glos 2G 19
Brocton. Staf 8H 35
Brodick. N Ayr 6K 57
Brodie. Mor 8K 79
Brodiesord. Abers 8E 80
Brodsworth. S Yor 7C 42
Brogaig. High 7F 76
Brogborough. C Beds 8G 29
Brokenborough. Wilts 5H 19
Broken Cross. Ches E 2G 35
Bromborough. Mers 1B 34
Bromdon. Shrp 3E 26
Brome. Suff 4H 31
Brome Street. Suff 4H 31
Bromeswell. Suff 6K 31
Bromfield. Cumb 7F 52
Bromfield. Shrp 4C 26
Bromford. W Mid 2K 27
Bromham. Bed 6H 29
Bromham. Wilts 7H 19
Bromley. G Lon 7M 21
Bromley. Herts 1M 21
Bromley. Shrp 2F 26
Bromley Cross. G Man 6F 40
Bromley Green. Kent 2F 12
Bromley Wood. Staf 7K 35
Brompton. Medw 7D 22
Brompton. N Yor
nr. Northallerton 6A 48
nr. Scarborough 7G 49
Brompton. Shrp 1D 26
Brompton-on-Swale. N Yor 6L 47
Brompton Ralph. Som 2K 7
Brompton Regis. Som 2J 7
Bromsash. Here 1E 18
Bromsberrow. Glos 8F 26
Bromsberrow Heath. Glos 8F 26
Bromsgrove. Worc 4H 27
Bromstead Heath. Staf 8F 34
Bromyard. Here 6E 26
Bromyard Downs. Here 6E 26
Bronaber. Gwyn 7G 33
Broncroft. Shrp 3D 26
Brongest. Cdgn 2K 15
Brongwyn. Cdgn 2J 15
Bronington. Wrex 6C 34
Bronllys. Powy 1L 17
Bronnant. Cdgn 6F 24
Bronwydd Arms. Carm 4L 15
Bronydd. Powy 8M 25
Bronygarth. Shrp 6A 34
Brook. Carm 6J 15
Brook. Hants
nr. Cadnam 4L 9
nr. Romsey 3M 9
Brook. IOW 7A 10
Brook. Kent 1G 13
Brook. Surr
nr. Guildford 1H 11
nr. Haslemere 2G 11
Brooke. Norf 2J 31
Brooke. Rut 1F 28
Brookeborough. Ferm 6C 92
Brookenby. Linc 8K 43
Brook End. Worc 7G 27
Brookend. Glos 3E 18
Brookfield. Lanc 4D 40
Brookfield. Ren 3C 58
Brookhouse. Lanc 1D 40
Brookhouse. S Yor 1C 36
Brookhouse Green. Ches E 3G 35
Brookhouses. Staf 5H 35
Brookhurst. Mers 1B 34
Brookland. Kent 3F 12
Brooklands. G Man 8F 40
Brooklands. Shrp 5D 34
Brookmans Park. Herts 3K 21
Brooks. Powy 3L 25
Brooksby. Leics 8D 36
Brooks Green. W Sus 3J 11
Brook Street. Essx 4B 22
Brook Street. Kent 2F 12
Brook Street. W Sus 3L 11
Brookthorpe. Glos 2G 19
Brookville. Norf 2D 30
Brookwood. Surr 8G 21
Broom. C Beds 7J 29
Broom. Fife 7G 67
Broom. Warw 6J 27
Broome. Norf 2K 31
Broome. Shrp
nr. Cardington 2D 26
nr. Craven Arms 3C 26
Broome. Worc 4H 27
Broomedge. Warr 1F 34
Broomend. Abers 4G 73
Broomer's Corner. W Sus 3J 11
Broomfield. Abers 2J 73
Broomfield. Essx 2D 22
Broomfield. Kent
nr. Herne Bay 7H 23
nr. Maidstone 8E 22
Broomfield. Som 2M 7
Broomfleet. E Yor 5F 42
Broom Green. Norf 7F 38
Broomhall. Ches E 5E 34
Broomhall. Wind 7G 21
Broomhaugh. Nmbd 5D 54
Broom Hill. Dors 5J 9
Broom Hill. Worc 4H 27
Broomhill. High
nr. Grantown-on-Spey 3K 71
nr. Invergordon 6H 79
Broomhill. Norf 1C 30
Broomhill. S Yor 7B 42
Broomhillbank. Dum 2F 52
Broomholm. Norf 6K 39
Broomlands. Dum 1E 52
Broomley. Nmbd 5D 54
Broom of Moy. Mor 8L 79
Broompark. Dur 7F 54
Broom's Green. Glos 8F 26
Brora. High 3K 79
Broseley. Shrp 1E 26
Brotherhouse Bar. Linc 8K 37
Brotheridge Green. Worc 7G 27
Brotherlee. Dur 8C 54
Brothertoft. Linc 5K 37
Brotherton. N Yor 5B 42
Brotton. Red C 4D 48
Broubster. High 5B 86
Brough. Cumb 4F 46
Brough. Derbs 1K 35
Brough. E Yor 5G 43
Brough. High 4D 86
Brough. Notts 4F 36
Brough. Orkn
nr. Finstown 8C 88
nr. St Margaret's Hope 3F 86
Brough. Shet
nr. Benston 2E 90
nr. Booth of Toft 6J 91
on Bressay 3F 90
on Whalsay 1F 90
Broughall. Shrp 5D 34
Brougham. Cumb 3D 46
Brough Lodge. Shet 4K 91
Broughshane. ME Ant 3G 93
Brough Sowerby. Cumb 4F 46
Broughton. Cambs 4K 29
Broughton. Flin 3B 34
Broughton. Hants 2M 9
Broughton. Lanc 4D 40
Broughton. Mil 8F 28
Broughton. Nptn 4F 28
Broughton. N Lin 7G 43
Broughton. N Yor
nr. Malton 8E 48
nr. Skipton 2H 41
Broughton. Orkn 5D 88
Broughton. Oxon 8B 28
Broughton. Bord 6K 59
Broughton. Staf 6F 34
Broughton. V Glam 7J 17
Broughton Astley. Leics 2C 28
Broughton Beck. Cumb 7A 46
Broughton Cross. Cumb 8E 52
Broughton Gifford. Wilts 7G 19
Broughton Green. Worc 5H 27
Broughton Hackett. Worc 6H 27
Broughton in Furness. Cumb 6M 45
Broughton Mills. Cumb 5M 45
Broughton Moor. Cumb 8E 52
Broughton Park. G Man 7G 41
Broughton Poggs. Oxon 3L 19
Broughtown. Orkn 5F 88
Broughty Ferry. D'dee 4H 67
Browland. Shet 2C 90
Brownbread Street. E Sus 4C 12
Brown Candover. Hants 2C 10
Brown Edge. Lanc 6B 40
Brown Edge. Staf 4H 35
Brownhill. Bkbn 4E 40
Brownhill. Shrp 7C 34
Brownhills. Shrp 6E 34
Brownhills. W Mid 1J 27
Brown Knowl. Ches W 4C 34
Brownlow. Ches E 3G 35
Brownlow Heath. Ches E 3G 35
Brown's Green. W Mid 2J 27
Brownshill. Glos 3G 19
Brownston. Devn 6J 5
Brownstone. Devn 5G 7
Browston Green. Norf 1L 31
Broxa. N Yor 6G 49
Broxbourne. Herts 3L 21
Broxburn. E Lot 2D 60
Broxburn. W Lot 2J 59
Broxholme. Linc 2G 37
Broxted. Essx 1B 22
Broxton. Ches W 4C 34
Broxwood. Here 6B 26
Broyle Side. E Sus 4A 12
Brù. W Isl 7G 83
Bruach Mairi. W Isl 8H 83
Bruairnis. W Isl 5D 74
Bruan. High 8E 86
Bruar Lodge. Per 8J 71
Brucehill. W Dun 2B 58
Brucklay. Abers 8J 81
Bruera. Ches W 3C 34
Bruern Abbey. Oxon 1L 19
Bruichladdich. Arg 3B 56
Bruisyard. Suff 5K 31
Bruisyard Street. Suff 5K 31
Brund. Staf 3K 35
Brundall. Norf 1K 31
Brundish. Norf 2K 31
Brundish. Suff 5J 31
Brundish Street. Suff 4J 31
Brunery. High 8J 69
Brunswick Village. Tyne 4F 54
Brunthwaite. W Yor 3J 41
Bruntingthorpe. Leics 2D 28
Brunton. Fife 5G 67
Brunton. Nmbd 7K 61
Brunton. Wilts 8L 19
Brushford. Devn 5F 6
Brushford. Som 3J 7
Brusta. W Isl 5L 75
Bruton. Som 2E 8
Bryansford. New M 7H 93
Bryanston. Dors 5G 9
Bryant's Bottom. Buck 4F 20
Brydekirk. Dum 4F 52
Brymbo. Cnwy 3H 33
Brymbo. Wrex 4A 34
Brympton D'Evercy. Som 4D 8
Bryn. Carm 6M 15
Bryn. G Man 7D 40
Bryn. Neat 5H 17
Bryn. Shrp 3A 26
Brynamman. Carm 3G 17
Brynberian. Pemb 3H 15
Brynbryddan. Neat 5G 17
Bryncae. Rhon 6J 17
Bryncethin. B'end 6J 17
Bryncir. Gwyn 6D 32
Bryncoch. Neat 5G 17
Bryncroes. Gwyn 7B 32
Bryncrug. Gwyn 2F 24
Bryn Du. IOA 3C 32
Bryn Eden. Gwyn 8G 33
Bryn Eglwys. Gwyn 4F 32
Bryneglwys. Den 6L 33
Brynford. Flin 3L 33
Bryn Gates. G Man 7D 40
Bryn Golau. Rhon 6K 17
Bryngwran. IOA 3C 32
Bryngwyn. Mon 3B 18
Bryngwyn. Powy 8L 25
Bryn-henllan. Pemb 3G 15
Brynhoffnant. Cdgn 1K 15
Bryn-llwyn. Den 2K 33
Brynllywarch. Powy 4L 25
Bryn-mawr. Gwyn 7B 32
Brynmawr. Blae 3L 17
Brynmenyn. B'end 6J 17
Brynmill. Swan 5F 16
Brynna. Rhon 6J 17
Brynrefail. Gwyn 4E 32
Brynrefail. IOA 2D 32
Brynsadler. Rhon 6K 17
Bryn-Saith Marchog. Den 5K 33
Brynsiencyn. IOA 4D 32
Brynteg. IOA 2D 32
Brynteg. Wrex 4B 34
Brynygwenyn. Mon 2B 18
Bryn-y-maen. Cnwy 3H 33
Buaile nam Bodach. W Isl 5D 74
Bualintur. High 3F 68
Bubbenhall. Warw 4A 28
Bubwith. E Yor 4E 42
Buccleuch. Bord 8M 59
Buchanan Smithy. Stir 1C 58
Buchanhaven. Abers 1L 73
Buchanty. Per 5C 66
Buchany. Stir 7M 65
Buchley. E Dun 2D 58
Buchlyvie. Stir 8K 65
Buckabank. Cumb 7H 53
Buckden. Cambs 5J 29
Buckden. N Yor 8H 47
Buckenham. Norf 1K 31
Buckerell. Devn 5L 7
Buckfast. Devn 5K 5
Buckfastleigh. Devn 5K 5
Buckhaven. Fife 8G 67
Buckholm. Bord 6B 60
Buckholt. Here 2D 18
Buckhorn Weston. Dors 3F 8
Buckhurst Hill. Essx 4M 21
Buckie. Mor 7D 80
Buckingham. Buck 8D 28
Buckland. Buck 2F 20
Buckland. Glos 8J 27
Buckland. Here 6D 26
Buckland. Herts 8L 29
Buckland. Kent 1K 13
Buckland. Oxon 4M 19
Buckland. Surr 8K 21
Buckland Brewer. Devn 3D 6
Buckland Common. Buck 3G 21
Buckland Dinham. Som 8F 18
Buckland Filleigh. Devn 5D 6
Buckland in the Moor. Devn 8G 7
Buckland Monachorum. Devn 5G 5
Buckland Newton. Dors 5E 8
Buckland Ripers. Dors 7E 8
Buckland St Mary. Som 4A 8
Buckland-tout-Saints. Devn 7K 5
Bucklebury. W Ber 6C 20
Bucklegate. Linc 6L 37
Buckleigh. Devn 3D 6
Buckler's Hard. Hants 6B 10
Bucklesham. Suff 7J 31
Buckley. Flin 3A 34
Buckley Green. Warw 5K 27
Buckley Hill. Mers 8B 40
Bucklow Hill. Ches E 1F 34
Buckminster. Leics 7F 36
Bucknall. Linc 3J 37
Bucknall. Stoke 5H 35
Bucknell. Oxon 1C 20
Bucknell. Shrp 4B 26
Buckpool. Mor 7D 80
Bucksburn. Aber 5H 73
Buck's Cross. Devn 3C 6
Bucks Green. W Sus 2H 11
Buckshaw Village. Lanc 5D 40
Bucks Hill. Herts 3H 21
Bucks Horn Oak. Hants 1F 10
Buck's Mills. Devn 3C 6
Buckton. E Yor 8J 49
Buckton. Here 4B 26
Buckton. Nmbd 6H 61
Buckton Vale. G Man 7H 41
Buckworth. Cambs 4J 29
Budby. Notts 3D 36
Bude. Corn 5B 6
Budge's Shop. Corn 6F 4
Budlake. Devn 5J 7
Budle. Nmbd 6J 61
Budleigh Salterton. Devn 7K 7
Budock Water. Corn 5L 3
Buerton. Ches E 5E 34
Buffler's Holt. Buck 8D 28
Bugbrooke. Nptn 6D 28
Buglawton. Ches E 3G 35
Bugle. Corn 6C 4
Bugthorpe. E Yor 2E 42
Buildwas. Shrp 1E 26
Builth Road. Powy 7K 25
Builth Wells. Powy 7K 25
Bulbourne. Herts 2G 21
Bulby. Linc 7H 37
Bulcote. Notts 5D 36
Buldoo. High 5A 86
Bulford. Wilts 1K 9
Bulford Camp. Wilts 1K 9
Bulkeley. Ches E 4D 34
Bulkington. Warw 3A 28
Bulkington. Wilts 8H 19
Bulkworthy. Devn 4C 6
Bullamoor. N Yor 6A 48
Bull Bay. IOA 1D 32
Bullbridge. Derbs 4A 36
Bullgill. Cumb 8E 52
Bull Hill. Hants 6M 9
Bullinghope. Here 8D 26
Bull's Green. Herts 2K 21
Bullwood. Arg 2L 57
Bulmer. Essx 7E 30
Bulmer. N Yor 1D 42
Bulmer Tye. Essx 8E 30
Bulphan. Thur 5C 22
Bulverhythe. E Sus 5D 12
Bulwark. Abers 1J 73
Bulwell. Nott 5C 36
Bulwick. Nptn 2G 29
Bumble's Green. Essx 3M 21
Bun Abhainn Eadarra. W Isl 3C 76
Bunacaimb. High 7H 69
Bun a' Mhuillinn. W Isl 4D 74
Bunarkaig. High 7B 70
Bunbury. Ches E 4D 34
Bunchrew. High 1G 71
Bundalloch. High 3K 69
Buness. Shet 3L 91
Bunessan. Arg 5J 63
Bungay. Suff 3K 31
Bunkegivie. High 4F 70
Bunker's Hill. Cambs 1M 29
Bunker's Hill. Suff 1M 31
Bunkers Hill. Linc 4K 37
Bunloit. High 3F 70
Bunnahabhain. Arg 2D 56
Bunny. Notts 7C 36
Bunoich. High 5D 70
Bunree. High 1E 64
Bunroy. High 7C 70
Buntait. High 2E 70
Buntingford. Herts 1L 21
Bunting's Green. Essx 8E 30
Bunwell. Norf 2H 31
Burbage. Derbs 2J 35
Burbage. Leics 2B 28
Burbage. Wilts 7L 19
Burcher. Here 5B 26
Burchett's Green. Wind 5F 20
Burcombe. Wilts 2J 9
Burcot. Oxon 4C 20
Burcot. Worc 4H 27
Burcote. Shrp 2F 26
Burcott. Buck 1F 20
Burcott. Som 1D 8
Burdale. N Yor 1F 42
Burdrop. Oxon 8A 28
Bures. Suff 8F 30
The Burf. Worc 5G 27
Burford. Oxon 2L 19
Burford. Shrp 5D 26
Burg. Arg 3J 63
Burgate Great Green. Suff 4G 31
Burgate Little Green. Suff 4G 31
Burgess Hill. W Sus 4L 11
Burgh. Suff 6J 31
Burgh by Sands. Cumb 6H 53
Burgh Castle. Norf 1L 31
Burghclere. Hants 7B 20
Burghead. Mor 7M 79
Burghfield. W Ber 7D 20
Burghfield Common. W Ber 7D 20
Burghfield Hill. W Ber 7D 20
Burgh Heath. Surr 8K 21
Burghill. Here 7C 26
Burgh le Marsh. Linc 3B 38
Burgh Muir. Abers 4G 73
Burgh next Aylsham. Norf 7J 39
Burgh on Bain. Linc 1K 37
Burgh St Margaret. Norf 8L 39
Burgh St Peter. Norf 2L 31
Burghwallis. S Yor 6C 42
Burham. Kent 7D 22
Buriton. Hants 3E 10
Burland. Ches E 4E 34
Burland. Shet 4D 90
Burlawn. Corn 5B 4
Burleigh. Glos 3G 19
Burleigh. Wind 6F 20
Burlescombe. Devn 4K 7
Burleston. Dors 6F 8
Burlestone. Devn 7L 5
Burley. Hants 5L 9
Burley. Rut 8F 36
Burley. W Yor 4L 41
Burleydam. Ches E 5E 34
Burley Gate. Here 7D 26
Burley in Wharfedale. W Yor 3K 41
Burley Street. Hants 5L 9
Burley Woodhead. W Yor 3K 41
Burlingjobb. Powy 6A 26
Burlington. Shrp 8F 34
Burlton. Shrp 7C 34
Burmantofts. W Yor 4M 41
Burmarsh. Kent 2H 13
Burmington. Warw 8L 27
Burn. N Yor 5C 42
Burnage. G Man 8G 41
Burnaston. Derbs 6L 35
Burnbanks. Cumb 4D 46
Burnby. E Yor 3F 42
Burncross. S Yor 8M 41
Burneside. Cumb 6D 46
Burness. Orkn 5F 88
Burneston. N Yor 7M 47
Burnett. Bath 7E 18
Burnfoot. E Ayr 1K 51
Burnfoot. Per 7C 66
Burnfoot. Bord
nr. Hawick 8C 60
nr. Roberton 8B 60
Burngreave. S Yor 1A 36
Burnham. Buck 5G 21
Burnham. N Lin 6H 43
Burnham Deepdale. Norf 5E 38
Burnham Green. Herts 2K 21
Burnham Market. Norf 5E 38
Burnham Norton. Norf 5E 38
Burnham-on-Crouch. Essx 4F 22
Burnham-on-Sea. Som 1B 8
Burnham Overy Staithe. Norf 5E 38
Burnham Overy Town. Norf 5E 38
Burnham Thorpe. Norf 5E 38
Burnhaven. Abers 1L 73
Burnhead. Dum 2C 52
Burnhervie. Abers 4G 73
Burnhill Green. Staf 1F 26
Burnhope. Dur 7E 54
Burnhouse. N Ayr 4B 58
Burniston. N Yor 6H 49
Burnlee. W Yor 7K 41
Burnley. Lanc 4G 41
Burnmouth. Bord 3G 61
Burn Naze. Lanc 3B 40
Burn of Cambus. Stir 7M 65
Burnopfield. Dur 6E 54
Burnsall. N Yor 1J 41
Burnside. Ang 2J 67
Burnside. Ant
nr. Antrim 4G 93
nr. Ballyclare 4H 93
Burnside. E Ayr 8D 58
Burnside. Per 7E 66
Burnside. Shet 6G 91
Burnside. S Lan 4E 58
Burnside. W Lot
nr. Broxburn 2J 59
nr. Winchburgh 2J 59
Burntcommon. Surr 8H 21
Burnt Heath. Essx 1G 23
Burntheath. Derbs 6L 35
Burnt Hill. W Ber 6C 20
Burnt Houses. Dur 3K 47
Burntisland. Fife 1L 59
Burnt Oak. G Lon 4K 21
Burnton. E Ayr 1K 51
Burntstalk. Norf 6D 38
Burntwood. Staf 1J 27
Burntwood Green. Staf 1J 27
Burnt Yates. N Yor 1L 41
Burnwynd. Edin 3K 59
Burpham. Surr 8H 21
Burpham. W Sus 5H 11
Burradon. Nmbd 1C 54
Burradon. Tyne 4F 54
Burrafirth. Shet 2L 91
Burragarth. Shet 3K 91
Burras. Corn 5K 3
Burraton. Corn 6G 5
Burravoe. Shet
nr. North Roe 5H 91
on Mainland 1D 90
on Yell 6K 91
Burray Village. Orkn 2F 86
Burrells. Cumb 4E 46
Burrelton. Per 4E 66
Burren. New M 7G 93
Burren Bridge. New M 7H 93
Burridge. Hants 4C 10
Burridge. Som 5B 8
Burrigill. High 8D 86
Burrill. N Yor 7L 47
Burringham. N Lin 7F 42
Burrington. Devn 4F 6
Burrington. Here 4C 26
Burrington. N Som 8C 18
Burrough End. Cambs 6C 30
Burrough Green. Cambs 6C 30
Burrough on the Hill. Leics 8E 36
Burroughston. Orkn 7E 88
Burrow. Devn 7K 7
Burrow. Som 1J 7
Burrowbridge. Som 3B 8
Burrowhill. Surr 7G 21
Burry. Swan 7L 15
Burry Green. Swan 7L 15
Burry Port. Carm 6L 15
Burscough. Lanc 6C 40
Burscough Bridge. Lanc 6C 40
Bursea. E Yor 4F 42
Burshill. E Yor 3H 43
Bursledon. Hants 5B 10
Burslem. Stoke 5G 35
Burstall. Suff 7G 31
Burstock. Dors 5C 8
Burston. Devn 5G 7
Burston. Norf 3H 31
Burston. Staf 6H 35
Burstow. Surr 1L 11
Burstwick. E Yor 5K 43
Burtersett. N Yor 7G 47
Burtholme. Cumb 5K 53
Burthorpe. Suff 5D 30
Burthwaite. Cumb 7J 53
Burtle. Som 1C 8
Burtoft. Linc 6K 37
Burton. Ches W
nr. Kelsall 3D 34
nr. Neston 2B 34
Burton. Dors
nr. Christchurch 6K 9
nr. Dorchester 6E 8
Burton. Nmbd 6J 61
Burton. Pemb 6F 14
Burton. Som 1L 7
Burton. Wilts
nr. Chippenham 6G 19
nr. Warminster 2G 9
Burton. Wrex 4B 34
Burton Agnes. E Yor 1J 43
Burton Bradstock. Dors 7C 8
Burton-by-Lincoln. Linc 2G 37
Burton Coggles. Linc 7G 37
Burton Constable. E Yor 4J 43
Burton Corner. Linc 5L 37
Burton End. Cambs 7C 30
Burton End. Essx 1B 22
Burton Fleming. E Yor 8H 49
Burton Green. Warw 4L 27
Burton Green. Wrex 4B 34
Burton Hastings. Warw 3B 28
Burton-in-Kendal. Cumb 8D 46
Burton in Lonsdale. N Yor 8E 46
Burton Joyce. Notts 5D 36
Burton Latimer. Nptn 4G 29
Burton Lazars. Leics 8E 36
Burton Leonard. N Yor 1M 41
Burton on the Wolds. Leics 7C 36
Burton Overy. Leics 2D 28
Burton Pedwardine. Linc 5J 37
Burton Pidsea. E Yor 4K 43
Burton Salmon. N Yor 5B 42
Burton's Green. Essx 1E 22
Burton Stather. N Lin 6F 42
Burton upon Stather. N Lin 6F 42
Burton upon Trent. Staf 7L 35
Burton Wolds. Leics 7D 36
Burtonwood. Warr 8D 40
Burwardsley. Ches W 4D 34
Burwarton. Shrp 3E 26
Burwash. E Sus 3C 12
Burwash Common. E Sus 3C 12
Burwash Weald. E Sus 3C 12
Burwell. Cambs 5B 30
Burwell. Linc 2L 37
Burwen. IOA 1D 32
Burwick. Orkn 3F 86
Bury. Cambs 3K 29
Bury. G Man 6G 41
Bury. Som 3J 7
Bury. W Sus 4H 11
Burybank. Staf 6G 35
Bury End. Worc 8J 27
Bury Green. Herts 1A 22
Bury St Edmunds. Suff 5E 30
Burythorpe. N Yor 1E 42
Busbridge. Surr 1G 11
Busby. E Ren 4D 58
Busby. Per 5D 66
Buscot. Oxon 4L 19
Bush. Corn 5B 6
The Bush. M Ulst 5F 93
Bush Bank. Here 6C 26
Bushbury. W Mid 1H 27
Bushby. Leics 1D 28
Bushey. Dors 7H 9
Bushey. Herts 4J 21
Bushey Heath. Herts 4J 21
Bush Green. Norf
nr. Attleborough 2G 31
nr. Harleston 3J 31
Bush Green. Suff 6F 30
Bushley. Worc 8G 27
Bushley Green. Worc 8G 27
Bushmead. Bed 5J 29
Bushmills. Caus 1F 93
Bushmoor. Shrp 3C 26
Bushton. Wilts 6J 19
Bushy Common. Norf 8F 38
Busk. Cumb 7L 53
Buslingthorpe. Linc 1H 37
Bussage. Glos 3G 19
Bussex. Som 2B 8
Busta. Shet 1D 90
Butcher's Cross. E Sus 3B 12
Butcombe. N Som 7D 18
Bute Town. Cphy 4L 17
Butleigh. Som 2D 8
Butleigh Wootton. Som 2D 8
Butlers Marston. Warw 7M 27
Butley. Suff 6K 31
Butley High Corner. Suff 7K 31
Butlocks Heath. Hants 5B 10
Butterburn. Cumb 4L 53
Buttercrambe. N Yor 2E 42
Butterknowle. Dur 3K 47
Butterleigh. Devn 5J 7
Buttermere. Cumb 3L 45
Buttermere. Wilts 7M 19
Buttershaw. W Yor 5K 41
Butterstone. Per 3D 66
Butterton. Staf
nr. Leek 4J 35
nr. Stoke-on-Trent 5G 35
Butterwick. Dur 3A 48
Butterwick. Linc 5L 37
Butterwick. N Yor
nr. Malton 8E 48
nr. Weaverthorpe 8G 49
Butteryhaugh. Nmbd 2L 53
Butt Green. Ches E 4E 34
Buttington. Powy 1A 26
Buttonbridge. Shrp 4F 26
Buttonoak. Shrp 4F 26
Buttsash. Hants 5B 10
Butt's Green. Essx 3D 22
Butt Yeats. Lanc 1D 40
Buxhall. Suff 6G 31
Buxted. E Sus 3A 12
Buxton. Derbs 2J 35
Buxton. Norf 7J 39
Buxworth. Derbs 1J 35
Bwcle. Flin 3A 34
Bwlch. Powy 2L 17
Bwlchderwin. Gwyn 6D 32
Bwlchgwyn. Wrex 4A 34
Bwlch-Llan. Cdgn 7E 24
Bwlchnewydd. Carm 4K 15
Bwlchtocyn. Gwyn 8C 32
Bwlch-y-cibau. Powy 1L 25
Bwlchyddar. Powy 8L 33
Bwlch-y-fadfa. Cdgn 2L 15
Bwlch-y-ffridd. Powy 3K 25
Bwlch y Garreg. Powy 3K 25
Bwlch-y-groes. Pemb 3J 15
Bwlch-y-sarnau. Powy 5K 25
Bybrook. Kent 1G 13
Byermoor. Tyne 6E 54
Byers Garth. Dur 7G 55
Byers Green. Dur 8F 54
Byfield. Nptn 6C 28
Byfleet. Surr 7H 21
Byford. Here 7B 26
Bygrave. Herts 8K 29
Byker. Tyne 5F 54
Byland Abbey. N Yor 8C 48
Bylchau. Cnwy 4J 33
Byley. Ches W 3F 34
Bynea. Carm 7M 15
Byram. N Yor 5B 42
Byrness. Nmbd 1A 54
Bystock. Devn 7K 7
Bythorn. Cambs 4H 29
Byton. Here 5B 26
Bywell. Nmbd 5D 54
Byworth. W Sus 3G 11

C

Cabharstadh. W Isl 2E 76
Cabourne. Linc 7J 43
Cabrach. Arg 3D 56
Cabrach. Mor 3C 72
Cabragh. M Ulst 5E 92
Cabus. Lanc 3C 40
Cadbury. Devn 5J 7
Cadder. E Dun 2E 58
Caddington. C Beds 2H 21
Caddonfoot. Bord 6B 60
Cadeby. Leics 1B 28
Cadeby. S Yor 7C 42
Cadeleigh. Devn 5J 7
Cade Street. E Sus 3C 12
Cadgwith. Corn 7L 3
Cadham. Fife 7F 66
Cadishead. G Man 8F 40
Cadle. Swan 5F 16
Cadley. Lanc 4D 40
Cadley. Wilts
nr. Ludgershall 8L 19
nr. Marlborough 7L 19
Cadmore End. Buck 4E 20
Cadnam. Hants 4L 9
Cadney. N Lin 7H 43
Cadole. Flin 4M 33
Cadoxton-juxta-Neath. Neat 5G 17
Cadwell. Herts 8J 29
Cadwst. Den 7K 33
Caeathro. Gwyn 4E 32
Caehopkin. Powy 3H 17
Caenby. Linc 1H 37
Caerau. B'end 5H 17
Caerau. Card 7L 17
Cae'r-bont. Powy 3H 17
Cae'r-bryn. Carm 3E 16
Caerdeon. Gwyn 1F 24
Caerdydd. Card 107 (7L 17)
Caerfarchell. Pemb 4D 14
Caerffili. Cphy 6L 17
Caerfyrddin. Carm 5L 15
Caergeiliog. IOA 3C 32
Caergwrle. Flin 4B 34
Caergybi. IOA 2B 32
Caerlaverock. Per 6B 66
Caerleon. Newp 4B 18
Caerlleon. Carm 4J 15
Caerllion. Newp 4B 18
Caernarfon. Gwyn 4D 32
Caerphilly. Cphy 6L 17
Caersws. Powy 3K 25
Caerwedros. Cdgn 1K 15
Caerwent. Mon 4C 18
Caerwys. Flin 3L 33
Caim. IOA 2F 32
Caio. Carm 1F 16
Cairinis. W Isl 7K 75
Cairisiadar. W Isl 8D 82
Cairminis. W Isl 5B 76
Cairnbaan. Arg 8C 64
Cairnbulg. Abers 7K 81
Cairncross. Ang 8D 72
Cairndow. Arg 6F 64
Cairness. Abers 7K 81
Cairneyhill. Fife 1J 59
Cairngarroch. Dum 7F 50
Cairnhill. Abers 2F 72
Cairnie. Abers 1D 72
Cairnorrie. Abers 1H 73
Cairnryan. Dum 5F 50
Cairston. Orkn 8B 88
Caister-on-Sea. Norf 8M 39
Caistor. Linc 7J 43
Caistor St Edmund. Norf 1J 31
Caistron. Nmbd 1C 54
Cakebole. Worc 4G 27
Calais Street. Suff 7F 30
Calanais. W Isl 8F 82
Calbost. W Isl 2F 76
Calbourne. IOW 7B 10
Calceby. Linc 2L 37
Calcot. Glos 2J 19
Calcot Row. W Ber 6D 20
Calcott. Kent 7H 23
Calcott. Shrp 8C 34
Caldback. Shet 3L 91
Caldbeck. Cumb 8H 53
Caldbergh. N Yor 7J 47
Caldecote. Cambs
nr. Cambridge 6L 29
nr. Peterborough 3J 29
Caldecote. Herts 8K 29
Caldecote. Nptn 6D 28
Caldecote. Warw 2A 28
Caldecott. Nptn 5G 29
Caldecott. Oxon 4B 20
Caldecott. Rut 2F 28
Calderbank. N Lan 3F 58
Calder Bridge. Cumb 4K 45
Calderbrook. G Man 6H 41
Caldercruix. N Lan 3G 59
Calder Grove. W Yor 6M 41
Calder Mains. High 6B 86
Caldermill. S Lan 5E 58
Calder Vale. Lanc 3D 40
Calderwood. S Lan 4E 58
Caldicot. Mon 5C 18
Caldwell. Derbs 8L 35
Caldwell. N Yor 4K 47
Caldy. Mers 2M 33
Calebrack. Cumb 8H 53
Caledon. M Ulst 6E 92
Calf Heath. Staf 1H 27
Calford Green. Suff 7C 30
Calfsound. Orkn 6E 88
Calgary. Arg 2J 63
Califer. Mor 8L 79
California. Cambs 3B 30
California. Falk 2H 59
California. Norf 8M 39
California. Suff 7H 31
Calke. Derbs 7A 36
Callakille. High 8H 77
Callaly. Nmbd 1D 54
Callander. Stir 7L 65
Callaughton. Shrp 2E 26
Callendoun. Arg 1B 58
Callestick. Corn 3L 3
Calligarry. High 5H 69
Callington. Corn 5F 4
Callingwood. Staf 7K 35
Callow. Here 8C 26
Callowell. Glos 3G 19
Callow End. Worc 7G 27
Callow Hill. Wilts 5J 19
Callow Hill. Worc
nr. Bewdley 4F 26
nr. Redditch 5J 27
Calmore. Hants 4M 9
Calmsden. Glos 3J 19
Calne. Wilts 6H 19
Calow. Derbs 2B 36
Calshot. Hants 5B 10
Calstock. Corn 5G 5
Calstone Wellington. Wilts 7J 19
Calthorpe. Norf 6H 39
Calthorpe Street. Norf 7L 39
Calthwaite. Cumb 7J 53
Calton. N Yor 2H 41
Calton. Staf 4K 35
Calveley. Ches E 4D 34
Calver. Derbs 2L 35
Calverhall. Shrp 6E 34
Calverleigh. Devn 4J 7
Calverley. W Yor 4L 41
Calvert. Buck 1D 20
Calverton. Mil 8E 28
Calverton. Notts 5D 36
Calvine. Per 1B 66
Calvo. Cumb 6F 52
Cam. Glos 4F 18
Camaghael. High 8B 70
Camas-luinie. High 3L 69
Camasnacroise. High 2C 64
Camastianavaig. High 2G 69
Camasunary. High 4G 69
Camault Muir. High 1F 70
Camb. Shet 4K 91
Camber. E Sus 4F 12
Camberley. Surr 7F 20
Camberwell. G Lon 6L 21
Camblesforth. N Yor 5D 42
Cambo. Nmbd 3D 54
Cambois. Nmbd 3G 55
Camborne. Corn 5K 3
Cambourne. Cambs 6L 29
Cambridge. Cambs 107 (6A 30)
Cambridge. Glos 3F 18
Cambrose. Corn 4K 3
Cambus. Clac 8B 66
Cambusbarron. Stir 8A 66
Cambuskenneth. Stir 8B 66
Cambuslang. S Lan 3E 58
Cambusnethan. N Lan 4G 59
Cambus o' May. Abers 6D 72
Camden Town. G Lon 5K 21
Cameley. Bath 8E 18
Camelford. Corn 3D 4
Camelon. Falk 1G 59
Camelsdale. W Sus 2F 10
Camer's Green. Worc 8F 26
Camerton. Bath 8E 18
Camerton. Cumb 8E 52
Camerton. E Yor 5K 43
Camghouran. Per 2K 65
Camlough. New M 7G 93
Cammachmore. Abers 6J 73
Cammeringham. Linc 1G 37
Camore. High 4H 79
The Camp. Glos 3H 19
Campbelton. N Ayr 4L 57
Campbeltown. Arg 7G 57
Campbeltown Airport. Arg 7F 56
Cample. Dum 2C 52
Campmuir. Per 4F 66
Campsall. S Yor 6C 42
Campsea Ashe. Suff 6K 31
Camps End. Cambs 7C 30
Campsey. Derr 2D 92
Campton. C Beds 8J 29
Camptoun. E Lot 2C 60
Camptown. Bord 8D 60
Camrose. Pemb 4F 14
Camserney. Per 3B 66
Camster. High 7D 86
Camus Croise. High 4H 69
Camuscross. High 4H 69
Camusdarach. High 6H 69
Camusnagaul. High
nr. Fort William 8A 70
nr. Little Loch Broom 5A 78
Camus Park. Derr 4C 92
Camusteel. High 1J 69
Camusterrach. High 1J 69
Camusvrachan. Per 3L 65
Canada. Hants 4L 9
Canadia. E Sus 4D 12
Canaston Bridge. Pemb 5G 15
Candlesby. Linc 3A 38
Candle Street. Suff 4G 31
Candy Mill. S Lan 5J 59
Cane End. Oxon 6D 20
Canewdon. Essx 4F 22
Canford Cliffs. Pool 7J 9
Canford Heath. Pool 6J 9
Canford Magna. Pool 6J 9
Cangate. Norf 8K 39
Canham's Green. Suff 5G 31
Canholes. Derbs 2J 35
Canisbay. High 4E 86
Canley. W Mid 4M 27
Cann. Dors 3G 9
Cann Common. Dors 3G 9
Cannich. High 2D 70
Cannington. Som 2A 8
Cannock. Staf 8H 35
Cannock Wood. Staf 8J 35
Canonbie. Dum 4H 53
Canon Bridge. Here 7C 26
Canon Frome. Here 7E 26
Canon Pyon. Here 7C 26
Canons Ashby. Nptn 6C 28
Canonstown. Corn 5J 3
Canterbury. Kent 107 (8H 23)
Cantley. Norf 1K 31
Cantley. S Yor 7D 42
Cantlop. Shrp 1D 26
Canton. Card 7L 17
Cantray. High 1H 71
Cantraybruich. High 1H 71
Cantraywood. High 1H 71
Cantsdam. Fife 8E 66
Cantsfield. Lanc 8E 46
Canvey Island. Essx 5D 22
Canwick. Linc 3G 37
Canworthy Water. Corn 6B 6
Caol. High 8B 70
Caolas. Arg 3F 62
Caolas. W Isl 6C 74
Caolas Liubharsaigh. W Isl 1E 74
Caolas Scalpaigh. W Isl 4D 76
Caolas Stocinis. W Isl 4C 76
Caol Ila. Arg 2D 56
Caol Loch Ailse. High 3J 69
Caol Reatha. High 3J 69
Capel. Kent 1C 12
Capel. Surr 1J 11
Capel Bangor. Cdgn 4F 24
Capel Betws Lleucu. Cdgn 7F 24
Capel Coch. IOA 2D 32
Capel Curig. Cnwy 5G 33
Capel Cynon. Cdgn 2K 15
Capel Dewi. Carm 4L 15
Capel Dewi. Cdgn
nr. Aberystwyth 4F 24
nr. Llandysul 2L 15
Capel Garmon. Cnwy 5H 33
Capel Green. Suff 7K 31
Capel Gwyn. IOA 3C 32
Capel Gwynfe. Carm 2G 17
Capel Hendre. Carm 3E 16
Capel Isaac. Carm 2E 16
Capel Iwan. Carm 3J 15
Capel-le-Ferne. Kent 2J 13
Capel Llanilltern. Card 7K 17
Capel Mawr. IOA 3D 32
Capel Newydd. Pemb 3J 15
Capel St Andrew. Suff 7K 31
Capel St Mary. Suff 8G 31
Capel Seion. Carm 5M 15
Capel Seion. Cdgn 5F 24
Capel Uchaf. Gwyn 6D 32
Capel-y-ffin. Powy 8A 26
Capenhurst. Ches W 2B 34
Capernwray. Lanc 8D 46
Capheaton. Nmbd 3D 54
Cappagh. M Ulst 5E 92
Cappercleuch. Bord 7L 59
Capplegill. Dum 1F 52
Capton. Devn 6L 5
Capton. Som 2K 7
Caputh. Per 4D 66
Caradon Town. Corn 8B 6
Carbis Bay. Corn 5J 3
Carbost. High
nr. Loch Harport 2E 68
nr. Portree 1F 68
Carbrook. S Yor 1A 36
Carbrooke. Norf 1F 30
Carburton. Notts 2D 36
Carcluie. S Ayr 8B 58
Car Colston. Notts 5E 36
Carcroft. S Yor 7C 42
Cardenden. Fife 8F 66
Cardeston. Shrp 8B 34
Cardewlees. Cumb 6H 53
Cardiff. Card 107 (7L 17)
Cardiff Airport. V Glam 8K 17
Cardigan. Cdgn 2H 15
Cardinal's Green. Cambs 7C 30
Cardington. Bed 7H 29
Cardington. Shrp 2D 26
Cardinham. Corn 5D 4
Cardno. Abers 7J 81
Cardow. Mor 1A 72
Cardross. Arg 2B 58
Cardurnock. Cumb 6F 52
Careby. Linc 8H 37
Careston. Ang 1J 67
Carew. Pemb 6G 15
Carew Cheriton. Pemb 6G 15
Carew Newton. Pemb 6G 15
Carey. Here 8D 26
Carfin. N Lan 4F 58
Carfrae. Bord 4C 60
Cargan. ME Ant 3G 93
Cargate Green. Norf 8K 39
Cargenbridge. Dum 4D 52
Cargill. Per 4E 66
Cargo. Cumb 6H 53
Cargreen. Corn 5G 5
Carham. Nmbd 6F 60
Carhampton. Som 1K 7
Carharrack. Corn 4L 3
Carie. Per
nr. Loch Rannah 2L 65
nr. Loch Tay 4L 65
Carisbrooke. IOW 7B 10
Cark. Cumb 8B 46
Carkeel. Corn 5G 5
Carlabhagh. W Isl 7F 82
Carland Cross. Corn 3M 3
Carlbury. Darl 4L 47
Carlby. Linc 8H 37
Carlecotes. S Yor 7K 41
Carleen. Corn 6K 3
Carlesmoor. N Yor 8K 47
Carleton. Cumb
nr. Carlisle 6J 53
nr. Egremont 4K 45
nr. Penrith 3D 46
Carleton. Lanc 3B 40
Carleton. N Yor 3H 41
Carleton. W Yor 5B 42
Carleton Forehoe. Norf 1G 31
Carleton Rode. Norf 2H 31
Carleton St Peter. Norf 1K 31
Carlidnack. Corn 6L 3
Carlingcott. Bath 8E 18
Carlin How. Red C 4E 48
Carlisle. Cumb 107 (6J 53)
Carloonan. Arg 6E 64
Carlops. Bord 4K 59
Carlton. Bed 6G 29
Carlton. Cambs 6C 30
Carlton. Leics 1A 28
Carlton. N Yor
nr. Helmsley 7D 48
nr. Middleham 7J 47
nr. Selby 5D 42
Carlton. Notts 5D 36
Carlton. S Yor 6A 42
Carlton. Stoc T 3A 48
Carlton. Suff 5K 31
Carlton. W Yor 5M 41
Carlton Colville. Suff 2M 31
Carlton Curlieu. Leics 2D 28
Carlton Husthwaite. N Yor 8B 48
Carlton in Cleveland. N Yor 5C 48
Carlton in Lindrick. Notts 1C 36
Carlton-le-Moorland. Linc 4G 37
Carlton Miniott. N Yor 7A 48
Carlton-on-Trent. Notts 3F 36

A-Z Great Britain Road Atlas 123

Carlton Scroop—Coddenham Green

Carlton Scroop. *Linc* 5G 37
Carluke. *S Lan* 4G 59
Carlyon Bay. *Corn* 6C 4
Carmarthen. *Carm* 5L 15
Carmel. *Carm* 3E 16
Carmel. *Flin* 3L 33
Carmel. *Gwyn* 5D 32
Carmel. *IOA* 2C 32
Carmichael. *S Lan* 6H 59
Carmunnock. *Glas* 4E 58
Carmyle. *Glas* 3E 58
Carmyllie. *Ang* 3J 67
Carnaby. *E Yor* 1J 43
Carnach. *High*
nr. Lochcarron 3M 69
nr. Ullapool 4M 77
Carnach. *Mor* 1L 71
Carnach. *W Isl* 4D 76
Carnachy. *High* 6K 85
Carnain. *Arg* 3C 56
Carnais. *W Isl* 8D 82
Carnan. *Arg* 3F 62
Carnan. *W Isl* 1D 74
Carnbee. *Fife* 7J 67
Carnbo. *Per* 7D 66
Carn Brea Village. *Corn* 4K 3
Carndu. *High* 3K 69
Carnduff. *Caus* 1G 93
Carne. *Corn* 8B 4
Carnell. *S Ayr* 6C 58
Carnforth. *Lanc* 8D 46
Carn-gorm. *High* 3L 69
Carnhedryn. *Pemb* 4E 14
Carnhell Green. *Corn* 5K 3
Carnie. *Abers* 5H 73
Carnkie. *Corn*
nr. Falmouth 5L 3
nr. Redruth 5K 3
Carnkief. *Corn* 3L 3
Carnlough. *ME Ant* 3H 93
Carnmoney. *Ant* 4H 93
Carno. *Powy* 3J 25
Carnock. *Fife* 1J 59
Carnon Downs. *Corn* 4L 3
Carnoustie. *Ang* 4J 67
Carnteel. *M Ulst* 6E 92
Carntyne. *Glas* 3E 58
Carnwath. *S Lan* 5H 59
Carnyorth. *Corn* 5G 3
Carol Green. *W Mid* 4L 27
Carpalla. *Corn* 6B 4
Carperby. *N Yor* 7J 47
Carradale. *Arg* 6H 57
Carragraich. *W Isl* 4C 76
Carrbridge. *High* 3K 71
Carr Cross. *Lanc* 6B 40
Carreglefn. *IOA* 2C 32
Carrhouse. *N Lin* 7E 42
Carrick Castle. *Arg* 8F 64
Carrickfergus. *ME Ant* 4J 93
Carrick Ho. *Orkn* 6E 88
Carrickmore. *Ferm* 5E 92
Carriden. *Falk* 1J 59
Carrington. *G Man* 8F 40
Carrington. *Linc* 4L 37
Carrington. *Midl* 3M 59
Carrog. *Cnwy* 6G 33
Carrog. *Den* 6L 33
Carron. *Falk* 1G 59
Carron. *Mor* 1B 72
Carronbridge. *Dum* 2C 52
Carronshore. *Falk* 1G 59
Carrowclare. *Caus* 2E 92
Carrowdore. *Ards* 5J 93
Carrow Hill. *Mon* 4C 18
Carr Shield. *Nmbd* 7B 54
Carrutherstown. *Dum* 4F 52
Carr Vale. *Derbs* 3B 36
Carrville. *Dur* 7G 55
Carryduff. *Lis* 5H 93
Carsaig. *Arg* 5L 63
Carscreugh. *Dum* 5H 51
Carsegowan. *Dum* 6K 51
Carse House. *Arg* 3G 57
Carseriggan. *Dum* 5J 51
Carsethorn. *Dum* 6D 52
Carshalton. *G Lon* 7K 21
Carsington. *Derbs* 4L 35
Carskiey. *Arg* 1B 50
Carsluith. *Dum* 6K 51
Carson Park. *New M* 6J 93
Carsphairn. *Dum* 2L 51
Carstairs. *S Lan* 5H 59
Carstairs Junction. *S Lan* 5H 59
Cartbridge. *Surr* 8H 21
Carterhaugh. *Ang* 3H 67
Carter's Clay. *Hants* 3M 9
Carterton. *Oxon* 3L 19
Carterway Heads. *Nmbd* 6D 54
Carthew. *Corn* 6C 4
Carthorpe. *N Yor* 7M 47
Cartington. *Nmbd* 1D 54
Cartland. *S Lan* 5G 59
Cartmel. *Cumb* 8B 46
Cartmel Fell. *Cumb* 7C 46
Cartworth. *W Yor* 7K 41
Carwath. *Cumb* 7H 53
Carway. *Carm* 6L 15
Carwinley. *Cumb* 4J 53
Cascob. *Powy* 6M 25
Cas-gwent. *Mon* 4D 18
Cash Feus. *Fife* 7F 66
Cashlie. *Per* 3J 65
Cashmoor. *Dors* 4H 9
Cas-Mael. *Pemb* 4G 15
Casnewydd. *Newp* 114 (5B 18)
Cassington. *Oxon* 2B 20
Cassop. *Dur* 8G 55
Castell. *Cnwy* 4G 33
Castell. *Den* 4L 33
Castell Hendre. *Pemb* 4G 15
Castell-Nedd. *Neat* 5G 17
Castell Newydd Emlyn.
Carm 2K 15
Castell-y-bwch. *Torf* 4A 18
Casterton. *Cumb* 8E 46
Castle. *Som* 1D 8
Castle Acre. *Norf* 8E 38
Castle Ashby. *Nptn* 6F 28
Castlebay. *W Isl* 6C 74
Castle Bolton. *N Yor* 6J 47
Castle Bromwich. *W Mid* 3K 27
Castle Bytham. *Linc* 8G 37
Castlebythe. *Pemb* 4G 15
Castle Caereinion. *Powy* 2L 25
Castle Camps. *Cambs* 7C 30
Castle Carrock. *Cumb* 6K 53
Castle Cary. *Som* 2E 8
Castlecary. *N Lan* 2F 58
Castlecaulfield. *M Ulst* 5E 92
Castle Combe. *Wilts* 6G 19
Castlecraig. *High* 7J 79
Castledawson. *M Ulst* 4F 93
Castlederg. *Derr* 4C 92
Castle Donington. *Leics* 7B 36
Castle Douglas. *Dum* 5B 52
Castle Eaton. *Swin* 4K 19
Castle Eden. *Dur* 8H 55
Castleford. *W Yor* 5B 42
Castle Frome. *Here* 7E 26
Castle Green. *Surr* 7G 21
Castle Green. *Warw* 4L 27
Castle Gresley. *Derbs* 8L 35
Castle Heaton. *Nmbd* 5G 61
Castle Hedingham. *Essx* 8D 30
Castle Hill. *Kent* 1C 12
Castle Hill. *Suff* 7H 31
Castlehill. *Per* 4F 66
Castlehill. *S Lan* 4G 59
Castlehill. *W Dun* 2B 58
Castle Kennedy. *Dum* 6G 51
Castle Lachlan. *Arg* 8E 64
Castlemartin. *Pemb* 7F 14
Castlemilk. *Glas* 4E 58
Castlemorris. *Pemb* 3F 14
Castlemorton. *Worc* 8F 26
Castle O'er. *Dum* 2G 53
Castle Park. *N Yor* 4F 48
Castlerigg. *Cumb* 3A 46
Castle Rising. *Norf* 7C 38
Castlerock. *Caus* 2E 92
Castleroe. *Caus* 2F 93
Castleside. *Dur* 7D 54
Castlethorpe. *Mil* 7E 28
Castleton. *Abers* 6A 72
Castleton. *Arg* 1H 57
Castleton. *Derbs* 1K 35
Castleton. *G Man* 6G 41
Castleton. *Mor* 3A 72
Castleton. *Newp* 5A 18
Castleton. *N Yor* 5D 48
Castleton. *Per* 6C 66
Castletown. *Cumb* 8K 53
Castletown. *Dors* 8E 8
Castletown. *High* 5C 86
Castletown. *IOM* 8B 44
Castletown. *Tyne* 6G 55
Castlewellan. *New M* 7H 93
Castley. *N Yor* 3L 41
Caston. *Norf* 2F 30
Castor. *Pet* 2J 29
Caswell. *Swan* 6E 16
Catacol. *N Ayr* 5J 57
Catbrook. *Mon* 3D 18
Catchems End. *Worc* 4F 26
Catchgate. *Dur* 6E 54
Catcleugh. *Nmbd* 1M 53
Catcliffe. *S Yor* 1B 36
Catcott. *Som* 2B 8
Caterham. *Surr* 8L 21
Catfield. *Norf* 7K 39
Catfield Common. *Norf* 7K 39
Catfirth. *Shet* 2E 90
Catford. *G Lon* 6L 21
Catforth. *Lanc* 4C 40
Cathcart. *Glas* 3D 58
Cathedine. *Powy* 2L 17
Catherine-de-Barnes. *W Mid* 3K 27
Catherington. *Hants* 4D 10
Catherston Leweston. *Dors* 6B 8
Catherton. *Shrp* 4E 26
Catisfield. *Hants* 5C 10
Catlodge. *High* 6G 71
Catlowdy. *Cumb* 4J 53
Catmore. *W Ber* 5B 20
Caton. *Devn* 8G 7
Caton. *Lanc* 1D 40
Catrine. *E Ayr* 7D 58
Cat's Ash. *Newp* 4B 18
Catsfield. *E Sus* 4D 12
Catsgore. *Som* 3D 8
Catshill. *Worc* 4H 27
Cattal. *N Yor* 2B 42
Cattawade. *Suff* 8H 31
Catterall. *Lanc* 3D 40
Catterick. *N Yor* 6L 47
Catterick Bridge. *N Yor* 6L 47
Catterick Garrison. *N Yor* 6K 47
Catterlen. *Cumb* 8J 53
Catterline. *Abers* 8H 73
Catterton. *N Yor* 3C 42
Catteshall. *Surr* 1G 11
Catthorpe. *Leics* 4C 28
Cattistock. *Dors* 6D 8
Catton. *Nmbd* 6B 54
Catton. *N Yor* 8A 48
Catwick. *E Yor* 3J 43
Catworth. *Cambs* 4H 29
Caudle Green. *Glos* 2H 19
Cauldhame. *Stir* 8L 65
Cauldmill. *Bord* 8C 60
Cauldon. *Staf* 5J 35
Cauldon Lowe. *Staf* 5J 35
Cauldwells. *Abers* 8G 81
Caulkerbush. *Dum* 6D 52
Caulside. *Dum* 3J 53
Caunsall. *Worc* 3G 27
Caunton. *Notts* 3E 36
Causewayend. *S Lan* 6J 59
Causewayhead. *Stir* 8B 66
Causey Park. *Nmbd* 2E 54
Caute. *Devn* 4D 6
Cautley. *Cumb* 6E 46
Cavendish. *Suff* 7E 30
Cavendish Bridge. *Leics* 7B 36
Cavenham. *Suff* 4D 30
Caversfield. *Oxon* 1C 20
Caversham. *Read* 6E 20
Caversham Heights. *Read* 6E 20
Caverswall. *Staf* 5H 35
Cawdor. *High* 1J 71
Cawkwell. *Linc* 1K 37
Cawood. *N Yor* 4C 42
Cawsand. *Corn* 6G 5
Cawston. *Norf* 7H 39
Cawston. *Warw* 4B 28
Cawthorne. *N Yor* 7E 48
Cawthorne. *S Yor* 7L 41
Cawthorpe. *Linc* 7H 37
Cawton. *N Yor* 8D 48
Caxton. *Cambs* 6L 29
Caynham. *Shrp* 4D 26
Caythorpe. *Linc* 5G 37
Caythorpe. *Notts* 5D 36
Cayton. *N Yor* 7H 49
Ceallan. *W Isl* 8K 75
Ceann a Bhaigh. *W Isl*
on North Uist 7J 75
on Scalpay 4D 76
on South Harris 4C 76
Ceann a Bhàigh. *W Isl* 5B 76
Ceannacroc Lodge. *High* 4C 70
Ceann a Deas Loch Baghasdail.
W Isl 4D 74
Ceann an Leothaid. *High* 7H 69
Ceann a Tuath Loch Baghasdail.
W Isl 3D 74
Ceann Loch Ailleart. *High* 7J 69
Ceann Loch Muideirt. *High* 8J 69
Ceann-na-Cleithe. *W Isl* 4C 76
Ceann Shiphoirt. *W Isl* 2D 76
Ceann Tarabhaigh. *W Isl* 2D 76
Cearsiadar. *W Isl* 1E 76
Ceathramh Meadhanach.
W Isl 6K 75
Cefn Berain. *Cnwy* 4J 33
Cefn-brith. *Cnwy* 5J 33
Cefn-bryn-brain. *Carm* 3G 17
Cefn Bychan. *Cphy* 5M 17
Cefn-bychan. *Flin* 4L 33
Cefncaeau. *Carm* 7M 15
Cefn Canol. *Powy* 7M 33
Cefn Coch. *Powy* 2K 25
Cefn-coch. *Powy* 8L 33
Cefn-coed-y-cymmer.
Mer T 4K 17
Cefn Cribwr. *B'end* 6H 17
Cefn-ddwysarn. *Gwyn* 7J 33
Cefn Einion. *Shrp* 3A 26
Cefneithin. *Carm* 3E 16
Cefn Glas. *B'end* 6H 17
Cefngorwydd. *Powy* 8J 25
Cefn Llwyd. *Cdgn* 4F 24
Cefn-mawr. *Wrex* 5A 34
Cefn-y-bedd. *Flin* 4B 34
Cefn-y-coed. *Powy* 3L 25
Cefn-y-pant. *Carm* 4H 15
Cegidfa. *Powy* 1M 25
Ceinewydd. *Cdgn* 1K 15
Cellan. *Cdgn* 8F 24
Cellardyke. *Fife* 7J 67
Cellarhead. *Staf* 5H 35
Cemaes. *IOA* 1C 32
Cemmaes. *Powy* 2H 25
Cemmaes Road. *Powy* 2H 25
Cenarth. *Cdgn* 2J 15
Cenin. *Gwyn* 6D 32
Ceos. *W Isl* 1E 76
Ceres. *Fife* 6H 67
Ceri. *Powy* 4L 25
Cerist. *Powy* 4J 25
Cerne Abbas. *Dors* 5E 8
Cerney Wick. *Glos* 4J 19
Cerrigceinwen. *IOA* 3D 32
Cerrigydrudion. *Cnwy* 6J 33
Cess. *Norf* 8L 39
Cessford. *Bord* 7E 60
Ceunant. *Gwyn* 4E 32
Chaceley. *Glos* 8G 27
Chacewater. *Corn* 4L 3
Chackmore. *Buck* 8D 28
Chacombe. *Nptn* 7B 28
Chadderton. *G Man* 7H 41
Chaddesden. *Derb* 6A 36
Chaddesden Common. *Derb* 6A 36
Chaddesley Corbett. *Worc* 4G 27
Chaddlehanger. *Devn* 8D 6
Chaddleworth. *W Ber* 6B 20
Chadlington. *Oxon* 1M 19
Chadshunt. *Warw* 6M 27
Chadstone. *Nptn* 6F 28
Chad Valley. *W Mid* 3J 27
Chadwell. *Leics* 7E 36
Chadwell. *Shrp* 8F 34
Chadwell Heath. *G Lon* 5A 22
Chadwell St Mary. *Thur* 6C 22
Chadwick End. *W Mid* 4L 27
Chadwick Green. *Mers* 8D 40
Chaffcombe. *Som* 4B 8
Chafford Hundred. *Thur* 6C 22
Chagford. *Devn* 7G 7
Chailey. *E Sus* 4L 11
Chain Bridge. *Linc* 5L 37
Chainbridge. *Cambs* 1M 29
Chainhurst. *Kent* 1D 12
Chalbury. *Dors* 5J 9
Chalbury Common. *Dors* 5J 9
Chaldon. *Surr* 8L 21
Chaldon Herring. *Dors* 7F 8
Chale. *IOW* 8B 10
Chale Green. *IOW* 8B 10
Chalfont Common. *Buck* 4H 21
Chalfont St Giles. *Buck* 4G 21
Chalfont St Peter. *Buck* 5H 21
Chalford. *Glos* 3G 19
Chalgrove. *Oxon* 4D 20
Chalk. *Kent* 6C 22
Chalk End. *Essx* 2C 22
Chalk Hill. *Glos* 1K 19
Challaborough. *Devn* 7J 5
Challacombe. *Devn* 1F 6
Challister. *Shet* 1F 90
Challoch. *Dum* 5J 51
Challock. *Kent* 8G 23
Chalton. *C Beds*
nr. Bedford 6J 29
nr. Luton 1H 21
Chalton. *Hants* 4E 10
Chalvington. *E Sus* 5B 12
Champany. *Falk* 2J 59
Chance Inn. *Fife* 6G 67
Chancery. *Cdgn* 5E 24
Chandler's Cross. *Herts* 4H 21
Chandler's Cross. *Worc* 8F 26
Chandler's Ford. *Hants* 3B 10
Chanlockfoot. *Dum* 1B 52
Channel's End. *Bed* 6J 29
Channel Tunnel. *Kent* 2H 13
Channerwick. *Shet* 5E 90
Chantry. *Som* 1F 8
Chantry. *Suff* 7H 31
Chapel. *Cumb* 8G 53
Chapel. *Fife* 8F 66
Chapel Allerton. *Som* 8C 18
Chapel Allerton. *W Yor* 4L 41
Chapel Amble. *Corn* 4B 4
Chapel Brampton. *Nptn* 5E 28
Chapelbridge. *Cambs* 2K 29
Chapel Chorlton. *Staf* 6G 35
Chapel Cleeve. *Som* 1K 7
Chapel End. *C Beds* 7H 29
Chapel-en-le-Frith. *Derbs* 1J 35
Chapelfield. *Abers* 1L 67
Chapelgate. *Linc* 7M 37
Chapel Green. *Warw*
nr. Coventry 3L 27
nr. Southam 5B 28
Chapel Haddlesey. *N Yor* 5C 42
Chapelhall. *N Lan* 3F 58
Chapel Hill. *Abers* 2K 73
Chapel Hill. *Linc* 4K 37
Chapel Hill. *Mon* 3D 18
Chapelhill. *Per*
nr. Glencarse 5F 66
nr. Harrietfield 4D 66
Chapelknowe. *Dum* 4H 53
Chapel Lawn. *Shrp* 4B 26
Chapel le Dale. *N Yor* 8F 46
Chapel Milton. *Derbs* 1J 35
Chapel of Garioch. *Abers* 3G 73
Chapel Row. *W Ber* 7C 20
Chapels. *Cumb* 6M 45
Chapel St Leonards. *Linc* 2B 38
Chapel Stile. *Cumb* 5B 46
Chapelthorpe. *W Yor* 6M 41
Chapelton. *Ang* 3K 67
Chapelton. *Devn* 3E 6
Chapelton. *High*
nr. Grantown-on-Spey 4K 71
nr. Inverness 8F 78
Chapelton. *S Lan* 5E 58
Chapel Town. *Corn* 6A 4
Chapeltown. *Bkbn* 6F 40
Chapeltown. *Mor* 3B 72
Chapeltown. *New M* 7J 93
Chapeltown. *S Yor* 8A 42
Chapmanslade. *Wilts* 1G 9
Chapmans Well. *Devn* 6C 6
Chapmore End. *Herts* 2L 21
Chappel. *Essx* 1E 22
Chard. *Som* 5B 8
Chard Junction. *Dors* 5B 8
Chardstock. *Devn* 5B 8
Charfield. *S Glo* 4F 18
Charing. *Kent* 1F 12
Charing Heath. *Kent* 1F 12
Charing Hill. *Kent* 8F 22
Charingworth. *Glos* 8L 27
Charlbury. *Oxon* 2A 20
Charlcombe. *Bath* 7F 18
Charlcutt. *Wilts* 6H 19
Charlecote. *Warw* 6L 27
Charlemont. *Arm* 6F 93
Charles. *Devn* 2F 6
Charlesfield. *Dum* 5F 52
Charleshill. *Surr* 1F 10
Charleston. *Ang* 3G 67
Charleston. *Ren* 3C 58
Charlestown. *Aber* 5J 73
Charlestown. *Abers* 7K 81
Charlestown. *Corn* 6C 4
Charlestown. *Dors* 8E 8
Charlestown. *Fife* 1J 59
Charlestown. *G Man* 7G 41
Charlestown. *High*
nr. Gairloch 6K 77
nr. Inverness 1G 71
Charlestown. *W Yor* 5H 41
Charlestown of Aberlour.
Mor 1B 72
Charles Tye. *Suff* 6G 31
Charlesworth. *Derbs* 8J 41
Charlton. *G Lon* 6M 21
Charlton. *Hants* 1A 10
Charlton. *Herts* 1J 21
Charlton. *Nptn* 8C 28
Charlton. *Nmbd* 3B 54
Charlton. *Oxon* 5B 20
Charlton. *Som*
nr. Radstock 8E 18
nr. Shepton Mallet 1E 8
nr. Taunton 3A 8
Charlton. *Telf* 8D 34
Charlton. *W Sus* 4F 10
Charlton. *Wilts*
nr. Malmesbury 5H 19
nr. Pewsey 8K 19
nr. Shaftesbury 3H 9
Charlton. *Worc*
nr. Evesham 7J 27
nr. Stourport-on-Severn 4G 27
Charlton Abbots. *Glos* 1J 19
Charlton Adam. *Som* 3D 8
Charlton All Saints. *Wilts* 3K 9
Charlton Down. *Dors* 6E 8
Charlton Horethorne. *Som* 3E 8
Charlton Kings. *Glos* 1H 19
Charlton Mackrell. *Som* 3D 8
Charlton Marshall. *Dors* 5H 9
Charlton Musgrove. *Som* 3F 8
Charlton-on-Otmoor. *Oxon* 2C 20
Charlton on the Hill. *Dors* 5G 9
Charlwood. *Hants* 2D 10
Charlwood. *Surr* 1K 11
Charlynch. *Som* 2M 7
Charminster. *Dors* 6E 8
Charmouth. *Dors* 6B 8
Charndon. *Buck* 1D 20
Charney Bassett. *Oxon* 4A 20
Charnock Green. *Lanc* 6D 40
Charnock Richard. *Lanc* 6D 40
Charsfield. *Suff* 6J 31
The Chart. *Kent* 8A 22
Chart Corner. *Kent* 8D 22
Charter Alley. *Hants* 8C 20
Charterhouse. *Som* 8C 18
Charterville Allotments.
Oxon 2M 19
Chartham. *Kent* 8H 23
Chartham Hatch. *Kent* 8H 23
Chartridge. *Buck* 3G 21
Chart Sutton. *Kent* 8D 22
Charvil. *Wok* 6E 20
Charwelton. *Nptn* 6C 28
Chase Terrace. *Staf* 1J 27
Chasetown. *Staf* 1J 27
Chastleton. *Oxon* 1L 19
Chasty. *Devn* 5C 6
Chatburn. *Lanc* 3F 40
Chatcull. *Staf* 6F 34
Chatham. *Medw*
Medway Towns 111 (7D 22)
Chatham Green. *Essx* 2D 22
Chathill. *Nmbd* 7J 61
Chatley. *Worc* 5G 27
Chattenden. *Medw* 6D 22
Chatteris. *Cambs* 3L 29
Chattisham. *Suff* 7G 31
Chatton. *Nmbd* 7H 61
Chatwall. *Shrp* 2D 26
Chaulden. *Herts* 3H 21
Chaul End. *C Beds* 1H 21
Chawleigh. *Devn* 4G 7
Chawley. *Oxon* 3B 20
Chawston. *Bed* 6J 29
Chawton. *Hants* 2E 10
Chaxhill. *Glos* 2F 18
Cheadle. *G Man* 1G 35
Cheadle. *Staf* 5J 35
Cheadle Hulme. *G Man* 1G 35
Cheam. *G Lon* 7K 21
Cheapside. *Wind* 7G 21
Chearsley. *Buck* 2E 20
Chebsey. *Staf* 7G 35
Checkendon. *Oxon* 5D 20
Checkley. *Ches E* 5F 34
Checkley. *Here* 8D 26
Checkley. *Staf* 6J 35
Chedburgh. *Suff* 6D 30
Cheddar. *Som* 8C 18
Cheddington. *Buck* 2G 21
Cheddleton. *Staf* 4H 35
Cheddon Fitzpaine. *Som* 3M 7
Chedglow. *Wilts* 4H 19
Chedgrave. *Norf* 2K 31
Chedington. *Dors* 5C 8
Chediston. *Suff* 4K 31
Chediston Green. *Suff* 4K 31
Chedworth. *Glos* 2J 19
Chedzoy. *Som* 2B 8
Cheeseman's Green. *Kent* 2G 13
Cheetham Hill. *G Man* 7G 41
Cheglinch. *Devn* 1E 6
Cheldon. *Devn* 4G 7
Chelford. *Ches E* 2G 35
Chellaston. *Derb* 6A 36
Chellington. *Bed* 6G 29
Chelmarsh. *Shrp* 3F 26
Chelmick. *Shrp* 2C 26
Chelmondiston. *Suff* 8J 31
Chelmorton. *Derbs* 3K 35
Chelmsford. *Essx* 3D 22
Chelsea. *G Lon* 6K 21
Chelsfield. *G Lon* 7A 22
Chelsham. *Surr* 8L 21
Chelston. *Som* 3L 7
Chelsworth. *Suff* 7F 30
Cheltenham. *Glos* 107 (1H 19)
Chelveston. *Nptn* 5G 29
Chelvey. *N Som* 7C 18
Chelwood. *Bath* 7E 18
Chelwood Common. *E Sus* 3M 11
Chelwood Gate. *E Sus* 3M 11
Chelworth. *Wilts* 4H 19
Chelworth Lower Green.
Wilts 4J 19
Chelworth Upper Green.
Wilts 4J 19
Chelynch. *Som* 1E 8
Cheney Longville. *Shrp* 3C 26
Chenies. *Buck* 4H 21
Chepstow. *Mon* 4D 18
Chequerfield. *W Yor* 5B 42
Chequers Corner. *Norf* 1A 30
Cherhill. *Wilts* 6J 19
Cherington. *Glos* 4H 19
Cherington. *Warw* 8L 27
Cheriton. *Devn* 1G 7
Cheriton. *Hants* 3C 10
Cheriton. *Kent* 2J 13
Cheriton. *Pemb* 7F 14
Cheriton. *Swan* 7L 15
Cheriton Bishop. *Devn* 6G 7
Cheriton Cross. *Devn* 6G 7
Cheriton Fitzpaine. *Devn* 5H 7
Cherrington. *Telf* 7E 34
Cherrybank. *Per* 5E 66
Cherry Burton. *E Yor* 3G 43
Cherry Green. *Herts* 1L 21
Cherry Hinton. *Cambs* 6A 30
Cherry Willingham. *Linc* 2H 37
Chertsey. *Surr* 7H 21
Cheselbourne. *Dors* 6F 8
Chesham. *Buck* 3G 21
Chesham. *G Man* 6G 41
Chesham Bois. *Buck* 4G 21
Cheshunt. *Herts* 3L 21
Cheslyn Hay. *Staf* 1H 27
Chessetts Wood. *Warw* 4K 27
Chessington. *G Lon* 7J 21
Chester. *Ches W* 108 (3C 34)
Chesterblade. *Som* 1E 8
Chesterfield. *Derbs* 2A 36
Chesterfield. *Staf* 1K 27
Chesterhope. *Nmbd* 3B 54
Chester-le-Street. *Dur* 6F 54
Chester Moor. *Dur* 7F 54
Chesters. *Bord* 8D 60
Chesterton. *Cambs*
nr. Cambridge 5A 30
nr. Peterborough 2J 29
Chesterton. *Glos* 3J 19
Chesterton. *Oxon* 1C 20
Chesterton. *Shrp* 2F 26
Chesterton. *Staf* 5G 35
Chesterton Green. *Warw* 6M 27
Chesterwood. *Nmbd* 5B 54
Chestfield. *Kent* 7H 23
Cheston. *Devn* 6J 5
Cheswardine. *Shrp* 6F 34
Cheswell. *Telf* 8F 34
Cheswick. *Nmbd* 5H 61
Cheswick Green. *W Mid* 4K 27
Chetnole. *Dors* 5E 8
Chettiscombe. *Devn* 4J 7
Chettisham. *Cambs* 3B 30
Chettle. *Dors* 4H 9
Chetton. *Shrp* 2E 26
Chetwode. *Buck* 1D 20
Chetwynd Aston. *Telf* 8F 34
Cheveley. *Cambs* 5C 30
Chevening. *Kent* 8A 22
Chevington. *Suff* 6D 30
Chevithorne. *Devn* 4J 7
Chew Magna. *Bath* 7D 18
Chew Moor. *G Man* 7E 40
Chew Stoke. *Bath* 7D 18
Chewton Keynsham. *Bath* 7E 18
Chewton Mendip. *Som* 8D 18
Chichacott. *Devn* 6F 6
Chicheley. *Mil* 7G 29
Chichester. *W Sus* 5F 10
Chickerell. *Dors* 7E 8
Chickering. *Suff* 4J 31
Chicklade. *Wilts* 2H 9
Chicksands. *C Beds* 8J 29
Chickward. *Here* 6A 26
Chidden. *Hants* 4D 10
Chiddingfold. *Surr* 2G 11
Chiddingly. *E Sus* 4B 12
Chiddingstone. *Kent* 1B 12
Chiddingstone Causeway.
Kent 1B 12
Chiddingstone Hoath. *Kent* 1A 12
Chideock. *Dors* 6C 8
Chidgley. *Som* 2K 7
Chidham. *W Sus* 5E 10
Chieveley. *W Ber* 6B 20
Chignal St James. *Essx* 3C 22
Chignal Smealy. *Essx* 2C 22
Chigwell. *Essx* 4M 21
Chigwell Row. *Essx* 4A 22
Chilbolton. *Hants* 1A 10
Chilcomb. *Hants* 3C 10
Chilcombe. *Dors* 6D 8
Chilcompton. *Som* 8E 18
Chilcote. *Leics* 8L 35
Childer Thornton. *Ches W* 2B 34
Child Okeford. *Dors* 4G 9
Childrey. *Oxon* 5A 20
Child's Ercall. *Shrp* 7E 34
Childswickham. *Worc* 8J 27
Childwall. *Mers* 1C 34
Childwick Green. *Herts* 2J 21
Chilfrome. *Dors* 6D 8
Chilgrove. *W Sus* 4F 10
Chilham. *Kent* 8G 23
Chilhampton. *Wilts* 2J 9
Chilla. *Devn* 5D 6
Chilland. *Hants* 2C 10
Chillaton. *Devn* 7D 6
Chillenden. *Kent* 8J 23
Chillerton. *IOW* 7B 10
Chillesford. *Suff* 6K 31
Chillingham. *Nmbd* 7H 61
Chillington. *Devn* 7K 5
Chillington. *Som* 4B 8
Chilmark. *Wilts* 2H 9
Chilmington Green. *Kent* 1F 12
Chilson. *Oxon* 2M 19
Chilsworthy. *Corn* 8D 6
Chilsworthy. *Devn* 5C 6
Chiltern Green. *C Beds* 2J 21
Chilthorne Domer. *Som* 4D 8
Chilton. *Buck* 2D 20
Chilton. *Devn* 5H 7
Chilton. *Dur* 3L 47
Chilton. *Oxon* 5B 20
Chilton Candover. *Hants* 1C 10
Chilton Cantelo. *Som* 3D 8
Chilton Foliat. *Wilts* 6M 19
Chilton Lane. *Dur* 8G 55
Chilton Polden. *Som* 2B 8
Chilton Street. *Suff* 7D 30
Chilton Trinity. *Som* 2A 8
Chilwell. *Notts* 6C 36
Chilworth. *Hants* 4B 10
Chilworth. *Surr* 1H 11
Chimney. *Oxon* 3A 20
Chimney Street. *Suff* 7D 30
Chineham. *Hants* 8D 20
Chingford. *G Lon* 4L 21
Chinley. *Derbs* 1J 35
Chinnor. *Oxon* 3E 20
Chipley. *Som* 3L 7
Chipnall. *Shrp* 6F 34
Chippenham. *Cambs* 5C 30
Chippenham. *Wilts* 6H 19
Chipperfield. *Herts* 3H 21
Chipping. *Herts* 8L 29
Chipping. *Lanc* 3E 40
Chipping Campden. *Glos* 8K 27
Chipping Hill. *Essx* 2E 22
Chipping Norton. *Oxon* 1M 19
Chipping Ongar. *Essx* 3B 22
Chipping Sodbury. *S Glo* 5F 18
Chipping Warden. *Nptn* 7B 28
Chipstable. *Som* 3K 7
Chipstead. *Kent* 8B 22
Chipstead. *Surr* 8K 21
Chirbury. *Shrp* 2A 26
Chirk. *Wrex* 6A 34
Chirmorie. *S Ayr* 4H 51
Chirnside. *Bord* 4F 60
Chirnsidebridge. *Bord* 4F 60
Chirton. *Wilts* 8J 19
Chisbridge Cross. *Buck* 5F 20
Chisbury. *Wilts* 7L 19
Chiselborough. *Som* 4C 8
Chiseldon. *Swin* 6K 19
Chiselhampton. *Oxon* 4C 20
Chiserley. *W Yor* 5J 41
Chislehurst. *G Lon* 6M 21
Chislet. *Kent* 7J 23
Chiswell. *Dors* 8E 8
Chiswell Green. *Herts* 3J 21
Chiswick. *G Lon* 6K 21
Chisworth. *Derbs* 8H 41
Chitcombe. *E Sus* 3E 12
Chithurst. *W Sus* 3F 10
Chittering. *Cambs* 5A 30
Chitterley. *Devn* 5J 7
Chitterne. *Wilts* 1H 9
Chittlehamholt. *Devn* 3F 6
Chittlehampton. *Devn* 3F 6
Chittoe. *Wilts* 7H 19
Chivelstone. *Devn* 8K 5
Chivenor. *Devn* 2E 6
Chobham. *Surr* 7G 21
Cholderton. *Wilts* 1L 9
Cholesbury. *Buck* 3G 21
Chollerford. *Nmbd* 4C 54
Chollerton. *Nmbd* 4C 54
Cholsey. *Oxon* 5C 20
Cholstrey. *Here* 6C 26
Chop Gate. *N Yor* 6C 48
Choppington. *Nmbd* 3F 54
Chopwell. *Tyne* 6E 54
Chorley. *Ches E* 4D 34
Chorley. *Lanc* 6D 40
Chorley. *Shrp* 3E 26
Chorley. *Staf* 8J 35
Chorleywood. *Herts* 4H 21
Chorlton. *Ches E* 4F 34
Chorlton-cum-Hardy.
G Man 8G 41
Chorlton Lane. *Ches W* 5C 34
Choulton. *Shrp* 3B 26
Chrishall. *Essx* 8M 29
Christchurch. *Cambs* 2A 30
Christchurch. *Dors* 6K 9
Christchurch. *Glos* 2D 18
Christian Malford. *Wilts* 6H 19
Christleton. *Ches W* 3C 34
Christmas Common. *Oxon* 4E 20
Christon. *N Som* 8B 18
Christon Bank. *Nmbd* 7K 61
Christow. *Devn* 7H 7
Chryston. *N Lan* 2E 58
Chuck Hatch. *E Sus* 2A 12
Chudleigh. *Devn* 8H 7
Chudleigh Knighton. *Devn* 8H 7
Chulmleigh. *Devn* 4F 6
Chunal. *Derbs* 8J 41
Church. *Lanc* 5F 40
Churcham. *Glos* 2F 18
Church Aston. *Telf* 8F 34
Church Brampton. *Nptn* 5E 28
Church Brough. *Cumb* 4F 46
Church Broughton. *Derbs* 6L 35
Church Corner. *Suff* 3L 31
Church Crookham. *Hants* 8F 20
Churchdown. *Glos* 1G 19
Church Eaton. *Staf* 8G 35
Church End. *Cambs*
nr. Cambridge 6A 30
nr. Over 4L 29
nr. Sawtry 3K 29
nr. Wisbech 1L 29
Church End. *C Beds*
nr. Stotfold 8J 29
nr. Totternhoe 1G 21
Church End. *E Yor* 2H 43
Church End. *Essx*
nr. Braintree 1D 22
nr. Great Dunmow 1C 22
nr. Saffron Walden 7B 30
Church End. *Glos* 3F 18
Church End. *Hants* 8D 20
Church End. *Linc*
nr. Donington 6K 37
nr. North Somercotes 8M 43
Church End. *Norf* 8B 38
Church End. *Warw*
nr. Coleshill 2L 27
nr. Nuneaton 2L 27
Church End. *Wilts* 6J 19
Churchend. *Essx* 4G 23
Church Enstone. *Oxon* 1A 20
Church Fenton. *N Yor* 4C 42
Church Green. *Devn* 6L 7
Church Gresley. *Derbs* 8L 35
Church Hanborough. *Oxon* 2B 20
Church Hill. *Ches W* 3E 34
Church Hill. *Worc* 5J 27
Church Hougham. *Kent* 1J 13
Church Houses. *N Yor* 6D 48
Churchill. *Devn*
nr. Axminster 5B 8
nr. Barnstaple 1E 6
Churchill. *N Som* 8C 18
Churchill. *Oxon* 1L 19
Churchill. *Worc*
nr. Kidderminster 4G 27
nr. Worcester 6H 27
Churchinford. *Som* 4M 7
Church Knowle. *Dors* 7H 9
Church Laneham. *Notts* 2F 36
Church Langley. *Essx* 3A 22
Church Langton. *Leics* 2E 28
Church Lawford. *Warw* 4B 28
Church Lawton. *Ches E* 4G 35
Church Leigh. *Staf* 6J 35
Church Lench. *Worc* 6J 27
Church Mayfield. *Staf* 5K 35
Church Minshull. *Ches E* 3E 34
Church Norton. *W Sus* 6F 10
Churchover. *Warw* 3C 28
Church Preen. *Shrp* 2D 26
Church Pulverbatch. *Shrp* 1C 26
Churchstanton. *Som* 4L 7
Church Stoke. *Powy* 2A 26
Churchstow. *Devn* 7K 5
Church Stowe. *Nptn* 6D 28
Church Street. *Kent* 6D 22
Church Stretton. *Shrp* 2C 26
Church Town. *Leics* 8A 36
Church Town. *N Lin* 7E 42
Churchtown. *Cumb* 7H 53
Churchtown. *Derbs* 3L 35
Churchtown. *Devn* 1F 6
Churchtown. *IOM* 5D 44
Churchtown. *Lanc* 3C 40
Churchtown. *Mers* 6B 40
Churchtown. *New M* 6J 93
Churchtown. *Shrp* 3A 26
Church Village. *Rhon* 6K 17
Church Warsop. *Notts* 3C 36
Church Westcote. *Glos* 1L 19
Church Wilne. *Derbs* 6B 36
Churnsike Lodge. *Nmbd* 4L 53
Churston Ferrers. *Torb* 6M 5
Churt. *Surr* 2F 10
Churton. *Ches W* 4C 34
Churwell. *W Yor* 5L 41
Chute Standen. *Wilts* 8M 19
Chwilog. *Gwyn* 7D 32
Chwittfordd. *Flin* 3L 33
Chyandour. *Corn* 5H 3
Cilan Uchaf. *Gwyn* 8B 32
Cilcain. *Flin* 4L 33
Cilcennin. *Cdgn* 6E 24
Cilfrew. *Neat* 4G 17
Cilfynydd. *Rhon* 5K 17
Cilgerran. *Pemb* 2H 15
Cilgeti. *Pemb* 6H 15
Cilgwyn. *Carm* 2G 17
Cilgwyn. *Pemb* 3G 15
Ciliau Aeron. *Cdgn* 1L 15
Cill Amhlaidh. *W Isl* 1D 74
Cill Donnain. *W Isl* 3D 74
Cille a' Bhacstair. *High* 7E 76
Cille Bhrighde. *W Isl* 4D 74
Cille Pheadair. *W Isl* 4D 74
Cilmaengwyn. *Neat* 4G 17
Cilmeri. *Powy* 7K 25
Cilmery. *Powy* 7K 25
Cilrhedyn. *Pemb* 3J 15
Cilsan. *Carm* 2E 16
Ciltalgarth. *Gwyn* 6H 33
Ciltwrch. *Powy* 8L 25
Cilybebyll. *Neat* 4G 17
Cilycwm. *Carm* 8G 25
Cimla. *Neat* 5G 17
Cinderford. *Glos* 2E 18
Cinderhill. *Derbs* 5A 36
Cippenham. *Slo* 5G 21
Cippyn. *Pemb* 2H 15
Cirbhig. *W Isl* 7E 82
Circebost. *W Isl* 8E 82
Cirencester. *Glos* 3J 19
City. *Powy* 3M 25
City. *V Glam* 7J 17
The City. *Buck* 4E 20
City Airport. *G Lon* 5M 21
City Centre. *Stoke*
Stoke 116 (5G 35)
City Dulas. *IOA* 2D 32
City of Derry Airport. *Derr* 2D 92
City of London. *G Lon*
London 113 (5L 21)
Civiltown. *Arm* 6G 93
Clabby. *Ferm* 6D 92
Clabhach. *Arg* 2G 63
Clachaig. *Arg* 1L 57
Clachaig. *High*
nr. Kinlochleven 2F 64
nr. Nethy Bridge 4L 71
Clachamish. *High* 8E 76
Clachan. *Arg*
on Kintyre 4G 57
on Lismore 3C 64
Clachan. *High*
nr. Bettyhill 5K 85
nr. Staffin 7F 76
nr. Uig 6F 76
on Raasay 2G 69
Clachan Farm. *Arg* 6F 64
Clachan na Luib. *W Isl* 7K 75
Clachan of Campsie. *E Dun* 2E 58
Clachan of Glendaruel. *Arg* 1J 57
Clachan-Seil. *Arg* 6B 64
Clachan Shannda. *W Isl* 6K 75
Clachan Strachur. *Arg* 7E 64
Clachbreck. *Arg* 2G 57
Clachnaharry. *High* 1G 71
Clachtoll. *High* 1M 77
Clackmannan. *Clac* 8C 66
Clackmannanshire Bridge.
Clac 1H 59
Clackmarras. *Mor* 8B 80
Clacton-on-Sea. *Essx* 2H 23
Cladach a Chaolais. *W Isl* 7J 75
Cladach Chairinis. *W Isl* 8K 75
Cladach Chireboist. *W Isl* 7J 75
Cladach Iolaraigh. *W Isl* 7J 75
Cladich. *Arg* 5E 64
Cladswell. *Worc* 6J 27
Clady. *Derr* 4C 92
Clady. *M Ulst* 3F 93
Claggan. *High*
nr. Fort William 8B 70
nr. Lochaline 2B 64
Claigan. *High* 8D 76
Clandown. *Bath* 8E 18
Clanfield. *Hants* 4D 10
Clanfield. *Oxon* 3L 19
Clanville. *Hants* 1M 9
Clanville. *Som* 2E 8
Claonaig. *Arg* 5J 57
Clapgate. *Dors* 5J 9
Clapgate. *Herts* 1M 21
Clapham. *Bed* 6H 29
Clapham. *Devn* 7H 7
Clapham. *G Lon* 6K 21
Clapham. *N Yor* 1F 40
Clapham. *W Sus* 5H 11
Clap Hill. *Kent* 2G 13
Clappers. *Bord* 4G 61
Clappersgate. *Cumb* 5B 46
Clapphoull. *Shet* 5E 90
Clapton. *Som*
nr. Crewkerne 5C 8
nr. Radstock 8E 18
Clapton in Gordano. *N Som* 6C 18
Clapton-on-the-Hill. *Glos* 2K 19
Clapworthy. *Devn* 3F 6
Clara Vale. *Tyne* 5E 54
Clarbeston. *Pemb* 4G 15
Clarbeston Road. *Pemb* 4G 15
Clarborough. *Notts* 1E 36
Clare. *Arm* 6G 93
Clare. *Suff* 7D 30
Clarebrand. *Dum* 5B 52
Clarencefield. *Dum* 5E 52
Clarilaw. *Bord* 8C 60
Clark's Green. *Surr* 2J 11
Clark's Hill. *Linc* 7L 37
Clarkston. *E Ren* 4D 58
Clasheddy. *High* 5J 85
Clashindarroch. *Abers* 2D 72
Clashmore. *High*
nr. Dornoch 5H 79
nr. Stoer 8C 84
Clashnessie. *High* 8C 84
Clashnoir. *Mor* 3B 72
Clate. *Shet* 1F 90
Clathick. *Per* 5B 66
Clathy. *Per* 6C 66
Clatt. *Abers* 3E 72
Clatter. *Powy* 3J 25
Clatterford. *IOW* 7B 10
Clatworthy. *Som* 2K 7
Claudy. *Derr* 3D 92
Claughton. *Lanc*
nr. Caton 1D 40
nr. Garstang 3D 40
Claughton. *Mers* 1A 34
Claverdon. *Warw* 5K 27
Claverham. *N Som* 7C 18
Clavering. *Essx* 8A 30
Claverley. *Shrp* 2F 26
Claverton. *Bath* 7F 18
Clawdd-côch. *V Glam* 7K 17
Clawdd-newydd. *Den* 5K 33
Clawson Hill. *Leics* 7E 36
Clawton. *Devn* 6C 6
Claxby. *Linc*
nr. Alford 2A 38
nr. Market Rasen 8J 43
Claxton. *Norf* 1K 31
Claxton. *N Yor* 1D 42
Claybrooke Magna. *Leics* 3B 28
Claybrooke Parva. *Leics* 3B 28
Clay Common. *Suff* 3L 31
Clay Coton. *Nptn* 4C 28
Clay Cross. *Derbs* 3A 36
Claydon. *Oxon* 6B 28
Claydon. *Suff* 6H 31
Clay End. *Herts* 1L 21
Claygate. *Dum* 4H 53
Claygate. *Kent* 1D 12
Claygate. *Surr* 7J 21
Claygate Cross. *Kent* 8C 22
Clayhall. *Hants* 6D 10
Clayhanger. *Devn* 3K 7
Clayhanger. *W Mid* 1J 27
Clayhidon. *Devn* 4L 7
Clay Hill. *Bris* 6E 18
Clayhill. *E Sus* 3E 12
Clayhill. *Hants* 5M 9
Clayhithe. *Cambs* 5B 30
Clayholes. *Ang* 4J 67
Clay Lake. *Linc* 7K 37
Clayock. *High* 6C 86
Claypits. *Glos* 3F 18
Claypole. *Linc* 5F 36
Claythorpe. *Linc* 2M 37
Clayton. *G Man* 8G 41
Clayton. *S Yor* 7B 42
Clayton. *Staf* 5G 35
Clayton. *W Sus* 4L 11
Clayton. *W Yor* 4K 41
Clayton Green. *Lanc* 5D 40
Clayton-le-Moors. *Lanc* 4F 40
Clayton-le-Woods. *Lanc* 5D 40
Clayton West. *W Yor* 6L 41
Clayworth. *Notts* 1E 36
Cleadale. *High* 7F 68
Cleadon. *Tyne* 5G 55
Clearbrook. *Devn* 5H 5
Clearwell. *Glos* 3D 18
Cleasby. *N Yor* 4L 47
Cleat. *Orkn*
nr. Braehead 5D 88
nr. St Margaret's Hope 3F 86
Cleatlam. *Dur* 4K 47
Cleator. *Cumb* 3K 45
Cleator Moor. *Cumb* 3K 45
Cleckheaton. *W Yor* 5K 41
Cleedownton. *Shrp* 3D 26
Cleehill. *Shrp* 4D 26
Cleekhimin. *N Lan* 4F 58
Clee St Margaret. *Shrp* 3D 26
Cleestanton. *Shrp* 4D 26
Cleethorpes. *NE Lin* 7L 43
Cleeton St Mary. *Shrp* 4E 26
Cleeve. *N Som* 7C 18
Cleeve. *Oxon* 5D 20
Cleeve Hill. *Glos* 1H 19
Cleeve Prior. *Worc* 7J 27
Clehonger. *Here* 8C 26
Cleigh. *Arg* 5C 64
Cleish. *Per* 8D 66
Cleland. *N Lan* 4G 59
Clench Common. *Wilts* 7K 19
Clenchwarton. *Norf* 7B 38
Clennell. *Nmbd* 1C 54
Clent. *Worc* 4H 27
Cleobury Mortimer. *Shrp* 4E 26
Cleobury North. *Shrp* 3E 26
Clephanton. *High* 8J 79
Clerkhill. *High* 5K 85
Clestrain. *Orkn* 1E 86
Clevancy. *Wilts* 6J 19
Clevedon. *N Som* 6C 18
Cleveley. *Oxon* 1A 20
Cleveleys. *Lanc* 3B 40
Clevelode. *Worc* 7G 27
Cleverton. *Wilts* 5H 19
Clewer. *Som* 8C 18
Cley next the Sea. *Norf* 5G 39
Cliaid. *W Isl* 5C 74
Cliasmol. *W Isl* 3B 76
Clibberswick. *Shet* 2L 91
Cliburn. *Cumb* 3D 46
Cliddesden. *Hants* 1D 10
Clieves Hills. *Lanc* 7B 40
Cliff. *Warw* 2L 27
Cliffburn. *Ang* 3K 67
Cliffe. *Medw* 6D 22
Cliffe. *N Yor*
nr. Darlington 4L 47
nr. Selby 4D 42
Cliff End. *E Sus* 4E 12
Cliffe Woods. *Medw* 6D 22
Clifford. *Here* 8M 25
Clifford. *W Yor* 3B 42
Clifford Chambers. *Warw* 6K 27
Clifford's Mesne. *Glos* 1F 18
Cliffsend. *Kent* 7K 23
Clifton. *Bris* 6D 18
Clifton. *C Beds* 8J 29
Clifton. *Cumb* 3D 46
Clifton. *Derbs* 5K 35
Clifton. *Devn* 1F 6
Clifton. *G Man* 7F 40
Clifton. *Lanc* 4C 40
Clifton. *Nmbd* 3F 54
Clifton. *N Yor* 3K 41
Clifton. *Nott* 6C 36
Clifton. *Oxon* 8B 28
Clifton. *S Yor* 8C 42
Clifton. *Stir* 4H 65
Clifton. *W Yor* 5K 41
Clifton. *Worc* 7G 27
Clifton. *York* 2C 42
Clifton Campville. *Staf* 8L 35
Clifton Hampden. *Oxon* 4C 20
Clifton Hill. *Worc* 5F 26
Clifton Reynes. *Mil* 6G 29
Clifton upon Dunsmore.
Warw 4C 28
Clifton upon Teme. *Worc* 5F 26
Cliftonville. *Kent* 6K 23
Cliftonville. *Norf* 6K 39
Climping. *W Sus* 5G 11
Climpy. *S Lan* 4H 59
Clink. *Som* 1F 8
Clint. *N Yor* 2L 41
Clint Green. *Norf* 8G 39
Clintmains. *Bord* 6D 60
Cliobh. *W Isl* 8D 82
Clipiau. *Gwyn* 1H 25
Clippesby. *Norf* 8L 39
Clippings Green. *Norf* 8G 39
Clipsham. *Rut* 8G 37
Clipston. *Nptn* 3E 28
Clipston. *Notts* 6D 36
Clipstone. *Notts* 3C 36
Clitheroe. *Lanc* 3F 40
Cliuthar. *W Isl* 4C 76
Clive. *Shrp* 7D 34
Clivocast. *Shet* 3K 91
Clixby. *Linc* 7H 43
Clocaenog. *Den* 5K 33
Clochan. *Mor* 7D 80
Clochforbie. *Abers* 8H 81
Clock Face. *Mers* 8D 40
Cloddiau. *Powy* 2M 25
Cloddymoss. *Mor* 7K 79
Clodock. *Here* 1B 18
Cloford. *Som* 1F 8
Clogh. *ME Ant* 3G 93
Clogher. *M Ulst* 6D 92
Cloghmills. *Caus* 3G 93
Clola. *Abers* 1K 73
Clonoe. *M Ulst* 5F 93
Clonvaraghan. *New M* 6H 93
Clophill. *C Beds* 8H 29
Clopton. *Nptn* 3H 29
Clopton Corner. *Suff* 6J 31
Clopton Green. *Suff* 6D 30
Closeburn. *Dum* 2C 52
Close Clark. *IOM* 7B 44
Closworth. *Som* 4D 8
Clothall. *Herts* 8K 29
Clotton. *Ches W* 3D 34
Clough. *G Man* 6H 41
Clough. *New M* 6J 93
Clough. *W Yor* 6J 41
Cloughey. *Ards* 6K 93
Clough Foot. *W Yor* 5H 41
Cloughton. *N Yor* 6H 49
Cloughton Newlands.
N Yor 6H 49
Clousta. *Shet* 2D 90
Clouston. *Orkn* 8B 88
Clova. *Abers* 3D 72
Clova. *Ang* 8C 72
Clovelly. *Devn* 3C 6
Clovenfords. *Bord* 6B 60
Clovenstone. *Abers* 4G 73
Clovullin. *High* 1E 64
Clowne. *Derbs* 2B 36
Clows Top. *Worc* 4F 26
Cloy. *Wrex* 5B 34
Cloyfin. *Caus* 2F 93
Cluanie Inn. *High* 4A 70
Cluanie Lodge. *High* 4A 70
Cluddley. *Telf* 8E 34
Clun. *Shrp* 3B 26
Y Clun. *Neat* 4H 17
Clunas. *High* 1J 71
Clunbury. *Shrp* 3B 26
Clunderwen. *Pemb* 5H 15
Clune. *High* 3H 71
Clunes. *High* 7C 70
Clungunford. *Shrp* 4B 26
Clunie. *Per* 3E 66
Clunton. *Shrp* 3B 26
Cluny. *Fife* 8F 66
Clutton. *Bath* 8E 18
Clutton. *Ches W* 4C 34
Clwt-y-bont. *Gwyn* 4E 32
Clwydfagwyr. *Mer T* 4K 17
Clydach. *Mon* 3M 17
Clydach. *Swan* 4F 16
Clydach Vale. *Rhon* 5J 17
Clydebank. *W Dun* 3D 58
Clydey. *Pemb* 3J 15
Clyffe Pypard. *Wilts* 6J 19
Clynder. *Arg* 1M 57
Clyne. *Neat* 4H 17
Clynelish. *High* 3J 79
Clynnog-fawr. *Gwyn* 6D 32
Clyro. *Powy* 8M 25
Clyst Honiton. *Devn* 6J 7
Clyst Hydon. *Devn* 5K 7
Clyst St George. *Devn* 7J 7
Clyst St Lawrence. *Devn* 5K 7
Clyst St Mary. *Devn* 6J 7
Clyth. *High* 8D 86
Cnip. *W Isl* 8D 82
Cnoc Amhlaigh. *W Isl* 8J 83
Cnwcau. *Pemb* 2J 15
Cnwch Coch. *Cdgn* 5F 24
Coad's Green. *Corn* 8B 6
Coagh. *M Ulst* 5F 93
Coal Aston. *Derbs* 2A 36
Coalbrookdale. *Telf* 1E 26
Coalbrookvale. *Blae* 4L 17
Coalburn. *S Lan* 6G 59
Coalburns. *Tyne* 5E 54
Coalcleugh. *Nmbd* 7B 54
Coaley. *Glos* 3F 18
Coalford. *Abers* 6H 73
Coalhall. *E Ayr* 8C 58
Coalhill. *Essx* 4D 22
Coalisland. *M Ulst* 5F 93
Coalpit Heath. *S Glo* 5E 18
Coal Pool. *W Mid* 1J 27
Coalport. *Telf* 1F 26
Coalsnaughton. *Clac* 8C 66
Coaltown of Balgonie. *Fife* 8G 67
Coaltown of Wemyss. *Fife* 8G 67
Coalville. *Leics* 8B 36
Coalway. *Glos* 2D 18
Coanwood. *Nmbd* 6L 53
Coat. *Som* 3C 8
Coatbridge. *N Lan* 3F 58
Coatdyke. *N Lan* 3F 58
Coate. *Swin* 5K 19
Coate. *Wilts* 7J 19
Coates. *Cambs* 2L 29
Coates. *Glos* 3H 19
Coates. *Linc* 1G 37
Coates. *W Sus* 4G 11
Coatham. *Red C* 3C 48
Coatham Mundeville. *Darl* 3L 47
Cobbaton. *Devn* 3F 6
Coberley. *Glos* 2H 19
Cobhall Common. *Here* 8C 26
Cobham. *Kent* 7C 22
Cobham. *Surr* 8J 21
Cobnash. *Here* 5C 26
Coburg. *Devn* 8H 7
Cockayne. *N Yor* 6D 48
Cockayne Hatley. *C Beds* 7K 29
Cock Bank. *Wrex* 5B 34
Cock Bridge. *Abers* 5B 72
Cockburnspath. *Bord* 2E 60
Cock Clarks. *Essx* 3E 22
Cockenzie and Port Seton.
E Lot 2B 60
Cockerham. *Lanc* 2C 40
Cockermouth. *Cumb* 8F 52
Cockernhoe. *Herts* 1J 21
Cockfield. *Dur* 3K 47
Cockfield. *Suff* 6F 30
Cockfosters. *G Lon* 4K 21
Cock Gate. *Here* 5C 26
Cock Green. *Essx* 2C 22
Cocking. *W Sus* 4F 10
Cocking Causeway. *W Sus* 4F 10
Cockington. *Torb* 5L 5
Cocklake. *Som* 1C 8
Cocklaw. *Abers* 1K 73
Cocklaw. *Nmbd* 4C 54
Cockley Beck. *Cumb* 4M 45
Cockley Cley. *Norf* 1D 30
Cockmuir. *Abers* 8J 81
Cockpole Green. *Wok* 5E 20
Cockshutford. *Shrp* 3D 26
Cockshutt. *Shrp* 7C 34
Cockthorpe. *Norf* 5F 38
Cockwood. *Devn* 7J 7
Cockyard. *Derbs* 2J 35
Cockyard. *Here* 8C 26
Codda. *Corn* 8A 6
Coddenham. *Suff* 6H 31
Coddenham Green. *Suff* 6H 31

Coddington—Cwmtillery

Coddington. *Ches W* 4C **34**
Coddington. *Here* 7F **26**
Coddington. *Notts* 4F **36**
Codford. *Wilts* 2H **9**
Codicote. *Herts* 2K **21**
Codmore Hill. *W Sus* 3H **11**
Codnor. *Derbs* 5B **36**
Codrington. *S Glo* 6F **18**
Codsall. *Staf* 1G **27**
Codsall Wood. *Staf* 1G **27**
Coed Duon. *Cphy* 5L **17**
Coedely. *Rhon* 6K **17**
Coedglasson. *Powy* 6K **25**
Coedkernew. *Newp* 5A **18**
Coed Morgan. *Mon* 2B **18**
Coedpoeth. *Wrex* 4A **34**
Coedway. *Powy* 8B **34**
Coed-y-bryn. *Cdgn* 2K **15**
Coed-y-paen. *Mon* 4B **18**
Coed Ystumgwern. *Gwyn* 8E **32**
Coelbren. *Powy* 3H **17**
Coffinswell. *Devn* 5L **5**
Cofton Hackett. *Worc* 4J **27**
Cogan. *V Glam* 7L **17**
Cogenhoe. *Nptn* 5F **28**
Cogges. *Oxon* 3A **20**
Coggeshall. *Essx* 1E **22**
Coggeshall Hamlet. *Essx* 1E **22**
Coggins Mill. *E Sus* 3B **12**
Coignafearn Lodge. *High* 4G **71**
Coig Peighinnean. *W Isl* 5J **83**
Coig Peighinnean Bhuirgh.
W Isl 6H **83**
Coilleag. *W Isl* 4D **74**
Coillemore. *High* 6G **79**
Coillore. *High* 2E **68**
Coire an Fhuarain. *W Isl* 8F **82**
Coity. *B'end* 6J **17**
Cokhay Green. *Derbs* 7L **35**
Col. *W Isl* 7H **83**
Colaboll. *High* 2F **78**
Colan. *Corn* 5A **4**
Colaton Raleigh. *Devn* 7K **7**
Colbost. *High* 1D **68**
Colburn. *N Yor* 6K **47**
Colby. *Cumb* 3E **46**
Colby. *IOM* 7B **44**
Colby. *Norf* 6J **39**
Colchester. *Essx* 1G **23**
Cold Ash. *W Ber* 7C **20**
Cold Ashby. *Nptn* 4D **28**
Cold Ashton. *S Glo* 6F **18**
Cold Aston. *Glos* 2K **19**
Coldbackie. *High* 6J **85**
Cold Blow. *Pemb* 5H **15**
Cold Brayfield. *Mil* 6G **29**
Cold Cotes. *N Yor* 8F **46**
Coldean. *Brig* 5L **11**
Coldeast. *Devn* 8H **7**
Colden. *W Yor* 5H **41**
Colden Common. *Hants* 3B **10**
Coldfair Green. *Suff* 5L **31**
Coldham. *Cambs* 1M **29**
Coldham. *Staf* 1G **27**
Cold Hanworth. *Linc* 1H **37**
Cold Harbour. *Dors* 6H **9**
Coldharbour. *Corn* 4L **3**
Coldharbour. *Glos* 3D **18**
Coldharbour. *Kent* 8B **22**
Coldharbour. *Surr* 1J **11**
Cold Hatton. *Telf* 7E **34**
Cold Hatton Heath. *Telf* 7E **34**
Cold Hesledon. *Dur* 7H **55**
Cold Hiendley. *W Yor* 6A **42**
Cold Higham. *Nptn* 6D **28**
Coldingham. *Bord* 3G **61**
Cold Kirby. *N Yor* 7C **48**
Coldmeece. *Staf* 6G **35**
Cold Northcott. *Corn* 7B **6**
Cold Norton. *Essx* 3E **22**
Cold Overton. *Leics* 8F **36**
Coldrain. *Per* 7D **66**
Coldred. *Kent* 1J **13**
Coldridge. *Devn* 5F **6**
Cold Row. *Lanc* 3B **40**
Coldstream. *Bord* 5F **60**
Coldwaltham. *W Sus* 4H **11**
Coldwell. *Here* 8C **26**
Coldwells. *Abers* 2L **73**
Coldwells Croft. *Abers* 3E **72**
Cole. *Shet* 1D **90**
Cole. *Som* 2E **8**
Colebatch. *Shrp* 3B **26**
Colebrook. *Devn* 5K **7**
Colebrooke. *Devn* 6G **7**
Coleburn. *Mor* 8B **80**
Coleby. *Linc* 3G **37**
Coleby. *N Lin* 6F **42**
Cole End. *Warw* 3L **27**
Coleford. *Devn* 5G **7**
Coleford. *Glos* 2D **18**
Coleford. *Som* 1E **8**
Colegate End. *Norf* 3H **31**
Cole Green. *Herts* 2K **21**
Cole Henley. *Hants* 8B **20**
Colehill. *Dors* 5J **9**
Coleman Green. *Herts* 2J **21**
Coleman's Hatch. *E Sus* 2A **12**
Colemere. *Shrp* 6C **34**
Colemore. *Hants* 2E **10**
Colemore Green. *Shrp* 2F **26**
Coleorton. *Leics* 8B **36**
Coleraine. *Caus* 2F **93**
Colerne. *Wilts* 6G **19**
Colesbourne. *Glos* 2J **19**
Colesden. *Bed* 6J **29**
Coles Green. *Worc* 6F **26**
Coleshill. *Buck* 4G **21**
Coleshill. *Oxon* 4L **19**
Coleshill. *Warw* 3L **27**
Colestocks. *Devn* 5K **7**
Colethrop. *Glos* 2G **19**
Coley. *Bath* 8D **18**
Colgate. *W Sus* 2K **11**
Colinsburgh. *Fife* 7H **67**
Colinton. *Edin* 3L **59**
Colintraive. *Arg* 2K **57**
Colkirk. *Norf* 7F **38**
Collace. *Per* 4F **66**
Collam. *W Isl* 4C **76**
Collaton. *Devn* 8K **5**
Collaton St Mary. *Torb* 5L **5**
College of Roseisle. *Mor* 7M **79**
Collessie. *Fife* 6F **66**
Collier Row. *G Lon* 4A **22**
Colliers End. *Herts* 1L **21**
Collier Street. *Kent* 1D **12**
Colliery Row. *Tyne* 7G **55**
Collieston. *Abers* 3K **73**
Collin. *Dum* 4E **52**
Collingbourne Ducis. *Wilts* 8L **19**
Collingbourne Kingston.
Wilts 8L **19**
Collingham. *Notts* 3F **36**
Collingham. *W Yor* 3A **42**
Collingtree. *Nptn* 6E **28**
Collins Green. *Warr* 8D **40**
Collins Green. *Worc* 6F **26**
Colliston. *Ang* 3K **67**
Colliton. *Devn* 5K **7**
Collydean. *Fife* 7F **66**
Collyweston. *Nptn* 1G **29**
Colmonell. *S Ayr* 3G **51**
Colmworth. *Bed* 6J **29**
Colnbrook. *Slo* 6H **21**
Colne. *Cambs* 4L **29**
Colne. *Lanc* 3G **41**
Colne Engaine. *Essx* 8E **30**
Colney. *Norf* 1H **31**
Colney Heath. *Herts* 3K **21**
Colney Street. *Herts* 3J **21**
Coln Rogers. *Glos* 3J **19**
Coln St Aldwyns. *Glos* 3K **19**
Coln St Dennis. *Glos* 2J **19**
Colpitts Grange. *Nmbd* 6C **54**
Colpy. *Abers* 2F **72**
Colscott. *Devn* 4C **6**
Colsterdale. *N Yor* 7K **47**
Colsterworth. *Linc* 7G **37**
Colston Bassett. *Notts* 6E **36**
Colstoun House. *E Lot* 2C **60**
Coltfield. *Mor* 7M **79**
Colthouse. *Cumb* 6B **46**
Coltishall. *Norf* 8J **39**
Coltness. *N Lan* 4G **59**
Colton. *Cumb* 7B **46**
Colton. *Norf* 1H **31**
Colton. *N Yor* 3C **42**
Colton. *Staf* 7J **35**
Colton. *W Yor* 4A **42**
Colt's Hill. *Kent* 1C **12**
Col Uarach. *W Isl* 8H **83**
Colvend. *Dum* 6C **52**
Colvister. *Shet* 4K **91**
Colwall. *Here* 7F **26**
Colwall Green. *Here* 7F **26**
Colwell. *Nmbd* 4C **54**
Colwich. *Staf* 7J **35**
Colwick. *Notts* 5D **36**
Colwinston. *V Glam* 7J **17**
Colworth. *W Sus* 5G **11**
Colwyn Bay. *Cnwy* 3H **33**
Colyford. *Devn* 6A **8**
Colyton. *Devn* 6M **7**
Combe. *Devn* 5K **5**
Combe. *Here* 5B **26**
Combe. *Oxon* 2B **20**
Combe. *W Ber* 7A **20**
Combe Almer. *Dors* 6H **9**
Combebow. *Devn* 7D **6**
Combe Down. *Bath* 7F **18**
Combe Fishacre. *Devn* 5L **5**
Combe Florey. *Som* 2L **7**
Combe Hay. *Bath* 7F **18**
Combeinteignhead. *Devn* 8J **7**
Combe Martin. *Devn* 1E **6**
Combe Moor. *Here* 5B **26**
Comber. *Ards* 5J **93**
Combe Raleigh. *Devn* 5L **7**
Comberbach. *Ches W* 2E **34**
Comberford. *Staf* 1K **27**
Comberton. *Cambs* 6L **29**
Comberton. *Here* 5C **26**
Combe St Nicholas. *Som* 4B **8**
Combpyne. *Devn* 6A **8**
Combridge. *Staf* 6J **35**
Combrook. *Warw* 6M **27**
Combs. *Derbs* 2J **35**
Combs. *Suff* 6G **31**
Combs Ford. *Suff* 6G **31**
Combwich. *Som* 1A **8**
Comers. *Abers* 5F **72**
Comhampton. *Worc* 5G **27**
Comins Coch. *Cdgn* 4F **24**
Comley. *Shrp* 2C **26**
Commercial End. *Cambs* 5B **30**
Commins. *Powy* 8L **33**
Commins Coch. *Powy* 2H **25**
The Common. *Wilts*
nr. Salisbury 2L **9**
nr. Swindon 5J **19**
Commondale. *N Yor* 4D **48**
Common End. *Cumb* 2K **45**
Common Hill. *Here* 8D **26**
Common Moor. *Corn* 5E **4**
Common Side. *Derbs* 2M **35**
Commonside. *Ches W* 2D **34**
Commonside. *Derbs* 5L **35**
Compstall. *G Man* 8H **41**
Compton. *Devn* 5L **5**
Compton. *Hants* 3B **10**
Compton. *Staf* 3G **27**
Compton. *Surr* 1G **11**
Compton. *W Ber* 6C **20**
Compton. *W Sus* 4E **10**
Compton. *Wilts* 8K **19**
Compton Abbas. *Dors* 4G **9**
Compton Abdale. *Glos* 2J **19**
Compton Bassett. *Wilts* 6J **19**
Compton Beauchamp. *Oxon* 5L **19**
Compton Bishop. *Som* 8B **18**
Compton Chamberlayne.
Wilts 3J **9**
Compton Dando. *Bath* 7E **18**
Compton Dundon. *Som* 2C **8**
Compton Greenfield. *S Glo* 5D **18**
Compton Martin. *Bath* 8D **18**
Compton Pauncefoot. *Som* 3E **8**
Compton Valence. *Dors* 6D **8**
Comrie. *Fife* 1J **59**
Comrie. *Per* 5A **66**
Conaglen. *High* 1E **64**
Conchra. *Arg* 1K **57**
Conchra. *High* 3K **69**
Conder Green. *Lanc* 2C **40**
Conderton. *Worc* 8H **27**
Condicote. *Glos* 1K **19**
Condorrat. *N Lan* 2F **58**
Condover. *Shrp* 1C **26**
Coneyhurst. *W Sus* 3J **11**
Coneyisland. *New M* 7J **93**
Coneysthorpe. *N Yor* 8E **48**
Coneythorpe. *N Yor* 2A **42**
Coney Weston. *Suff* 4F **30**
Conford. *Hants* 2F **10**
Congdon's Shop. *Corn* 8B **6**
Congerstone. *Leics* 1A **28**
Congham. *Norf* 7D **38**
Congleton. *Ches E* 3G **35**
Congl-y-wal. *Gwyn* 6G **33**
Congresbury. *N Som* 7C **18**
Congreve. *Staf* 8H **35**
Conham. *S Glo* 6E **18**
Conicaval. *Mor* 8K **79**
Coningsby. *Linc* 4K **37**
Conington. *Cambs*
nr. Fenstanton 5L **29**
nr. Sawtry 3J **29**
Conisbrough. *S Yor* 8C **42**
Conisby. *Arg* 3B **56**
Conisholme. *Linc* 8M **43**
Coniston. *Cumb* 6B **46**
Coniston. *E Yor* 4J **43**
Coniston Cold. *N Yor* 2H **41**
Conistone. *N Yor* 1H **41**
Conlig. *Ards* 5J **93**
Connah's Quay. *Flin* 2A **34**
Connel. *Arg* 4D **64**
Connel Park. *E Ayr* 8E **58**
Connista. *High* 6F **76**
Connor. *ME Ant* 4G **93**
Connor Downs. *Corn* 5J **3**
Conock. *Wilts* 8J **19**
Conon Bridge. *High* 8F **78**
Cononley. *N Yor* 3H **41**
Cononsyth. *Ang* 3J **67**
Conordan. *High* 2G **69**
Consall. *Staf* 5H **35**
Consett. *Dur* 6E **54**
Constable Burton. *N Yor* 6K **47**
Constantine. *Corn* 6L **3**
Constantine Bay. *Corn* 4A **4**
Contin. *High* 8E **78**
Contullich. *High* 6G **79**
Conwy. *Cnwy* 3G **33**
Conyer. *Kent* 7F **22**
Conyer's Green. *Suff* 5E **30**
Cooden. *E Sus* 5D **12**
Cooil. *IOM* 7C **44**
Cookbury. *Devn* 5D **6**
Cookbury Wick. *Devn* 5C **6**
Cookham. *Wind* 5F **20**
Cookham Dean. *Wind* 5F **20**
Cookham Rise. *Wind* 5F **20**
Cookhill. *Worc* 6J **27**
Cookley. *Suff* 4K **31**
Cookley. *Worc* 3G **27**
Cookley Green. *Oxon* 4D **20**
Cookney. *Abers* 6H **73**
Cooksbridge. *E Sus* 4M **11**
Cooksey Green. *Worc* 5H **27**
Cookshill. *Staf* 5H **35**
Cooksmill Green. *Essx* 3C **22**
Cookstown. *M Ulst* 5F **93**
Coolham. *W Sus* 3J **11**
Cooling. *Medw* 6D **22**
Cooling Street. *Medw* 6D **22**
Coombe. *Corn*
nr. Bude 4B **6**
nr. St Austell 6B **4**
nr. Truro 4M **3**
Coombe. *Devn*
nr. Sidmouth 6L **7**
nr. Teignmouth 8J **7**
Coombe. *Glos* 4F **18**
Coombe. *Hants* 3D **10**
Coombe. *Wilts* 8K **19**
Coombe Bissett. *Wilts* 3K **9**
Coombe Hill. *Glos* 1G **19**
Coombe Keynes. *Dors* 7G **9**
Coombes. *W Sus* 5J **11**
Coopersale. *Essx* 3A **22**
Coopersale Street. *Essx* 3A **22**
Cooper's Corner. *Kent* 1A **12**
Cooper Street. *Kent* 8K **23**
Cootham. *W Sus* 4H **11**
Copalder Corner. *Cambs* 2L **29**
Copdock. *Suff* 7H **31**
Copford. *Essx* 1F **22**
Copford Green. *Essx* 1F **22**
Copgrove. *N Yor* 1M **41**
Copister. *Shet* 6J **91**
Cople. *Bed* 7J **29**
Copley. *Dur* 3J **47**
Coplow Dale. *Derbs* 2K **35**
Copmanthorpe. *York* 3C **42**
Copp. *Lanc* 4C **40**
Coppathorne. *Corn* 5B **6**
Coppenhall. *Ches E* 4F **34**
Coppenhall. *Staf* 8H **35**
Coppenhall Moss. *Ches E* 4F **34**
Copperhouse. *Corn* 5J **3**
Coppicegate. *Shrp* 3F **26**
Coppingford. *Cambs* 3J **29**
Copplestone. *Devn* 5G **7**
Coppull. *Lanc* 6D **40**
Coppull Moor. *Lanc* 6D **40**
Copsale. *W Sus* 3J **11**
Copshaw Holm. *Bord* 3J **53**
Copster Green. *Lanc* 4E **40**
Copston Magna. *Warw* 3B **28**
Copt Green. *Warw* 5K **27**
Copthall Green. *Essx* 3M **21**
Copt Heath. *W Mid* 4K **27**
Copt Hewick. *N Yor* 8M **47**
Copthill. *Dur* 7B **54**
Copthorne. *W Sus* 2L **11**
Coptiviney. *Shrp* 6C **34**
Copy's Green. *Norf* 6F **38**
Copythorne. *Hants* 4M **9**
Corbridge. *Nmbd* 5C **54**
Corby. *Nptn* 3F **28**
Corby Glen. *Linc* 7G **37**
Cordon. *N Ayr* 6K **57**
Coreley. *Shrp* 4E **26**
Corfe. *Som* 4M **7**
Corfe Castle. *Dors* 7H **9**
Corfe Mullen. *Dors* 6H **9**
Corfton. *Shrp* 3C **26**
Corgarff. *Abers* 5B **72**
Corhampton. *Hants* 3D **10**
Corkey. *Caus* 2G **93**
Corlae. *Dum* 2A **52**
Corlannau. *Neat* 5G **17**
Corley. *Warw* 3M **27**
Corley Ash. *Warw* 3L **27**
Corley Moor. *Warw* 3L **27**
Cormiston. *S Lan* 6J **59**
Cornaa. *IOM* 6D **44**
Cornaigbeg. *Arg* 3E **62**
Cornaigmore. *Arg*
on Coll 1H **63**
on Tiree 3E **62**
Corner Row. *Lanc* 4C **40**
Corney. *Cumb* 5L **45**
Cornforth. *Dur* 8G **55**
Cornhill. *Abers* 8E **80**
Cornhill. *High* 4F **78**
Cornhill-on-Tweed. *Nmbd* 6F **60**
Cornholme. *W Yor* 5H **41**
Cornish Hall End. *Essx* 8C **30**
Cornquoy. *Orkn* 1G **87**
Cornriggs. *Dur* 7B **54**
Cornsay. *Dur* 7E **54**
Cornsay Colliery. *Dur* 7E **54**
Corntown. *High* 8F **78**
Corntown. *V Glam* 7J **17**
Cornwall Airport Newquay.
Corn 5A **4**
Cornwell. *Oxon* 1L **19**
Cornwood. *Devn* 6J **5**
Cornworthy. *Devn* 6L **5**
Corpach. *High* 8A **70**
Corpusty. *Norf* 7H **39**
Corra. *Dum* 5C **52**
Corran. *High*
nr. Arnisdale 1E **64**
nr. Fort William 5K **69**
Corrany. *IOM* 6D **44**
Corribeg. *High* 8L **69**
Corrie. *N Ayr* 5K **57**
Corrie Common. *Dum* 3G **53**
Corriecravie. *N Ayr* 7J **57**
Corriekinloch. *High* 1D **78**
Corriemoillie. *High* 7D **78**
Corrievarkie Lodge. *Per* 8F **70**
Corrievorrie. *High* 3H **71**
Corrigall. *Orkn* 8C **88**
Corrimony. *High* 2D **70**
Corringham. *Linc* 8F **42**
Corringham. *Thur* 5D **22**
Corris. *Gwyn* 2G **25**
Corris Uchaf. *Gwyn* 2G **25**
Corrour Shooting Lodge.
High 1J **65**
Corry. *High* 3H **69**
Corrybrough. *High* 3J **71**
Corrygills. *N Ayr* 6K **57**
Corry of Ardnagrask. *High* 1F **70**
Corsback. *High*
nr. Dunnet 4D **86**
nr. Halkirk 6D **86**
Corscombe. *Dors* 5D **8**
Corse. *Abers* 1F **72**
Corse. *Glos* 1F **18**
Corsehill. *Abers* 8J **81**
Corse Lawn. *Worc* 8G **27**
Corse of Kinnoir. *Abers* 1E **72**
Corsham. *Wilts* 6G **19**
Corsley. *Wilts* 1G **9**
Corsley Heath. *Wilts* 1G **9**
Corsock. *Dum* 4B **52**
Corston. *Bath* 7E **18**
Corston. *Wilts* 5H **19**
Corstorphine. *Edin* 2L **59**
Cortachy. *Ang* 2G **67**
Corton. *Suff* 2M **31**
Corton. *Wilts* 1H **9**
Corton Denham. *Som* 3E **8**
Corwar House. *S Ayr* 3H **51**
Corwen. *Den* 6K **33**
Coryates. *Dors* 7E **8**
Coryton. *Devn* 7D **6**
Coryton. *Thur* 5D **22**
Cosby. *Leics* 2C **28**
Coscote. *Oxon* 5C **20**
Coseley. *W Mid* 2H **27**
Cosgrove. *Nptn* 7E **28**
Cosham. *Port* 5D **10**
Cosheston. *Pemb* 6G **15**
Coskills. *N Lin* 6H **43**
Cosmeston. *V Glam* 8L **17**
Cossall. *Notts* 5B **36**
Cossington. *Leics* 8D **36**
Cossington. *Som* 1B **8**
Costa. *Orkn* 7C **88**
Costessey. *Norf* 8H **39**
Costock. *Notts* 7C **36**
Coston. *Leics* 7F **36**
Coston. *Norf* 1G **31**
Cote. *Oxon* 3A **20**
Cotebrook. *Ches W* 3D **34**
Cotehill. *Cumb* 6J **53**
Cotes. *Cumb* 7C **46**
Cotes. *Leics* 7C **36**
Cotes. *Staf* 6G **35**
Cotesbach. *Leics* 3C **28**
Cotes Heath. *Staf* 6G **35**
Cotford St Luke. *Som* 3L **7**
Cotgrave. *Notts* 6D **36**
Cothal. *Abers* 4H **73**
Cotham. *Notts* 5E **36**
Cothelstone. *Som* 2L **7**
Cotheridge. *Worc* 6F **26**
Cotherstone. *Dur* 4J **47**
Cothill. *Oxon* 4B **20**
Cotland. *Mon* 3D **18**
Cotleigh. *Devn* 5M **7**
Cotmanhay. *Derbs* 5B **36**
Coton. *Cambs* 6M **29**
Coton. *Nptn* 4D **28**
Coton. *Staf*
nr. Gnosall 7G **35**
nr. Stone 6H **35**
nr. Tamworth 1K **27**
Coton Clanford. *Staf* 7G **35**
Coton Hayes. *Staf* 6H **35**
Coton Hill. *Shrp* 8C **34**
Coton in the Clay. *Staf* 7K **35**
Coton in the Elms. *Derbs* 8L **35**
Cotonwood. *Shrp* 6D **34**
Cotonwood. *Staf* 7G **35**
Cott. *Devn* 5K **5**
Cott. *Orkn* 7F **88**
Cottam. *E Yor* 1G **43**
Cottam. *Lanc* 4D **40**
Cottam. *Notts* 2F **36**
Cottartown. *High* 2L **71**
Cottarville. *Nptn* 5E **28**
Cottenham. *Cambs* 5A **30**
Cotterdale. *N Yor* 6G **47**
Cottered. *Herts* 1L **21**
Cotterstock. *Nptn* 2H **29**
Cottesbrooke. *Nptn* 4E **28**
Cottesmore. *Rut* 8G **37**
Cotteylands. *Devn* 4J **7**
Cottingham. *E Yor* 4H **43**
Cottingham. *Nptn* 2F **28**
Cottingley. *W Yor* 4K **41**
Cottisford. *Oxon* 8C **28**
Cotton. *Staf* 5J **35**
Cotton. *Suff* 5G **31**
Cotton End. *Bed* 7H **29**
Cottown. *Abers* 1H **73**
Cotts. *Devn* 5G **5**
Cotwalton. *Staf* 6H **35**
Couch's Mill. *Corn* 6D **4**
Coughton. *Here* 1D **18**
Coughton. *Warw* 5J **27**
Coulags. *High* 1L **69**
Coulby Newham. *Midd* 4C **48**
Coulderton. *Cumb* 4J **45**
Coulin Lodge. *High* 8M **77**
Coull. *Abers* 5E **72**
Coulport. *Arg* 1M **57**
Coulsdon. *G Lon* 8K **21**
Coulston. *Wilts* 8H **19**
Coulter. *S Lan* 6J **59**
Coultings. *Som* 1M **7**
Coulton. *N Yor* 8D **48**
Cound. *Shrp* 1D **26**
Coundon. *Dur* 3L **47**
Coundon Grange. *Dur* 3L **47**
Countersett. *N Yor* 7H **47**
Countess. *Wilts* 1K **9**
Countess Cross. *Essx* 8E **30**
Countesthorpe. *Leics* 2C **28**
Countisbury. *Devn* 1G **7**
Coupar Angus. *Per* 3F **66**
Coupe Green. *Lanc* 5D **40**
Coupland. *Cumb* 4F **46**
Coupland. *Nmbd* 6G **61**
Cour. *Arg* 5H **57**
Courance. *Dum* 2E **52**
Court-at-Street. *Kent* 2G **13**
Courteachan. *High* 6H **69**
Courteenhall. *Nptn* 6E **28**
Court Henry. *Carm* 2E **16**
Courtsend. *Essx* 4G **23**
Courtway. *Som* 2M **7**
Cousland. *Midl* 3A **60**
Cousley Wood. *E Sus* 2C **12**
Coustonn. *Arg* 2K **57**
Cove. *Arg* 1M **57**
Cove. *Devn* 4J **7**
Cove. *Hants* 8F **20**
Cove. *High* 4K **77**
Cove. *Bord* 2E **60**
Cove Bay. *Aber* 5J **73**
Covehithe. *Suff* 3M **31**
Coven. *Staf* 1H **27**
Coveney. *Cambs* 3A **30**
Covenham St Bartholomew.
Linc 8L **43**
Covenham St Mary. *Linc* 8L **43**
Coven Heath. *Staf* 1H **27**
Coventry. *W Mid* **108** (4M **27**)
Coverack. *Corn* 7L **3**
Coverham. *N Yor* 7K **47**
Covesea. *Mor* 6A **80**
Covingham. *Swin* 5K **19**
Covington. *Cambs* 4H **29**
Covington. *S Lan* 6H **59**
Cowan Bridge. *Lanc* 8E **46**
Cowan Head. *Cumb* 6C **46**
Cowbar. *Red C* 4E **48**
Cowbeech. *E Sus* 4C **12**
Cowbit. *Linc* 8K **37**
Cowbridge. *V Glam* 7J **17**
Cowden. *Kent* 1A **12**
Cowdenbeath. *Fife* 8E **66**
Cowdenburn. *Bord* 4L **59**
Cowdenend. *Fife* 8E **66**
Cowers Lane. *Derbs* 5M **35**
Cowes. *IOW* 6B **10**
Cowesby. *N Yor* 7B **48**
Cowfold. *W Sus* 3K **11**
Cowfords. *Mor* 7C **80**
Cowgill. *Cumb* 7F **46**
Cowie. *Abers* 7H **73**
Cowie. *Stir* 1G **59**
Cowlam. *E Yor* 1G **43**
Cowley. *Devn* 6J **7**
Cowley. *Glos* 2H **19**
Cowley. *G Lon* 5H **21**
Cowley. *Oxon* 3C **20**
Cowley. *Staf* 8G **35**
Cowleymoor. *Devn* 4J **7**
Cowling. *Lanc* 6D **40**
Cowling. *N Yor*
nr. Bedale 7L **47**
nr. Glusburn 3H **41**
Cowlinge. *Suff* 6D **30**
Cowmes. *W Yor* 6K **41**
Cowpe. *Lanc* 5G **41**
Cowpen. *Nmbd* 3F **54**
Cowpen Bewley. *Stoc T* 3B **48**
Cowplain. *Hants* 4D **10**
Cowshill. *Dur* 7B **54**
Cowslip Green. *N Som* 7C **18**
Cowstrandburn. *Fife* 8D **66**
Cowthorpe. *N Yor* 2B **42**
Coxall. *Here* 4B **26**
Coxbank. *Ches E* 5E **34**
Coxbench. *Derbs* 5A **36**
Cox Common. *Suff* 3L **31**
Coxford. *Norf* 7E **38**
Cox Green. *Surr* 2H **11**
Cox Green. *Tyne* 6G **55**
Coxgreen. *Staf* 3G **27**
Coxheath. *Kent* 8D **22**
Coxhoe. *Dur* 8G **55**
Coxley. *Som* 1D **8**
Coxwold. *N Yor* 8C **48**
Coychurch. *B'end* 6J **17**
Coylton. *S Ayr* 8C **58**
Coylumbridge. *High* 4K **71**
Coynach. *Abers* 5D **72**
Coynachie. *Abers* 2D **72**
Coytrahen. *B'end* 6H **17**
Crabbs Cross. *Worc* 5J **27**
Crabgate. *Norf* 7G **39**
Crab Orchard. *Dors* 5J **9**
Crabtree. *W Sus* 3K **11**
Crabtree Green. *Wrex* 5B **34**
Crackaig. *High* 2K **79**
Crackenthorpe. *Cumb* 3E **46**
Crackington Haven. *Corn* 2D **4**
Crackley. *Staf* 4G **35**
Crackley. *Warw* 4L **27**
Crackleybank. *Shrp* 8F **34**
Crackpot. *N Yor* 6H **47**
Cracoe. *N Yor* 1H **41**
Craddock. *Devn* 4K **7**
Cradhlastadh. *W Isl* 8D **82**
Cradley. *Here* 7F **26**
Cradley. *W Mid* 3H **27**
Cradoc. *Powy* 1K **17**
Crafthole. *Corn* 6F **4**
Crafton. *Buck* 2F **20**
Cragabus. *Arg* 5C **56**
Crag Foot. *Lanc* 8C **46**
Craggan. *High* 3L **71**
Cragganmore. *Mor* 2A **72**
Cragganvallie. *High* 2F **70**
Craggie. *High* 2J **79**
Craggiemore. *High* 2H **71**
Cragg Vale. *W Yor* 5J **41**
Craghead. *Dur* 6F **54**
Crai. *Powy* 2H **17**
Craichie. *Ang* 3J **67**
Craig. *Arg* 4E **64**
Craig. *Dum* 4A **52**
Craig. *High*
nr. Achnashellach 1M **69**
nr. Lower Diabaig 7J **77**
nr. Stromeferry 2K **69**
Craiganour Lodge. *Per* 2L **65**
Craigavon. *Arm* 6G **93**
Craigbrack. *Arg* 8F **64**
Craig-Cefn-Parc. *Swan* 4F **16**
Craigdallie. *Per* 5F **66**
Craigdam. *Abers* 2H **73**
Craigdarragh. *Derr* 3D **92**
Craigdarroch. *E Ayr* 1M **51**
Craigdarroch. *High* 8E **78**
Craigdhu. *High* 1E **70**
Craigearn. *Abers* 4G **73**
Craigellachie. *Mor* 1B **72**
Craigend. *Per* 5E **66**
Craigendoran. *Arg* 1B **58**
Craigends. *Ren* 3C **58**
Craigenputtock. *Dum* 3B **52**
Craigens. *E Ayr* 8D **58**
Craighall. *Edin* 2K **59**
Craighead. *Fife* 6K **67**
Craighouse. *Arg* 3E **56**
Craigie. *Abers* 4J **73**
Craigie. *D'dee* 4H **67**
Craigie. *Per*
nr. Blairgowrie 3E **66**
nr. Perth 5E **66**
Craigie. *S Ayr* 6C **58**
Craigielaw. *E Lot* 2B **60**
Craiglemine. *Dum* 8K **51**
Craig-llwyn. *Shrp* 8M **33**
Craiglockhart. *Edin* 2L **59**
Craig Lodge. *Arg* 2K **57**
Craigmalloch. *E Ayr* 2K **51**
Craigmaud. *Abers* 8H **81**
Craigmill. *Stir* 8B **66**
Craigmillar. *Edin* 2L **59**
Craigmore. *Arg* 3L **57**
Craigmuie. *Dum* 3B **52**
Craignair. *Dum* 5C **52**
Craignant. *Shrp* 6A **34**
Craigneuk. *N Lan*
nr. Airdrie 3F **58**
nr. Motherwell 4F **58**
Craignure. *Arg* 4B **64**
Craigo. *Ang* 1K **67**
Craigrory. *High* 1G **71**
Craigrothie. *Fife* 6G **67**
Craigs. *Dum* 4G **53**
The Craigs. *High* 4E **78**
Craigshill. *W Lot* 3J **59**
Craigton. *Aber* 5H **73**
Craigton. *Abers* 5G **73**
Craigton. *Ang*
nr. Carnoustie 4J **67**
nr. Kirriemuir 2G **67**
Craigton. *High* 1G **71**
Craigtown. *High* 6L **85**
Craig-y-Duke. *Neat* 4G **17**
Craig-y-nos. *Powy* 3H **17**
Craik. *Bord* 1H **53**
Crail. *Fife* 7K **67**
Crailing. *Bord* 7D **60**
Crailinghall. *Bord* 7D **60**
Crakehill. *N Yor* 8B **48**
Crakemarsh. *Staf* 6J **35**
Crambe. *N Yor* 1E **42**
Crambeck. *N Yor* 1E **42**
Cramlington. *Nmbd* 4F **54**
Cramond. *Edin* 2K **59**
Cramond Bridge. *Edin* 2K **59**
Cranage. *Ches E* 3F **34**
Cranagh. *Derr* 4D **92**
Cranberry. *Staf* 6G **35**
Cranborne. *Dors* 4J **9**
Cranbourne. *Brac* 6G **21**
Cranbrook. *Devn* 6K **7**
Cranbrook. *Kent* 2D **12**
Cranbrook Common. *Kent* 2D **12**
Crane Moor. *S Yor* 7M **41**
Crane's Corner. *Norf* 8F **38**
Cranfield. *C Beds* 7G **29**
Cranford. *G Lon* 6J **21**
Cranford St Andrew. *Nptn* 4G **29**
Cranford St John. *Nptn* 4G **29**
Cranham. *Glos* 2G **19**
Cranham. *G Lon* 5B **22**
Crank. *Mers* 8D **40**
Cranleigh. *Surr* 2H **11**
Cranley. *Suff* 4H **31**
Cranloch. *Mor* 8B **80**
Cranmer Green. *Suff* 4G **31**
Cranmore. *IOW* 6B **10**
Cranmore. *Linc* 1J **29**
Crannich. *Arg* 3L **63**
Crannoch. *Mor* 8D **80**
Cranoe. *Leics* 2E **28**
Cransford. *Suff* 5K **31**
Cranshaws. *Bord* 3D **60**
Cranstal. *IOM* 4D **44**
Crantock. *Corn* 2L **3**
Cranwell. *Linc* 5H **37**
Cranwich. *Norf* 2D **30**
Cranworth. *Norf* 1F **30**
Craobh Haven. *Arg* 7B **64**
Craobhnaclag. *High* 1E **70**
Crapstone. *Devn* 5H **5**
Crarae. *Arg* 8D **64**
Crask. *High*
nr. Bettyhill 5K **85**
nr. Lairg 1F **78**
Crask of Aigas. *High* 1E **70**
Craster. *Nmbd* 7K **61**
Craswall. *Here* 8A **26**
Cratfield. *Suff* 4K **31**
Crathes. *Abers* 6G **73**
Crathie. *Abers* 6B **72**
Crathie. *High* 6F **70**
Crathorne. *N Yor* 5B **48**
Craven Arms. *Shrp* 3C **26**
Crawcrook. *Tyne* 5E **54**
Crawford. *Lanc* 7C **40**
Crawford. *S Lan* 7H **59**
Crawforddyke. *S Lan* 4G **59**
Crawfordjohn. *S Lan* 7G **59**
Crawfordsburn. *Ards* 4J **93**
Crawick. *Dum* 8F **58**
Crawley. *Devn* 5A **8**
Crawley. *Hants* 2B **10**
Crawley. *Oxon* 2M **19**
Crawley. *W Sus* 2K **11**
Crawley Down. *W Sus* 2L **11**
Crawley End. *Essx* 7M **29**
Crawley Side. *Dur* 7C **54**
Crawshawbooth. *Lanc* 5G **41**
Crawton. *Abers* 7H **73**
Cray. *N Yor* 8H **47**
Cray. *Per* 1E **66**
Crayford. *G Lon* 6B **22**
Crayke. *N Yor* 8C **48**
Craymere Beck. *Norf* 6G **39**
Crays Hill. *Essx* 4D **22**
Cray's Pond. *Oxon* 5D **20**
Crazies Hill. *Wok* 5E **20**
Creacombe. *Devn* 4H **7**
Creagan. *Arg* 3D **64**
Creag Aoil. *High* 8B **70**
Creag Ghoraidh. *W Isl* 1D **74**
Creaguaineach Lodge. *High* 1H **65**
Creamore Bank. *Shrp* 6D **34**
Creaton. *Nptn* 4E **28**
Creca. *Dum* 4G **53**
Credenhill. *Here* 7C **26**
Crediton. *Devn* 5H **7**
Creebridge. *Dum* 5K **51**
Creech. *Dors* 7H **9**
Creech Heathfield. *Som* 3A **8**
Creech St Michael. *Som* 3A **8**
Creed. *Corn* 7B **4**
Creekmoor. *Pool* 6H **9**
Creekmouth. *G Lon* 5A **22**
Creeting St Mary. *Suff* 6G **31**
Creeting St Peter. *Suff* 6G **31**
Creeton. *Linc* 7H **37**
Creetown. *Dum* 6K **51**
Creggan. *Ferm* 5E **92**
Creggan. *New M* 7F **93**
Creggans. *Arg* 7E **64**
Cregneash. *IOM* 8A **44**
Cregrina. *Powy* 7L **25**
Creich. *Arg* 5J **63**
Creich. *Fife* 5G **67**
Creighton. *Staf* 6J **35**
Creigiau. *Card* 6K **17**
Cremyll. *Corn* 6G **5**
Crendell. *Dors* 4J **9**
Crepkill. *High* 1F **68**
Cressage. *Shrp* 1D **26**
Cressbrook. *Derbs* 2K **35**
Cresselly. *Pemb* 6G **15**
Cressing. *Essx* 1D **22**
Cresswell. *Nmbd* 2F **54**
Cresswell. *Staf* 6H **35**
Cresswell Quay. *Pemb* 6G **15**
Creswell. *Derbs* 2C **36**
Creswell Green. *Staf* 8J **35**
Cretingham. *Suff* 5J **31**
Crewe. *Ches E* 4F **34**
Crewe-by-Farndon. *Ches W* 4C **34**
Crewgreen. *Powy* 8B **34**
Crewkerne. *Som* 5C **8**
Crews Hill. *G Lon* 3L **21**
Crewton. *Derb* 6A **36**
Crianlarich. *Stir* 5H **65**
Cribbs Causeway. *S Glo* 5D **18**
Cribyn. *Cdgn* 1M **15**
Criccieth. *Gwyn* 7D **32**
Crich. *Derbs* 4A **36**
Crichton. *Midl* 3A **60**
Crick. *Mon* 4C **18**
Crick. *Nptn* 4C **28**
Crickadarn. *Powy* 8K **25**
Cricket Hill. *Hants* 7F **20**
Cricket Malherbie. *Som* 4B **8**
Cricket St Thomas. *Som* 5B **8**
Crickham. *Som* 1C **8**
Crickheath. *Shrp* 7A **34**
Crickhowell. *Powy* 3M **17**
Cricklade. *Wilts* 4K **19**
Cricklewood. *G Lon* 5K **21**
Cridling Stubbs. *N Yor* 5C **42**
Crieff. *Per* 5B **66**
Criftins. *Shrp* 6B **34**
Criggion. *Powy* 8A **34**
Crigglestone. *W Yor* 6M **41**
Crimchard. *Som* 5B **8**
Crimdon Park. *Dur* 8H **55**
Crimond. *Abers* 8K **81**
Crimonmogate. *Abers* 8K **81**
Crimplesham. *Norf* 1C **30**
Crimscote. *Warw* 7L **27**
Crinan. *Arg* 8B **64**
Cringleford. *Norf* 1H **31**
Crinow. *Pemb* 5H **15**
Cripplesease. *Corn* 5J **3**
Cripplestyle. *Dors* 4J **9**
Cripp's Corner. *E Sus* 3D **12**
Croanford. *Corn* 4C **4**
Crockenhill. *Kent* 7B **22**
Crocker End. *Oxon* 5E **20**
Crockerhill. *Hants* 5C **10**
Crockernwell. *Devn* 6G **7**
Crocker's Ash. *Here* 2D **18**
Crockerton. *Wilts* 1G **9**
Crocketford. *Dum* 4C **52**
Crockey Hill. *York* 3D **42**
Crockham Hill. *Kent* 8M **21**
Crockhurst Street. *Kent* 1C **12**
Crockleford Heath. *Essx* 1G **23**
Croeserw. *Neat* 5H **17**
Croes-Goch. *Pemb* 3E **14**
Croes Hywel. *Mon* 2B **18**
Croes-lan. *Cdgn* 2K **15**
Croesor. *Gwyn* 6F **32**
Croesoswallt. *Shrp* 7A **34**
Croesyceiliog. *Carm* 5L **15**
Croesyceiliog. *Torf* 4B **18**
Croes-y-mwyalch. *Torf* 4B **18**
Croesywaun. *Gwyn* 5E **32**
Croford. *Som* 3L **7**
Croft. *Leics* 2C **28**
Croft. *Linc* 3B **38**
Croft. *Warr* 8E **40**
Croftamie. *Stir* 1C **58**
Croftfoot. *Glas* 3D **58**
Croftmill. *Per* 4B **66**
Crofton. *Cumb* 6H **53**
Crofton. *W Yor* 6A **42**
Crofton. *Wilts* 7L **19**
Croft-on-Tees. *N Yor* 5L **47**
Crofts. *Dum* 4B **52**
Crofts of Benachielt. *High* 8C **86**
Crofts of Dipple. *Mor* 8C **80**
Crofty. *Swan* 7M **15**
Croggan. *Arg* 5B **64**
Croglin. *Cumb* 7K **53**
Croich. *High* 4E **78**
Croick. *High* 6L **85**
Croig. *Arg* 2J **63**
Cromarty. *High* 7H **79**
Crombie. *Fife* 1J **59**
Cromdale. *High* 3L **71**
Cromer. *Herts* 1K **21**
Cromer. *Norf* 5J **39**
Cromford. *Derbs* 4L **35**
Cromhall. *S Glo* 4E **18**
Cromor. *W Isl* 1F **76**
Cromra. *High* 7F **70**
Cromwell. *Notts* 3E **36**
Cronberry. *E Ayr* 7E **58**
Crondall. *Hants* 1E **10**
The Cronk. *IOM* 5C **44**
Cronk-y-Voddy. *IOM* 6C **44**
Cronton. *Mers* 1C **34**
Crook. *Cumb* 6C **46**
Crook. *Dur* 8E **54**
Crookdake. *Cumb* 7F **52**
Crooke. *G Man* 7D **40**
Crookedholm. *E Ayr* 6C **58**
Crooked Soley. *Wilts* 6M **19**
Crookes. *S Yor* 1M **35**
Crookgate Bank. *Dur* 6E **54**
Crookhall. *Dur* 6E **54**
Crookham. *Nmbd* 6G **61**
Crookham. *W Ber* 7C **20**
Crookham Village. *Hants* 8E **20**
Crooklands. *Cumb* 7D **46**
Crook of Devon. *Per* 7D **66**
Crookston. *Glas* 3D **58**
Cropredy. *Oxon* 7B **28**
Cropston. *Leics* 8C **36**
Cropthorne. *Worc* 7H **27**
Cropton. *N Yor* 7E **48**
Cropwell Bishop. *Notts* 6D **36**
Cropwell Butler. *Notts* 6D **36**
Cros. *W Isl* 5J **83**
Crosbie. *N Ayr* 4M **57**
Crosbost. *W Isl* 1E **76**
Crosby. *Cumb* 8E **52**
Crosby. *IOM* 7C **44**
Crosby. *Mers* 8B **40**
Crosby. *N Lin* 6F **42**
Crosby Court. *N Yor* 6A **48**
Crosby Garrett. *Cumb* 5F **46**
Crosby Ravensworth. *Cumb* 4E **46**
Crosby Villa. *Cumb* 8E **52**
Croscombe. *Som* 1D **8**
Crosland Moor. *W Yor* 6K **41**
Cross. *Som* 8C **18**
Crossaig. *Arg* 4H **57**
Crossapol. *Arg* 3E **62**
Cross Ash. *Mon* 2C **18**
Cross-at-Hand. *Kent* 1D **12**
Crossbush. *W Sus* 5H **11**
Crosscanonby. *Cumb* 8E **52**
Crossdale Street. *Norf* 6J **39**
Cross End. *Essx* 8E **30**
Crossens. *Mers* 5B **40**
Crossford. *Fife* 1J **59**
Crossford. *S Lan* 5G **59**
Cross Foxes. *Gwyn* 1G **25**
Crossgar. *New M* 6J **93**
Crossgate. *Orkn* 8D **88**
Crossgate. *Staf* 6H **35**
Crossgatehall. *E Lot* 3A **60**
Cross Gates. *W Yor* 4A **42**
Crossgates. *Fife* 1K **59**
Crossgates. *N Yor* 7H **49**
Crossgates. *Powy* 6K **25**
Crossgill. *Lanc* 1D **40**
Cross Green. *Devn* 7C **6**
Cross Green. *Staf* 1H **27**
Cross Green. *Suff*
nr. Cockfield 6E **30**
nr. Hitcham 6F **30**
Cross Hands. *Carm* 3E **16**
Crosshands. *Carm* 4H **15**
Crosshands. *E Ayr* 6C **58**
Cross Hill. *Derbs* 5B **36**
Cross Hill. *Glos* 4D **18**
Crosshill. *E Ayr* 7C **58**
Crosshill. *Fife* 8E **66**
Crosshill. *S Ayr* 1J **51**
Cross Hills. *N Yor* 3J **41**
Crosshills. *High* 6G **79**
Cross Holme. *N Yor* 6C **48**
Crosshouse. *E Ayr* 6B **58**
Cross Houses. *Shrp* 1D **26**
Crossings. *Cumb* 4K **53**
Cross in Hand. *E Sus* 3B **12**
Cross Inn. *Cdgn*
nr. Aberaeron 6E **24**
nr. New Quay 1K **15**
Cross Inn. *Rhon* 6K **17**
Crosskeys. *Cphy* 5M **17**
Crosskirk. *High* 5B **86**
Crosslands. *Cumb* 7B **46**
Cross Lane Head. *Shrp* 2F **26**
Cross Lanes. *Corn* 6K **3**
Cross Lanes. *Dur* 4J **47**
Cross Lanes. *N Yor* 1C **42**
Cross Lanes. *Wrex* 5B **34**
Crosslanes. *Shrp* 8B **34**
Crosslee. *Ren* 3C **58**
Crossmaglen. *New M* 7F **93**
Crossmichael. *Dum* 5B **52**
Crossmoor. *Lanc* 4C **40**
Crossnacreevy. *Lis* 5H **93**
Cross Oak. *Powy* 2L **17**
Cross of Jackston. *Abers* 2G **73**
Cross o' th' Hands. *Derbs* 5L **35**
Crossroads. *Abers*
nr. Aberdeen 5J **73**
nr. Banchory 6G **73**
Crossroads. *E Ayr* 6C **58**
Cross Side. *Devn* 3H **7**
Cross Street. *Suff* 4H **31**
Crosston. *Ang* 2J **67**
Cross Town. *Ches E* 2F **34**
Crossway. *Mon* 2C **18**
Crossway. *Powy* 7K **25**
Crossway Green. *Mon* 4D **18**
Crossway Green. *Worc* 5G **27**
Crossways. *Dors* 7F **8**
Crosswell. *Pemb* 3H **15**
Crosswood. *Cdgn* 5F **24**
Crosthwaite. *Cumb* 6C **46**
Croston. *Lanc* 6C **40**
Crostwick. *Norf* 8J **39**
Crostwight. *Norf* 7K **39**
Crothair. *W Isl* 8E **82**
Crouch. *Kent* 8C **22**
Croucheston. *Wilts* 3J **9**
Crouch Hill. *Dors* 4F **8**
Croughton. *Nptn* 8C **28**
Crovie. *Abers* 7H **81**
Crow. *Hants* 5K **9**
Crowan. *Corn* 5K **3**
Crowborough. *E Sus* 2B **12**
Crowcombe. *Som* 2L **7**
Crowcroft. *Worc* 6F **26**
Crowdecote. *Derbs* 3K **35**
Crowden. *Derbs* 8J **41**
Crowden. *Devn* 6D **6**
Crowdhill. *Hants* 4B **10**
Crowdon. *N Yor* 6G **49**
Crow Edge. *S Yor* 7K **41**
Crow End. *Cambs* 6L **29**
Crowfield. *Nptn* 7D **28**
Crowfield. *Suff* 6H **31**
Crow Green. *Essx* 4B **22**
Crow Hill. *Here* 1E **18**
Crowhurst. *E Sus* 4D **12**
Crowhurst. *Surr* 1L **11**
Crowhurst Lane End. *Surr* 1L **11**
Crowland. *Linc* 8K **37**
Crowland. *Suff* 4G **31**
Crowlas. *Corn* 5J **3**
Crowle. *N Lin* 6E **42**
Crowle. *Worc* 6H **27**
Crowle Green. *Worc* 6H **27**
Crowmarsh Gifford. *Oxon* 5D **20**
Crown Corner. *Suff* 4J **31**
Crownthorpe. *Norf* 1G **31**
Crowntown. *Corn* 5K **3**
Crows-an-wra. *Corn* 6G **3**
Crowshill. *Norf* 1F **30**
Crowthorne. *Brac* 7F **20**
Crowton. *Ches W* 2D **34**
Croxall. *Staf* 8K **35**
Croxby. *Linc* 8J **43**
Croxdale. *Dur* 8F **54**
Croxden. *Staf* 6J **35**
Croxley Green. *Herts* 4H **21**
Croxton. *Cambs* 5K **29**
Croxton. *Norf*
nr. Fakenham 6F **38**
nr. Thetford 3E **30**
Croxton. *N Lin* 6H **43**
Croxton. *Staf* 6F **34**
Croxtonbank. *Staf* 6F **34**
Croxton Green. *Ches E* 4D **34**
Croxton Kerrial. *Leics* 7F **36**
Croy. *High* 1H **71**
Croy. *N Lan* 2F **58**
Croyde. *Devn* 2D **6**
Croydon. *Cambs* 7L **29**
Croydon. *G Lon* 7L **21**
Crubenbeg. *High* 6G **71**
Crubenmore Lodge. *High* 6G **71**
Cruckmeole. *Shrp* 1C **26**
Cruckton. *Shrp* 8C **34**
Cruden Bay. *Abers* 2K **73**
Crudgington. *Telf* 8E **34**
Crudie. *Abers* 8G **81**
Crudwell. *Wilts* 4H **19**
Cruft. *Devn* 6E **6**
Crug. *Powy* 5L **25**
Crughywel. *Powy* 3M **17**
Crugmeer. *Corn* 4B **4**
Crugybar. *Carm* 1F **16**
Crug-y-byddar. *Powy* 4L **25**
Crulabhig. *W Isl* 8E **82**
Crumlin. *Ant* 5G **93**
Crumlin. *Cphy* 5M **17**
Crumpsall. *G Man* 7G **41**
Crumpsbrook. *Shrp* 4E **26**
Crundale. *Kent* 1G **13**
Crundale. *Pemb* 5F **14**
Cruwys Morchard. *Devn* 4H **7**
Crux Easton. *Hants* 8B **20**
Cruxton. *Dors* 6E **8**
Crwbin. *Carm* 5L **15**
Cryers Hill. *Buck* 4F **20**
Crymych. *Pemb* 3H **15**
Crynant. *Neat* 4G **17**
Crystal Palace. *G Lon* 6L **21**
Cuaich. *High* 7G **71**
Cuaig. *High* 8J **77**
Cuan. *Arg* 6B **64**
Cubbington. *Warw* 5M **27**
Cubert. *Corn* 3L **3**
Cubley. *S Yor* 7L **41**
Cubley Common. *Derbs* 6K **35**
Cublington. *Buck* 1F **20**
Cublington. *Here* 8B **26**
Cuckfield. *W Sus* 3L **11**
Cucklington. *Som* 3F **8**
Cuckney. *Notts* 2C **36**
Cuckron. *Shet* 2E **90**
Cuddesdon. *Oxon* 3D **20**
Cuddington. *Buck* 2E **20**
Cuddington. *Ches W* 2E **34**
Cuddington Heath. *Ches W* 5C **34**
Cuddy Hill. *Lanc* 4C **40**
Cudham. *G Lon* 8M **21**
Cudlipptown. *Devn* 8E **6**
Cudworth. *Som* 4B **8**
Cudworth. *S Yor* 7A **42**
Cudworth. *Surr* 1K **11**
Cuerdley Cross. *Warr* 1D **34**
Cuffley. *Herts* 3L **21**
Cuidhir. *W Isl* 5C **74**
Cuidhsiadar. *W Isl* 6J **83**
Cuidhtinis. *W Isl* 5B **76**
Culbo. *High* 7G **79**
Culbokie. *High* 8G **79**
Culburnie. *High* 1E **70**
Culcabock. *High* 1G **71**
Culcavy. *Lis* 5H **93**
Culcharry. *High* 8J **79**
Culcheth. *Warr* 8E **40**
Culduie. *High* 1J **69**
Culeave. *High* 4F **78**
Culford. *Suff* 4E **30**
Culgaith. *Cumb* 3E **46**
Culham. *Oxon* 4C **20**
Culkein. *High* 8C **84**
Culkein Drumbeg. *High* 8D **84**
Culkerton. *Glos* 4H **19**
Cullaville. *New M* 7F **93**
Cullen. *Mor* 7E **80**
Cullercoats. *Tyne* 4G **55**
Cullicudden. *High* 7G **79**
Cullingworth. *W Yor* 4J **41**
Cullipool. *Arg* 6B **64**
Cullivoe. *Shet* 3K **91**
Culloch. *Per* 6A **66**
Culloden. *High* 1H **71**
Cullompton. *Devn* 5K **7**
Cullybackey. *ME Ant* 3G **93**
Cullycapple. *Caus* 2F **93**
Cullyhanna. *New M* 7F **93**
Culm Davy. *Devn* 4L **7**
Culmington. *Shrp* 3C **26**
Culmore. *Derr* 2D **92**
Culmstock. *Devn* 4L **7**
Cul na Caepaich. *High* 7H **69**
Culnacnoc. *High* 7G **77**
Culnacraig. *High* 3A **78**
Culnady. *M Ulst* 3F **93**
Culrain. *High* 4F **78**
Culross. *Fife* 1H **59**
Culroy. *S Ayr* 8B **58**
Culswick. *Shet* 3C **90**
Cults. *Aber* 5H **73**
Cults. *Abers* 2E **72**
Cults. *Fife* 7G **67**
Cultybraggan Camp. *Per* 5A **66**
Culver. *Devn* 6H **7**
Culverlane. *Devn* 5K **5**
Culverstone Green. *Kent* 7C **22**
Culverthorpe. *Linc* 5H **37**
Culworth. *Nptn* 7C **28**
Culzie Lodge. *High* 6F **78**
Cumberlow Green. *Herts* 8L **29**
Cumbernauld. *N Lan* 2F **58**
Cumbernauld Village. *N Lan* 2F **58**
Cumberworth. *Linc* 2B **38**
Cumdivock. *Cumb* 7H **53**
Cuminestown. *Abers* 8H **81**
Cumledge Mill. *Bord* 4E **60**
Cumlewick. *Shet* 5E **90**
Cummersdale. *Cumb* 6H **53**
Cummertrees. *Dum* 5F **52**
Cummingstown. *Mor* 7M **79**
Cumnock. *E Ayr* 7D **58**
Cumnor. *Oxon* 3B **20**
Cumrew. *Cumb* 6K **53**
Cumwhinton. *Cumb* 6J **53**
Cumwhitton. *Cumb* 6K **53**
Cundall. *N Yor* 8B **48**
Cunninghamhead. *N Ayr* 5B **58**
Cunning Park. *S Ayr* 8B **58**
Cunningsburgh. *Shet* 5E **90**
Cunnister. *Shet* 4K **91**
Cupar. *Fife* 6G **67**
Cupar Muir. *Fife* 6G **67**
Cupernham. *Hants* 3A **10**
Curbar. *Derbs* 2L **35**
Curborough. *Staf* 8K **35**
Curbridge. *Hants* 4C **10**
Curbridge. *Oxon* 3M **19**
Curdridge. *Hants* 4C **10**
Curdworth. *Warw* 2K **27**
Curland. *Som* 4A **8**
Curland Common. *Som* 4A **8**
Curran. *M Ulst* 4F **93**
Curridge. *W Ber* 6B **20**
Currie. *Edin* 3K **59**
Curry Mallet. *Som* 3B **8**
Curry Rivel. *Som* 3B **8**
Curtisden Green. *Kent* 1D **12**
Curtisknowle. *Devn* 6K **5**
Cury. *Corn* 6K **3**
Cusgarne. *Corn* 4L **3**
Cushendall. *Caus* 2H **93**
Cushendun. *Caus* 2H **93**
Cusop. *Here* 8M **25**
Cusworth. *S Yor* 7C **42**
Cutcombe. *Som* 2J **7**
Cuthill. *E Lot* 2A **60**
Cutiau. *Gwyn* 1F **24**
Cutlers Green. *Essx* 8B **30**
Cutmadoc. *Corn* 5C **4**
Cutnall Green. *Worc* 5G **27**
Cutsdean. *Glos* 8J **27**
Cutthorpe. *Derbs* 2M **35**
Cuttiford's Door. *Som* 4B **8**
Cuttivett. *Corn* 5F **4**
Cutts. *Shet* 4D **90**
Cuttybridge. *Pemb* 5F **14**
Cuttyhill. *Abers* 8K **81**
Cuxham. *Oxon* 4D **20**
Cuxton. *Medw* 7D **22**
Cuxwold. *Linc* 7J **43**
Cwm. *Blae* 4L **17**
Cwm. *Den* 3K **33**
Cwm. *Powy* 2A **26**
Cwmafan. *Neat* 5G **17**
Cwmaman. *Rhon* 5J **17**
Cwmann. *Carm* 8E **24**
Cwmbach. *Carm* 4J **15**
Cwmbach. *Powy* 1L **17**
Cwmbach. *Rhon* 4K **17**
Cwmbach Llechrhyd. *Powy* 7K **25**
Cwmbelan. *Powy* 4J **25**
Cwmbran. *Torf* 4A **18**
Cwmbrwyno. *Cdgn* 4G **25**
Cwm Capel. *Carm* 6L **15**
Cwmcarn. *Cphy* 5M **17**
Cwmcarvan. *Mon* 3C **18**
Cwm-celyn. *Blae* 4M **17**
Cwmcerdinen. *Swan* 4F **16**
Cwm-Cewydd. *Gwyn* 1H **25**
Cwm-cou. *Cdgn* 2J **15**
Cwmcych. *Pemb* 3J **15**
Cwmdare. *Rhon* 4J **17**
Cwmdu. *Carm* 1F **16**
Cwmdu. *Powy* 2L **17**
Cwmduad. *Carm* 3K **15**
Cwm Dulais. *Swan* 4F **16**
Cwmerfyn. *Cdgn* 4F **24**
Cwmfelin. *B'end* 6H **17**
Cwmfelin Boeth. *Carm* 5H **15**
Cwmfelinfach. *Cphy* 5L **17**
Cwmfelin Mynach. *Carm* 4J **15**
Cwmffrwd. *Carm* 5L **15**
Cwmgiedd. *Powy* 3G **17**
Cwmgors. *Neat* 3G **17**
Cwmgwili. *Carm* 3E **16**
Cwmgwrach. *Neat* 4H **17**
Cwmhiraeth. *Carm* 3K **15**
Cwmifor. *Carm* 2F **16**
Cwmisfael. *Carm* 5L **15**
Cwm-Llinau. *Powy* 2H **25**
Cwmllynfell. *Neat* 3G **17**
Cwm-mawr. *Carm* 5M **15**
Cwm-miles. *Carm* 4H **15**
Cwmorgan. *Carm* 3J **15**
Cwmparc. *Rhon* 5J **17**
Cwm Penmachno. *Cnwy* 6G **33**
Cwmpennar. *Rhon* 4K **17**
Cwm Plysgog. *Pemb* 2H **15**
Cwmrhos. *Powy* 2L **17**
Cwmsychpant. *Cdgn* 2L **15**
Cwmsyfiog. *Cphy* 4L **17**
Cwmsymlog. *Cdgn* 4F **24**
Cwmtillery. *Blae* 4M **17**

Cwm-twrch Isaf—East Hagbourne

Cwm-twrch Isaf. Powy 4G 17
Cwm-twrch Uchaf. Powy 3G 17
Cwmwysg. Powy 2H 17
Cwm-y-glo. Gwyn 4E 32
Cwmyoy. Mon 1B 18
Cwmystwyth. Cdgn 5G 25
Cwrt. Gwyn 2F 24
Cwrtnewydd. Cdgn 2L 15
Cwrt-y-Cadno. Carm 8F 24
Cydweli. Carm 6L 15
Cyffylliog. Den 5K 33
Cymau. Flin 4A 34
Cymer. Neat 5H 17
Cymmer. Neat 5H 17
Cymmer. Rhon 5K 17
Cyncoed. Card 6L 17
Cynghordy. Carm 1H 17
Cynheidre. Carm 6L 15
Cynonville. Neat 5H 17
Cynwyd. Den 6K 33
Cynwyl Elfed. Carm 4K 15
Cywarch. Gwyn 1H 25

D

Dacre. Cumb 3C 46
Dacre. N Yor 1K 41
Dacre Banks. N Yor 1K 41
Daddry Shield. Dur 8B 54
Dadford. Buck 8D 28
Dadlington. Leics 2B 28
Dafen. Carm 6M 15
Daffy Green. Norf 1F 30
Dagdale. Staf 6J 35
Dagenham. G Lon 5A 22
Daggons. Dors 4K 9
Daglingworth. Glos 3H 19
Dagnall. Buck 2G 21
Dagtail End. Worc 5J 27
Dail. Arg 4E 64
Dail Beag. W Isl 7F 82
Dail bho Dheas. W Isl 5H 83
Dailly. S Ayr 1H 51
Dail Mor. W Isl 7F 82
Dairsie. Fife 6H 67
Daisy Bank. W Mid 2J 27
Daisy Hill. G Man 7E 40
Daisy Hill. W Yor 4K 41
Dalabrog. W Isl 3D 74
Dalavich. Arg 6D 64
Dalbeattie. Dum 5C 52
Dalblair. E Ayr 8E 58
Dalbury. Derbs 6L 35
Dalby. IOM 7B 44
Dalby Wolds. Leics 7D 36
Dalchalm. High 3K 79
Dalcharn. High 6J 85
Dalchork. High 2F 78
Dalchreichart. High 4C 70
Dalchruin. Per 6M 65
Dalcross. High 1H 71
Dalderby. Linc 3K 37
Dale. Cumb 7K 53
Dale. Pemb 6E 14
Dale Abbey. Derbs 6B 36
Dalebank. Derbs 3A 36
Dale Bottom. Cumb 3A 46
Dale Head. Cumb 4C 46
Dalehouse. N Yor 4E 48
Dalelia. High 1B 64
Dale of Walls. Shet 2B 90
Dalgarven. N Ayr 5A 58
Dalgety Bay. Fife 1K 59
Dalginross. Per 5A 66
Dalguise. Per 3C 66
Dalhalvaig. High 6L 85
Dalham. Suff 5D 30
Dalintart. Arg 5C 64
Dalkeith. Midl 3M 59
Dallas. Mor 8M 79
Dalleagles. E Ayr 8D 58
Dall House. Per 2K 65
Dallinghoo. Suff 6J 31
Dallington. E Sus 4C 12
Dallow. N Yor 8K 47
Dalmally. Arg 5F 64
Dalmarnock. Glas 3E 58
Dalmellington. E Ayr 1K 51
Dalmeny. Edin 2K 59
Dalmigavie. High 4H 71
Dalmilling. S Ayr 7B 58
Dalmore. High
nr. Alness 7G 79
nr. Rogart 3H 79
Dalmuir. W Dun 2C 58
Dalmunach. Mor 1B 72
Dalnabreck. High 1B 64
Dalnacardoch Lodge. Per 8H 71
Dalnamein Lodge. Per 1A 66
Dalnaspidal Lodge. Per 8G 71
Dalnatrat. High 2D 64
Dalnavie. High 6G 79
Dalnawillan Lodge. High 7B 86
Dalness. High 2F 64
Dalnessie. High 2G 79
Dalqueich. Per 7D 66
Dalquhairn. S Ayr 2J 51
Dalreavoch. High 3H 79
Dalreoch. Per 6D 66
Dalry. Edin 2L 59
Dalry. N Ayr 5A 58
Dalrymple. E Ayr 8B 58
Dalscote. Nptn 6D 28
Dalserf. S Lan 4G 59
Dalsmirren. Arg 8F 56
Dalston. Cumb 6H 53
Dalswinton. Dum 3D 52
Dalton. Dum 4F 52
Dalton. Lanc 7C 40
Dalton. Nmbd
nr. Hexham 6C 54
nr. Ponteland 4E 54
Dalton. N Yor
nr. Richmond 5K 47
nr. Thirsk 8B 48
Dalton. S Lan 4E 58
Dalton. S Yor 8B 42
Dalton-in-Furness. Cumb 7M 45
Dalton-le-Dale. Dur 7H 55
Dalton Magna. S Yor 8B 42
Dalton-on-Tees. N Yor 5L 47
Dalton Piercy. Hart 8H 55
Daltot. Arg 1G 57
Dalvey. High 2M 71
Dalwhinnie. High 7G 71
Dalwood. Devn 5A 8
Damerham. Hants 4K 9
Damgate. Norf
nr. Acle 1L 31
nr. Martham 8L 39
Dam Green. Norf 3G 31
Damhead. Mor 8L 79
Danaway. Kent 7E 22
Danbury. Essx 3D 22
Danby. N Yor 5E 48
Danby Botton. N Yor 5D 48
Danby Wiske. N Yor 6M 47
Danderhall. Midl 3M 59
Danebank. Ches E 1H 35
Danebridge. Ches E 3H 35
Dane End. Herts 1L 21
Danehill. E Sus 3M 11
Danesford. Shrp 2F 26
Daneshill. Hants 8D 20
Danesmoor. Derbs 3B 36
Danestone. Aber 4J 73
Dangerous Corner. Lanc 6D 40
Daniel's Water. Kent 1F 12
Dan's Castle. Dur 8E 54
Danzey Green. Warw 5K 27
Dapple Heath. Staf 7J 35
Daren. Powy 3M 17
Darenth. Kent 6B 22
Daresbury. Hal 1D 34
Darfield. S Yor 7B 42
Dargate. Kent 7G 23
Dargill. Per 6B 66
Darite. Corn 5E 4
Darkley. Arm 7F 93
Darlaston. W Mid 2H 27
Darley. N Yor 2L 41
Darley Abbey. Derb 6M 35
Darley Bridge. Derbs 3L 35
Darley Dale. Derbs 3L 35
Darley Head. N Yor 2K 41
Darlingscott. Warw 7L 27
Darlington. Darl 4L 47
Darliston. Shrp 6D 34
Darlton. Notts 2E 36
Darmsden. Suff 6G 31
Darnall. S Yor 1A 36
Darnford. Abers 6G 73
Darnford. Staf 1K 27
Darnhall. Ches W 3E 34
Darnick. Bord 6C 60
Darowen. Powy 2H 25
Darra. Abers 1G 73
Darracott. Devn 2D 6
Darragh Cross. New M 6J 93
Darras Hall. Nmbd 4E 54
Darrington. W Yor 5B 42
Darrow Green. Norf 3J 31
Darsham. Suff 5L 31
Dartfield. Abers 8K 81
Dartford. Kent 6B 22
Dartford-Thurrock River Crossing.
Kent 6B 22
Dartington. Devn 5K 5
Dartmeet. Devn 8F 6
Dartmouth. Devn 6L 5
Darton. S Yor 6M 41
Darvel. E Ayr 6D 58
Darwen. Bkbn 5E 40
Dassels. Herts 1L 21
Datchet. Wind 6G 21
Datchworth. Herts 2K 21
Datchworth Green. Herts 2K 21
Daubhill. G Man 7F 40
Dauntsey. Wilts 5H 19
Dauntsey Green. Wilts 5H 19
Dauntsey Lock. Wilts 5H 19
Dava. Mor 2L 71
Davenham. Ches W 2E 34
Daventry. Nptn 5C 28
Davidson's Mains. Edin 2L 59
Davidston. High 7H 79
Davidstow. Corn 7A 6
David's Well. Powy 5K 25
Davington. Dum 1G 53
Daviot. Abers 3G 73
Daviot. High 2H 71
Davyhulme. G Man 8F 40
Daw Cross. N Yor 2L 41
Dawdon. Dur 7H 55
Dawesgreen. Surr 1K 11
Dawley. Telf 1E 26
Dawlish. Devn 8J 7
Dawlish Warren. Devn 8J 7
Dawn. Cnwy 3H 33
Daws Heath. Essx 5E 22
Dawshill. Worc 6G 27
Daw's House. Corn 7C 6
Dawsmere. Linc 6M 37
Dayhills. Staf 6H 35
Dayhouse Bank. Worc 4H 27
Daylesford. Glos 1L 19
Daywall. Shrp 6A 34
Ddol. Flin 3L 33
Ddol Cownwy. Powy 1K 25
Deadman's Cross. C Beds 7J 29
Deadwater. Nmbd 2L 53
Deaf Hill. Dur 8G 55
Deal. Kent 8K 23
Dean. Cumb 2K 45
Dean. Devn
nr. Combe Martin 1F 6
nr. Lynton 1G 7
Dean. Dors 4H 9
Dean. Hants
nr. Bishop's Waltham 4C 10
nr. Winchester 2B 10
Dean. Oxon 1M 19
Dean. Som 1E 8
Dean Bank. Dur 8F 54
Deanburnhaugh. Bord 8A 60
Dean Cross. Devn 1E 6
Deane. Hants 8C 20
Deanich Lodge. High 5D 78
Deanland. Dors 4H 9
Deanlane End. W Sus 4E 10
Dean Park. Shrp 5E 26
Dean Prior. Devn 5K 5
Dean Row. Ches E 1G 35
Deans. W Lot 3J 59
Deanscales. Cumb 2K 45
Deanshanger. Nptn 7E 28
Deanston. Stir 7M 65
Dearham. Cumb 8E 52
Dearne Valley. S Yor 7A 42
Debach. Suff 6J 31
Debden. Essx 8B 30
Debden Green. Essx
nr. Loughton 4M 21
nr. Saffron Walden 8B 30
Debenham. Suff 5H 31
Dechmont. W Lot 2J 59
Deddington. Oxon 8B 28
Dedham. Essx 8G 31
Dedham Heath. Essx 8G 31
Deebank. Abers 6F 72
Deene. Nptn 2G 29
Deenethorpe. Nptn 2G 29
Deepcar. S Yor 8L 41
Deepcut. Surr 8G 21
Deepdale. Cumb 7F 46
Deepdale. N Lin 6H 43
Deepdale. N Yor 8G 47
Deeping Gate. Pet 1J 29
Deeping St James. Linc 8J 37
Deeping St Nicholas. Linc 8K 37
Deerhill. Mor 8D 80
Deerhurst. Glos 1G 19
Deerhurst Walton. Glos 1G 19
Deerness. Orkn 1G 87
Defford. Worc 7H 27
Defynnog. Powy 2J 17
Deganwy. Cnwy 3G 33
Deighton. N Yor 5A 48
Deighton. W Yor 6K 41
Deighton. York 3D 42
Deiniolen. Gwyn 4E 32
Delabole. Corn 3C 4
Delamere. Ches W 3D 34
Delfour. High 5J 71
The Dell. Suff 2L 31
Delliefure. High 2L 71
Delly End. Oxon 2A 20
Delny. High 6H 79
Delph. G Man 7H 41
Delves. Dur 7E 54
The Delves. W Mid 2J 27
Delvin End. Essx 8D 30
Dembleby. Linc 6H 37
Demelza. Corn 5B 4
The Den. N Ayr 4B 58
Denaby Main. S Yor 8B 42
Denbeath. Fife 8G 67
Denbigh. Den 4K 33
Denbury. Devn 5L 5
Denby. Derbs 5A 36
Denby Common. Derbs 5B 36
Denby Dale. W Yor 7L 41
Denchworth. Oxon 4A 20
Dendron. Cumb 7M 45
Deneside. Dur 7H 55
Denford. Nptn 4G 29
Dengie. Essx 3F 22
Denham. Buck 5H 21
Denham. Suff
nr. Bury St Edmunds 5D 30
nr. Eye 4H 31
Denham Green. Buck 5H 21
Denham Street. Suff 4H 31
Denhead. Abers
nr. Ellon 2J 73
nr. Strichen 8J 81
Denhead. Fife 6H 67
Denholm. Bord 8C 60
Denholme. W Yor 4J 41
Denholme Clough. W Yor 4J 41
Denholme Gate. W Yor 4J 41
Denio. Gwyn 7C 32
Denmead. Hants 4D 10
Dennington. Suff 5J 31
Denny. Falk 1G 59
Denny End. Cambs 5A 30
Dennyloanhead. Falk 1G 59
Den of Lindores. Fife 6F 66
Denshaw. G Man 6H 41
Denside. Abers 6H 73
Densole. Kent 1J 13
Denston. Suff 6D 30
Denstone. Staf 5K 35
Denstroude. Kent 7H 23
Dent. Cumb 7F 46
Denton. Cambs 3J 29
Denton. Darl 4L 47
Denton. E Sus 5A 12
Denton. G Man 8H 41
Denton. Kent 1J 13
Denton. Linc 6F 36
Denton. Norf 3J 31
Denton. Nptn 6F 28
Denton. N Yor 3K 41
Denton. Oxon 3C 20
Denver. Norf 1C 30
Denwick. Nmbd 8K 61
Deopham. Norf 1G 31
Deopham Green. Norf 2G 31
Depden. Suff 6D 30
Depden Green. Suff 6D 30
Deptford. G Lon 6L 21
Deptford. Wilts 2J 9
Derby. Derb 108 (6A 36)
Derbyhaven. IOM 8B 44
Derculich. Per 2B 66
Dereham. Norf 8F 38
Deri. Cphy 4L 17
Derril. Devn 5C 6
Derringstone. Kent 1J 13
Derrington. Shrp 2E 26
Derrington. Staf 7G 35
Derriton. Devn 5C 6
Derry. Derr 3D 92
Derryboye. New M 6J 93
Derrycrin. M Ulst 5F 93
Derrygonnelly. Ferm 6B 92
Derryguaig. Arg 4K 63
Derry Hill. Wilts 6H 19
Derrykeighan. Caus 2F 93
Derrylin. Ferm 7C 92
Derrymacash. Arm 6G 93
Derrythorpe. N Lin 7F 42
Derrytrasna. Arm 5F 93
Dersingham. Norf 6C 38
Dervaig. Arg 2K 63
Dervock. Caus 2F 93
Derwen. Den 5K 33
Derwen Gam. Cdgn 1L 15
Derwenlas. Powy 3G 25
Desborough. Nptn 3F 28
Desertmartin. M Ulst 4F 93
Desford. Leics 1B 28
Detchant. Nmbd 6H 61
Dethick. Derbs 4M 35
Detling. Kent 8D 22
Deuchar. Ang 1H 67
Deuddwr. Powy 1M 25
Devauden. Mon 4C 18
Devil's Bridge. Cdgn 5G 25
Devitts Green. Warw 2L 27
Devizes. Wilts 7J 19
Devonport. Plym 6G 5
Devonside. Clac 8C 66
Devoran. Corn 5L 3
Dewartown. Midl 3A 60
Dewlish. Dors 6F 8
Dewsall Court. Here 8C 26
Dewsbury. W Yor 5L 41
Dexbeer. Devn 5B 6
Dhoon. IOM 6D 44
Dhoor. IOM 5D 44
Dhowin. IOM 4D 44
Dial Green. W Sus 3G 11
Dial Post. W Sus 4J 11
The Diamond. M Ulst 5F 93
Dibberford. Dors 5C 8
Dibden. Hants 5B 10
Dibden Purlieu. Hants 5B 10
Dickleburgh. Norf 3H 31
Didbrook. Glos 8J 27
Didcot. Oxon 4C 20
Diddington. Cambs 5J 29
Diddlebury. Shrp 3D 26
Didley. Here 8C 26
Didling. W Sus 4F 10
Didmarton. Glos 5G 19
Didsbury. G Man 8G 41
Didworthy. Devn 5J 5
Digby. Linc 4H 37
Digg. High 7F 76
Diggle. G Man 7J 41
Digmoor. Lanc 7C 40
Digswell. Herts 2K 21
Dihewyd. Cdgn 1L 15
Dilham. Norf 7K 39
Dilhorne. Staf 5H 35
Dillarburn. S Lan 5G 59
Dillington. Cambs 5J 29
Dilston. Nmbd 5C 54
Dilton Marsh. Wilts 1G 9
Dilwyn. Here 6C 26
Dimmer. Som 2E 8
Dimple. G Man 6F 40
Dinas. Carm 3J 15
Dinas. Gwyn
nr. Caernarfon 5D 32
nr. Tudweiliog 7B 32
Dinas Cross. Pemb 3G 15
Dinas Dinlle. Gwyn 5D 32
Dinas Mawddwy. Gwyn 1H 25
Dinas Powys. V Glam 7L 17
Dinbych. Den 4K 33
Dinbych-y-Pysgod. Pemb 6H 15
Dinckley. Lanc 4E 40
Dinder. Som 1D 8
Dinedor. Here 8D 26
Dinedor Cross. Here 8D 26
Dingestow. Mon 2C 18
Dingle. Mers 1B 34
Dingleden. Kent 2E 12
Dingleton. Bord 6C 60
Dingley. Nptn 3E 28
Dingwall. High 8F 78
Dinmael. Cnwy 6K 33
Dinnet. Abers 6D 72
Dinnington. Som 4C 8
Dinnington. S Yor 1C 36
Dinnington. Tyne 4F 54
Dinorwig. Gwyn 4E 32
Dinton. Buck 2E 20
Dinton. Wilts 2J 9
Dinworthy. Devn 4C 6
Dipley. Hants 8E 20
Dippen. Arg 6G 57
Dippenhall. Surr 1F 10
Dippertown. Devn 7D 6
Dippin. N Ayr 7K 57
Dipple. S Ayr 1H 51
Diptford. Devn 6K 5
Dipton. Dur 6E 54
Dirleton. E Lot 1C 60
Dirt Pot. Nmbd 7B 54
Discoed. Powy 5A 26
Diseworth. Leics 7B 36
Dishes. Orkn 7F 88
Dishforth. N Yor 8A 48
Disley. Ches E 1H 35
Diss. Norf 4H 31
Disserth. Powy 7K 25
Distington. Cumb 2K 45
Ditchampton. Wilts 2J 9
Ditcheat. Som 2E 8
Ditchingham. Norf 2K 31
Ditchling. E Sus 4L 11
Ditteridge. Wilts 7G 19
Dittisham. Devn 6L 5
Ditton. Hal 1C 34
Ditton. Kent 8D 22
Ditton Green. Cambs 6C 30
Ditton Priors. Shrp 3E 26
Divach. High 3E 70
Dixonfield. High 5C 86
Dixton. Glos 8H 27
Dixton. Mon 2D 18
Dizzard. Corn 6A 6
Doagh. Ant 4H 93
Dobcross. G Man 7H 41
Dobs Hill. Flin 3B 34
Dobson's Bridge. Shrp 6C 34
Dobwalls. Corn 5E 4
Doccombe. Devn 7G 7
Dochgarroch. High 1G 71
Docking. Norf 6D 38
Docklow. Here 6D 26
Dockray. Cumb 3B 46
Doc Penfro. Pemb 6F 14
Dodbrooke. Devn 7K 5
Doddenham. Worc 6F 26
Doddinghurst. Essx 4B 22
Doddington. Cambs 2L 29
Doddington. Kent 8F 22
Doddington. Linc 2G 37
Doddington. Nmbd 6G 61
Doddington. Shrp 4E 26
Doddiscombsleigh. Devn 7H 7
Doddshill. Norf 6D 38
Dodford. Nptn 5D 28
Dodford. Worc 4H 27
Dodington. Som 1L 7
Dodington. S Glo 5F 18
Dodleston. Ches W 3B 34
Dods Leigh. Staf 6J 35
Dodworth. S Yor 7M 41
Doe Lea. Derbs 3B 36
Dogdyke. Linc 4K 37
Dogmersfield. Hants 8E 20
Dogsthorpe. Pet 1K 29
Dog Village. Devn 6J 7
Dolanog. Powy 1K 25
Dolau. Powy 6L 25
Dolau. Rhon 6K 17
Dolbenmaen. Gwyn 6E 32
Doley. Staf 7F 34
Dol-fâch. Powy 2J 25
Dolfach. Powy 5J 25
Dolfor. Powy 4L 25
Dolgarrog. Cnwy 4G 33
Dolgellau. Gwyn 1G 25
Dolgoch. Gwyn 2F 24
Dol-gran. Carm 3L 15
Dolhelfa. Powy 5J 25
Doll. High 3J 79
Dollar. Clac 8C 66
Dolley Green. Powy 5A 26
Dollingstown. Arm 6G 93
Dollwen. Cdgn 4F 24
Dolphin. Flin 3L 33
Dolphinholme. Lanc 2D 40
Dolphinton. S Lan 5K 59
Dolton. Devn 4E 6
Dolwen. Cnwy 3H 33
Dolwyddelan. Cnwy 5G 33
Dol-y-Bont. Cdgn 4F 24
Dolyhir. Powy 7M 25
Domgay. Powy 8A 34
Donagh. Ferm 7C 92
Donaghadee. Ards 5J 93
Donaghcloney. Arm 6G 93
Donaghmore. M Ulst 5E 92
Doncaster. S Yor 7C 42
Doncaster Sheffield Airport.
S Yor 8D 42
Donhead St Andrew. Wilts 3H 9
Donhead St Mary. Wilts 3H 9
Doniford. Som 1K 7
Donington. Linc 6K 37
Donington. Shrp 1G 27
Donington Eaudike. Linc 6K 37
Donington le Heath. Leics 8B 36
Donington on Bain. Linc 1K 37
Donington South Ing. Linc 6K 37
Donisthorpe. Leics 8M 35
Donkey Street. Kent 2H 13
Donkey Town. Surr 7G 21
Donna Nook. Linc 8M 43
Donnington. Glos 1K 19
Donnington. Here 8F 26
Donnington. Shrp 1D 26
Donnington. Telf 8F 34
Donnington. W Ber 7B 20
Donnington. W Sus 5F 10
Donyatt. Som 4B 8
Doomsday Green. W Sus 3J 11
Doonfoot. S Ayr 8B 58
Doonholm. S Ayr 8B 58
Dorback Lodge. High 4L 71
Dorchester. Dors 6E 8
Dorchester on Thames.
Oxon 4C 20
Dordon. Warw 1L 27
Dore. S Yor 1M 35
Dores. High 2F 70
Dorking. Surr 1J 11
Dorking Tye. Suff 8F 30
Dormansland. Surr 1M 11
Dormans Park. Surr 1L 11
Dormanstown. Red C 3C 48
Dormington. Here 7D 26
Dormston. Worc 6H 27
Dorn. Glos 8L 27
Dorney. Buck 6G 21
Dornie. High 3K 69
Dornoch. High 5H 79
Dornock. Dum 5G 53
Dorrery. High 6B 86
Dorridge. W Mid 4K 27
Dorrington. Linc 4H 37
Dorrington. Shrp 1C 26
Dorsington. Warw 7K 27
Dorstone. Here 7B 26
Dorton. Buck 2D 20
Dosthill. Staf 1L 27
Dotham. IOA 3C 32
Dottery. Dors 6C 8
Doublebois. Corn 5D 4
Dougarie. N Ayr 6H 57
Doughton. Glos 4G 19
Douglas. IOM 7C 44
Douglas. S Lan 6G 59
Douglas Bridge. Derr 4C 92
Douglastown. Ang 3H 67
Douglas Water. S Lan 6G 59
Doulting. Som 1E 8
Dounby. Orkn 7B 88
Doune. High
nr. Kingussie 4J 71
nr. Lairg 3E 78
Doune. Stir 7M 65
Dounie. High
nr. Bonar Bridge 4F 78
nr. Tain 5G 79
Dounreay, Upper & Lower.
High 5A 86
Doura. N Ayr 5B 58
Dousland. Devn 5H 5
Dovaston. Shrp 7B 34
Dove Holes. Derbs 2J 35
Dovenby. Cumb 8E 52
Dover. Kent 108 (1K 13)
Dovercourt. Essx 8J 31
Doverdale. Worc 5G 27
Doveridge. Derbs 6K 35
Doversgreen. Surr 1K 11
Dowally. Per 3D 66
Dowbridge. Lanc 4C 40
Dowdeswell. Glos 2J 19
Dowlais. Mer T 4K 17
Dowland. Devn 4E 6
Dowlands. Devn 6A 8
Dowles. Worc 4F 26
Dowlesgreen. Wok 7F 20
Dowlish Wake. Som 4B 8
The Down. Shrp 2E 26
Downall Green. Mers 7D 40
Down Ampney. Glos 4K 19
Downderry. Corn
nr. Looe 6F 4
nr. St Austell 6B 4
Downe. G Lon 7M 21
Downend. IOW 7C 10
Downend. S Glo 6E 18
Downend. W Ber 6B 20
Down Field. Cambs 4C 30
Downfield. D'dee 4G 67
Downgate. Corn
nr. Kelly Bray 8C 6
nr. Upton Cross 8B 6
Downham. Essx 4D 22
Downham. Lanc 3F 40
Downham. Nmbd 6F 60
Downham Market. Norf 1C 30
Down Hatherley. Glos 1G 19
Downhead. Som
nr. Frome 1E 8
nr. Yeovil 3D 8
Downhill. Caus 2E 92
Downholland Cross. Lanc 7B 40
Downholme. N Yor 6K 47
Downies. Abers 6J 73
Downley. Buck 4F 20
Downpatrick. New M 6J 93
Down St Mary. Devn 5G 7
Downside. Som
nr. Chilcompton 8E 18
nr. Shepton Mallet 1E 8
Downside. Surr 8J 21
Down Thomas. Devn 6H 5
Downton. Hants 6L 9
Downton. Wilts 3K 9
Downton on the Rock.
Here 4C 26
Dowsby. Linc 7J 37
Dowsdale. Linc 8K 37
Dowthwaitehead. Cumb 3B 46
Doxey. Staf 7H 35
Doxford. Nmbd 7J 61
Doynton. S Glo 6F 18
Drabblegate. Norf 7J 39
Draethen. Cphy 6M 17
Draffan. S Lan 5F 58
Dragonby. N Lin 6G 43
Dragon's Green. W Sus 3J 11
Drakelow. Worc 3G 27
Drakemyre. N Ayr 4A 58
Drakes Broughton. Worc 7H 27
Drakes Cross. Worc 4J 27
Drakewalls. Corn 8D 6
Draperstown. M Ulst 4E 92
Draughton. Nptn 4E 28
Draughton. N Yor 2J 41
Drax. N Yor 5D 42
Draycot. Oxon 3D 20
Draycote. Warw 4B 28
Draycot Foliat. Swin 6K 19
Draycott. Derbs 6B 36
Draycott. Glos 8K 27
Draycott. Shrp 2G 27
Draycott. Som
nr. Cheddar 8C 18
nr. Yeovil 3D 8
Draycott. Worc 7G 27
Draycott in the Clay. Staf 7K 35
Draycott in the Moors. Staf 5H 35
Drayford. Devn 4G 7
Drayton. Leics 2F 28
Drayton. Linc 6K 37
Drayton. Norf 8H 39
Drayton. Nptn 5C 28
Drayton. Oxon
nr. Abingdon 4B 20
nr. Banbury 7B 28
Drayton. Port 5D 10
Drayton. Som 3C 8
Drayton. Warw 6K 27
Drayton. Worc 4H 27
Drayton Bassett. Staf 1K 27
Drayton Beauchamp. Buck 2G 21
Drayton Parslow. Buck 1F 20
Drayton St Leonard. Oxon 4C 20
Drebley. N Yor 2J 41
Dreenhill. Pemb 5F 14
Y Dref. Gwyn 7D 32
Drefach. Carm
nr. Meidrim 5M 15
nr. Newcastle Emlyn 3K 15
nr. Tumble 4J 15
Drefach. Cdgn 2L 15
Dreghorn. N Ayr 6B 58
Drellingore. Kent 1J 13
Drem. E Lot 2C 60
Y Drenewydd. Powy 3L 25
Dreumasdal. W Isl 2D 74
Drewsteignton. Devn 6G 7
Driby. Linc 2L 37
Driffield. E Yor 2H 43
Driffield. Glos 4J 19
Drift. Corn 6H 3
Drigg. Cumb 5K 45
Drighlington. W Yor 5L 41
Drimnin. High 2L 63
Drimpton. Dors 5C 8
Dringhoe. E Yor 2J 43
Drinisiadar. W Isl 4C 76
Drinkstone. Suff 5F 30
Drinkstone Green. Suff 5F 30
Drointon. Staf 7J 35
Droitwich Spa. Worc 5G 27
Droman. High 6D 84
Dromara. Lis 6H 93
Dromore. Arm 6H 93
Dromore. Ferm 5C 92
Dron. Per 6E 66
Dronfield. Derbs 2A 36
Dronfield Woodhouse.
Derbs 2M 35
Drongan. E Ayr 8C 58
Dronley. Ang 4G 67
Droop. Dors 5F 8
Drope. V Glam 7L 17
Droxford. Hants 4D 10
Droylsden. G Man 8G 41
Druggers End. Worc 8F 26
Druid. Den 6K 33
Druid's Heath. W Mid 1J 27
Druidston. Pemb 5E 14
Druim. High 8K 79
Druimarbin. High 8A 70
Druim Fhearna. High 4H 69
Druimindarroch. High 7H 69
Druim Saighdinis. W Isl 7K 75
Drum. Per 7D 66
Drumaness. New M 6H 93
Drumaroad. New M 6H 93
Drumbeg. High 8D 84
Drumblade. Abers 1E 72
Drumbo. Lis 5H 93
Drumbuie. Dum 3L 51
Drumbuie. High 2J 69
Drumburgh. Cumb 6G 53
Drumburn. Dum 5D 52
Drumchapel. Glas 2D 58
Drumchardine. High 1F 70
Drumchork. High 5K 77
Drumclog. S Lan 6E 58
Drumeldrie. Fife 7H 67
Drumelzier. Bord 6K 59
Drumfearn. High 4H 69
Drumgask. High 6G 71
Drumgelloch. N Lan 3F 58
Drumgley. Ang 2H 67
Drumguish. High 6H 71
Drumin. Mor 2A 72
Drumindorsair. High 1E 70
Drumintee. New M 7G 93
Drumlamford House. S Ayr 4H 51
Drumlasie. Abers 5F 72
Drumlemble. Arg 8F 56
Drumlithie. Abers 7G 73
Drummoddie. Dum 7J 51
Drummond. High 7G 79
Drummore. Dum 8G 51
Drummuir. Mor 1C 72
Drumnacanvy. Arm 6G 93
Drumnadrochit. High 2F 70
Drumnagorrach. Mor 8E 80
Drumnakilly. Ferm 5D 92
Drumoak. Abers 6G 73
Drumquin. Ferm 5C 92
Drumraighland. Caus 2E 92
Drumrunie. High 3B 78
Drumry. W Dun 2D 58
Drums. Abers 3J 73
Drumsleet. Dum 4D 52
Drumsmittal. High 1G 71
Drums of Park. Abers 8E 80
Drumsturdy. Ang 4H 67
Drumsurn. Caus 3E 92
Drumtochty Castle. Abers 7F 72
Drumuie. High 1F 68
Drumuillie. High 3K 71
Drumvaich. Stir 7L 65
Drumwhindle. Abers 2J 73
Drunkendub. Ang 3K 67
Drury. Flin 3A 34
Drury Square. Norf 8F 38
Drybeck. Cumb 4E 46
Drybridge. Mor 7D 80
Drybridge. N Ayr 6B 58
Drybrook. Glos 2E 18
Drybrook. Here 2D 18
Dryburgh. Bord 6C 60
Dry Doddington. Linc 5F 36
Dry Drayton. Cambs 5L 29
Drym. Corn 5K 3
Drymen. Stir 1C 58
Drymuir. Abers 1J 73
Drynachan Lodge. High 2J 71
Drynie Park. High 8F 78
Drynoch. High 2F 68
Dry Sandford. Oxon 3B 20
Dryslwyn. Carm 2E 16
Dry Street. Essx 5C 22
Dryton. Shrp 1D 26
Dubford. Abers 7G 81
Dubiton. Abers 8F 80
Dubton. Ang 2J 67
Duchally. High 2D 78
Duck End. Essx 1C 22
Duckington. Ches W 4C 34
Ducklington. Oxon 3A 20
Duckmanton. Derbs 2B 36
Duck Street. Hants 1M 9
Dudbridge. Glos 3G 19
Duddenhoe End. Essx 8A 30
Duddingston. Edin 2L 59
Duddington. Nptn 1G 29
Duddleswell. E Sus 3A 12
Duddo. Nmbd 5G 61
Duddon. Ches W 3D 34
Duddon Bridge. Cumb 6L 45
Dudleston. Shrp 6B 34
Dudleston Heath. Shrp 6B 34
Dudley. Tyne 4F 54
Dudley. W Mid 3H 27
Dudston. Shrp 3M 25
Dudwells. Pemb 4F 14
Duffield. Derbs 5M 35
Duffryn. Neat 5H 17
Dufftown. Mor 1C 72
Duffus. Mor 7A 80
Dufton. Cumb 3E 46
Duggleby. N Yor 1F 42
Duirinish. High 2J 69
Duisdalemore. High 4H 69
Duisdeil Mòr. High 4H 69
Duisky. High 8M 69
Dukesfield. Nmbd 6C 54
Dukestown. Blae 4L 17
Dukinfield. G Man 8H 41
Dulas. IOA 2D 32
Dulcote. Som 1D 8
Dulford. Devn 5K 7
Dull. Per 3B 66
Dullatur. N Lan 2F 58
Dullingham. Cambs 6C 30
Dullingham Ley. Cambs 6C 30
Dulnain Bridge. High 3K 71
Duloe. Bed 5J 29
Duloe. Corn 6E 4
Dulverton. Som 3J 7
Dulwich. G Lon 6L 21
Dumbarton. W Dun 2C 58
Dumbleton. Glos 8J 27
Dumfin. Arg 1B 58
Dumfries. Dum 108 (4D 52)
Dumgoyne. Stir 1D 58
Dummer. Hants 1C 10
Dumpford. W Sus 3F 10
Dun. Ang 1K 67
Dunadry. Ant 4G 93
Dunaghy. Caus 2F 93
Dunagoil. Arg 4K 57
Dunalastair. Per 2M 65
Dunan. High 3G 69
Dunball. Som 1B 8
Dunbar. E Lot 2D 60
Dunbeath. High 1A 80
Dunbeg. Arg 4C 64
Dunblane. Stir 7A 66
Dunbog. Fife 6F 66
Dunbridge. Hants 3M 9
Duncanston. Abers 3E 72
Duncanston. High 8F 78
Dun Charlabhaigh. W Isl 7E 82
Dunchideock. Devn 7H 7
Dunchurch. Warw 4B 28
Duncote. Nptn 6D 28
Duncow. Dum 3D 52
Duncrievie. Per 7E 66
Duncton. W Sus 4G 11
Dundee. D'dee 108 (4H 67)
Dundee Airport. D'dee 5G 67
Dundon. Som 2C 8
Dundonald. Lis 5J 93
Dundonald. S Ayr 6B 58
Dundonnell. High 5A 78
Dundraw. Cumb 7G 53
Dundreggan. High 4D 70
Dundrennan. Dum 7B 52
Dundridge. Hants 4C 10
Dundrod. Lis 5H 93
Dundrum. New M 7J 93
Dundry. N Som 7D 18
Dunecht. Abers 5G 73
Dunfermline. Fife 1J 59
Dunford Bridge. S Yor 7K 41
Dungannon. M Ulst 5E 92
Dungate. Kent 8F 22
Dunge. Wilts 8G 19
Dungeness. Kent 4G 13
Dungiven. Caus 3E 92
Dungworth. S Yor 1L 35
Dunham-on-the-Hill.
Ches W 2C 34
Dunham-on-Trent. Notts 2F 36
Dunhampton. Worc 5G 27
Dunham Town. G Man 1F 34
Dunham Woodhouses.
G Man 1F 34
Dunholme. Linc 2H 37
Dunino. Fife 6J 67
Dunipace. Falk 1G 59
Dunira. Per 5M 65
Dunkeld. Per 3D 66
Dunkerton. Bath 8F 18
Dunkeswell. Devn 5L 7
Dunkeswick. N Yor 3M 41
Dunkirk. Kent 8G 23
Dunkirk. S Glo 5F 18
Dunkirk. Staf 4G 35
Dunkirk. Wilts 7H 19
Dunk's Green. Kent 8C 22
Dunlappie. Ang 1J 67
Dunley. Hants 8B 20
Dunley. Worc 5F 26
Dunlichity Lodge. High 2G 71
Dunlop. E Ayr 5C 58
Dunloy. Caus 3G 93
Dunmaglass Lodge. High 3F 70
Dunmore. Arg 3G 57
Dunmore. Falk 1G 59
Dunmore. High 1F 70
Dunmurry. Bel 5H 93
Dunnamanagh. Derr 3D 92
Dunnaval. New M 7H 93
Dunnet. High 4D 86
Dunnichen. Ang 3J 67
Dunning. Per 6D 66
Dunnington. E Yor 2J 43
Dunnington. Warw 6J 27
Dunnington. York 2D 42
Dunningwell. Cumb 6L 45
Dunnockshaw. Lanc 5G 41
Dunoon. Arg 2L 57
Dunphail. Mor 1L 71
Dunragit. Dum 6G 51
Dunrostan. Arg 1G 57
Duns. Bord 4E 60
Dunsby. Linc 7J 37
Dunscar. G Man 6F 40
Dunscore. Dum 3C 52
Dunscroft. S Yor 7D 42
Dunsdale. Red C 4D 48
Dunsden Green. Oxon 6E 20
Dunsfold. Surr 2H 11
Dunsford. Devn 7H 7
Dunshalt. Fife 6F 66
Dunshillock. Abers 1J 73
Dunsley. N Yor 4F 48
Dunsley. Staf 3G 27
Dunsmore. Buck 3F 20
Dunsop Bridge. Lanc 2E 40
Dunstable. C Beds 1H 21
Dunstal. Staf 7J 35
Dunstall. Staf 7K 35
Dunstall Green. Suff 5D 30
Dunstall Hill. W Mid 1H 27
Dunstan. Nmbd 8K 61
Dunster. Som 1J 7
Duns Tew. Oxon 1B 20
Dunston. Linc 3H 37
Dunston. Norf 1J 31
Dunston. Staf 8H 35
Dunston. Tyne 5F 54
Dunstone. Devn 6H 5
Dunston Heath. Staf 8H 35
Dunsville. S Yor 7D 42
Dunswell. E Yor 4H 43
Dunsyre. S Lan 5J 59
Dunterton. Devn 8C 6
Duntisbourne Abbots. Glos 3H 19
Duntisbourne Leer. Glos 3H 19
Duntisbourne Rouse. Glos 3H 19
Duntish. Dors 5E 8
Duntocher. W Dun 2C 58
Dunton. Buck 1F 20
Dunton. C Beds 7K 29
Dunton. Norf 6E 38
Dunton Bassett. Leics 2C 28
Dunton Green. Kent 8B 22
Dunton Patch. Norf 6E 38
Duntulm. High 6F 76
Dunure. S Ayr 8A 58
Dunvant. Swan 5E 16
Dunvegan. High 1D 68
Dunwich. Suff 4L 31
Dunwood. Staf 4H 35
Durdar. Cumb 6J 53
Durgates. E Sus 2C 12
Durham. Dur 108 (7F 54)
Durham Tees Valley Airport.
Darl 4A 48
Durisdeer. Dum 1C 52
Durisdeermill. Dum 1C 52
Durkar. W Yor 6M 41
Durleigh. Som 2A 8
Durley. Hants 4C 10
Durley. Wilts 7L 19
Durley Street. Hants 4C 10
Durlow Common. Here 8E 26
Durnamuck. High 4M 77
Durness. High 5G 85
Durno. Abers 3G 73
Durns Town. Hants 6L 9
Duror. High 2D 64
Durran. Arg 7D 64
Durran. High 5C 86
Durrant Green. Kent 2E 12
Durrants. Hants 4E 10
Durrington. W Sus 5J 11
Durrington. Wilts 1K 9
Dursley. Glos 4F 18
Dursley Cross. Glos 2E 18
Durston. Som 3A 8
Durweston. Dors 5G 9
Dury. Shet 2E 90
Duston. Nptn 5E 28
Duthil. High 3K 71
Dutlas. Powy 5M 25
Duton Hill. Essx 1C 22
Dutson. Corn 7C 6
Dutton. Ches W 2D 34
Duxford. Cambs 7A 30
Duxford. Oxon 4A 20
Dwygyfylchi. Cnwy 3G 33
Dwyran. IOA 4D 32
Dyce. Aber 4H 73
Dyffryn. B'end 5H 17
Dyffryn. Carm 4K 15
Dyffryn. Pemb 3F 14
Dyffryn. V Glam 7K 17
Dyffryn Ardudwy. Gwyn 8E 32
Dyffryn Castell. Cdgn 4G 25
Dyffryn Ceidrych. Carm 2G 17
Dyffryn Cellwen. Neat 4H 17
Dyke. Linc 7J 37
Dyke. Mor 8K 79
Dykehead. Ang 1G 67
Dykehead. N Lan 3G 59
Dykehead. Stir 8K 65
Dykend. Ang 2F 66
Dykesfield. Cumb 6H 53
Dylife. Powy 3H 25
Dymchurch. Kent 3H 13
Dymock. Glos 8F 26
Dyrham. S Glo 6F 18
Dysart. Fife 8G 67
Dyserth. Den 3K 33

E

Eachwick. Nmbd 4E 54
Eadar Dha Fhadhail. W Isl 8D 82
Eagland Hill. Lanc 3C 40
Eagle. Linc 3F 36
Eagle Barnsdale. Linc 3F 36
Eagle Moor. Linc 3F 36
Eaglescliffe. Stoc T 4B 48
Eaglesfield. Cumb 2K 45
Eaglesfield. Dum 4G 53
Eaglesham. E Ren 4D 58
Eaglethorpe. Nptn 2H 29
Eagley. G Man 6F 40
Eairy. IOM 7B 44
Eakley Lanes. Mil 6F 28
Eakring. Notts 3D 36
Ealand. N Lin 6E 42
Ealing. G Lon 5J 21
Eallabus. Arg 3C 56
Eals. Nmbd 6L 53
Eamont Bridge. Cumb 3D 46
Earby. Lanc 3H 41
Earcroft. Bkbn 5E 40
Eardington. Shrp 2F 26
Eardisland. Here 6C 26
Eardisley. Here 7B 26
Eardiston. Shrp 7B 34
Eardiston. Worc 5E 26
Earith. Cambs 4L 29
Earlais. High 7E 76
Earle. Nmbd 7G 61
Earlesfield. Linc 6G 37
Earlestown. Mers 8D 40
Earley. Wok 6E 20
Earlham. Norf 1H 31
Earlish. High 7E 76
Earls Barton. Nptn 5F 28
Earls Colne. Essx 1E 22
Earls Common. Worc 6H 27
Earl's Croome. Worc 7G 27
Earlsdon. W Mid 4M 27
Earlsferry. Fife 7H 67
Earlsford. Abers 2H 73
Earl's Green. Suff 5G 31
Earlsheaton. W Yor 5L 41
Earl Shilton. Leics 2B 28
Earl Soham. Suff 5J 31
Earl Sterndale. Derbs 3J 35
Earlston. E Ayr 6C 58
Earlston. Bord 6C 60
Earl Stonham. Suff 6H 31
Earlstoun. Dum 3M 51
Earlswood. Mon 4C 18
Earlswood. Warw 4K 27
Earlyvale. Bord 4L 59
Earnley. W Sus 6F 10
Earsairidh. W Isl 6D 74
Earsdon. Tyne 4G 55
Earsham. Norf 3K 31
Earsham Street. Suff 4J 31
Earswick. York 2D 42
Eartham. W Sus 5G 11
Earthcott Green. S Glo 5E 18
Easby. N Yor
nr. Great Ayton 5C 48
nr. Richmond 5K 47
Easdale. Arg 6B 64
Easebourne. W Sus 3F 10
Easenhall. Warw 4B 28
Eashing. Surr 1G 11
Easington. Buck 2D 20
Easington. Dur 7H 55
Easington. E Yor 6L 43
Easington. Nmbd 6J 61
Easington. Oxon
nr. Banbury 8B 28
nr. Watlington 4D 20
Easington. Red C 4E 48
Easington Colliery. Dur 7H 55
Easington Lane. Tyne 7G 55
Easingwold. N Yor 8C 48
Eassie. Ang 3G 67
Eassie and Nevay. Ang 3G 67
East Aberthaw. V Glam 8K 17
Eastacombe. Devn 3E 6
Eastacott. Devn 3F 6
East Allington. Devn 7K 5
East Anstey. Devn 3H 7
East Anton. Hants 1A 10
East Appleton. N Yor 6L 47
East Ardsley. W Yor 5M 41
East Ashley. Devn 4F 6
East Ashling. W Sus 5F 10
East Aston. Hants 1B 10
East Ayton. N Yor 7G 49
East Barkwith. Linc 1J 37
East Barnby. N Yor 4F 48
East Barnet. G Lon 4K 21
East Barns. E Lot 2E 60
East Barsham. Norf 6F 38
East Beach. W Sus 6F 10
East Beckham. Norf 6H 39
East Bedfont. G Lon 6H 21
East Bennan. N Ayr 7J 57
East Bergholt. Suff 8G 31
East Bierley. W Yor 5L 41
East Bilney. Norf 8F 38
East Blatchington. E Sus 5A 12
East Bloxworth. Dors 6G 9
East Boldre. Hants 5A 10
East Bolton. Nmbd 8J 61
Eastbourne. Darl 4L 47
Eastbourne. E Sus 108 (6C 12)
East Brent. Som 8B 18
East Bridge. Suff 5L 31
East Bridgford. Notts 5D 36
East Briscoe. Dur 4H 47
East Buckland. Devn
nr. Barnstaple 2F 6
nr. Thurlestone 7J 5
East Budleigh. Devn 7K 7
Eastburn. W Yor 3J 41
East Burnham. Buck 5G 21
East Burrafirth. Shet 2D 90
East Burton. Dors 7G 9
Eastbury. Herts 4H 21
Eastbury. W Ber 6M 19
East Butsfield. Dur 7E 54
East Butterleigh. Devn 5J 7
East Butterwick. N Lin 7F 42
Eastby. N Yor 2J 41
East Calder. W Lot 3J 59
East Carleton. Norf 1H 31
East Carlton. Nptn 3F 28
East Carlton. W Yor 3L 41
East Chaldon. Dors 7F 8
East Challow. Oxon 5A 20
East Charleton. Devn 7K 5
East Chelborough. Dors 5D 8
East Chiltington. E Sus 4L 11
East Chinnock. Som 4C 8
East Chisenbury. Wilts 8K 19
Eastchurch. Kent 6F 22
East Clandon. Surr 8H 21
East Claydon. Buck 1E 20
East Clevedon. N Som 6C 18
East Clyne. High 3J 79
East Clyth. High 8D 86
East Coker. Som 4D 8
East Combe. Som 2L 7
Eastcombe. Glos 3G 19
East Common. N Yor 4D 42
East Compton. Som 1E 8
East Cornworthy. Devn 6L 5
Eastcote. G Lon 5J 21
Eastcote. Nptn 6D 28
Eastcote. W Mid 4K 27
Eastcott. Corn 4B 6
Eastcott. Wilts 8J 19
East Cottingwith. E Yor 3E 42
Eastcourt. Wilts
nr. Pewsey 7L 19
nr. Tetbury 4H 19
East Cowes. IOW 6C 10
East Cowick. E Yor 5D 42
East Cowton. N Yor 5M 47
East Cramlington. Nmbd 4F 54
East Cranmore. Som 1E 8
East Creech. Dors 7H 9
East Croachy. High 3G 71
East Dean. E Sus 6B 12
East Dean. Glos 1E 18
East Dean. Hants 3L 9
East Dean. W Sus 4G 11
East Down. Devn 1F 6
East Drayton. Notts 2E 36
East Dundry. N Som 7D 18
East Ella. Hull 5H 43
East End. Cambs 4L 29
East End. Dors 6H 9
East End. E Yor
nr. Ulrome 2J 43
nr. Withernsea 5K 43
East End. Hants
nr. Lymington 6A 10
nr. Newbury 7B 20
East End. Herts 1A 22
East End. Kent
nr. Minster 6F 22
nr. Tenterden 2E 12
East End. N Som 6C 18
East End. Oxon 2A 20
East End. Som 8D 18
East End. Suff 8H 31
Easter Ardross. High 6G 79
Easter Balgedie. Per 7E 66
Easter Balmoral. Abers 6B 72
Easter Brae. High 7G 79
Easter Buckieburn. Stir 1F 58
Easter Compton. S Glo 5D 18
Easter Fearn. High 5G 79
Easter Galcantray. High 1J 71
Eastergate. W Sus 5G 11
Easterhouse. Glas 3E 58
Easter Howgate. Midl 3L 59
Easter Kinkell. High 8F 78
Easter Lednathie. Ang 1G 67
Easter Ogil. Ang 1H 67
Easter Ord. Abers 5H 73
Easter Quarff. Shet 4E 90
Easter Rhynd. Per 6E 66
Easter Skeld. Shet 3D 90
Easter Suddie. High 8G 79
Easterton. Wilts 8J 19
Eastertown. Som 8B 18
Easter Tulloch. Abers 8G 73
East Everleigh. Wilts 8L 19
East Farleigh. Kent 8D 22
East Farndon. Nptn 3E 28
East Ferry. Linc 8F 42
Eastfield. N Lan
nr. Caldercruix 3G 59
nr. Harthill 3G 59
Eastfield. N Yor 7H 49
Eastfield. S Lan 3E 58
Eastfield Hall. Nmbd 1F 54
East Fortune. E Lot 2C 60
East Garforth. W Yor 4B 42
East Garston. W Ber 6A 20
Eastgate. Dur 8C 54
Eastgate. Norf 7H 39
East Ginge. Oxon 5B 20
East Gores. Essx 1E 22
East Goscote. Leics 8D 36
East Grafton. Wilts 7L 19
East Green. Suff 6C 30
East Grimstead. Wilts 3L 9
East Grinstead. W Sus 2L 11
East Guldeford. E Sus 3F 12
East Haddon. Nptn 5D 28
East Hagbourne. Oxon 5C 20

Ford—Great Hockham

Ford. Nmbd 6G 61
Ford. Plym 6G 5
Ford. Shrp 8C 34
Ford. Som
nr. Wells 8D 18
nr. Wiveliscombe 3K 7
Ford. Staf 4J 35
Ford. W Sus 5H 11
Ford. Wilts
nr. Chippenham 6G 19
nr. Salisbury 2K 9
Forda. Devn 2D 6
Ford Barton. Devn 4J 7
Fordcombe. Kent 1B 12
Fordell. Fife 1K 59
Forden. Powy 2M 25
Ford End. Essx 2C 22
Forder Green. Devn 5K 5
Ford Green. Lanc 3C 40
Fordham. Cambs 4C 30
Fordham. Essx 1F 22
Fordham. Norf 2C 30
Fordham Heath. Essx 1F 22
Ford Heath. Shrp 8C 34
Fordhouses. W Mid 1H 27
Fordie. Per 5A 66
Fordingbridge. Hants 4K 9
Fordington. Linc 2M 37
Fordon. E Yor 8H 49
Fordoun. Abers 8G 73
Ford Street. Essx 1F 22
Ford Street. Som 4L 7
Fordton. Devn 6H 7
Fordwells. Oxon 2M 19
Fordwich. Kent 8H 23
Fordyce. Abers 7E 80
Forebridge. Staf 7H 35
Foreglen. Caus 3E 92
Foremark. Derbs 7M 35
Forest. N Yor 5L 47
Forestburn Gate. Nmbd 2D 54
Foresterseat. Mor 8A 80
Forest Green. Glos 4G 19
Forest Green. Surr 1J 11
Forest Hall. Cumb 5D 46
Forest Head. Cumb 6K 53
Forest Hill. Oxon 3C 20
Forest-in-Teesdale. Dur 3G 47
Forest Lodge. Per 8K 71
Forest Mill. Clac 8C 66
Forest Row. E Sus 2M 11
Forestside. W Sus 4E 10
Forest Town. Notts 3C 36
Forfar. Ang 2H 67
Forgandenny. Per 6D 66
Forge. Powy 3G 25
The Forge. Here 6B 26
Forge Side. Torf 4M 17
Forgewood. N Lan 4F 58
Forgie. Mor 8C 80
Forgue. Abers 1F 72
Forkill. New M 7G 93
Formby. Mers 7B 40
Forncett End. Norf 2H 31
Forncett St Mary. Norf 2H 31
Forncett St Peter. Norf 2H 31
Forneth. Per 3D 66
Fornham All Saints. Suff 5E 30
Fornham St Martin. Suff 5E 30
Forres. Mor 8L 79
Forrestfield. N Lan 3G 59
Forrest Lodge. Dum 3L 51
Forsbrook. Staf 5H 35
Forse. High 8D 86
Forsinard. High 7L 85
Forss. High 5B 86
The Forstal. Kent 2G 13
Forston. Dors 6E 8
Fort Augustus. High 5D 70
Forteviot. Per 6D 66
Fort George. High 8H 79
Forth. S Lan 4H 59
Forthampton. Glos 8G 27
Forthay. Glos 4F 18
Fortingall. Per 3M 65
Fort Matilda. Inv 2A 58
Forton. Hants 1B 10
Forton. Lanc 2C 40
Forton. Shrp 8C 34
Forton. Som 5B 8
Forton. Staf 7F 34
Forton Heath. Shrp 8C 34
Fortrie. Abers 1F 72
Fortrose. High 8H 79
Fortuneswell. Dors 8E 8
Fort William. High 8B 70
Forty Green. Buck 4G 21
Forty Hill. G Lon 4L 21
Forward Green. Suff 6G 31
Fosbury. Wilts 8M 19
Foscot. Oxon 1L 19
Fosdyke. Linc 6L 37
Foss. Per 2A 66
Fossebridge. Glos 2J 19
Foster Street. Essx 3A 22
Foston. Derbs 6K 35
Foston. Leics 2D 28
Foston. Linc 5F 36
Foston. N Yor 1D 42
Foston on the Wolds. E Yor 2J 43
Fotherby. Linc 8L 43
Fothergill. Cumb 8E 52
Fotheringhay. Nptn 2H 29
Foubister. Orkn 1G 87
Foula Airport. Shet 4B 90
Foul Anchor. Cambs 8A 38
Foulbridge. Cumb 7J 53
Foulden. Norf 2D 30
Foulden. Bord 4G 61
Foul Mile. E Sus 4C 12
Foulridge. Lanc 3G 41
Foulsham. Norf 7G 39
Fountainhall. Bord 5B 60
The Four Alls. Shrp 6E 34
Four Ashes. Staf
nr. Cannock 1H 27
nr. Kinver 3G 27
Four Ashes. Suff 4G 31
Four Crosses. Powy
nr. Llanerfyl 2K 25
nr. Llanymynech 8A 34
Four Crosses. Staf 1H 27
Four Elms. Kent 1A 12
Four Forks. Som 2M 7
Four Gotes. Cambs 8A 38
Four Lane End. S Yor 7L 41
Four Lane Ends. Lanc 2D 40
Four Lanes. Corn 5K 3
Fourlanes End. Ches E 4G 35
Four Marks. Hants 2D 10
Four Mile Bridge. IOA 3B 32
Four Oaks. E Sus 3E 12
Four Oaks. Glos 1E 18
Four Oaks. W Mid 3L 27
Four Roads. Carm 6L 15
Four Roads. IOM 8B 44
Fourstones. Nmbd 5B 54
Four Throws. Kent 3D 12
Fovant. Wilts 3J 9
Foveran. Abers 3J 73
Fowey. Corn 6D 4
Fowlershill. Aber 4J 73
Fowley Common. Warr 8E 40
Fowlis. Ang 4G 67
Fowlis Wester. Per 5C 66
Fowlmere. Cambs 7M 29
Fownhope. Here 8D 26
Fox Corner. Surr 8G 21
Foxcote. Glos 2J 19
Foxcote. Som 8F 18
Foxdale. IOM 7B 44
Foxearth. Essx 7E 30
Foxfield. Cumb 6M 45
Foxham. Wilts 6H 19
Fox Hatch. Essx 4B 22
Foxhole. Corn 6B 4
Foxholes. N Yor 8H 49
Foxhunt Green. E Sus 4B 12
Fox Lane. Hants 8F 20
Foxley. Norf 7G 39
Foxley. Nptn 6D 28
Foxley. Wilts 5G 19
Foxlydiate. Worc 5J 27
Fox Street. Essx 1G 23
Foxt. Staf 5J 35
Foxton. Cambs 7M 29
Foxton. Dur 3A 48
Foxton. Leics 3D 28
Foxton. N Yor 6B 48
Foxup. N Yor 8G 47
Foxwist Green. Ches W 3E 34
Foxwood. Shrp 4E 26
Foy. Here 1D 18
Foyers. High 3E 70
Foynesfield. High 8J 79
Fraddam. Corn 5J 3
Fraddon. Corn 6B 4
Fradley. Staf 8K 35
Fradley South. Staf 8K 35
Fradswell. Staf 6H 35
Fraisthorpe. E Yor 1J 43
Framfield. E Sus 3A 12
Framingham Earl. Norf 1J 31
Framingham Pigot. Norf 1J 31
Framlingham. Suff 5J 31
Frampton. Dors 6E 8
Frampton. Linc 6L 37
Frampton Cotterell. S Glo 5E 18
Frampton Mansell. Glos 3H 19
Frampton on Severn. Glos 3F 18
Frampton West End. Linc 5K 37
Framsden. Suff 6H 31
Framwellgate Moor. Dur 7F 54
Franche. Worc 4G 27
Frandley. Ches W 2E 34
Frankby. Mers 2M 33
Frankfort. Norf 7K 39
Frankley. Worc 3H 27
Frank's Bridge. Powy 7L 25
Frankton. Warw 4B 28
Frankwell. Shrp 8C 34
Frant. E Sus 2B 12
Fraserburgh. Abers 7J 81
Frating Green. Essx 1G 23
Fratton. Port 5D 10
Freathy. Corn 6G 5
Freckenham. Suff 4C 30
Freckleton. Lanc 5C 40
Freeby. Leics 7F 36
Freefolk Priors. Hants 1B 10
Freehay. Staf 5J 35
Freeland. Oxon 2B 20
Freester. Shet 2E 90
Freethorpe. Norf 1L 31
Freiston. Linc 5L 37
Freiston Shore. Linc 5L 37
Fremington. Devn 2E 6
Fremington. N Yor 6J 47
Frenchay. S Glo 6E 18
Frenchbeer. Devn 7F 6
Frenich. Stir 7J 65
Frensham. Surr 1F 10
Frenze. Norf 3H 31
Fresgoe. High 5A 86
Freshfield. Mers 7A 40
Freshford. Bath 7F 18
Freshwater. IOW 7M 9
Freshwater Bay. IOW 7M 9
Freshwater East. Pemb 7G 15
Fressingfield. Suff 4J 31
Freston. Suff 8H 31
Freswick. High 5E 86
Fretherne. Glos 3F 18
Frettenham. Norf 8J 39
Freuchie. Fife 7F 66
Freystrop. Pemb 5F 14
Friar's Gate. E Sus 2A 12
Friar Waddon. Dors 7E 8
Friday Bridge. Cambs 1A 30
Friday Street. E Sus 5C 12
Friday Street. Surr 1J 11
Fridaythorpe. E Yor 2F 42
Friden. Derbs 3K 35
Friern Barnet. G Lon 4K 21
Friesthorpe. Linc 1H 37
Frieston. Linc 5G 37
Frieth. Buck 4E 20
Friezeland. Notts 4B 36
Frilford. Oxon 4B 20
Frilsham. W Ber 6C 20
Frimley. Surr 8F 20
Frimley Green. Surr 8F 20
Frindsbury. Medw 7D 22
Fring. Norf 6D 38
Fringford. Oxon 1D 20
Frinsted. Kent 8E 22
Frinton-on-Sea. Essx 2J 23
Friockheim. Ang 3J 67
Friog. Gwyn 1F 24
Frisby. Leics 1E 28
Frisby on the Wreake.
Leics 8D 36
Friskney. Linc 4A 38
Friskney Eaudyke. Linc 4A 38
Friston. E Sus 6B 12
Friston. Suff 5L 31
Fritchley. Derbs 4A 36
Fritham. Hants 4L 9
Frith Bank. Linc 5L 37
Frith Common. Worc 5E 26
Frithelstock. Devn 4D 6
Frithelstock Stone. Devn 4D 6
Frithsden. Herts 3H 21
Frithville. Linc 4L 37
Frittenden. Kent 1E 12
Frittiscombe. Devn 7L 5
Fritton. Norf
nr. Great Yarmouth 1L 31
nr. Long Stratton 2J 31
Fritwell. Oxon 1C 20
Frizinghall. W Yor 4K 41
Frizington. Cumb 3K 45
Frobost. W Isl 3D 74
Frocester. Glos 3F 18
Frochas. Powy 2L 25
Frodesley. Shrp 1D 26
Frodingham. N Lin 6G 43
Frodsham. Ches W 2D 34
Froggatt. Derbs 2L 35
Froghall. Staf 5J 35
Frogham. Hants 4K 9
Frogham. Kent 8J 23
Frogmore. Devn 7K 5
Frogmore. Hants 7F 20
Frogmore. Herts 3J 21
Frognall. Linc 8J 37
Frogshall. Norf 6J 39
Frogwell. Corn 5F 4
Frolesworth. Leics 2C 28
Frome. Som 1F 8
Fromefield. Som 1F 8
Frome St Quintin. Dors 5D 8
Fromes Hill. Here 7E 26
Fron. Gwyn 7C 32
Fron. Powy
nr. Llandrindod Wells 6K 25
nr. Newtown 3L 25
nr. Welshpool 2M 25
Y Fron. Gwyn 5E 32
Froncysyllte. Wrex 5A 34
Frongoch. Gwyn 7J 33
Fron Isaf. Wrex 5A 34
Fronoleu. Gwyn 7G 33
Frosterley. Dur 8D 54
Frotoft. Orkn 7D 88
Froxfield. C Beds 8G 29
Froxfield. Wilts 7L 19
Froxfield Green. Hants 3E 10
Fryern Hill. Hants 3B 10
Fryerning. Essx 3C 22
Fryton. N Yor 8D 48
Fugglestone St Peter. Wilts 2K 9
Fulbeck. Linc 4G 37
Fulbourn. Cambs 6B 30
Fulbrook. Oxon 2L 19
Fulflood. Hants 2B 10
Fulford. Som 3M 7
Fulford. Staf 6H 35
Fulford. York 3D 42
Fulham. G Lon 6K 21
Fulking. W Sus 4K 11
Fuller's Moor. Ches W 4C 34
Fuller Street. Essx 2D 22
Fullerton. Hants 2A 10
Fulletby. Linc 2K 37
Full Sutton. E Yor 2E 42
Fullwood. E Ayr 4C 58
Fulmer. Buck 5G 21
Fulmodestone. Norf 6F 38
Fulnetby. Linc 2H 37
Fulney. Linc 7K 37
Fulstow. Linc 8L 43
Fulthorpe. Stoc T 3B 48
Fulwell. Tyne 6G 55
Fulwood. Lanc 4D 40
Fulwood. Notts 4B 36
Fulwood. Som 4M 7
Fulwood. S Yor 1L 35
Fundenhall. Norf 2H 31
Funtington. W Sus 5F 10
Funtley. Hants 5C 10
Funzie. Shet 4L 91
Furley. Devn 5A 8
Furnace. Arg 7E 64
Furnace. Carm 6M 15
Furnace. Cdgn 3F 24
Furner's Green. E Sus 3M 11
Furness Vale. Derbs 1J 35
Furneux Pelham. Herts 1M 21
Furzebrook. Dors 7H 9
Furzehill. Devn 1G 7
Furzehill. Dors 5J 9
Furzeley Corner. Hants 4D 10
Furzey Lodge. Hants 5A 10
Furzley. Hants 4L 9
Fyfield. Essx 3B 22
Fyfield. Glos 3L 19
Fyfield. Hants 1L 9
Fyfield. Oxon 4B 20
Fyfield. Wilts 7K 19
The Fylde. Lanc 4B 40
Fylingthorpe. N Yor 5G 49
Fyning. W Sus 3F 10
Fyvie. Abers 2G 73

G

Gabhsann bho Dheas.
W Isl 6H 83
Gabhsann bho Thuath.
W Isl 6H 83
Gabroc Hill. E Ayr 4C 58
Gadbrook. Surr 1K 11
Gaddesby. Leics 8D 36
Gadfa. IOA 2D 32
Gadgirth. S Ayr 7C 58
Gaer. Powy 2L 17
Gaerwen. IOA 3D 32
Gagingwell. Oxon 1B 20
Gaick Lodge. High 7H 71
Gailey. Staf 8H 35
Gainford. Dur 4K 47
Gainsborough. Linc 8F 42
Gainsborough. Suff 7H 31
Gainsford End. Essx 8D 30
Gairletter. Arg 1L 57
Gairloch. Abers 5G 73
Gairloch. High 6K 77
Gairlochy. High 7B 70
Gairney Bank. Per 8E 66
Gairnshiel Lodge. Abers 5B 72
Gaisgill. Cumb 5E 46
Gaitsgill. Cumb 7H 53
Galashiels. Bord 6B 60
Galgate. Lanc 2C 40
Galgorm. ME Ant 3G 93
Galhampton. Som 3E 8
Gallatown. Fife 8F 66
Galley Common. Warw 2M 27
Galleyend. Essx 3D 22
Galleywood. Essx 3D 22
Gallin. Per 3K 65
Gallowfauld. Ang 3H 67
Gallowhill. Per 4E 66
Gallowhill. Ren 3C 58
Gallowhills. Abers 8K 81
Gallows Green. Staf 5J 35
Gallows Green. Worc 5H 27
Gallowstree Common.
Oxon 5D 20
Galltair. High 3K 69
Gallt Melyd. Den 2K 33
Galmington. Som 3M 7
Galmisdale. High 7F 68
Galmpton. Devn 7J 5
Galmpton. Torb 6L 5
Galmpton Warborough. Torb 6L 5
Galphay. N Yor 8L 47
Galston. E Ayr 6C 58
Galton. Dors 7F 8
Galtrigill. High 8C 76
Gamblesby. Cumb 8L 53
Gamblestown. Arm 6G 93
Gamelsby. Cumb 6G 53
Gamesley. Derbs 8J 41
Gamlingay. Cambs 6K 29
Gamlingay Cinques. Cambs 6K 29
Gamlingay Great Heath.
Cambs 6K 29
Gammaton. Devn 3D 6
Gammersgill. N Yor 7J 47
Gamston. Notts
nr. Nottingham 6D 36
nr. Retford 2E 36
Ganarew. Here 2D 18
Ganavan. Arg 4C 64
Ganborough. Glos 1K 19
Gang. Corn 5F 4
Ganllwyd. Gwyn 8G 33
Gannochy. Ang 8E 72
Gannochy. Per 5E 66
Gansclet. High 7E 86
Ganstead. E Yor 4J 43
Ganthorpe. N Yor 8D 48
Ganton. N Yor 8G 49
Gants Hill. G Lon 5M 21
Gappah. Devn 8H 7
Garafad. High 7F 76
Garboldisham. Norf 3G 31
Garden City. Flin 3B 34
Gardeners Green. Wok 7F 20
Gardenstown. Abers 7H 81
Garden Village. S Yor 8L 41
Garden Village. Swan 5E 16
Garderhouse. Shet 3D 90
Gardham. E Yor 3G 43
Gardie. Shet
on Papa Stour 1B 90
on Unst 2L 91
Gardie Ho. Shet 3E 90
Gare Hill. Wilts 1F 8
Garelochhead. Arg 8G 65
Garford. Oxon 4B 20
Garforth. W Yor 4B 42
Gargrave. N Yor 2H 41
Gargunnock. Stir 8M 65
Garleffin. S Ayr 3F 50
Garlieston. Dum 7K 51
Garlinge Green. Kent 8H 23
Garlogie. Abers 5G 73
Garmelow. Staf 7F 34
Garmond. Abers 8H 81
Garmondsway. Dur 8G 55
Garmony. Arg 3A 64
Garmouth. Mor 7C 80
Garmston. Shrp 1E 26
Garnant. Carm 3F 16
Garndiffaith. Torf 3A 18
Garndolbenmaen. Gwyn 6D 32
Garnett Bridge. Cumb 6D 46
Garnfadryn. Gwyn 7B 32
Garnkirk. N Lan 3E 58
Garnlydan. Blae 3L 17
Garnsgate. Linc 7M 37
Garnswllt. Swan 4F 16
Garn yr Erw. Torf 3M 17
Garrabost. W Isl 8J 83
Garrallan. E Ayr 8D 58
Garras. Corn 6L 3
Garreg. Gwyn 6F 32
Garrigill. Cumb 7M 53
Garrison. Ferm 6A 92
Garriston. N Yor 6K 47
Garrogie Lodge. High 4F 70
Garros. High 7F 76
Garrow. Per 3B 66
Garsdale. Cumb 7F 46
Garsdale Head. Cumb 6F 46
Garsdon. Wilts 5H 19
Garshall Green. Staf 6H 35
Garsington. Oxon 3C 20
Garstang. Lanc 3C 40
Garston. Mers 1C 34
Garswood. Mers 8D 40
Gartcosh. N Lan 3E 58
Garth. B'end 5H 17
Garth. Cdgn 4F 24
Garth. Gwyn 7E 32
Garth. IOM 7C 44
Garth. Powy
nr. Builth Wells 8J 25
nr. Knighton 4A 26
Garth. Shet
nr. Sandness 2C 90
nr. Skellister 2E 90
Garth. Wrex 5A 34
Garthamlock. Glas 3E 58
Garthbrengy. Powy 1K 17
Gartheli. Cdgn 7E 24
Garthmyl. Powy 3L 25
Garthorpe. Leics 7F 36
Garthorpe. N Lin 6F 42
Garth Owen. Powy 3L 25
Garth Place. Cphy 6L 17
Garth Row. Cumb 6D 46
Gartly. Abers 2E 72
Gartmore. Stir 8K 65
Gartness. N Lan 3F 58
Gartness. Stir 1D 58
Gartocharn. W Dun 1C 58
Garton. E Yor 4K 43
Garton-on-the-Wolds.
E Yor 2G 43
Gartsherrie. N Lan 3F 58
Gartymore. High 2L 79
Garvagh. Caus 3F 93
Garvaghy. Ferm 5D 92
Garvald. E Lot 2C 60
Garvamore. High 6F 70
Garvard. Arg 8J 63
Garvault. High 8K 85
Garve. High 7D 78
Garvestone. Norf 1G 31
Garvetagh. Derr 4C 92
Garvie. Arg 8E 64
Garvock. Abers 8G 73
Garvock. Inv 2A 58
Garway. Here 1C 18
Garway Common. Here 1C 18
Garway Hill. Here 1C 18
Garwick. Linc 5J 37
Gaskan. High 8K 69
Gasper. Wilts 2F 8
Gastard. Wilts 7G 19
Gasthorpe. Norf 3F 30
Gatcombe. IOW 7B 10
Gateacre. Mers 1C 34
Gatebeck. Cumb 7D 46
Gate Burton. Linc 1F 36
Gateforth. N Yor 5C 42
Gatehead. E Ayr 6B 58
Gate Helmsley. N Yor 2D 42
Gatehouse. Nmbd 3A 54
Gatehouse of Fleet. Dum 6M 51
Gatelawbridge. Dum 2D 52
Gateley. Norf 7F 38
Gatenby. N Yor 7M 47
Gatesgarth. Cumb 3L 45
Gateshead. Tyne 5F 54
Gatesheath. Ches W 3C 34
Gateside. Ang
nr. Forfar 3H 67
nr. Kirriemuir 3G 67
Gateside. Fife 7E 66
Gateside. N Ayr 4B 58
Gathurst. G Man 7D 40
Gatley. G Man 1G 35
Gatton. Surr 8K 21
Gattonside. Bord 6C 60
Gatwick Airport.
W Sus 119 (1K 11)
Gaufron. Powy 6J 25
Gaulby. Leics 1D 28
Gauldry. Fife 5G 67
Gaultree. Norf 1A 30
Gaunt's Common. Dors 5J 9
Gaunt's Earthcott. S Glo 5E 18
Gautby. Linc 2J 37
Gavinton. Bord 4E 60
Gawber. S Yor 7M 41
Gawcott. Buck 8D 28
Gawsworth. Ches E 3G 35
Gawthorpe. W Yor 5L 41
Gawthrop. Cumb 7E 46
Gawthwaite. Cumb 7A 46
Gay Bowers. Essx 3D 22
Gaydon. Warw 6A 28
Gayfield. Orkn 4D 88
Gayhurst. Mil 7F 28
Gayle. N Yor 7G 47
Gayles. N Yor 5K 47
Gay Street. W Sus 3H 11
Gayton. Mers 1A 34
Gayton. Norf 8D 38
Gayton. Nptn 6E 28
Gayton. Staf 7H 35
Gayton le Marsh. Linc 1M 37
Gayton le Wold. Linc 1K 37
Gayton Thorpe. Norf 8D 38
Gaywood. Norf 7C 38
Gazeley. Suff 5D 30
Geanies. High 6J 79
Gearraidh Bhailteas. W Isl 3D 74
Gearraidh Bhaird. W Isl 2E 76
Gearraidh ma Monadh.
W Isl 4D 74
Gearraidh na h-Aibhne.
W Isl 8F 82
Geary. High 7D 76
Geddes. High 8J 79
Gedding. Suff 6F 30
Geddington. Nptn 3F 28
Gedintailor. High 2G 69
Gedling. Notts 5D 36
Gedney. Linc 7M 37
Gedney Broadgate. Linc 7M 37
Gedney Drove End. Linc 7A 38
Gedney Dyke. Linc 7M 37
Gedney Hill. Linc 8L 37
Gee Cross. G Man 8H 41
Geeston. Rut 1G 29
Geilston. Arg 2B 58
Geirinis. W Isl 1D 74
Geise. High 5C 86
Geisiadar. W Isl 8E 82
Gelder Shiel. Abers 7B 72
Geldeston. Norf 2K 31
Gell. Cnwy 4H 33
Gelli. Pemb 5G 15
Gelli. Rhon 5J 17
Gellifor. Den 4L 33
Gelligaer. Cphy 5L 17
Y Gelli Gandryll. Powy 8M 25
Gellilydan. Gwyn 7F 32
Gellinudd. Neat 4G 17
Gellyburn. Per 4D 66
Gellywen. Carm 4J 15
Gelston. Dum 6B 52
Gelston. Linc 5G 37
Gembling. E Yor 2J 43
Geneva. Cdgn 1L 15
Gentleshaw. Staf 8J 35
Geocrab. W Isl 4C 76
George Best Belfast City Airport.
Bel 5H 93
George Green. Buck 5G 21
Georgeham. Devn 2D 6
George Nympton. Devn 3G 7
Georgetown. Blae 4L 17
Georgetown. Ren 3C 58
Georth. Orkn 7C 88
Gerlan. Gwyn 4F 32
Germansweek. Devn 6D 6
Germoe. Corn 6J 3
Gerrans. Corn 8A 4
Gerrard's Bromley. Staf 6F 34
Gerrards Cross. Buck 5G 21
Gerston. High 6C 86
Gestingthorpe. Essx 8E 30
Gethsemane. Pemb 2G 15
Geuffordd. Powy 1M 25
Gibraltar. Buck 2E 20
Gibraltar. Linc 4B 38
Gibraltar. Suff 6H 31
Gibsmere. Notts 5E 36
Giddeahall. Wilts 6G 19
Gidea Park. G Lon 5B 22
Gidleigh. Devn 7F 6
Giffnock. E Ren 4D 58
Gifford. E Lot 3C 60
Giffordtown. Fife 6F 66
Giggetty. Staf 2G 27
Giggleswick. N Yor 1G 41
Gignog. Pemb 4E 14
Gilberdyke. E Yor 5F 42
Gilbert's End. Worc 7G 27
Gilbert's Green. Warw 4K 27
Gilchriston. E Lot 3B 60
Gilcrux. Cumb 8F 52
Gildersome. W Yor 5L 41
Gildingwells. S Yor 1C 36
Gilesgate Moor. Dur 7F 54
Gileston. V Glam 8K 17
Gilfach. Cphy 5L 17
Gilfach Goch. Rhon 6J 17
Gilfachreda. Cdgn 1L 15
Gilford. Arm 6G 93
Gilgarran. Cumb 2K 45
Gillamoor. N Yor 6D 48
Gillan. Corn 6L 3
Gillar's Green. Mers 8C 40
Gillen. High 8D 76
Gilling East. N Yor 8D 48
Gillingham. Dors 3G 9
Gillingham. Medw
Medway Towns 111 (7D 22)
Gillingham. Norf 2L 31
Gilling West. N Yor 5K 47
Gillock. High 6D 86
Gillow Heath. Staf 4G 35
Gills. High 4E 86
Gill's Green. Kent 2D 12
Gilmanscleuch. Bord 7M 59
Gilmerton. Edin 3L 59
Gilmerton. Per 5B 66
Gilmonby. Dur 4H 47
Gilmorton. Leics 3C 28
Gilsland. Nmbd 5L 53
Gilsland Spa. Cumb 5L 53
Gilston. Bord 4B 60
Giltbrook. Notts 5B 36
Gilwern. Mon 3M 17
Gimingham. Norf 6J 39
Giosla. W Isl 1C 76
Gipping. Suff 5G 31
Gipsey Bridge. Linc 5K 37
Gipton. W Yor 4M 41
Girdle Toll. N Ayr 5B 58
Girlsta. Shet 2E 90
Girsby. N Yor 5A 48
Girthon. Dum 6M 51
Girton. Cambs 5M 29
Girton. Notts 3F 36
Girvan. S Ayr 2G 51
Gisburn. Lanc 3G 41
Gisleham. Suff 3M 31
Gislingham. Suff 4G 31
Gissing. Norf 3H 31
Gittisham. Devn 6L 7
Gladestry. Powy 7M 25
Gladsmuir. E Lot 2B 60
Glaichbea. High 2F 70
Glais. Swan 4G 17
Glaisdale. N Yor 5E 48
Glame. High 1G 69
Glamis. Ang 3G 67
Glanaman. Carm 3F 16
Glan-Conwy. Cnwy 5H 33
Glandford. Norf 5G 39
Glan Duar. Carm 2M 15
Glandwr. Blae 4M 17
Glandwr. Pemb 4H 15
Glan-Dwyfach. Gwyn 6D 32
Glandy Cross. Carm 4H 15
Glandyfi. Cdgn 3F 24
Glangrwyney. Powy 3M 17
Glanmule. Powy 3L 25
Glan-rhyd. Pemb 3H 15
Glan-rhyd. Powy 4G 17
Glanrhyd. Gwyn 7B 32
Glanrhyd. Pemb 2H 15
Glanton. Nmbd 8H 61
Glanton Pyke. Nmbd 8H 61
Glanvilles Wootton. Dors 5E 8
Glan-y-don. Flin 3L 33
Glan-y-nant. Powy 4J 25
Glan-yr-afon. Gwyn 6K 33
Glan-yr-afon. IOA 2F 32
Glan-yr-afon. Powy 2K 25
Glan-y-wern. Gwyn 7F 32
Glapthorn. Nptn 2H 29
Glapwell. Derbs 3B 36
Glarryford. ME Ant 3G 93
Glas Aird. Arg 8J 63
Glas-allt Shiel. Abers 7B 72
Glasbury. Powy 1L 17
Glaschoil. High 2L 71
Glascoed. Den 3J 33
Glascoed. Mon 3B 18
Glascote. Staf 1L 27
Glascwm. Powy 7L 25
Glasfryn. Cnwy 5J 33
Glasgow. Glas 109 (3D 58)
Glasgow Airport. Ren 119 (3C 58)
Glasgow Prestwick Airport.
S Ayr 7B 58
Glashvin. High 7F 76
Glasinfryn. Gwyn 4E 32
Glas na Cardaich. High 6H 69
Glasnacardoch. High 6H 69
Glasnakille. High 4G 69
Glaspwll. Cdgn 3G 25
Glassburn. High 2D 70
Glassenbury. Kent 2D 12
Glasserton. Dum 8K 51
Glassford. S Lan 5F 58
Glassgreen. Mor 7B 80
Glasshouse. Glos 1F 18
Glasshouses. N Yor 1K 41
Glasson. Cumb 5G 53
Glasson. Lanc 2C 40
Glassonby. Cumb 8K 53
Glasswater. New M 6J 93
Glasterlaw. Ang 2J 67
Glaston. Rut 1F 28
Glastonbury. Som 2C 8
Glatton. Cambs 3J 29
Glazebrook. Warr 8E 40
Glazebury. Warr 8E 40
Glazeley. Shrp 3F 26
Gleadless. S Yor 1A 36
Gleadsmoss. Ches E 3G 35
Gleann Dail bho Dheas.
W Isl 4D 74
Gleann Tholastaidh. W Isl 7J 83
Gleann Uige. High 8H 69
Gleaston. Cumb 8A 46
Glebe. Derr 4C 92
Glecknabae. Arg 3K 57
Gledrid. Shrp 6A 34
Gleiniant. Powy 3J 25
Glemsford. Suff 7E 30
Glen. Dum 6L 51
Glenancross. High 6H 69
Glenanne. Arm 7F 93
Glenariff. Caus 2H 93
Glenarm. ME Ant 3H 93
Glen Auldyn. IOM 5D 44
Glenavy. Lis 5G 93
Glenbarr. Arg 6F 56
Glenbeg. High 1L 63
Glen Bernisdale. High 1F 68
Glenbervie. Abers 7G 73
Glenboig. N Lan 3F 58
Glenborrodale. High 1M 63
Glenbranter. Arg 8F 64
Glenbreck. Bord 7J 59
Glenbrein Lodge. High 4E 70
Glenbrittle. High 3F 68
Glenbuchat Lodge. Abers 4C 72
Glenbuck. E Ayr 7F 58
Glenburn. Ren 3C 58
Glencalvie Lodge. High 5E 78
Glencaple. Dum 5D 52
Glencarron Lodge. High 8A 78
Glencarse. Per 5E 66
Glencassley Castle. High 3E 78
Glencat. Abers 6E 72
Glencoe. High 2F 64
Glen Cottage. High 7H 69
Glencraig. Fife 8E 66
Glendale. High 1C 68
Glendevon. Per 7C 66
Glendoebeg. High 5E 70
Glendoick. Per 5F 66
Glendoune. S Ayr 2G 51
Glenduckie. Fife 6F 66
Gleneagles. Per 7C 66
Glenegedale. Arg 4C 56
Glenegedale Lots. Arg 4C 56
Glenelg. High 4K 69
Glenernie. Mor 1L 71
Glenesslin. Dum 3C 52
Glenfarg. Per 6E 66
Glenfarquhar Lodge. Abers 7G 73
Glenferness Mains. High 1K 71
Glenfeshie Lodge. High 6J 71
Glenfiddich Lodge. Mor 2C 72
Glenfield. Leics 1C 28
Glenfinnan. High 7L 69
Glenfintaig Lodge. High 7C 70
Glenfoot. Per 6E 66
Glenfyne Lodge. Arg 6G 65
Glengap. Dum 6A 52
Glengarnock. N Ayr 4B 58
Glengolly. High 5C 86
Glengorm Castle. Arg 2K 63
Glengormley. Ant 4H 93
Glengrasco. High 1F 68
Glenhead Farm. Ang 1F 66
Glenholm. Bord 6K 59
Glen House. Bord 6L 59
Glenhurich. High 1C 64
Glenkerry. Bord 8L 59
Glenkiln. Dum 4C 52
Glenkindie. Abers 4D 72
Glenkinglass Lodge. Arg 4F 64
Glenkirk. Bord 7J 59
Glenlean. Arg 1K 57
Glenlee. Dum 3M 51
Glenleraig. High 8D 84
Glenlichorn. Per 6A 66
Glenlivet. Mor 3A 72
Glenlochar. Dum 5B 52
Glenlochsie Lodge. Per 8L 71
Glenluce. Dum 6G 51
Glenmarksie. High 8D 78
Glenmassan. Arg 1L 57
Glenmavis. N Lan 3F 58
Glen Maye. IOM 7B 44
Glenmazeran Lodge. High 3H 71
Glenmidge. Dum 3C 52
Glen Mona. IOM 6D 44
Glenmore. High
nr. Glenborrodale 1L 63
nr. Kingussie 5K 71
on Isle of Skye 1F 68
Glenmoy. Ang 1H 67
Glennoe. Arg 4E 64
Glen of Coachford. Abers 1D 72
Glenogil. Ang 1H 67
Glen Parva. Leics 2C 28
Glenprosen Village. Ang 1G 67
Glenree. N Ayr 7J 57
Glenridding. Cumb 4B 46
Glenrosa. N Ayr 6K 57
Glenrothes. Fife 7F 66
Glensanda. High 3C 64
Glensaugh. Abers 8F 72
Glenshero Lodge. High 6F 70
Glensluain. Arg 8E 64
Glenstockadale. Dum 5F 50
Glenstriven. Arg 2K 57
Glen Tanar House. Abers 6D 72
Glentham. Linc 8H 43
Glenton. Abers 3F 72
Glentress. Bord 6L 59
Glentromie Lodge. High 6H 71
Glentrool Lodge. Dum 3K 51
Glentrool Village. Dum 4J 51
Glentruim House. High 6G 71
Glentworth. Linc 1G 37
Glenuig. High 8H 69
Glen View. New M 7G 93
Glen Village. Falk 2G 59
Glen Vine. IOM 7C 44
Glenwhilly. Dum 4G 51
Glenzierfoot. Dum 4H 53
Glespin. S Lan 7G 59
Gletness. Shet 2E 90
Glewstone. Here 1D 18
Glib Cheois. W Isl 1E 76
Glinton. Pet 1J 29
Glooston. Leics 2E 28
Glossop. Derbs 8J 41
Gloster Hill. Nmbd 1F 54
Gloucester. Glos 109 (2G 19)
Gloucestershire Airport.
Glos 1G 19
Gloup. Shet 3K 91
Glusburn. N Yor 3J 41
Glutt Lodge. High 8A 86
Glutton Bridge. Derbs 3J 35
Gluvian. Corn 5B 4
Glympton. Oxon 1B 20
Glyn. Cnwy 3H 33
Glynarthen. Cdgn 2K 15
Glynbrochan. Powy 4J 25
Glyn Ceiriog. Wrex 7M 33
Glyncoch. Rhon 5K 17
Glyncorrwg. Neat 5H 17
Glynde. E Sus 5A 12
Glyndebourne. E Sus 4A 12
Glyndyfrdwy. Den 6L 33
Glyn Ebwy. Blae 4L 17
Glynllan. B'end 6J 17
Glynn. ME Ant 4J 93
Glyn-neath. Neat 4H 17
Glynogwr. B'end 6J 17
Glyntaff. Rhon 6K 17
Glyntawe. Powy 3H 17
Glynteg. Carm 3K 15
Gnosall. Staf 7G 35
Gnosall Heath. Staf 7G 35
Goadby. Leics 2E 28
Goadby Marwood. Leics 7E 36
Goatacre. Wilts 6J 19
Goathill. Dors 4E 8
Goathland. N Yor 5F 48
Goathurst. Som 2A 8
Goathurst Common. Kent 8A 22
Goat Lees. Kent 1G 13
Gobernuisgach Lodge. High 7G 85
Gobernuisgeach. High 8A 86
Gobhaig. W Isl 3B 76
Gobowen. Shrp 6B 34
Godalming. Surr 1G 11
Goddard's Corner. Suff 5J 31
Goddard's Green. Kent
nr. Benenden 2E 12
nr. Cranbrook 2D 12
Goddards' Green. W Sus 3K 11
Godford Cross. Devn 5L 7
Godleybrook. Staf 5H 35
Godmanchester. Cambs 4K 29
Godmanstone. Dors 6E 8
Godmersham. Kent 8G 23
Godolphin Cross. Corn 5K 3
Godre'r-graig. Neat 4G 17
Godshill. Hants 4K 9
Godshill. IOW 7C 10
Godstone. Staf 6J 35
Godstone. Surr 8L 21
Goetre. Mon 3B 18
Goff's Oak. Herts 3L 21
Gogar. Edin 2K 59
Goginan. Cdgn 4F 24
Golan. Gwyn 6E 32
Golant. Corn 6D 4
Golberdon. Corn 8C 6
Golborne. G Man 8E 40
Golcar. W Yor 6J 41
Goldcliff. Newp 5B 18
Golden Cross. E Sus 4B 12
Golden Green. Kent 1C 12
Golden Grove. Carm 3E 16
Golden Grove. N Yor 5F 48
Golden Hill. Pemb 4F 14
Goldenhill. Stoke 4G 35
Golden Pot. Hants 1E 10
Golden Valley. Glos 1H 19
Golders Green. G Lon 5K 21
Goldhanger. Essx 3F 22
Gold Hill. Norf 2B 30
Golding. Shrp 1D 26
Goldington. Bed 6H 29
Goldsborough. N Yor
nr. Harrogate 2A 42
nr. Whitby 4F 48
Goldsithney. Corn 5J 3
Goldstone. Kent 7J 23
Goldstone. Shrp 7F 34
Goldthorpe. S Yor 7B 42
Goldworthy. Devn 3C 6
Golfa. Powy 8L 33
Gollanfield. High 8J 79
Gollinglith Foot. N Yor 7K 47
Golsoncott. Som 2K 7
Golspie. High 4J 79
Gomeldon. Wilts 2K 9
Gomersal. W Yor 5L 41
Gometra House. Arg 3J 63
Gomshall. Surr 1H 11
Gonalston. Notts 5D 36
Gonerby Hill Foot. Linc 6G 37
Gonfirth. Shet 1D 90
Good Easter. Essx 2C 22
Gooderstone. Norf 1D 30
Goodleigh. Devn 2F 6
Goodmanham. E Yor 3F 42
Goodmayes. G Lon 5A 22
Goodnestone. Kent
nr. Aylesham 8J 23
nr. Faversham 7G 23
Goodrich. Here 2D 18
Goodrington. Torb 6L 5
Goodshaw. Lanc 5G 41
Goodshaw Fold. Lanc 5G 41
Goodstone. Devn 8G 7
Goodwick. Pemb 3F 14
Goodworth Clatford. Hants 1A 10
Goole. E Yor 5E 42
Goom's Hill. Worc 6J 27
Goonabarn. Corn 6B 4
Goonbell. Corn 4L 3
Goonhavern. Corn 3L 3
Goonlaze. Corn 5L 3
Goonvrea. Corn 4L 3
Goose Green. Cumb 7D 46
Goose Green. S Glo 5F 18
Gooseham. Corn 4B 6
Goosewell. Plym 6H 5
Goosey. Oxon 4A 20
Goosnargh. Lanc 4D 40
Goostrey. Ches E 2F 34
Gorcott Hill. Warw 5J 27
Gord. Shet 5E 90
Gordon. Bord 5D 60
Gordonbush. High 3J 79
Gordonstown. Abers
nr. Cornhill 8E 80
nr. Fyvie 2G 73
Gorebridge. Midl 3M 59
Gorefield. Cambs 8M 37
Gores. Wilts 8K 19
Gorgie. Edin 2L 59
Goring. Oxon 5D 20
Goring-by-Sea. W Sus 5J 11
Goring Heath. Oxon 6D 20
Gorleston-on-Sea. Norf 1M 31
Gornalwood. W Mid 2H 27
Gorran Churchtown. Corn 7B 4
Gorran Haven. Corn 7C 4
Gorran High Lanes. Corn 7B 4
Gors. Cdgn 5F 24
Gorsedd. Flin 3L 33
Gorseinon. Swan 5E 16
Gorseness. Orkn 8D 88
Gorseybank. Derbs 4L 35
Gorsgoch. Cdgn 1L 15
Gorslas. Carm 3E 16
Gorsley. Glos 1E 18
Gorsley Common. Here 1E 18
Gorstan. High 7D 78
Gorstella. Ches W 3B 34
Gorsty Common. Here 8C 26
Gorsty Hill. Staf 7K 35
Gortantaoid. Arg 2C 56
Gorteneorn. High 1M 63
Gortenfern. High 1M 63
Gortin. Ferm 4D 92
Gortnahey. Caus 3E 92
Gorton. G Man 8G 41
Gosbeck. Suff 6H 31
Gosberton. Linc 6K 37
Gosberton Cheal. Linc 7K 37
Gosberton Clough. Linc 7J 37
Goseley Dale. Derbs 7M 35
Gosfield. Essx 1D 22
Gosford. Oxon 2C 20
Gosforth. Cumb 4K 45
Gosforth. Tyne 5F 54
Gosmore. Herts 1J 21
Gospel End. Staf 2G 27
Gosport. Hants 6D 10
Gossabrough. Shet 5K 91
Gossington. Glos 3F 18
Gossops Green. W Sus 2K 11
Goswick. Nmbd 5H 61
Gotham. Notts 6C 36
Gotherington. Glos 1H 19
Gott. Arg 3F 62
Gott. Shet 3E 90
Goudhurst. Kent 2D 12
Goulceby. Linc 2K 37
Gourdon. Abers 8H 73
Gourock. Inv 2M 57
Govan. Glas 3D 58
Govanhill. Glas 3D 58
Goverton. Notts 5E 36
Goveton. Devn 7K 5
Govilon. Mon 2A 18
Gowanhill. Abers 7K 81
Gowdall. E Yor 5D 42
Gowdystown. Arm 6G 93
Gowerton. Swan 5E 16
Gowkhall. Fife 1J 59
Gowthorpe. E Yor 2E 42
Goxhill. E Yor 3J 43
Goxhill. N Lin 5J 43
Goxhill Haven. N Lin 5J 43
Goytre. Neat 6G 17
Grabhair. W Isl 2E 76
Graby. Linc 7H 37
Gracehill. ME Ant 3G 93
Graffham. W Sus 4G 11
Grafham. Cambs 5J 29
Grafham. Surr 1H 11
Grafton. Here 8C 26
Grafton. N Yor 1B 42
Grafton. Oxon 3L 19
Grafton. Shrp 8C 34
Grafton. Worc
nr. Evesham 8H 27
nr. Leominster 5D 26
Grafton Flyford. Worc 6H 27
Grafton Regis. Nptn 7E 28
Grafton Underwood. Nptn 3G 29
Grafty Green. Kent 1E 12
Graianrhyd. Den 5M 33
Graig. Carm 6L 15
Graig. Cnwy 3H 33
Graig. Den 3K 33
Graig-fechan. Den 5L 33
Graig Penllyn. V Glam 7J 17
Grain. Medw 6E 22
Grainsby. Linc 8K 43
Grainthorpe. Linc 8L 43
Grainthorpe Fen. Linc 8L 43
Graiselound. N Lin 8E 42
Gramasdail. W Isl 8K 75
Grampound. Corn 7B 4
Grampound Road. Corn 6B 4
Granborough. Buck 1E 20
Granby. Notts 6E 36
Grandborough. Warw 5B 28
Grandpont. Oxon 3C 20
Grandtully. Per 2C 66
Grange. Cumb 4A 46
Grange. E Ayr 6C 58
Grange. Here 4C 26
Grange. Mers 2M 33
Grange. Per 5F 66
The Grange. N Yor 6C 48
Grange Corner. ME Ant 4G 93
Grange Crossroads. Mor 8D 80
Grange Hill. Essx 4M 21
Grangemill. Derbs 4L 35
Grange Moor. W Yor 6L 41
Grangemouth. Falk 1H 59
Grange of Lindores. Fife 6F 66
Grange-over-Sands. Cumb 8C 46
Grangepans. Falk 1J 59
Grange Park. New M 6J 93
Grangetown. Card 7L 17
Grangetown. Red C 3C 48
Grange Villa. Dur 6F 54
Granish. High 4J 71
Gransmoor. E Yor 2J 43
Granston. Pemb 3E 14
Grantchester. Cambs 6M 29
Grantham. Linc 6G 37
Grantley. N Yor 1L 41
Grantlodge. Abers 4G 73
Granton. Edin 2L 59
Grantown-on-Spey. High 3L 71
Grantshouse. Bord 3F 60
Grappenhall. Warr 1E 34
Grasby. Linc 7H 43
Grasmere. Cumb 5B 46
Grasscroft. G Man 7H 41
Grassendale. Mers 1B 34
Grassgarth. Cumb 7H 53
Grassholme. Dur 3H 47
Grassington. N Yor 1J 41
Grassmoor. Derbs 3B 36
Grassthorpe. Notts 3E 36
Grateley. Hants 1L 9
Gratton. Devn 4C 6
Gratton. Staf 4H 35
Gratwich. Staf 6J 35
Graveley. Cambs 5K 29
Graveley. Herts 1K 21
Gravelhill. Shrp 8C 34
Gravel Hole. G Man 7H 41
Gravelly Hill. W Mid 2K 27
Graven. Shet 6J 91
Graveney. Kent 7G 23
Gravesend. Kent 6C 22
Grayingham. Linc 8G 43
Grayrigg. Cumb 6D 46
Grays. Thur 6C 22
Grayshott. Hants 2F 10
Grayson Green. Cumb 2J 45
Grayswood. Surr 2G 11
Graythorp. Hart 3C 48
Grazeley. Wok 7D 20
Grealin. High 7G 77
Greasbrough. S Yor 8B 42
Greasby. Mers 1A 34
Great Abington. Cambs 7B 30
Great Addington. Nptn 4G 29
Great Alne. Warw 6K 27
Great Altcar. Lanc 7B 40
Great Amwell. Herts 2L 21
Great Asby. Cumb 4E 46
Great Ashfield. Suff 5F 30
Great Ayton. N Yor 4C 48
Great Baddow. Essx 3D 22
Great Bardfield. Essx 8C 30
Great Barford. Bed 6J 29
Great Barr. W Mid 2J 27
Great Barrington. Glos 2L 19
Great Barrow. Ches W 3C 34
Great Barton. Suff 5E 30
Great Barugh. N Yor 8E 48
Great Bavington. Nmbd 3C 54
Great Bealings. Suff 7J 31
Great Bedwyn. Wilts 7L 19
Great Bentley. Essx 1H 23
Great Billing. Nptn 5F 28
Great Bircham. Norf 6D 38
Great Blakenham. Suff 6H 31
Great Blencow. Cumb 8J 53
Great Bolas. Telf 7E 34
Great Bookham. Surr 8J 21
Great Bosullow. Corn 5H 3
Great Bourton. Oxon 7B 28
Great Bowden. Leics 3E 28
Great Bradley. Suff 6C 30
Great Braxted. Essx 2E 22
Great Bricett. Suff 6G 31
Great Brickhill. Buck 8G 29
Great Bridgeford. Staf 7G 35
Great Brington. Nptn 5D 28
Great Bromley. Essx 1G 23
Great Broughton. Cumb 8E 52
Great Broughton. N Yor 5C 48
Great Budworth. Ches W 2E 34
Great Burdon. Darl 4M 47
Great Burstead. Essx 4C 22
Great Busby. N Yor 5C 48
Great Canfield. Essx 2B 22
Great Carlton. Linc 1M 37
Great Casterton. Rut 1G 29
Great Chalfield. Wilts 7G 19
Great Chart. Kent 1F 12
Great Chatwell. Staf 8F 34
Great Chesterford. Essx 7B 30
Great Cheverell. Wilts 8H 19
Great Chilton. Dur 8F 54
Great Chishill. Cambs 8M 29
Great Clacton. Essx 2H 23
Great Cliff. W Yor 6M 41
Great Clifton. Cumb 2K 45
Great Coates. NE Lin 6K 43
Great Comberton. Worc 7H 27
Great Corby. Cumb 6J 53
Great Cornard. Suff 7E 30
Great Cowden. E Yor 3K 43
Great Coxwell. Oxon 4L 19
Great Crakehall. N Yor 6L 47
Great Cransley. Nptn 4F 28
Great Cressingham. Norf 1E 30
Great Crosby. Mers 7B 40
Great Cubley. Derbs 6K 35
Great Dalby. Leics 8E 36
Great Doddington. Nptn 5F 28
Great Doward. Here 2D 18
Great Dunham. Norf 8E 38
Great Dunmow. Essx 1C 22
Great Durnford. Wilts 2K 9
Great Easton. Essx 1C 22
Great Easton. Leics 2F 28
Great Eccleston. Lanc 3C 40
Great Edstone. N Yor 7E 48
Great Ellingham. Norf 2G 31
Great Elm. Som 1F 8
Great Eppleton. Tyne 7G 55
Great Eversden. Cambs 6L 29
Great Fencote. N Yor 6L 47
Great Finborough. Suff 6G 31
Greatford. Linc 8H 37
Great Fransham. Norf 8E 38
Great Gaddesden. Herts 2H 21
Great Gate. Staf 5J 35
Great Gidding. Cambs 3J 29
Great Givendale. E Yor 2F 42
Great Glemham. Suff 5K 31
Great Glen. Leics 2D 28
Great Gonerby. Linc 6F 36
Great Gransden. Cambs 6K 29
Great Green. Norf 3J 31
Great Green. Suff
nr. Lavenham 6F 30
nr. Palgrave 4H 31
Great Habton. N Yor 8E 48
Great Hale. Linc 5J 37
Great Hallingbury. Essx 2B 22
Greatham. Hants 2E 10
Greatham. Hart 3B 48
Greatham. W Sus 4H 11
Great Hampden. Buck 3F 20
Great Harrowden. Nptn 4F 28
Great Harwood. Lanc 4F 40
Great Haseley. Oxon 3D 20
Great Hatfield. E Yor 3J 43
Great Haywood. Staf 7H 35
Great Heath. W Mid 3M 27
Great Heck. N Yor 5C 42
Great Henny. Essx 8E 30
Great Hinton. Wilts 8H 19
Great Hockham. Norf 2F 30

Great Holland—Hendomen

Great Holland. Essx 2J 23
Great Horkesley. Essx 8F 30
Great Hormead. Herts 8M 29
Great Horton. W Yor 4K 41
Great Horwood. Buck 8E 28
Great Houghton. Nptn 6E 28
Great Houghton. S Yor 7B 42
Great Hucklow. Derbs 2K 35
Great Kelk. E Yor 2J 43
Great Kendale. E Yor 1H 43
Great Kimble. Buck 3F 20
Great Kingshill. Buck 4F 20
Great Langdale. Cumb 5A 46
Great Langton. N Yor 6L 47
Great Leighs. Essx 2D 22
Great Limber. Linc 7J 43
Great Linford. Mil 7F 28
Great Livermere. Suff 4E 30
Great Longstone. Derbs 2L 35
Great Lumley. Dur 7F 54
Great Lyth. Shrp 1C 26
Great Malvern. Worc 7F 26
Great Maplestead. Essx 8E 30
Great Marton. Bkpl 4B 40
Great Massingham. Norf 7D 38
Great Melton. Norf 1H 31
Great Milton. Oxon 3D 20
Great Missenden. Buck 3F 20
Great Mitton. Lanc 4F 40
Great Mongeham. Kent 8K 23
Great Moulton. Norf 2H 31
Great Munden. Herts 1L 21
Great Musgrave. Cumb 4F 46
Great Ness. Shrp 8B 34
Great Notley. Essx 1D 22
Great Oak. Mon 3B 18
Great Oakley. Essx 1H 23
Great Oakley. Nptn 3F 28
Great Offley. Herts 1J 21
Great Ormside. Cumb 4F 46
Great Orton. Cumb 6H 53
Great Ouseburn. N Yor 1B 42
Great Oxendon. Nptn 3E 28
Great Oxney Green. Essx 3C 22
Great Parndon. Essx 3M 21
Great Paxton. Cambs 5K 29
Great Plumpton. Lanc 4B 40
Great Plumstead. Norf 8K 39
Great Ponton. Linc 6G 37
Great Potheridge. Devn 4E 6
Great Preston. W Yor 5B 42
Great Raveley. Cambs 3K 29
Great Rissington. Glos 2K 19
Great Rollright. Oxon 8M 27
Great Ryburgh. Norf 7F 38
Great Ryle. Nmbd 8H 61
Great Ryton. Shrp 1C 26
Great Saling. Essx 1D 22
Great Salkeld. Cumb 8K 53
Great Sampford. Essx 8C 30
Great Sankey. Warr 1D 34
Great Saredon. Staf 1H 27
Great Saxham. Suff 5D 30
Great Shefford. W Ber 6A 20
Great Shelford. Cambs 6A 30
Great Shoddesden. Hants 1L 9
Great Smeaton. N Yor 5M 47
Great Snoring. Norf 6F 38
Great Somerford. Wilts 5H 19
Great Stainton. Darl 3M 47
Great Stambridge. Essx 4E 22
Great Staughton. Cambs 5J 29
Great Steeping. Linc 3M 37
Great Stonar. Kent 8K 23
Greatstone-on-Sea. Kent 3G 13
Great Strickland. Cumb 3D 46
Great Stukeley. Cambs 4K 29
Great Sturton. Linc 2K 37
Great Sutton. Ches W 2B 34
Great Sutton. Shrp 3D 26
Great Swinburne. Nmbd 4C 54
Great Tew. Oxon 1A 20
Great Tey. Essx 1E 22
Great Thirkleby. N Yor 8B 48
Great Thorness. IOW 6B 10
Great Thurlow. Suff 6C 30
Great Torr. Devn 7J 5
Great Torrington. Devn 4D 6
Great Tosson. Nmbd 1D 54
Great Totham North. Essx 2E 22
Great Totham South. Essx 2E 22
Great Tows. Linc 8K 43
Great Urswick. Cumb 8A 46
Great Wakering. Essx 5F 22
Great Waldingfield. Suff 7F 30
Great Walsingham. Norf 6F 38
Great Waltham. Essx 2C 22
Great Warley. Essx 4B 22
Great Washbourne. Glos 8H 27
Great Wenham. Suff 8G 31
Great Whelnetham. Suff 6E 30
Great Whittington. Nmbd 4D 54
Great Wigborough. Essx 2F 22
Great Wilbraham. Cambs 6B 30
Great Wilne. Derbs 6B 36
Great Wishford. Wilts 2J 9
Great Witchingham. Norf 7H 39
Great Witcombe. Glos 2H 19
Great Witley. Worc 5F 26
Great Wolford. Warw 8L 27
Greatworth. Nptn 7C 28
Great Wratting. Suff 7C 30
Great Wymondley. Herts 1K 21
Great Wyrley. Staf 1H 27
Great Wytheford. Shrp 8D 34
Great Yarmouth. Norf 1M 31
Great Yeldham. Essx 8D 30
Grebby. Linc 3M 37
Greeba Castle. IOM 6C 44
The Green. Cumb 6L 45
The Green. Wilts 2G 9
Greenbank. Shet 3K 91
Greenbottom. Corn 4L 3
Greenburn. W Lot 3H 59
Greencastle. Ferm 4D 92
Greencroft. Dur 6E 54
Greendown. Som 8D 18
Greendykes. Nmbd 7H 61
Green End. Bed
nr. Bedford 7H 29
nr. Little Staughton 5J 29
Green End. Herts
nr. Buntingford 8L 29
nr. Stevenage 1L 21
Green End. N Yor 5F 48
Green End. Warw 3L 27
Greenfield. Arg 8G 65
Greenfield. C Beds 8H 29
Greenfield. Flin 3L 33
Greenfield. G Man 7H 41
Greenfield. Oxon 4E 20
Greenfoot. N Lan 3F 58
Greenford. G Lon 5J 21
Greengairs. N Lan 2F 58
Greengate. Norf 8G 39
Greengill. Cumb 8F 52
Greenhalgh. Lanc 4C 40
Greenham. Dors 5C 8
Greenham. Som 3K 7
Greenham. W Ber 7B 20
Green Hammerton. N Yor 2B 42
Greenhaugh. Nmbd 3A 54
Greenhead. Nmbd 5L 53
Green Heath. Staf 8H 35
Greenhill. Dum 4F 52
Greenhill. Falk 2G 59
Greenhill. Kent 7H 23
Greenhill. S Yor 1M 35
Greenhill. Worc 4G 27
Greenhills. N Ayr 4B 58
Greenhithe. Kent 6B 22
Greenholm. E Ayr 6D 58
Greenhow Hill. N Yor 1K 41
Greenigoe. Orkn 1F 86
Greenisland. ME Ant 4H 93
Greenland. High 5D 86
Greenland Mains. High 5D 86
Greenlands. Worc 5J 27
Green Lane. Shrp 7E 34
Green Lane. Worc 5J 27
Greenlaw. Bord 5E 60
Greenlea. Dum 4E 52
Greenloaning. Per 7B 66
Greenmount. G Man 6F 40
Greenmow. Shet 5E 90
Greenock. Inv 2A 58
Greenock Mains. E Ayr 7E 58
Greenodd. Cumb 7B 46
Green Ore. Som 8D 18
Greenrow. Cumb 6F 52
Greens. Abers 1H 73
Greensgate. Norf 8H 39
Greenside. Tyne 5E 54
Greensidehill. Nmbd 8G 61
Greens Norton. Nptn 7D 28
Greenstead Green. Essx 1E 22
Greensted Green. Essx 3B 22
Green Street. Herts 4J 21
Green Street. Suff 4H 31
Green Street Green. G Lon 7A 22
Green Street Green. Kent 6B 22
Greenstreet Green. Suff 7G 31
Green Tye. Herts 2M 21
Greenwall. Orkn 1G 87
Greenway. Pemb 3G 15
Greenway. V Glam 7K 17
Greenwell. Cumb 6K 53
Greenwich. G Lon 6L 21
Greet. Glos 8J 27
Greete. Shrp 4D 26
Greetham. Linc 2L 37
Greetham. Rut 8G 37
Greetland. W Yor 5J 41
Gregson Lane. Lanc 5D 40
Grein. W Isl 5C 74
Greinetobht. W Isl 6K 75
Greinton. Som 2C 8
Gremista. Shet 3E 90
Grenaby. IOM 7B 44
Grendon. Nptn 5F 28
Grendon. Warw 2L 27
Grendon Common. Warw 2L 27
Grendon Green. Here 6D 26
Grendon Underwood. Buck 1D 20
Grenofen. Devn 8D 6
Grenoside. S Yor 8M 41
Greosabhagh. W Isl 4C 76
Gresford. Wrex 4B 34
Gresham. Norf 6H 39
Greshornish. High 8E 76
Gressenhall. Norf 8F 38
Gressingham. Lanc 1D 40
Greta Bridge. Dur 4J 47
Gretna. Dum 5H 53
Gretna Green. Dum 5H 53
Gretton. Glos 8J 27
Gretton. Nptn 2G 29
Gretton. Shrp 2D 26
Grewelthorpe. N Yor 8L 47
Greyabbey. Ards 5J 93
Greygarth. N Yor 8K 47
Grey Green. N Lin 7E 42
Greylake. Som 2B 8
Greysouthen. Cumb 2K 45
Greysteel. Caus 2D 92
Greystoke. Cumb 8J 53
Greystoke Gill. Cumb 3C 46
Greystone. Ang 3J 67
Greystones. S Yor 1M 35
Greywell. Hants 8E 20
Griais. W Isl 7H 83
Grianan. W Isl 8H 83
Gribthorpe. E Yor 4E 42
Gribun. Arg 4K 63
Griff. Warw 3A 28
Griffithstown. Torf 4A 18
Griffydam. Leics 8B 36
Griggs Green. Hants 2F 10
Grimbister. Orkn 8C 88
Grimeford Village. Lanc 6E 40
Grimeston. Orkn 8C 88
Grimethorpe. S Yor 7B 42
Griminis. W Isl
on Benbecula 8J 75
on North Uist 6J 75
Grimister. Shet 4J 91
Grimley. Worc 5G 27
Grimness. Orkn 2F 86
Grimoldby. Linc 1L 37
Grimpo. Shrp 7B 34
Grimsargh. Lanc 4D 40
Grimsbury. Oxon 7B 28
Grimsby. NE Lin 7K 43
Grimscote. Nptn 6D 28
Grimscott. Corn 5B 6
Grimshaw. Bkbn 5F 40
Grimshaw Green. Lanc 6C 40
Grimsthorpe. Linc 7H 37
Grimston. E Yor 4K 43
Grimston. Leics 7D 36
Grimston. Norf 7D 38
Grimston. York 2D 42
Grimstone. Dors 6E 8
Grimstone End. Suff 5F 30
Grinacombe Moor. Devn 6D 6
Grindale. E Yor 8J 49
Grindhill. Devn 6D 6
Grindiscol. Shet 4E 90
Grindle. Shrp 1F 26
Grindleford. Derbs 2L 35
Grindleton. Lanc 3F 40
Grindley. Staf 7J 35
Grindley Brook. Shrp 5D 34
Grindlow. Derbs 2K 35
Grindon. Nmbd 5G 61
Grindon. Staf 4J 35
Gringley on the Hill. Notts 8E 42
Grinsdale. Cumb 6H 53
Grinshill. Shrp 7D 34
Grinton. N Yor 6J 47
Griomsidar. W Isl 1F 76
Grishipoll. Arg 2G 63
Grisling Common. E Sus 3M 11
Gristhorpe. N Yor 7H 49
Griston. Norf 2F 30
Gritley. Orkn 1G 87
Grittenham. Wilts 5J 19
Grittleton. Wilts 5G 19
Grizebeck. Cumb 6M 45
Grizedale. Cumb 6B 46
Grobister. Orkn 7F 88
Grobsness. Shet 1D 90
Groby. Leics 1C 28
Groes. Cnwy 4K 33
Groes. Neat 6G 17
Groes-faen. Rhon 6K 17
Groesffordd. Gwyn 7B 32
Groesffordd. Powy 2K 17
Groeslon. Gwyn 5D 32
Groes-lwyd. Powy 1M 25
Groes-wen. Cphy 6L 17
Grogport. Arg 5H 57
Groigearraidh. W Isl 1D 74
Gromford. Suff 6K 31
Gronant. Flin 2K 33
Groombridge. E Sus 2B 12
Groomsport. Ards 4J 93
Grosmont. Mon 1C 18
Grosmont. N Yor 5F 48
Groton. Suff 7F 30
Grove. Dors 8E 8
Grove. Kent 7J 23
Grove. Notts 2E 36
Grove. Oxon 4A 20
The Grove. Dum 4D 52
The Grove. Worc 7G 27
Grovehill. E Yor 4H 43
Grove Park. G Lon 6M 21
Grovesend. Swan 4E 16
Grub Street. Staf 7F 34
Grudie. High 7D 78
Gruids. High 3F 78
Gruinard House. High 4L 77
Gruinart. Arg 3B 56
Grulinbeg. Arg 3B 56
Gruline. Arg 3L 63
Grummore. High 8J 85
Grundisburgh. Suff 6J 31
Gruting. Shet 3C 90
Grutness. Shet 7E 90
Gualachulain. High 3F 64
Gualin House. High 6F 84
Guardbridge. Fife 6H 67
Guarlford. Worc 7G 27
Guay. Per 3D 66
Gubblecote. Herts 2G 21
Guestling Green. E Sus 4E 12
Guestling Thorn. E Sus 4E 12
Guestwick. Norf 7G 39
Guestwick Green. Norf 7G 39
Guide. Bkbn 5F 40
Guide Post. Nmbd 3F 54
Guilden Down. Shrp 3B 26
Guilden Morden. Cambs 7K 29
Guilden Sutton. Ches W 3C 34
Guildford. Surr 109 (1G 11)
Guildtown. Per 4E 66
Guilsborough. Nptn 4D 28
Guilsfield. Powy 1M 25
Guineaford. Devn 2E 6
Guisborough. Red C 4D 48
Guiseley. W Yor 3K 41
Guist. Norf 7F 38
Guiting Power. Glos 1J 19
Gulberwick. Shet 4E 90
Gulladuff. M Ulst 4F 93
Gullane. E Lot 1B 60
Gulling Green. Suff 6E 30
Gulval. Corn 5H 3
Gulworthy. Devn 8D 6
Gumfreston. Pemb 6H 15
Gumley. Leics 2D 28
Gunby. E Yor 4E 42
Gunby. Linc 7G 37
Gundleton. Hants 2D 10
Gun Green. Kent 2D 12
Gun Hill. E Sus 4B 12
Gunn. Devn 2F 6
Gunnerside. N Yor 6H 47
Gunnerton. Nmbd 4C 54
Gunness. N Lin 6F 42
Gunnislake. Corn 8D 6
Gunnista. Shet 3E 90
Gunsgreenhill. Bord 3G 61
Gunstone. Staf 1G 27
Gunthorpe. Norf 6G 39
Gunthorpe. N Lin 8F 42
Gunthorpe. Notts 5D 36
Gunthorpe. Pet 1J 29
Gunville. IOW 7B 10
Gupworthy. Som 2J 7
Gurnard. IOW 6B 10
Gurney Slade. Som 1E 8
Gurnos. Powy 4G 17
Gussage All Saints. Dors 4J 9
Gussage St Andrew. Dors 4H 9
Gussage St Michael. Dors 4H 9
Guston. Kent 1K 13
Gutcher. Shet 4K 91
Guthram Gowt. Linc 7J 37
Guthrie. Ang 2J 67
Guyhirn. Cambs 1M 29
Guyhirn Gull. Cambs 1L 29
Guy's Head. Linc 7A 38
Guy's Marsh. Dors 3G 9
Guyzance. Nmbd 1F 54
Gwaelod-y-garth. Card 6L 17
Gwaenynog Bach. Den 4K 33
Gwaenysgor. Flin 2K 33
Gwalchmai. IOA 3C 32
Gwastad. Pemb 4G 15
Gwaun-Cae-Gurwen. Neat 3G 17
Gwbert. Cdgn 2H 15
Gweek. Corn 6L 3
Gwehelog. Mon 3B 18
Gwenddwr. Powy 8K 25
Gwennap. Corn 4L 3
Gwenter. Corn 7L 3
Gwernaffield. Flin 4M 33
Gwernesney. Mon 3C 18
Gwernogle. Carm 3M 15
Gwern-y-go. Powy 3M 25
Gwernymynydd. Flin 4M 33
Gwersyllt. Wrex 4B 34
Gwespyr. Flin 2L 33
Gwinear. Corn 5J 3
Gwithian. Corn 4J 3
Gwredog. IOA 2D 32
Gwyddelwern. Den 6K 33
Gwyddgrug. Carm 3L 15
Gwynfryn. Wrex 4A 34
Gwystre. Powy 6K 25
Gwytherin. Cnwy 4H 33
Gyfelia. Wrex 5B 34
Gyffin. Cnwy 3G 33

H

Haa of Houlland. Shet 3K 91
Habberley. Shrp 1C 26
Habblesthorpe. Notts 1E 36
Habergham. Lanc 4G 41
Habin. W Sus 3F 10
Habrough. NE Lin 6J 43
Haceby. Linc 6H 37
Hacheston. Suff 6K 31
Hackenthorpe. S Yor 1B 36
Hackford. Norf 1G 31
Hackforth. N Yor 6L 47
Hackland. Orkn 7C 88
Hackleton. Nptn 6F 28
Hackman's Gate. Worc 4G 27
Hackness. N Yor 6G 49
Hackness. Orkn 2E 86
Hackney. G Lon 5L 21
Hackthorn. Linc 1G 37
Hackthorpe. Cumb 3D 46
Haclait. W Isl 1E 74
Haconby. Linc 7J 37
Hadden. Bord 6E 60
Haddenham. Buck 3E 20
Haddenham. Cambs 4A 30
Haddenham End Field.
Cambs 4A 30
Haddington. E Lot 2C 60
Haddington. Linc 3G 37
Haddiscoe. Norf 2L 31
Haddo. Abers 2H 73
Haddon. Cambs 2J 29
Hademore. Staf 1K 27
Hadfield. Derbs 8J 41
Hadham Cross. Herts 2M 21
Hadham Ford. Herts 1M 21
Hadleigh. Essx 5E 22
Hadleigh. Suff 7G 31
Hadleigh Heath. Suff 7F 30
Hadley. Telf 8E 34
Hadley. Worc 5G 27
Hadley End. Staf 7K 35
Hadley Wood. G Lon 4K 21
Hadlow. Kent 1C 12
Hadlow Down. E Sus 3B 12
Hadnall. Shrp 7D 34
Hadstock. Essx 7B 30
Hadston. Nmbd 1F 54
Hady. Derbs 2A 36
Hadzor. Worc 5H 27
Haffenden Quarter. Kent 1E 12
Haggate. Lanc 4G 41
Haggbeck. Cumb 4J 53
Haggersta. Shet 3D 90
Haggerston. Nmbd 5H 61
Haggrister. Shet 6H 91
Hagley. Here 7D 26
Hagley. Worc 3H 27
Hagnaby. Linc 3L 37
Hagworthingham. Linc 3L 37
Haigh. G Man 7E 40
Haigh Moor. W Yor 5L 41
Haighton Green. Lanc 4D 40
Haile. Cumb 4K 45
Hailes. Glos 8J 27
Hailey. Herts 2L 21
Hailey. Oxon 2A 20
Hailsham. E Sus 5B 12
Hail Weston. Cambs 5J 29
Hainault. G Lon 4A 22
Hainford. Norf 8J 39
Hainton. Linc 1J 37
Hainworth. W Yor 4J 41
Haisthorpe. E Yor 1J 43
Hakin. Pemb 6E 14
Halam. Notts 4D 36
Halbeath. Fife 1K 59
Halberton. Devn 4K 7
Halcro. High 5D 86
Hale. Cumb 8D 46
Hale. G Man 1F 34
Hale. Hal 1C 34
Hale. Hants 4K 9
Hale. Surr 1F 10
Hale Bank. Hal 1C 34
Halebarns. G Man 1F 34
Hales. Norf 2K 31
Hales. Staf 6F 34
Halesgate. Linc 7L 37
Hales Green. Derbs 5K 35
Halesowen. W Mid 3H 27
Hale Street. Kent 1C 12
Halesworth. Suff 4K 31
Halewood. Mers 1C 34
Halford. Shrp 3C 26
Halford. Warw 7L 27
Halfpenny. Cumb 7D 46
Halfpenny Furze. Carm 5J 15
Halfpenny Green. Staf 2G 27
Halfway. Carm
nr. Llandeilo 1F 16
nr. Llandovery 1H 17
Halfway. S Yor 1B 36
Halfway. W Ber 7B 20
Halfway House. Shrp 8B 34
Halfway Houses. Kent 6F 22
Halgabron. Corn 3C 4
Halifax. W Yor 5J 41
Halistra. High 8D 76
Halket. E Ayr 4C 58
Halkirk. High 6C 86
Halkyn. Flin 3M 33
Hall. E Ren 4C 58
Hallam Fields. Derbs 5B 36
Halland. E Sus 4B 12
The Hallands. N Lin 5H 43
Hallaton. Leics 2E 28
Hallatrow. Bath 8E 18
Hallbank. Cumb 6E 46
Hallbankgate. Cumb 6K 53
Hall Dunnerdale. Cumb 5M 45
Hallen. S Glo 5D 18
Hall End. Bed 7H 29
Hallgarth. Dur 7G 55
Hall Green. Ches E 4G 35
Hall Green. Norf 3H 31
Hall Green. W Mid 3K 27
Hall Green. W Yor 6M 41
Hall Green. Wrex 5C 34
Halliburton. Bord 5D 60
Hallin. High 8D 76
Halling. Medw 7D 22
Hallington. Linc 1L 37
Hallington. Nmbd 4C 54
Halloughton. Notts 4D 36
Hallow. Worc 6G 27
Hallow Heath. Worc 6G 27
Hallowsgate. Ches W 3D 34
Hallsands. Devn 8L 5
Hall's Green. Herts 1K 21
Hallspill. Devn 3D 6
Hallthwaites. Cumb 6L 45
Hall Waberthwaite. Cumb 5L 45
Hallwood Green. Glos 8E 26
Hallworthy. Corn 7A 6
Hallyne. Bord 5K 59
Halmer End. Staf 5G 35
Halmond's Frome. Here 7E 26
Halmore. Glos 3E 18
Halnaker. W Sus 5G 11
Halsall. Lanc 6B 40
Halse. Nptn 7C 28
Halse. Som 3L 7
Halsetown. Corn 5J 3
Halsham. E Yor 5K 43
Halsinger. Devn 2E 6
Halstead. Essx 8E 30
Halstead. Kent 7A 22
Halstead. Leics 1E 28
Halstock. Dors 5D 8
Halsway. Som 2L 7
Haltcliff Bridge. Cumb 8H 53
Haltham. Linc 3K 37
Haltoft End. Linc 5L 37
Halton. Buck 3F 20
Halton. Hal 1D 34
Halton. Lanc 1D 40
Halton. Nmbd 5C 54
Halton. W Yor 4A 42
Halton. Wrex 6B 34
Halton East. N Yor 2J 41
Halton Fenside. Linc 3M 37
Halton Gill. N Yor 8G 47
Halton Holegate. Linc 3M 37
Halton Lea Gate. Nmbd 6L 53
Halton Moor. W Yor 4M 41
Halton Shields. Nmbd 5D 54
Halton West. N Yor 2G 41
Haltwhistle. Nmbd 5M 53
Halvergate. Norf 1L 31
Halwell. Devn 6K 5
Halwill. Devn 6D 6
Halwill Junction. Devn 6D 6
Ham. Devn 5M 7
Ham. Glos 4E 18
Ham. G Lon 6J 21
Ham. High 4D 86
Ham. Kent 8K 23
Ham. Plym 6G 5
Ham. Shet 4B 90
Ham. Som
nr. Ilminster 4A 8
nr. Taunton 3A 8
nr. Wellington 3L 7
Ham. Wilts 7M 19
Hambleden. Buck 5E 20
Hambledon. Hants 4D 10
Hambledon. Surr 2G 11
Hamble-le-Rice. Hants 5B 10
Hambleton. Lanc 3B 40
Hambleton. N Yor 4C 42
Hambridge. Som 3B 8
Hambrook. S Glo 6E 18
Hambrook. W Sus 5E 10
Ham Common. Dors 3G 9
Hameringham. Linc 3L 37
Hamerton. Cambs 4J 29
Ham Green. Here 7F 26
Ham Green. Kent 7E 22
Ham Green. N Som 6D 18
Ham Green. Worc 5J 27
Ham Hill. Kent 7C 22
Hamilton. Leic 1D 28
Hamilton. S Lan 4F 58
Hamiltonsbawn. Arm 6F 93
Hamister. Shet 1F 90
Hammer. W Sus 2F 10
Hammersmith. G Lon 6K 21
Hammerwich. Staf 1J 27
Hammerwood. E Sus 2M 11
Hammill. Kent 8J 23
Hammond Street. Herts 3L 21
Hammoon. Dors 4G 9
Hamnavoe. Shet
nr. Braehoulland 5G 91
nr. Burland 4D 90
nr. Lunna 6J 91
on Yell 5J 91
Hamp. Som 2B 8
Hampden Park. E Sus 5B 12
Hampen. Glos 2J 19
Hamperden End. Essx 8B 30
Hamperley. Shrp 3C 26
Hampnett. Glos 2J 19
Hampole. S Yor 6C 42
Hampreston. Dors 6J 9
Hampstead. G Lon 5K 21
Hampstead Norreys. W Ber 6C 20
Hampsthwaite. N Yor 2L 41
Hampton. Devn 6A 8
Hampton. G Lon 6J 21
Hampton. Kent 7H 23
Hampton. Shrp 3F 26
Hampton. Swin 4K 19
Hampton. Worc 7J 27
Hampton Bishop. Here 8D 26
Hampton Fields. Glos 4G 19
Hampton Hargate. Pet 2J 29
Hampton Heath. Ches W 5D 34
Hampton in Arden. W Mid 3L 27
Hampton Loade. Shrp 3F 26
Hampton Lovett. Worc 5G 27
Hampton Lucy. Warw 6L 27
Hampton Magna. Warw 5L 27
Hampton on the Hill. Warw 5L 27
Hampton Poyle. Oxon 2C 20
Hampton Wick. G Lon 7J 21
Hamptworth. Wilts 4L 9
Hamrow. Norf 7F 38
Hamsey. E Sus 4M 11
Hamsey Green. Surr 8L 21
Hamstall Ridware. Staf 8K 35
Hamstead. IOW 6B 10
Hamstead. W Mid 2J 27
Hamstead Marshall. W Ber 7B 20
Hamsterley. Dur
nr. Consett 6E 54
nr. Wolsingham 8E 54
Hamsterley Mill. Dur 6E 54
Ham Street. Som 2D 8
Hamstreet. Kent 2G 13
Hamworthy. Pool 6H 9
Hanbury. Staf 7K 35
Hanbury. Worc 5H 27
Hanbury Woodend. Staf 7K 35
Hanby. Linc 6H 37
Hanchurch. Staf 5G 35
Hand and Pen. Devn 6K 7
Handbridge. Ches W 3C 34
Handcross. W Sus 2K 11
Handforth. Ches E 1G 35
Handley. Ches W 4C 34
Handley. Derbs 3A 36
Handsacre. Staf 8J 35
Handsworth. S Yor 1B 36
Handsworth. W Mid 2J 27
Handy Cross. Buck 4F 20
Hanford. Dors 4G 9
Hanford. Stoke 5G 35
Hangersley. Hants 5K 9
Hanging Houghton. Nptn 4E 28
Hanging Langford. Wilts 2J 9
Hangleton. Brig 5K 11
Hangleton. W Sus 5H 11
Hanham. S Glo 6E 18
Hanham Green. S Glo 6E 18
Hankelow. Ches E 5E 34
Hankerton. Wilts 4H 19
Hankham. E Sus 5C 12
Hanley. Stoke **Stoke 116** (5G 35)
Hanley Castle. Worc 7G 27
Hanley Childe. Worc 5E 26
Hanley Swan. Worc 7G 27
Hanley William. Worc 5E 26
Hanlith. N Yor 1H 41
Hanmer. Wrex 6C 34
Hannaborough. Devn 5E 6
Hannaford. Devn 3F 6
Hannah. Linc 2B 38
Hannington. Hants 8C 20
Hannington. Nptn 4F 28
Hannington. Swin 4K 19
Hannington Wick. Swin 4K 19
Hanscombe End. C Beds 8J 29
Hanslope. Mil 7F 28
Hanthorpe. Linc 7H 37
Hanwell. G Lon 5J 21
Hanwell. Oxon 7B 28
Hanwood. Shrp 1C 26
Hanworth. G Lon 6J 21
Hanworth. Norf 6H 39
Happas. Ang 3H 67
Happendon. S Lan 6G 59
Happisburgh. Norf 6K 39
Happisburgh Common.
Norf 7K 39
Hapsford. Ches W 2C 34
Hapton. Lanc 4F 40
Hapton. Norf 2H 31
Harberton. Devn 6K 5
Harbertonford. Devn 6K 5
Harbledown. Kent 8H 23
Harborne. W Mid 3J 27
Harborough Magna. Warw 4B 28
Harbottle. Nmbd 1C 54
Harbourneford. Devn 5K 5
Harbours Hill. Worc 5H 27
Harbridge. Hants 4K 9
Harbury. Warw 5A 28
Harby. Leics 6E 36
Harby. Notts 2F 36
Harcombe. Devn 6L 7
Harcombe Bottom. Devn 6B 8
Harcourt. Corn 5M 3
Harden. W Yor 4J 41
Hardenhuish. Wilts 6H 19
Hardgate. Abers 5G 73
Hardgate. Dum 5C 52
Hardham. W Sus 4H 11
Hardingham. Norf 1G 31
Hardingstone. Nptn 6E 28
Hardings Wood. Staf 4G 35
Hardington. Som 8F 18
Hardington Mandeville. Som 4D 8
Hardington Marsh. Som 5D 8
Hardington Moor. Som 4D 8
Hardley. Hants 5B 10
Hardley Street. Norf 1K 31
Hardmead. Mil 7G 29
Hardraw. N Yor 6G 47
Hardstoft. Derbs 3B 36
Hardway. Hants 5D 10
Hardway. Som 2F 8
Hardwick. Buck 2F 20
Hardwick. Cambs 6L 29
Hardwick. Norf 3J 31
Hardwick. Nptn 5F 28
Hardwick. Oxon
nr. Bicester 1C 20
nr. Witney 3A 20
Hardwick. Shrp 2B 26
Hardwick. S Yor 1B 36
Hardwick. Stoc T 3B 48
Hardwick. W Mid 2J 27
Hardwicke. Glos
nr. Cheltenham 1H 19
nr. Gloucester 2F 18
Hardwicke. Here 7A 26
Hardwick Village. Notts 2D 36
Hardy's Green. Essx 1F 22
Hare. Som 4A 8
Hareby. Linc 3L 37
Hareden. Lanc 2E 40
Harefield. G Lon 4H 21
Hare Green. Essx 1G 23
Hare Hatch. Wok 6F 20
Harehill. Derbs 6K 35
Harehills. W Yor 4M 41
Harehope. Nmbd 7H 61
Harelaw. Dum 4J 53
Harelaw. Dur 6E 54
Hareplain. Kent 2E 12
Haresceugh. Cumb 7L 53
Harescombe. Glos 2G 19
Haresfield. Glos 2G 19
Haresfinch. Mers 8D 40
Hareshaw. N Lan 3G 59
Hare Street. Essx 3M 21
Hare Street. Herts 1L 21
Harewood. W Yor 3M 41
Harewood End. Here 1D 18
Harford. Devn 6J 5
Hargate. Norf 2H 31
Hargatewall. Derbs 2K 35
Hargrave. Ches W 3C 34
Hargrave. Nptn 4H 29
Hargrave. Suff 6D 30
Harker. Cumb 5H 53
Harkland. Shet 5J 91
Harkstead. Suff 8H 31
Harlaston. Staf 8L 35
Harlaxton. Linc 6F 36
Harlech. Gwyn 7E 32
Harlequin. Notts 6D 36
Harlescott. Shrp 8D 34
Harleston. Devn 7K 5
Harleston. Norf 3J 31
Harleston. Suff 5G 31
Harlestone. Nptn 5E 28
Harley. Shrp 1D 26
Harley. S Yor 8A 42
Harling Road. Norf 3F 30
Harlington. C Beds 8H 29
Harlington. G Lon 6H 21
Harlington. S Yor 7B 42
Harlosh. High 1D 68
Harlow. Essx 2M 21
Harlow Hill. Nmbd 5D 54
Harlsey Castle. N Yor 6B 48
Harlthorpe. E Yor 4E 42
Harlton. Cambs 6L 29
Harlyn Bay. Corn 4A 4
Harman's Cross. Dors 7H 9
Harmby. N Yor 7K 47
Harmer Green. Herts 2K 21
Harmer Hill. Shrp 7C 34
Harmondsworth. G Lon 6H 21
Harmston. Linc 3G 37
Harnage. Shrp 1D 26
Harnham. Nmbd 3D 54
Harnham. Wilts 3K 9
Harnhill. Glos 3J 19
Harold Hill. G Lon 4B 22
Haroldston West. Pemb 5E 14
Haroldswick. Shet 2L 91
Harold Wood. G Lon 4B 22
Harome. N Yor 7D 48
Harpenden. Herts 2J 21
Harpford. Devn 6K 7
Harpham. E Yor 1H 43
Harpley. Norf 7D 38
Harpley. Worc 5E 26
Harpole. Nptn 5D 28
Harpsdale. High 6C 86
Harpsden. Oxon 5E 20
Harpswell. Linc 1G 37
Harpurhey. G Man 7G 41
Harpur Hill. Derbs 2J 35
Harraby. Cumb 6J 53
Harracott. Devn 3E 6
Harrapool. High 3H 69
Harrapul. High 3H 69
Harrietfield. Per 5C 66
Harrietsham. Kent 8E 22
Harrington. Cumb 2J 45
Harrington. Linc 2L 37
Harrington. Nptn 3E 28
Harringworth. Nptn 2G 29
Harriseahead. Staf 4G 35
Harriston. Cumb 7F 52
Harrogate. N Yor 110 (2M 41)
Harrold. Bed 6G 29
Harrop Dale. G Man 7J 41
Harrow. G Lon 5J 21
Harrowbarrow. Corn 5F 4
Harrowden. Bed 7H 29
Harrowgate Hill. Darl 4L 47
Harrow on the Hill. G Lon 5J 21
Harrow Weald. G Lon 4J 21
Harry Stoke. S Glo 6E 18
Harston. Cambs 6M 29
Harston. Leics 6F 36
Harswell. E Yor 3F 42
Hart. Hart 8H 55
Hartburn. Nmbd 3D 54
Hartburn. Stoc T 4B 48
Hartest. Suff 6E 30
Hartfield. E Sus 2A 12
Hartford. Cambs 4K 29
Hartford. Ches W 2E 34
Hartford. Som 3J 7
Hartford Bridge. Hants 8E 20
Hartford End. Essx 2C 22
Harthill. Ches W 4D 34
Harthill. N Lan 3H 59
Harthill. S Yor 1B 36
Hartington. Derbs 3K 35
Hartland. Devn 3B 6
Hartland Quay. Devn 3B 6
Hartle. Worc 4H 27
Hartlebury. Worc 4G 27
Hartlepool. Hart 8J 55
Hartley. Cumb 5F 46
Hartley. Kent
nr. Cranbrook 2D 12
nr. Dartford 7C 22
Hartley. Nmbd 4G 55
Hartley Green. Staf 7H 35
Hartley Mauditt. Hants 2E 10
Hartley Wespall. Hants 8D 20
Hartley Wintney. Hants 8E 20
Hartlip. Kent 7E 22
Hartmount Holdings. High 6H 79
Hartoft End. N Yor 6E 48
Harton. N Yor 1E 42
Harton. Shrp 3C 26
Harton. Tyne 5G 55
Hartpury. Glos 1G 19
Hartshead. W Yor 5K 41
Hartshill. Warw 2M 27
Hartshorne. Derbs 7M 35
Hartsop. Cumb 4C 46
Hart Station. Hart 8H 55
Hartswell. Som 3K 7
Hartwell. Nptn 6E 28
Hartwood. Lanc 6D 40
Hartwood. N Lan 4G 59
Harvel. Kent 7C 22
Harvington. Worc
nr. Evesham 7J 27
nr. Kidderminster 4G 27
Harwell. Oxon 5B 20
Harwich. Essx 118 (8J 31)
Harwood. Dur 8B 54
Harwood. G Man 6F 40
Harwood Dale. N Yor 6G 49
Harworth. Notts 8D 42
Hascombe. Surr 2G 11
Haselbech. Nptn 4E 28
Haselbury Plucknett. Som 4C 8
Haseley. Warw 5L 27
Hasfield. Glos 1G 19
Hasguard. Pemb 6E 14
Haskayne. Lanc 7B 40
Hasketon. Suff 6J 31
Hasland. Derbs 3A 36
Haslemere. Surr 2G 11
Haslingden. Lanc 5F 40
Haslingfield. Cambs 6M 29
Haslington. Ches E 4F 34
Hassall. Ches E 4F 34
Hassall Green. Ches E 4F 34
Hassell Street. Kent 1G 13
Hassendean. Bord 7C 60
Hassingham. Norf 1K 31
Hassness. Cumb 3L 45
Hassocks. W Sus 4L 11
Hassop. Derbs 2L 35
Haster. High 6E 86
Hasthorpe. Linc 3A 38
Hastigrow. High 5D 86
Hastingleigh. Kent 1G 13
Hastings. E Sus 5E 12
Hastingwood. Essx 3A 22
Hastoe. Herts 3G 21
Haston. Shrp 7D 34
Haswell. Dur 7G 55
Haswell Plough. Dur 7G 55
Hatch. C Beds 7J 29
Hatch Beauchamp. Som 3B 8
Hatch End. G Lon 4J 21
Hatch Green. Som 4B 8
Hatching Green. Herts 2J 21
Hatchmere. Ches W 2D 34
Hatch Warren. Hants 1D 10
Hatcliffe. NE Lin 7K 43
Hatfield. Here 6D 26
Hatfield. Herts 3K 21
Hatfield. S Yor 7D 42
Hatfield. Worc 6G 27
Hatfield Broad Oak. Essx 2B 22
Hatfield Garden Village.
Herts 3K 21
Hatfield Heath. Essx 2B 22
Hatfield Hyde. Herts 2K 21
Hatfield Peverel. Essx 2D 22
Hatfield Woodhouse. S Yor 7D 42
Hatford. Oxon 4M 19
Hatherden. Hants 8M 19
Hatherleigh. Devn 5E 6
Hathern. Leics 7B 36
Hatherop. Glos 3K 19
Hathersage. Derbs 1L 35
Hathersage Booths. Derbs 1L 35
Hatherton. Ches E 5E 34
Hatherton. Staf 8H 35
Hatley St George. Cambs 6K 29
Hatt. Corn 5F 4
Hattersley. G Man 8H 41
Hattingley. Hants 2D 10
Hatton. Abers 2K 73
Hatton. Derbs 6L 35
Hatton. G Lon 6H 21
Hatton. Linc 2J 37
Hatton. Shrp 2C 26
Hatton. Warr 1E 34
Hatton. Warw 5L 27
Hattoncrook. Abers 3H 73
Hatton Heath. Ches W 3C 34
Hatton of Fintray. Abers 4H 73
Haugh. E Ayr 7C 58
Haugh. Linc 2M 37
Haugham. Linc 1L 37
Haugh Head. Nmbd 7H 61
Haughley. Suff 5G 31
Haughley Green. Suff 5G 31
Haugh of Ballechin. Per 2C 66
Haugh of Glass. Mor 2D 72
Haugh of Urr. Dum 5C 52
Haughton. Ches E 4D 34
Haughton. Notts 2D 36
Haughton. Shrp
nr. Bridgnorth 2E 26
nr. Oswestry 7B 34
nr. Shifnal 1F 26
nr. Shrewsbury 8D 34
Haughton. Staf 7G 35
Haughton Green. G Man 8H 41
Haughton le Skerne. Darl 4M 47
Haultwick. Herts 1L 21
Haunn. Arg 3J 63
Haunn. W Isl 4D 74
Haunton. Staf 8L 35
Hauxton. Cambs 6M 29
Havannah. Ches E 3G 35
Havant. Hants 5E 10
Haven. Here 6C 26
The Haven. W Sus 2H 11
Haven Bank. Linc 4K 37
Havenstreet. IOW 6C 10
Havercroft. W Yor 6A 42
Haverfordwest. Pemb 5F 14
Haverhill. Suff 7C 30
Haverigg. Cumb 7L 45
Havering-Atte-Bower.
G Lon 4B 22
Havering's Grove. Essx 4C 22
Haversham. Mil 7F 28
Haverthwaite. Cumb 7B 46
Haverton Hill. Stoc T 3B 48
Havyatt. Som 2D 8
Hawarden. Flin 3B 34
Hawbridge. Worc 7H 27
Hawcoat. Cumb 7M 45
Hawcross. Glos 8F 26
Hawen. Cdgn 2K 15
Hawes. N Yor 7G 47
Hawes Green. Norf 2J 31
Hawick. Bord 8C 60
Hawkchurch. Devn 5B 8
Hawkedon. Suff 6D 30
Hawkenbury. Kent 1E 12
Hawkeridge. Wilts 8G 19
Hawkerland. Devn 7K 7
Hawkesbury. S Glo 5F 18
Hawkesbury. Warw 3A 28
Hawkesbury Upton. S Glo 5F 18
Hawkes End. W Mid 3L 27
Hawk Green. G Man 1H 35
Hawkhurst. Kent 2D 12
Hawkhurst Common. E Sus 4B 12
Hawkinge. Kent 1J 13
Hawkley. Hants 3E 10
Hawkridge. Som 2H 7
Hawksdale. Cumb 7H 53
Hawkshaw. G Man 6F 40
Hawkshead. Cumb 6B 46
Hawkshead Hill. Cumb 6B 46
Hawkswick. N Yor 8H 47
Hawksworth. Notts 5E 36
Hawksworth. W Yor 3K 41
Hawkwell. Essx 4E 22
Hawley. Hants 8F 20
Hawley. Kent 6B 22
Hawling. Glos 1J 19
Hawnby. N Yor 7C 48
Haworth. W Yor 4J 41
Hawstead. Suff 6E 30
Hawthorn. Dur 7H 55
Hawthorn Hill. Brac 6F 20
Hawthorn Hill. Linc 4K 37
Hawthorpe. Linc 7H 37
Hawton. Notts 4E 36
Haxby. York 2D 42
Haxey. N Lin 8E 42
Haybridge. Shrp 4E 26
Haybridge. Som 1D 8
Haydock. Mers 8D 40
Haydon. Bath 8E 18
Haydon. Dors 4E 8
Haydon. Som 3A 8
Haydon Bridge. Nmbd 5B 54
Haydon Wick. Swin 5K 19
Haye. Corn 5F 4
Hayes. G Lon
nr. Bromley 7M 21
Hayes. G Lon
nr. Uxbridge 5H 21
Hayfield. Derbs 1J 35
Hay Green. Norf 8B 38
Hayhill. E Ayr 8C 58
Haylands. IOW 6C 10
Hayle. Corn 5J 3
Hayley Green. W Mid 3H 27
Hayling Island. Hants 6E 10
Hayne. Devn 5H 7
Haynes. C Beds 7H 29
Haynes West End. C Beds 7H 29
Hay-on-Wye. Powy 8M 25
Hayscastle. Pemb 4E 14
Hayscastle Cross. Pemb 4F 14
Hayshead. Ang 3K 67
Hay Street. Herts 1L 21
Hayton. Aber 5J 73
Hayton. Cumb
nr. Aspatria 7F 52
nr. Brampton 6K 53
Hayton. E Yor 3F 42
Hayton. Notts 1E 36
Hayton's Bent. Shrp 3D 26
Haytor Vale. Devn 8G 7
Haytown. Devn 4C 6
Haywards Heath. W Sus 3L 11
Haywood. S Lan 4H 59
Hazelbank. S Lan 5G 59
Hazelbury Bryan. Dors 5F 8
Hazeleigh. Essx 3E 22
Hazeley. Hants 8E 20
Hazel Grove. G Man 1H 35
Hazelhead. S Yor 7K 41
Hazelslade. Staf 8J 35
Hazel Street. Kent 2C 12
Hazelton Walls. Fife 5G 67
Hazelwood. Derbs 5M 35
Hazlemere. Buck 4F 20
Hazler. Shrp 2C 26
Hazlerigg. Tyne 4F 54
Hazles. Staf 5J 35
Hazleton. Glos 2J 19
Hazon. Nmbd 1E 54
Heacham. Norf 6C 38
Headbourne Worthy. Hants 2B 10
Headcorn. Kent 1E 12
Headingley. W Yor 4L 41
Headington. Oxon 3C 20
Headlam. Dur 4K 47
Headless Cross. Worc 5J 27
Headley. Hants
nr. Haslemere 2F 10
nr. Kingsclere 7C 20
Headley. Surr 8K 21
Headley Down. Hants 2F 10
Headley Heath. Worc 4J 27
Headley Park. Bris 7D 18
Head of Muir. Falk 1G 59
Headon. Notts 2E 36
Heads Nook. Cumb 6J 53
Heage. Derbs 4A 36
Healaugh. N Yor
nr. Grinton 6J 47
nr. York 3C 42
Heald Green. G Man 1G 35
Heale. Devn 1F 6
Healey. G Man 6G 41
Healey. Nmbd 6D 54
Healey. N Yor 7K 47
Healeyfield. Dur 7D 54
Healing. NE Lin 6K 43
Heamoor. Corn 5H 3
Heanish. Arg 3F 62
Heanor. Derbs 5B 36
Heanton Punchardon. Devn 2E 6
Heapham. Linc 1F 36
Heartsease. Powy 6L 25
Heasley Mill. Devn 2G 7
Heaste. High 4H 69
Heath. Derbs 3B 36
The Heath. Norf
nr. Buxton 7J 39
nr. Fakenham 7F 38
nr. Hevingham 7H 39
The Heath. Staf 6J 35
The Heath. Suff 8H 31
Heath and Reach. C Beds 1G 21
Heath Common. W Sus 4J 11
Heathcote. Derbs 3K 35
Heath Cross. Devn 6G 7
Heathencote. Nptn 7E 28
Heath End. Hants 7C 20
Heath End. Leics 7A 36
Heath End. W Mid 1J 27
Heather. Leics 8A 36
Heatherfield. High 1F 68
Heatherton. Derb 6M 35
Heathfield. Cambs 7A 30
Heathfield. Cumb 7F 52
Heathfield. Devn 8H 7
Heathfield. E Sus 3B 12
Heathfield. Ren 3B 58
Heathfield. Som
nr. Lydeard St Lawrence 2L 7
nr. Norton Fitzwarren 3L 7
Heath Green. Worc 4J 27
Heathhall. Dum 4D 52
Heath Hayes. Staf 8J 35
Heath Hill. Shrp 8F 34
Heath House. Som 1C 8
Heathrow Airport. G Lon 119 (6H 21)
Heathstock. Devn 5M 7
Heathton. Shrp 2G 27
Heathtop. Derbs 6L 35
Heath Town. W Mid 2H 27
Heatley. Staf 7J 35
Heatley. Warr 1F 34
Heaton. Lanc 1C 40
Heaton. Staf 3H 35
Heaton. Tyne 5F 54
Heaton. W Yor 4K 41
Heaton Moor. G Man 8G 41
Heaton's Bridge. Lanc 6C 40
Heaverham. Kent 8B 22
Heavitree. Devn 6J 7
Hebburn. Tyne 5G 55
Hebden. N Yor 1J 41
Hebden Bridge. W Yor 5H 41
Hebden Green. Ches W 3E 34
Hebing End. Herts 1L 21
Hebron. Carm 4H 15
Hebron. Nmbd 3E 54
Heck. Dum 3E 52
Heckdyke. Notts 8E 42
Heckfield. Hants 7E 20
Heckfield Green. Suff 4H 31
Heckfordbridge. Essx 1F 22
Heckington. Linc 5J 37
Heckmondwike. W Yor 5L 41
Heddington. Wilts 7H 19
Heddle. Orkn 8C 88
Heddon. Devn 3F 6
Heddon-on-the-Wall. Nmbd 5E 54
Hedenham. Norf 2K 31
Hedge End. Hants 4B 10
Hedgerley. Buck 5G 21
Hedging. Som 3B 8
Hedley on the Hill. Nmbd 6D 54
Hednesford. Staf 8J 35
Hedon. E Yor 5J 43
Hegdon Hill. Here 6D 26
Heglibister. Shet 2D 90
Heighington. Darl 3L 47
Heighington. Linc 3H 37
Heightington. Worc 4F 26
Heights of Brae. High 7F 78
Heights of Fodderty. High 7F 78
Heights of Kinlochewe.
High 7A 78
Heiton. Bord 6E 60
Hele. Devn
nr. Exeter 5J 7
nr. Holsworthy 6C 6
nr. Ilfracombe 1E 6
Hele. Torb 5M 5
Helen's Bay. Ards 4J 93
Helensburgh. Arg 1A 58
Helford. Corn 6L 3
Helhoughton. Norf 7E 38
Helions Bumpstead. Essx 7C 30
Helland. Corn 4C 4
Helland. Som 3B 8
Hellandbridge. Corn 4C 4
Hellesdon. Norf 8J 39
Hellesveor. Corn 4J 3
Hellidon. Nptn 6C 28
Hellifield. N Yor 2G 41
Hellingly. E Sus 4B 12
Hellington. Norf 1K 31
Hellister. Shet 3D 90
Helmdon. Nptn 7C 28
Helmingham. Suff 6H 31
Helmington Row. Dur 8E 54
Helmsdale. High 2L 79
Helmshore. Lanc 5F 40
Helmsley. N Yor 7D 48
Helperby. N Yor 1B 42
Helperthorpe. N Yor 8G 49
Helpringham. Linc 5J 37
Helpston. Pet 1J 29
Helsby. Ches W 2C 34
Helsey. Linc 2B 38
Helston. Corn 6K 3
Helstone. Corn 3C 4
Helton. Cumb 3D 46
Helwith. N Yor 5J 47
Helwith Bridge. N Yor 1G 41
Helygain. Flin 3M 33
The Hem. Shrp 1F 26
Hemblington. Norf 8K 39
Hemel Hempstead. Herts 3H 21
Hemerdon. Devn 6H 5
Hemingbrough. N Yor 4D 42
Hemingby. Linc 2K 37
Hemingfield. S Yor 7A 42
Hemingford Abbots.
Cambs 4K 29
Hemingford Grey. Cambs 4K 29
Hemingstone. Suff 6H 31
Hemington. Leics 7B 36
Hemington. Nptn 3H 29
Hemington. Som 8F 18
Hemley. Suff 7J 31
Hemlington. Midd 4B 48
Hempholme. E Yor 2H 43
Hempnall. Norf 2J 31
Hempnall Green. Norf 2J 31
Hempriggs. High 7E 86
Hemp's Green. Essx 1F 22
Hempstead. Essx 8C 30
Hempstead. Medw 7D 22
Hempstead. Norf
nr. Holt 6H 39
nr. Stalham 7L 39
Hempsted. Glos 2G 19
Hempton. Norf 7F 38
Hempton. Oxon 8B 28
Hemsby. Norf 8L 39
Hemswell. Linc 8G 43
Hemswell Cliff. Linc 1G 37
Hemsworth. Dors 5H 9
Hemsworth. W Yor 6B 42
Hemyock. Devn 4L 7
Henallt. Carm 4L 15
Henbury. Bris 6D 18
Henbury. Ches E 2G 35
Hendomen. Powy 3M 25

Incheril—Lanark

Incheril. High 7M 77
Inchinnan. Ren 3C 58
Inchlaggan. High 5B 70
Inchmichael. Per 5F 66
Inchnadamph. High 1C 78
Inchree. High 1E 64
Inchture. Per 5F 66
Inchyra. Per 5E 66
Indian Queens. Corn 6B 4
Ingatestone. Essx 4C 22
Ingbirchworth. S Yor 7L 41
Ingestre. Staf 7H 35
Ingham. Linc 1G 37
Ingham. Norf 7K 39
Ingham. Suff 4E 30
Ingham Corner. Norf 7K 39
Ingleborough. Norf 8A 38
Ingleby. Derbs 7M 35
Ingleby Arncliffe. N Yor 5B 48
Ingleby Barwick. Stoc T 4B 48
Ingleby Greenhow. N Yor 5C 48
Ingleigh Green. Devn 5F 6
Inglemire. Hull 4H 43
Inglesbatch. Bath 7F 18
Ingleton. Dur 3K 47
Ingleton. N Yor 8E 46
Inglewhite. Lanc 3D 40
Ingoe. Nmbd 4D 54
Ingol. Lanc 4D 40
Ingoldisthorpe. Norf 6C 38
Ingoldmells. Linc 3B 38
Ingoldsby. Linc 6H 37
Ingon. Warw 6L 27
Ingram. Nmbd 8H 61
Ingrave. Essx 4C 22
Ingrow. W Yor 4J 41
Ings. Cumb 6C 46
Ingst. S Glo 5D 18
Ingthorpe. Rut 1G 29
Ingworth. Norf 7H 39
Inishrush. M Ulst 3F 93
Inkberrow. Worc 6J 27
Inkford. Worc 4J 27
Inkpen. W Ber 7A 20
Inkstack. High 4D 86
Innellan. Arg 3L 57
Inner Hope. Devn 8J 5
Innerleith. Fife 6F 66
Innerleithen. Bord 6M 59
Innerleven. Fife 7G 67
Innermessan. Dum 5F 50
Innerwick. E Lot 2E 60
Innerwick. Per 3K 65
Innsworth. Glos 1G 19
Insch. Abers 3F 72
Insh. High 5J 71
Inshegra. High 6E 84
Inshore. High 4F 84
Inskip. Lanc 4C 40
Instow. Devn 2D 6
Intwood. Norf 1H 31
Inver. Abers 6B 72
Inver. High 5J 79
Inver. Per 3D 66
Inverailort. High 7J 69
Inveralligin. High 8K 77
Inverallochy. Abers 7K 81
Inveramsay. Abers 3G 73
Inveran. High 4F 78
Inveraray. Arg 7E 64
Inverarish. High 2G 69
Inverarity. Ang 3H 67
Inverarnan. Stir 6H 65
Inverarnie. High 2G 71
Inverbeg. Arg 8H 65
Inverbervie. Abers 8H 73
Inverboyndie. Abers 7F 80
Invercassley. High 3E 78
Invercharnan. High 3F 64
Inverchoran. High 8C 78
Invercreran. Arg 3E 64
Inverdruie. High 4K 71
Inverebrie. Abers 2J 73
Invereck. Arg 1L 57
Inveresk. E Lot 2M 59
Inveresragan. Arg 4D 64
Inverey. Abers 7L 71
Inverfarigaig. High 3F 70
Invergarry. High 5D 70
Invergeldie. Per 5M 65
Invergordon. High 7H 79
Invergowrie. Per 4G 67
Inverguseran. High 5J 69
Inverharroch. Mor 2C 72
Inverie. High 5J 69
Inverinan. Arg 6D 64
Inverinate. High 3L 69
Inverkeilor. Ang 3K 67
Inverkeithing. Fife 1K 59
Inverkeithny. Abers 1F 72
Inverkip. Inv 2M 57
Inverkirkaig. High 2A 78
Inverlael. High 5B 78
Inverliever Lodge. Arg 7C 64
Inverliver. Arg 4E 64
Inverlochlarig. Stir 6J 65
Inverlochy. High 8B 70
Inverlussa. Arg 1F 56
Inver Mallie. High 7B 70
Invermarkie. Abers 2D 72
Invermoriston. High 4E 70
Invernaver. High 5K 85
Inverneil House. Arg 1H 57
Inverness. High 110 (1G 71)
Inverness Airport. High 8H 79
Invernettie. Abers 1L 73
Inverpolly Lodge. High 2A 78
Inverquhomery. Abers 1K 73
Inverroy. High 7C 70
Inversanda. High 2D 64
Invershiel. High 4L 69
Invershin. High 4F 78
Invershore. High 8D 86
Inversnaid. Stir 7H 65
Inverugie. Abers 1L 73
Inveruglas. Arg 7H 65
Inverurie. Abers 3G 73
Invervar. Per 3L 65
Inverythan. Abers 1G 73
Inwardleigh. Devn 6E 6
Inworth. Essx 2E 22
Iochdar. W Isl 1D 74
Iping. W Sus 3F 10
Ipplepen. Devn 5L 5
Ipsden. Oxon 5D 20
Ipstones. Staf 5J 35
Ipswich. Suff 110 (7H 31)
Irby. Mers 1A 34
Irby in the Marsh. Linc 3A 38
Irby upon Humber. NE Lin 7J 43
Irchester. Nptn 5G 29
Ireby. Cumb 8G 53
Ireby. Lanc 8E 46
Ireland. Shet 5D 90
Ireleth. Cumb 7M 45
Ireshopeburn. Dur 8B 54
Ireton Wood. Derbs 5L 35
Irlam. G Man 8F 40
Irnham. Linc 7H 37
Iron Acton. S Glo 5E 18
Iron Bridge. Cambs 2A 30
Ironbridge. Telf 1E 26
Iron Cross. Warw 6J 27
Ironville. Derbs 4B 36
Irstead. Norf 7K 39
Irthington. Cumb 5J 53
Irthlingborough. Nptn 4G 29
Irton. N Yor 7H 49
Irvine. N Ayr 6B 58
Irvine Mains. N Ayr 6B 58
Irvinestown. Ferm 6C 92
Isabella Pit. Nmbd 3G 55
Isauld. High 5A 86
Isbister. Orkn 8C 88
Isbister. Shet
on Mainland 4H 91
on Whalsay 1F 90
Isfield. E Sus 4A 12
Isham. Nptn 4F 28
Island Carr. N Lin 7G 43
Islay Airport. Arg 4C 56
Isle Abbotts. Som 3B 8
Isle Brewers. Som 3B 8
Isleham. Cambs 4C 30
Isle of Man Airport. IOM 8B 44
Isle of Thanet. Kent 7K 23
Isle of Whithorn. Dum 8K 51
Isle of Wight. IOW 7B 10
Isleornsay. High 4J 69
Islesburgh. Shet 1D 90
Isles of Scilly Airport. IOS 1H 3
Islesteps. Dum 4D 52
Isleworth. G Lon 6J 21
Isley Walton. Leics 7B 36
Islibhig. W Isl 1A 76
Islington. G Lon 5L 21
Islington. Telf 7F 34
Islip. Nptn 4G 29
Islip. Oxon 2C 20
Isombridge. Telf 8E 34
Istead Rise. Kent 7C 22
Itchen. Sotn 4B 10
Itchen Abbas. Hants 2C 10
Itchenor. W Sus 5E 10
Itchen Stoke. Hants 2C 10
Itchingfield. W Sus 3J 11
Itchington. S Glo 5E 18
Itlaw. Abers 8F 80
Itteringham. Norf 6H 39
Itteringham Common. Norf 7H 39
Itton. Devn 6F 6
Itton Common. Mon 4C 18
Ivegill. Cumb 7J 53
Ivelet. N Yor 6H 47
Iverchaolain. Arg 2K 57
Iver Heath. Buck 5H 21
Iveston. Dur 6E 54
Ivetsey Bank. Staf 8G 35
Ivinghoe. Buck 2G 21
Ivinghoe Aston. Buck 2G 21
Ivington. Here 6C 26
Ivington Green. Here 6C 26
Ivybridge. Devn 6J 5
Ivychurch. Kent 3G 13
Ivy Hatch. Kent 8B 22
Ivy Todd. Norf 1E 30
Iwade. Kent 7F 22
Iwerne Courtney. Dors 4G 9
Iwerne Minster. Dors 4G 9
Ixworth. Suff 4F 30
Ixworth Thorpe. Suff 4F 30

J

Jackfield. Shrp 1E 26
Jack Hill. N Yor 2K 41
Jacksdale. Notts 4B 36
Jackton. S Lan 4D 58
Jacobstow. Corn 6A 6
Jacobstowe. Devn 5E 6
Jacobs Well. Surr 8G 21
Jameston. Pemb 7G 15
Jamestown. Dum 2H 53
Jamestown. Fife 1K 59
Jamestown. High 8E 78
Jamestown. W Dun 1B 58
Janetstown. High
nr. Thurso 5B 86
nr. Wick 6E 86
Jarrow. Tyne 5G 55
Jarvis Brook. E Sus 3B 12
Jasper's Green. Essx 1D 22
Jaywick. Essx 2H 23
Jedburgh. Bord 7D 60
Jeffreyston. Pemb 6G 15
Jemimaville. High 7H 79
Jenkins Park. High 5D 70
Jersey Marine. Neat 5G 17
Jesmond. Tyne 5F 54
Jevington. E Sus 5B 12
Jingle Street. Mon 2C 18
Jockey End. Herts 2H 21
Jodrell Bank. Ches E 2F 34
Johnby. Cumb 8J 53
John O'Gaunts. W Yor 5M 41
John o' Groats. High 4E 86
John's Cross. E Sus 3D 12
Johnshaven. Abers 1L 67
Johnson Street. Norf 8K 39
Johnston. Pemb 5F 14
Johnstone. Ren 3C 58
Johnstonebridge. Dum 2E 52
Johnstown. Carm 5L 15
Johnstown. Wrex 5B 34
Jonesborough. New M 7G 93
Joppa. Edin 2M 59
Joppa. S Ayr 8C 58
Jordan Green. Norf 7G 39
Jordans. Buck 4G 21
Jordanston. Pemb 3F 14
Jump. S Yor 7A 42
Jumpers Common. Dors 6K 9
Juniper. Nmbd 6C 54
Juniper Green. Edin 3K 59
Jurby East. IOM 5C 44
Jurby West. IOM 5C 44
Jury's Gap. E Sus 4F 12

K

Kaber. Cumb 4F 46
Kaimend. S Lan 5H 59
Kaimes. Edin 3L 59
Kaimrig End. Bord 5J 59
Kames. Arg 2J 57
Kames. E Ayr 7E 58
Katesbridge. Arm 6H 93
Kea. Corn 4M 3
Keadby. N Lin 6F 42
Keady. Arm 7F 93
Keal Cotes. Linc 3L 37
Kearsley. G Man 7F 40
Kearsney. Kent 1J 13
Kearstwick. Cumb 7E 46
Kearton. N Yor 6H 47
Kearvaig. High 4E 84
Keasden. N Yor 1F 40
Keason. Corn 5F 4
Keckwick. Hal 1D 34
Keddington. Linc 1L 37
Keddington Corner. Linc 1L 37
Kedington. Suff 7D 30
Kedleston. Derbs 5M 35
Kedlock Feus. Fife 6G 67
Keekle. Cumb 3K 45
Keelby. Linc 6J 43
Keele. Staf 5G 35
Keeley Green. Bed 7H 29
Keeston. Pemb 5F 14
Keevil. Wilts 8H 19
Kegworth. Leics 7B 36
Kehelland. Corn 4K 3
Keig. Abers 4F 72
Keighley. W Yor 3J 41
Keilarsbrae. Clac 8B 66
Keillmore. Arg 1F 56
Keillor. Per 3F 66
Keillour. Per 5C 66
Keills. Arg 3D 56
Keiloch. Abers 6A 72
Keils. Arg 3E 56
Keinton Mandeville. Som 2D 8
Keir Mill. Dum 2C 52
Keirsleywell Row. Nmbd 6A 54
Keisby. Linc 7H 37
Keisley. Cumb 3F 46
Keiss. High 5E 86
Keith. Mor 8D 80
Keith Inch. Abers 1L 73
Kelbrook. Lanc 3H 41
Kelby. Linc 5H 37
Keld. Cumb 4D 46
Keld. N Yor 5G 47
Keldholme. N Yor 7E 48
Kelfield. N Lin 7F 42
Kelfield. N Yor 4C 42
Kelham. Notts 4E 36
Kellacott. Devn 7D 6
Kellan. Arg 3L 63
Kellas. Ang 4H 67
Kellas. Mor 8A 80
Kellaton. Devn 8L 5
Kelleth. Cumb 5E 46
Kelling. Norf 5G 39
Kellingley. N Yor 5C 42
Kellington. N Yor 5C 42
Kelloe. Dur 8G 55
Kelloholm. Dum 8F 58
Kells. Cumb 3J 45
Kells. ME Ant 4G 93
Kelly. Devn 7C 6
Kelly Bray. Corn 8C 6
Kelmarsh. Nptn 4E 28
Kelmscott. Oxon 4L 19
Kelsale. Suff 5K 31
Kelsall. Ches W 3D 34
Kelshall. Herts 8L 29
Kelsick. Cumb 6F 52
Kelso. Bord 6E 60
Kelstedge. Derbs 3M 35
Kelstern. Linc 8K 43
Kelsterton. Flin 2A 34
Kelston. Bath 7F 18
Keltneyburn. Per 3A 66
Kelton. Dum 4D 52
Kelton Hill. Dum 6B 52
Kelty. Fife 8E 66
Kelvedon. Essx 2E 22
Kelvedon Hatch. Essx 4B 22
Kelvinside. Glas 3D 58
Kelynack. Corn 5G 3
Kemback. Fife 6H 67
Kemberton. Shrp 1F 26
Kemble. Glos 4H 19
Kemerton. Worc 8H 27
Kemeys Commander. Mon 3B 18
Kemnay. Abers 4G 73
Kempe's Corner. Kent 1G 13
Kempley. Glos 1E 18
Kempley Green. Glos 1E 18
Kempsey. Worc 7G 27
Kempsford. Glos 4K 19
Kemps Green. Warw 4K 27
Kempshott. Hants 1D 10
Kempston. Bed 7H 29
Kempston Hardwick. Bed 7H 29
Kempton. Shrp 3B 26
Kemp Town. Brig 5L 11
Kemsing. Kent 8B 22
Kemsley. Kent 7F 22
Kenardington. Kent 2F 12
Kenchester. Here 7C 26
Kencot. Oxon 3L 19
Kendal. Cumb 6D 46
Kendleshire. S Glo 6E 18
Kendray. S Yor 7A 42
Kenfig. B'end 6H 17
Kenfig Hill. B'end 6H 17
Kengharair. Arg 3K 63
Kenilworth. Warw 4L 27
Kenknock. Stir 4J 65
Kenley. G Lon 8L 21
Kenley. Shrp 1D 26
Kenmore. High 8J 77
Kenmore. Per 3A 66
Kenn. Devn 7J 7
Kenn. N Som 7C 18
Kennacraig. Arg 3H 57
Kenneggy Downs. Corn 6J 3
Kennerleigh. Devn 5H 7
Kennet. Clac 8C 66
Kennethmont. Abers 3E 72
Kennett. Cambs 5D 30
Kennford. Devn 7J 7
Kenninghall. Norf 3G 31
Kennington. Kent 1G 13
Kennington. Oxon 3C 20
Kennoway. Fife 7G 67
Kennyhill. Suff 4C 30
Kennythorpe. N Yor 1E 42
Kenovay. Arg 3E 62
Kensaleyre. High 8F 76
Kensington. G Lon 6K 21
Kenstone. Shrp 7D 34
Kensworth. C Beds 2H 21
Kensworth Common.
C Beds 2H 21
Kentallen. High 2E 64
Kentchurch. Here 1C 18
Kentford. Suff 5D 30
Kentisbeare. Devn 5K 7
Kentisbury. Devn 1F 6
Kentisbury Ford. Devn 1F 6
Kentmere. Cumb 5C 46
Kenton. Devn 7J 7
Kenton. G Lon 5J 21
Kenton. Suff 5H 31
Kenton Bankfoot. Tyne 5F 54
Kentra. High 1M 63
Kentrigg. Cumb 6D 46
Kents Bank. Cumb 8B 46
Kent's Green. Glos 1F 18
Kent's Oak. Hants 3M 9
Kent Street. E Sus 4D 12
Kent Street. Kent 8C 22
Kent Street. W Sus 3K 11
Kenwick. Shrp 6C 34
Kenwyn. Corn 4M 3
Kenyon. Warr 8E 40
Keoldale. High 5F 84
Keppoch. High 3L 69
Kepwick. N Yor 6B 48
Keresley. W Mid 3M 27
Keresley Newland. Warw 3M 27
Keristal. IOM 7C 44
Kerne Bridge. Here 2D 18
Kerridge. Ches E 2H 35
Kerris. Corn 6H 3
Kerrow. High 2D 70
Kerry. Powy 4L 25
Kerrycroy. Arg 3L 57
Kerry's Gate. Here 8B 26
Kersall. Notts 3E 36
Kersbrook. Devn 7K 7
Kerse. Ren 4B 58
Kersey. Suff 7G 31
Kershopefoot. Cumb 3J 53
Kersoe. Worc 7H 27
Kerswell. Devn 5K 7
Kerswell Green. Worc 7G 27
Kesgrave. Suff 7J 31
Kesh. Ferm 5B 92
Kessingland. Suff 3M 31
Kessingland Beach. Suff 3M 31
Kestle. Corn 7B 4
Kestle Mill. Corn 6A 4
Keston. G Lon 7M 21
Keswick. Cumb 3A 46
Keswick. Norf
nr. North Walsham 6K 39
nr. Norwich 1J 31
Ketsby. Linc 2L 37
Kettering. Nptn 4F 28
Ketteringham. Norf 1H 31
Kettins. Per 4F 66
Kettlebaston. Suff 6F 30
Kettlebridge. Fife 7G 67
Kettlebrook. Staf 1L 27
Kettleburgh. Suff 5J 31
Kettleholm. Dum 4F 52
Kettleness. N Yor 4F 48
Kettleshulme. Ches E 2H 35
Kettlesing. N Yor 2L 41
Kettlesing Bottom. N Yor 2L 41
Kettlestone. Norf 6F 38
Kettlethorpe. Linc 2F 36
Kettletoft. Orkn 6F 88
Kettlewell. N Yor 8H 47
Ketton. Rut 1G 29
Kew. G Lon 6J 21
Kewaigue. IOM 7C 44
Kewstoke. N Som 7B 18
Kexbrough. S Yor 7L 41
Kexby. Linc 1F 36
Kexby. York 2E 42
Keyford. Som 1F 8
Key Green. Ches E 3G 35
Key Green. N Yor 5F 48
Keyham. Leics 1D 28
Keyhaven. Hants 6M 9
Keyhead. Abers 8K 81
Keyingham. E Yor 5K 43
Keymer. W Sus 4L 11
Keynsham. Bath 7E 18
Keysoe. Bed 5H 29
Keysoe Row. Bed 5H 29
Key's Toft. Linc 4A 38
Keyston. Cambs 4H 29
Key Street. Kent 7E 22
Keyworth. Notts 6D 36
Kibblesworth. Tyne 6F 54
Kibworth Beauchamp.
Leics 2D 28
Kibworth Harcourt. Leics 2D 28
Kidbrooke. G Lon 6M 21
Kidburngill. Cumb 2K 45
Kiddemore Green. Staf 1G 27
Kidderminster. Worc 4G 27
Kiddington. Oxon 1B 20
Kidd's Moor. Norf 1H 31
Kidlington. Oxon 2B 20
Kidmore End. Oxon 6D 20
Kidnal. Ches W 5C 34
Kidsgrove. Staf 4G 35
Kidstones. N Yor 7H 47
Kidwelly. Carm 6L 15
Kiel Crofts. Arg 4D 64
Kielder. Nmbd 2L 53
Kilbagie. Fife 8C 66
Kilbarchan. Ren 3C 58
Kilbeg. High 5H 69
Kilberry. Arg 3G 57
Kilbirnie. N Ayr 4B 58
Kilbride. Arg 5C 64
Kilbride. High 3G 69
Kilbucho Place. Bord 6J 59
Kilburn. Derbs 5A 36
Kilburn. G Lon 5K 21
Kilburn. N Yor 8C 48
Kilby. Leics 2D 28
Kilchattan. Arg 8J 63
Kilchattan Bay. Arg 4L 57
Kilchenzie. Arg 7F 56
Kilcheran. Arg 4C 64
Kilchiaran. Arg 3B 56
Kilchoan. High
nr. Inverie 6J 69
nr. Tobermory 1K 63
Kilchoman. Arg 3B 56
Kilchrenan. Arg 5E 64
Kilclief. New M 6J 93
Kilconquhar. Fife 7H 67
Kilcoo. New M 7H 93
Kilcot. Glos 1E 18
Kilcoy. High 8F 78
Kilcreggan. Arg 1M 57
Kildale. N Yor 5D 48
Kildary. High 6H 79
Kildermorie Lodge. High 6F 78
Kildonan. Dum 6F 50
Kildonan. High
nr. Helmsdale 1K 79
on Isle of Skye 8E 76
Kildonan. N Ayr 7K 57
Kildonnan. High 7F 68
Kildrummy. Abers 4D 72
Kildwick. N Yor 3J 41
Kilfillan. Dum 6H 51
Kilfinan. Arg 2J 57
Kilfinnan. High 6C 70
Kilgetty. Pemb 6H 15
Kilgour. Fife 7F 66
Kilgrammie. S Ayr 1H 51
Kilham. E Yor 1H 43
Kilham. Nmbd 6F 60
Kilkeel. New M 7H 93
Kilkenneth. Arg 3E 62
Kilkhampton. Corn 4B 6
Killadeas. Ferm 6C 92
Killamarsh. Derbs 1B 36
Killandrist. Arg 3C 64
Killay. Swan 5F 16
Killean. Arg 5F 56
Killearn. Stir 1D 58
Killeen. M Ulst 5F 93
Killellan. Arg 8F 56
Killen. Derr 4C 92
Killen. High 8G 79
Killerby. Darl 4K 47
Killeter. Derr 4C 92
Killichonan. Per 2K 65
Killiechronan. Arg 3L 63
Killiecrankie. Per 1C 66
Killilan. High 2L 69
Killimster. High 6E 86
Killin. Stir 4K 65
Killinchy. Ards 5J 93
Killinghall. N Yor 2L 41
Killington. Cumb 7E 46
Killingworth. Tyne 4F 54
Killin Lodge. High 5F 70
Killinochonoch. Arg 8C 64
Killochyett. Bord 5B 60
Killough. New M 7J 93
Killowen. New M 7G 93
Killundine. High 3L 63
Killylea. Arm 6E 92
Killyleagh. New M 6J 93
Killyrammer. Caus 2F 93
Kilmacolm. Inv 3B 58
Kilmahog. Stir 7L 65
Kilmahumaig. Arg 8B 64
Kilmalieu. High 2C 64
Kilmaluag. High 6F 76
Kilmany. Fife 5G 67
Kilmarie. High 4G 69
Kilmarnock. E Ayr 110 (6C 58)
Kilmaron. Fife 6G 67
Kilmartin. Arg 8C 64
Kilmaurs. E Ayr 5C 58
Kilmelford. Arg 6C 64
Kilmeny. Arg 3C 56
Kilmersdon. Som 8E 18
Kilmeston. Hants 3C 10
Kilmichael Glassary. Arg 8C 64
Kilmichael of Inverlussa.
Arg 1G 57
Kilmington. Devn 6A 8
Kilmington. Wilts 2F 8
Kilmoluaig. Arg 3E 62
Kilmorack. High 1E 70
Kilmore. Arg 5C 64
Kilmore. Arm 6F 93
Kilmore. High 5H 69
Kilmore. New M 6J 93
Kilmory. Arg 2G 57
Kilmory. High
nr. Kilchoan 8G 69
on Rùm 5E 68
Kilmory. N Ayr 7J 57
Kilmory Lodge. Arg 7B 64
Kilmote. High 2K 79
Kilmuir. High
nr. Dunvegan 1D 68
nr. Invergordon 6H 79
nr. Inverness 1G 71
nr. Uig 6E 76
Kilmun. Arg 1L 57
Kilnave. Arg 2B 56
Kilncadzow. S Lan 5G 59
Kilndown. Kent 2D 12
Kiln Green. Here 2E 18
Kiln Green. Wok 6F 20
Kilnhill. Cumb 8G 53
Kilnhurst. S Yor 8B 42
Kilninian. Arg 3J 63
Kilninver. Arg 5C 64
Kiln Pit Hill. Nmbd 6D 54
Kilnsea. E Yor 6M 43
Kilnsey. N Yor 1H 41
Kilnwick. E Yor 3G 43
Kiloran. Arg 8J 63
Kilpatrick. N Ayr 7J 57
Kilpeck. Here 8C 26
Kilpin. E Yor 5E 42
Kilpin Pike. E Yor 5E 42
Kilrea. Caus 3F 93
Kilrenny. Fife 7J 67
Kilsby. Nptn 4C 28
Kilspindie. Per 5F 66
Kilsyth. N Lan 2F 58
Kiltarlity. High 1F 70
Kilton. Som 1L 7
Kilton Thorpe. Red C 4D 48
Kilvaxter. High 7E 76
Kilve. Som 1L 7
Kilvington. Notts 5F 36
Kilwinning. N Ayr 5A 58
Kimberley. Norf 1G 31
Kimberley. Notts 5B 36
Kimblesworth. Dur 7F 54
Kimble Wick. Buck 3F 20
Kimbolton. Cambs 5H 29
Kimbolton. Here 5D 26
Kimcote. Leics 3C 28
Kimmeridge. Dors 8H 9
Kimmerston. Nmbd 6G 61
Kimpton. Hants 1L 9
Kimpton. Herts 2J 21
Kinallen. Arm 6H 93
Kinawley. Ferm 7C 92
Kinbeachie. High 7G 79
Kinbrace. High 8L 85
Kinbuck. Stir 7A 66
Kincaple. Fife 6H 67
Kincardine. Fife 1H 59
Kincardine. High 5G 79
Kincardine Bridge. Falk 1H 59
Kincardine O'Neil. Abers 6E 72
Kinchrackine. Arg 5F 64
Kincorth. Aber 5J 73
Kincraig. High 5J 71
Kincraigie. Per 3C 66
Kindallachan. Per 2C 66
Kineton. Glos 1J 19
Kineton. Warw 6M 27
Kinfauns. Per 5E 66
Kingairloch. High 2C 64
Kingarth. Arg 4K 57
Kingcoed. Mon 3C 18
King Edward. Abers 8G 81
Kingerby. Linc 8H 43
Kingham. Oxon 1L 19
Kingholm Quay. Dum 4D 52
Kinghorn. Fife 1L 59
Kingie. High 5B 70
Kinglassie. Fife 8F 66
Kingledores. Bord 7K 59
King o' Muirs. Clac 8B 66
Kingoodie. Per 5G 67
King's Acre. Here 7C 26
Kingsand. Corn 6G 5
Kingsash. Buck 3F 20
Kingsbarns. Fife 6J 67
Kingsbridge. Devn 7K 5
Kingsbridge. Som 2J 7
King's Bromley. Staf 8K 35
Kingsburgh. High 8E 76
Kingsbury. G Lon 5J 21
Kingsbury. Warw 2L 27
Kingsbury Episcopi. Som 3C 8
Kings Caple. Here 1D 18
Kingscavil. W Lot 2J 59
Kingsclere. Hants 8C 20
King's Cliffe. Nptn 2H 29
Kings Clipstone. Notts 3D 36
Kingscote. Glos 4G 19
Kingscott. Devn 4E 6
Kings Coughton. Warw 6J 27
Kingscross. N Ayr 7K 57
Kingsdon. Som 3D 8
Kingsdown. Kent 1K 13
Kingsdown. Swin 5K 19
Kingsdown. Wilts 7G 19
Kingseat. Fife 8E 66
Kingsey. Buck 3E 20
Kingsfold. Lanc 5D 40
Kingsfold. W Sus 2J 11
Kingsford. E Ayr 5C 58
Kingsford. Worc 3G 27
Kingsforth. N Lin 6H 43
Kingsgate. Kent 6K 23
King's Green. Glos 8F 26
Kingshall Street. Suff 5F 30
Kingsheanton. Devn 2E 6
King's Heath. W Mid 3J 27
Kings Hill. Kent 8C 22
Kingsholm. Glos 2G 19
Kingshouse. High 2G 65
Kingshouse. Stir 5K 65
Kingshurst. W Mid 3K 27
Kingskerswell. Devn 5L 5
Kingskettle. Fife 7G 67
Kingsland. Here 5C 26
Kingsland. IOA 2B 32
Kings Langley. Herts 3H 21
Kingsley. Ches W 2D 34
Kingsley. Hants 2E 10
Kingsley. Staf 5J 35
Kingsley Green. W Sus 2F 10
Kingsley Holt. Staf 5J 35
King's Lynn. Norf 7C 38
King's Meaburn. Cumb 3E 46
Kings Moss. Mers 7D 40
Kings Muir. Bord 6L 59
Kingsmuir. Ang 3H 67
Kingsmuir. Fife 7J 67
King's Newnham. Warw 4B 28
King's Newton. Derbs 7A 36
Kingsnorth. Kent 2G 13
Kingsnorth. Medw 6E 22
King's Norton. Leics 1D 28
King's Norton. W Mid 4J 27
King's Nympton. Devn 4F 6
King's Pyon. Here 6C 26
Kings Ripton. Cambs 4K 29
King's Somborne. Hants 2A 10
King's Stag. Dors 4F 8
King's Stanley. Glos 3G 19
King's Sutton. Nptn 8B 28
Kingstanding. W Mid 2J 27
Kingsteignton. Devn 8H 7
Kingsteps. High 8K 79
King Sterndale. Derbs 2J 35
King's Thorn. Here 8D 26
Kingsthorpe. Nptn 5E 28
Kingston. Cambs 6L 29
Kingston. Devn 7J 5
Kingston. Dors
nr. Sturminster Newton 5F 8
nr. Swanage 8H 9
Kingston. E Lot 1C 60
Kingston. Hants 5K 9
Kingston. IOW 7B 10
Kingston. Kent 8H 23
Kingston. Mor 7C 80
Kingston. W Sus 5H 11
Kingston Bagpuize. Oxon 4B 20
Kingston Blount. Oxon 4E 20
Kingston by Sea. W Sus 5K 11
Kingston Deverill. Wilts 2G 9
Kingstone. Here 8C 26
Kingstone. Som 4B 8
Kingstone. Staf 7J 35
Kingston Lisle. Oxon 5M 19
Kingston Maurward. Dors 6F 8
Kingston near Lewes.
E Sus 5L 11
Kingston on Soar. Notts 7C 36
Kingston Russell. Dors 6D 8
Kingston St Mary. Som 3M 7
Kingston Seymour. N Som 7C 18
Kingston Stert. Oxon 3E 20
Kingston upon Hull.
Hull 110 (5J 43)
Kingston upon Thames.
G Lon 7J 21
King's Walden. Herts 1J 21
Kingswear. Devn 6L 5
Kingswells. Aber 5H 73
Kingswinford. W Mid 3G 27
Kingswood. Buck 2D 20
Kingswood. Glos 4F 18
Kingswood. Here 6A 26
Kingswood. Kent 8E 22
Kingswood. Per 4D 66
Kingswood. Powy 2M 25
Kingswood. Som 2L 7
Kingswood. S Glo 6E 18
Kingswood. Surr 8K 21
Kingswood. Warw 4K 27
Kingswood Common. Staf 1G 27
Kings Worthy. Hants 2B 10
Kingthorpe. Linc 2J 37
Kington. Here 6A 26
Kington. S Glo 4E 18
Kington. Worc 6H 27
Kington Langley. Wilts 6H 19
Kington Magna. Dors 3F 8
Kington St Michael. Wilts 6H 19
Kingussie. High 5H 71
Kingweston. Som 2D 8
Kinharrachie. Abers 2J 73
Kinhrive. High 6G 79
Kinkell Bridge. Per 6C 66
Kinknockie. Abers 1K 73
Kinkry Hill. Cumb 4K 53
Kinlet. Shrp 3F 26
Kinloch. High
nr. Lochaline 2A 64
nr. Loch More 8F 84
on Rùm 6E 68
Kinloch. Per 3E 66
Kinlochard. Stir 7J 65
Kinlochbervie. High 6E 84
Kinlocheil. High 8L 69
Kinlochewe. High 7M 77
Kinloch Hourn. High 5L 69
Kinloch Laggan. High 7F 70
Kinlochleven. High 1F 64
Kinloch Lodge. High 6H 85
Kinlochmoidart. High 8J 69
Kinlochmore. High 1F 64
Kinloch Rannoch. Per 2L 65
Kinlochspelve. Arg 5A 64
Kinloid. High 7H 69
Kinloss. Mor 7L 79
Kinmel Bay. Cnwy 2J 33
Kinmuck. Abers 4H 73
Kinnadie. Abers 1J 73
Kinnaird. Per 5F 66
Kinneff. Abers 8H 73
Kinnelhead. Dum 1E 52
Kinnell. Ang 2K 67
Kinnerley. Shrp 7B 34
Kinnernie. Abers 5G 73
Kinnersley. Here 7B 26
Kinnersley. Worc 7G 27
Kinnerton. Powy 6M 25
Kinnerton. Shrp 2B 26
Kinnesswood. Per 7E 66
Kinninvie. Dur 3J 47
Kinnordy. Ang 2G 67
Kinoulton. Notts 6D 36
Kinross. Per 7E 66
Kinrossie. Per 4E 66
Kinsbourne Green. Herts 2J 21
Kinsey Heath. Ches E 5E 34
Kinsham. Here 5B 26
Kinsham. Worc 8H 27
Kinsley. W Yor 6B 42
Kinson. Bour 6J 9
Kintbury. W Ber 7A 20
Kintessack. Mor 7L 79
Kintillo. Per 6E 66
Kinton. Here 4C 26
Kinton. Shrp 8B 34
Kintore. Abers 4G 73
Kintour. Arg 4D 56
Kintra. Arg 5J 63
Kintraw. Arg 7C 64
Kinveachy. High 4K 71
Kinver. Staf 3G 27
Kinwarton. Warw 6K 27
Kiplingcotes. E Yor 3G 43
Kippax. W Yor 4B 42
Kippen. Stir 8L 65
Kippford. Dum 6C 52
Kipping's Cross. Kent 1C 12
Kirbister. Orkn
nr. Hobbister 1E 86
nr. Quholm 8B 88
Kirbuster. Orkn 7F 88
Kirby Bedon. Norf 1J 31
Kirby Bellars. Leics 8E 36
Kirby Cane. Norf 2K 31
Kirby Cross. Essx 1J 23
Kirby Fields. Leics 1C 28
Kirby Green. Norf 2K 31
Kirby Grindalythe. N Yor 1G 43
Kirby Hill. N Yor
nr. Richmond 5K 47
nr. Ripon 1A 42
Kirby Knowle. N Yor 7B 48
Kirby-le-Soken. Essx 1J 23
Kirby Misperton. N Yor 8E 48
Kirby Muxloe. Leics 1C 28
Kirby Sigston. N Yor 6B 48
Kirby Underdale. E Yor 2F 42
Kirby Wiske. N Yor 7A 48
Kircubbin. Ards 5K 93
Kirdford. W Sus 3H 11
Kirk. High 6D 86
Kirkabister. Shet
on Bressay 4E 90
on Mainland 2E 90
Kirkandrews. Dum 7M 51
Kirkandrews-on-Eden.
Cumb 6H 53
Kirkapol. Arg 3F 62
Kirkbampton. Cumb 6H 53
Kirkbean. Dum 6D 52
Kirk Bramwith. S Yor 6D 42
Kirkbride. Cumb 6G 53
Kirkbridge. N Yor 6L 47
Kirkbuddo. Ang 3J 67
Kirkburn. E Yor 2G 43
Kirkburton. W Yor 6K 41
Kirkby. Linc 8H 43
Kirkby. Mers 8C 40
Kirkby. N Yor 5C 48
Kirkby Fenside. Linc 3L 37
Kirkby Fleetham. N Yor 6L 47
Kirkby Green. Linc 4H 37
Kirkby-in-Ashfield. Notts 4C 36
Kirkby-in-Furness. Cumb 6M 45
Kirkby la Thorpe. Linc 5J 37
Kirkby Lonsdale. Cumb 8E 46
Kirkby Malham. N Yor 1G 41
Kirkby Mallory. Leics 1B 28
Kirkby Malzeard. N Yor 8L 47
Kirkby Mills. N Yor 7E 48
Kirkbymoorside. N Yor 7D 48
Kirkby on Bain. Linc 3K 37
Kirkby Overblow. N Yor 3M 41
Kirkby Stephen. Cumb 5F 46
Kirkby Thore. Cumb 3E 46
Kirkby Underwood. Linc 7H 37
Kirkby Wharfe. N Yor 3C 42
Kirkcaldy. Fife 8F 66
Kirkcambeck. Cumb 5K 53
Kirkcolm. Dum 5F 50
Kirkconnel. Dum 8F 58
Kirkconnell. Dum 5D 52
Kirkcowan. Dum 5J 51
Kirkcudbright. Dum 6A 52
Kirkdale. Mers 8B 40
Kirk Deighton. N Yor 2A 42
Kirk Ella. E Yor 5H 43
Kirkfieldbank. S Lan 5G 59
Kirkforthar Feus. Fife 7F 66
Kirkgunzeon. Dum 5C 52
Kirk Hallam. Derbs 5B 36
Kirkham. Lanc 4C 40
Kirkham. N Yor 1E 42
Kirkhamgate. W Yor 5L 41
Kirk Hammerton. N Yor 2B 42
Kirkharle. Nmbd 3D 54
Kirkheaton. Nmbd 4D 54
Kirkheaton. W Yor 6K 41
Kirkhill. Ang 1K 67
Kirkhill. High 1F 70
Kirkhope. S Lan 1D 52
Kirkhouse. Bord 6M 59
Kirkibost. High 4G 69
Kirkinch. Ang 3G 67
Kirkinner. Dum 6K 51
Kirkintilloch. E Dun 2E 58
Kirk Ireton. Derbs 4L 35
Kirkland. Cumb
nr. Cleator Moor 3K 45
nr. Penrith 8L 53
nr. Wigton 7G 53
Kirkland. Dum
nr. Kirkconnel 8F 58
nr. Moniaive 2C 52
Kirkland Guards. Cumb 7F 52
Kirk Langley. Derbs 6L 35
Kirklauchline. Dum 6F 50
Kirkleatham. Red C 3C 48
Kirklevington. Stoc T 5B 48
Kirkley. Suff 2M 31
Kirklington. N Yor 7M 47
Kirklington. Notts 4D 36
Kirklinton. Cumb 5J 53
Kirkliston. Edin 2K 59
Kirkmabreck. Dum 6K 51
Kirkmaiden. Dum 8G 51
Kirk Merrington. Dur 8F 54
Kirk Michael. IOM 5C 44
Kirkmichael. Per 1D 66
Kirkmichael. S Ayr 1J 51
Kirkmuirhill. S Lan 5F 58
Kirknewton. Nmbd 6G 61
Kirknewton. W Lot 3J 59
Kirkney. Abers 2E 72
Kirk of Shotts. N Lan 3G 59
Kirkoswald. Cumb 7K 53
Kirkoswald. S Ayr 1H 51
Kirkpatrick. Dum 2D 52
Kirkpatrick Durham. Dum 4B 52
Kirkpatrick-Fleming. Dum 4G 53
Kirk Sandall. S Yor 7D 42
Kirksanton. Cumb 6L 45
Kirk Smeaton. N Yor 6C 42
Kirkstall. W Yor 4L 41
Kirkstile. Dum 2H 53
Kirkstyle. High 4E 86
Kirkthorpe. W Yor 5A 42
Kirkton. Abers
nr. Alford 4F 72
nr. Insch 3F 72
nr. Turriff 1H 73
Kirkton. Ang
nr. Dundee 4H 67
nr. Forfar 3H 67
nr. Tarfside 7D 72
Kirkton. Dum 3D 52
Kirkton. Fife 5G 67
Kirkton. High
nr. Golspie 4H 79
nr. Kyle of Lochalsh 3K 69
nr. Lochcarron 1L 69
Kirkton. Bord 8C 60
Kirkton. S Lan 7H 59
Kirktonhill. W Dun 2B 58
Kirkton Manor. Bord 6L 59
Kirkton of Airlie. Ang 2G 67
Kirkton of Auchterhouse.
Ang 4G 67
Kirkton of Bourtie. Abers 3H 73
Kirkton of Collace. Per 4E 66
Kirkton of Craig. Ang 2L 67
Kirkton of Culsalmond.
Abers 2F 72
Kirkton of Durris. Abers 6G 73
Kirkton of Glenbuchat.
Abers 4C 72
Kirkton of Glenisla. Ang 1F 66
Kirkton of Kingoldrum. Ang 2G 67
Kirkton of Largo. Fife 7H 67
Kirkton of Lethendy. Per 3E 66
Kirkton of Logie Buchan.
Abers 3J 73
Kirkton of Maryculter.
Abers 6H 73
Kirkton of Menmuir. Ang 1J 67
Kirkton of Monikie. Ang 4J 67
Kirkton of Oyne. Abers 3F 72
Kirkton of Rayne. Abers 2F 72
Kirkton of Skene. Abers 5H 73
Kirktown. Abers
nr. Fraserburgh 7J 81
nr. Peterhead 8K 81
Kirktown of Alvah. Abers 7F 80
Kirktown of Auchterless.
Abers 1G 73
Kirktown of Deskford. Mor 7E 80
Kirktown of Fetteresso.
Abers 7H 73
Kirktown of Mortlach. Mor 2C 72
Kirktown of Slains. Abers 3K 73
Kirkurd. Bord 5K 59
Kirkwall. Orkn 8D 88
Kirkwall Airport. Orkn 1F 86
Kirkwhelpington. Nmbd 3C 54
Kirk Yetholm. Bord 7F 60
Kirmington. N Lin 6J 43
Kirmond le Mire. Linc 8J 43
Kirn. Arg 2L 57
Kirriemuir. Ang 2G 67
Kirstead Green. Norf 2J 31
Kirtlebridge. Dum 4G 53
Kirtleton. Dum 4G 53
Kirtling. Cambs 6C 30
Kirtling Green. Cambs 6C 30
Kirtlington. Oxon 2C 20
Kirtomy. High 5K 85
Kirton. Linc 6L 37
Kirton. Notts 3D 36
Kirton. Suff 8J 31
Kirton End. Linc 5K 37
Kirton Holme. Linc 5K 37
Kirton in Lindsey. N Lin 8G 43
Kishorn. High 1K 69
Kislingbury. Nptn 6D 28
Kites Hardwick. Warw 5B 28
Kittisford. Som 3K 7
Kittle. Swan 6E 16
Kittybrewster. Aber 5J 73
Kitwood. Hants 2D 10
Kivernoll. Here 8C 26
Kiveton Park. S Yor 1B 36
Knaith. Linc 1F 36
Knaith Park. Linc 1F 36
Knaphill. Surr 8G 21
Knapp. Hants 3B 10
Knapp. Per 4F 66
Knapp. Som 3B 8
Knapperfield. High 6D 86
Knapton. Norf 6K 39
Knapton. York 2C 42
Knapton Green. Here 6C 26
Knapwell. Cambs 5L 29
Knaresborough. N Yor 2A 42
Knarsdale. Nmbd 6L 53
Knatts Valley. Kent 7B 22
Knaven. Abers 1H 73
Knayton. N Yor 7B 48
Knebworth. Herts 1K 21
Knedlington. E Yor 5E 42
Kneesall. Notts 3E 36
Kneesworth. Cambs 7L 29
Kneeton. Notts 5E 36
Knelston. Swan 8L 15
Knenhall. Staf 6H 35
Knightacott. Devn 2F 6
Knightcote. Warw 6B 28
Knightcott. N Som 8B 18
Knightley. Staf 7G 35
Knightley Dale. Staf 7G 35
Knightlow Hill. Warw 4B 28
Knighton. Devn 7H 5
Knighton. Dors 4E 8
Knighton. Leic 1C 28
Knighton. Powy 4A 26
Knighton. Som 1L 7
Knighton. Staf
nr. Eccleshall 7F 34
nr. Woore 5F 34
Knighton. Wilts 6L 19
Knighton. Worc 6J 27
Knighton Common. Worc 4E 26
Knight's End. Cambs 2M 29
Knightswood. Glas 3D 58
Knightwick. Worc 6F 26
Knill. Here 5A 26
Knipton. Leics 6F 36
Knitsley. Dur 7E 54
Kniveton. Derbs 4L 35
Knock. Arg 4L 63
Knock. Cumb 3E 46
Knock. Mor 8E 80
Knockally. High 1M 79
Knockan. Arg 5K 63
Knockan. High 2C 78
Knockandhu. Mor 3B 72
Knockando. Mor 1A 72
Knockarthur. High 3H 79
Knockbain. High 8G 79
Knockbreck. High 7D 76
Knockcloghrim. M Ulst 4F 93
Knockdee. High 5C 86
Knockdolian. S Ayr 3G 51
Knockdon. S Ayr 8B 58
Knockdown. Glos 5G 19
Knockenbaird. Abers 3F 72
Knockenkelly. N Ayr 7K 57
Knockentiber. E Ayr 6B 58
Knockfarrel. High 8F 78
Knockglass. High 5B 86
Knockholt. Kent 8A 22
Knockholt Pound. Kent 8A 22
Knockie Lodge. High 4E 70
Knockin. Shrp 7B 34
Knockinlaw. E Ayr 6C 58
Knockinnon. High 8C 86
Knocknacarry. Caus 2H 93
Knockrome. Arg 2E 56
Knocksharry. IOM 6B 44
Knockshinnoch. E Ayr 8C 58
Knockvennie. Dum 4B 52
Knockvologan. Arg 6J 63
Knodishall. Suff 5L 31
Knole. Som 3C 8
Knollbury. Mon 5C 18
Knolls Green. Ches E 2G 35
Knolton. Wrex 6B 34
Knook. Wilts 1H 9
Knossington. Leics 1F 28
Knott. High 8E 76
Knott End-on-Sea. Lanc 3B 40
Knotting. Bed 5H 29
Knotting Green. Bed 5H 29
Knottingley. W Yor 5B 42
Knotts. Cumb 3C 46
Knotty Ash. Mers 8C 40
Knotty Green. Buck 4G 21
Knowbury. Shrp 4D 26
Knowe. Dum 4J 51
Knowefield. Cumb 6J 53
Knowehead. Dum 2M 51
Knowes. E Lot 2D 60
Knowesgate. Nmbd 3C 54
Knoweside. S Ayr 8A 58
Knowes of Elrick. Abers 8F 80
Knowle. Bris 6E 18
Knowle. Devn
nr. Braunton 2D 6
nr. Budleigh Salterton 7K 7
nr. Crediton 5G 7
Knowle. Shrp 4D 26
Knowle. W Mid 4K 27
Knowle Green. Lanc 4E 40
Knowle St Giles. Som 4B 8
Knowlesands. Shrp 2F 26
Knowle Village. Hants 5C 10
Knowl Hill. Wind 6F 20
Knowlton. Kent 8J 23
Knowsley. Mers 8C 40
Knowstone. Devn 3H 7
Knucklas. Powy 4A 26
Knuston. Nptn 5G 29
Knutsford. Ches E 2F 34
Knypersley. Staf 4G 35
Krumlin. W Yor 6J 41
Kuggar. Corn 7L 3
Kyleakin. High 3J 69
Kyle of Lochalsh. High 3J 69
Kylerhea. High 3J 69
Kylesku. High 8E 84
Kyles Lodge. W Isl 5A 76
Kylesmorar. High 6K 69
Kylestrome. High 8E 84
Kymin. Mon 2D 18
Kynaston. Here 8E 26
Kynaston. Shrp 7B 34
Kynnersley. Telf 8E 34
Kyre Green. Worc 5E 26
Kyre Park. Worc 5E 26
Kyrewood. Worc 5E 26

L

Labost. W Isl 7F 82
Lacasaidh. W Isl 1E 76
Lacasdail. W Isl 8H 83
Laceby. NE Lin 7K 43
Lacey Green. Buck 3F 20
Lach Dennis. Ches W 2F 34
Lache. Ches W 3B 34
Lack. Ferm 5C 92
Lackagh. Caus 3E 92
Lackford. Suff 4D 30
Lacock. Wilts 7H 19
Ladbroke. Warw 6B 28
Laddingford. Kent 1C 12
Lade Bank. Linc 4L 37
Ladock. Corn 6A 4
Lady. Orkn 5F 88
Ladybank. Fife 6G 67
Ladycross. Corn 7C 6
Lady Green. Mers 7B 40
Lady Hall. Cumb 6L 45
Ladykirk. Bord 5F 60
Ladysford. Abers 7J 81
Ladywood. W Mid 3J 27
Ladywood. Worc 5G 27
Laga. High 1M 63
Lagavulin. Arg 5D 56
Lagg. Arg 2E 56
Lagg. N Ayr 7J 57
Laggan. Arg 4B 56
Laggan. High
nr. Fort Augustus 6C 70
nr. Newtonmore 6G 71
Laggan. Mor 2C 72
Lagganlia. High 5J 71
Lagganulva. Arg 3K 63
Laghey Corner. M Ulst 5F 93
Laglingarten. Arg 7F 64
Lagness. W Sus 5F 10
Laid. High 6G 85
Laide. High 4K 77
Laigh Fenwick. E Ayr 5C 58
Laindon. Essx 5C 22
Lairg. High 3F 78
Lairg Muir. High 3F 78
Laithes. Cumb 8J 53
Laithkirk. Dur 3H 47
Lake. Devn 2E 6
Lake. IOW 7C 10
Lake. Wilts 2K 9
Lakenham. Norf 1J 31
Lakenheath. Suff 3D 30
Lakesend. Norf 2B 30
Lakeside. Cumb 7B 46
Laleham. Surr 7H 21
Laleston. B'end 6H 17
Lamancha. Bord 4L 59
Lamarsh. Essx 8E 30
Lamas. Norf 7J 39
Lamb Corner. Essx 8G 31
Lambden. Bord 5E 60
Lamberhead Green. G Man 7D 40
Lamberhurst. Kent 2C 12
Lamberhurst Quarter. Kent 2C 12
Lamberton. Bord 4G 61
Lambeth. G Lon 6L 21
Lambfell Moar. IOM 6B 44
Lambhill. Glas 3D 58
Lambley. Nmbd 6L 53
Lambley. Notts 5D 36
Lambourn. W Ber 6M 19
Lambourne End. Essx 4A 22
Lambourn Woodlands.
W Ber 6M 19
Lambs Green. Dors 6H 9
Lambs Green. W Sus 2K 11
Lambston. Pemb 5F 14
Lamellion. Corn 5E 4
Lamerton. Devn 8D 6
Lamesley. Tyne 6F 54
Laminess. Orkn 6F 88
Lamington. High 6H 79
Lamington. S Lan 6H 59
Lamlash. N Ayr 6K 57
Lamonby. Cumb 8J 53
Lamorick. Corn 5C 4
Lamorna. Corn 6H 3
Lamorran. Corn 7A 4
Lampeter. Cdgn 8E 24
Lampeter Velfrey. Pemb 5H 15
Lamphey. Pemb 6G 15
Lamplugh. Cumb 2K 45
Lamport. Nptn 4E 28
Lamyatt. Som 2E 8
Lana. Devn
nr. Ashwater 6C 6
nr. Holsworthy 5C 6
Lanark. S Lan 5G 59

Lanarth—Llansanffraid Glan Conwy

Lanarth. *Corn* 6L 3
Lancaster. *Lanc* 1C 40
Lanchester. *Dur* 7E 54
Lancing. *W Sus* 5J 11
Landbeach. *Cambs* 5A 30
Landcross. *Devn* 3D 6
Landerberry. *Abers* 5G 73
Landford. *Wilts* 4L 9
Land Gate. *G Man* 7D 40
Landhallow. *High* 8C 86
Landimore. *Swan* 7L 15
Landkey. *Devn* 2E 6
Landkey Newland. *Devn* 2E 6
Landore. *Swan* 5F 16
Landport. *Port* 5D 10
Landrake. *Corn* 5F 4
Landscove. *Devn* 5K 5
Land's End Airport. *Corn* 6G 3
Landshipping. *Pemb* 5G 15
Landulph. *Corn* 5G 5
Landywood. *Staf* 1H 27
Lane. *Corn* 2M 3
Laneast. *Corn* 7B 6
Lane Bottom. *Lanc* 4G 41
Lane End. *Buck* 4F 20
Lane End. *Hants* 3C 10
Lane End. *IOW* 7D 10
Lane End. *Wilts* 1G 9
Lane Ends. *Derbs* 6L 35
Lane Ends. *Dur* 8E 54
Lane Ends. *Lanc* 2F 40
Laneham. *Notts* 2F 36
Lane Head. *Dur*
nr. Hutton Magna 4K 47
nr. Woodland 3J 47
Lane Head. *G Man* 8E 40
Lane Head. *W Yor* 7K 41
Lanehead. *Dur* 7B 54
Lanehead. *Nmbd* 3A 54
Lane Heads. *Lanc* 4C 40
Lanercost. *Cumb* 5K 53
Laneshaw Bridge. *Lanc* 3H 41
Laney Green. *Staf* 1H 27
Langais. *W Isl* 7K 75
Langal. *High* 1B 64
Langar. *Notts* 6E 36
Langbank. *Ren* 2B 58
Langbar. *N Yor* 2J 41
Langburnshiels. *Bord* 1K 53
Langcliffe. *N Yor* 1G 41
Langdale End. *N Yor* 6G 49
Langdon. *Corn* 6B 6
Langdon Beck. *Dur* 8B 54
Langdon Cross. *Corn* 7C 6
Langdon Hills. *Essx* 5C 22
Langdown. *Hants* 5B 10
Langdyke. *Fife* 7G 67
Langenhoe. *Essx* 2G 23
Langford. *C Beds* 7J 29
Langford. *Devn* 5K 7
Langford. *Essx* 3E 22
Langford. *Notts* 4F 36
Langford. *Oxon* 3L 19
Langford. *Som* 3M 7
Langford Budville. *Som* 3L 7
Langham. *Dors* 3F 8
Langham. *Essx* 8G 31
Langham. *Norf* 5G 39
Langham. *Rut* 8F 36
Langham. *Suff* 5F 30
Langho. *Lanc* 4F 40
Langholm. *Dum* 3H 53
Langland. *Swan* 6F 16
Langleeford. *Nmbd* 7G 61
Langley. *Ches E* 2H 35
Langley. *Derbs* 5B 36
Langley. *Essx* 8M 29
Langley. *Glos* 1J 19
Langley. *Hants* 5B 10
Langley. *Herts* 1K 21
Langley. *Kent* 8E 22
Langley. *Nmbd* 5B 54
Langley. *Slo* 6H 21
Langley. *Som* 3K 7
Langley. *Warw* 5K 27
Langley. *W Sus* 3F 10
Langley Burrell. *Wilts* 6H 19
Langleybury. *Herts* 3H 21
Langley Common. *Derbs* 6L 35
Langley Green. *Derbs* 6L 35
Langley Green. *Norf* 1K 31
Langley Green. *Warw* 5K 27
Langley Green. *W Sus* 2K 11
Langley Heath. *Kent* 8E 22
Langley Marsh. *Som* 3K 7
Langley Moor. *Dur* 7F 54
Langley Park. *Dur* 7F 54
Langley Street. *Norf* 1K 31
Langney. *E Sus* 5C 12
Langold. *Notts* 1C 36
Langore. *Corn* 7B 6
Langport. *Som* 3C 8
Langrick. *Linc* 5K 37
Langridge. *Bath* 7F 18
Langridgeford. *Devn* 3E 6
Langrigg. *Cumb* 7F 52
Langrish. *Hants* 3E 10
Langsett. *S Yor* 7L 41
Langshaw. *Bord* 6C 60
Langstone. *Hants* 5E 10
Langthorne. *N Yor* 6L 47
Langthorpe. *N Yor* 1A 42
Langthwaite. *N Yor* 5J 47
Langtoft. *E Yor* 1H 43
Langtoft. *Linc* 8J 37
Langton. *Dur* 4K 47
Langton. *Linc*
nr. Horncastle 3K 37
nr. Spilsby 2L 37
Langton. *N Yor* 1E 42
Langton by Wragby. *Linc* 2J 37
Langton Green. *Kent* 2B 12
Langton Herring. *Dors* 7E 8
Langton Long Blandford.
Dors 5G 9
Langton Matravers. *Dors* 8H 9
Langtree. *Devn* 4D 6
Langwathby. *Cumb* 8K 53
Langwith. *Derbs* 2C 36
Langworth. *Linc* 2H 37
Lanivet. *Corn* 5C 4
Lanjeth. *Corn* 6B 4
Lank. *Corn* 4C 4
Lanlivery. *Corn* 6C 4
Lanner. *Corn* 5L 3
Lanreath. *Corn* 6D 4
Lansallos. *Corn* 6D 4
Lansdown. *Bath* 7F 18
Lansdown. *Glos* 1H 19
Lanteglos Highway. *Corn* 6D 4
Lanton. *Nmbd* 6G 61
Lanton. *Bord* 7D 60
Lapford. *Devn* 5G 7
Lapford Cross. *Devn* 5G 7
Laphroaig. *Arg* 5C 56
Lapley. *Staf* 8G 35
Lapworth. *Warw* 4K 27
Larachbeg. *High* 3A 64
Larbert. *Falk* 1G 59
Larden Green. *Ches E* 4D 34
Larel. *High* 6C 86
Largie. *Abers* 2F 72
Largiemore. *Arg* 1J 57
Largoward. *Fife* 7H 67
Largs. *N Ayr* 4M 57
Largue. *Abers* 1F 72
Largybeg. *N Ayr* 7K 57
Largymeanoch. *N Ayr* 7K 57
Largymore. *N Ayr* 7K 57
Larkfield. *Inv* 2M 57
Larkfield. *Kent* 8D 22
Larkhall. *Bath* 7F 18
Larkhall. *S Lan* 4F 58
Larkhill. *Wilts* 1K 9
Larling. *Norf* 3F 30
Larne. *ME Ant* 3J 93
Larport. *Here* 8D 26
Lartington. *Dur* 4J 47
Lary. *Abers* 5C 72
Lasham. *Hants* 1D 10
Lashenden. *Kent* 1E 12
Lasswade. *Midl* 3M 59
Lastingham. *N Yor* 6E 48
Latchford. *Herts* 1L 21
Latchford. *Oxon* 3D 20
Latchingdon. *Essx* 3E 22
Latchley. *Corn* 8D 6
Latchmere Green. *Hants* 8D 20
Lathbury. *Mil* 7F 28
Latheron. *High* 8C 86
Latheronwheel. *High* 8C 86
Lathom. *Lanc* 7C 40
Lathones. *Fife* 7H 67
Latimer. *Buck* 4H 21
Latteridge. *S Glo* 5E 18
Lattiford. *Som* 3E 8
Latton. *Wilts* 4J 19
Laudale House. *High* 2B 64
Lauder. *Bord* 5C 60
Laugharne. *Carm* 5K 15
Laughterton. *Linc* 2F 36
Laughton. *E Sus* 4B 12
Laughton. *Leics* 3D 28
Laughton. *Linc*
nr. Gainsborough 8F 42
nr. Grantham 6H 37
Laughton Common. *S Yor* 1C 36
Laughton en le Morthen.
S Yor 1C 36
Launcells. *Corn* 5B 6
Launceston. *Corn* 7C 6
Launcherley. *Som* 1D 8
Launton. *Oxon* 1D 20
Laurelvale. *Arm* 6G 93
Laurencekirk. *Abers* 8G 73
Laurieston. *Dum* 5A 52
Laurieston. *Falk* 2H 59
Lavendon. *Mil* 6G 29
Lavenham. *Suff* 7F 30
Laverhay. *Dum* 2F 52
Laversdale. *Cumb* 5J 53
Laverstock. *Wilts* 2K 9
Laverstoke. *Hants* 1B 10
Laverton. *Glos* 8J 27
Laverton. *N Yor* 8L 47
Laverton. *Som* 8F 18
Lavister. *Wrex* 4B 34
Law. *S Lan* 4G 59
Lawers. *Per* 4L 65
Lawford. *Essx* 8G 31
Lawhitton. *Corn* 7C 6
Lawkland. *N Yor* 1F 40
Lawley. *Telf* 1E 26
Lawnhead. *Staf* 7G 35
Lawrencetown. *Arm* 6G 93
Lawrenny. *Pemb* 6G 15
Lawshall. *Suff* 6E 30
Lawton. *Here* 6C 26
Laxey. *IOM* 6D 44
Laxfield. *Suff* 4J 31
Laxfirth. *Shet* 2E 90
Laxo. *Shet* 1E 90
Laxton. *E Yor* 5E 42
Laxton. *Nptn* 2G 29
Laxton. *Notts* 3E 36
Laycock. *W Yor* 3J 41
Layer Breton. *Essx* 2F 22
Layer-de-la-Haye. *Essx* 1F 22
Layer Marney. *Essx* 2F 22
Laymore. *Dors* 5B 8
Laysters Pole. *Here* 5D 26
Layter's Green. *Buck* 4G 21
Laytham. *E Yor* 4E 42
Lazenby. *Red C* 4C 48
Lazonby. *Cumb* 8K 53
Lea. *Derbs* 4M 35
Lea. *Here* 1E 18
Lea. *Linc* 1F 36
Lea. *Shrp*
nr. Bishop's Castle 3B 26
nr. Shrewsbury 1C 26
Lea. *Wilts* 5H 19
Leabrooks. *Derbs* 4B 36
Leac a Li. *W Isl* 4C 76
Leachd. *Arg* 8E 64
Leachkin. *High* 1G 71
Leachpool. *Pemb* 5F 14
Leadburn. *Midl* 4L 59
Leadenham. *Linc* 4G 37
Leaden Roding. *Essx* 2B 22
Leaderfoot. *Bord* 6C 60
Leadgate. *Cumb* 7M 53
Leadgate. *Dur* 6E 54
Leadgate. *Nmbd* 6E 54
Leadhills. *S Lan* 8G 59
Leadingcross Green. *Kent* 8E 22
Lea End. *Worc* 4J 27
Leafield. *Oxon* 2M 19
Leagrave. *Lutn* 1H 21
Lea Hall. *W Mid* 3K 27
Lea Heath. *Staf* 7J 35
Leake. *N Yor* 6B 48
Leake Common Side. *Linc* 4L 37
Leake Fold Hill. *Linc* 4M 37
Leake Hurn's End. *Linc* 5M 37
Lealholm. *N Yor* 5E 48
Lealt. *Arg* 8A 64
Lealt. *High* 7G 77
Leam. *Derbs* 2L 35
Lea Marston. *Warw* 2L 27
Leamington Hastings.
Warw 5B 28
Leamington Spa, Royal.
Warw 5M 27
Leamonsley. *Staf* 1K 27
Leamside. *Dur* 7G 55
Leargybreck. *Arg* 2E 56
Lease Rigg. *N Yor* 5F 48
Leasgill. *Cumb* 7C 46
Leasingham. *Linc* 5H 37
Leasingthorne. *Dur* 8F 54
Leasowe. *Mers* 8A 40
Leatherhead. *Surr* 8J 21
Leathley. *N Yor* 3L 41
Leaths. *Dum* 5B 52
Leaton. *Shrp* 8C 34
Leaton. *Telf* 8E 34
Lea Town. *Lanc* 4C 40
Leaveland. *Kent* 8G 23
Leavenheath. *Suff* 8F 30
Leavening. *N Yor* 1E 42
Leaves Green. *G Lon* 7M 21
Lea Yeat. *Cumb* 7F 46
Leazes. *Dur* 6E 54
Lebberston. *N Yor* 7H 49
Lechlade on Thames. *Glos* 4L 19
Leck. *Lanc* 8E 46
Leckford. *Hants* 2A 10
Leckfurin. *High* 6K 85
Leckgruinart. *Arg* 3B 56
Leckhampstead. *Buck* 8E 28
Leckhampstead. *W Ber* 6B 20
Leckhampton. *Glos* 2H 19
Leckmelm. *High* 4B 78
Leckwith. *V Glam* 7L 17
Leconfield. *E Yor* 3H 43
Ledaig. *Arg* 4D 64
Ledburn. *Buck* 1G 21
Ledbury. *Here* 8F 26
Ledgemoor. *Here* 6C 26
Ledgowan. *High* 8B 78
Ledicot. *Here* 5C 26
Ledmore. *High* 2C 78
Lednabirichen. *High* 4H 79
Lednagullin. *High* 5L 85
Ledsham. *Ches W* 2B 34
Ledsham. *W Yor* 5B 42
Ledston. *W Yor* 5B 42
Ledstone. *Devn* 7K 5
Ledwell. *Oxon* 1B 20
Lee. *Devn*
nr. Ilfracombe 1D 6
nr. South Molton 3H 7
Lee. *G Lon* 6L 21
Lee. *Hants* 4A 10
Lee. *Lanc* 2D 40
Lee. *Shrp* 6C 34
The Lee. *Buck* 3G 21
Leeans. *Shet* 3D 90
Leebotten. *Shet* 5E 90
Leebotwood. *Shrp* 2C 26
Lee Brockhurst. *Shrp* 7D 34
Leece. *Cumb* 8M 45
Leechpool. *Mon* 5D 18
Lee Clump. *Buck* 3G 21
Leeds. *Kent* 8E 22
Leeds. *W Yor* 110 (4L 41)
Leeds Bradford Airport.
W Yor 3L 41
Leedstown. *Corn* 5K 3
Leegomery. *Telf* 8E 34
Lee Head. *Derbs* 8J 41
Leek. *Staf* 4H 35
Leekbrook. *Staf* 4H 35
Leek Wootton. *Warw* 5L 27
Lee Mill. *Devn* 6H 5
Leeming. *N Yor* 7L 47
Leeming Bar. *N Yor* 6L 47
Lee Moor. *Devn* 5H 5
Lee Moor. *W Yor* 5M 41
Lee-on-the-Solent. *Hants* 5C 10
Lees. *Derbs* 6L 35
Lees. *G Man* 7H 41
Lees. *W Yor* 4J 41
The Lees. *Kent* 8G 23
Leeswood. *Flin* 3A 34
Leetown. *Per* 5F 66
Leftwich. *Ches W* 2E 34
Legbourne. *Linc* 1L 37
Legburthwaite. *Cumb* 4B 46
Legerwood. *Bord* 5C 60
Legsby. *Linc* 1J 37
Leicester. *Leic* 110 (1C 28)
Leicester Forest East. *Leics* 1C 28
Leigh. *Dors* 5E 8
Leigh. *G Man* 7E 40
Leigh. *Kent* 1B 12
Leigh. *Shrp* 1B 26
Leigh. *Surr* 1K 11
Leigh. *Wilts* 4J 19
Leigh. *Worc* 6F 26
The Leigh. *Glos* 1G 19
Leigham. *Plym* 6H 5
Leigh Beck. *Essx* 5E 22
Leigh Common. *Som* 3F 8
Leigh Delamere. *Wilts* 6G 19
Leigh Green. *Kent* 2F 12
Leighland Chapel. *Som* 2K 7
Leigh-on-Sea. *S'end* 5E 22
Leigh Park. *Hants* 5E 10
Leigh Sinton. *Worc* 6F 26
Leighterton. *Glos* 4G 19
Leighton. *N Yor* 8K 47
Leighton. *Powy* 2M 25
Leighton. *Shrp* 1E 26
Leighton. *Som* 1F 8
Leighton Bromswold.
Cambs 4J 29
Leighton Buzzard. *C Beds* 1G 21
Leigh-upon-Mendip. *Som* 1E 8
Leinthall Earls. *Here* 5C 26
Leinthall Starkes. *Here* 5C 26
Leintwardine. *Here* 4C 26
Leire. *Leics* 2C 28
Leirinmore. *High* 5G 85
Leishmore. *High* 1E 70
Leiston. *Suff* 5L 31
Leitfie. *Per* 3F 66
Leith. *Edin* 2L 59
Leitholm. *Bord* 5E 60
Leitrim. *New M* 7H 93
Lelant. *Corn* 5J 3
Lelant Downs. *Corn* 5J 3
Lelley. *E Yor* 4K 43
Lem Hill. *Shrp* 4F 26
Lemington. *Tyne* 5E 54
Lempitlaw. *Bord* 6E 60
Lemsford. *Herts* 2K 21
Lenacre. *Cumb* 7E 46
Lenchie. *Abers* 2E 72
Lenchwick. *Worc* 7J 27
Lendalfoot. *S Ayr* 3G 51
Lendrick. *Stir* 7K 65
Lenham. *Kent* 8E 22
Lenham Heath. *Kent* 1F 12
Lenimore. *N Ayr* 5H 57
Lennel. *Bord* 5F 60
Lennoxtown. *E Dun* 2E 58
Lenton. *Linc* 6H 37
Lentran. *High* 1F 70
Lenwade. *Norf* 8G 39
Lenzie. *E Dun* 2E 58
Leochel Cushnie. *Abers* 4E 72
Leogh. *Shet* 2M 89
Leominster. *Here* 6C 26
Leonard Stanley. *Glos* 3G 19
Lepe. *Hants* 6B 10
Lephenstrath. *Arg* 1B 50
Lephin. *High* 1C 68
Lephinchapel. *Arg* 8D 64
Lephinmore. *Arg* 8D 64
Leppington. *N Yor* 1E 42
Lepton. *W Yor* 6L 41
Lerryn. *Corn* 6D 4
Lerwick. *Shet* 3E 90
Lerwick (Tingwall) Airport.
Shet 3E 90
Lesbury. *Nmbd* 8K 61
Leslie. *Abers* 3E 72
Leslie. *Fife* 7F 66
Lesmahagow. *S Lan* 6G 59
Lesnewth. *Corn* 2D 4
Lessingham. *Norf* 7K 39
Lessonhall. *Cumb* 6G 53
Leswalt. *Dum* 5F 50
Letchmore Heath. *Herts* 4J 21
Letchworth Garden City.
Herts 8K 29
Letcombe Bassett. *Oxon* 5A 20
Letcombe Regis. *Oxon* 5A 20
Letham. *Ang* 3J 67
Letham. *Falk* 1G 59
Letham. *Fife* 6G 67
Lethanhill. *E Ayr* 8C 58
Lethenty. *Abers* 1H 73
Letheringham. *Suff* 6J 31
Letheringsett. *Norf* 6G 39
Lettaford. *Devn* 7G 7
Lettan. *Orkn* 5G 89
Letter. *Abers* 4G 73
Letterewe. *High* 6L 77
Letterfearn. *High* 3K 69
Lettermore. *Arg* 3K 63
Letters. *High* 5B 78
Lettershendoney. *Derr* 3D 92
Letterston. *Pemb* 4F 14
Letton. *Here*
nr. Kington 7B 26
nr. Leintwardine 4B 26
Letty Green. *Herts* 2K 21
Letwell. *S Yor* 1C 36
Leuchars. *Fife* 5H 67
Leumrabhagh. *W Isl* 2E 76
Leusdon. *Devn* 8G 7
Levaneap. *Shet* 1E 90
Levedale. *Staf* 8G 35
Leven. *E Yor* 3J 43
Leven. *Fife* 7G 67
Levencorroch. *N Ayr* 7K 57
Levenhall. *E Lot* 2A 60
Levens. *Cumb* 7C 46
Levens Green. *Herts* 1L 21
Levenshulme. *G Man* 8G 41
Levenwick. *Shet* 5E 90
Leverburgh. *W Isl* 5B 76
Leverington. *Cambs* 8M 37
Leverton. *Linc* 5L 37
Leverton. *W Ber* 6M 19
Leverton Lucasgate. *Linc* 5M 37
Leverton Outgate. *Linc* 5M 37
Levington. *Suff* 8J 31
Levisham. *N Yor* 6F 48
Levishie. *High* 4E 70
Lew. *Oxon* 3M 19
Lewaigue. *IOM* 5D 44
Lewannick. *Corn* 7B 6
Lewdown. *Devn* 7D 6
Lewes. *E Sus* 4M 11
Leweston. *Pemb* 4F 14
Lewisham. *G Lon* 6L 21
Lewiston. *High* 3F 70
Lewistown. *B'end* 6J 17
Lewknor. *Oxon* 4E 20
Leworthy. *Devn*
nr. Barnstaple 2F 6
nr. Holsworthy 5C 6
Lewson Street. *Kent* 7F 22
Lewthorn Cross. *Devn* 8G 7
Lewtrenchard. *Devn* 7D 6
Ley. *Corn* 5D 4
Leybourne. *Kent* 8C 22
Leyburn. *N Yor* 6K 47
Leycett. *Staf* 5F 34
Leyfields. *Staf* 1L 27
Ley Green. *Herts* 1J 21
Ley Hill. *Buck* 3G 21
Leyland. *Lanc* 5D 40
Leylodge. *Abers* 4G 73
Leymoor. *W Yor* 6K 41
Leys. *Per* 4F 66
Leysdown-on-Sea. *Kent* 6G 23
Leysmill. *Ang* 3K 67
Leyton. *G Lon* 5L 21
Leytonstone. *G Lon* 5M 21
Lezant. *Corn* 8C 6
Leziate. *Norf* 8C 38
Lhanbryde. *Mor* 7B 80
The Lhen. *IOM* 4C 44
Liatrie. *High* 2C 70
Libanus. *Powy* 2J 17
Libberton. *S Lan* 5H 59
Libbery. *Worc* 6H 27
Liberton. *Edin* 3L 59
Liceasto. *W Isl* 4C 76
Lichfield. *Staf* 1K 27
Lickey. *Worc* 4H 27
Lickey End. *Worc* 4H 27
Lickfold. *W Sus* 3G 11
Liddaton. *Devn* 7D 6
Liddington. *Swin* 5L 19
Liddle. *Orkn* 3F 86
Lidgate. *Suff* 6D 30
Lidgett. *Notts* 3D 36
Lidham Hill. *E Sus* 4E 12
Lidlington. *C Beds* 8G 29
Lidsey. *W Sus* 5G 11
Lidstone. *Oxon* 1A 20
Lienassie. *High* 3L 69
Liff. *Ang* 4G 67
Lifford. *W Mid* 3J 27
Lifton. *Devn* 7C 6
Liftondown. *Devn* 7C 6
Lighthorne. *Warw* 6M 27
Light Oaks. *Stoke* 4H 35
Lightwater. *Surr* 7G 21
Lightwood. *Staf* 5J 35
Lightwood. *Stoke* 5H 35
Lightwood Green. *Ches E* 5E 34
Lightwood Green. *Wrex* 5B 34
Lilbourne. *Nptn* 4C 28
Lilburn Tower. *Nmbd* 7H 61
Lillesdon. *Som* 3B 8
Lilleshall. *Telf* 8F 34
Lilley. *Herts* 1J 21
Lilliesleaf. *Bord* 7C 60
Lillingstone Dayrell. *Buck* 8E 28
Lillingstone Lovell. *Buck* 7E 28
Lillington. *Dors* 4E 8
Lilstock. *Som* 1L 7
Lilybank. *Inv* 2B 58
Lilyhurst. *Shrp* 8F 34
Limavady. *Caus* 2E 92
Limbrick. *Lanc* 6E 40
Limbury. *Lutn* 1H 21
Limekilnburn. *S Lan* 4F 58
Limekilns. *Fife* 1J 59
Limerigg. *Falk* 2G 59
Limestone Brae. *Nmbd* 7A 54
Lime Street. *Worc* 8G 27
Limington. *Som* 3D 8
Limpenhoe. *Norf* 1K 31
Limpley Stoke. *Wilts* 7F 18
Limpsfield. *Surr* 8M 21
Limpsfield Chart. *Surr* 8M 21
Linburn. *W Lot* 3K 59
Linby. *Notts* 4C 36
Linchmere. *W Sus* 2F 10
Lincluden. *Dum* 4D 52
Lincoln. *Linc* 111 (2G 37)
Lincomb. *Worc* 5G 27
Lindale. *Cumb* 7C 46
Lindal in Furness. *Cumb* 8A 46
Lindean. *Bord* 6B 60
Linden. *Glos* 2G 19
Lindfield. *W Sus* 3L 11
Lindford. *Hants* 2F 10
Lindores. *Fife* 6F 66
Lindridge. *Worc* 5E 26
Lindsell. *Essx* 1C 22
Lindsey. *Suff* 7F 30
Lindsey Tye. *Suff* 7F 30
Linford. *Hants* 5K 9
Linford. *Thur* 6C 22
Lingague. *IOM* 7B 44
Lingdale. *Red C* 4D 48
Lingen. *Here* 5B 26
Lingfield. *Surr* 1L 11
Lingreabhagh. *W Isl* 5B 76
Lingwood. *Norf* 1K 31
Lingy Close. *Cumb* 6H 53
Linicro. *High* 7E 76
Linkend. *Worc* 8G 27
Linkenholt. *Hants* 8A 20
Linkinhorne. *Corn* 8C 6
Linklater. *Orkn* 3F 86
Linksness. *Orkn* 8E 88
Linktown. *Fife* 8F 66
Linkwood. *Mor* 7B 80
Linley. *Shrp*
nr. Bishop's Castle 2B 26
nr. Bridgnorth 2E 26
Linley Green. *Here* 6E 26
Linlithgow. *W Lot* 2H 59
Linlithgow Bridge. *Falk* 2H 59
Linneraineach. *High* 3B 78
Linshiels. *Nmbd* 1B 54
Linsiadar. *W Isl* 8F 82
Linsidemore. *High* 4F 78
Linslade. *C Beds* 1G 21
Linstead Parva. *Suff* 4K 31
Linstock. *Cumb* 6J 53
Linthwaite. *W Yor* 6K 41
Lintlaw. *Bord* 4F 60
Lintmill. *Mor* 7E 80
Linton. *Cambs* 7B 30
Linton. *Derbs* 8L 35
Linton. *Here* 1E 18
Linton. *Kent* 1D 12
Linton. *N Yor* 1H 41
Linton. *Bord* 7E 60
Linton. *W Yor* 3A 42
Linton Colliery. *Nmbd* 2F 54
Linton Hill. *Here* 1E 18
Linton-on-Ouse. *N Yor* 1B 42
Lintzford. *Dur* 6E 54
Lintzgarth. *Dur* 7C 54
Linwood. *Hants* 5K 9
Linwood. *Linc* 1J 37
Linwood. *Ren* 3C 58
Lionacleit. *W Isl* 1D 74
Lionacro. *High* 7E 76
Lionacuidhe. *W Isl* 1D 74
Lional. *W Isl* 5J 83
Liphook. *Hants* 2F 10
Lipley. *Shrp* 6F 34
Lipyeate. *Som* 8E 18
Liquo. *N Lan* 4G 59
Lisbane. *Ards* 5J 93
Lisbellaw. *Ferm* 6C 92
Lisburn. *Lis* 5H 93
Liscard. *Mers* 8B 40
Liscolman. *Caus* 2F 93
Liscombe. *Som* 2H 7
Lishahawley. *Derr* 2D 92
Liskeard. *Corn* 5E 4
Lislea. *New M* 7G 93
Lisle Court. *Hants* 6M 9
Lisnarick. *Ferm* 6B 92
Lisnaskea. *Ferm* 7C 92
Liss. *Hants* 3E 10
Lissett. *E Yor* 2J 43
Liss Forest. *Hants* 3E 10
Lissington. *Linc* 1J 37
Liston. *Essx* 7E 30
Listooder. *New M* 6J 93
Lisvane. *Card* 6L 17
Liswerry. *Newp* 5B 18
Litcham. *Norf* 8E 38
Litchard. *B'end* 6J 17
Litchborough. *Nptn* 6D 28
Litchfield. *Hants* 8B 20
Litherland. *Mers* 8B 40
Litlington. *Cambs* 7L 29
Litlington. *E Sus* 5B 12
Littemill. *Nmbd* 8K 61
Litterty. *Abers* 8G 81
Little Abington. *Cambs* 7B 30
Little Addington. *Nptn* 4G 29
Little Airmyn. *N Yor* 5E 42
Little Alne. *Warw* 5K 27
Little Ardo. *Abers* 2H 73
Little Asby. *Cumb* 5E 46
Little Aston. *Staf* 1J 27
Little Atherfield. *IOW* 7B 10
Little Ayton. *N Yor* 4C 48
Little Baddow. *Essx* 3D 22
Little Badminton. *S Glo* 5G 19
Little Ballinluig. *Per* 2C 66
Little Bampton. *Cumb* 6G 53
Little Bardfield. *Essx* 8C 30
Little Barford. *Bed* 6J 29
Little Barningham. *Norf* 6H 39
Little Barrington. *Glos* 2L 19
Little Barrow. *Ches W* 3C 34
Little Barugh. *N Yor* 8E 48
Little Bavington. *Nmbd* 4C 54
Little Bealings. *Suff* 7J 31
Littlebeck. *Cumb* 4E 46
Little Bedwyn. *Wilts* 7L 19
Little Bentley. *Essx* 1H 23
Little Berkhamsted. *Herts* 3K 21
Little Billing. *Nptn* 5F 28
Little Billington. *C Beds* 1G 21
Little Birch. *Here* 8D 26
Little Bispham. *Bkpl* 3B 40
Little Blakenham. *Suff* 7H 31
Little Blencow. *Cumb* 8J 53
Little Bognor. *W Sus* 3H 11
Little Bolas. *Shrp* 7E 34
Little Bollington. *Ches E* 1F 34
Little Bookham. *Surr* 8J 21
Littleborough. *Devn* 4H 7
Littleborough. *G Man* 6H 41
Littleborough. *Notts* 1F 36
Littlebourne. *Kent* 8J 23
Little Bourton. *Oxon* 7B 28
Little Bowden. *Leics* 3E 28
Little Bradley. *Suff* 6C 30
Little Brampton. *Shrp* 3B 26
Little Brechin. *Ang* 1J 67
Littlebredy. *Dors* 7D 8
Little Brickhill. *Mil* 8G 29
Little Bridgeford. *Staf* 7G 35
Little Brington. *Nptn* 5D 28
Little Bromley. *Essx* 1G 23
Little Broughton. *Cumb* 8E 52
Little Budworth. *Ches W* 3D 34
Little Burstead. *Essx* 4C 22
Little Burton. *E Yor* 3J 43
Littlebury. *Essx* 8B 30
Littlebury Green. *Essx* 8A 30
Little Bytham. *Linc* 8H 37
Little Canfield. *Essx* 1B 22
Little Canford. *Dors* 6J 9
Little Carlton. *Linc* 1L 37
Little Carlton. *Notts* 4E 36
Little Casterton. *Rut* 1H 29
Little Catwick. *E Yor* 3J 43
Little Catworth. *Cambs* 4J 29
Little Cawthorpe. *Linc* 1L 37
Little Chalfont. *Buck* 4G 21
Little Chart. *Kent* 1F 12
Little Chesterford. *Essx* 7B 30
Little Cheverell. *Wilts* 8H 19
Little Chishill. *Cambs* 8M 29
Little Clacton. *Essx* 2H 23
Little Clanfield. *Oxon* 3L 19
Little Clifton. *Cumb* 2K 45
Little Coates. *NE Lin* 7K 43
Little Comberton. *Worc* 7H 27
Little Common. *E Sus* 5D 12
Little Compton. *Warw* 8L 27
Little Cornard. *Suff* 8E 30
Littlecote. *Buck* 1F 20
Littlecott. *Wilts* 8K 19
Little Cowarne. *Here* 6E 26
Little Coxwell. *Oxon* 4L 19
Little Crakehall. *N Yor* 6L 47
Little Crawley. *Mil* 7G 29
Little Creich. *High* 5G 79
Little Cressingham. *Norf* 1E 30
Little Crosby. *Mers* 7B 40
Little Crosthwaite. *Cumb* 2M 45
Little Cubley. *Derbs* 6K 35
Little Dalby. *Leics* 8E 36
Little Dawley. *Telf* 1E 26
Littledean. *Glos* 2E 18
Little Dens. *Abers* 1K 73
Little Dewchurch. *Here* 8D 26
Little Ditton. *Cambs* 6C 30
Little Down. *Hants* 8A 20
Little Downham. *Cambs* 3B 30
Little Drayton. *Shrp* 6E 34
Little Driffield. *E Yor* 2H 43
Little Dunham. *Norf* 8E 38
Little Dunkeld. *Per* 3D 66
Little Dunmow. *Essx* 1C 22
Little Easton. *Essx* 1C 22
Little Eaton. *Derbs* 5A 36
Little Eccleston. *Lanc* 3C 40
Little Ellingham. *Norf* 2G 31
Little Elm. *Som* 1F 8
Little End. *Essx* 3B 22
Little Everdon. *Nptn* 6C 28
Little Eversden. *Cambs* 6L 29
Little Faringdon. *Oxon* 3L 19
Little Fencote. *N Yor* 6L 47
Little Fenton. *N Yor* 4C 42
Littleferry. *High* 4J 79
Little Fransham. *Norf* 8F 38
Little Gaddesden. *Herts* 2G 21
Little Garway. *Here* 1C 18
Little Gidding. *Cambs* 3J 29
Little Glemham. *Suff* 6K 31
Little Glenshee. *Per* 4C 66
Little Gransden. *Cambs* 6K 29
Little Green. *Suff* 4G 31
Little Green. *Wrex* 5C 34
Little Grimsby. *Linc* 8L 43
Little Habton. *N Yor* 8E 48
Little Hadham. *Herts* 1M 21
Little Hale. *Linc* 5J 37
Little Hallingbury. *Essx* 2A 22
Littleham. *Devn*
nr. Bideford 3D 6
nr. Exmouth 7K 7
Little Hampden. *Buck* 3F 20
Littlehampton. *W Sus* 5H 11
Little Haresfield. *Glos* 3G 19
Little Harrowden. *Nptn* 4F 28
Little Haseley. *Oxon* 3D 20
Little Hatfield. *E Yor* 3J 43
Little Hautbois. *Norf* 7J 39
Little Haven. *Pemb* 5E 14
Little Hay. *Staf* 1K 27
Little Hayfield. *Derbs* 1J 35
Little Haywood. *Staf* 7J 35
Little Heath. *W Mid* 3M 27
Little Heck. *N Yor* 5C 42
Littlehempston. *Devn* 5L 5
Little Herbert's. *Glos* 2H 19
Little Hereford. *Here* 5D 26
Little Horkesley. *Essx* 8F 30
Little Hormead. *Herts* 1L 21
Little Horsted. *E Sus* 4A 12
Little Horton. *W Yor* 4K 41
Little Horwood. *Buck* 8E 28
Little Houghton. *Nptn* 6F 28
Little Houghton. *S Yor* 7B 42
Littlehoughton. *Nmbd* 8K 61
Little Hucklow. *Derbs* 2K 35
Little Hulton. *G Man* 7F 40
Little Irchester. *Nptn* 5G 29
Little Kelk. *E Yor* 1H 43
Little Kimble. *Buck* 3F 20
Little Kineton. *Warw* 6M 27
Little Kingshill. *Buck* 4F 20
Little Langdale. *Cumb* 5B 46
Little Langford. *Wilts* 2J 9
Little Laver. *Essx* 3B 22
Little Lawford. *Warw* 4B 28
Little Leigh. *Ches W* 2E 34
Little Leighs. *Essx* 2D 22
Little Leven. *E Yor* 3H 43
Little Lever. *G Man* 7F 40
Little Linford. *Mil* 7F 28
Little London. *Buck* 2D 20
Little London. *E Sus* 4B 12
Little London. *Hants*
nr. Andover 1A 10
nr. Basingstoke 8D 20
Little London. *Linc*
nr. Long Sutton 7M 37
nr. Spalding 7K 37
Little London. *Norf*
nr. North Walsham 6J 39
nr. Northwold 2D 30
nr. Saxthorpe 6H 39
nr. Southery 2C 30
Little London. *Powy* 4K 25
Little Longstone. *Derbs* 2K 35
Little Malvern. *Worc* 7F 26
Little Maplestead. *Essx* 8E 30
Little Marcle. *Here* 8E 26
Little Marlow. *Buck* 5F 20
Little Massingham. *Norf* 7D 38
Little Melton. *Norf* 1H 31
Little Mill. *Mon* 3B 18
Littlemill. *Abers* 6C 72
Littlemill. *E Ayr* 8C 58
Littlemill. *High* 1K 71
Little Milton. *Oxon* 3D 20
Little Missenden. *Buck* 4G 21
Littlemoor. *Derbs* 3A 36
Littlemoor. *Dors* 7E 8
Littlemore. *Oxon* 3C 20
Little Mountain. *Flin* 3A 34
Little Musgrave. *Cumb* 4F 46
Little Ness. *Shrp* 8C 34
Little Neston. *Ches W* 2A 34
Little Newcastle. *Pemb* 4F 14
Little Newsham. *Dur* 4K 47
Little Oakley. *Essx* 1J 23
Little Oakley. *Nptn* 3F 28
Little Onn. *Staf* 8G 35
Little Ormside. *Cumb* 4F 46
Little Orton. *Cumb* 6H 53
Little Orton. *Leics* 1M 27
Little Ouse. *Cambs* 3C 30
Little Ouseburn. *N Yor* 1B 42
Littleover. *Derb* 6M 35
Little Packington. *Warw* 3L 27
Little Paxton. *Cambs* 5J 29
Little Petherick. *Corn* 4B 4
Little Plumpton. *Lanc* 4B 40
Little Plumstead. *Norf* 8K 39
Little Ponton. *Linc* 6G 37
Littleport. *Cambs* 3B 30
Little Posbrook. *Hants* 5C 10
Little Potheridge. *Devn* 4E 6
Little Preston. *Nptn* 6C 28
Little Raveley. *Cambs* 4K 29
Little Reynoldston. *Swan* 8L 15
Little Ribston. *N Yor* 2A 42
Little Rissington. *Glos* 2K 19
Little Rogart. *High* 3H 79
Little Rollright. *Oxon* 8L 27
Little Ryburgh. *Norf* 7F 38
Little Ryle. *Nmbd* 8H 61
Little Ryton. *Shrp* 1C 26
Little Salkeld. *Cumb* 8K 53
Little Sampford. *Essx* 8C 30
Little Sandhurst. *Brac* 7F 20
Little Saredon. *Staf* 1H 27
Little Saxham. *Suff* 5D 30
Little Scatwell. *High* 8D 78
Little Shelford. *Cambs* 6A 30
Little Shoddesden. *Hants* 1L 9
Little Singleton. *Lanc* 4B 40
Little Smeaton. *N Yor* 6C 42
Little Snoring. *Norf* 6F 38
Little Sodbury. *S Glo* 5F 18
Little Somborne. *Hants* 2A 10
Little Somerford. *Wilts* 5H 19
Little Soudley. *Shrp* 7F 34
Little Stainforth. *N Yor* 1G 41
Little Stainton. *Darl* 4M 47
Little Stanney. *Ches W* 2C 34
Little Staughton. *Bed* 5J 29
Little Steeping. *Linc* 3M 37
Littlester. *Shet* 5K 91
Little Stoke. *Staf* 6H 35
Littlestone-on-Sea. *Kent* 3G 13
Little Stonham. *Suff* 5H 31
Little Stretton. *Leics* 1D 28
Little Stretton. *Shrp* 2C 26
Little Strickland. *Cumb* 4D 46
Little Stukeley. *Cambs* 4K 29
Little Sugnall. *Staf* 6G 35
Little Sutton. *Ches W* 2B 34
Little Sutton. *Linc* 7A 38
Little Swinburne. *Nmbd* 4C 54
Little Tew. *Oxon* 1A 20
Little Tey. *Essx* 1E 22
Little Thetford. *Cambs* 4B 30
Little Thirkleby. *N Yor* 8B 48
Little Thornage. *Norf* 6G 39
Little Thornton. *Lanc* 3B 40
Little Thorpe. *W Yor* 5K 41
Littlethorpe. *Leics* 2C 28
Littlethorpe. *N Yor* 1M 41
Little Thurlow. *Suff* 6C 30
Little Thurrock. *Thur* 6C 22
Littleton. *Ches W* 3C 34
Littleton. *Hants* 2B 10
Littleton. *Som* 2C 8
Littleton. *Surr*
nr. Guildford 1G 11
nr. Staines 7H 21
Littleton Drew. *Wilts* 5G 19
Littleton Pannell. *Wilts* 8J 19
Littleton-upon-Severn.
S Glo 5D 18
Little Torboll. *High* 4H 79
Little Torrington. *Devn* 4D 6
Little Totham. *Essx* 2E 22
Little Town. *Cumb* 3M 45
Little Town. *Lanc* 4E 40
Littletown. *Dur* 7G 55
Littletown. *High* 5H 79
Little Twycross. *Leics* 1M 27
Little Urswick. *Cumb* 8A 46
Little Wakering. *Essx* 5F 22
Little Walden. *Essx* 7B 30
Little Waldingfield. *Suff* 7F 30
Little Walsingham. *Norf* 6F 38
Little Waltham. *Essx* 2D 22
Little Warley. *Essx* 4C 22
Little Weighton. *E Yor* 4G 43
Little Wenham. *Suff* 8G 31
Little Wenlock. *Telf* 1E 26
Little Whelnetham. *Suff* 5E 30
Little Whittingham Green.
Suff 4J 31
Littlewick Green. *Wind* 6F 20
Little Wilbraham. *Cambs* 6B 30
Littlewindsor. *Dors* 5C 8
Little Wisbeach. *Linc* 6J 37
Little Witcombe. *Glos* 2H 19
Little Witley. *Worc* 5F 26
Little Wittenham. *Oxon* 4C 20
Little Wolford. *Warw* 8L 27
Littleworth. *Bed* 7H 29
Littleworth. *Glos* 8K 27
Littleworth. *Oxon* 4M 19
Littleworth. *Staf*
nr. Cannock 8J 35
nr. Eccleshall 7F 34
nr. Stafford 7H 35
Littleworth. *W Sus* 3J 11
Littleworth. *Worc*
nr. Redditch 5H 27
nr. Worcester 6G 27
Little Wratting. *Suff* 7C 30
Little Wymondley. *Herts* 1K 21
Little Wyrley. *Staf* 1J 27
Little Yeldham. *Essx* 8D 30
Littley Green. *Essx* 2C 22
Litton. *Derbs* 2K 35
Litton. *N Yor* 8H 47
Litton. *Som* 8D 18
Litton Cheney. *Dors* 6D 8
Liurbost. *W Isl* 1E 76
Liverpool. *Mers* 111 (8B 40)
Liverpool John Lennon Airport.
Mers 1C 34
Liversedge. *W Yor* 5K 41
Liverton. *Devn* 8H 7
Liverton. *Red C* 4E 48
Liverton Mines. *Red C* 4E 48
Livingston. *W Lot* 3J 59
Livingston Village. *W Lot* 3J 59
Lixwm. *Flin* 3L 33
Lizard. *Corn* 7L 3
Llaingoch. *IOA* 2B 32
Llaithddu. *Powy* 4K 25
Llampha. *V Glam* 7J 17
Llan. *Powy* 2H 25
Llanaber. *Gwyn* 1F 24
Llanaelhaearn. *Gwyn* 6C 32
Llanaeron. *Cdgn* 6D 24
Llanafan. *Cdgn* 5F 24
Llanafan-fawr. *Powy* 7J 25
Llanafan-fechan. *Powy* 7J 25
Llanallgo. *IOA* 2D 32
Llanandras. *Powy* 5B 26
Llananno. *Powy* 5K 25
Llanarmon. *Gwyn* 7D 32
Llanarmon Dyffryn Ceiriog.
Wrex 7L 33
Llanarmon-yn-Ial. *Den* 5L 33
Llanarth. *Cdgn* 1L 15
Llanarth. *Mon* 2B 18
Llanarthne. *Carm* 4M 15
Llanasa. *Flin* 2L 33
Llanbabo. *IOA* 2C 32
Llanbadarn Fawr. *Cdgn* 4F 24
Llanbadarn Fynydd. *Powy* 5L 25
Llanbadarn-y-garreg. *Powy* 8L 25
Llanbadoc. *Mon* 3B 18
Llanbadrig. *IOA* 1C 32
Llanbeder. *Newp* 4B 18
Llanbedr. *Gwyn* 8E 32
Llanbedr. *Powy*
nr. Crickhowell 2M 17
nr. Hay-on-Wye 8L 25
Llanbedr-Dyffryn-Clwyd.
Den 5L 33
Llanbedrgoch. *IOA* 2E 32
Llanbedrog. *Gwyn* 7C 32
Llanbedr Pont Steffan.
Cdgn 8E 24
Llanbedr-y-cennin. *Cnwy* 4G 33
Llanberis. *Gwyn* 4E 32
Llanbethery. *V Glam* 8K 17
Llanbister. *Powy* 5L 25
Llanblethian. *V Glam* 7J 17
Llanboidy. *Carm* 4J 15
Llanbradach. *Cphy* 5L 17
Llanbrynmair. *Powy* 2H 25
Llanbydderi. *V Glam* 8K 17
Llancadle. *V Glam* 8K 17
Llancarfan. *V Glam* 7K 17
Llancatal. *V Glam* 8K 17
Llancayo. *Mon* 3B 18
Llancloudy. *Here* 1C 18
Llancoch. *Powy* 5M 25
Llancynfelyn. *Cdgn* 3F 24
Llandaff. *Card* 7L 17
Llandanwg. *Gwyn* 8E 32
Llandarcy. *Neat* 5G 17
Llandawke. *Carm* 5J 15
Llanddaniel Fab. *IOA* 3D 32
Llanddarog. *Carm* 5M 15
Llanddeiniol. *Cdgn* 5E 24
Llanddeiniolen. *Gwyn* 4E 32
Llandderfel. *Gwyn* 7J 33
Llanddeusant. *Carm* 2G 17
Llanddeusant. *IOA* 2C 32
Llanddew. *Powy* 1K 17
Llanddewi. *Swan* 8L 15
Llanddewi Brefi. *Cdgn* 7F 24
Llanddewi'r Cwm. *Powy* 8K 25
Llanddewi Rhydderch. *Mon* 2B 18
Llanddewi Velfrey. *Pemb* 5H 15
Llanddewi Ystradenni.
Powy 6L 25
Llanddoged. *Cnwy* 4H 33
Llanddona. *IOA* 3E 32
Llanddowror. *Carm* 5J 15
Llanddulas. *Cnwy* 3J 33
Llanddwywe. *Gwyn* 8E 32
Llanddyfnan. *IOA* 3E 32
Llandecwyn. *Gwyn* 7F 32
Llandefaelog Fach. *Powy* 1K 17
Llandefaelog-tre'r-graig.
Powy 1L 17
Llandefalle. *Powy* 1L 17
Llandegfan. *IOA* 3E 32
Llandegla. *Den* 5L 33
Llandegley. *Powy* 6L 25
Llandegveth. *Mon* 4B 18
Llandeilo. *Carm* 2F 16
Llandeilo Graban. *Powy* 8K 25
Llandeilo'r Fan. *Powy* 1H 17
Llandeloy. *Pemb* 4E 14
Llandenny. *Mon* 3C 18
Llandevaud. *Newp* 4C 18
Llandevenny. *Mon* 5C 18
Llandilo. *Pemb* 4H 15
Llandinabo. *Here* 1D 18
Llandinam. *Powy* 4K 25
Llandissilio. *Pemb* 4H 15
Llandogo. *Mon* 3D 18
Llandough. *V Glam*
nr. Cowbridge 7J 17
nr. Penarth 7L 17
Llandovery. *Carm* 1G 17
Llandow. *V Glam* 7J 17
Llandre. *Cdgn* 4F 24
Llandrillo. *Den* 7K 33
Llandrillo-yn-Rhos. *Cnwy* 2H 33
Llandrindod. *Powy* 6K 25
Llandrindod Wells. *Powy* 6K 25
Llandrinio. *Powy* 8A 34
Llandudno. *Cnwy* 2G 33
Llandudno Junction. *Cnwy* 3G 33
Llandudoch. *Pemb* 2H 15
Llandw. *V Glam* 7J 17
Llandwrog. *Gwyn* 5D 32
Llandybie. *Carm* 3F 16
Llandyfaelog. *Carm* 5L 15
Llandyfan. *Carm* 3F 16
Llandyfriog. *Cdgn* 2K 15
Llandyfrydog. *IOA* 2D 32
Llandygai. *Gwyn* 3F 32
Llandygwydd. *Cdgn* 2J 15
Llandynan. *Den* 6L 33
Llandyrnog. *Den* 4L 33
Llandysilio. *Powy* 8A 34
Llandyssil. *Powy* 3L 25
Llandysul. *Cdgn* 2L 15
Llanedeyrn. *Card* 6M 17
Llaneglwys. *Powy* 1K 17
Llanegryn. *Gwyn* 2F 24
Llanegwad. *Carm* 4M 15
Llaneilian. *IOA* 1D 32
Llanelian-yn-Rhos. *Cnwy* 3H 33
Llanelidan. *Den* 5L 33
Llanelieu. *Powy* 1L 17
Llanellen. *Mon* 2B 18
Llanelli. *Carm* 7M 15
Llanelltyd. *Gwyn* 1G 25
Llanelly. *Mon* 3M 17
Llanelly Hill. *Mon* 3M 17
Llanelwedd. *Powy* 7K 25
Llan-Elwy. *Den* 3K 33
Llanenddwyn. *Gwyn* 8E 32
Llanengan. *Gwyn* 8B 32
Llanerch. *Powy* 2B 26
Llanerchymedd. *IOA* 2D 32
Llanerfyl. *Powy* 2K 25
Llaneuddog. *IOA* 2D 32
Llanfachraeth. *IOA* 2C 32
Llanfachreth. *Gwyn* 8G 33
Llanfaelog. *IOA* 3C 32
Llanfaelrhys. *Gwyn* 8B 32
Llanfaenor. *Mon* 2C 18
Llanfaes. *IOA* 3F 32
Llanfaes. *Powy* 2K 17
Llanfaethlu. *IOA* 2C 32
Llanfaglan. *Gwyn* 4D 32
Llanfair. *Gwyn* 8E 32
Llanfair. *Here* 7A 26
Llanfair Caereinion. *Powy* 2L 25
Llanfair Clydogau. *Cdgn* 7F 24
Llanfair Dyffryn Clwyd. *Den* 5L 33
Llanfairfechan. *Cnwy* 3F 32
Llanfair-Nant-Gwyn. *Pemb* 3H 15
Llanfair Pwllgwyngyll. *IOA* 3E 32
Llanfair Talhaiarn. *Cnwy* 3J 33
Llanfair Waterdine. *Shrp* 5M 25
Llanfair-ym-Muallt. *Powy* 7K 25
Llanfairyneubwll. *IOA* 3C 32
Llanfairynghornwy. *IOA* 1C 32
Llanfallteg. *Carm* 5H 15
Llanfallteg West. *Carm* 5H 15
Llanfaredd. *Powy* 7K 25
Llanfarian. *Cdgn* 5E 24
Llanfechain. *Powy* 8L 33
Llanfechell. *IOA* 1C 32
Llanfendigaid. *Gwyn* 2E 24
Llanferres. *Den* 4L 33
Llan Ffestiniog. *Gwyn* 6G 33
Llanfflewyn. *IOA* 2C 32
Llanfihangel-ar-Arth. *Carm* 3L 15
Llanfihangel Glyn Myfyr.
Cnwy 6J 33
Llanfihangel Nant Bran.
Powy 1J 17
Llanfihangel-Nant-Melan.
Powy 7L 25
Llanfihangel near Rogiet.
Mon 5C 18
Llanfihangel Rhydithon.
Powy 6L 25
Llanfihangel Tal-y-llyn.
Powy 2L 17
Llanfihangel-uwch-Gwili.
Carm 4L 15
Llanfihangel-y-Creuddyn.
Cdgn 5F 24
Llanfihangel-yng-Ngwynfa.
Powy 1K 25
Llanfihangel yn Nhowyn.
IOA 3C 32
Llanfihangel-y-pennant.
*Gwyn*nr. Golan 6E 32
nr. Tywyn 2F 24
Llanfihangel-y-traethau.
Gwyn 7E 32
Llanfilo. *Powy* 1L 17
Llanfleiddan. *V Glam* 7J 17
Llanfoist. *Mon* 2A 18
Llanfor. *Gwyn* 7J 33
Llanfrechfa. *Torf* 4B 18
Llanfrothen. *Gwyn* 6F 32
Llanfrynach. *Powy* 2K 17
Llanfwrog. *Den* 5L 33
Llanfwrog. *IOA* 2C 32
Llanfyllin. *Powy* 1L 25
Llanfynydd. *Carm* 2E 16
Llanfynydd. *Flin* 4A 34
Llanfyrnach. *Pemb* 3J 15
Llangadfan. *Powy* 1K 25
Llangadog. *Carm*
nr. Llandovery 2G 17
nr. Llanelli 6L 15
Llangadwaladr. *IOA* 4C 32
Llangadwaladr. *Powy* 7L 33
Llangaffo. *IOA* 4D 32
Llangain. *Carm* 5K 15
Llangammarch Wells. *Powy* 8J 25
Llangan. *V Glam* 7J 17
Llangarron. *Here* 1D 18
Llangasty-Talyllyn. *Powy* 2L 17
Llangathen. *Carm* 2E 16
Llangattock. *Powy* 3M 17
Llangattock Lingoed. *Mon* 1B 18
Llangattock-Vibon-Avel.
Mon 2C 18
Llangedwyn. *Powy* 8L 33
Llangefni. *IOA* 3D 32
Llangeinor. *B'end* 6J 17
Llangeitho. *Cdgn* 7F 24
Llangeler. *Carm* 3K 15
Llangelynin. *Gwyn* 2E 24
Llangendeirne. *Carm* 5L 15
Llangennech. *Carm* 4E 16
Llangennith. *Swan* 7L 15
Llangenny. *Powy* 3M 17
Llangernyw. *Cnwy* 4H 33
Llangian. *Gwyn* 8B 32
Llangiwg. *Neat* 4G 17
Llangloffan. *Pemb* 3F 14
Llanglydwen. *Carm* 4H 15
Llangoed. *IOA* 3F 32
Llangoedmor. *Cdgn* 2H 15
Llangollen. *Den* 6M 33
Llangolman. *Pemb* 4H 15
Llangorse. *Powy* 2L 17
Llangorwen. *Cdgn* 4F 24
Llangovan. *Mon* 3C 18
Llangower. *Gwyn* 7J 33
Llangranog. *Cdgn* 1K 15
Llangristiolus. *IOA* 3D 32
Llangrove. *Here* 2D 18
Llangua. *Mon* 1B 18
Llangunllo. *Powy* 5M 25
Llangunnor. *Carm* 4L 15
Llangurig. *Powy* 5J 25
Llangwm. *Cnwy* 6J 33
Llangwm. *Mon* 3C 18
Llangwm. *Pemb* 6F 14
Llangwm-isaf. *Mon* 3C 18
Llangwnnadl. *Gwyn* 7B 32
Llangwyfan. *Den* 4L 33
Llangwyfan-isaf. *IOA* 4C 32
Llangwyllog. *IOA* 3D 32
Llangwyryfon. *Cdgn* 5F 24
Llangybi. *Cdgn* 7F 24
Llangybi. *Gwyn* 6D 32
Llangybi. *Mon* 4B 18
Llangyfelach. *Swan* 5F 16
Llangynhafal. *Den* 4L 33
Llangynidr. *Powy* 3L 17
Llangynin. *Carm* 5J 15
Llangynog. *Carm* 5K 15
Llangynog. *Powy* 8K 33
Llangynwyd. *B'end* 6H 17
Llanhamlach. *Powy* 2K 17
Llanharan. *Rhon* 6K 17
Llanharry. *Rhon* 6K 17
Llanhennock. *Mon* 4B 18
Llanhilleth. *Blae* 4M 17
Llanidloes. *Powy* 4J 25
Llaniestyn. *Gwyn* 7B 32
Llanigon. *Powy* 8M 25
Llanilar. *Cdgn* 5F 24
Llanilid. *Rhon* 6J 17
Llanilltud Fawr. *V Glam* 8J 17
Llanishen. *Card* 6L 17
Llanishen. *Mon* 3C 18
Llanllawddog. *Carm* 4L 15
Llanllechid. *Gwyn* 4F 32
Llanllowell. *Mon* 4B 18
Llanllugan. *Powy* 2K 25
Llanllwch. *Carm* 5K 15
Llanllwchaiarn. *Powy* 3L 25
Llanllwni. *Carm* 3L 15
Llanllyfni. *Gwyn* 5D 32
Llanmadoc. *Swan* 7L 15
Llanmaes. *V Glam* 8J 17
Llanmartin. *Newp* 5B 18
Llanmerwig. *Powy* 3L 25
Llanmihangel. *V Glam* 7J 17
Llan-mill. *Pemb* 5H 15
Llanmiloe. *Carm* 6J 15
Llanmorlais. *Swan* 7M 15
Llannefydd. *Cnwy* 3J 33
Llan-non. *Cdgn* 6E 24
Llannon. *Carm* 6M 15
Llannor. *Gwyn* 7C 32
Llanover. *Mon* 3B 18
Llanpumsaint. *Carm* 4L 15
Llanrhaeadr. *Den* 4K 33
Llanrhaeadr-ym-Mochnant.
Powy 8L 33
Llanrhian. *Pemb* 3E 14
Llanrhidian. *Swan* 7L 15
Llanrhos. *Cnwy* 2G 33
Llanrhyddlad. *IOA* 2C 32
Llanrhystud. *Cdgn* 6E 24
Llanrothal. *Here* 2C 18
Llanrug. *Gwyn* 4E 32
Llanrumney. *Card* 6M 17
Llanrwst. *Cnwy* 4G 33
Llansadurnen. *Carm* 5J 15
Llansadwrn. *Carm* 1F 16
Llansadwrn. *IOA* 3E 32
Llansaint. *Carm* 6K 15
Llansamlet. *Swan* 5F 16
Llansanffraid Glan Conwy.
Cnwy 3H 33

Llansannan—Meadgate

Llansannan. Cnwy 4J 33
Llansannor. V Glam 7J 17
Llansantffraed. Cdgn 6E 24
Llansantffraed. Powy 2L 17
Llansantffraed Cwmdeuddwr. Powy 6J 25
Llansantffraed-in-Elwel. Powy 7K 25
Llansantffraid-ym-Mechain. Powy 8M 33
Llansawel. Carm 1F 16
Llansawel. Neat 5G 17
Llansilin. Powy 8M 33
Llansoy. Mon 3C 18
Llanspyddid. Powy 2K 17
Llanstadwell. Pemb 6F 14
Llansteffan. Carm 5K 15
Llanstephan. Powy 8L 25
Llantarnam. Torf 4B 18
Llanteg. Pemb 5H 15
Llanthony. Mon 1A 18
Llantilio Crossenny. Mon 2B 18
Llantilio Pertholey. Mon 2B 18
Llantood. Pemb 2H 15
Llantrisant. Mon 4B 18
Llantrisant. Rhon 6K 17
Llantrithyd. V Glam 7K 17
Llantwit Fardre. Rhon 6K 17
Llantwit Major. V Glam 8J 17
Llanuwchllyn. Gwyn 7H 33
Llanvaches. Newp 4C 18
Llanvair Discoed. Mon 4C 18
Llanvapley. Mon 2B 18
Llanvetherine. Mon 2B 18
Llanveynoe. Here 8B 26
Llanvihangel Crucorney. Mon 1B 18
Llanvihangel Gobion. Mon 3B 18
Llanvihangel Ystern-Llewern. Mon 2C 18
Llanwarne. Here 1D 18
Llanwddyn. Powy 1K 25
Llanwenarth. Mon 2A 18
Llanwenog. Cdgn 2L 15
Llanwern. Newp 5B 18
Llanwinio. Carm 4J 15
Llanwnda. Gwyn 5D 32
Llanwnda. Pemb 3F 14
Llanwnnen. Cdgn 2M 15
Llanwnog. Powy 3K 25
Llanwrda. Carm 1G 17
Llanwrin. Powy 2G 25
Llanwrthwl. Powy 6J 25
Llanwrtud. Powy 8H 25
Llanwrtyd. Powy 8H 25
Llanwrtyd Wells. Powy 8H 25
Llanwyddelan. Powy 2K 25
Llanyblodwel. Shrp 8M 33
Llanybri. Carm 5K 15
Llanybydder. Carm 2M 15
Llanycefn. Pemb 4G 15
Llanychaer. Pemb 3F 14
Llanycil. Gwyn 7J 33
Llanymawddwy. Gwyn 1J 25
Llanymddyfri. Carm 1G 17
Llanymynech. Powy 7A 34
Llanynghenedl. IOA 2C 32
Llanynys. Den 4L 33
Llan-y-pwll. Wrex 4B 34
Llanyrafon. Torf 4B 18
Llanyre. Powy 6K 25
Llanystumdwy. Gwyn 7D 32
Llanywern. Powy 2L 17
Llawhaden. Pemb 5G 15
Llawndy. Flin 2L 33
Llawnt. Shrp 6A 34
Llawr Dref. Gwyn 8B 32
Llawryglyn. Powy 3J 25
Llay. Wrex 4B 34
Llechfaen. Powy 2K 17
Llechryd. Cphy 4L 17
Llechryd. Cdgn 2J 15
Llechrydau. Wrex 7M 33
Lledrod. Cdgn 5F 24
Llethrid. Swan 7M 15
Llidiad-Nenog. Carm 3M 15
Llidiardau. Gwyn 7H 33
Llidiart y Parc. Den 6L 33
Llithfaen. Gwyn 6C 32
Lloc. Flin 3L 33
Llong. Flin 3A 34
Llowes. Powy 8L 25
Lloyney. Powy 5M 25
Llundain-fach. Cdgn 7E 24
Llwydcoed. Rhon 4J 17
Llwyncelyn. Cdgn 1L 15
Llwyncelyn. Swan 4F 16
Llwyndafydd. Cdgn 1K 15
Llwynderw. Powy 2M 25
Llwyn-du. Mon 2A 18
Llwyngwril. Gwyn 2E 24
Llwynhendy. Carm 7M 15
Llwynmawr. Wrex 7M 33
Llwyn-on Village. Mer T 3K 17
Llwyn-têg. Carm 4E 16
Llwyn-y-brain. Carm 5H 15
Llwynygog. Powy 3H 25
Llwyn-y-groes. Cdgn 7E 24
Llwynypia. Rhon 5J 17
Llynclys. Shrp 7A 34
Llynfaes. IOA 3D 32
Llysfaen. Cnwy 3H 33
Llyswen. Powy 1L 17
Llysworney. V Glam 7J 17
Llys-y-fran. Pemb 4G 15
Llywel. Powy 1H 17
Llywernog. Cdgn 4G 25
Loan. Falk 2H 59
Loanend. Nmbd 4G 61
Loanhead. Midl 3L 59
Loaningfoot. Dum 6D 52
Loanreoch. High 6G 79
Loans. S Ayr 6B 58
Loansdean. Nmbd 3E 54
Lobb. Devn 2D 6
Lobhillcross. Devn 7D 6
Lochaber. Mor 8L 79
Loch a Charnain. W Isl 1E 74
Loch a Ghainmhich. W Isl 1D 76
Lochailort. High 7J 69
Lochaline. High 3A 64
Lochans. Dum 6F 50
Locharbriggs. Dum 3D 52
Lochardil. High 1G 71
Lochassynt Lodge. High 1B 78
Lochavich. Arg 6D 64
Lochawe. Arg 5F 64
Loch Baghasdail. W Isl 4D 74
Lochboisdale. W Isl 4D 74
Lochbuie. Arg 5M 63
Lochcarron. High 2K 69
Loch Choire Lodge. High 8J 85
Lochdochart House. Stir 5J 65
Lochdon. Arg 4B 64
Lochearnhead. Stir 5K 65
Lochee. D'dee 4G 67
Lochend. High
nr. Inverness 2F 70
nr. Thurso 5D 86
Locherben. Dum 2D 52
Loch Euphort. W Isl 7K 75
Lochfoot. Dum 4C 52
Lochgair. Arg 8D 64
Lochgarthside. High 4F 70
Lochgelly. Fife 8E 66
Lochgilphead. Arg 1H 57
Lochgoilhead. Arg 7F 64
Loch Head. Dum 7J 51
Lochhill. Mor 7B 80
Lochindorb Lodge. High 2K 71
Lochinver. High 1A 78
Lochlane. Per 5B 66
Loch Lomond. Arg 7H 65
Loch Loyal Lodge. High 7J 85
Lochluichart. High 7D 78
Lochmaben. Dum 3E 52
Lochmaddy. W Isl 7L 75
Loch nam Madadh. W Isl 7L 75
Lochore. Fife 8E 66
Lochportain. W Isl 6L 75
Lochranza. N Ayr 4J 57
Loch Sgioport. W Isl 2E 74
Lochside. Abers 1L 67
Lochside. High
nr. Achentoul 8L 85
nr. Nairn 8J 79
Lochslin. High 5J 79
Lochstack Lodge. High 7E 84
Lochton. Abers 6G 73
Lochty. Fife 7J 67
Lochuisge. High 2B 64
Lochussie. High 8E 78
Lochwinnoch. Ren 4B 58
Lochyside. High 8B 70
Lockengate. Corn 5C 4
Lockerbie. Dum 3F 52
Lockeridge. Wilts 7K 19
Lockerley. Hants 3L 9
Lockhills. Cumb 7K 53
Locking. N Som 8B 18
Lockington. E Yor 3G 43
Lockington. Leics 7B 36
Lockleywood. Shrp 7E 34
Locksgreen. IOW 6B 10
Locks Heath. Hants 5C 10
Lockton. N Yor 6F 48
Loddington. Leics 1E 28
Loddington. Nptn 4F 28
Loddiswell. Devn 7K 5
Loddon. Norf 2K 31
Lode. Cambs 5B 30
Loders. Dors 6C 8
Lodsworth. W Sus 3G 11
Lofthouse. N Yor 8K 47
Lofthouse. W Yor 5M 41
Lofthouse Gate. W Yor 5M 41
Loftus. Red C 4E 48
Logan. E Ayr 7D 58
Loganlea. W Lot 3H 59
Logaston. Here 6B 26
Loggerheads. Den 4L 33
Loggerheads. Staf 6F 34
Loggie. High 4B 78
Logie. Ang 1K 67
Logie. Fife 5H 67
Logie. Mor 8L 79
Logie Coldstone. Abers 5D 72
Logie Pert. Ang 1K 67
Logierait. Per 2C 66
Login. Carm 4H 15
Lolworth. Cambs 5L 29
Lonbain. High 8H 77
Londesborough. E Yor 3F 42
London. G Lon 112-113 (5L 21)
London Apprentice. Corn 6C 4
London Ashford Airport. Kent 3G 13
London City Airport. G Lon 5M 21
London Colney. Herts 3J 21
Londonderry. Derr 3D 92
Londonderry. N Yor 7M 47
London Gatwick Airport. W Sus 119 (1K 11)
London Heathrow Airport. G Lon 119 (6H 21)
London Luton Airport. Lutn 119 (1J 21)
London Southend Airport. Essx 5E 22
London Stansted Airport. Essx 119 (1B 22)
Londonthorpe. Linc 6G 37
Londubh. High 5K 77
Lone. High 7F 84
Lonemore. High
nr. Dornoch 5H 79
nr. Gairloch 6J 77
Long Ashton. N Som 6D 18
Long Bank. Worc 4F 26
Longbar. N Ayr 4B 58
Long Bennington. Linc 5F 36
Longbenton. Tyne 5F 54
Longborough. Glos 1K 19
Long Bredy. Dors 6D 8
Longbridge. Warw 5L 27
Longbridge. W Mid 4J 27
Longbridge Deverill. Wilts 1G 9
Long Buckby. Nptn 5D 28
Long Buckby Wharf. Nptn 5D 28
Longburgh. Cumb 6H 53
Longburton. Dors 4E 8
Long Clawson. Leics 7E 36
Longcliffe. Derbs 4L 35
Long Common. Hants 4C 10
Long Compton. Staf 7G 35
Long Compton. Warw 8L 27
Longcot. Oxon 4L 19
Long Crendon. Buck 3D 20
Long Crichel. Dors 4H 9
Longcroft. Cumb 6G 53
Longcroft. Falk 2F 58
Longcross. Surr 7G 21
Longdale. Cumb 5E 46
Longdales. Cumb 7K 53
Longden. Shrp 1C 26
Longden Common. Shrp 1C 26
Long Ditton. Surr 7J 21
Longdon. Staf 8J 35
Longdon. Worc 8G 27
Longdon Green. Staf 8J 35
Longdon on Tern. Telf 8E 34
Longdown. Devn 6H 7
Longdowns. Corn 5L 3
Long Drax. N Yor 5D 42
Long Duckmanton. Derbs 2B 36
Long Eaton. Derbs 6B 36
Longfield. Kent 7C 22
Longfield. Shet 6D 90
Longfield Hill. Kent 7C 22
Longford. Derbs 6L 35
Longford. Glos 1G 19
Longford. G Lon 6H 21
Longford. Shrp 6E 34
Longford. Telf 8F 34
Longford. W Mid 3A 28
Longforgan. Per 4G 67
Longformacus. Bord 4D 60
Longframlington. Nmbd 1E 54
Long Gardens. Essx 8E 30
Long Green. Ches W 2C 34
Long Green. Worc 8G 27
Longham. Dors 6J 9
Longham. Norf 8F 38
Long Hanborough. Oxon 2B 20
Longhedge. Wilts 1G 9
Longhill. Abers 8K 81
Longhirst. Nmbd 3F 54
Longhope. Glos 2E 18
Longhope. Orkn 2E 86
Longhorsley. Nmbd 2E 54
Longhoughton. Nmbd 8K 61
Long Itchington. Warw 5B 28
Longlands. Cumb 8G 53
Long Lane. Telf 8E 34
Longlane. Derbs 6L 35
Longlane. W Ber 6B 20
Long Lawford. Warw 4B 28
Long Lease. N Yor 5G 49
Longley Green. Worc 6F 26
Long Load. Som 3C 8
Longmanhill. Abers 7G 81
Long Marston. Herts 2F 20
Long Marston. N Yor 2C 42
Long Marston. Warw 7K 27
Long Marton. Cumb 3E 46
Long Meadow. Cambs 5B 30
Long Meadowend. Shrp 3C 26
Long Melford. Suff 7E 30
Longmoor Camp. Hants 2E 10
Longmorn. Mor 8B 80
Longmoss. Ches E 2G 35
Long Newnton. Glos 4H 19
Long Newton. Stoc T 4A 48
Longnewton. Bord 7C 60
Longney. Glos 2F 18
Longniddry. E Lot 2B 60
Longnor. Shrp 1C 26
Longnor. Staf
nr. Leek 3J 35
nr. Stafford 8G 35
Longparish. Hants 1B 10
Longpark. Cumb 5J 53
Long Preston. N Yor 2G 41
Longridge. Lanc 4E 40
Longridge. Staf 8H 35
Longridge. W Lot 3H 59
Longriggend. N Lan 2G 59
Long Riston. E Yor 3J 43
Longrock. Corn 5J 3
Longsdon. Staf 4H 35
Longshaw. G Man 7D 40
Longshaw. Staf 5J 35
Longside. Abers 1K 73
Longslow. Shrp 6E 34
Longstanton. Cambs 5L 29
Longstock. Hants 2A 10
Longstowe. Cambs 6L 29
Long Stratton. Norf 2H 31
Long Street. Mil 7E 28
Longstreet. Wilts 8K 19
Long Sutton. Hants 1E 10
Long Sutton. Linc 7M 37
Long Sutton. Som 3C 8
Longthorpe. Pet 2J 29
Long Thurlow. Suff 5G 31
Longthwaite. Cumb 3C 46
Longton. Lanc 5C 40
Longton. Stoke 5H 35
Longtown. Cumb 5H 53
Longtown. Here 1B 18
Longville in the Dale. Shrp 2D 26
Long Whatton. Leics 7B 36
Longwick. Buck 3E 20
Long Wittenham. Oxon 4C 20
Longwitton. Nmbd 3D 54
Longworth. Oxon 4A 20
Longyester. E Lot 3C 60
Lonmore. High 1D 68
Looe. Corn 6E 4
Loose. Kent 8D 22
Loosegate. Linc 7L 37
Loosley Row. Buck 3F 20
Lopcombe Corner. Wilts 2L 9
Lopen. Som 4C 8
Loppington. Shrp 7C 34
Lorbottle. Nmbd 1D 54
Lordington. W Sus 5E 10
Loscoe. Derbs 5B 36
Loscombe. Dors 6D 8
Losgaintir. W Isl 4B 76
Lossiemouth. Mor 7B 80
Lossit. Arg 4A 56
Lostock Gralam. Ches W 2E 34
Lostock Green. Ches W 2E 34
Lostock Hall. Lanc 5D 40
Lostock Junction. G Man 7E 40
Lostwithiel. Corn 6D 4
Lothbeg. High 2K 79
Lothersdale. N Yor 3H 41
Lothianbridge. Midl 3M 59
Lothianburn. Midl 3L 59
Lothmore. High 2K 79
Lottisham. Som 2D 8
Loudwater. Buck 4G 21
Loughborough. Leics 8C 36
Loughbrickland. Arm 6G 93
Loughgall. Arm 6F 93
Loughguile. Caus 2G 93
Loughinisland. New M 6J 93
Loughmacrory. Ferm 5D 92
Loughor. Swan 5E 16
Loughries. Ards 5J 93
Loughton. Essx 4M 21
Loughton. Mil 8F 28
Loughton. Shrp 3E 26
Lound. Linc 8H 37
Lound. Notts 1D 36
Lound. Suff 2M 31
Lount. Leics 8A 36
The Loup. M Ulst 4F 93
Louth. Linc 1L 37
Love Clough. Lanc 5G 41
Lovedean. Hants 4D 10
Lover. Wilts 3L 9
Loversall. S Yor 8C 42
Loves Green. Essx 3C 22
Loveston. Pemb 6G 15
Lovington. Som 2D 8
Low Ackworth. W Yor 6B 42
Low Angerton. Nmbd 3D 54
Low Ardwell. Dum 7F 50
Low Ballochdowan. S Ayr 4F 50
Lowbands. Glos 8F 26
Low Barlings. Linc 2H 37
Low Bell End. N Yor 6E 48
Low Bentham. N Yor 1E 40
Low Borrowbridge. Cumb 5E 46
Low Bradfield. S Yor 8L 41
Low Bradley. N Yor 3J 41
Low Braithwaite. Cumb 7J 53
Low Brunton. Nmbd 4C 54
Low Burnham. N Lin 7E 42
Lowca. Cumb 2J 45
Low Catton. E Yor 2E 42
Low Coniscliffe. Darl 4L 47
Low Coylton. S Ayr 8C 58
Low Crosby. Cumb 6J 53
Low Dalby. N Yor 7F 48
Lowdham. Notts 5D 36
Low Dinsdale. Darl 4M 47
Lowe. Shrp 6D 34
Low Ellington. N Yor 7L 47
Lower Amble. Corn 4B 4
Lower Ansty. Dors 5F 8
Lower Arboll. High 5J 79
Lower Arncott. Oxon 2D 20
Lower Ashton. Devn 7H 7
Lower Assendon. Oxon 5E 20
Lower Auchenreath. Mor 7C 80
Lower Badcall. High 7D 84
Lower Ballam. Lanc 4B 40
Lower Ballinderry. Lis 5G 93
Lower Basildon. W Ber 6D 20
Lower Beeding. W Sus 3K 11
Lower Benefield. Nptn 3G 29
Lower Bentley. Worc 5H 27
Lower Beobridge. Shrp 2F 26
Lower Bockhampton. Dors 6F 8
Lower Boddington. Nptn 6B 28
Lower Bordean. Hants 3D 10
Lower Brailes. Warw 8M 27
Lower Breakish. High 3H 69
Lower Broadheath. Worc 6G 27
Lower Brynamman. Neat 3G 17
Lower Bullingham. Here 8D 26
Lower Bullington. Hants 1B 10
Lower Burgate. Hants 4K 9
Lower Cam. Glos 3F 18
Lower Catesby. Nptn 6C 28
Lower Chapel. Powy 1K 17
Lower Cheriton. Devn 5L 7
Lower Chicksgrove. Wilts 2H 9
Lower Chute. Wilts 8M 19
Lower Clopton. Warw 6K 27
Lower Common. Hants 1D 10
Lower Crossings. Derbs 1J 35
Lower Cumberworth. W Yor 7L 41
Lower Darwen. Bkbn 5E 40
Lower Dean. Bed 5H 29
Lower Dean. Devn 5K 5
Lower Diabaig. High 7J 77
Lower Dicker. E Sus 4B 12
Lower Dounreay. High 5A 86
Lower Down. Shrp 3B 26
Lower Dunsforth. N Yor 1B 42
Lower East Carleton. Norf 1H 31
Lower Egleton. Here 7E 26
Lower Ellastone. Staf 5K 35
Lower End. Nptn 5F 28
Lower Everleigh. Wilts 8K 19
Lower Eype. Dors 6C 8
Lower Failand. N Som 6D 18
Lower Faintree. Shrp 3E 26
Lower Farringdon. Hants 2E 10
Lower Foxdale. IOM 7B 44
Lower Frankton. Shrp 6B 34
Lower Froyle. Hants 1E 10
Lower Gabwell. Devn 5M 5
Lower Gledfield. High 4F 78
Lower Godney. Som 1C 8
Lower Gravenhurst. C Beds 8J 29
Lower Green. Essx 8M 29
Lower Green. Norf 6F 38
Lower Green. W Ber 7A 20
Lower Halstow. Kent 7E 22
Lower Hardres. Kent 8H 23
Lower Hardwick. Here 6C 26
Lower Hartshay. Derbs 4A 36
Lower Hawthwaite. Cumb 6M 45
Lower Haysden. Kent 1B 12
Lower Hayton. Shrp 3D 26
Lower Hergest. Here 6A 26
Lower Heyford. Oxon 1B 20
Lower Heysham. Lanc 1C 40
Lower Higham. Kent 6D 22
Lower Holbrook. Suff 8H 31
Lower Holditch. Dors 5B 8
Lower Hordley. Shrp 7B 34
Lower Horncroft. W Sus 4H 11
Lower Horsebridge. E Sus 4B 12
Lower Kilcott. Glos 5F 18
Lower Killeyan. Arg 5B 56
Lower Kingcombe. Dors 6D 8
Lower Kingswood. Surr 8K 21
Lower Kinnerton. Ches W 3B 34
Lower Langford. N Som 7C 18
Lower Largo. Fife 7H 67
Lower Layham. Suff 7G 31
Lower Ledwyche. Shrp 4D 26
Lower Leigh. Staf 6J 35
Lower Lemington. Glos 8L 27
Lower Lenie. High 3F 70
Lower Ley. Glos 2F 18
Lower Llanfadog. Powy 6J 25
Lower Lode. Glos 8G 27
Lower Lovacott. Devn 3E 6
Lower Loxhore. Devn 2F 6
Lower Loxley. Staf 6J 35
Lower Lydbrook. Glos 2D 18
Lower Lye. Here 5C 26
Lower Machen. Newp 6M 17
Lower Maes-coed. Here 8B 26
Lower Meend. Glos 3D 18
Lower Midway. Derbs 7M 35
Lower Milovaig. High 8C 76
Lower Moor. Worc 7H 27
Lower Morton. S Glo 4E 18
Lower Mountain. Flin 4B 34
Lower Nazeing. Essx 3L 21
Lower Netchwood. Shrp 2E 26
Lower Nyland. Dors 3F 8
Lower Oakfield. Fife 8E 66
Lower Oddington. Glos 1L 19
Lower Ollach. High 2G 69
Lower Penarth. V Glam 8L 17
Lower Penn. Staf 2G 27
Lower Pennington. Hants 6M 9
Lower Peover. Ches W 2F 34
Lower Pilsley. Derbs 3B 36
Lower Pitkerrie. High 6J 79
Lower Place. G Man 6H 41
Lower Quinton. Warw 7K 27
Lower Rainham. Medw 7E 22
Lower Raydon. Suff 8G 31
Lower Seagry. Wilts 5H 19
Lower Shelton. C Beds 7G 29
Lower Shiplake. Oxon 6E 20
Lower Shuckburgh. Warw 5B 28
Lower Sketty. Swan 5F 16
Lower Slade. Devn 1E 6
Lower Slaughter. Glos 1K 19
Lower Soudley. Glos 2E 18
Lower Stanton St Quintin. Wilts 5H 19
Lower Stoke. Medw 6E 22
Lower Stondon. C Beds 8J 29
Lower Stonnall. Staf 1J 27
Lower Stow Bedon. Norf 2F 30
Lower Street. Norf 6J 39
Lower Strensham. Worc 7H 27
Lower Sundon. C Beds 1H 21
Lower Swanwick. Hants 5B 10
Lower Swell. Glos 1K 19
Lower Tale. Devn 5K 7
Lower Tean. Staf 6J 35
Lower Thurlton. Norf 2L 31
Lower Thurnham. Lanc 2C 40
Lower Thurvaston. Derbs 6L 35
Lower Town. Here 7E 26
Lower Town. IOS 1H 3
Lower Town. Pemb 3F 14
Lowertown. Corn 6K 3
Lowertown. Orkn 2F 86
Lower Tysoe. Warw 7M 27
Lower Upham. Hants 4C 10
Lower Upnor. Medw 6D 22
Lower Vexford. Som 2L 7
Lower Walton. Warr 1E 34
Lower Wear. Devn 7J 7
Lower Weare. Som 8C 18
Lower Welson. Here 6A 26
Lower Whatcombe. Dors 5G 9
Lower Whitley. Ches W 2E 34
Lower Wield. Hants 1D 10
Lower Withington. Ches E 3G 35
Lower Woodend. Buck 5F 20
Lower Woodford. Wilts 2K 9
Lower Wraxall. Dors 5D 8
Lower Wych. Ches W 5C 34
Lower Wyche. Worc 7F 26
Lowesby. Leics 1E 28
Lowestoft. Suff 2M 31
Loweswater. Cumb 2L 45
Low Etherley. Dur 3K 47
Lowfield Heath. W Sus 1K 11
Lowford. Hants 4B 10
Low Fulney. Linc 7K 37
Low Gate. Nmbd 5C 54
Lowgill. Cumb 6E 46
Lowgill. Lanc 1E 40
Low Grantley. N Yor 8L 47
Low Green. N Yor 2L 41
Low Habberley. Worc 4G 27
Low Ham. Som 3C 8
Low Hameringham. Linc 3L 37
Low Hawsker. N Yor 5G 49
Low Hesket. Cumb 7J 53
Low Hesleyhurst. Nmbd 2D 54
Lowick. Cumb 7A 46
Lowick. Nptn 3G 29
Lowick. Nmbd 6H 61
Lowick Bridge. Cumb 7A 46
Lowick Green. Cumb 7A 46
Low Knipe. Cumb 3D 46
Low Leighton. Derbs 1J 35
Low Lorton. Cumb 2L 45
Low Marishes. N Yor 8F 48
Low Marnham. Notts 3F 36
Low Mill. N Yor 6D 48
Low Moor. Lanc 3F 40
Low Moor. W Yor 5K 41
Low Moorsley. Tyne 7G 55
Low Newton-by-the-Sea. Nmbd 7K 61
Lownie Moor. Ang 3H 67
Lowood. Bord 6C 60
Low Row. Cumb
nr. Brampton 5K 53
nr. Wigton 7F 52
Low Row. N Yor 6H 47
Lowsonford. Warw 5K 27
Low Street. Norf 1G 31
Lowther. Cumb 3D 46
Lowthorpe. E Yor 1H 43
Lowton. Devn 5F 6
Lowton. G Man 8E 40
Lowton. Som 4L 7
Lowton Common. G Man 8E 40
Low Torry. Fife 1J 59
Low Toynton. Linc 2K 37
Low Valleyfield. Fife 1H 59
Low Westwood. Dur 6E 54
Low Whinnow. Cumb 6H 53
Low Wood. Cumb 7B 46
Low Worsall. N Yor 5A 48
Low Wray. Cumb 5B 46
Loxbeare. Devn 4J 7
Loxhill. Surr 2H 11
Loxhore. Devn 2F 6
Loxley. S Yor 1M 35
Loxley. Warw 6L 27
Loxley Green. Staf 6J 35
Loxton. N Som 8B 18
Loxwood. W Sus 2H 11
Lubcroy. High 3D 78
Lubenham. Leics 3E 28
Lubinvullin. High 5H 85
Luccombe. Som 1J 7
Luccombe Village. IOW 7C 10
Lucker. Nmbd 6J 61
Luckett. Corn 8C 6
Luckington. Wilts 5G 19
Lucklawhill. Fife 5H 67
Luckwell Bridge. Som 2J 7
Lucton. Here 5C 26
Ludag. W Isl 4D 74
Ludborough. Linc 8K 43
Ludchurch. Pemb 5H 15
Luddenden. W Yor 5J 41
Luddenden Foot. W Yor 5J 41
Luddenham. Kent 7F 22
Ludderburn. Cumb 6C 46
Luddesdown. Kent 7C 22
Luddington. N Lin 6F 42
Luddington. Warw 6K 27
Luddington in the Brook. Nptn 3J 29
Ludford. Linc 1J 37
Ludford. Shrp 4D 26
Ludgershall. Buck 2D 20
Ludgershall. Wilts 8L 19
Ludgvan. Corn 5J 3
Ludham. Norf 8K 39
Ludlow. Shrp 4D 26
Ludstone. Shrp 2G 27
Ludwell. Wilts 3H 9
Ludworth. Dur 7G 55
Luffenhall. Herts 1K 21
Luffincott. Devn 6C 6
Lugar. E Ayr 7D 58
Luggate Burn. E Lot 2D 60
Lugg Green. Here 5C 26
Luggiebank. N Lan 2F 58
Lugton. E Ayr 4C 58
Lugwardine. Here 7D 26
Luib. High 3G 69
Luib. Stir 5J 65
Lulham. Here 7C 26
Lullington. Derbs 8L 35
Lullington. E Sus 5B 12
Lullington. Som 8F 18
Lulsgate Bottom. N Som 7D 18
Lulsley. Worc 6F 26
Lulworth Camp. Dors 7G 9
Lumb. Lanc 5G 41
Lumby. N Yor 4B 42
Lumphanan. Abers 5E 72
Lumphinnans. Fife 8E 66
Lumsdaine. Bord 3F 60
Lumsden. Abers 3D 72
Lunan. Ang 2K 67
Lunanhead. Ang 2H 67
Luncarty. Per 5D 66
Lund. E Yor 3G 43
Lund. N Yor 4D 42
Lundie. Ang 4F 66
Lundin Links. Fife 7H 67
Lundy Green. Norf 2J 31
Lunna. Shet 1E 90
Lunning. Shet 1F 90
Lunnon. Swan 8M 15
Lunsford. Kent 8C 22
Lunsford's Cross. E Sus 4D 12
Lunt. Mers 7B 40
Luppitt. Devn 5L 7
Lupridge. Devn 6K 5
Lupset. W Yor 6M 41
Lupton. Cumb 7D 46
Lurgan. Arm 6G 93
Lurganare. New M 7G 93
Lurgashall. W Sus 3G 11
Lurley. Devn 4J 7
Lusby. Linc 3L 37
Luscombe. Devn 6K 5
Luson. Devn 7J 5
Luss. Arg 8H 65
Lussagiven. Arg 1F 56
Lusta. High 8D 76
Lustleigh. Devn 7G 7
Luston. Here 5C 26
Luthermuir. Abers 1K 67
Luthrie. Fife 6G 67
Lutley. Staf 3G 27
Luton. Devn
nr. Honiton 5K 7
nr. Teignmouth 8J 7
Luton. Lutn 1H 21
Luton Airport. Lutn 119 (1J 21)
Lutterworth. Leics 3C 28
Lutton. Devn
nr. Ivybridge 6H 5
nr. South Brent 5J 5
Lutton. Linc 7M 37
Lutton. Nptn 3J 29
Lutton Gowts. Linc 7M 37
Lutworthy. Devn 4G 7
Luxborough. Som 2J 7
Luxley. Glos 1E 18
Luxulyan. Corn 6C 4
Lybster. High 8D 86
Lydbury North. Shrp 3B 26
Lydcott. Devn 2F 6
Lydd. Kent 3G 13
Lydd Airport. Kent 3G 13
Lydden. Kent
nr. Dover 1J 13
nr. Margate 7K 23
Lyddington. Rut 2F 28
Lydd-on-Sea. Kent 3G 13
Lydeard St Lawrence. Som 2L 7
Lyde Green. Hants 8E 20
Lydford. Devn 7E 6
Lydford Fair Place. Som 2D 8
Lydgate. G Man 7H 41
Lydgate. W Yor 5H 41
Lydham. Shrp 2B 26
Lydiard Millicent. Wilts 5J 19
Lydiate. Mers 7B 40
Lydiate Ash. Worc 4H 27
Lydlinch. Dors 4F 8
Lydmarsh. Som 5B 8
Lydney. Glos 3E 18
Lydstep. Pemb 7G 15
Lye. W Mid 3H 27
The Lye. Shrp 2E 26
Lye Green. Buck 3G 21
Lye Green. E Sus 2B 12
Lye Head. Worc 4F 26
Lyford. Oxon 4A 20
Lyham. Nmbd 6H 61
Lylestone. N Ayr 5B 58
Lymbridge Green. Kent 1H 13
Lyme Regis. Dors 6B 8
Lyminge. Kent 1H 13
Lymington. Hants 6M 9
Lyminster. W Sus 5H 11
Lymm. Warr 1E 34
Lymore. Hants 6L 9
Lympne. Kent 2H 13
Lympsham. Som 8B 18
Lympstone. Devn 7J 7
Lynaberack Lodge. High 6H 71
Lynbridge. Devn 1G 7
Lynch. Som 1J 7
Lynchat. High 5H 71
Lynch Green. Norf 1H 31
Lyndhurst. Hants 5M 9
Lyndon. Rut 1G 29
Lyne. Bord 5L 59
Lyne. Surr 7H 21
Lyneal. Shrp 6C 34
Lyne Down. Here 8E 26
Lyneham. Oxon 1L 19
Lyneham. Wilts 6J 19
Lyneholmeford. Cumb 4K 53
Lynemouth. Nmbd 2F 54
Lyne of Gorthleck. High 3F 70
Lyne of Skene. Abers 4G 73
Lynesack. Dur 3J 47
Lyness. Orkn 2E 86
Lyng. Norf 8G 39
Lyngate. Norf
nr. North Walsham 6J 39
nr. Worstead 7K 39
Lynmouth. Devn 1G 7
Lynn. Staf 1J 27
Lynn. Telf 8F 34
Lynsted. Kent 7F 22
Lynstone. Corn 5B 6
Lynton. Devn 1G 7
Lynwilg. High 4J 71
Lyon's Gate. Dors 5E 8
Lyonshall. Here 6B 26
Lytchett Matravers. Dors 6H 9
Lytchett Minster. Dors 6H 9
Lyth. High 5D 86
Lytham. Lanc 5B 40
Lytham St Anne's. Lanc 5B 40
Lythe. N Yor 4F 48
Lythes. Orkn 3F 86
Lythmore. High 5B 86

M

Mabe Burnthouse. Corn 5L 3
Mabie. Dum 4D 52
Mablethorpe. Linc 1B 38
Macbiehill. Bord 4K 59
Macclesfield. Ches E 2H 35
Macclesfield Forest. Ches E 2H 35
Macduff. Abers 7G 81
Machan. S Lan 4F 58
Macharioch. Arg 1C 50
Machen. Cphy 6M 17
Machrie. N Ayr 6H 57
Machrihanish. Arg 7F 56
Machroes. Gwyn 8C 32
Machynlleth. Powy 2G 25
Mackerye End. Herts 2J 21
Mackworth. Derb 6M 35
Macmerry. E Lot 2B 60
Macosquin. Caus 2F 93
Madderty. Per 5C 66
Maddington. Wilts 1J 9
Maddiston. Falk 2H 59
Madehurst. W Sus 4G 11
Madeley. Staf 5F 34
Madeley. Telf 1E 26
Madeley Heath. Staf 5F 34
Madeley Heath. Worc 4H 27
Madford. Devn 4L 7
Madingley. Cambs 5L 29
Madley. Here 8C 26
Madresfield. Worc 7G 27
Madron. Corn 5H 3
Maenaddwyn. IOA 2D 32
Maenclochog. Pemb 4G 15
Maendy. V Glam 7K 17
Maenporth. Corn 6L 3
Maentwrog. Gwyn 6F 32
Maen-y-groes. Cdgn 1K 15
Maer. Staf 6F 34
Maerdy. Carm 2F 16
Maerdy. Cnwy 6K 33
Maerdy. Rhon 5J 17
Maesbrook. Shrp 7B 34
Maesbury. Shrp 7B 34
Maesbury Marsh. Shrp 7B 34
Maes-glas. Flin 3L 33
Maesgwyn-Isaf. Powy 1L 25
Maeshafn. Den 4M 33
Maes Llyn. Cdgn 2K 15
Maesmynis. Powy 8K 25
Maesteg. B'end 5H 17
Maestir. Cdgn 8E 24
Maesybont. Carm 3E 16
Maesycrugiau. Carm 2L 15
Maesycwmmer. Cphy 5L 17
Maesyrhandir. Powy 3K 25
Magdalen Laver. Essx 3B 22
Maggieknockater. Mor 1C 72
Maghaberry. Lis 5G 93
Magham Down. E Sus 4C 12
Maghera. M Ulst 3F 93
Maghera. New M 7H 93
Magherafelt. M Ulst 4F 93
Magheralin. Arm 6G 93
Magheramason. Derr 3C 92
Magheraveely. Ferm 7D 92
Maghery. Arm 5F 93
Maghull. Mers 7B 40
Magna Park. Leics 3C 28
Magor. Mon 5C 18
Magpie Green. Suff 4G 31
Maguiresbridge. Ferm 7C 92
Magwyr. Mon 5C 18
Maidenbower. W Sus 2K 11
Maiden Bradley. Wilts 2G 9
Maidencombe. Torb 5M 5
Maidenhayne. Devn 6A 8
Maidenhead. Wind 5F 20
Maiden Law. Dur 7E 54
Maiden Newton. Dors 6D 8
Maidens. S Ayr 1H 51
Maiden's Green. Brac 6F 20
Maidensgrove. Oxon 5E 20
Maidenwell. Corn 4D 4
Maidenwell. Linc 2L 37
Maiden Wells. Pemb 7F 14
Maidford. Nptn 6D 28
Maids Moreton. Buck 8E 28
Maidstone. Kent 8D 22
Maidwell. Nptn 4E 28
Mail. Shet 5E 90
Maindee. Newp 5B 18
Mainsforth. Dur 8G 55
Mains of Auchindachy. Mor 1D 72
Mains of Auchnagatt. Abers 1J 73
Mains of Drum. Abers 6H 73
Mains of Edingight. Mor 8E 80
Mainsriddle. Dum 6D 52
Mainstone. Shrp 3A 26
Maisemore. Glos 1G 19
Major's Green. Worc 4K 27
Makeney. Derbs 5A 36
Makerstoun. Bord 6D 60
Malacleit. W Isl 6J 75
Malaig. High 6H 69
Malaig Bheag. High 6H 69
Malborough. Devn 8K 5
Malcoff. Derbs 1J 35
Malcolmburn. Mor 8C 80
Malden Rushett. G Lon 7J 21
Maldon. Essx 3E 22
Malham. N Yor 1H 41
Maligar. High 7F 76
Malinslee. Telf 1E 26
Mallaig. High 6H 69
Malleny Mills. Edin 3K 59
Mallows Green. Essx 1A 22
Malltraeth. IOA 4D 32
Mallusk. Ant 4H 93
Mallwyd. Gwyn 1H 25
Malmesbury. Wilts 5H 19
Malmsmead. Devn 1G 7
Malpas. Ches W 5C 34
Malpas. Corn 4M 3
Malpas. Newp 4B 18
Malswick. Glos 1F 18
Maltby. S Yor 8C 42
Maltby. Stoc T 4B 48
Maltby le Marsh. Linc 1A 38
Malt Lane. Arg 7E 64
Maltman's Hill. Kent 1F 12
Malton. N Yor 8E 48
Malvern Link. Worc 7F 26
Malvern Wells. Worc 7F 26
Mamble. Worc 4E 26
Mamhilad. Mon 3B 18
Manaccan. Corn 6L 3
Manafon. Powy 2L 25
Manais. W Isl 5C 76
Manaton. Devn 7G 7
Manby. Linc 1L 37
Mancetter. Warw 2M 27
Manchester. G Man 111 (8G 41)
Manchester Airport. G Man 119 (1G 35)
Mancot. Flin 3B 34
Manea. Cambs 3A 30
Maney. W Mid 2K 27
Manfield. N Yor 4L 47
Mangotsfield. S Glo 6E 18
Mangurstadh. W Isl 8D 82
Mankinholes. W Yor 5H 41
Manley. Ches W 2D 34
Manmoel. Cphy 4L 17
Mannal. Arg 3E 62
Mannerston. Falk 2J 59
Manningford Bohune. Wilts 8K 19
Manningford Bruce. Wilts 8K 19
Manningham. W Yor 4K 41
Mannings Heath. W Sus 3K 11
Mannington. Dors 5J 9
Manningtree. Essx 8H 31
Mannofield. Aber 5J 73
Manorbier. Pemb 7G 15
Manorbier Newton. Pemb 7G 15
Manordeilo. Carm 2F 16
Manorowen. Pemb 3F 14
Manor Park. G Lon 5M 21
Mansell Gamage. Here 7B 26
Mansell Lacy. Here 7C 26
Mansergh. Cumb 7E 46
Mansewood. Glas 3D 58
Mansfield. E Ayr 8E 58
Mansfield. Notts 3C 36
Mansfield Woodhouse. Notts 3C 36
Mansriggs. Cumb 7A 46
Manston. Dors 4G 9
Manston. Kent 7K 23
Manston. W Yor 4A 42
Manswood. Dors 5H 9
Manthorpe. Linc
nr. Bourne 8H 37
nr. Grantham 6G 37
Manton. N Lin 7G 43
Manton. Notts 2C 36
Manton. Rut 1F 28
Manton. Wilts 7K 19
Manuden. Essx 1A 22
Maperton. Som 3E 8
Maplebeck. Notts 3E 36
Maple Cross. Herts 4H 21
Mapledurham. Oxon 6D 20
Mapledurwell. Hants 8D 20
Maplehurst. W Sus 3J 11
Maplescombe. Kent 7B 22
Mapleton. Derbs 5K 35
Mapperley. Derbs 5B 36
Mapperley. Nott 5C 36
Mapperley Park. Nott 5C 36
Mapperton. Dors
nr. Beaminster 6D 8
nr. Poole 6H 9
Mappleborough Green. Warw 5J 27
Mappleton. E Yor 3K 43
Mapplewell. S Yor 7M 41
Mappowder. Dors 5F 8
Maraig. W Isl 3D 76
Marazion. Corn 5J 3
Marbhig. W Isl 2F 76
Marbury. Ches E 5D 34
March. Cambs 2M 29
Marcham. Oxon 4B 20
Marchamley. Shrp 7D 34
Marchington. Staf 6K 35
Marchington Woodlands. Staf 7K 35
Marchwiel. Wrex 5B 34
Marchwood. Hants 4A 10
Marcross. V Glam 8J 17
Marden. Here 7D 26
Marden. Kent 1D 12
Marden. Wilts 8J 19
Marden Beech. Kent 1D 12
Marden Thorn. Kent 1D 12
Mardu. Shrp 3A 26
Mardy. Mon 2B 18
Marefield. Leics 1E 28
Mareham le Fen. Linc 3K 37
Mareham on the Hill. Linc 3K 37
Marehay. Derbs 5B 36
Marehill. W Sus 4H 11
Maresfield. E Sus 3A 12
Marfleet. Hull 5J 43
Marford. Wrex 4B 34
Margam. Neat 6G 17
Margaret Marsh. Dors 4G 9
Margaret Roding. Essx 2B 22
Margaretting. Essx 3C 22
Margaretting Tye. Essx 3C 22
Margate. Kent 6K 23
Margery. Surr 8K 21
Margnaheglish. N Ayr 6K 57
Marham. Norf 1D 30
Marhamchurch. Corn 5B 6
Marholm. Pet 1J 29
Marian Cwm. Den 3K 33
Mariandyrys. IOA 2F 32
Marian-glas. IOA 2E 32
Mariansleigh. Devn 3G 7
Marian-y-de. Gwyn 7C 32
Marian-y-mor. Gwyn 7C 32
Marine Town. Kent 6F 22
Marishader. High 7F 76
Marjoriebanks. Dum 3E 52
Mark. Dum 6G 51
Mark. Som 1B 8
Markbeech. Kent 1A 12
Markby. Linc 2A 38
Mark Causeway. Som 1B 8
Mark Cross. E Sus 2B 12
Markeaton. Derb 6M 35
Market Bosworth. Leics 1B 28
Market Deeping. Linc 8J 37
Market Drayton. Shrp 6E 34
Market End. Warw 3M 27
Market Harborough. Leics 3E 28
Markethill. Arm 7F 93
Markethill. Per 4F 66
Market Lavington. Wilts 8J 19
Market Overton. Rut 8F 36
Market Rasen. Linc 1J 37
Market Stainton. Linc 1K 37
Market Weighton. E Yor 3F 42
Market Weston. Suff 4F 30
Markfield. Leics 8B 36
Markham. Cphy 4L 17
Markinch. Fife 7F 66
Markington. N Yor 1L 41
Marksbury. Bath 7E 18
Mark's Corner. IOW 6B 10
Marks Tey. Essx 1F 22
Markwell. Corn 6F 4
Markyate. Herts 2H 21
Marlborough. Wilts 7K 19
Marlcliff. Warw 6J 27
Marldon. Devn 5L 5
Marle Green. E Sus 4B 12
Marlesford. Suff 6K 31
Marley Green. Ches E 5D 34
Marley Hill. Tyne 6F 54
Marlingford. Norf 1H 31
Mar Lodge. Abers 7L 71
Marloes. Pemb 6D 14
Marlow. Buck 5F 20
Marlow. Here 4B 26
Marlow Bottom. Buck 5F 20
Marlow Common. Buck 5F 20
Marlpit Hill. Kent 1M 11
Marlpits. E Sus 3M 11
Marlpool. Derbs 5B 36
Marnhull. Dors 4F 8
Marnoch. Abers 8E 80
Marnock. N Lan 3F 58
Marple. G Man 1H 35
Marr. S Yor 7C 42
Marrel. High 2L 79
Marrick. N Yor 6J 47
Marrister. Shet 1F 90
Marros. Carm 6J 15
Marsden. Tyne 5G 55
Marsden. W Yor 6J 41
Marsett. N Yor 7H 47
Marsh. Buck 3F 20
Marsh. Devn 4A 8
The Marsh. Powy 2B 26
The Marsh. Shrp 7E 34
Marshall Meadows. Nmbd 4G 61
Marshalsea. Dors 5B 8
Marshalswick. Herts 3J 21
Marsham. Norf 7H 39
Marshaw. Lanc 2D 40
Marsh Baldon. Oxon 4C 20
Marsh Benham. W Ber 7B 20
Marshborough. Kent 8K 23
Marshbrook. Shrp 3C 26
Marshchapel. Linc 8L 43
Marshfield. Newp 5A 18
Marshfield. S Glo 6F 18
Marshgate. Corn 6A 6
Marsh Gibbon. Buck 1D 20
Marsh Green. Devn 6K 7
Marsh Green. Kent 1M 11
Marsh Green. Staf 4G 35
Marsh Green. Telf 8E 34
Marsh Lane. Derbs 2B 36
Marsh Side. Norf 5D 38
Marshside. Kent 7J 23
Marshside. Mers 6B 40
Marsh Street. Som 1J 7
Marshwood. Dors 6B 8
Marske. N Yor 5K 47
Marske-by-the-Sea. Red C 3D 48
Marston. Ches W 2E 34
Marston. Here 6B 26
Marston. Linc 5F 36
Marston. Oxon 3C 20
Marston. Staf
nr. Stafford 7H 35
nr. Wheaton Aston 8G 35
Marston. Warw 2L 27
Marston. Wilts 8H 19
Marston Doles. Warw 6B 28
Marston Green. W Mid 3K 27
Marston Hill. Glos 4K 19
Marston Jabbett. Warw 3A 28
Marston Magna. Som 3D 8
Marston Meysey. Wilts 4K 19
Marston Montgomery. Derbs 6K 35
Marston Moretaine. C Beds 7G 29
Marston on Dove. Derbs 7L 35
Marston St Lawrence. Nptn 7C 28
Marston Stannett. Here 6D 26
Marston Trussell. Nptn 3D 28
Marstow. Here 2D 18
Marsworth. Buck 2G 21
Marten. Wilts 8L 19
Marthall. Ches E 2G 35
Martham. Norf 8L 39
Marthwaite. Cumb 6E 46
Martin. Hants 4J 9
Martin. Kent 1K 13
Martin. Linc
nr. Horncastle 3K 37
nr. Metheringham 4J 37
Martindale. Cumb 4C 46
Martin Dales. Linc 3J 37
Martin Drove End. Hants 3J 9
Martinhoe. Devn 1F 6
Martinhoe Cross. Devn 1F 6
Martin Hussingtree. Worc 5G 27
Martin Mill. Kent 1K 13
Martinscroft. Warr 1E 34
Martin's Moss. Ches E 3G 35
Martinstown. Dors 7E 8
Martinstown. ME Ant 3G 93
Martlesham. Suff 7J 31
Martlesham Heath. Suff 7J 31
Martletwy. Pemb 5G 15
Martley. Worc 5F 26
Martock. Som 4C 8
Marton. Ches E 3G 35
Marton. Cumb 7M 45
Marton. E Yor
nr. Bridlington 1K 43
nr. Hull 4J 43
Marton. Linc 1F 36
Marton. Midd 4C 48
Marton. N Yor
nr. Boroughbridge 1B 42
nr. Pickering 7E 48
Marton. Shrp
nr. Myddle 7C 34
nr. Worthen 1A 26
Marton. Warw 5B 28
Marton Abbey. N Yor 1C 42
Marton-le-Moor. N Yor 8A 48
Martyr's Green. Surr 8H 21
Martyr Worthy. Hants 2C 10
Marwick. Orkn 7B 88
Marwood. Devn 2E 6
Marybank. High
nr. Dingwall 8E 78
nr. Invergordon 6H 79
Maryburgh. High 8F 78
Maryfield. Corn 6G 5
Maryhill. Glas 3D 58
Marykirk. Abers 1K 67
Marylebone. G Lon 5K 21
Marylebone. G Man 7D 40
Marypark. Mor 2A 72
Maryport. Cumb 8E 52
Maryport. Dum 8G 51
Marystow. Devn 7D 6
Mary Tavy. Devn 8E 6
Maryton. Ang
nr. Kirriemuir 2G 67
nr. Montrose 2K 67
Marywell. Abers 6E 72
Marywell. Ang 3K 67
Masham. N Yor 7L 47
Mashbury. Essx 2C 22
Masongill. N Yor 8E 46
Masons Lodge. Abers 5H 73
Mastin Moor. Derbs 2B 36
Mastrick. Aber 5J 73
Matching. Essx 2B 22
Matching Green. Essx 2B 22
Matching Tye. Essx 2B 22
Matfen. Nmbd 4D 54
Matfield. Kent 1C 12
Mathern. Mon 4D 18
Mathon. Here 7F 26
Mathry. Pemb 3E 14
Matlaske. Norf 6H 39
Matlock. Derbs 4L 35
Matlock Bath. Derbs 4L 35
Matterdale End. Cumb 3B 46
Mattersey. Notts 1D 36
Mattersey Thorpe. Notts 1D 36
Mattingley. Hants 8E 20
Mattishall. Norf 8G 39
Mattishall Burgh. Norf 8G 39
Mauchline. E Ayr 7C 58
Maud. Abers 1J 73
Maudlin. Corn 5C 4
Maugersbury. Glos 1K 19
Maughold. IOM 5D 44
Maulden. C Beds 8H 29
Maulds Meaburn. Cumb 4E 46
Maunby. N Yor 7A 48
Maund Bryan. Here 6D 26
Mautby. Norf 8L 39
Mavesyn Ridware. Staf 8J 35
Mavis Enderby. Linc 3L 37
Mawbray. Cumb 7E 52
Mawdesley. Lanc 6C 40
Mawdlam. B'end 6H 17
Mawgan. Corn 6L 3
Mawgan Porth. Corn 2M 3
Maw Green. Ches E 4F 34
Mawla. Corn 4L 3
Mawnan. Corn 6L 3
Mawnan Smith. Corn 6L 3
Mawsley Village. Nptn 4E 28
Mawthorpe. Linc 2A 38
Maxey. Pet 1J 29
Maxstoke. Warw 3L 27
Maxted Street. Kent 1H 13
Maxton. Kent 1J 13
Maxton. Bord 6D 60
Maxwellheugh. Bord 6E 60
Maxwelltown. Dum 4D 52
Maxworthy. Corn 6B 6
Mayals. Swan 6F 16
Maybole. S Ayr 8B 58
Maybush. Sotn 4A 10
Maydown. Derr 3D 92
Mayes Green. Surr 2J 11
Mayfield. E Sus 3B 12
Mayfield. Midl 3A 60
Mayfield. Per 5D 66
Mayfield. Staf 5K 35
Mayford. Surr 8G 21
Mayhill. Swan 5F 16
Mayland. Essx 3F 22
Maylandsea. Essx 3F 22
Maynard's Green. E Sus 4B 12
Mayobridge. New M 7G 93
Maypole. IOS 1H 3
Maypole. Kent 7J 23
Maypole. Mon 2C 18
Maypole Green. Norf 2L 31
Maypole Green. Suff 6F 30
Maywick. Shet 5D 90
Mazetown. Lis 5H 93
Mead. Devn 4B 6
Meadgate. Bath 8E 18

Otley—Poundland

Otley. Suff 6J 31
Otley. W Yor 3L 41
Otterbourne. Hants 3B 10
Otterburn. Nmbd 2B 54
Otterburn. N Yor 2G 41
Otterburn Camp. Nmbd 2B 54
Otterburn Hall. Nmbd 2B 54
Otter Ferry. Arg 1J 57
Otterford. Som 4M 7
Otterham. Corn 6A 6
Otterhampton. Som 1M 7
Otterham Quay. Medw 7E 22
Ottershaw. Surr 7H 21
Otterspool. Mers 1B 34
Otterswick. Shet 5K 91
Otterton. Devn 7K 7
Otterwood. Hants 5B 10
Ottery St Mary. Devn 6K 7
Ottinge. Kent 1H 13
Ottringham. E Yor 5K 43
Oughterby. Cumb 6G 53
Oughtershaw. N Yor 7G 47
Oughterside. Cumb 7F 52
Oughtibridge. S Yor 8M 41
Oughtrington. Warr 1E 34
Oulston. N Yor 8C 48
Oulton. Cumb 6G 53
Oulton. Norf 7H 39
Oulton. Staf
nr. Gnosall Heath 7F 34
nr. Stone 6H 35
Oulton. Suff 2M 31
Oulton. W Yor 5A 42
Oulton Broad. Suff 2M 31
Oulton Street. Norf 7H 39
Oundle. Nptn 3H 29
Ousby. Cumb 8L 53
Ousdale. High 2L 79
Ousden. Suff 6D 30
Ousefleet. E Yor 5F 42
Ouston. Dur 6F 54
Ouston. Nmbd
nr. Bearsbridge 6A 54
nr. Stamfordham 4D 54
Outer Hope. Devn 7J 5
Outertown. Orkn 8B 88
Outgate. Cumb 6B 46
Outhgill. Cumb 5F 46
Outlands. Staf 6F 34
Outlane. W Yor 6J 41
Out Newton. E Yor 5L 43
Out Rawcliffe. Lanc 3C 40
Outwell. Norf 1B 30
Outwick. Hants 4K 9
Outwood. Surr 1L 11
Outwood. W Yor 5M 41
Outwood. Worc 4H 27
Outwoods. Leics 8B 36
Outwoods. Staf 8F 34
Ouzlewell Green. W Yor 5M 41
Ovenden. W Yor 5J 41
Over. Cambs 4L 29
Over. Ches W 3E 34
Over. Glos 2G 19
Over. S Glo 5D 18
Overbister. Orkn 5F 88
Over Burrows. Derbs 6L 35
Overbury. Worc 8H 27
Overcombe. Dors 7E 8
Over Compton. Dors 4D 8
Over End. Cambs 2H 29
Over Finlarg. Ang 3H 67
Over Green. Warw 2K 27
Overgreen. Derbs 2M 35
Over Haddon. Derbs 3L 35
Over Hulton. G Man 7E 40
Over Kellet. Lanc 8D 46
Over Kiddington. Oxon 1B 20
Overleigh. Som 2C 8
Overley. Staf 8K 35
Over Monnow. Mon 2D 18
Over Norton. Oxon 1M 19
Over Peover. Ches E 2F 34
Overpool. Ches W 2B 34
Overscaig. High 1E 78
Overseal. Derbs 8L 35
Over Silton. N Yor 6B 48
Oversland. Kent 8G 23
Overstone. Nptn 5F 28
Over Stowey. Som 2L 7
Overstrand. Norf 5J 39
Over Stratton. Som 4C 8
Over Street. Wilts 2J 9
Overthorpe. Nptn 7B 28
Overton. Aber 4H 73
Overton. Ches W 2D 34
Overton. Hants 1C 10
Overton. High 8D 86
Overton. Lanc 2C 40
Overton. N Yor 2C 42
Overton. Shrp
nr. Bridgnorth 3E 26
nr. Ludlow 4D 26
Overton. Swan 8L 15
Overton. W Yor 6L 41
Overton. Wrex 5B 34
Overtown. Lanc 8E 46
Overtown. N Lan 4G 59
Overtown. Swin 6K 19
Over Wallop. Hants 2L 9
Over Whitacre. Warw 2L 27
Over Worton. Oxon 1B 20
Oving. Buck 1E 20
Oving. W Sus 5G 11
Ovingdean. Brig 5L 11
Ovingham. Nmbd 5D 54
Ovington. Dur 4K 47
Ovington. Essx 7D 30
Ovington. Hants 2C 10
Ovington. Norf 1F 30
Ovington. Nmbd 5D 54
Owen's Bank. Staf 7L 35
Ower. Hants
nr. Holbury 5B 10
nr. Totton 4M 9
Owermoigne. Dors 7F 8
Owlbury. Shrp 2B 26
Owler Bar. Derbs 2L 35
Owlerton. S Yor 8M 41
Owlsmoor. Brac 7F 20
Owlswick. Buck 3E 20
Owmby. Linc 7H 43
Owmby-by-Spital. Linc 1H 37
Ownham. W Ber 6B 20
Owrytn. Wrex 5B 34
Owslebury. Hants 3C 10
Owston. Leics 1E 28
Owston. S Yor 6C 42
Owston Ferry. N Lin 7F 42
Owstwick. E Yor 4K 43
Owthorne. E Yor 5L 43
Owthorpe. Notts 6D 36
Owton Manor. Hart 3B 48
Oxborough. Norf 1D 30
Oxbridge. Dors 6C 8
Oxcombe. Linc 2L 37
Oxen End. Essx 1C 22
Oxenhall. Glos 1F 18
Oxenholme. Cumb 6D 46
Oxenhope. W Yor 4J 41
Oxen Park. Cumb 7B 46
Oxenpill. Som 1C 8
Oxenton. Glos 8H 27
Oxenwood. Wilts 8M 19
Oxford. Oxon 114 (3C 20)
Oxgangs. Edin 3L 59
Oxhey. Herts 4J 21
Oxhill. Warw 7M 27
Oxley. W Mid 1H 27
Oxley Green. Essx 2F 22
Oxley's Green. E Sus 3C 12
Oxlode. Cambs 3A 30
Oxnam. Bord 8E 60
Oxshott. Surr 7J 21
Oxspring. S Yor 7L 41
Oxted. Surr 8L 21
Oxton. Mers 1B 34
Oxton. N Yor 3C 42
Oxton. Notts 4D 36
Oxton. Bord 4B 60
Oxwich. Swan 8L 15
Oxwich Green. Swan 8L 15
Oxwick. Norf 7F 38
Oykel Bridge. High 3D 78
Oyne. Abers 3F 72
Oystermouth. Swan 6F 16
Ozleworth. Glos 4F 18

P

Pabail Iarach. W Isl 8J 83
Pabail Uarach. W Isl 8J 83
Pachesham Park. Surr 8J 21
Packers Hill. Dors 4F 8
Packington. Leics 8A 36
Packmoor. Stoke 4G 35
Packmores. Warw 5L 27
Packwood. W Mid 4K 27
Packwood Gullet. W Mid 4K 27
Padanaram. Ang 2H 67
Padbury. Buck 8E 28
Paddington. G Lon 5K 21
Paddington. Warr 1E 34
Paddlesworth. Kent 2H 13
Paddock. Kent 8F 22
Paddockhole. Dum 3G 53
Paddock Wood. Kent 1C 12
Paddolgreen. Shrp 6D 34
Padeswood. Flin 3A 34
Padiham. Lanc 4F 40
Padside. N Yor 2K 41
Padson. Devn 6E 6
Padstow. Corn 4B 4
Padworth. W Ber 7D 20
Page Bank. Dur 8F 54
Pagham. W Sus 6F 10
Paglesham Churchend.
Essx 4F 22
Paglesham Eastend. Essx 4F 22
Paibeil. W Isl
on North Uist 7J 75
on Taransay 4B 76
Paiblesgearraidh. W Isl 7J 75
Paignton. Torb 5L 5
Pailton. Warw 3B 28
Paine's Corner. E Sus 3C 12
Painleyhill. Staf 6J 35
Painscastle. Powy 8L 25
Painshawfield. Nmbd 5D 54
Painsthorpe. E Yor 2F 42
Painswick. Glos 3G 19
Painter's Forstal. Kent 8F 22
Painthorpe. W Yor 6M 41
Pairc Shiaboist. W Isl 7F 82
Paisley. Ren 3C 58
Pakefield. Suff 2M 31
Pakenham. Suff 5F 30
Pale. Gwyn 7J 33
Palehouse Common. E Sus 4A 12
Palestine. Hants 1L 9
Paley Street. Wind 6F 20
Palgowan. Dum 3J 51
Palgrave. Suff 4H 31
Pallington. Dors 6F 8
Palmarsh. Kent 2H 13
Palmer Moor. Derbs 6K 35
Palmers Cross. W Mid 1G 27
Palmerstown. V Glam 8L 17
Palnackie. Dum 6C 52
Palnure. Dum 5K 51
Palterton. Derbs 3B 36
Pamber End. Hants 8D 20
Pamber Green. Hants 8D 20
Pamber Heath. Hants 7D 20
Pamington. Glos 8H 27
Pamphill. Dors 5H 9
Pampisford. Cambs 7A 30
Panborough. Som 1C 8
Panbride. Ang 4J 67
Pancrasweek. Devn 5B 6
Pandy. Gwyn
nr. Bala 7H 33
nr. Tywyn 2F 24
Pandy. Mon 1B 18
Pandy. Powy 2J 25
Pandy. Wrex 7L 33
Pandy Tudur. Cnwy 4H 33
Panfield. Essx 1D 22
Pangbourne. W Ber 6D 20
Pannal. N Yor 2M 41
Pannal Ash. N Yor 2L 41
Pannanich. Abers 6C 72
Pant. Shrp 7A 34
Pant. Wrex 5A 34
Pantasaph. Flin 3L 33
Pant Glas. Gwyn 6D 32
Pant-glas. Shrp 6A 34
Pantgwyn. Carm 2E 16
Pantgwyn. Cdgn 2J 15
Pant-lasau. Swan 4F 16
Panton. Linc 2J 37
Pant-pastynog. Den 4K 33
Pantperthog. Gwyn 2G 25
Pant-teg. Carm 4L 15
Pant-y-Caws. Carm 4H 15
Pant-y-dwr. Powy 5J 25
Pant-y-ffridd. Powy 2L 25
Pantyffynnon. Carm 3F 16
Pantygasseg. Torf 3A 18
Pant-y-llyn. Carm 3F 16
Pant-yr-awel. B'end 6J 17
Pant y Wacco. Flin 3L 33
Panxworth. Norf 8K 39
Papa Stour Airport. Shet 2B 90
Papa Westray Airport. Orkn 4D 88
Papcastle. Cumb 8F 52
Papigoe. High 6E 86
Papil. Shet 4D 90
Papple. E Lot 2C 60
Papplewick. Notts 4C 36
Papworth Everard. Cambs 5K 29
Papworth St Agnes. Cambs 5K 29
Par. Corn 6C 4
Paramour Street. Kent 7J 23
Parbold. Lanc 6C 40
Parbrook. Som 2D 8
Parbrook. W Sus 3H 11
Parc. Gwyn 7H 33
Parcllyn. Cdgn 1J 15
Parc-Seymour. Newp 4C 18
Pardown. Hants 1C 10
Pardshaw. Cumb 2K 45
Parham. Suff 5K 31
Park. Abers 6G 73
Park. Arg 3D 64
Park. Derr 3D 92
Park. Dum 2D 52
Park Bottom. Corn 4K 3
Parkburn. Abers 2G 73
Park Corner. E Sus 2B 12
Park Corner. Oxon 5D 20
Park End. Nmbd 4B 54
Parkend. Glos 3E 18
Parkeston. Essx 8J 31
Parkfield. Corn 5F 4
Park Gate. Hants 5C 10
Park Gate. Worc 4H 27
Parkgate. Ant 4H 93
Parkgate. Ches W 2A 34
Parkgate. Cumb 7G 53
Parkgate. Dum 3E 52
Parkgate. Surr 1K 11
Parkhall. W Dun 2C 58
Parkham. Devn 3C 6
Parkham Ash. Devn 3C 6
Parkhead. Cumb 7H 53
Parkhead. Glas 3E 58
Park Hill. Mers 7C 40
Parkhouse. Mon 3D 18
Parkhurst. IOW 6B 10
Park Lane. G Man 7F 40
Park Lane. Staf 1G 27
Park Mill. W Yor 6L 41
Parkmill. Swan 8M 15
Parkneuk. Abers 8G 73
Parkside. N Lan 4G 59
Parkstone. Pool 6J 9
Park Street. Herts 3J 21
Park Street. W Sus 2J 11
Park Town. Oxon 3C 20
Park Village. Nmbd 5L 53
Parkway. Here 8F 26
Parley Cross. Dors 6J 9
Parmoor. Buck 5E 20
Parr. Mers 8D 40
Parracombe. Devn 1F 6
Parrog. Pemb 3G 15
Parsonage Green. Essx 2D 22
Parsonby. Cumb 8F 52
Parson Cross. S Yor 8M 41
Parson Drove. Cambs 1L 29
Partick. Glas 3D 58
Partington. G Man 8F 40
Partney. Linc 3M 37
Parton. Cumb
nr. Whitehaven 2J 45
nr. Wigton 6G 53
Parton. Dum 4A 52
Partridge Green. W Sus 4J 11
Parwich. Derbs 4K 35
Passenham. Nptn 8E 28
Passfield. Hants 2F 10
Passingford Bridge. Essx 4B 22
Paston. Norf 6K 39
Pasturefields. Staf 7H 35
Patchacott. Devn 6D 6
Patcham. Brig 5L 11
Patchetts Green. Herts 4J 21
Patching. W Sus 5H 11
Patchole. Devn 1F 6
Patchway. S Glo 5E 18
Pateley Bridge. N Yor 1K 41
Pathe. Som 2B 8
Pathfinder Village. Devn 6H 7
Pathhead. Abers 1L 67
Pathhead. E Ayr 8E 58
Pathhead. Fife 8F 66
Pathhead. Midl 3A 60
Pathlow. Warw 6K 27
Path of Condie. Per 6D 66
Pathstruie. Per 6D 66
Patmore Heath. Herts 1M 21
Patna. E Ayr 8C 58
Patney. Wilts 8J 19
Patrick. IOM 6B 44
Patrick Brompton. N Yor 6L 47
Patrington. E Yor 5L 43
Patrington Haven. E Yor 5L 43
Patrixbourne. Kent 8H 23
Patterdale. Cumb 4B 46
Pattiesmuir. Fife 1J 59
Pattingham. Staf 2G 27
Pattishall. Nptn 6D 28
Pattiswick. Essx 1E 22
Patton Bridge. Cumb 6D 46
Paul. Corn 6H 3
Paulerspury. Nptn 7E 28
Paull. E Yor 5J 43
Paulton. Bath 8E 18
Pauperhaugh. Nmbd 2E 54
Pave Lane. Telf 8F 34
Pavenham. Bed 6G 29
Pawlett. Som 1A 8
Pawston. Nmbd 6F 60
Paxford. Glos 8K 27
Paxton. Bord 4G 61
Payhembury. Devn 5K 7
Paythorne. Lanc 2G 41
Payton. Som 3L 7
Peacehaven. E Sus 5M 11
Peak Dale. Derbs 2J 35
Peak Forest. Derbs 2K 35
Peak Hill. Linc 8K 37
Peakirk. Pet 1J 29
Pearsie. Ang 2G 67
Peasedown St John. Bath 8F 18
Peaseland Green. Norf 8G 39
Peasemore. W Ber 6B 20
Peasenhall. Suff 5K 31
Pease Pottage. W Sus 2K 11
Peaslake. Surr 1H 11
Peasley Cross. Mers 8D 40
Peasmarsh. E Sus 3E 12
Peasmarsh. Som 4B 8
Peasmarsh. Surr 1G 11
Peaston. E Lot 3B 60
Peastonbank. E Lot 3B 60
Peathill. Abers 7J 81
Peat Inn. Fife 7H 67
Peatling Magna. Leics 2C 28
Peatling Parva. Leics 3C 28
Peaton. Arg 1M 57
Peaton. Shrp 3D 26
Peats Corner. Suff 5H 31
Pebmarsh. Essx 8E 30
Pebworth. Worc 7K 27
Pecket Well. W Yor 5H 41
Peckforton. Ches E 4D 34
Peckham Bush. Kent 8C 22
Peckleton. Leics 1B 28
Pedair-ffordd. Powy 8L 33
Pedham. Norf 8K 39
Pedlinge. Kent 2H 13
Pedmore. W Mid 3H 27
Pedwell. Som 2C 8
Peebles. Bord 5L 59
Peel. IOM 6B 44
Peel. Bord 6B 60
Peel Common. Hants 5C 10
Peening Quarter. Kent 3E 12
Peggs Green. Leics 8B 36
Pegsdon. C Beds 8J 29
Pegswood. Nmbd 3F 54
Peinchorran. High 2G 69
Peinlich. High 8F 76
Pelaw. Tyne 5F 54
Pelcomb Bridge. Pemb 5F 14
Pelcomb Cross. Pemb 5F 14
Peldon. Essx 2F 22
Pelsall. W Mid 1J 27
Pelton. Dur 6F 54
Pelutho. Cumb 7F 52
Pelynt. Corn 6E 4
Pemberton. Carm 6M 15
Pembrey. Carm 6L 15
Pembridge. Here 6B 26
Pembroke. Pemb 6F 14
Pembroke Dock.
Pemb 118 (6F 14)
Pembroke Ferry. Pemb 6F 14
Pembury. Kent 1C 12
Penallt. Mon 2D 18
Penally. Pemb 7H 15
Penalt. Here 1D 18
Penalum. Pemb 7H 15
Penare. Corn 7B 4
Penarth. V Glam 7L 17
Penbeagle. Corn 5J 3
Penberth. Corn 6H 3
Pen-bont Rhydybeddau.
Cdgn 4F 24
Penbryn. Cdgn 1J 15
Pencader. Carm 3L 15
Pen-cae. Cdgn 1L 15
Pencaenewydd. Gwyn 6D 32
Pencaerau. Neat 5G 17
Pencaitland. E Lot 3B 60
Pencarnisiog. IOA 3C 32
Pencarreg. Carm 2M 15
Pencarrow. Corn 3D 4
Pencelli. Powy 2K 17
Pen-clawdd. Swan 7M 15
Pencoed. B'end 6J 17
Pencombe. Here 6D 26
Pencraig. Here 1D 18
Pencraig. Powy 8K 33
Pendeen. Corn 5G 3
Pendeford. W Mid 1G 27
Penderyn. Rhon 4J 17
Pendine. Carm 6J 15
Pendlebury. G Man 7F 40
Pendleton. G Man 8G 41
Pendleton. Lanc 4F 40
Pendock. Worc 8F 26
Pendoggett. Corn 4C 4
Pendomer. Som 4D 8
Pendoylan. V Glam 7K 17
Pendre. B'end 6J 17
Penegoes. Powy 2G 25
Penelewey. Corn 4M 3
Penffordd. Pemb 4G 15
Penffordd-Lâs. Powy 3H 25
Penfro. Pemb 6F 14
Pengam. Cphy 5L 17
Pengam. Card 7M 17
Penge. G Lon 7L 21
Pengelly. Corn 3C 4
Pengenffordd. Powy 1L 17
Pengersick. Corn 6J 3
Pengorffwysfa. IOA 1D 32
Pengover Green. Corn 5E 4
Pengwern. Den 3K 33
Penhale. Corn
nr. Mullion 7K 3
nr. St Austell 6B 4
Penhale Camp. Corn 3L 3
Penhallow. Corn 3L 3
Penhalvean. Corn 5L 3
Penhelig. Gwyn 3F 24
Penhill. Swin 5K 19
Penhow. Newp 4C 18
Penhurst. E Sus 4C 12
Peniarth. Gwyn 2F 24
Penicuik. Midl 3L 59
Peniel. Carm 4L 15
Penifiler. High 1F 68
Peninver. Arg 7G 57
Penisa'r Waun. Gwyn 4E 32
Penistone. S Yor 7L 41
Penketh. Warr 1D 34
Penkill. S Ayr 2H 51
Penkridge. Staf 8H 35
Penley. Wrex 6C 34
Penllech. Gwyn 7B 32
Penllergaer. Swan 5F 16
Pen-llyn. IOA 2C 32
Penmachno. Cnwy 5G 33
Penmaen. Swan 8M 15
Penmaenmawr. Cnwy 3G 33
Penmaenpool. Gwyn 1F 24
Penmaen Rhos. Cnwy 3H 33
Pen-marc. V Glam 8K 17
Penmark. V Glam 8K 17
Penmarth. Corn 5L 3
Penmon. IOA 2F 32
Penmorfa. Gwyn 6E 32
Penmynydd. IOA 3E 32
Penn. Buck 4G 21
Penn. Dors 6B 8
Penn. W Mid 2G 27
Pennal. Gwyn 2G 25
Pennan. Abers 7H 81
Pennant. Cdgn 6E 24
Pennant. Den 7K 33
Pennant. Gwyn 8J 33
Pennant. Powy 3H 25
Pennant Melangell. Powy 8K 33
Pennar. Pemb 6F 14
Pennard. Swan 6E 16
Pennerley. Shrp 2B 26
Pennington. Cumb 8A 46
Pennington. G Man 8E 40
Pennington. Hants 6M 9
Pennorth. Powy 2L 17
Penn Street. Buck 4G 21
Pennsylvania. Devn 6J 7
Pennsylvania. S Glo 6F 18
Penny Bridge. Cumb 7B 46
Pennycross. Plym 6G 5
Pennygate. Norf 7K 39
Pennyghael. Arg 5L 63
Penny Hill. Linc 7L 37
Pennylands. Lanc 7C 40
Pennymoor. Devn 4H 7
Pennyvenie. E Ayr 1K 51
Pennywell. Tyne 6G 55
Penparc. Cdgn 2J 15
Penparcau. Cdgn 4E 24
Pen-pedair-heol. Cphy 5L 17
Penperlleni. Mon 3B 18
Penpillick. Corn 6C 4
Penpol. Corn 5M 3
Penpoll. Corn 6D 4
Penponds. Corn 5K 3
Penpont. Corn 4C 4
Penpont. Dum 2C 52
Penpont. Powy 2J 17
Penprysg. B'end 6J 17
Penquit. Devn 6J 5
Penrherber. Carm 3J 15
Penrhiw. Pemb 2J 15
Penrhiwceiber. Rhon 5K 17
Pen Rhiw-fawr. Neat 3G 17
Penrhiw-llan. Cdgn 2K 15
Penrhiw-pal. Cdgn 2K 15
Penrhos. Gwyn 7C 32
Penrhos. Here 6B 26
Penrhos. IOA 2B 32
Penrhos. Mon 2C 18
Penrhos. Powy 3H 17
Penrhos Garnedd. Gwyn 3E 32
Penrhyn. IOA 1C 32
Penrhyn Bay. Cnwy 2H 33
Penrhyn-coch. Cdgn 4F 24
Penrhyndeudraeth. Gwyn 7F 32
Penrhyn-side. Cnwy 2H 33
Penrice. Swan 8L 15
Penrith. Cumb 3D 46
Penrose. Corn 4A 4
Penruddock. Cumb 3C 46
Penryn. Corn 5L 3
Pen-sarn. Carm 5L 15
Pen-sarn. Gwyn 8E 32
Pensax. Worc 5F 26
Pensby. Mers 1A 34
Penselwood. Som 2F 8
Pensford. Bath 7E 18
Pensham. Worc 7H 27
Penshaw. Tyne 6G 55
Penshurst. Kent 1B 12
Pensilva. Corn 5E 4
Pensnett. W Mid 3H 27
Penston. E Lot 2B 60
Penstone. Devn 5G 7
Pentewan. Corn 7C 4
Pentir. Gwyn 4E 32
Pentire. Corn 2L 3
Pentlepoir. Pemb 6H 15
Pentlow. Essx 7E 30
Pentney. Norf 8D 38
Penton Mewsey. Hants 1M 9
Pentraeth. IOA 3E 32
Pentre. Powy
nr. Church Stoke 2A 26
nr. Kerry 4L 25
nr. Mochdre 4K 25
Pentre. Rhon 5J 17
Pentre. Shrp 8B 34
Pentre. Wrex
nr. Chirk 5A 34
nr. Llanarmon Dyffryn Ceiriog
7L 33
Pentre-bach. Cdgn 2M 15
Pentre-bach. Powy 1J 17
Pentrebach. Carm 1H 17
Pentrebach. Mer T 4K 17
Pentrebach. Swan 4F 16
Pentre Berw. IOA 3D 32
Pentre-bont. Cnwy 5G 33
Pentrecagal. Carm 2K 15
Pentre-celyn. Den 5L 33
Pentre-clawdd. Shrp 6A 34
Pentreclwydau. Neat 4H 17
Pentre-cwrt. Carm 3K 15
Pentre Dolau Honddu.
Powy 8J 25
Pentre-dwr. Swan 5F 16
Pentrefelin. Carm 2E 16
Pentrefelin. Cdgn 8F 24
Pentrefelin. Cnwy 3H 33
Pentrefelin. Gwyn 7E 32
Pentrefoelas. Cnwy 5H 33
Pentre Galar. Pemb 3H 15
Pentregat. Cdgn 1K 15
Pentre Gwenlais. Carm 3F 16
Pentre Gwynfryn. Gwyn 8E 32
Pentre Halkyn. Flin 3M 33
Pentre Hodre. Shrp 4B 26
Pentre-Llanrhaeadr. Den 4K 33
Pentre Llifior. Powy 3L 25
Pentrellwyn. IOA 2E 32
Pentre-llwyn-llwyd. Powy 7J 25
Pentre-llyn-cymmer. Cnwy 5J 33
Pentre Meyrick. V Glam 7J 17
Pentre-piod. Gwyn 7H 33
Pentre-poeth. Newp 5A 18
Pentre'r beirdd. Powy 1L 25
Pentre'r-felin. Powy 1J 17
Pentre-tafarn-y-fedw. Cnwy 4H 33
Pentre-ty-gwyn. Carm 1H 17
Pentre-uchaf. Gwyn 7C 32
Pentrich. Derbs 4A 36
Pentridge. Dors 4J 9
Pen-twyn. Cphy 4M 17
Pentwyn. Cphy 4L 17
Pentwyn. Card 6M 17
Pentyrch. Card 6L 17
Pentywyn. Carm 6J 15
Penuwch. Cdgn 6E 24
Penwithick. Corn 6C 4
Penwyllt. Powy 3H 17
Pen-y-banc. Carm 2F 16
Penybanc. Carm 3F 16
Pen-y-bont. Carm 4K 15
Pen-y-bont. Powy 8M 33
Penybont. Powy 6L 25
Pen-y-Bont Ar Ogwr. B'end 6J 17
Penybontfawr. Powy 8K 33
Pen-y-bryn. Pemb 2H 15
Pen-y-bryn. Wrex 5A 34
Penybryn. Cphy 5L 17
Pen-y-cae. Powy 3H 17
Penycae. Wrex 5A 34
Pen-y-cae mawr. Mon 4C 18
Penycaerau. Gwyn 8A 32
Pen-y-cefn. Flin 3L 33
Pen-y-clawdd. Mon 3C 18
Pen-y-coedcae. Rhon 6K 17
Penycwm. Pemb 4E 14
Pen-y-Darren. Mer T 4K 17
Pen-y-fai. B'end 6H 17
Pen-y-ffordd. Flin 2L 33
Penyffordd. Flin 3B 34
Penyffridd. Gwyn 5E 32
Pen-y-garn. Cdgn 4F 24
Pen-y-garnedd. IOA 3E 32
Penygarnedd. Powy 8L 33
Pen-y-graig. Gwyn 7B 32
Penygraig. Rhon 5J 17
Penygraigwen. IOA 2D 32
Pen-y-groes. Carm 3E 16
Penygroes. Gwyn 5D 32
Penygroes. Pemb 3H 15
Pen-y-Mynydd. Carm 6L 15
Penymynydd. Flin 3B 34
Pen-yr-heol. Mon 2C 18
Penyrheol. Cphy 6L 17
Penyrheol. Swan 5E 16
Penysarn. IOA 1D 32
Pen-y-stryt. Den 5L 33
Penywaun. Rhon 4J 17
Penzance. Corn 5H 3
Peopleton. Worc 6H 27
Peover Heath. Ches E 2F 34
Peper Harow. Surr 1G 11
Peplow. Shrp 7E 34
Pepper Arden. N Yor 5L 47
Perceton. N Ayr 5B 58
Percyhorner. Abers 7J 81
Perham Down. Wilts 1L 9
Periton. Som 1J 7
Perkinsville. Dur 6F 54
Perlethorpe. Notts 2D 36
Perranarworthal. Corn 5L 3
Perranporth. Corn 3L 3
Perranuthnoe. Corn 6J 3
Perranwell. Corn 5L 3
Perranzabuloe. Corn 3L 3
Perrott's Brook. Glos 3J 19
Perry. W Mid 2J 27
Perry Barr. W Mid 2J 27
Perry Crofts. Staf 1L 27
Perry Green. Essx 1E 22
Perry Green. Herts 2M 21
Perry Green. Wilts 5H 19
Perry Street. Kent 6C 22
Perry Street. Som 5B 8
Perrywood. Kent 8G 23
Pershall. Staf 7G 35
Pershore. Worc 7H 27
Pertenhall. Bed 5H 29
Perth. Per 115 (5E 66)
Perthy. Shrp 6B 34
Perton. Staf 2G 27
Pertwood. Wilts 2G 9
Peterborough. Pet 115 (2J 29)
Peterburn. High 5J 77
Peterchurch. Here 8B 26
Peterculter. Aber 5H 73
Peterhead. Abers 1L 73
Peterlee. Dur 7H 55
Petersfield. Hants 3E 10
Petersfinger. Wilts 3K 9
Peters Green. Herts 2J 21
Peters Marland. Devn 4D 6
Peterstone Wentlooge.
Newp 5A 18
Peterston-super-Ely.
V Glam 7K 17
Peterstow. Here 1D 18
Peters Village. Kent 7D 22
Peter Tavy. Devn 8E 6
Petertown. Orkn 1E 86
Petham. Kent 8H 23
Petherwin Gate. Corn 7B 6
Petrockstowe. Devn 5E 6
Petsoe End. Mil 7F 28
Pett. E Sus 4E 12
Pettaugh. Suff 6H 31
Pett Bottom. Kent 8H 23
Petteridge. Kent 1C 12
Pettinain. S Lan 5H 59
Pettistree. Suff 6J 31
Petton. Devn 3K 7
Petton. Shrp 7C 34
Petts Wood. G Lon 7M 21
Pettycur. Fife 1L 59
Pettywell. Norf 7G 39
Petworth. W Sus 3G 11
Pevensey. E Sus 5C 12
Pevensey Bay. E Sus 5C 12
Pewsey. Wilts 7K 19
Pheasants Hill. Buck 5E 20
Philadelphia. Tyne 6G 55
Philham. Devn 3B 6
Philiphaugh. Bord 7B 60
Phillack. Corn 5J 3
Philleigh. Corn 8A 4
Philpstoun. W Lot 2J 59
Phocle Green. Here 1E 18
Phoenix Green. Hants 8E 20
Pibsbury. Som 3C 8
Pibwrlwyd. Carm 5L 15
Pica. Cumb 2K 45
Piccadilly. Warw 2L 27
Piccadilly Corner. Norf 3J 31
Piccotts End. Herts 3H 21
Pickering. N Yor 7E 48
Picket Piece. Hants 1A 10
Picket Post. Hants 5K 9
Pickford. W Mid 3L 27
Pickhill. N Yor 7M 47
Picklenash. Glos 1F 18
Picklescott. Shrp 2C 26
Pickletillem. Fife 5H 67
Pickmere. Ches E 2E 34
Pickstock. Telf 7F 34
Pickwell. Devn 1D 6
Pickwell. Leics 8E 36
Pickworth. Linc 6H 37
Pickworth. Rut 8G 37
Picton. Ches W 2C 34
Picton. Flin 2L 33
Picton. N Yor 5B 48
Pict's Hill. Som 3C 8
Piddinghoe. E Sus 5M 11
Piddington. Buck 4F 20
Piddington. Nptn 6F 28
Piddington. Oxon 2D 20
Piddlehinton. Dors 6F 8
Piddletrenthide. Dors 5F 8
Pidley. Cambs 4L 29
Pidney. Dors 5F 8
Pie Corner. Here 5E 26
Piercebridge. Darl 4L 47
Pierowall. Orkn 5D 88
Pigdon. Nmbd 3E 54
Pightley. Som 2M 7
Pikehall. Derbs 4K 35
Pikeshill. Hants 5L 9
Pilford. Dors 5J 9
Pilgrims Hatch. Essx 4B 22
Pilham. Linc 8F 42
Pill. N Som 6D 18
The Pill. Mon 5C 18
Pillaton. Corn 5F 4
Pillaton. Staf 8H 35
Pillerton Hersey. Warw 7M 27
Pillerton Priors. Warw 7L 27
Pilleth. Powy 5A 26
Pilley. Hants 6M 9
Pilley. S Yor 7M 41
Pillgwenlly. Newp 5B 18
Pilling. Lanc 3C 40
Pilling Lane. Lanc 3B 40
Pillowell. Glos 3E 18
Pillwell. Dors 4F 8
Pilning. S Glo 5D 18
Pilsbury. Derbs 3K 35
Pilsdon. Dors 6C 8
Pilsgate. Pet 1H 29
Pilsley. Derbs
nr. Bakewell 2L 35
nr. Clay Cross 3B 36
Pilson Green. Norf 8K 39
Piltdown. E Sus 3M 11
Pilton. Edin 2L 59
Pilton. Nptn 3H 29
Pilton. Rut 1G 29
Pilton. Som 1D 8
Pilton Green. Swan 8L 15
Pimperne. Dors 5H 9
Pinchbeck. Linc 7K 37
Pinchbeck Bars. Linc 7J 37
Pinchbeck West. Linc 7K 37
Pinfold. Lanc 6B 40
Pinford End. Suff 6E 30
Pinged. Carm 6L 15
Pinhoe. Devn 6J 7
Pinkerton. E Lot 2E 60
Pinkneys Green. Wind 5F 20
Pinley. W Mid 4A 28
Pinley Green. Warw 5L 27
Pinmill. Suff 8J 31
Pinmore. S Ayr 2H 51
Pinner. G Lon 5J 21
Pins Green. Worc 7F 26
Pinsley Green. Ches E 5D 34
Pinvin. Worc 7H 27
Pinwherry. S Ayr 3G 51
Pinxton. Derbs 4B 36
Pipe and Lyde. Here 7D 26
Pipe Aston. Here 4C 26
Pipe Gate. Shrp 5F 34
Pipehill. Staf 1J 27
Piperhill. High 8J 79
Pipe Ridware. Staf 8J 35
Pipers Pool. Corn 7B 6
Pipewell. Nptn 3F 28
Pippacott. Devn 2E 6
Pipton. Powy 1L 17
Pirbright. Surr 8G 21
Pirnmill. N Ayr 5H 57
Pirton. Herts 8J 29
Pirton. Worc 7G 27
Pisgah. Stir 7A 66
Pishill. Oxon 5E 20
Pistyll. Gwyn 6C 32
Pitagowan. Per 1B 66
Pitcairn. Per 2B 66
Pitcairngreen. Per 5D 66
Pitcalnie. High 6J 79
Pitcaple. Abers 3G 73
Pitchcombe. Glos 3G 19
Pitchcott. Buck 1E 20
Pitchford. Shrp 1D 26
Pitch Green. Buck 3E 20
Pitch Place. Surr 8G 21
Pitcombe. Som 2E 8
Pitcox. E Lot 2D 60
Pitcur. Per 4F 66
Pitfichie. Abers 4F 72
Pitgrudy. High 4H 79
Pitkennedy. Ang 2J 67
Pitlessie. Fife 7G 67
Pitlochry. Per 2C 66
Pitmachie. Abers 3F 72
Pitmaduthy. High 6H 79
Pitmedden. Abers 3H 73
Pitminster. Som 4M 7
Pitnacree. Per 2C 66
Pitney. Som 3C 8
Pitroddie. Per 5F 66
Pitscottie. Fife 6H 67
Pitsea. Essx 5D 22
Pitsford. Nptn 5E 28
Pitsford Hill. Som 2L 7
Pitsmoor. S Yor 1A 36
Pitstone. Buck 2G 21
Pitt. Hants 3B 10
Pitt Court. Glos 4F 18
Pittentrail. High 3H 79
Pittenweem. Fife 7J 67
Pittington. Dur 7G 55
Pitton. Swan 8L 15
Pitton. Wilts 2L 9
Pittswood. Kent 1C 12
Pittulie. Abers 7J 81
Pittville. Glos 1H 19
Pitversie. Per 6E 66
Pity Me. Dur 7F 54
Pityme. Corn 4B 4
Pixey Green. Suff 4J 31
Pixley. Here 8E 26
Place Newton. N Yor 8F 48
Plaidy. Abers 8G 81
Plaidy. Corn 6E 4
Plain Dealings. Pemb 5G 15
Plains. N Lan 3F 58
Plainsfield. Som 2L 7
Plaish. Shrp 2D 26
Plaistow. Here 8E 26
Plaistow. W Sus 2H 11
Plaitford. Wilts 4L 9
Plastow Green. Hants 7C 20
Plas yn Cefn. Den 3K 33
The Platt. E Sus 2B 12
Platt Bridge. G Man 7E 40
Platt Lane. Shrp 6D 34
Platts Common. S Yor 7A 42
Platt's Heath. Kent 8E 22
Plawsworth. Dur 7F 54
Plaxtol. Kent 8C 22
Playden. E Sus 3F 12
Playford. Suff 7J 31
Play Hatch. Oxon 6E 20
Playing Place. Corn 4M 3
Playley Green. Glos 8F 26
Plealey. Shrp 1C 26
Plean. Stir 1G 59
Pleasington. Bkbn 5E 40
Pleasley. Derbs 3C 36
Pledgdon Green. Essx 1B 22
Plenmeller. Nmbd 5M 53
Pleshey. Essx 2C 22
Plockton. High 2K 69
Plocrapol. W Isl 4C 76
Ploughfield. Here 7B 26
Plowden. Shrp 3B 26
Ploxgreen. Shrp 1B 26
Pluckley. Kent 1F 12
Plucks Gutter. Kent 7J 23
Plumbland. Cumb 8F 52
Plumbridge. Derr 4D 92
Plumgarths. Cumb 6C 46
Plumley. Ches E 2F 34
Plummers Plain. W Sus 3K 11
Plumpton. Cumb 8J 53
Plumpton. E Sus 4L 11
Plumpton. Nptn 7C 28
Plumpton Foot. Cumb 8J 53
Plumpton Green. E Sus 4L 11
Plumpton Head. Cumb 8K 53
Plumstead. G Lon 6M 21
Plumstead. Norf 6H 39
Plumtree. Notts 6D 36
Plumtree Park. Notts 6D 36
Plungar. Leics 6E 36
Plush. Dors 5F 8
Plushabridge. Corn 8C 6
Plwmp. Cdgn 1K 15
Plymouth. Plym 115 (6G 5)
Plympton. Plym 6H 5
Plymstock. Plym 6H 5
Plymtree. Devn 5K 7
Pockley. N Yor 7D 48
Pocklington. E Yor 3F 42
Pode Hole. Linc 7K 37
Podimore. Som 3D 8
Podington. Bed 5G 29
Podmore. Staf 6F 34
Poffley End. Oxon 2A 20
Point Clear. Essx 2G 23
Pointon. Linc 6J 37
Pokesdown. Bour 6K 9
Polbae. Dum 4H 51
Polbain. High 3M 77
Polbathic. Corn 6F 4
Polbeth. W Lot 3J 59
Polbrock. Corn 5C 4
Polchar. High 5J 71
Polebrook. Nptn 3H 29
Pole Elm. Worc 7G 27
Polegate. E Sus 5B 12
Pole Moor. W Yor 6J 41
Poles. High 4H 79
Polesworth. Warw 1L 27
Polglass. High 3M 77
Polgooth. Corn 6B 4
Poling. W Sus 5H 11
Poling Corner. W Sus 5H 11
Polio. High 6H 79
Polkerris. Corn 6C 4
Polla. High 6F 84
Pollard Street. Norf 6K 39
Pollicott. Buck 2E 20
Pollington. E Yor 6D 42
Polloch. High 1B 64
Pollok. Glas 3D 58
Pollokshaws. Glas 3D 58
Pollokshields. Glas 3D 58
Polmaily. High 2E 70
Polmassick. Corn 7B 4
Polmont. Falk 2H 59
Polnessan. E Ayr 8C 58
Polnish. High 7J 69
Polperro. Corn 6E 4
Polruan. Corn 6D 4
Polscoe. Corn 5D 4
Polsham. Som 1D 8
Polskeoch. Dum 1A 52
Polstead. Suff 8F 30
Polstead Heath. Suff 7F 30
Poltesco. Corn 7L 3
Poltimore. Devn 6J 7
Polton. Midl 3L 59
Polwarth. Bord 4E 60
Polyphant. Corn 7B 6
Polzeath. Corn 4B 4
Pomeroy. M Ulst 5E 92
Ponde. Powy 1L 17
Pondersbridge. Cambs 2K 29
Ponders End. G Lon 4L 21
Pond Street. Essx 8A 30
Pondtail. Hants 8F 20
Ponsanooth. Corn 5L 3
Ponsongath. Corn 7L 3
Ponsworthy. Devn 8G 7
Pontamman. Carm 3F 16
Pontantwn. Carm 5L 15
Pontardawe. Neat 4G 17
Pontarddulais. Swan 4E 16
Pontarfynach. Cdgn 5G 25
Pont-ar-gothi. Carm 4M 15
Pont ar Hydfer. Powy 2H 17
Pontarllechau. Carm 2G 17
Pontarsais. Carm 4L 15
Pontblyddyn. Flin 3A 34
Pontbren Llwyd. Rhon 4J 17
Pont-Cyfyng. Cnwy 5G 33
Pontdolgoch. Powy 3K 25
Pontefract. W Yor 5B 42
Ponteland. Nmbd 4E 54
Ponterwyd. Cdgn 4G 25
Pontesbury. Shrp 1C 26
Pontesford. Shrp 1C 26
Pontfadog. Wrex 7M 33
Pont-Faen. Shrp 6A 34
Pont-faen. Powy 1J 17
Pontfaen. Pemb 3G 15
Pontgarreg. Cdgn 1K 15
Pont-Henri. Carm 6L 15
Ponthir. Torf 4B 18
Ponthirwaun. Cdgn 2J 15
Pont-iets. Carm 6L 15
Pontllanfraith. Cphy 5L 17
Pontlliw. Swan 4F 16
Pont Llogel. Powy 1K 25
Pontllyfni. Gwyn 5D 32
Pontlottyn. Cphy 4L 17
Pontneddfechan. Powy 4J 17
Pont-newydd. Carm 6L 15
Pont-newydd. Flin 4L 33
Pontnewydd. Torf 4A 18
Ponton. Shet 2D 90
Pont Pen-y-benglog. Gwyn 4F 32
Pontrhydfendigaid. Cdgn 6G 25
Pont Rhyd-y-cyff. B'end 6H 17
Pontrhydyfen. Neat 5G 17
Pont-rhyd-y-groes. Cdgn 5G 25
Pontrhydyrun. Torf 4A 18
Pont-Rhythallt. Gwyn 4E 32
Pontrilas. Here 1B 18
Pontrilas Road. Here 1B 18
Pontrobert. Powy 1L 25
Pont-rug. Gwyn 4E 32
Ponts Green. E Sus 4C 12
Pontshill. Here 1E 18
Pont-Sian. Cdgn 2L 15
Pontsticill. Mer T 3K 17
Pont-Walby. Neat 4H 17
Pontwelly. Carm 3L 15
Pontwgan. Cnwy 3G 33
Pontyates. Carm 6L 15
Pontyberem. Carm 5M 15
Pontybodkin. Flin 4A 34
Pontyclun. Rhon 6K 17
Pontycymer. B'end 5J 17
Pontyglazier. Pemb 3H 15
Pontygwaith. Rhon 5K 17
Pont-y-pant. Cnwy 5G 33
Pontypool. Torf 4A 18
Pontypridd. Rhon 6K 17
Pontypwl. Torf 4A 18
Pontywaun. Cphy 5M 17
Pooksgreen. Hants 4A 10
Pool. Corn 4K 3
Pool. W Yor 3L 41
Poole. N Yor 4B 42
Poole. Pool 118 (6J 9)
Poole. Som 3L 7
Poole Keynes. Glos 4H 19
Poolend. Staf 4H 35
Poolewe. High 5K 77
Pooley Bridge. Cumb 3C 46
Poolfold. Staf 4G 35
Pool Head. Here 6D 26
Pool Hey. Lanc 6B 40
Poolhill. Glos 1F 18
Poolmill. Here 1D 18
Pool o' Muckhart. Clac 7D 66
Pool Quay. Powy 8A 34
Poolsbrook. Derbs 2B 36
Pool Street. Essx 8D 30
Pootings. Kent 1A 12
Pope Hill. Pemb 5F 14
Pope's Hill. Glos 2E 18
Popeswood. Brac 7F 20
Popham. Hants 1C 10
Poplar. G Lon 5L 21
Popley. Hants 8D 20
Porchfield. IOW 6B 10
Porin. High 8D 78
Poringland. Norf 1J 31
Porkellis. Corn 5K 3
Porlock. Som 1H 7
Porlock Weir. Som 1H 7
Portachoillan. Arg 4G 57
Port Adhair Bheinn na Faoghla.
W Isl 8J 75
Port Adhair Thirlodh. Arg 3F 62
Portadown. Arm 6G 93
Portaferry. Ards 6J 93
Port Ann. Arg 1J 57
Port Appin. Arg 3D 64
Port Asgaig. Arg 3D 56
Port Askaig. Arg 3D 56
Portavadie. Arg 3J 57
Portavogie. Ards 5K 93
Portballintrae. Caus 1F 93
Port Bannatyne. Arg 3K 57
Portbury. N Som 6D 18
Port Carlisle. Cumb 5G 53
Port Charlotte. Arg 4B 56
Portchester. Hants 5D 10
Port Clarence. Stoc T 3B 48
Port Driseach. Arg 2J 57
Port Dundas. Glas 3D 58
Port Ellen. Arg 5C 56
Port Elphinstone. Abers 3G 73
Portencalzie. Dum 4F 50
Portencross. N Ayr 5L 57
Port Erin. IOM 8A 44
Port Erroll. Abers 2K 73
Porter's Fen Corner. Norf 1B 30
Portesham. Dors 7E 8
Portessie. Mor 7D 80
Port e Vullen. IOM 5D 44
Port-Eynon. Swan 8L 15
Portfield. Som 3C 8
Portfield Gate. Pemb 5F 14
Portgate. Devn 7D 6
Port Gaverne. Corn 3C 4
Port Glasgow. Inv 2B 58
Portglenone. ME Ant 3F 93
Portgordon. Mor 7C 80
Portgower. High 2L 79
Porth. Corn 2M 3
Porth. Rhon 5K 17
Porthaethwy. IOA 3E 32
Porthallow. Corn
nr. Looe 6E 4
nr. St Keverne 6L 3
Porthcawl. B'end 7H 17
Porthceri. V Glam 8K 17
Porthcothan. Corn 4A 4
Porthcurno. Corn 6G 3
Port Henderson. High 6J 77
Porthgain. Pemb 3E 14
Porthgwarra. Corn 6G 3
Porthill. Shrp 8C 34
Porthkerry. V Glam 8K 17
Porthleven. Corn 6K 3
Porthllechog. IOA 1D 32
Porthmadog. Gwyn 7E 32
Porthmeor. Corn 5H 3
Porth Navas. Corn 6L 3
Portholland. Corn 7B 4
Porthoustock. Corn 6M 3
Porthtowan. Corn 4K 3
Porth Tywyn. Carm 6L 15
Porth-y-felin. IOA 2B 32
Porthyrhyd. Carm
nr. Carmarthen 5M 15
nr. Llandovery 1G 17
Porth-y-waen. Shrp 7A 34
Portincaple. Arg 8G 65
Portington. E Yor 4E 42
Portinnisherrich. Arg 6D 64
Portinscale. Cumb 3A 46
Port Isaac. Corn 3B 4
Portishead. N Som 6C 18
Portknockie. Mor 7D 80
Port Lamont. Arg 2K 57
Portlethen. Abers 6J 73
Portlethen Village. Abers 6J 73
Portling. Dum 6C 52
Port Lion. Pemb 6F 14
Portloe. Corn 8B 4
Port Logan. Dum 7F 50
Portmahomack. High 5K 79
Portmead. Swan 5F 16
Portmeirion. Gwyn 7E 32
Portmellon. Corn 7C 4
Port Mholair. W Isl 8J 83
Port Mor. High 8F 68
Portmore. Hants 6M 9
Port Mulgrave. N Yor 4E 48
Portnacroish. Arg 3D 64
Portnahaven. Arg 4A 56
Portnalong. High 2E 68
Portnaluchaig. High 7H 69
Portnancon. High 5G 85
Port Nan Giuran. W Isl 8J 83
Port nan Long. W Isl 6K 75
Port Nis. W Isl 5J 83
Portobello. Edin 2M 59
Portobello. W Yor 6M 41
Port of Menteith. Stir 7K 65
Porton. Wilts 2K 9
Portormin. High 1A 80
Portpatrick. Dum 6F 50
Port Quin. Corn 3B 4
Port Ramsay. Arg 3C 64
Portreath. Corn 4K 3
Portree. High 1F 68
Port Righ. High 1F 68
Portrush. Caus 2F 93
Port St Mary. IOM 8B 44
Portscatho. Corn 8A 4
Portsea. Port 5D 10
Port Seton. E Lot 2B 60
Portskerra. High 5L 85
Portskewett. Mon 5D 18
Portslade-by-Sea. Brig 5K 11
Portsmouth. Port 115 (5D 10)
Portsmouth. W Yor 5H 41
Port Soderick. IOM 7C 44
Port Solent. Port 5D 10
Portsonachan. Arg 5E 64
Portsoy. Abers 7E 80
Portstewart. Caus 2F 93
Port Sunlight. Mers 1B 34
Portswood. Sotn 4B 10
Port Talbot. Neat 6G 17
Porttannachy. Mor 7C 80
Port Tennant. Swan 5F 16
Portuairk. High 1K 63
Portway. Here 7C 26
Portway. Worc 4J 27
Port Wemyss. Arg 4A 56
Port William. Dum 7J 51
Portwrinkle. Corn 6F 4
Poslingford. Suff 7D 30
Postbridge. Devn 8F 6
Postcombe. Oxon 4E 20
Post Green. Dors 6H 9
Postling. Kent 2H 13
Postlip. Glos 1J 19
Post-Mawr. Cdgn 1L 15
Postwick. Norf 1J 31
Potarch. Abers 6F 72
Potsgrove. C Beds 1G 21
Potten End. Herts 3H 21
Potter Brompton. N Yor 8G 49
Pottergate Street. Norf 2H 31
Potterhanworth. Linc 3H 37
Potterhanworth Booths.
Linc 3H 37
Potter Heigham. Norf 8L 39
Potter Hill. Leics 7E 36
The Potteries. Stoke 5G 35
Potterne. Wilts 8H 19
Potterne Wick. Wilts 8J 19
Potternewton. W Yor 4M 41
Potters Bar. Herts 3K 21
Potters Brook. Lanc 2C 40
Potter's Cross. Staf 3G 27
Potters Crouch. Herts 3J 21
Potter Somersal. Derbs 6K 35
Potterspury. Nptn 7E 28
Potter Street. Essx 3A 22
Potterton. Abers 4J 73
Potthorpe. Norf 7F 38
Pottle Street. Wilts 1G 9
Potto. N Yor 5B 48
Potton. C Beds 7K 29
Pott Row. Norf 7D 38
Pott Shrigley. Ches E 2H 35
Poughill. Corn 5B 6
Poughill. Devn 5H 7
Poulner. Hants 5K 9
Poulshot. Wilts 8H 19
Poulton. Glos 3K 19
Poulton-le-Fylde. Lanc 4B 40
Pound Bank. Worc 4F 26
Poundbury. Dors 6E 8
Poundfield. E Sus 2B 12
Poundgate. E Sus 3A 12
Pound Green. E Sus 3B 12
Pound Green. Suff 6D 30
Pound Hill. W Sus 2K 11
Poundland. S Ayr 3G 51

Poundon—St Albans

Poundon. *Buck* 1D 20
Poundsgate. *Devn* 8G 7
Poundstock. *Corn* 6B 6
Pound Street. *Hants* 7B 20
Pounsley. *E Sus* 3B 12
Powburn. *Nmbd* 8H 61
Powderham. *Devn* 7J 7
Powerstock. *Dors* 6D 8
Powfoot. *Dum* 5F 52
Powick. *Worc* 6G 27
Powmill. *Per* 8D 66
Poxwell. *Dors* 7F 8
Poyle. *Slo* 6H 21
Poynings. *W Sus* 4K 11
Poyntington. *Dors* 3E 8
Poynton. *Ches E* 1H 35
Poynton. *Telf* 8D 34
Poynton Green. *Telf* 8D 34
Poyntz Pass. *Arm* 7G 93
Poystreet Green. *Suff* 6F 30
Praa Sands. *Corn* 6J 3
Pratt's Bottom. *G Lon* 7A 22
Praze-an-Beeble. *Corn* 5K 3
Prees. *Shrp* 6D 34
Preesall. *Lanc* 3B 40
Preesall Park. *Lanc* 3B 40
Prees Green. *Shrp* 6D 34
Prees Higher Heath. *Shrp* 6D 34
Prendergast. *Pemb* 5F 14
Prendwick. *Nmbd* 8H 61
Pren-gwyn. *Cdgn* 2L 15
Prenteg. *Gwyn* 6E 32
Prenton. *Mers* 1B 34
Prescot. *Mers* 8C 40
Prescott. *Devn* 4K 7
Prescott. *Shrp* 7C 34
Preshute. *Wilts* 7K 19
Pressen. *Nmbd* 6F 60
Prestatyn. *Den* 2K 33
Prestbury. *Ches E* 2H 35
Prestbury. *Glos* 1H 19
Presteigne. *Powy* 5B 26
Presthope. *Shrp* 2D 26
Prestleigh. *Som* 1E 8
Preston. *Brig* 5L 11
Preston. *Devn* 8H 7
Preston. *Dors* 7F 8
Preston. *E Lot*
nr. East Linton 2C 60
nr. Prestonpans 2A 60
Preston. *E Yor* 4J 43
Preston. *Glos* 3J 19
Preston. *Herts* 1J 21
Preston. *Kent*
nr. Canterbury 7J 23
nr. Faversham 7G 23
Preston. *Lanc* 115 (5D 40)
Preston. *Nmbd* 7J 61
Preston. *Rut* 1F 28
Preston. *Bord* 4E 60
Preston. *Shrp* 8D 34
Preston. *Suff* 6F 30
Preston. *Wilts*
nr. Aldbourne 6L 19
nr. Lyneham 6J 19
Preston Bagot. *Warw* 5K 27
Preston Bissett. *Buck* 1D 20
Preston Bowyer. *Som* 3L 7
Preston Brockhurst. *Shrp* 7D 34
Preston Brook. *Hal* 1D 34
Preston Candover. *Hants* 1D 10
Preston Capes. *Nptn* 6C 28
Preston Cross. *Glos* 8E 26
Preston Gubbals. *Shrp* 8C 34
Preston-le-Skerne. *Dur* 3M 47
Preston Marsh. *Here* 7D 26
Prestonmill. *Dum* 6D 52
Preston on Stour. *Warw* 7L 27
Preston on the Hill. *Hal* 1D 34
Preston on Wye. *Here* 7B 26
Prestonpans. *E Lot* 2A 60
Preston Plucknett. *Som* 4D 8
Preston-under-Scar. *N Yor* 6J 47
Preston upon the Weald Moors. *Telf* 8E 34
Preston Wynne. *Here* 7D 26
Prestwich. *G Man* 7G 41
Prestwick. *Nmbd* 4E 54
Prestwick. *S Ayr* 7B 58
Prestwold. *Leics* 7C 36
Prestwood. *Buck* 3F 20
Prestwood. *Staf* 5K 35
Price Town. *B'end* 5J 17
Prickwillow. *Cambs* 3B 30
Priddy. *Som* 8D 18
Priestcliffe. *Derbs* 2K 35
Priesthill. *Glas* 3D 58
Priest Hutton. *Lanc* 8D 46
Priestland. *E Ayr* 6D 58
Priest Weston. *Shrp* 2A 26
Priestwood. *Brac* 6F 20
Priestwood. *Kent* 7C 22
Primethorpe. *Leics* 2C 28
Primrose Green. *Norf* 8G 39
Primrose Hill. *Glos* 3E 18
Primrose Hill. *Lanc* 7B 40
Primrose Valley. *N Yor* 8J 49
Primsidemill. *Bord* 7F 60
Princes Gate. *Pemb* 5H 15
Princes Risborough. *Buck* 3F 20
Princethorpe. *Warw* 4B 28
Princetown. *Devn* 8E 6
Prinsted. *W Sus* 5E 10
Prion. *Den* 4K 33
Prior Muir. *Fife* 6J 67
Prior's Frome. *Here* 8D 26
Priors Halton. *Shrp* 4C 26
Priors Hardwick. *Warw* 6B 28
Priorslee. *Telf* 8F 34
Priors Marston. *Warw* 6B 28
Prior's Norton. *Glos* 1G 19
The Priory. *W Ber* 7M 19
Priory Wood. *Here* 7A 26
Priston. *Bath* 7E 18
Pristow Green. *Norf* 3H 31
Prittlewell. *S'end* 5E 22
Privett. *Hants* 3D 10
Prixford. *Devn* 2E 6
Probus. *Corn* 7A 4
Prospect. *Cumb* 7F 52
Prospect Village. *Staf* 8J 35
Provanmill. *Glas* 3E 58
Prudhoe. *Nmbd* 5D 54
Publow. *Bath* 7E 18
Puckeridge. *Herts* 1L 21
Puckington. *Som* 4B 8
Pucklechurch. *S Glo* 6E 18
Puckrup. *Glos* 8G 27
Puddinglake. *Ches W* 3F 34
Puddington. *Ches W* 2B 34
Puddington. *Devn* 4H 7
Puddlebrook. *Glos* 2E 18
Puddledock. *Norf* 2G 31
Puddletown. *Dors* 6F 8
Pudleston. *Here* 6D 26
Pudsey. *W Yor* 4L 41
Pulborough. *W Sus* 4H 11
Puleston. *Telf* 7F 34
Pulford. *Ches W* 4B 34
Pulham. *Dors* 5F 8
Pulham Market. *Norf* 3H 31
Pulham St Mary. *Norf* 3J 31
Pulley. *Shrp* 1C 26
Pulloxhill. *C Beds* 8H 29
Pulpit Hill. *Arg* 5C 64
Pulverbatch. *Shrp* 1C 26
Pumpherston. *W Lot* 3J 59
Pumsaint. *Carm* 8F 24
Puncheston. *Pemb* 4G 15
Puncknowle. *Dors* 7D 8
Punnett's Town. *E Sus* 3C 12
Purbrook. *Hants* 5D 10
Purfleet. *Thur* 6B 22
Puriton. *Som* 1B 8
Purleigh. *Essx* 3E 22
Purley. *G Lon* 7L 21
Purley on Thames. *W Ber* 6D 20
Purlogue. *Shrp* 4A 26
Purl's Bridge. *Cambs* 3A 30
Purse Caundle. *Dors* 4E 8
Purslow. *Shrp* 3B 26
Purston Jaglin. *W Yor* 6B 42
Purtington. *Som* 5B 8
Purton. *Glos*
nr. Lydney 3E 18
nr. Sharpness 3E 18
Purton. *Wilts* 5J 19
Purton Stoke. *Wilts* 4J 19
Pury End. *Nptn* 7E 28
Pusey. *Oxon* 4A 20
Putley. *Here* 8E 26
Putney. *G Lon* 6K 21
Putsborough. *Devn* 1D 6
Puttenham. *Herts* 2F 20
Puttenham. *Surr* 1G 11
Puttock End. *Essx* 7E 30
Puttock's End. *Essx* 2B 22
Puxey. *Dors* 4F 8
Puxton. *N Som* 7C 18
Pwll. *Carm* 6L 15
Pwll. *Powy* 2L 25
Pwllcrochan. *Pemb* 6F 14
Pwll-glas. *Den* 5L 33
Pwllgloyw. *Powy* 1K 17
Pwllheli. *Gwyn* 7C 32
Pwllmeyric. *Mon* 4D 18
Pwlltrap. *Carm* 5J 15
Pwll-y-glaw. *Neat* 5G 17
Pyecombe. *W Sus* 4K 11
Pye Corner. *Herts* 2M 21
Pye Corner. *Newp* 5B 18
Pye Green. *Staf* 8H 35
Pyewipe. *NE Lin* 6K 43
Pyle. *B'end* 6H 17
Pyle. *IOW* 8B 10
Pyle Hill. *Surr* 8G 21
Pylle. *Som* 2E 8
Pymoor. *Cambs* 3A 30
Pymore. *Dors* 6C 8
Pyrford. *Surr* 8H 21
Pyrford Village. *Surr* 8H 21
Pyrton. *Oxon* 4D 20
Pytchley. *Nptn* 4F 28
Pyworthy. *Devn* 5C 6

Q

Quabbs. *Shrp* 4M 25
Quadring. *Linc* 6K 37
Quadring Eaudike. *Linc* 6K 37
Quainton. *Buck* 1E 20
Quaking Houses. *Dur* 6E 54
Quarley. *Hants* 1L 9
Quarndon. *Derbs* 5M 35
Quarrendon. *Buck* 2F 20
Quarrier's Village. *Inv* 3B 58
Quarrington. *Linc* 5H 37
Quarrington Hill. *Dur* 8G 55
The Quarry. *Glos* 4F 18
Quarry Bank. *W Mid* 3H 27
Quarrywood. *Mor* 7A 80
Quartalehouse. *Abers* 1J 73
Quarter. *N Ayr* 3L 57
Quarter. *S Lan* 4F 58
Quatford. *Shrp* 2F 26
Quatt. *Shrp* 3F 26
Quebec. *Dur* 7E 54
Quedgeley. *Glos* 2G 19
Queen Adelaide. *Cambs* 3B 30
Queenborough. *Kent* 6F 22
Queen Camel. *Som* 3D 8
Queen Charlton. *Bath* 7E 18
Queen Dart. *Devn* 4H 7
Queenhill. *Worc* 8G 27
Queen Oak. *Dors* 2F 8
Queensbury. *W Yor* 4K 41
Queensferry. *Flin* 3B 34
Queensferry Crossing. *Edin* 2K 59
Queenstown. *Bkpl* 4B 40
Queen Street. *Kent* 1C 12
Queenzieburn. *N Lan* 2E 58
Quemerford. *Wilts* 7J 19
Quendale. *Shet* 6D 90
Quendon. *Essx* 8B 30
Queniborough. *Leics* 8D 36
Quenington. *Glos* 3K 19
Quernmore. *Lanc* 1D 40
Quethiock. *Corn* 5F 4
Quholm. *Orkn* 8B 88
Quick's Green. *W Ber* 6C 20
Quidenham. *Norf* 3G 31
Quidhampton. *Hants* 8C 20
Quidhampton. *Wilts* 2K 9
Quilquox. *Abers* 2J 73
Quina Brook. *Shrp* 6D 34
Quindry. *Orkn* 2F 86
Quine's Hill. *IOM* 7C 44
Quinton. *Nptn* 6E 28
Quinton. *W Mid* 3H 27
Quintrell Downs. *Corn* 2M 3
Quixhill. *Staf* 5K 35
Quoditch. *Devn* 6D 6
Quorn. *Leics* 8C 36
Quorndon. *Leics* 8C 36
Quothquan. *S Lan* 6H 59
Quoyloo. *Orkn* 7B 88
Quoyness. *Orkn* 1D 86
Quoys. *Shet*
on Mainland 1E 90
on Unst 2L 91

R

Rableyheath. *Herts* 2K 21
Raby. *Cumb* 6F 52
Raby. *Mers* 2B 34
Rachan Mill. *Bord* 6K 59
Rachub. *Gwyn* 4F 32
Rack End. *Oxon* 3B 20
Rackenford. *Devn* 4H 7
Rackham. *W Sus* 4H 11
Rackheath. *Norf* 8J 39
Racks. *Dum* 4E 52
Rackwick. *Orkn*
on Hoy 2D 86
on Westray 5D 88
Radbourne. *Derbs* 6L 35
Radcliffe. *G Man* 7F 40
Radcliffe. *Nmbd* 1F 54
Radcliffe on Trent. *Notts* 6D 36
Radclive. *Buck* 8D 28
Radernie. *Fife* 7H 67
Radfall. *Kent* 7H 23
Radford. *Bath* 8E 18
Radford. *Nott* 5C 36
Radford. *Oxon* 1B 20
Radford. *W Mid* 3M 27
Radford. *Worc* 6J 27
Radford Semele. *Warw* 5M 27
Radipole. *Dors* 7E 8
Radlett. *Herts* 4J 21
Radley. *Oxon* 4C 20
Radnage. *Buck* 4E 20
Radstock. *Bath* 8E 18
Radstone. *Nptn* 7C 28
Radway. *Warw* 7A 28
Radway Green. *Ches E* 4F 34
Radwell. *Bed* 6H 29
Radwell. *Herts* 8K 29
Radwinter. *Essx* 8C 30
Radyr. *Card* 6L 17
RAF Coltishall. *Norf* 7J 39
Rafford. *Mor* 8L 79
Raffrey. *New M* 6J 93
Ragdale. *Leics* 8D 36
Ragdon. *Shrp* 2C 26
Ragged Appleshaw. *Hants* 1M 9
Raggra. *High* 7E 86
Raglan. *Mon* 3C 18
Ragnall. *Notts* 2F 36
Raholp. *New M* 6J 93
Raigbeg. *High* 3J 71
Rainford. *Mers* 7C 40
Rainford Junction. *Mers* 7C 40
Rainham. *G Lon* 5B 22
Rainham. *Medw* 7E 22
Rainhill. *Mers* 8C 40
Rainow. *Ches E* 2H 35
Rainton. *N Yor* 8A 48
Rainworth. *Notts* 4C 36
Raisbeck. *Cumb* 5E 46
Raise. *Cumb* 7M 53
Rait. *Per* 5F 66
Raithby. *Linc* 1L 37
Raithby by Spilsby. *Linc* 3L 37
Raithwaite. *N Yor* 4F 48
Rake. *W Sus* 3F 10
Rake End. *Staf* 8J 35
Rakeway. *Staf* 5J 35
Rakewood. *G Man* 6H 41
Ralia. *High* 6H 71
Ram Alley. *Wilts* 7L 19
Ramasaig. *High* 1C 68
Rame. *Corn*
nr. Millbrook 7G 5
nr. Penryn 5L 3
Ram Lane. *Kent* 1F 12
Ramnageo. *Shet* 3L 91
Rampisham. *Dors* 5D 8
Rampside. *Cumb* 8M 45
Rampton. *Cambs* 5M 29
Rampton. *Notts* 2E 36
Ramsbottom. *G Man* 6F 40
Ramsburn. *Mor* 8E 80
Ramsbury. *Wilts* 6L 19
Ramscraigs. *High* 1M 79
Ramsdean. *Hants* 3E 10
Ramsdell. *Hants* 8C 20
Ramsden. *Oxon* 2A 20
Ramsden. *Worc* 7H 27
Ramsden Bellhouse. *Essx* 4D 22
Ramsden Heath. *Essx* 4D 22
Ramsey. *Cambs* 3K 29
Ramsey. *Essx* 8J 31
Ramsey. *IOM* 5D 44
Ramsey Forty Foot. *Cambs* 3L 29
Ramsey Heights. *Cambs* 3K 29
Ramsey Island. *Essx* 3F 22
Ramsey Mereside. *Cambs* 3K 29
Ramsey St Mary's. *Cambs* 3K 29
Ramsgate. *Kent* 7K 23
Ramsgill. *N Yor* 8K 47
Ramshaw. *Dur* 7C 54
Ramshorn. *Staf* 5J 35
Ramsley. *Devn* 6F 6
Ramsnest Common. *Surr* 2G 11
Ramstone. *Abers* 4F 72
Ranais. *W Isl* 1F 76
Ranby. *Linc* 2K 37
Ranby. *Notts* 1D 36
Rand. *Linc* 2J 37
Randalstown. *Ant* 4G 93
Randwick. *Glos* 3G 19
Ranfurly. *Ren* 3B 58
Rangag. *High* 7C 86
Rangemore. *Staf* 7K 35
Rangeworthy. *S Glo* 5E 18
Rankinston. *E Ayr* 8C 58
Rank's Green. *Essx* 2D 22
Ranmore Common. *Surr* 8J 21
Rannoch Station. *Per* 2J 65
Ranochan. *High* 7K 69
Ranskill. *Notts* 1D 36
Ranton. *Staf* 7G 35
Ranton Green. *Staf* 7G 35
Ranworth. *Norf* 8K 39
Raploch. *Stir* 8A 66
Rapness. *Orkn* 5E 88
Rapps. *Som* 4B 8
Rascal Moor. *E Yor* 4F 42
Rascarrel. *Dum* 7B 52
Rasharkin. *Caus* 3F 93
Rashfield. *Arg* 1L 57
Rashwood. *Worc* 5H 27
Raskelf. *N Yor* 8B 48
Rassau. *Blae* 3L 17
Rastrick. *W Yor* 5K 41
Ratagan. *High* 4L 69
Ratby. *Leics* 1C 28
Ratcliffe Culey. *Leics* 2M 27
Ratcliffe on Soar. *Notts* 7B 36
Ratcliffe on the Wreake. *Leics* 8D 36
Rathen. *Abers* 7K 81
Rathfriland. *Arm* 7G 93
Rathillet. *Fife* 5G 67
Rathmell. *N Yor* 1G 41
Ratho. *Edin* 2K 59
Ratho Station. *Edin* 2K 59
Rathven. *Mor* 7D 80
Ratley. *Hants* 3M 9
Ratley. *Warw* 7A 28
Ratlinghope. *Shrp* 2C 26
Rattar. *High* 4D 86
Ratten Row. *Cumb* 7H 53
Ratten Row. *Lanc* 3C 40
Rattery. *Devn* 5K 5
Rattlesden. *Suff* 6F 30
Ratton Village. *E Sus* 5B 12
Rattray. *Abers* 8K 81
Rattray. *Per* 3E 66
Raughton. *Cumb* 7H 53
Raughton Head. *Cumb* 7H 53
Raunds. *Nptn* 4G 29
Ravenfield. *S Yor* 8B 42
Ravenfield Common. *S Yor* 8B 42
Ravenglass. *Cumb* 5K 45
Ravenhills Green. *Worc* 6F 26
Raveningham. *Norf* 2K 31
Ravenscar. *N Yor* 5G 49
Ravensdale. *IOM* 5C 44
Ravensden. *Bed* 6H 29
Ravenseat. *N Yor* 5G 47
Ravenshead. *Notts* 4C 36
Ravensmoor. *Ches E* 4E 34
Ravensthorpe. *Nptn* 4D 28
Ravensthorpe. *W Yor* 5L 41
Ravenstone. *Leics* 8B 36
Ravenstone. *Mil* 6F 28
Ravenstonedale. *Cumb* 5F 46
Ravenstown. *Cumb* 8B 46
Ravenstruther. *S Lan* 5H 59
Ravensworth. *N Yor* 5K 47
Ravernet. *Lis* 5H 93
Raw. *N Yor* 5G 49
Rawcliffe. *E Yor* 5D 42
Rawcliffe. *York* 2C 42
Rawcliffe Bridge. *E Yor* 5D 42
Rawdon. *W Yor* 4L 41
Rawgreen. *Nmbd* 6C 54
Rawmarsh. *S Yor* 8B 42
Rawnsley. *Staf* 8J 35
Rawreth. *Essx* 4D 22
Rawridge. *Devn* 5M 7
Rawson Green. *Derbs* 5A 36
Rawtenstall. *Lanc* 5G 41
Raydon. *Suff* 8G 31
Raylees. *Nmbd* 2C 54
Rayleigh. *Essx* 4E 22
Raymond's Hill. *Devn* 6B 8
Rayne. *Essx* 1D 22
Rayners Lane. *G Lon* 5J 21
Reach. *Cambs* 5B 30
Read. *Lanc* 4F 40
Reading. *Read* 115 (6E 20)
Reading Green. *Suff* 4H 31
Reading Street. *Kent* 2F 12
Readymoney. *Corn* 6D 4
Reagill. *Cumb* 4E 46
Rearquhar. *High* 4H 79
Rearsby. *Leics* 8D 36
Reasby. *Linc* 2H 37
Reaseheath. *Ches E* 4E 34
Reaster. *High* 5D 86
Reawick. *Shet* 3D 90
Reay. *High* 5A 86
Rechullin. *High* 8K 77
Reculver. *Kent* 7J 23
Redberth. *Pemb* 6G 15
Redbourn. *Herts* 2J 21
Redbourne. *N Lin* 7G 43
Redbrook. *Glos* 3D 18
Redbrook. *Wrex* 5D 34
Redburn. *High* 1K 71
Redburn. *Nmbd* 5A 54
Redcar. *Red C* 3D 48
Redcastle. *High* 1F 70
Redcliffe Bay. *N Som* 6C 18
Red Dial. *Cumb* 7G 53
Redding. *Falk* 2H 59
Reddingmuirhead. *Falk* 2H 59
The Reddings. *Glos* 1H 19
Reddish. *G Man* 8G 41
Redditch. *Worc* 5J 27
Rede. *Suff* 6E 30
Redenhall. *Norf* 3J 31
Redesdale Camp. *Nmbd* 2B 54
Redesmouth. *Nmbd* 3B 54
Redford. *Ang* 3J 67
Redford. *Dur* 8D 54
Redford. *W Sus* 3F 10
Redfordgreen. *Bord* 8A 60
Redgate. *Corn* 5E 4
Redgrave. *Suff* 4G 31
Red Hill. *Warw* 6K 27
Red Hill. *W Yor* 5B 42
Redhill. *Abers* 5G 73
Redhill. *Herts* 8K 29
Redhill. *N Som* 7D 18
Redhill. *Shrp* 8F 34
Redhill. *Surr* 8K 21
Redhouses. *Arg* 3C 56
Redisham. *Suff* 3L 31
Redland. *Bris* 6D 18
Redland. *Orkn* 7C 88
Redlingfield. *Suff* 4H 31
Red Lodge. *Suff* 4C 30
Redlynch. *Som* 2F 8
Redlynch. *Wilts* 3L 9
Redmain. *Cumb* 8F 52
Redmarley. *Worc* 5F 26
Redmarley D'Abitot. *Glos* 8F 26
Redmarshall. *Stoc T* 3A 48
Redmile. *Leics* 6E 36
Redmire. *N Yor* 6J 47
Rednal. *Shrp* 7B 34
Redpath. *Bord* 6C 60
Redpoint. *High* 7J 77
Red Post. *Corn* 5B 6
Red Rock. *G Man* 7D 40
Red Roses. *Carm* 5J 15
Red Row. *Nmbd* 2F 54
Redruth. *Corn* 4L 3
Red Street. *Staf* 4G 35
Redvales. *G Man* 7G 41
Red Wharf Bay. *IOA* 2E 32
Redwick. *Newp* 5C 18
Redwick. *S Glo* 5D 18
Redworth. *Darl* 3L 47
Reed. *Herts* 8L 29
Reed End. *Herts* 8L 29
Reedham. *Linc* 4K 37
Reedham. *Norf* 1L 31
Reedness. *E Yor* 5F 42
Reeds Beck. *Linc* 3K 37
Reemshill. *Abers* 1G 73
Reepham. *Linc* 2H 37
Reepham. *Norf* 7G 39
Reeth. *N Yor* 6J 47
Regaby. *IOM* 5D 44
Regil. *N Som* 7D 18
Regoul. *High* 8J 79
Reiff. *High* 2L 77
Reigate. *Surr* 8K 21
Reighton. *N Yor* 8J 49
Reilth. *Shrp* 3A 26
Reinigeadal. *W Isl* 3D 76
Reisque. *Abers* 4H 73
Reiss. *High* 6E 86
Rejerrah. *Corn* 3L 3
Releath. *Corn* 5K 3
Relubbus. *Corn* 5J 3
Relugas. *Mor* 1K 71
Remenham. *Wok* 5E 20
Remenham Hill. *Wok* 5E 20
Rempstone. *Notts* 7C 36
Rendcomb. *Glos* 3J 19
Rendham. *Suff* 5K 31
Rendlesham. *Suff* 6K 31
Renfrew. *Ren* 3D 58
Renhold. *Bed* 6H 29
Renishaw. *Derbs* 2B 36
Rennington. *Nmbd* 8K 61
Renton. *W Dun* 2B 58
Renwick. *Cumb* 7K 53
Repps. *Norf* 8L 39
Repton. *Derbs* 7M 35
Rescassa. *Corn* 7B 4
Rescobie. *Ang* 2J 67
Rescorla. *Corn*
nr. Penwithick 6C 4
nr. Sticker 7B 4
Resipole. *High* 1B 64
Resolfen. *Neat* 4H 17
Resolis. *High* 7G 79
Resolven. *Neat* 4H 17
Rest and be thankful. *Arg* 7G 65
Reston. *Bord* 3F 60
Restrop. *Wilts* 5J 19
Retford. *Notts* 1E 36
Retire. *Corn* 5C 4
Rettendon. *Essx* 4D 22
Revesby. *Linc* 3K 37
Rew. *Devn* 8K 5
Rewe. *Devn* 6J 7
Rew Street. *IOW* 6B 10
Rexon. *Devn* 7D 6
Reybridge. *Wilts* 7H 19
Reydon. *Suff* 4M 31
Reymerston. *Norf* 1G 31
Reynalton. *Pemb* 6G 15
Reynoldston. *Swan* 8L 15
Rezare. *Corn* 8C 6
Rhadyr. *Mon* 3B 18
Rhaeadr Gwy. *Powy* 6J 25
Rhandirmwyn. *Carm* 8G 25
Rhayader. *Powy* 6J 25
Rheindown. *High* 1F 70
Rhemore. *High* 2L 63
Rhenetra. *High* 8F 76
Rhewl. *Den*
nr. Llangollen 6L 33
nr. Ruthin 4L 33
Rhewl. *Shrp* 6B 34
Rhewl-Mostyn. *Flin* 2L 33
Rhian. *High* 2F 78
Rhian Breck. *High* 3F 78
Rhicarn. *High* 1A 78
Rhiconich. *High* 6E 84
Rhicullen. *High* 6G 79
Rhidorroch. *High* 4B 78
Rhifail. *High* 7K 85
Rhigos. *Rhon* 4J 17
Rhilochan. *High* 3H 79
Rhiroy. *High* 5B 78
Rhitongue. *High* 6J 85
Rhiw. *Gwyn* 8B 32
Rhiwabon. *Wrex* 5B 34
Rhiwbina. *Card* 6L 17
Rhiwbryfdir. *Gwyn* 6F 32
Rhiwderin. *Newp* 5A 18
Rhiwlas. *Gwyn*
nr. Bala 7J 33
nr. Bangor 4E 32
Rhiwlas. *Powy* 7L 33
Rhodes. *G Man* 7G 41
Rhodesia. *Notts* 1C 36
Rhodes Minnis. *Kent* 1H 13
Rhodiad-y-Brenin. *Pemb* 4D 14
Rhondda. *Rhon* 5J 17
Rhonehouse. *Dum* 6B 52
Rhoose. *V Glam* 8K 17
Rhos. *Carm* 3K 15
Rhos. *Neat* 4G 17
The Rhos. *Pemb* 5G 15
Rhosaman. *Carm* 3G 17
Rhoscefnhir. *IOA* 3E 32
Rhoscolyn. *IOA* 3B 32
Rhos Common. *Powy* 8A 34
Rhoscrowther. *Pemb* 6F 14
Rhos-ddu. *Gwyn* 7B 32
Rhosdylluan. *Gwyn* 8H 33
Rhosesmor. *Flin* 4M 33
Rhos-fawr. *Gwyn* 7C 32
Rhosgadfan. *Gwyn* 5E 32
Rhosgoch. *IOA* 2D 32
Rhosgoch. *Powy* 8L 25
Rhos Haminiog. *Cdgn* 6E 24
Rhos-hill. *Pemb* 2H 15
Rhoshirwaun. *Gwyn* 8A 32
Rhoslan. *Gwyn* 6D 32
Rhoslefain. *Gwyn* 2E 24
Rhosllanerchrugog. *Wrex* 5A 34
Rhôs Lligwy. *IOA* 2D 32
Rhosmaen. *Carm* 2F 16
Rhosmeirch. *IOA* 3D 32
Rhosneigr. *IOA* 3C 32
Rhôs-on-Sea. *Cnwy* 2H 33
Rhossili. *Swan* 8L 15
Rhosson. *Pemb* 4D 14
Rhostrenwfa. *IOA* 3D 32
Rhostryfan. *Gwyn* 5D 32
Rhostyllen. *Wrex* 5B 34
Rhoswiel. *Shrp* 6A 34
Rhosybol. *IOA* 2D 32
Rhos-y-brithdir. *Powy* 8L 33
Rhos-y-garth. *Cdgn* 5F 24
Rhos-y-gwaliau. *Gwyn* 7J 33
Rhos-y-llan. *Gwyn* 7B 32
Rhos-y-meirch. *Powy* 5A 26
Rhu. *Arg* 1A 58
Rhualt. *Den* 3K 33
Rhubha Stoer. *High* 8C 84
Rhubodach. *Arg* 2K 57
Rhuddall Heath. *Ches W* 3D 34
Rhuddlan. *Cdgn* 2L 15
Rhuddlan. *Den* 3K 33
Rhue. *High* 4A 78
Rhulen. *Powy* 8L 25
Rhunahaorine. *Arg* 5G 57
Rhuthun. *Den* 5L 33
Rhuvoult. *High* 6E 84
Y Rhws. *V Glam* 8K 17
Rhyd. *Gwyn* 6F 32
Rhydaman. *Carm* 3F 16
Rhydargaeau. *Carm* 4L 15
Rhydcymerau. *Carm* 1E 16
Rhydd. *Worc* 7G 27
Rhyd-Ddu. *Gwyn* 5E 32
Rhydding. *Neat* 5G 17
Rhydfudr. *Cdgn* 6E 24
Rhydlanfair. *Cnwy* 5H 33
Rhydlewis. *Cdgn* 2K 15
Rhydlios. *Gwyn* 7A 32
Rhydlydan. *Cnwy* 5H 33
Rhyd-meirionydd. *Cdgn* 4F 24
Rhydowen. *Cdgn* 2L 15
Rhyd-Rosser. *Cdgn* 6E 24
Rhydspence. *Here* 8M 25
Rhydtalog. *Flin* 5M 33
Rhyd-uchaf. *Gwyn* 7J 33
Rhydwyn. *IOA* 2C 32
Rhyd-y-clafdy. *Gwyn* 7C 32
Rhydycroesau. *Powy* 7M 33
Rhydyfelin. *Cdgn* 5E 24
Rhydyfelin. *Rhon* 6K 17
Rhyd-y-foel. *Cnwy* 3J 33
Rhyd-y-fro. *Neat* 4G 17
Rhydymain. *Gwyn* 8H 33
Rhyd-y-meudwy. *Den* 5L 33
Rhydymwyn. *Flin* 4M 33
Rhyd-yr-onen. *Gwyn* 2F 24
Rhyd-y-sarn. *Gwyn* 6F 32
Rhyl. *Den* 2K 33
Rhymney. *Cphy* 4L 17
Rhymni. *Cphy* 4L 17
Rhynd. *Per* 5E 66
Rhynie. *Abers* 3D 72
Ribbesford. *Worc* 4F 26
Ribbleton. *Lanc* 4D 40
Ribby. *Lanc* 4C 40
Ribchester. *Lanc* 4E 40
Riber. *Derbs* 4M 35
Ribigill. *High* 6H 85
Riby. *Linc* 7J 43
Riccall. *N Yor* 4D 42
Riccarton. *E Ayr* 6C 58
Richards Castle. *Here* 5C 26
Richborough Port. *Kent* 7K 23
Richhill. *Arm* 6F 93
Richings Park. *Buck* 6H 21
Richmond. *G Lon* 6J 21
Richmond. *N Yor* 5K 47
Rickarton. *Abers* 7H 73
Rickerby. *Cumb* 6J 53
Rickerscote. *Staf* 7H 35
Rickford. *N Som* 8C 18
Rickham. *Devn* 8K 5
Rickinghall. *Suff* 4G 31
Rickleton. *Tyne* 6F 54
Rickling. *Essx* 8A 30
Rickling Green. *Essx* 1B 22
Rickmansworth. *Herts* 4H 21
Riddings. *Derbs* 4B 36
Riddlecombe. *Devn* 4F 6
Riddlesden. *W Yor* 3J 41
Ridge. *Dors* 7H 9
Ridge. *Herts* 3K 21
Ridge. *Wilts* 2H 9
Ridgebourne. *Powy* 6K 25
Ridge Lane. *Warw* 2L 27
Ridgeway. *Derbs*
nr. Alfreton 4A 36
nr. Sheffield 1B 36
Ridgeway. *Staf* 4G 35
Ridgeway Cross. *Here* 7F 26
Ridgeway Moor. *Derbs* 1B 36
Ridgewell. *Essx* 7D 30
Ridgewood. *E Sus* 3A 12
Ridgmont. *C Beds* 8G 29
Ridgwardine. *Shrp* 6E 34
Riding Mill. *Nmbd* 5D 54
Ridley. *Kent* 7C 22
Ridley. *Nmbd* 5A 54
Ridlington. *Norf* 6K 39
Ridlington. *Rut* 1F 28
Ridsdale. *Nmbd* 3C 54
Riemore Lodge. *Per* 3D 66
Rievaulx. *N Yor* 7C 48
Rift House. *Hart* 8H 55
Rigg. *Dum* 5G 53
Riggend. *N Lan* 2F 58
Rigsby. *Linc* 2M 37
Rigside. *S Lan* 6G 59
Riley Green. *Lanc* 5E 40
Rileyhill. *Staf* 8K 35
Rilla Mill. *Corn* 8B 6
Rillington. *N Yor* 8F 48
Rimington. *Lanc* 3G 41
Rimpton. *Som* 3E 8
Rimsdale. *High* 7K 85
Rimswell. *E Yor* 5L 43
Ringasta. *Shet* 6D 90
Ringford. *Dum* 6A 52
Ringing Hill. *Leics* 8B 36
Ringinglow. *S Yor* 1L 35
Ringland. *Norf* 8H 39
Ringlestone. *Kent* 8E 22
Ringmer. *E Sus* 4M 11
Ringmore. *Devn*
nr. Kingsbridge 7J 5
nr. Teignmouth 8J 7
Ring o' Bells. *Lanc* 6C 40
Ring's End. *Cambs* 1L 29
Ringsfield. *Suff* 3L 31
Ringsfield Corner. *Suff* 3L 31
Ringshall. *Buck* 2G 21
Ringshall. *Suff* 6G 31
Ringshall Stocks. *Suff* 6G 31
Ringstead. *Norf* 5D 38
Ringstead. *Nptn* 4G 29
Ringwood. *Hants* 5K 9
Ringwould. *Kent* 1K 13
Rinmore. *Abers* 4D 72
Rinnigill. *Orkn* 2E 86
Rinsey. *Corn* 6J 3
Riof. *W Isl* 8E 82
Ripe. *E Sus* 4B 12
Ripley. *Derbs* 4B 36
Ripley. *Hants* 6K 9
Ripley. *N Yor* 1L 41
Ripley. *Surr* 8H 21
Riplingham. *E Yor* 4G 43
Ripon. *N Yor* 8M 47
Rippingale. *Linc* 7H 37
Ripple. *Kent* 1K 13
Ripple. *Worc* 8G 27
Ripponden. *W Yor* 6J 41
Rireavach. *High* 4M 77
Risabus. *Arg* 5C 56
Risbury. *Here* 6D 26
Risby. *E Yor* 4H 43
Risby. *N Lin* 6G 43
Risby. *Suff* 5D 30
Risca. *Cphy* 5M 17
Rise. *E Yor* 3J 43
Riseden. *E Sus* 2C 12
Riseden. *Kent* 2D 12
Rise End. *Derbs* 4L 35
Risegate. *Linc* 7K 37
Riseholme. *Linc* 2G 37
Riseley. *Bed* 5H 29
Riseley. *Wok* 7E 20
Rishangles. *Suff* 5H 31
Rishton. *Lanc* 4F 40
Rishworth. *W Yor* 6J 41
Risley. *Derbs* 6B 36
Risley. *Warr* 8E 40
Risplith. *N Yor* 1L 41
Rispond. *High* 5G 85
Rivar. *Wilts* 7M 19
Rivenhall. *Essx* 2E 22
Rivenhall End. *Essx* 2E 22
River. *Kent* 1J 13
River. *W Sus* 3G 11
River Bank. *Cambs* 5B 30
Riverhead. *Kent* 8B 22
Rivington. *Lanc* 6E 40
Roach Bridge. *Lanc* 5D 40
Roachill. *Devn* 3H 7
Roade. *Nptn* 6E 28
Road Green. *Norf* 2J 31
Roadhead. *Cumb* 4K 53
Roadmeetings. *S Lan* 5G 59
Roadside. *High* 5C 86
Roadside of Catterline. *Abers* 8H 73
Roadside of Kinneff. *Abers* 8H 73
Roadwater. *Som* 2K 7
Road Weedon. *Nptn* 6D 28
Roag. *High* 1D 68
Roa Island. *Cumb* 8M 45
Roath. *Card* 7L 17
Roberton. *Bord* 8B 60
Roberton. *S Lan* 7H 59
Robertsbridge. *E Sus* 3D 12
Robertstown. *Mor* 1B 72
Robertstown. *Rhon* 4J 17
Roberttown. *W Yor* 5K 41
Robeston Back. *Pemb* 5G 15
Robeston Wathen. *Pemb* 5G 15
Robeston West. *Pemb* 6E 14
Robin Hood. *Lanc* 6D 40
Robin Hood. *W Yor* 5M 41
Robinhood End. *Essx* 8D 30
Robin Hood's Bay. *N Yor* 5G 49
Roborough. *Devn*
nr. Great Torrington 4E 6
nr. Plymouth 5H 5
Rob Roy's House. *Arg* 6F 64
Roby Mill. *Lanc* 7D 40
Rocester. *Staf* 6K 35
Roch. *Pemb* 4E 14
Rochdale. *G Man* 6G 41
Roche. *Corn* 5B 4
Rochester. *Medw* **Medway Towns 111** (7D 22)
Rochester. *Nmbd* 2B 54
Rochford. *Essx* 4E 22
Rock. *Corn* 4B 4
Rock. *Nmbd* 7K 61
Rock. *W Sus* 4J 11
Rock. *Worc* 4F 26
The Rock. *M Ulst* 5E 92
Rockbeare. *Devn* 6K 7
Rockbourne. *Hants* 4K 9
Rockcliffe. *Cumb* 5H 53
Rockcliffe. *Dum* 6C 52
Rockcliffe Cross. *Cumb* 5H 53
Rock Ferry. *Mers* 1B 34
Rockfield. *High* 5K 79
Rockfield. *Mon* 2C 18
Rockford. *Hants* 5K 9
Rockgreen. *Shrp* 4D 26
Rockhampton. *S Glo* 4E 18
Rockhead. *Corn* 3C 4
Rockingham. *Nptn* 2F 28
Rockland All Saints. *Norf* 2F 30
Rockland St Mary. *Norf* 1K 31
Rockland St Peter. *Norf* 2F 30
Rockley. *Wilts* 6K 19
Rockwell End. *Buck* 5E 20
Rockwell Green. *Som* 4L 7
Rodborough. *Glos* 3G 19
Rodbourne. *Wilts* 5H 19
Rodd. *Here* 5B 26
Roddam. *Nmbd* 7H 61
Rodden. *Dors* 7E 8
Roddenloft. *E Ayr* 7C 58
Roddymoor. *Dur* 8E 54
Rode. *Som* 8G 19
Rode Heath. *Ches E* 4G 35
Rodeheath. *Ches E* 3G 35
Rodel. *W Isl* 5B 76
Roden. *Telf* 8D 34
Rodhuish. *Som* 2K 7
Rodington. *Telf* 8D 34
Rodington Heath. *Telf* 8D 34
Rodley. *Glos* 2F 18
Rodmarton. *Glos* 4H 19
Rodmell. *E Sus* 5M 11
Rodmersham. *Kent* 7F 22
Rodmersham Green. *Kent* 7F 22
Rodney Stoke. *Som* 1C 8
Rodsley. *Derbs* 5L 35
Rodway. *Som* 2A 8
Rodway. *Telf* 8E 34
Rodwell. *Dors* 8E 8
Roecliffe. *N Yor* 1A 42
Roe Green. *Herts* 8L 29
Roehampton. *G Lon* 6K 21
Roesound. *Shet* 1D 90
Roffey. *W Sus* 2J 11
Rogart. *High* 3H 79
Rogate. *W Sus* 3F 10
Roger Ground. *Cumb* 6B 46
Rogerstone. *Newp* 5A 18
Rogiet. *Mon* 5C 18
Rogue's Alley. *Cambs* 1L 29
Roke. *Oxon* 4D 20
Rokemarsh. *Oxon* 4D 20
Roker. *Tyne* 6H 55
Rollesby. *Norf* 8L 39
Rolleston. *Leics* 1E 28
Rolleston. *Notts* 4E 36
Rolleston on Dove. *Staf* 7L 35
Rolston. *E Yor* 3K 43
Rolvenden. *Kent* 2E 12
Rolvenden Layne. *Kent* 2E 12
Romaldkirk. *Dur* 3H 47
Roman Bank. *Shrp* 2D 26
Romanby. *N Yor* 6A 48
Romannobridge. *Bord* 5K 59
Romansleigh. *Devn* 3G 7
Romers Common. *Worc* 5D 26
Romesdal. *High* 8F 76
Romford. *Dors* 5J 9
Romford. *G Lon* 5B 22
Romiley. *G Man* 8H 41
Romsey. *Hants* 3A 10
Romsley. *Shrp* 3F 26
Romsley. *Worc* 4H 27
Ronague. *IOM* 7B 44
Ronaldsvoe. *Orkn* 2F 86
Rookby. *Cumb* 4G 47
Rookhope. *Dur* 7C 54
Rooking. *Cumb* 4C 46
Rookley. *IOW* 7C 10
Rooks Bridge. *Som* 8B 18
Rooksey Green. *Suff* 6F 30
Rook's Nest. *Som* 2K 7
Rookwood. *W Sus* 6E 10
Roos. *E Yor* 4K 43
Roosebeck. *Cumb* 8M 45
Roosecote. *Cumb* 8M 45
Rootfield. *High* 8F 78
Rootham's Green. *Bed* 6J 29
Rootpark. *S Lan* 4H 59
Ropley. *Hants* 2D 10
Ropley Dean. *Hants* 2D 10
Ropsley. *Linc* 6G 37
Rora. *Abers* 8K 81
Rorandle. *Abers* 4F 72
Rorrington. *Shrp* 1B 26
Rose. *Corn* 3L 3
Roseacre. *Lanc* 4C 40
Rose Ash. *Devn* 3G 7
Rosebank. *S Lan* 5G 59
Rosebush. *Pemb* 4G 15
Rosedale Abbey. *N Yor* 6E 48
Roseden. *Nmbd* 7H 61
Rose Green. *Essx* 1E 22
Rose Green. *Suff* 7F 30
Rosehall. *High* 3E 78
Rosehearty. *Abers* 7J 81
Rose Hill. *E Sus* 4A 12
Rose Hill. *Lanc* 4G 41
Rosehill. *Shrp*
nr. Market Drayton 6E 34
nr. Shrewsbury 8C 34
Roseisle. *Mor* 7M 79
Rosemarket. *Pemb* 6F 14
Rosemarkie. *High* 8H 79
Rosemary Lane. *Devn* 4L 7
Rosemount. *Per* 3E 66
Rosenannon. *Corn* 5B 4
Roser's Cross. *E Sus* 3B 12
Rosevean. *Corn* 6C 4
Rosewell. *Midl* 3L 59
Roseworth. *Stoc T* 3B 48
Roseworthy. *Corn* 5K 3
Rosgill. *Cumb* 4D 46
Roshven. *High* 8J 69
Roskhill. *High* 1D 68
Roskorwell. *Corn* 6L 3
Rosley. *Cumb* 7H 53
Roslin. *Midl* 3L 59
Rosliston. *Derbs* 8L 35
Rosneath. *Arg* 1A 58
Ross. *Dum* 7M 51
Ross. *Nmbd* 6J 61
Ross. *Per* 5A 66
Ross. *Bord* 3G 61
Rossendale. *Lanc* 5F 40
Rossett. *Wrex* 4B 34
Rossington. *S Yor* 8D 42
Rosskeen. *High* 7G 79
Rossland. *Ren* 2C 58
Rosslea. *Ferm* 7D 92
Ross-on-Wye. *Here* 1E 18
Roster. *High* 8D 86
Rostherne. *Ches E* 1F 34
Rostholme. *S Yor* 7C 42
Rosthwaite. *Cumb* 4A 46
Roston. *Derbs* 5K 35
Rostrevor. *New M* 7G 93
Rosudgeon. *Corn* 6J 3
Rosyth. *Fife* 1K 59
Rothbury. *Nmbd* 1D 54
Rotherby. *Leics* 8D 36
Rotherfield. *E Sus* 3B 12
Rotherfield Greys. *Oxon* 5E 20
Rotherfield Peppard. *Oxon* 5E 20
Rotherham. *S Yor* 8B 42
Rothersthorpe. *Nptn* 6E 28
Rotherwick. *Hants* 8E 20
Rothes. *Mor* 1B 72
Rothesay. *Arg* 3K 57
Rothienorman. *Abers* 2G 73
Rothiesholm. *Orkn* 7F 88
Rothley. *Leics* 8C 36
Rothley. *Nmbd* 3D 54
Rothwell. *Linc* 8J 43
Rothwell. *Nptn* 3F 28
Rothwell. *W Yor* 5M 41
Rotsea. *E Yor* 2H 43
Rottal. *Ang* 1G 67
Rotten End. *Suff* 5K 31
Rotten Row. *Norf* 8G 39
Rotten Row. *W Ber* 6C 20
Rotten Row. *W Mid* 4K 27
Rottingdean. *Brig* 5L 11
Rottington. *Cumb* 3J 45
Roud. *IOW* 7C 10
Rougham. *Norf* 7E 38
Rougham. *Suff* 5F 30
Rough Close. *Staf* 6H 35
Rough Common. *Kent* 8H 23
Roughcote. *Staf* 5H 35
Roughfort. *Ant* 4H 93
Rough Haugh. *High* 7K 85
Rough Hay. *Staf* 7L 35
Roughlee. *Lanc* 3G 41
Roughley. *W Mid* 2K 27
Roughsike. *Cumb* 4K 53
Roughton. *Linc* 3K 37
Roughton. *Norf* 6J 39
Roughton. *Shrp* 2F 26
Roundbush Green. *Essx* 2B 22
Roundham. *Som* 5C 8
Roundhay. *W Yor* 4M 41
Round Hill. *Torb* 5L 5
Roundhurst. *W Sus* 2G 11
Round Maple. *Suff* 7F 30
Round Oak. *Shrp* 3B 26
Roundstreet Common. *W Sus* 3H 11
Roundthwaite. *Cumb* 5E 46
Roundway. *Wilts* 7J 19
Roundyhill. *Ang* 2G 67
Rousdon. *Devn* 6A 8
Rousham. *Oxon* 1B 20
Rousky. *Ferm* 4D 92
Rous Lench. *Worc* 6J 27
Routh. *E Yor* 3H 43
Rout's Green. *Buck* 4E 20
Row. *Corn* 4C 4
Row. *Cumb*
nr. Kendal 7C 46
nr. Penrith 8L 53
The Row. *Lanc* 8C 46
Rowanburn. *Dum* 4J 53
Rowanhill. *Abers* 8K 81
Rowardennan. *Stir* 8H 65
Rowarth. *Derbs* 1J 35
Row Ash. *Hants* 4C 10
Rowberrow. *Som* 8C 18
Rowde. *Wilts* 7H 19
Rowden. *Devn* 6F 6
Rowen. *Cnwy* 3G 33
Rowfoot. *Nmbd* 5L 53
Row Green. *Essx* 1D 22
Row Heath. *Essx* 2H 23
Rowhedge. *Essx* 1G 23
Rowhook. *W Sus* 2J 11
Rowington. *Warw* 5L 27
Rowland. *Derbs* 2L 35
Rowlands Castle. *Hants* 4E 10
Rowlands Gill. *Tyne* 6E 54
Rowledge. *Hants* 1F 10
Rowley. *Dur* 7D 54
Rowley. *E Yor* 4G 43
Rowley. *Shrp* 1B 26
Rowley Hill. *W Yor* 6K 41
Rowley Regis. *W Mid* 3H 27
Rowlstone. *Here* 1B 18
Rowly. *Surr* 1H 11
Rowner. *Hants* 5C 10
Rowney Green. *Worc* 4J 27
Rownhams. *Hants* 4A 10
Rowrah. *Cumb* 3K 45
Rowsham. *Buck* 2F 20
Rowsley. *Derbs* 3L 35
Rowstock. *Oxon* 5B 20
Rowston. *Linc* 4H 37
Rowthorne. *Derbs* 3B 36
Rowton. *Ches W* 3C 34
Rowton. *Shrp*
nr. Ludlow 3C 26
nr. Shrewsbury 8B 34
Rowton. *Telf* 8E 34
Row Town. *Surr* 7H 21
Roxburgh. *Bord* 6E 60
Roxby. *N Lin* 6G 43
Roxby. *N Yor* 4E 48
Roxhill. *Ant* 4G 93
Roxton. *Bed* 6J 29
Roxwell. *Essx* 3C 22
Royal Leamington Spa. *Warw* 5M 27
Royal Oak. *Darl* 3L 47
Royal Oak. *Lanc* 7C 40
Royal Oak. *N Yor* 8J 49
Royal's Green. *Ches E* 5E 34
Royal Sutton Coldfield. *W Mid* 2K 27
Royal Tunbridge Wells. *Kent* 2B 12
Royal Wootton Bassett. *Wilts* 5J 19
Roybridge. *High* 7C 70
Roydon. *Essx* 2M 21
Roydon. *Norf*
nr. Diss 3G 31
nr. King's Lynn 7D 38
Roydon Hamlet. *Essx* 3M 21
Royston. *Herts* 7L 29
Royston. *S Yor* 6A 42
Royston Water. *Som* 4M 7
Royton. *G Man* 7H 41
Ruabon. *Wrex* 5B 34
Ruaig. *Arg* 3F 62
Ruan High Lanes. *Corn* 8B 4
Ruan Lanihorne. *Corn* 7A 4
Ruan Major. *Corn* 7L 3
Ruan Minor. *Corn* 7L 3
Ruarach. *High* 3L 69
Ruardean. *Glos* 2E 18
Ruardean Hill. *Glos* 2E 18
Ruardean Woodside. *Glos* 2E 18
Rubane. *Ards* 5K 93
Rubery. *Worc* 4H 27
Ruchazie. *Glas* 3E 58
Ruckcroft. *Cumb* 7K 53
Ruckinge. *Kent* 2G 13
Ruckland. *Linc* 2L 37
Rucklers Lane. *Herts* 3H 21
Ruckley. *Shrp* 1D 26
Rudbaxton. *Pemb* 4F 14
Rudby. *N Yor* 5B 48
Ruddington. *Notts* 6C 36
Rudford. *Glos* 1F 18
Rudge. *Shrp* 2G 27
Rudge. *Wilts* 8G 19
Rudge Heath. *Shrp* 2F 26
Rudgeway. *S Glo* 5E 18
Rudgwick. *W Sus* 2H 11
Rudhall. *Here* 1E 18
Rudheath. *Ches W* 2E 34
Rudley Green. *Essx* 3E 22
Rudloe. *Wilts* 6G 19
Rudry. *Cphy* 6M 17
Rudston. *E Yor* 1H 43
Rudyard. *Staf* 4H 35
Rufford. *Lanc* 6C 40
Rufforth. *York* 2C 42
Rugby. *Warw* 4C 28
Rugeley. *Staf* 8J 35
Ruglen. *S Ayr* 1H 51
Ruilick. *High* 1F 70
Ruisaurie. *High* 1E 70
Ruishton. *Som* 3A 8
Ruisigearraidh. *W Isl* 5L 75
Ruislip. *G Lon* 5H 21
Ruislip Common. *G Lon* 5H 21
Rumbling Bridge. *Per* 8D 66
Rumburgh. *Suff* 3K 31
Rumford. *Corn* 4A 4
Rumford. *Falk* 2H 59
Rumney. *Card* 7M 17
Rumwell. *Som* 3L 7
Runcorn. *Hal* 1D 34
Runcton. *W Sus* 5F 10
Runcton Holme. *Norf* 1C 30
Rundlestone. *Devn* 8E 6
Runfold. *Surr* 1F 10
Runhall. *Norf* 1G 31
Runham. *Norf* 8L 39
Runnington. *Som* 3L 7
Runshaw Moor. *Lanc* 6D 40
Runswick. *N Yor* 4F 48
Runtaleave. *Ang* 1F 66
Runwell. *Essx* 4D 22
Ruscombe. *Wok* 6E 20
Rushall. *Here* 8E 26
Rushall. *Norf* 3H 31
Rushall. *W Mid* 1J 27
Rushall. *Wilts* 8K 19
Rushbrooke. *Suff* 5E 30
Rushbury. *Shrp* 2D 26
Rushden. *Herts* 8L 29
Rushden. *Nptn* 5G 29
Rushenden. *Kent* 6F 22
Rushford. *Devn* 8D 6
Rushford. *Suff* 3F 30
Rush Green. *Herts* 1K 21
Rushlake Green. *E Sus* 4C 12
Rushmere. *Suff* 3L 31
Rushmere St Andrew. *Suff* 7J 31
Rushmoor. *Surr* 1F 10
Rushock. *Worc* 4G 27
Rusholme. *G Man* 8G 41
Rushton. *Ches W* 3D 34
Rushton. *Nptn* 3F 28
Rushton. *Shrp* 1E 26
Rushton Spencer. *Staf* 3H 35
Rushwick. *Worc* 6G 27
Rushyford. *Dur* 3L 47
Ruskie. *Stir* 7L 65
Ruskington. *Linc* 4H 37
Rusland. *Cumb* 7B 46
Rusper. *W Sus* 2K 11
Ruspidge. *Glos* 2E 18
Russell's Water. *Oxon* 5E 20
Russel's Green. *Suff* 4J 31
Russ Hill. *Surr* 1K 11
Russland. *Orkn* 8C 88
Rusthall. *Kent* 2B 12
Rustington. *W Sus* 5H 11
Ruston. *N Yor* 7G 49
Ruston Parva. *E Yor* 1H 43
Ruswarp. *N Yor* 5F 48
Rutherglen. *S Lan* 3E 58
Ruthernbridge. *Corn* 5C 4
Ruthin. *Den* 5L 33
Ruthin. *V Glam* 7J 17
Ruthrieston. *Aber* 5J 73
Ruthven. *Abers* 1E 72
Ruthven. *Ang* 3F 66
Ruthven. *High*
nr. Inverness 2J 71
nr. Kingussie 6H 71
Ruthvoes. *Corn* 5B 4
Ruthwaite. *Cumb* 8G 53
Ruthwell. *Dum* 5F 52
Ruxton Green. *Here* 2D 18
Ruyton-XI-Towns. *Shrp* 7B 34
Ryal. *Nmbd* 4D 54
Ryall. *Dors* 6C 8
Ryall. *Worc* 7G 27
Ryarsh. *Kent* 8C 22
Rychraggan. *High* 2E 70
Rydal. *Cumb* 5B 46
Ryde. *IOW* 6C 10
Rye. *E Sus* 3F 12
Ryecroft Gate. *Staf* 3H 35
Ryeford. *Here* 1E 18
Rye Foreign. *E Sus* 3F 12
Rye Harbour. *E Sus* 4F 12
Ryehill. *E Yor* 5K 43
Rye Street. *Worc* 8F 26
Ryhall. *Rut* 8H 37
Ryhill. *W Yor* 6A 42
Ryhope. *Tyne* 6H 55
Ryhope Colliery. *Tyne* 6H 55
Rylands. *Notts* 6C 36
Rylstone. *N Yor* 2H 41
Ryme Intrinseca. *Dors* 4D 8
Ryther. *N Yor* 4C 42
Ryton. *Glos* 8F 26
Ryton. *N Yor* 8E 48
Ryton. *Shrp* 1F 26
Ryton. *Tyne* 5E 54
Ryton. *Warw* 3B 28
Ryton-on-Dunsmore. *Warw* 4A 28
Ryton Woodside. *Tyne* 5E 54

S

Saasaig. *High* 5H 69
Sabden. *Lanc* 4F 40
Sacombe. *Herts* 2L 21
Sacriston. *Dur* 7F 54
Sadberge. *Darl* 4M 47
Saddell. *Arg* 6G 57
Saddington. *Leics* 2D 28
Saddle Bow. *Norf* 8C 38
Saddlescombe. *W Sus* 4K 11
Saddleworth. *G Man* 7H 41
Sadgill. *Cumb* 5C 46
Saffron Walden. *Essx* 8B 30
Sageston. *Pemb* 6G 15
Saham Hills. *Norf* 1F 30
Saham Toney. *Norf* 1E 30
Saighdinis. *W Isl* 7K 75
Saighton. *Ches W* 3C 34
Sain Dunwyd. *V Glam* 8J 17
Sain Hilari. *V Glam* 7K 17
St Abbs. *Bord* 3G 61
St Agnes. *Corn* 3L 3
St Albans. *Herts* 3J 21

St Allen—Slaley

St Allen. *Corn* 3M 3
St Andrews. *Fife* 6J 67
St Andrews Major. *V Glam* 7L 17
St Anne's. *Lanc* 5B 40
St Ann's. *Dum* 2E 52
St Ann's Chapel. *Corn* 8D 6
St Ann's Chapel. *Devn* 7J 5
St Anthony. *Corn* 8A 4
St Anthony-in-Meneage.
Corn 6L 3
St Arvans. *Mon* 4D 18
St Asaph. *Den* 3K 33
Sain Tathan. *V Glam* 8K 17
St Athan. *V Glam* 8K 17
St Austell. *Corn* 6C 4
St Bartholomew's Hill. *Wilts* 3H 9
St Bees. *Cumb* 3J 45
St Blazey. *Corn* 6C 4
St Blazey Gate. *Corn* 6C 4
St Boswells. *Bord* 6C 60
St Breock. *Corn* 4B 4
St Breward. *Corn* 4C 4
St Briavels. *Glos* 3D 18
St Brides. *Pemb* 5D 14
St Brides Major. *V Glam* 7H 17
St Bride's Netherwent. *Mon* 5C 18
St Bride's-super-Ely.
V Glam 7K 17
St Brides Wentlooge. *Newp* 5A 18
St Budeaux. *Plym* 6G 5
Saintbury. *Glos* 8K 27
St Buryan. *Corn* 6H 3
St Catherine. *Bath* 6F 18
St Catherines. *Arg* 7F 64
St Clears. *Carm* 5J 15
St Cleer. *Corn* 5E 4
St Clement. *Corn* 7A 4
St Clether. *Corn* 7B 6
St Colmac. *Arg* 3K 57
St Columb Major. *Corn* 5B 4
St Columb Minor. *Corn* 2M 3
St Columb Road. *Corn* 6B 4
St Combs. *Abers* 7K 81
St Cross. *Hants* 3B 10
St Cross South Elmham.
Suff 3J 31
St Cyrus. *Abers* 1L 67
St David's. *Per* 5C 66
St Davids. *Pemb* 4D 14
St Day. *Corn* 4L 3
St Dennis. *Corn* 6B 4
St Dogmaels. *Pemb* 2H 15
St Dominick. *Corn* 5F 4
St Donat's. *V Glam* 8J 17
St Edith's Marsh. *Wilts* 7H 19
St Endellion. *Corn* 4B 4
St Enoder. *Corn* 6A 4
St Erme. *Corn* 4M 3
St Erney. *Corn* 6F 4
St Erth. *Corn* 5J 3
St Erth Praze. *Corn* 5J 3
St Ervan. *Corn* 4A 4
St Eval. *Corn* 5A 4
St Ewe. *Corn* 7B 4
St Fagans. *Card* 7L 17
St Fergus. *Abers* 8K 81
Saintfield. *New M* 6J 93
St Fillans. *Per* 5L 65
St Florence. *Pemb* 6G 15
St Gennys. *Corn* 6A 6
St George. *Cnwy* 3J 33
St George's. *N Som* 7B 18
St Georges. *V Glam* 7K 17
St George's Hill. *Surr* 7H 21
St Germans. *Corn* 6F 4
St Giles in the Wood. *Devn* 4E 6
St Giles on the Heath. *Devn* 6C 6
St Giles's Hill. *Hants* 3B 10
St Gluvias. *Corn* 5L 3
St Harmon. *Powy* 5J 25
St Helena. *Warw* 1L 27
St Helen Auckland. *Dur* 3K 47
St Helen's. *E Sus* 4E 12
St Helens. *Cumb* 8E 52
St Helens. *IOW* 7D 10
St Helens. *Mers* 8D 40
St Hilary. *Corn* 5J 3
St Hilary. *V Glam* 7K 17
Saint Hill. *Devn* 5K 7
Saint Hill. *W Sus* 2L 11
St Illtyd. *Blae* 4M 17
St Ippolyts. *Herts* 1J 21
St Ishmael. *Carm* 6K 15
St Ishmael's. *Pemb* 6E 14
St Issey. *Corn* 4B 4
St Ive. *Corn* 5F 4
St Ives. *Cambs* 4L 29
St Ives. *Corn* 4J 3
St Ives. *Dors* 5K 9
St James' End. *Nptn* 5E 28
St James South Elmham.
Suff 3K 31
St Jidgey. *Corn* 5B 4
St John. *Corn* 6G 5
St John's. *IOM* 6B 44
St John's. *Worc* 6G 27
St John's Chapel. *Devn* 3E 6
St John's Chapel. *Dur* 8B 54
St John's Fen End. *Norf* 8B 38
St John's Town of Dalry.
Dum 3M 51
St Judes. *IOM* 5C 44
St Just. *Corn* 5G 3
St Just in Roseland. *Corn* 8A 4
St Katherines. *Abers* 2G 73
St Keverne. *Corn* 6L 3
St Kew. *Corn* 4C 4
St Kew Highway. *Corn* 4C 4
St Keyne. *Corn* 5E 4
St Lawrence. *Corn* 5C 4
St Lawrence. *Essx* 3F 22
St Lawrence. *IOW* 8C 10
St Leonards. *Buck* 3G 21
St Leonards. *Dors* 5K 9
St Leonards. *E Sus* 5D 12
St Levan. *Corn* 6G 3
St Lythans. *V Glam* 7L 17
St Mabyn. *Corn* 4C 4
St Madoes. *Per* 5E 66
St Margaret's. *Herts* 2H 21
St Margaret's. *Wilts* 7L 19
St Margarets. *Here* 8B 26
St Margarets. *Herts* 2L 21
St Margaret's at Cliffe. *Kent* 1K 13
St Margaret's Hope. *Orkn* 2F 86
St Margaret South Elmham.
Suff 3K 31
St Mark's. *IOM* 7B 44
St Martin. *Corn*
nr. Helston 6L 3
nr. Looe 6E 4
St Martin's. *Shrp* 6B 34
St Martins. *Per* 4E 66
St Mary Bourne. *Hants* 8B 20
St Mary Church. *V Glam* 7K 17
St Marychurch. *Torb* 5M 5
St Mary Cray. *G Lon* 7A 22
St Mary Hill. *V Glam* 7J 17
St Mary Hoo. *Medw* 6E 22
St Mary in the Marsh. *Kent* 3G 13
St Mary's. *Orkn* 1F 86
St Mary's Airport. *IOS* 1H 3
St Mary's Bay. *Kent* 3G 13
St Marys Platt. *Kent* 8C 22
St Maughan's Green. *Mon* 2C 18
St Mawes. *Corn* 5M 3
St Mawgan. *Corn* 5A 4
St Mellion. *Corn* 5F 4
St Mellons. *Card* 6M 17
St Merryn. *Corn* 4A 4
St Mewan. *Corn* 6B 4
St Michael Caerhays. *Corn* 7B 4
St Michael Penkevil. *Corn* 7A 4
St Michaels. *Kent* 2E 12
St Michaels. *Torb* 6L 5
St Michaels. *Worc* 5D 26
St Michael's on Wyre. *Lanc* 3C 40
St Michael South Elmham.
Suff 3K 31
St Minver. *Corn* 4B 4
St Monans. *Fife* 7J 67
St Neot. *Corn* 5D 4
St Neots. *Cambs* 5J 29
St Newlyn East. *Corn* 3M 3
St Nicholas. *Pemb* 3E 14
St Nicholas. *V Glam* 7K 17
St Nicholas at Wade. *Kent* 7J 23
St Nicholas South Elmham.
Suff 3K 31
St Ninians. *Stir* 8A 66
St Olaves. *Norf* 2L 31
St Osyth. *Essx* 2H 23
St Osyth Heath. *Essx* 2H 23
St Owen's Cross. *Here* 1D 18
St Paul's Cray. *G Lon* 7A 22
St Paul's Walden. *Herts* 1J 21
St Peter's. *Kent* 7K 23
St Peter The Great. *Worc* 6G 27
St Petrox. *Pemb* 7F 14
St Pinnock. *Corn* 5E 4
St Quivox. *S Ayr* 7B 58
St Ruan. *Corn* 7L 3
St Stephen. *Corn* 6B 4
St Stephens. *Corn*
nr. Launceston 7C 6
nr. Saltash 6G 5
St Teath. *Corn* 3C 4
St Thomas. *Devn* 6J 7
St Thomas. *Swan* 5F 16
St Tudy. *Corn* 4C 4
St Twynnells. *Pemb* 7F 14
St Veep. *Corn* 6D 4
St Vigeans. *Ang* 3K 67
St Wenn. *Corn* 5B 4
St Weonards. *Here* 1C 18
St Winnolls. *Corn* 6F 4
St Winnow. *Corn* 6D 4
Salcombe. *Devn* 8K 5
Salcombe Regis. *Devn* 7L 7
Salcott. *Essx* 2F 22
Sale. *G Man* 8F 40
Saleby. *Linc* 2A 38
Sale Green. *Worc* 6H 27
Salehurst. *E Sus* 3D 12
Salem. *Carm* 2F 16
Salem. *Cdgn* 4F 24
Salen. *Arg* 3L 63
Salen. *High* 1A 64
Salesbury. *Lanc* 4E 40
Saleway. *Worc* 6H 27
Salford. *C Beds* 8G 29
Salford.
G Man
Manchester 111 (8G 41)
Salford. *Oxon* 1L 19
Salford Priors. *Warw* 6J 27
Salfords. *Surr* 1K 11
Salhouse. *Norf* 8K 39
Saligo. *Arg* 3B 56
Saline. *Fife* 8D 66
Salisbury. *Wilts* **115** (2K 9)
Salkeld Dykes. *Cumb* 8K 53
Sallachan. *High* 1D 64
Sallachy. *High*
nr. Lairg 3F 78
nr. Stromeferry 2L 69
Salle. *Norf* 7H 39
Salmonby. *Linc* 2L 37
Salmond's Muir. *Ang* 4J 67
Salperton. *Glos* 1J 19
Salph End. *Bed* 6H 29
Salsburgh. *N Lan* 3G 59
Salt. *Staf* 7H 35
Salta. *Cumb* 7E 52
Saltaire. *W Yor* 4K 41
Saltash. *Corn* 6G 5
Saltburn. *High* 7H 79
Saltburn-by-the-Sea. *Red C* 3D 48
Saltby. *Leics* 7F 36
Saltcoats. *Cumb* 5K 45
Saltcoats. *N Ayr* 5M 57
Saltdean. *Brig* 5L 11
Salt End. *E Yor* 5J 43
Salter. *Lanc* 1E 40
Salterforth. *Lanc* 3G 41
Salters Lode. *Norf* 1B 30
Salterswall. *Ches W* 3E 34
Salterton. *Wilts* 2K 9
Saltfleet. *Linc* 8M 43
Saltfleetby All Saints. *Linc* 1A 38
Saltfleetby St Clements.
Linc 1A 38
Saltfleetby St Peter. *Linc* 1M 37
Saltford. *Bath* 7E 18
Salthouse. *Norf* 5G 39
Saltmarshe. *E Yor* 5E 42
Saltness. *Orkn* 3D 86
Saltness. *Shet* 3C 90
Saltney. *Flin* 3B 34
Salton. *N Yor* 8E 48
Saltrens. *Devn* 3D 6
Saltwick. *Nmbd* 4E 54
Saltwood. *Kent* 2H 13
Salum. *Arg* 3F 62
Salwarpe. *Worc* 5G 27
Salwayash. *Dors* 6C 8
Samalaman. *High* 8H 69
Sambourne. *Warw* 5J 27
Sambourne. *Wilts* 1G 9
Sambrook. *Telf* 7F 34
Samhia. *W Isl* 7J 75
Samlesbury. *Lanc* 4D 40
Samlesbury Bottoms. *Lanc* 5E 40
Sampford Arundel. *Som* 4L 7
Sampford Brett. *Som* 1K 7
Sampford Courtenay. *Devn* 5F 6
Sampford Peverell. *Devn* 4K 7
Sampford Spiney. *Devn* 8E 6
Samsonslane. *Orkn* 7F 88
Samuelston. *E Lot* 2B 60
Sanaigmore. *Arg* 2B 56
Sancreed. *Corn* 6H 3
Sancton. *E Yor* 4G 43
Sand. *High* 4L 77
Sand. *Shet* 3D 90
Sand. *Som* 1C 8
Sandaig. *Arg* 3E 62
Sandaig. *High* 5J 69
Sandale. *Cumb* 7G 53
Sandal Magna. *W Yor* 6M 41
Sandavore. *High* 7F 68
Sanday Airport. *Orkn* 5F 88
Sandbach. *Ches E* 3F 34
Sandbank. *Arg* 1L 57
Sandbanks. *Pool* 7J 9
Sandend. *Abers* 7E 80
Sanderstead. *G Lon* 7L 21
Sandfields. *Neat* 5G 17
Sandford. *Cumb* 4F 46
Sandford. *Devn* 5H 7
Sandford. *Dors* 7H 9
Sandford. *Hants* 5K 9
Sandford. *IOW* 7C 10
Sandford. *N Som* 8C 18
Sandford. *Shrp*
nr. Oswestry 7B 34
nr. Whitchurch 6D 34
Sandford. *S Lan* 5F 58
Sandfordhill. *Abers* 1L 73
Sandford-on-Thames.
Oxon 3C 20
Sandford Orcas. *Dors* 3E 8
Sandford St Martin. *Oxon* 1B 20
Sandgate. *Kent* 2H 13
Sandgreen. *Dum* 6L 51
Sandhaven. *Abers* 7J 81
Sandhead. *Dum* 6F 50
Sandhill. *Cambs* 3B 30
Sandhills. *Dors* 4E 8
Sandhills. *Oxon* 3C 20
Sandhills. *Surr* 2G 11
Sandhoe. *Nmbd* 5C 54
Sand Hole. *E Yor* 4F 42
Sandholes. *M Ulst* 5E 92
Sandholme. *E Yor* 4F 42
Sandholme. *Linc* 6L 37
Sandhurst. *Brac* 7F 20
Sandhurst. *Glos* 1G 19
Sandhurst. *Kent* 3D 12
Sandhurst Cross. *Kent* 3D 12
Sand Hutton. *N Yor* 2D 42
Sandhutton. *N Yor* 7A 48
Sandiacre. *Derbs* 6B 36
Sandilands. *Linc* 1B 38
Sandiway. *Ches W* 2E 34
Sandleheath. *Hants* 4K 9
Sandling. *Kent* 8D 22
Sandlow Green. *Ches E* 3F 34
Sandness. *Shet* 2B 90
Sandon. *Essx* 3D 22
Sandon. *Herts* 8L 29
Sandon. *Staf* 7H 35
Sandonbank. *Staf* 7H 35
Sandown. *IOW* 7C 10
Sandplace. *Corn* 6E 4
Sandridge. *Herts* 2J 21
Sandringham. *Norf* 7C 38
The Sands. *Surr* 1F 10
Sandsend. *N Yor* 4F 48
Sandside. *Cumb* 8B 46
Sandsound. *Shet* 3D 90
Sandtoft. *N Lin* 7E 42
Sandvoe. *Shet* 4H 91
Sandway. *Kent* 8E 22
Sandwich. *Kent* 8K 23
Sandwick. *Cumb* 4C 46
Sandwick. *Orkn*
on Mainland 8B 88
on South Ronaldsay 3F 86
Sandwick. *Shet*
on Mainland 5E 90
on Whalsay 1F 90
Sandwith. *Cumb* 3J 45
Sandy. *Carm* 6L 15
Sandy. *C Beds* 7J 29
Sandy Bank. *Linc* 4K 37
Sandycroft. *Flin* 3B 34
Sandy Cross. *Here* 6E 26
Sandygate. *Devn* 8H 7
Sandygate. *IOM* 5C 44
Sandy Haven. *Pemb* 6E 14
Sandyhills. *Dum* 6C 52
Sandylands. *Lanc* 1C 40
Sandy Lane. *Wilts* 7H 19
Sandylane. *Swan* 6E 16
Sandystones. *Bord* 7C 60
Sandyway. *Here* 1C 18
Sangobeg. *High* 5G 85
Sangomore. *High* 5G 85
Sankyn's Green. *Worc* 5F 26
Sanna. *High* 1K 63
Sanndabhaig. *W Isl*
on Isle of Lewis 8H 83
on South Uist 1E 74
Sannox. *N Ayr* 5K 57
Sanquhar. *Dum* 8F 58
Santon. *Cumb* 4K 45
Santon Bridge. *Cumb* 4L 45
Santon Downham. *Suff* 3E 30
Sapcote. *Leics* 2B 28
Sapey Common. *Here* 5F 26
Sapiston. *Suff* 4F 30
Sapley. *Cambs* 4K 29
Sapperton. *Derbs* 6K 35
Sapperton. *Glos* 3H 19
Sapperton. *Linc* 6H 37
Saracen's Head. *Linc* 7L 37
Sarclet. *High* 7E 86
Sardis. *Carm* 4E 16
Sardis. *Pemb*
nr. Milford Haven 6F 14
nr. Tenby 6H 15
Sarisbury Green. *Hants* 5C 10
Sarn. *B'end* 6J 17
Sarn. *Powy* 3M 25
Sarnau. *Carm* 4L 15
Sarnau. *Cdgn* 1K 15
Sarnau. *Gwyn* 7J 33
Sarnau. *Powy*
nr. Brecon 1K 17
nr. Welshpool 1M 25
Sarn Bach. *Gwyn* 8C 32
Sarnesfield. *Here* 6B 26
Sarn Meyllteyrn. *Gwyn* 7B 32
Saron. *Carm*
nr. Ammanford 3F 16
nr. Newcastle Emlyn 3K 15
Saron. *Gwyn*
nr. Bethel 4E 32
nr. Bontnewydd 5D 32
Sarratt. *Herts* 4H 21
Sarre. *Kent* 7J 23
Sarsden. *Oxon* 1L 19
Satley. *Dur* 7E 54
Satron. *N Yor* 6H 47
Satterleigh. *Devn* 3F 6
Satterthwaite. *Cumb* 6B 46
Satwell. *Oxon* 5E 20
Sauchen. *Abers* 4F 72
Saucher. *Per* 4E 66
Saughall. *Ches W* 2B 34
Saughtree. *Bord* 2K 53
Saul. *Glos* 3F 18
Saul. *New M* 6J 93
Saundby. *Notts* 1E 36
Saundersfoot. *Pemb* 6H 15
Saunderton. *Buck* 3E 20
Saunderton Lee. *Buck* 4F 20
Saunton. *Devn* 2D 6
Sausthorpe. *Linc* 3L 37
Saval. *High* 3F 78
Saverley Green. *Staf* 6H 35
Sawbridge. *Warw* 5C 28
Sawbridgeworth. *Herts* 2A 22
Sawdon. *N Yor* 7G 49
Sawley. *Derbs* 6B 36
Sawley. *Lanc* 3F 40
Sawley. *N Yor* 1L 41
Sawston. *Cambs* 7A 30
Sawtry. *Cambs* 3J 29
Saxby. *Leics* 7F 36
Saxby. *Linc* 1H 37
Saxby All Saints. *N Lin* 6G 43
Saxelby. *Leics* 7D 36
Saxelbye. *Leics* 7D 36
Saxham Street. *Suff* 5G 31
Saxilby. *Linc* 2F 36
Saxlingham. *Norf* 6G 39
Saxlingham Green. *Norf* 2J 31
Saxlingham Nethergate.
Norf 2J 31
Saxlingham Thorpe. *Norf* 2J 31
Saxmundham. *Suff* 5K 31
Saxondale. *Notts* 5D 36
Saxon Street. *Cambs* 6C 30
Saxtead. *Suff* 5J 31
Saxtead Green. *Suff* 5J 31
Saxthorpe. *Norf* 6H 39
Saxton. *N Yor* 4B 42
Sayers Common. *W Sus* 4K 11
Scackleton. *N Yor* 8D 48
Scadabhagh. *W Isl* 4C 76
Scaddy. *New M* 6J 93
Scaftworth. *Notts* 8D 42
Scagglethorpe. *N Yor* 8F 48
Scaitcliffe. *Lanc* 5F 40
Scaladal. *W Isl* 2C 76
Scalasaig. *Arg* 8J 63
Scalby. *E Yor* 5F 42
Scalby. *N Yor* 6H 49
Scalby Mills. *N Yor* 6H 49
Scaldwell. *Nptn* 4E 28
Scaleby. *Cumb* 5J 53
Scaleby Hill. *Cumb* 5J 53
Scale Houses. *Cumb* 7K 53
Scales. *Cumb*
nr. Barrow-in-Furness 8A 46
nr. Keswick 3B 46
Scalford. *Leics* 7E 36
Scaling. *N Yor* 4E 48
Scaling Dam. *Red C* 4E 48
Scalloway. *Shet* 4E 90
Scalpaigh. *W Isl* 4D 76
Scalpay House. *High* 3H 69
Scamblesby. *Linc* 2K 37
Scamodale. *High* 8K 69
Scampston. *N Yor* 8F 48
Scampton. *Linc* 2G 37
Scaniport. *High* 2G 71
Scapa. *Orkn* 1F 86
Scapegoat Hill. *W Yor* 6J 41
Scar. *Orkn* 5F 88
Scarasta. *W Isl* 4B 76
Scarborough. *N Yor* 7H 49
Scarcliffe. *Derbs* 3B 36
Scarcroft. *W Yor* 3A 42
Scardroy. *High* 8C 78
Scarfskerry. *High* 4D 86
Scargill. *Dur* 4J 47
Scarinish. *Arg* 3F 62
Scarisbrick. *Lanc* 6B 40
Scarning. *Norf* 8F 38
Scarrington. *Notts* 5E 36
Scarth Hill. *Lanc* 7C 40
Scartho. *NE Lin* 7K 43
Scarva. *Arm* 6G 93
Scarvister. *Shet* 3D 90
Scatness. *Shet* 7D 90
Scatwell. *High* 8D 78
Scaur. *Dum* 6C 52
Scawby. *N Lin* 7G 43
Scawby Brook. *N Lin* 7G 43
Scawsby. *S Yor* 7C 42
Scawton. *N Yor* 7C 48
Scaynes Hill. *W Sus* 3L 11
Scethrog. *Powy* 2L 17
Scholar Green. *Ches E* 4G 35
Scholes. *G Man* 7D 40
Scholes. *W Yor*
nr. Bradford 5K 41
nr. Holmfirth 7K 41
nr. Leeds 4A 42
Scholey Hill. *W Yor* 5A 42
School Aycliffe. *Darl* 3L 47
School Green. *Ches W* 3E 34
School Green. *Essx* 8D 30
Scissett. *W Yor* 6L 41
Scleddau. *Pemb* 3F 14
Scofton. *Notts* 1D 36
Scole. *Norf* 4H 31
Scollogstown. *New M* 7J 93
Scolpaig. *W Isl* 6J 75
Scolton. *Pemb* 4F 14
Scone. *Per* 5E 66
Sconser. *High* 2G 69
Scoonie. *Fife* 7G 67
Scopwick. *Linc* 4H 37
Scoraig. *High* 4M 77
Scorborough. *E Yor* 3H 43
Scorrier. *Corn* 4L 3
Scorriton. *Devn* 5K 5
Scorton. *Lanc* 3D 40
Scorton. *N Yor* 5L 47
Sco Ruston. *Norf* 7J 39
Scotbheinn. *W Isl* 8K 75
Scotby. *Cumb* 6J 53
Scotch Corner. *N Yor* 5L 47
Scotch Street. *Arm* 6F 93
Scotforth. *Lanc* 1C 40
Scot Hay. *Staf* 5G 35
Scothern. *Linc* 2H 37
Scotland End. *Oxon* 8A 28
Scotlandwell. *Per* 7E 66
Scot Lane End. *G Man* 7E 40
Scotsburn. *High* 6H 79
Scotsburn. *Mor* 7B 80
Scotsdike. *Cumb* 4H 53
Scot's Gap. *Nmbd* 3D 54
Scotstoun. *Glas* 3D 58
Scotstown. *High* 1C 64
Scotswood. *Tyne* 5F 54
Scottas. *High* 5J 69
Scotter. *Linc* 7F 42
Scotterthorpe. *Linc* 7F 42
Scottlethorpe. *Linc* 7H 37
Scotton. *Linc* 8F 42
Scotton. *N Yor*
nr. Catterick Garrison 6K 47
nr. Harrogate 2M 41
Scottow. *Norf* 7J 39
Scoulton. *Norf* 1F 30
Scounslow Green. *Staf* 7J 35
Scourie. *High* 7D 84
Scourie More. *High* 7D 84
Scousburgh. *Shet* 6D 90
Scout Green. *Cumb* 5D 46
Scouthead. *G Man* 7H 41
Scrabster. *High* 4B 86
Scrafield. *Linc* 3L 37
Scrainwood. *Nmbd* 1C 54
Scrane End. *Linc* 5L 37
Scraptoft. *Leics* 1D 28
Scratby. *Norf* 8M 39
Scrayingham. *N Yor* 1E 42
Scredington. *Linc* 5H 37
Scremby. *Linc* 3M 37
Scremerston. *Nmbd* 5H 61
Screveton. *Notts* 5E 36
Scrivelsby. *Linc* 3K 37
Scriven. *N Yor* 2A 42
Scronkey. *Lanc* 3C 40
Scrooby. *Notts* 8D 42
Scropton. *Derbs* 6K 35
Scrub Hill. *Linc* 4K 37
Scruton. *N Yor* 6L 47
Scuggate. *Cumb* 4J 53
Sculamus. *High* 3H 69
Sculcoates. *Hull* 4H 43
Sculthorpe. *Norf* 6F 38
Scunthorpe. *N Lin* 6F 42
Scurlage. *Swan* 8L 15
Sea. *Som* 4B 8
Seaborough. *Dors* 5C 8
Seabridge. *Staf* 5G 35
Seabrook. *Kent* 2H 13
Seaburn. *Tyne* 5H 55
Seacombe. *Mers* 8B 40
Seacroft. *Linc* 3B 38
Seacroft. *W Yor* 4M 41
Seadyke. *Linc* 6L 37
Seafield. *High* 5K 79
Seafield. *Midl* 3L 59
Seafield. *S Ayr* 7B 58
Seafield. *W Lot* 3J 59
Seaford. *E Sus* 6A 12
Seaforde. *New M* 6J 93
Seaforth. *Mers* 8B 40
Seagrave. *Leics* 8D 36
Seaham. *Dur* 7H 55
Seahouses. *Nmbd* 6K 61
Seal. *Kent* 8B 22
Sealand. *Flin* 3B 34
Seale. *Surr* 1F 10
Seamer. *N Yor*
nr. Scarborough 7H 49
nr. Stokesley 4B 48
Seamill. *N Ayr* 5M 57
Sea Mills. *Bris* 6D 18
Sea Palling. *Norf* 7L 39
Seapatrick. *Arm* 6G 93
Searby. *Linc* 7H 43
Seasalter. *Kent* 7G 23
Seascale. *Cumb* 4K 45
Seaside. *Per* 5F 66
Seater. *High* 4E 86
Seathorne. *Linc* 3B 38
Seathwaite. *Cumb*
nr. Buttermere 3M 45
nr. Ulpha 5M 45
Seatle. *Cumb* 7B 46
Seatoller. *Cumb* 3M 45
Seaton. *Corn* 6F 4
Seaton. *Cumb* 8E 52
Seaton. *Devn* 6M 7
Seaton. *Dur* 6G 55
Seaton. *E Yor* 3J 43
Seaton. *Nmbd* 4G 55
Seaton. *Rut* 2G 29
Seaton Burn. *Tyne* 4F 54
Seaton Carew. *Hart* 3C 48
Seaton Delaval. *Nmbd* 4G 55
Seaton Junction. *Devn* 6A 8
Seaton Ross. *E Yor* 3E 42
Seaton Sluice. *Nmbd* 4G 55
Seatown. *Abers* 7E 80
Seatown. *Dors* 6C 8
Seatown. *Mor*
nr. Cullen 7E 80
nr. Lossiemouth 6B 80
Seave Green. *N Yor* 5C 48
Seaview. *IOW* 6D 10
Seaville. *Cumb* 6F 52
Seavington St Mary. *Som* 4C 8
Seavington St Michael. *Som* 4C 8
Seawick. *Essx* 2H 23
Sebastopol. *Torf* 4A 18
Sebergham. *Cumb* 7H 53
Seckington. *Warw* 1L 27
Second Coast. *High* 4L 77
Sedbergh. *Cumb* 6E 46
Sedbury. *Glos* 4D 18
Sedbusk. *N Yor* 6G 47
Sedgeberrow. *Worc* 8J 27
Sedgebrook. *Linc* 6F 36
Sedgefield. *Dur* 3A 48
Sedgeford. *Norf* 6D 38
Sedgehill. *Wilts* 3G 9
Sedgley. *W Mid* 2H 27
Sedgwick. *Cumb* 7D 46
Sedlescombe. *E Sus* 4D 12
Seend. *Wilts* 7H 19
Seend Cleeve. *Wilts* 7H 19
Seer Green. *Buck* 4G 21
Seething. *Norf* 2K 31
Sefster. *Shet* 2D 90
Sefton. *Mers* 7B 40
Sefton Park. *Mers* 1B 34
Segensworth. *Hants* 5C 10
Seggat. *Abers* 1G 73
Seghill. *Nmbd* 4F 54
Seifton. *Shrp* 3C 26
Seighford. *Staf* 7G 35
Seilebost. *W Isl* 4B 76
Seisdon. *Staf* 2G 27
Seisiadar. *W Isl* 8J 83
Selattyn. *Shrp* 6A 34
Selborne. *Hants* 2E 10
Selby. *N Yor* 4D 42
Selham. *W Sus* 3G 11
Selkirk. *Bord* 7B 60
Sellack. *Here* 1D 18
Sellafirth. *Shet* 4K 91
Sellick's Green. *Som* 4M 7
Sellindge. *Kent* 2H 13
Selling. *Kent* 8G 23
Sells Green. *Wilts* 7H 19
Selly Oak. *W Mid* 3J 27
Selmeston. *E Sus* 5B 12
Selsdon. *G Lon* 7L 21
Selsey. *W Sus* 6F 10
Selsfield Common. *W Sus* 2L 11
Selside. *Cumb* 6D 46
Selside. *N Yor* 8F 46
Selsley. *Glos* 3G 19
Selsted. *Kent* 1J 13
Selston. *Notts* 4B 36
Selworthy. *Som* 1J 7
Semblister. *Shet* 2D 90
Semer. *Suff* 7G 31
Semington. *Wilts* 7G 19
Semley. *Wilts* 3G 9
Sempringham. *Linc* 6J 37
Send. *Surr* 8H 21
Send Marsh. *Surr* 8H 21
Senghenydd. *Cphy* 5L 17
Sennen. *Corn* 6G 3
Sennen Cove. *Corn* 6G 3
Sennybridge. *Powy* 2J 17
Serlby. *Notts* 1D 36
Seskinore. *Ferm* 5D 92
Sessay. *N Yor* 8B 48
Setchey. *Norf* 8C 38
Setley. *Hants* 5M 9
Setter. *Shet* 5J 91
Settiscarth. *Orkn* 8C 88
Settle. *N Yor* 1G 41
Settrington. *N Yor* 8F 48
Seven Ash. *Som* 2L 7
Sevenhampton. *Glos* 1J 19
Sevenhampton. *Swin* 4L 19
Sevenoaks. *Kent* 8B 22
Sevenoaks Weald. *Kent* 8B 22
Seven Sisters. *Neat* 4H 17
Seven Springs. *Glos* 2H 19
Severn Beach. *S Glo* 5D 18
Severn Stoke. *Worc* 7G 27
Sevington. *Kent* 1G 13
Sewards End. *Essx* 8B 30
Sewardstone. *Essx* 4L 21
Sewell. *C Beds* 1G 21
Sewerby. *E Yor* 1K 43
Seworgan. *Corn* 5L 3
Sewstern. *Leics* 7F 36
Sgallairidh. *W Isl* 6C 74
Sgarasta Mhor. *W Isl* 4B 76
Sgiogarstaigh. *W Isl* 5J 83
Sgreadan. *Arg* 8J 63
Shabbington. *Buck* 3D 20
Shackerley. *Shrp* 1G 27
Shackerstone. *Leics* 1A 28
Shackleford. *Surr* 1G 11
Shadforth. *Dur* 7G 55
Shadingfield. *Suff* 3L 31
Shadoxhurst. *Kent* 2F 12
Shadsworth. *Bkbn* 5F 40
Shadwell. *Norf* 3F 30
Shadwell. *W Yor* 4M 41
Shaftesbury. *Dors* 3G 9
Shafton. *S Yor* 6A 42
Shafton Two Gates. *S Yor* 6A 42
Shaggs. *Dors* 7G 9
Shakesfield. *Glos* 8E 26
Shalbourne. *Wilts* 7M 19
Shalcombe. *IOW* 7A 10
Shalden. *Hants* 1D 10
Shaldon. *Devn* 8J 7
Shalfleet. *IOW* 7B 10
Shalford. *Essx* 1D 22
Shalford. *Surr* 1H 11
Shalford Green. *Essx* 1D 22
Shallowford. *Devn* 1G 7
Shallowford. *Staf* 7G 35
Shalmsford Street. *Kent* 8G 23
Shalstone. *Buck* 8D 28
Shamley Green. *Surr* 1H 11
Shandon. *Arg* 1A 58
Shandwick. *High* 6J 79
Shangton. *Leics* 2E 28
Shankhouse. *Nmbd* 4F 54
Shanklin. *IOW* 7C 10
Shannochie. *N Ayr* 7J 57
Shap. *Cumb* 4D 46
Shapwick. *Dors* 5H 9
Shapwick. *Som* 2C 8
Sharcott. *Wilts* 8K 19
Shardlow. *Derbs* 6B 36
Shareshill. *Staf* 1H 27
Sharlston. *W Yor* 6A 42
Sharlston Common. *W Yor* 6A 42
Sharnal Street. *Medw* 6D 22
Sharnbrook. *Bed* 6G 29
Sharneyford. *Lanc* 5G 41
Sharnford. *Leics* 2B 28
Sharnhill Green. *Dors* 5F 8
Sharoe Green. *Lanc* 4D 40
Sharow. *N Yor* 8M 47
Sharpenhoe. *C Beds* 8H 29
Sharperton. *Nmbd* 1C 54
Sharpness. *Glos* 3E 18
Sharp Street. *Norf* 7K 39
Sharpthorne. *W Sus* 2L 11
Sharrington. *Norf* 6G 39
Shatterford. *Worc* 3F 26
Shatton. *Derbs* 1K 35
Shaugh Prior. *Devn* 5H 5
Shavington. *Ches E* 4F 34
Shaw. *G Man* 7H 41
Shaw. *W Ber* 7B 20
Shaw. *Wilts* 7G 19
Shawbirch. *Telf* 8E 34
Shawbury. *Shrp* 7D 34
Shawell. *Leics* 3C 28
Shawford. *Hants* 3B 10
Shawforth. *Lanc* 5G 41
Shaw Green. *Lanc* 6D 40
Shawhead. *Dum* 4C 52
Shaw Mills. *N Yor* 1L 41
Shawwood. *E Ayr* 7D 58
Shearington. *Dum* 5E 52
Shearsby. *Leics* 2D 28
Shearston. *Som* 2A 8
Shebbear. *Devn* 5D 6
Shebdon. *Staf* 7F 34
Shebster. *High* 5B 86
Sheddocksley. *Aber* 5H 73
Shedfield. *Hants* 4C 10
Shedog. *N Ayr* 6J 57
Sheen. *Staf* 3K 35
Sheepbridge. *Derbs* 2A 36
Sheep Hill. *Dur* 6E 54
Sheepscar. *W Yor* 4M 41
Sheepscombe. *Glos* 2G 19
Sheepstor. *Devn* 5H 5
Sheepwash. *Devn* 5D 6
Sheepwash. *Nmbd* 3F 54
Sheepway. *N Som* 6C 18
Sheepy Magna. *Leics* 1M 27
Sheepy Parva. *Leics* 1M 27
Sheering. *Essx* 2B 22
Sheerness. *Kent* 6F 22
Sheerwater. *Surr* 7H 21
Sheet. *Hants* 3E 10
Sheffield. *S Yor* **116** (1A 36)
Sheffield Bottom. *W Ber* 7D 20
Sheffield Green. *E Sus* 3M 11
Shefford. *C Beds* 8J 29
Shefford Woodlands.
W Ber 6A 20
Sheigra. *High* 5D 84
Sheinton. *Shrp* 1E 26
Shelderton. *Shrp* 4C 26
Sheldon. *Derbs* 3K 35
Sheldon. *Devn* 5L 7
Sheldon. *W Mid* 3K 27
Sheldwich. *Kent* 8G 23
Sheldwich Lees. *Kent* 8G 23
Shelf. *W Yor* 5K 41
Shelfanger. *Norf* 3H 31
Shelfield. *Warw* 5K 27
Shelfield. *W Mid* 1J 27
Shelford. *Notts* 5D 36
Shelford. *Warw* 3B 28
Shell. *Worc* 6H 27
Shelley. *Suff* 8G 31
Shelley. *W Yor* 6L 41
Shell Green. *Hal* 1D 34
Shellingford. *Oxon* 4M 19
Shellow Bowells. *Essx* 3C 22
Shelsley Beauchamp. *Worc* 5F 26
Shelsley Walsh. *Worc* 5F 26
Shelthorpe. *Leics* 8C 36
Shelton. *Bed* 5H 29
Shelton. *Norf* 2J 31
Shelton. *Notts* 5E 36
Shelton. *Shrp* 8C 34
Shelton Green. *Norf* 2J 31
Shelton Lock. *Derb* 6A 36
Shelve. *Shrp* 2B 26
Shelwick. *Here* 7D 26
Shelwick Green. *Here* 7D 26
Shenfield. *Essx* 4C 22
Shenington. *Oxon* 7A 28
Shenley. *Herts* 3J 21
Shenley Brook End. *Mil* 8F 28
Shenleybury. *Herts* 3J 21
Shenley Church End. *Mil* 8F 28
Shenmore. *Here* 8B 26
Shennanton. *Dum* 5J 51
Shenstone. *Staf* 1K 27
Shenstone. *Worc* 4G 27
Shenstone Woodend. *Staf* 1K 27
Shenton. *Leics* 1A 28
Shenval. *Mor* 3B 72
Shepeau Stow. *Linc* 8L 37
Shephall. *Herts* 1K 21
Shepherd's Bush. *G Lon* 5K 21
Shepherd's Gate. *Norf* 8B 38
Shepherd's Green. *Oxon* 5E 20
Shepherd's Port. *Norf* 6C 38
Shepherdswell. *Kent* 1J 13
Shepley. *W Yor* 7K 41
Sheppardstown. *High* 7C 86
Shepperdine. *S Glo* 4E 18
Shepperton. *Surr* 7H 21
Shepreth. *Cambs* 7L 29
Shepshed. *Leics* 8B 36
Shepton Beauchamp. *Som* 4C 8
Shepton Mallet. *Som* 1E 8
Shepton Montague. *Som* 2E 8
Shepway. *Kent* 8D 22
Sheraton. *Dur* 8H 55
Sherborne. *Dors* 4E 8
Sherborne. *Glos* 2K 19
Sherborne. *Som* 8D 18
Sherborne Causeway. *Dors* 3G 9
Sherborne St John. *Hants* 8D 20
Sherbourne. *Warw* 5L 27
Sherburn. *Dur* 7G 55
Sherburn. *N Yor* 8G 49
Sherburn Hill. *Dur* 7G 55
Sherburn in Elmet. *N Yor* 4B 42
Shere. *Surr* 1H 11
Shereford. *Norf* 7E 38
Sherfield English. *Hants* 3L 9
Sherfield on Loddon. *Hants* 8D 20
Sherford. *Devn* 7K 5
Sherford. *Dors* 6H 9
Sheriffhales. *Shrp* 8F 34
Sheriff Hutton. *N Yor* 1D 42
Sheriffston. *Mor* 7B 80
Sheringham. *Norf* 5H 39
Sherington. *Mil* 7F 28
Shermanbury. *W Sus* 4K 11
Shernal Green. *Worc* 5H 27
Shernborne. *Norf* 6D 38
Sherrington. *Wilts* 2H 9
Sherston. *Wilts* 5G 19
Sherwood. *Nott* 5C 36
Sherwood Green. *Devn* 3E 6
Shettleston. *Glas* 3E 58
Shevington. *G Man* 7D 40
Shevington Moor. *G Man* 6D 40
Shevington Vale. *G Man* 7D 40
Sheviock. *Corn* 6F 4
Shide. *IOW* 7B 10
Shiel Bridge. *High* 4L 69
Shieldaig. *High*
nr. Charlestown 6K 77
nr. Torridon 8K 77
Shieldhill. *Dum* 3E 52
Shieldhill. *Falk* 2G 59
Shieldhill. *S Lan* 5J 59
Shieldmuir. *N Lan* 4F 58
Shielfoot. *High* 8H 69
Shielhill. *Abers* 8K 81
Shielhill. *Ang* 2H 67
Shifnal. *Shrp* 1F 26
Shilbottle. *Nmbd* 1E 54
Shilbottle Grange. *Nmbd* 1F 54
Shildon. *Dur* 3L 47
Shillford. *E Ren* 4C 58
Shillingford. *Devn* 3J 7
Shillingford. *Oxon* 4C 20
Shillingford St George. *Devn* 7J 7
Shillingstone. *Dors* 4G 9
Shillington. *C Beds* 8J 29
Shillmoor. *Nmbd* 1B 54
Shilton. *Oxon* 3L 19
Shilton. *Warw* 3B 28
Shilvinghampton. *Dors* 7E 8
Shilvington. *Nmbd* 3E 54
Shimpling. *Norf* 3H 31
Shimpling. *Suff* 6E 30
Shimpling Street. *Suff* 6E 30
Shincliffe. *Dur* 7F 54
Shiney Row. *Tyne* 6G 55
Shinfield. *Wok* 7E 20
Shingay. *Cambs* 7L 29
Shingham. *Norf* 1D 30
Shingle Street. *Suff* 7K 31
Shinner's Bridge. *Devn* 5K 5
Shinness. *High* 2F 78
Shipbourne. *Kent* 8B 22
Shipdham. *Norf* 1F 30
Shipham. *Som* 8C 18
Shiphay. *Torb* 5L 5
Shiplake. *Oxon* 6E 20
Shipley. *Derbs* 5B 36
Shipley. *Nmbd* 8J 61
Shipley. *Shrp* 2G 27
Shipley. *W Sus* 3J 11
Shipley. *W Yor* 4K 41
Shipley Bridge. *Surr* 1L 11
Shipmeadow. *Suff* 3K 31
Shippon. *Oxon* 4B 20
Shipston-on-Stour. *Warw* 7L 27
Shipton. *Buck* 1E 20
Shipton. *Glos* 2J 19
Shipton. *N Yor* 2C 42
Shipton. *Shrp* 2D 26
Shipton Bellinger. *Hants* 1L 9
Shipton Gorge. *Dors* 6C 8
Shipton Green. *W Sus* 6F 10
Shipton Moyne. *Glos* 5G 19
Shipton-on-Cherwell. *Oxon* 2B 20
Shiptonthorpe. *E Yor* 3F 42
Shipton-under-Wychwood.
Oxon 2L 19
Shirburn. *Oxon* 4D 20
Shirdley Hill. *Lanc* 6B 40
Shire. *Cumb* 8L 53
Shirebrook. *Derbs* 3C 36
Shiregreen. *S Yor* 8A 42
Shirehampton. *Bris* 6D 18
Shiremoor. *Tyne* 4G 55
Shirenewton. *Mon* 4C 18
Shireoaks. *Notts* 1C 36
Shires Mill. *Fife* 1J 59
Shirkoak. *Kent* 2F 12
Shirland. *Derbs* 4A 36
Shirley. *Derbs* 5L 35
Shirley. *Sotn* 4A 10
Shirley. *W Mid* 4K 27
Shirleywich. *Staf* 7H 35
Shirl Heath. *Here* 6C 26
Shirrell Heath. *Hants* 4C 10
Shirwell. *Devn* 2E 6
Shiskine. *N Ayr* 7J 57
Shobdon. *Here* 5B 26
Shobnall. *Staf* 7L 35
Shobrooke. *Devn* 5H 7
Shoby. *Leics* 7D 36
Shocklach. *Ches W* 5C 34
Shoeburyness. *S'end* 5F 22
Sholden. *Kent* 8K 23
Sholing. *Sotn* 4B 10
Sholver. *G Man* 7H 41
Shoot Hill. *Shrp* 8C 34
Shop. *Corn*
nr. Bude 4B 6
nr. Padstow 4A 4
Shop. *Devn* 4C 6
Shopford. *Cumb* 4K 53
Shoreditch. *G Lon* 5L 21
Shoreditch. *Som* 3M 7
Shoregill. *Cumb* 5F 46
Shoreham. *Kent* 7B 22
Shoreham-by-Sea. *W Sus* 5K 11
Shoresdean. *Nmbd* 5G 61
Shoreswood. *Nmbd* 5G 61
Shorncote. *Glos* 4J 19
Shorne. *Kent* 6C 22
Shorne Ridgeway. *Kent* 6C 22
Shortacombe. *Devn* 7E 6
Shortbridge. *E Sus* 3A 12
Shortgate. *E Sus* 4A 12
Short Green. *Norf* 3G 31
Shorthampton. *Oxon* 1M 19
Short Heath. *Derbs* 8M 35
Short Heath. *W Mid*
nr. Erdington 2J 27
nr. Wednesfield 1H 27
Shortlanesend. *Corn* 4M 3
Shorton. *Torb* 5L 5
Shortstown. *Bed* 7H 29
Shortwood. *S Glo* 6E 18
Shorwell. *IOW* 7B 10
Shoscombe. *Bath* 8F 18
Shotesham. *Norf* 2J 31
Shotgate. *Essx* 4D 22
Shotley. *Suff* 8J 31
Shotley Bridge. *Dur* 6D 54
Shotleyfield. *Nmbd* 6D 54
Shotley Gate. *Suff* 8J 31
Shottenden. *Kent* 8G 23
Shottermill. *Surr* 2F 10
Shottery. *Warw* 6K 27
Shotteswell. *Warw* 7B 28
Shottisham. *Suff* 7K 31
Shottle. *Derbs* 5M 35
Shotton. *Dur*
nr. Peterlee 8H 55
nr. Sedgefield 3A 48
Shotton. *Flin* 3B 34
Shotton. *Nmbd*
nr. Morpeth 4F 54
nr. Town Yetholm 6F 60
Shotton Colliery. *Dur* 7G 55
Shotts. *N Lan* 3G 59
Shotwick. *Ches W* 2B 34
Shouldham. *Norf* 1C 30
Shouldham Thorpe. *Norf* 1C 30
Shoulton. *Worc* 6G 27
Shrawardine. *Shrp* 8C 34
Shrawley. *Worc* 5G 27
Shreding Green. *Buck* 5H 21
Shrewley. *Warw* 5L 27
Shrewsbury. *Shrp* **116** (8C 34)
Shrewton. *Wilts* 1J 9
Shrigley. *New M* 6J 93
Shripney. *W Sus* 5G 11
Shrivenham. *Oxon* 5L 19
Shropham. *Norf* 2F 30
Shroton. *Dors* 4G 9
Shrub End. *Essx* 1F 22
Shucknall. *Here* 7D 26
Shudy Camps. *Cambs* 7C 30
Shulishadermor. *High* 1F 68
Shulista. *High* 6F 76
Shurdington. *Glos* 2H 19
Shurlock Row. *Wind* 6F 20
Shurrery. *High* 6B 86
Shurton. *Som* 1M 7
Shustoke. *Warw* 2L 27
Shute. *Devn*
nr. Axminster 6A 8
nr. Crediton 5H 7
Shutford. *Oxon* 7A 28
Shut Heath. *Staf* 7G 35
Shuthonger. *Glos* 8G 27
Shutlanehead. *Staf* 5G 35
Shutlanger. *Nptn* 7E 28
Shutt Green. *Staf* 1G 27
Shuttington. *Warw* 1L 27
Shuttlewood. *Derbs* 2B 36
Shuttleworth. *G Man* 6G 41
Siabost. *W Isl* 7F 82
Siabost bho Dheas. *W Isl* 7F 82
Siabost bho Thuath. *W Isl* 7F 82
Siadar. *W Isl* 6G 83
Siadar Uarach. *W Isl* 6G 83
Sibbaldbie. *Dum* 3F 52
Sibbertoft. *Nptn* 3D 28
Sibdon Carwood. *Shrp* 3C 26
Sibertswold. *Kent* 1J 13
Sibford Ferris. *Oxon* 8A 28
Sibford Gower. *Oxon* 8A 28
Sible Hedingham. *Essx* 8D 30
Sibsey. *Linc* 4L 37
Sibsey Fen Side. *Linc* 4L 37
Sibson. *Cambs* 2H 29
Sibson. *Leics* 1A 28
Sibster. *High* 6E 86
Sibthorpe. *Notts* 5E 36
Sibton. *Suff* 5K 31
Sicklesmere. *Suff* 5E 30
Sicklinghall. *N Yor* 3A 42
Sid. *Devn* 7L 7
Sidbury. *Devn* 6L 7
Sidbury. *Shrp* 3E 26
Sidcot. *N Som* 8C 18
Sidcup. *G Lon* 6A 22
Siddick. *Cumb* 8E 52
Siddington. *Ches E* 2G 35
Siddington. *Glos* 4J 19
Side of the Moor. *G Man* 6F 40
Sidestrand. *Norf* 6J 39
Sidford. *Devn* 6L 7
Sidlesham. *W Sus* 6F 10
Sidley. *E Sus* 5D 12
Sidlow. *Surr* 1K 11
Sidmouth. *Devn* 7L 7
Sigford. *Devn* 8G 7
Sigglesthorne. *E Yor* 3J 43
Sighthill. *Edin* 2K 59
Sigingstone. *V Glam* 7J 17
Signet. *Oxon* 2L 19
Silchester. *Hants* 7D 20
Sildinis. *W Isl* 2D 76
Sileby. *Leics* 8D 36
Silecroft. *Cumb* 6L 45
Silfield. *Norf* 2H 31
Silian. *Cdgn* 7E 24
Silkstone. *S Yor* 7L 41
Silkstone Common. *S Yor* 7L 41
Silksworth. *Tyne* 6G 55
Silk Willoughby. *Linc* 5H 37
Silloth. *Cumb* 6F 52
Sills. *Nmbd* 1B 54
Sillyearn. *Mor* 8E 80
Silpho. *N Yor* 6G 49
Silsden. *W Yor* 3J 41
Silsoe. *C Beds* 8H 29
Silverbank. *Abers* 6G 73
Silverbridge. *New M* 7F 93
Silverburn. *Midl* 3L 59
Silverdale. *Lanc* 8C 46
Silverdale. *Staf* 5G 35
Silverdale Green. *Lanc* 8C 46
Silver End. *Essx* 2E 22
Silver End. *W Mid* 3H 27
Silvergate. *Norf* 7H 39
Silver Green. *Norf* 2J 31
Silverhillocks. *Abers* 7G 81
Silverley's Green. *Suff* 4J 31
Silverstone. *Nptn* 7D 28
Silverton. *Devn* 5J 7
Silverton. *W Dun* 2C 58
Silvington. *Shrp* 4E 26
Simm's Cross. *Hal* 1D 34
Simm's Lane End. *Mers* 7D 40
Simonburn. *Nmbd* 4B 54
Simonsbath. *Som* 2G 7
Simonstone. *Lanc* 4F 40
Simprim. *Bord* 5F 60
Simpson. *Pemb* 5E 14
Simpson Cross. *Pemb* 5E 14
Sinclairston. *E Ayr* 8C 58
Sinclairtown. *Fife* 8F 66
Sinderby. *N Yor* 7M 47
Sinderhope. *Nmbd* 6B 54
Sindlesham. *Wok* 7E 20
Sinfin. *Derb* 6M 35
Singleborough. *Buck* 8E 28
Singleton. *Kent* 1F 12
Singleton. *Lanc* 4B 40
Singleton. *W Sus* 4F 10
Singlewell. *Kent* 6C 22
Sinkhurst Green. *Kent* 1E 12
Sinnahard. *Abers* 4D 72
Sinnington. *N Yor* 7E 48
Sinton Green. *Worc* 5G 27
Sion Mills. *Derr* 4C 92
Sipson. *G Lon* 6H 21
Sirhowy. *Blae* 3L 17
Sisland. *Norf* 2K 31
Sissinghurst. *Kent* 2D 12
Siston. *S Glo* 6E 18
Sithney. *Corn* 6K 3
Sittingbourne. *Kent* 7F 22
Six Ashes. *Staf* 3F 26
Six Bells. *Blae* 4M 17
Six Hills. *Leics* 7D 36
Sixhills. *Linc* 1J 37
Six Mile Bottom. *Cambs* 6B 30
Sixmilecross. *Ferm* 5D 92
Sixpenny Handley. *Dors* 4H 9
Sizewell. *Suff* 5L 31
Skail. *High* 7K 85
Skaill. *Orkn* 8B 88
Skaills. *Orkn* 1G 87
Skares. *E Ayr* 8D 58
Skateraw. *E Lot* 2E 60
Skaw. *Shet* 1F 90
Skeabost. *High* 1F 68
Skeabrae. *Orkn* 7B 88
Skeeby. *N Yor* 5K 47
Skeffington. *Leics* 1E 28
Skeffling. *E Yor* 6L 43
Skegby. *Notts*
nr. Mansfield 3B 36
nr. Tuxford 2E 36
Skegness. *Linc* 3B 38
Skelberry. *Shet*
nr. Boddam 6D 90
nr. Housetter 5H 91
Skelbo. *High* 4H 79
Skelbo Street. *High* 4H 79
Skelbrooke. *S Yor* 6C 42
Skeldyke. *Linc* 6L 37
Skelfhill. *Bord* 1J 53
Skellingthorpe. *Linc* 2G 37
Skellister. *Shet* 2E 90
Skellorn Green. *Ches E* 1H 35
Skellow. *S Yor* 6C 42
Skelmanthorpe. *W Yor* 6L 41
Skelmersdale. *Lanc* 7C 40
Skelmorlie. *N Ayr* 3L 57
Skelpick. *High* 6K 85
Skelton. *Cumb* 8J 53
Skelton. *E Yor* 5E 42
Skelton. *N Yor*
nr. Richmond 5J 47
nr. Ripon 1A 42
Skelton. *Red C* 4D 48
Skelton. *York* 2C 42
Skelton Green. *Red C* 4D 48
Skelwick. *Orkn* 5D 88
Skelwith Bridge. *Cumb* 5B 46
Skendleby. *Linc* 3M 37
Skendleby Psalter. *Linc* 2M 37
Skenfrith. *Mon* 1C 18
Skerne. *E Yor* 2H 43
Skeroblingarry. *Arg* 7G 57
Skerray. *High* 5J 85
Skerricha. *High* 6E 84
Skerries Airport. *Shet* 6L 91
Skerton. *Lanc* 1C 40
Sketchley. *Leics* 2B 28
Sketty. *Swan* 5F 16
Skewen. *Neat* 5G 17
Skewsby. *N Yor* 8D 48
Skeyton. *Norf* 7J 39
Skeyton Corner. *Norf* 7J 39
Skiall. *High* 5B 86
Skidbrooke. *Linc* 8M 43
Skidbrooke North End.
Linc 8M 43
Skidby. *E Yor* 4H 43
Skilgate. *Som* 3J 7
Skillington. *Linc* 7F 36
Skinburness. *Cumb* 6F 52
Skinflats. *Falk* 1H 59
Skinidin. *High* 1D 68
Skinnet. *High* 5H 85
Skinningrove. *Red C* 4E 48
Skipness. *Arg* 4H 57
Skippool. *Lanc* 3B 40
Skiprigg. *Cumb* 7H 53
Skipsea. *E Yor* 2J 43
Skipsea Brough. *E Yor* 2J 43
Skipton. *N Yor* 2H 41
Skipton-on-Swale. *N Yor* 8A 48
Skipwith. *N Yor* 4D 42
Skirbeck. *Linc* 5L 37
Skirbeck Quarter. *Linc* 5L 37
Skirlaugh. *E Yor* 4J 43
Skirling. *Bord* 6J 59
Skirmett. *Buck* 4E 20
Skirpenbeck. *E Yor* 2E 42
Skirwith. *Cumb* 8L 53
Skirwith. *N Yor* 8F 46
Skirza. *High* 5E 86
Skitby. *Cumb* 5J 53
Skitham. *Lanc* 3C 40
Skittle Green. *Buck* 3E 20
Skroo. *Shet* 2M 89
Skulamus. *High* 3H 69
Skullomie. *High* 5J 85
Skyborry Green. *Shrp* 4A 26
Skye Green. *Essx* 1E 22
Skye of Curr. *High* 3K 71
Slack. *W Yor* 5H 41
The Slack. *Dur* 3K 47
Slackhall. *Derbs* 1J 35
Slack Head. *Cumb* 8C 46
Slackhead. *Mor* 7D 80
Slackholme End. *Linc* 2B 38
Slacks of Cairnbanno.
Abers 1H 73
Slad. *Glos* 3G 19
Slade. *Swan* 8L 15
The Slade. *W Ber* 7C 20
Slade End. *Oxon* 4C 20
Slade Field. *Cambs* 3L 29
Slade Green. *G Lon* 6B 22
Slade Heath. *Staf* 1H 27
Slade Hooton. *S Yor* 1C 36
Sladesbridge. *Corn* 4C 4
Slaggyford. *Nmbd* 6L 53
Slaidburn. *Lanc* 2F 40
Slaid Hill. *W Yor* 3M 41
Slaithwaite. *W Yor* 6J 41
Slaley. *Derbs* 4L 35

Slaley—Sudbrook

Slaley. Nmbd 6C 54
Slamannan. Falk 2G 59
Slapton. Buck 1G 21
Slapton. Devn 7L 5
Slapton. Nptn 7D 28
Slattocks. G Man 7G 41
Slaugham. W Sus 3K 11
Slaughterbridge. Corn 3D 4
Slaughterford. Wilts 6G 19
Slawston. Leics 2E 28
Sleaford. Hants 2F 10
Sleaford. Linc 5H 37
Sleagill. Cumb 4D 46
Sleap. Shrp 7C 34
Sledmere. E Yor 1G 43
Sleightholme. Dur 4H 47
Sleights. N Yor 5F 48
Slepe. Dors 6H 9
Slickly. High 5D 86
Sliddery. N Ayr 7J 57
Sligachan. High 3F 68
Slimbridge. Glos 3F 18
Slindon. Staf 6G 35
Slindon. W Sus 5G 11
Slinfold. W Sus 2J 11
Slingsby. N Yor 8D 48
Slip End. C Beds 2H 21
Slipton. Nptn 4G 29
Slitting Mill. Staf 8J 35
Slochd. High 3J 71
Slockavullin. Arg 8C 64
Sloley. Norf 7J 39
Sloncombe. Devn 7G 7
Slothby. Linc 2A 38
Slough. Slo 6G 21
Slough Green. Som 3A 8
Slough Green. W Sus 3K 11
Sluggan. High 3J 71
Slyne. Lanc 1C 40
Smailholm. Bord 6D 60
Smallbridge. G Man 6H 41
Smallbrook. Devn 6H 7
Smallburgh. Norf 7K 39
Smallburn. E Ayr 7E 58
Smalldale. Derbs 2J 35
Small Dole. W Sus 4K 11
Smalley. Derbs 5B 36
Smallfield. Surr 1L 11
Small Heath. W Mid 3J 27
Smallholm. Dum 4F 52
Small Hythe. Kent 2E 12
Smallrice. Staf 6H 35
Smallridge. Devn 5B 8
Smallwood Hey. Lanc 3B 40
Smallworth. Norf 3G 31
Smannell. Hants 1A 10
Smardale. Cumb 5F 46
Smarden. Kent 1E 12
Smarden Bell. Kent 1E 12
Smart's Hill. Kent 1B 12
Smeatharpe. Devn 4M 7
Smeeth. Kent 2G 13
The Smeeth. Norf 8B 38
Smeeton Westerby. Leics 2D 28
Smeircleit. W Isl 4D 74
Smerral. High 8C 86
Smestow. Staf 2G 27
Smethwick. W Mid 3J 27
Smirisary. High 8H 69
Smisby. Derbs 8M 35
Smitham Hill. Bath 8D 18
Smith End Green. Worc 6F 26
Smithfield. Cumb 5J 53
Smith Green. Lanc 2C 40
The Smithies. Shrp 2E 26
Smithincott. Devn 4K 7
Smith's Green. Essx 1B 22
Smithstown. High 6J 77
Smithton. High 1H 71
Smithwood Green. Suff 6F 30
Smithy Bridge. G Man 6H 41
Smithy Green. Ches E 2F 34
Smithy Lane Ends. Lanc 6C 40
Smockington. Leics 3B 28
Smoogro. Orkn 1E 86
Smythe's Green. Essx 2F 22
Snaigow House. Per 3D 66
Snailbeach. Shrp 1B 26
Snailwell. Cambs 5C 30
Snainton. N Yor 7G 49
Snaith. E Yor 5D 42
Snape. N Yor 7L 47
Snape. Suff 6K 31
Snape Green. Lanc 6B 40
Snapper. Devn 2E 6
Snarestone. Leics 1M 27
Snarford. Linc 1H 37
Snargate. Kent 3F 12
Snave. Kent 3G 13
Sneachill. Worc 6H 27
Snead. Powy 2B 26
Snead Common. Worc 5F 26
Sneaton. N Yor 5F 48
Sneatonthorpe. N Yor 5G 49
Snelland. Linc 1H 37
Snelston. Derbs 5K 35
Snetterton. Norf 2F 30
Snettisham. Norf 6C 38
Snibston. Leics 8B 36
Sniseabhal. W Isl 2D 74
Snitter. Nmbd 1D 54
Snitterby. Linc 8G 43
Snitterfield. Warw 6L 27
Snitton. Shrp 4D 26
Snodhill. Here 7B 26
Snodland. Kent 7D 22
Snods Edge. Nmbd 6D 54
Snowshill. Glos 8J 27
Snow Street. Norf 3G 31
Snydale. W Yor 5B 42
Soake. Hants 4D 10
Soar. Carm 2F 16
Soar. Gwyn 7F 32
Soar. IOA 3C 32
Soar. Powy 1J 17
Soberton. Hants 4D 10
Soberton Heath. Hants 4D 10
Sockbridge. Cumb 3D 46
Sockburn. Darl 5M 47
Sodom. Den 3K 33
Sodom. Shet 1F 90
Soham. Cambs 4B 30
Soham Cotes. Cambs 4B 30
Solas. W Isl 6K 75
Soldon Cross. Devn 4C 6
Soldridge. Hants 2D 10
Solent Breezes. Hants 5C 10
Sole Street. Kent
nr. Meopham 7C 22
nr. Waltham 1G 13
Solihull. W Mid 3K 27
Sollers Dilwyn. Here 6C 26
Sollers Hope. Here 8E 26
Sollom. Lanc 6C 40
Solva. Pemb 4D 14
Somerby. Leics 8E 36
Somerby. Linc 7H 43
Somercotes. Derbs 4B 36
Somerford. Dors 6K 9
Somerford. Staf 1G 27
Somerford Keynes. Glos 4J 19
Somerley. W Sus 6F 10
Somerleyton. Suff 2L 31
Somersal Herbert. Derbs 6K 35
Somersby. Linc 2L 37
Somersham. Cambs 4L 29
Somersham. Suff 7G 31
Somerton. Oxon 1B 20
Somerton. Som 3C 8
Somerton. Suff 6E 30
Sompting. W Sus 5J 11
Sonning. Wok 6E 20
Sonning Common. Oxon 5E 20
Sonning Eye. Oxon 6E 20
Sookholme. Notts 3C 36
Sopley. Hants 6K 9
Sopworth. Wilts 5G 19
Sorbie. Dum 7K 51
Sordale. High 5C 86
Sorisdale. Arg 1H 63
Sorn. E Ayr 7D 58
Sornhill. E Ayr 6D 58
Sortat. High 5D 86
Sotby. Linc 2K 37
Sots Hole. Linc 3J 37
Sotterley. Suff 3L 31
Soudley. Shrp
nr. Church Stretton 2C 26
nr. Market Drayton 7F 34
Soughton. Flin 4M 33
Soulbury. Buck 1F 20
Soulby. Cumb
nr. Appleby 4F 46
nr. Penrith 3C 46
Souldern. Oxon 8C 28
Souldrop. Bed 5G 29
Sound. Ches E 5E 34
Sound. Shet
nr. Lerwick 3E 90
nr. Tresta 2D 90
Soundwell. S Glo 6E 18
Sourhope. Bord 7F 60
Sourin. Orkn 6D 88
Sour Nook. Cumb 7H 53
Sourton. Devn 6E 6
Soutergate. Cumb 6M 45
South Acre. Norf 8E 38
Southall. G Lon 6J 21
South Allington. Devn 8K 5
South Alloa. Falk 8B 66
Southam. Glos 1H 19
Southam. Warw 5B 28
South Ambersham. W Sus 3G 11
Southampton. Sotn 116 (4B 10)
Southampton Airport.
Hants 4B 10
Southannan. N Ayr 4M 57
South Anston. S Yor 1C 36
South Ascot. Wind 7G 21
South Baddesley. Hants 6A 10
South Balfern. Dum 6K 51
South Ballachulish. High 2E 64
South Bank. Red C 3C 48
South Barrow. Som 3E 8
South Benfleet. Essx 5D 22
South Bents. Tyne 5H 55
South Bersted. W Sus 5G 11
Southborough. Kent 1B 12
Southbourne. Bour 6K 9
Southbourne. W Sus 5E 10
South Bowood. Dors 6C 8
South Brent. Devn 6J 5
South Brewham. Som 2F 8
South Broomage. Falk 1G 59
South Broomhill. Nmbd 2F 54
Southburgh. Norf 1F 30
South Burlingham. Norf 1K 31
Southburn. E Yor 2G 43
South Cadbury. Som 3E 8
South Carlton. Linc 2G 37
South Cave. E Yor 4G 43
South Cerney. Glos 4J 19
South Chailey. E Sus 4L 11
South Chard. Som 5B 8
South Charlton. Nmbd 7J 61
South Cheriton. Som 3E 8
South Church. Dur 3L 47
Southchurch. S'end 5F 22
South Cleatlam. Dur 4K 47
South Cliffe. E Yor 4F 42
South Clifton. Notts 2F 36
South Clunes. High 1F 70
South Cockerington. Linc 1L 37
South Common. Devn 5B 8
South Cornelly. B'end 6H 17
Southcott. Devn
nr. Great Torrington 4D 6
nr. Okehampton 6E 6
Southcott. Wilts 8K 19
Southcourt. Buck 2F 20
South Cove. Suff 3L 31
South Creagan. Arg 3D 64
South Creake. Norf 6E 38
South Crosland. W Yor 6K 41
South Croxton. Leics 8D 36
South Dalton. E Yor 3G 43
South Darenth. Kent 7B 22
Southdean. Bord 1L 53
Southdown. Bath 7F 18
South Duffield. N Yor 4D 42
Southease. E Sus 5M 11
South Elkington. Linc 1K 37
South Elmsall. W Yor 6B 42
South End. Cumb 8M 45
South End. N Lin 5J 43
Southend. Arg 1B 50
Southend. Glos 4F 18
Southend. W Ber 6C 20
Southend Airport. Essx 5E 22
Southend-on-Sea. S'end 5E 22
Southerfield. Cumb 7F 52
Southerhouse. Shet 4D 90
Southerly. Devn 7E 6
Southernden. Kent 1E 12
Southerndown. V Glam 7H 17
Southerness. Dum 6D 52
South Erradale. High 6J 77
Southerton. Devn 6K 7
Southery. Norf 2C 30
Southey Green. Essx 8D 30
South Fambridge. Essx 4E 22
South Fawley. W Ber 5A 20
South Feorline. N Ayr 7J 57
South Ferriby. N Lin 5G 43
South Field. E Yor 5H 43
Southfleet. Kent 6C 22
South Garvan. High 8L 69
Southgate. Cdgn 4E 24
Southgate. G Lon 4L 21
Southgate. Norf
nr. Aylsham 7H 39
nr. Fakenham 6E 38
Southgate. Swan 6E 16
South Gluss. Shet 6H 91
South Godstone. Surr 1L 11
South Gorley. Hants 4K 9
South Green. Essx
nr. Billericay 4C 22
nr. Colchester 2G 23
South Green. Kent 7E 22
South Hanningfield. Essx 4D 22
South Harting. W Sus 4E 10
South Hayling. Hants 6E 10
South Hazelrigg. Nmbd 6H 61
South Heath. Buck 3G 21
South Heath. Essx 2H 23
South Heighton. E Sus 5M 11
South Hetton. Dur 7G 55
South Hiendley. W Yor 6A 42
South Hill. Corn 8C 6
South Hill. Som 3C 8
South Hinksey. Oxon 3C 20
South Hole. Devn 3B 6
South Holme. N Yor 8E 48
South Holmwood. Surr 1J 11
South Hornchurch. G Lon 5B 22
South Huish. Devn 7J 5
South Hykeham. Linc 3G 37
South Hylton. Tyne 6G 55
Southill. C Beds 7J 29
Southington. Hants 1C 10
South Kelsey. Linc 8H 43
South Kessock. High 1G 71
South Killingholme. N Lin 6J 43
South Kilvington. N Yor 7B 48
South Kilworth. Leics 3D 28
South Kirkby. W Yor 6B 42
South Kirkton. Abers 5G 73
South Knighton. Devn 8H 7
South Kyme. Linc 5J 37
South Lancing. W Sus 5J 11
South Ledaig. Arg 4D 64
South Leigh. Oxon 3A 20
Southleigh. Devn 6M 7
South Leverton. Notts 1E 36
South Littleton. Worc 7J 27
South Lopham. Norf 3G 31
South Luffenham. Rut 1G 29
South Malling. E Sus 4M 11
South Marston. Swin 5K 19
South Middleton. Nmbd 7G 61
South Milford. N Yor 4B 42
South Milton. Devn 7K 5
South Mimms. Herts 3K 21
Southminster. Essx 4F 22
South Molton. Devn 3G 7
South Moor. Dur 6E 54
Southmoor. Oxon 4A 20
South Moreton. Oxon 5C 20
South Mundham. W Sus 5F 10
South Muskham. Notts 4E 36
South Newbald. E Yor 4G 43
South Newington. Oxon 8B 28
South Newsham. Nmbd 4G 55
South Newton. N Ayr 4J 57
South Newton. Wilts 2J 9
South Normanton. Derbs 4B 36
South Norwood. G Lon 7L 21
South Nutfield. Surr 1L 11
South Ockendon. Thur 5B 22
Southoe. Cambs 5J 29
Southolt. Suff 5H 31
South Ormsby. Linc 2L 37
Southorpe. Pet 1H 29
South Otterington. N Yor 7A 48
South Owersby. Linc 8H 43
Southowram. W Yor 5K 41
South Oxhey. Herts 4J 21
South Perrott. Dors 5C 8
South Petherton. Som 4C 8
South Petherwin. Corn 7C 6
South Pickenham. Norf 1E 30
South Pool. Devn 7K 5
South Poorton. Dors 6D 8
South Port. Arg 5E 64
Southport. Mers 6B 40
Southpunds. Shet 6E 90
South Queensferry. Edin 2K 59
South Radworthy. Devn 2G 7
South Rauceby. Linc 5H 37
South Raynham. Norf 7E 38
Southrepps. Norf 6J 39
South Reston. Linc 1M 37
Southrey. Linc 3J 37
Southrop. Glos 3K 19
Southrope. Hants 1D 10
South Runcton. Norf 1C 30
South Scarle. Notts 3F 36
Southsea. Port 6D 10
South Shields. Tyne 5G 55
South Shore. Bkpl 4B 40
Southside. Orkn 7E 88
South Somercotes. Linc 8M 43
South Stainley. N Yor 1M 41
South Stainmore. Cumb 4G 47
South Stifford. Thur 6B 22
South Stoke. Bath 7F 18
South Stoke. Oxon 5C 20
South Stoke. W Sus 5H 11
South Street. E Sus 4L 11
South Street. Kent
nr. Faversham 8G 23
nr. Whitstable 7H 23
South Tawton. Devn 6F 6
South Thoresby. Linc 2M 37
South Tidworth. Wilts 1L 9
South Town. Devn 7J 7
South Town. Hants 2D 10
Southtown. Norf 1M 31
Southtown. Orkn 2F 86
South View. Shet 3D 90
Southwaite. Cumb 7J 53
South Walsham. Norf 8K 39
South Warnborough. Hants 1E 10
Southwater. W Sus 3J 11
Southwater Street. W Sus 3J 11
Southway. Som 1D 8
South Weald. Essx 4B 22
South Weirs. Hants 5L 9
Southwell. Dors 8E 8
Southwell. Notts 4E 36
South Weston. Oxon 4E 20
South Wheatley. Corn 6B 6
South Wheatley. Notts 1E 36
Southwick. Hants 5D 10
Southwick. Nptn 2H 29
Southwick. Tyne 6G 55
Southwick. W Sus 5K 11
Southwick. Wilts 8G 19
South Widcombe. Bath 8D 18
South Wigston. Leics 2C 28
South Willingham. Linc 1J 37
South Wingfield. Derbs 4A 36
South Witham. Linc 8G 37
Southwold. Suff 4M 31
South Wonston. Hants 2B 10
Southwood. Norf 1K 31
Southwood. Som 2D 8
South Woodham Ferrers.
Essx 4E 22
South Wootton. Norf 7C 38
South Wraxall. Wilts 7G 19
South Zeal. Devn 6F 6
Soval Lodge. W Isl 1E 76
Sowerby. N Yor 7B 48
Sowerby. W Yor 5J 41
Sowerby Bridge. W Yor 5J 41
Sowerby Row. Cumb 7H 53
Sower Carr. Lanc 3B 40
Sowley Green. Suff 6D 30
Sowood. W Yor 6J 41
Sowton. Devn 6J 7
Soyal. High 4F 78
Soyland Town. W Yor 5J 41
The Spa. New M 6H 93
Spacey Houses. N Yor 2M 41
Spa Common. Norf 6J 39
Spalding. Linc 7K 37
Spaldington. E Yor 4E 42
Spaldwick. Cambs 4J 29
Spalford. Notts 3F 36
Spamount. Derr 4C 92
Spanby. Linc 6H 37
Sparham. Norf 8G 39
Sparhamhill. Norf 8G 39
Spark Bridge. Cumb 7B 46
Sparket. Cumb 3C 46
Sparkford. Som 3E 8
Sparkwell. Devn 6H 5
Sparrow Green. Norf 8F 38
Sparrowpit. Derbs 1J 35
Sparrow's Green. E Sus 2C 12
Sparsholt. Hants 2B 10
Sparsholt. Oxon 5M 19
Spartylea. Nmbd 7B 54
Spath. Staf 6J 35
Spaunton. N Yor 7E 48
Spaxton. Som 2M 7
Spean Bridge. High 7C 70
Spear Hill. W Sus 4J 11
Speen. Buck 4F 20
Speen. W Ber 7B 20
Speeton. N Yor 8J 49
Speke. Mers 1C 34
Speldhurst. Kent 1B 12
Spellbrook. Herts 2A 22
Spelsbury. Oxon 1A 20
Spencers Wood. Wok 7E 20
Spennithorne. N Yor 7K 47
Spennymoor. Dur 8F 54
Spernall. Warw 5J 27
Sperrin. Derr 4E 92
Spetchley. Worc 6G 27
Spetisbury. Dors 5H 9
Spexhall. Suff 3K 31
Speybank. High 5J 71
Spey Bay. Mor 7C 80
Speybridge. High 3L 71
Speyview. Mor 1B 72
Spilsby. Linc 3M 37
Spindlestone. Nmbd 6J 61
Spinkhill. Derbs 2B 36
Spinney Hills. Leic 1D 28
Spinningdale. High 5G 79
Spital. Mers 1B 34
Spitalhill. Derbs 5K 35
Spital in the Street. Linc 8G 43
Spithurst. E Sus 4M 11
Spittal. Dum 6J 51
Spittal. E Lot 2B 60
Spittal. High 6C 86
Spittal. Nmbd 4H 61
Spittal. Pemb 4F 14
Spittalfield. Per 3E 66
Spittal of Glenmuick. Abers 7C 72
Spittal of Glenshee. Per 8M 71
Spittal-on-Rule. Bord 7C 60
Spixworth. Norf 8J 39
Splatt. Corn 7B 6
Spofforth. N Yor 2A 42
Spondon. Derb 6B 36
Spon End. W Mid 4M 27
Spooner Row. Norf 2G 31
Sporle. Norf 8E 38
Spott. E Lot 2D 60
Spratton. Nptn 4E 28
Spreakley. Surr 1F 10
Spreyton. Devn 6G 7
Spridlington. Linc 1H 37
Springburn. Glas 3E 58
Springfield. Dum 5H 53
Springfield. Ferm 6B 92
Springfield. Fife 6G 67
Springfield. High 7G 79
Springfield. W Mid 3J 27
Spring Hill. W Mid 2G 27
Springhill. Staf 1H 27
Springholm. Dum 5C 52
Springside. N Ayr 6B 58
Springthorpe. Linc 1F 36
Spring Vale. IOW 6D 10
Spring Valley. IOM 7C 44
Springwell. Tyne 6F 54
Sproatley. E Yor 4J 43
Sproston Green. Ches W 3F 34
Sprotbrough. S Yor 7C 42
Sproughton. Suff 7H 31
Sprouston. Bord 6E 60
Sprowston. Norf 8J 39
Sproxton. Leics 7F 36
Sproxton. N Yor 7D 48
Sprunston. Cumb 7J 53
Spurstow. Ches E 4D 34
Squires Gate. Bkpl 4B 40
Sraid Ruadh. Arg 3E 62
Srannda. W Isl 5B 76
Sron an t-Sithein. High 1C 64
Sronphadruig Lodge. Per 8H 71
Sruth Mor. W Isl 7L 75
Stableford. Shrp 2F 26
Stackhouse. N Yor 1G 41
Stackpole. Pemb 7F 14
Stackpole Elidor. Pemb 7F 14
Stacksford. Norf 2G 31
Stacksteads. Lanc 5G 41
Staddiscombe. Plym 6H 5
Staddlethorpe. E Yor 5F 42
Staddon. Devn 5C 6
Stadhampton. Oxon 4D 20
Stadhlaigearraidh. W Isl 2D 74
Stafainn. High 7F 76
Staffield. Cumb 7K 53
Staffin. High 7F 76
Stafford. Staf 7H 35
Stafford Park. Telf 1F 26
Stagden Cross. Essx 2C 22
Stagsden. Bed 7G 29
Stag's Head. Devn 3F 6
Stainburn. Cumb 2K 45
Stainburn. N Yor 3L 41
Stainby. Linc 7G 37
Staincliffe. W Yor 5L 41
Staincross. S Yor 6M 41
Staindrop. Dur 3K 47
Staines-upon-Thames.
Surr 6H 21
Stainfield. Linc
nr. Bourne 7H 37
nr. Lincoln 2J 37
Stainforth. N Yor 1G 41
Stainforth. S Yor 6D 42
Staining. Lanc 4B 40
Stainland. W Yor 6J 41
Stainsacre. N Yor 5G 49
Stainton. Cumb
nr. Carlisle 6H 53
nr. Kendal 7D 46
nr. Penrith 3C 46
Stainton. Dur 4J 47
Stainton. Midd 4B 48
Stainton. N Yor 6K 47
Stainton. S Yor 8C 42
Stainton by Langworth.
Linc 2H 37
Staintondale. N Yor 6G 49
Stainton le Vale. Linc 8J 43
Stainton with Adgarley.
Cumb 8A 46
Stair. Cumb 2M 45
Stair. E Ayr 7C 58
Stairhaven. Dum 6H 51
Staithes. N Yor 4E 48
Stakeford. Nmbd 3F 54
Stake Pool. Lanc 3C 40
Stakes. Hants 5D 10
Stalbridge. Dors 4F 8
Stalbridge Weston. Dors 4F 8
Stalham. Norf 7K 39
Stalham Green. Norf 7K 39
Stalisfield Green. Kent 8F 22
Stallen. Dors 4E 8
Stallingborough. NE Lin 6K 43
Stalling Busk. N Yor 7H 47
Stallington. Staf 6H 35
Stalmine. Lanc 3B 40
Stalybridge. G Man 8H 41
Stambourne. Essx 8D 30
Stamford. Linc 1H 29
Stamford. Nmbd 8K 61
Stamford Bridge. Ches W 3C 34
Stamford Bridge. E Yor 2E 42
Stamfordham. Nmbd 4D 54
Stamperland. E Ren 4D 58
Stanah. Lanc 3B 40
Stanborough. Herts 2K 21
Stanbridge. C Beds 1G 21
Stanbridge. Dors 5J 9
Stanbury. W Yor 4J 41
Stand. N Lan 3F 58
Standburn. Falk 2H 59
Standeford. Staf 1H 27
Standen. Kent 1E 12
Standen Street. Kent 2E 12
Standerwick. Som 8G 19
Standford. Hants 2F 10
Standford Bridge. Telf 7F 34
Standingstone. Cumb 7G 53
Standish. Glos 3G 19
Standish. G Man 6D 40
Standish Lower Ground.
G Man 7D 40
Standlake. Oxon 3A 20
Standon. Hants 3B 10
Standon. Herts 1L 21
Standon. Staf 6G 35
Standon Green End. Herts 2L 21
Stane. N Lan 4G 59
Stanecastle. N Ayr 6B 58
Stanfield. Norf 7F 38
Stanfield. Suff 6D 30
Stanford. C Beds 7J 29
Stanford. Kent 2H 13
Stanford Bishop. Here 6E 26
Stanford Bridge. Worc 5F 26
Stanford Dingley. W Ber 6C 20
Stanford in the Vale. Oxon 4M 19
Stanford-le-Hope. Thur 5C 22
Stanford on Avon. Nptn 4C 28
Stanford on Soar. Notts 7C 36
Stanford on Teme. Worc 5F 26
Stanford Rivers. Essx 3B 22
Stanfree. Derbs 2B 36
Stanghow. Red C 4D 48
Stanground. Pet 2K 29
Stanhoe. Norf 6E 38
Stanhope. Dur 8C 54
Stanhope. Bord 7K 59
Stanion. Nptn 3G 29
Stanley. Derbs 5B 36
Stanley. Dur 6E 54
Stanley. Per 4E 66
Stanley. Shrp 3F 26
Stanley. Staf 4H 35
Stanley. W Yor 5M 41
Stanley Common. Derbs 5B 36
Stanley Crook. Dur 8E 54
Stanley Hill. Here 7E 26
Stanlow. Ches W 2C 34
Stanmer. Brig 5L 11
Stanmore. G Lon 4J 21
Stanmore. Hants 3B 10
Stanmore. W Ber 6B 20
Stannersburn. Nmbd 3M 53
Stanningfield. Suff 6E 30
Stannington. Nmbd 4F 54
Stannington. S Yor 1M 35
Stansbatch. Here 5B 26
Stanshope. Staf 4K 35
Stanstead. Suff 7E 30
Stanstead Abbotts. Herts 2L 21
Stansted. Kent 7C 22
Stansted Airport. Essx 119 (1B 22)
Stansted Mountfitchet.
Essx 1B 22
Stanthorne. Ches W 3E 34
Stanton. Derbs 8L 35
Stanton. Glos 8J 27
Stanton. Nmbd 2E 54
Stanton. Staf 5K 35
Stanton. Suff 4F 30
Stanton by Bridge. Derbs 7A 36
Stanton-by-Dale. Derbs 6B 36
Stanton Chare. Suff 4F 30
Stanton Drew. Bath 7D 18
Stanton Fitzwarren. Swin 4K 19
Stanton Harcourt. Oxon 3B 20
Stanton Hill. Notts 3B 36
Stanton in Peak. Derbs 3L 35
Stanton Lacy. Shrp 4C 26
Stanton Long. Shrp 2D 26
Stanton-on-the-Wolds.
Notts 6D 36
Stanton Prior. Bath 7E 18
Stanton St Bernard. Wilts 7J 19
Stanton St John. Oxon 3C 20
Stanton St Quintin. Wilts 6H 19
Stanton Street. Suff 5F 30
Stanton under Bardon.
Leics 8B 36
Stanton upon Hine Heath.
Shrp 7D 34
Stanton Wick. Bath 7E 18
Stanwardine in the Fields.
Shrp 7C 34
Stanwardine in the Wood.
Shrp 7C 34
Stanway. Essx 1F 22
Stanway. Glos 8J 27
Stanwell. Surr 6H 21
Stanwell Green. Suff 4H 31
Stanwell Moor. Surr 6H 21
Stanwick. Nptn 4G 29
Stanydale. Shet 2C 90
Staoinebrig. W Isl 2D 74
Stape. N Yor 6E 48
Stapehill. Dors 5J 9
Stapeley. Ches E 5E 34
Stapenhill. Staf 7L 35
Staple. Kent 8J 23
Staple Cross. Devn 3K 7
Staplecross. E Sus 3D 12
Staplefield. W Sus 3K 11
Staple Fitzpaine. Som 4A 8
Stapleford. Cambs 6A 30
Stapleford. Herts 2L 21
Stapleford. Leics 8F 36
Stapleford. Linc 4F 36
Stapleford. Notts 6B 36
Stapleford. Wilts 2J 9
Stapleford Abbotts. Essx 4B 22
Stapleford Tawney. Essx 4B 22
Staplegrove. Som 3M 7
Staplehay. Som 3M 7
Staple Hill. S Glo 6E 18
Staplehurst. Kent 1D 12
Staplers. IOW 7C 10
Stapleton. Bris 6E 18
Stapleton. Cumb 4K 53
Stapleton. Here 5B 26
Stapleton. Leics 2B 28
Stapleton. N Yor 4L 47
Stapleton. Shrp 1C 26
Stapleton. Som 3C 8
Stapley. Som 4L 7
Staploe. Bed 5J 29
Staplow. Here 7E 26
Star. Fife 7G 67
Star. Pemb 3J 15
Starbeck. N Yor 2M 41
Starbotton. N Yor 8H 47
Starcross. Devn 7J 7
Stareton. Warw 4M 27
Starkholmes. Derbs 4M 35
Starling. G Man 6F 40
Starling's Green. Essx 8A 30
Starston. Norf 3J 31
Start. Devn 7L 5
Startforth. Dur 4J 47
Start Hill. Essx 1B 22
Startley. Wilts 5H 19
Stathe. Som 3B 8
Stathern. Leics 6E 36
Station Town. Dur 8H 55
Staughton Green. Cambs 5J 29
Staughton Highway.
Cambs 5J 29
Staunton. Glos
nr. Cheltenham 1F 18
nr. Monmouth 2D 18
Staunton in the Vale.
Notts 5F 36
Staunton on Arrow. Here 5B 26
Staunton on Wye. Here 7B 26
Staveley. Cumb 6C 46
Staveley. Derbs 2B 36
Staveley. N Yor 1A 42
Staveley-in-Cartmel. Cumb 7B 46
Staverton. Devn 5K 5
Staverton. Glos 1G 19
Staverton. Nptn 5C 28
Staverton. Wilts 7G 19
Stawell. Som 2B 8
Stawley. Som 3K 7
Staxigoe. High 6E 86
Staxton. N Yor 8H 49
Staylittle. Powy 3H 25
Staynall. Lanc 3B 40
Staythorpe. Notts 4E 36
Stean. N Yor 8J 47
Stearsby. N Yor 8D 48
Steart. Som 1A 8
Stebbing. Essx 1C 22
Stebbing Green. Essx 1C 22
Stedham. W Sus 3F 10
Steel. Nmbd 6C 54
Steel Cross. E Sus 2B 12
Steelend. Fife 8D 66
Steele Road. Bord 2K 53
Steel Heath. Shrp 6D 34
Steen's Bridge. Here 6D 26
Steep. Hants 3E 10
Steep Lane. W Yor 5J 41
Steeple. Dors 7H 9
Steeple. Essx 3F 22
Steeple Ashton. Wilts 8H 19
Steeple Aston. Oxon 1B 20
Steeple Barton. Oxon 1B 20
Steeple Bumpstead. Essx 7C 30
Steeple Claydon. Buck 1D 20
Steeple Gidding. Cambs 3J 29
Steeple Langford. Wilts 2J 9
Steeple Morden. Cambs 7K 29
Steeton. W Yor 3J 41
Stein. High 8D 76
Steinmanhill. Abers 1G 73
Stelling Minnis. Kent 1H 13
Stembridge. Som 3C 8
Stemster. High
nr. Halkirk 5C 86
nr. Westfield 5B 86
Stenalees. Corn 6C 4
Stenhill. Devn 4K 7
Stenhouse. Edin 2L 59
Stenhousemuir. Falk 1G 59
Stenigot. Linc 1K 37
Stenscholl. High 7F 76
Stenso. Orkn 7C 88
Stenson. Derbs 7M 35
Stenson Fields. Derbs 6M 35
Stenton. E Lot 2D 60
Stenwith. Linc 6F 36
Steòrnabhagh. W Isl 8H 83
Stepaside. Pemb 6H 15
Stepford. Dum 3C 52
Stepney. G Lon 5L 21
Steppingley. C Beds 8H 29
Stepps. N Lan 3E 58
Sterndale Moor. Derbs 3K 35
Sternfield. Suff 5K 31
Stert. Wilts 8J 19
Stetchworth. Cambs 6C 30
Stevenage. Herts 1K 21
Stevenston. N Ayr 5A 58
Stevenstone. Devn 4E 6
Steventon. Hants 1C 10
Steventon. Oxon 4B 20
Steventon End. Essx 7B 30
Stevington. Bed 6G 29
Stewartby. Bed 7H 29
Stewarton. Arg 8F 56
Stewarton. E Ayr 5C 58
Stewartstown. M Ulst 5F 93
Stewkley. Buck 1F 20
Stewkley Dean. Buck 1F 20
Stewley. Som 4B 8
Stewton. Linc 1L 37
Steyning. W Sus 4J 11
Steynton. Pemb 6F 14
Stibb. Corn 4B 6
Stibbard. Norf 7F 38
Stibb Cross. Devn 4D 6
Stibb Green. Wilts 7L 19
Stibbington. Cambs 2H 29
Stichill. Bord 6E 60
Sticker. Corn 6B 4
Stickford. Linc 3L 37
Sticklepath. Devn 6F 6
Sticklinch. Som 2D 8
Stickling Green. Essx 8A 30
Stickney. Linc 4L 37
Stiffkey. Norf 5F 38
Stifford's Bridge. Here 7F 26
Stileway. Som 1C 8
Stillingfleet. N Yor 3C 42
Stillington. N Yor 1C 42
Stillington. Stoc T 3A 48
Stilton. Cambs 3J 29
Stinchcombe. Glos 4F 18
Stinsford. Dors 6F 8
Stiperstones. Shrp 1B 26
Stirchley. Telf 1F 26
Stirchley. W Mid 3J 27
Stirling. Abers 1L 73
Stirling. Stir 116 (8A 66)
Stirton. N Yor 2H 41
Stisted. Essx 1D 22
Stitchcombe. Wilts 7L 19
Stithians. Corn 5L 3
Stittenham. High 6G 79
Stivichall. W Mid 4M 27
Stixwould. Linc 3J 37
Stoak. Ches W 2C 34
Stobo. Bord 6K 59
Stobo Castle. Bord 6K 59
Stoborough. Dors 7H 9
Stoborough Green. Dors 7H 9
Stobs Castle. Bord 1K 53
Stobswood. Nmbd 2F 54
Stock. Essx 4C 22
Stockbridge. Hants 2A 10
Stockbridge. W Yor 3J 41
Stockbury. Kent 7E 22
Stockcross. W Ber 7B 20
Stockdalewath. Cumb 7H 53
Stocker's Head. Kent 8F 22
Stockerston. Leics 2F 28
Stock Green. Worc 6H 27
Stocking. Here 8E 26
Stockingford. Warw 2M 27
Stocking Green. Essx 8B 30
Stocking Pelham. Herts 1A 22
Stockland. Devn 5M 7
Stockland Bristol. Som 1M 7
Stockleigh English. Devn 5H 7
Stockleigh Pomeroy. Devn 5H 7
Stockley. Wilts 7J 19
Stocklinch. Som 4B 8
Stockport. G Man 1G 35
The Stocks. Kent 3F 12
Stocksbridge. S Yor 8L 41
Stocksfield. Nmbd 5D 54
Stockstreet. Essx 1E 22
Stockton. Here 5D 26
Stockton. Norf 2K 31
Stockton. Shrp
nr. Bridgnorth 2F 26
nr. Chirbury 1A 26
Stockton. Telf 8F 34
Stockton. Warw 5B 28
Stockton. Wilts 2H 9
Stockton Brook. Staf 4H 35
Stockton Cross. Here 5D 26
Stockton Heath. Warr 1E 34
Stockton-on-Tees. Stoc T 4B 48
Stockton on Teme. Worc 5F 26
Stockton-on-the-Forest.
York 2D 42
Stockwell Heath. Staf 7J 35
Stock Wood. Worc 6J 27
Stockwood. Bris 7E 18
Stodmarsh. Kent 7J 23
Stody. Norf 6G 39
Stoer. High 1M 77
Stoford. Som 4D 8
Stoford. Wilts 2J 9
Stogumber. Som 2K 7
Stogursey. Som 1M 7
Stoke. Devn 3B 6
Stoke. Hants
nr. Andover 8B 20
nr. South Hayling 5E 10
Stoke. Medw 6E 22
Stoke. W Mid 4A 28
Stoke Abbott. Dors 5C 8
Stoke Albany. Nptn 3F 28
Stoke Ash. Suff 4H 31
Stoke Bardolph. Notts 5D 36
Stoke Bliss. Worc 5E 26
Stoke Bruerne. Nptn 7E 28
Stoke by Clare. Suff 7D 30
Stoke-by-Nayland. Suff 8F 30
Stoke Canon. Devn 6J 7
Stoke Charity. Hants 2B 10
Stoke Climsland. Corn 8C 6
Stoke Cross. Here 6E 26
Stoke D'Abernon. Surr 8J 21
Stoke Doyle. Nptn 3H 29
Stoke Dry. Rut 2F 28
Stoke Edith. Here 7E 26
Stoke Farthing. Wilts 3J 9
Stoke Ferry. Norf 1D 30
Stoke Fleming. Devn 7L 5
Stokeford. Dors 7G 9
Stoke Gabriel. Devn 6L 5
Stoke Gifford. S Glo 6E 18
Stoke Golding. Leics 2A 28
Stoke Goldington. Mil 7F 28
Stokeham. Notts 2E 36
Stoke Hammond. Buck 1F 20
Stoke Heath. Shrp 7E 34
Stoke Holy Cross. Norf 1J 31
Stokeinteignhead. Devn 8J 7
Stoke Lacy. Here 7E 26
Stoke Lyne. Oxon 1C 20
Stoke Mandeville. Buck 2F 20
Stokenchurch. Buck 4E 20
Stoke Newington. G Lon 5L 21
Stokenham. Devn 7L 5
Stoke on Tern. Shrp 7E 34
Stoke-on-Trent.
Stoke 116 (5G 35)
Stoke Orchard. Glos 1H 19
Stoke Pero. Som 1H 7
Stoke Poges. Buck 5G 21
Stoke Prior. Here 6D 26
Stoke Prior. Worc 5H 27
Stoke Rivers. Devn 2F 6
Stoke Rochford. Linc 7G 37
Stoke Row. Oxon 5D 20
Stoke St Gregory. Som 3B 8
Stoke St Mary. Som 3A 8
Stoke St Michael. Som 1E 8
Stoke St Milborough. Shrp 3D 26
Stokesay. Shrp 3C 26
Stokesby. Norf 8L 39
Stokesley. N Yor 5C 48
Stoke sub Hamdon. Som 4C 8
Stoke Talmage. Oxon 4D 20
Stoke Town. Stoke 116 (5G 35)
Stoke Trister. Som 3F 8
Stoke Wake. Dors 5F 8
Stolford. Som 1M 7
Stondon Massey. Essx 3B 22
Stone. Buck 2E 20
Stone. Glos 4E 18
Stone. Kent 6B 22
Stone. Som 2D 8
Stone. Staf 6H 35
Stone. Worc 4G 27
Stonea. Cambs 2A 30
Stoneacton. Shrp 2D 26
Stone Allerton. Som 8C 18
Ston Easton. Som 8E 18
Stonebridge. N Som 8B 18
Stonebridge. Surr 1J 11
Stone Bridge Corner. Pet 1K 29
Stonebroom. Derbs 4B 36
Stonebyres Holdings.
S Lan 5G 59
Stone Chair. W Yor 5K 41
Stone Cross. E Sus 5C 12
Stone Cross. Kent 2B 12
Stone-edge Batch. N Som 6C 18
Stoneferry. Hull 4H 43
Stonefield. Arg 4D 64
Stonefield. S Lan 4E 58
Stonegate. E Sus 3C 12
Stonegate. N Yor 5E 48
Stonegrave. N Yor 8D 48
Stonehall. Worc 7G 27
Stonehaugh. Nmbd 4A 54
Stonehaven. Abers 7H 73
Stone Heath. Staf 6H 35
Stone Hill. Kent 2G 13
Stone House. Cumb 7F 46
Stonehouse. Glos 3G 19
Stonehouse. Nmbd 6L 53
Stonehouse. S Lan 5F 58
Stone in Oxney. Kent 3F 12
Stoneleigh. Warw 4M 27
Stoneley Green. Ches E 4E 34
Stonely. Cambs 5J 29
Stonepits. Worc 6J 27
Stoner Hill. Hants 3E 10
Stonesby. Leics 7F 36
Stonesfield. Oxon 2A 20
Stones Green. Essx 1H 23
Stone Street. Kent 8B 22
Stone Street. Suff
nr. Boxford 8F 30
nr. Halesworth 3K 31
Stonethwaite. Cumb 4A 46
Stoneyburn. W Lot 3H 59
Stoney Cross. Hants 4L 9
Stoneyford. Devn 5K 7
Stoneygate. Leic 1D 28
Stoneyhills. Essx 4F 22
Stoneykirk. Dum 6F 50
Stoney Middleton. Derbs 2L 35
Stoney Stanton. Leics 2B 28
Stoney Stoke. Som 2F 8
Stoney Stratton. Som 2E 8
Stoney Stretton. Shrp 1B 26
Stoneywood. Aber 4H 73
Stonham Aspal. Suff 6H 31
Stonnall. Staf 1J 27
Stonor. Oxon 5E 20
Stonton Wyville. Leics 2E 28
Stonybreck. Shet 2M 89
Stony Cross. Devn 3E 6
Stony Cross. Here
nr. Great Malvern 7F 26
nr. Leominster 5D 26
Stonyford. Lis 5H 93
Stony Houghton. Derbs 3B 36
Stony Stratford. Mil 7E 28
Stoodleigh. Devn
nr. Barnstaple 2F 6
nr. Tiverton 4J 7
Stopham. W Sus 4H 11
Stopsley. Lutn 1J 21
Stoptide. Corn 4B 4
Storeton. Mers 1B 34
Stormontfield. Per 5E 66
Stornoway. W Isl 8H 83
Stornoway Airport. W Isl 8H 83
Storridge. Here 7F 26
Storrington. W Sus 4H 11
Storrs. Cumb 6B 46
Storth. Cumb 7C 46
Storwood. E Yor 3E 42
Stotfield. Mor 6B 80
Stotfold. C Beds 8K 29
Stottesdon. Shrp 3E 26
Stoughton. Leics 1D 28
Stoughton. Surr 8G 21
Stoughton. W Sus 4F 10
Stoul. High 6J 69
Stoulton. Worc 7H 27
Stourbridge. W Mid 3G 27
Stourpaine. Dors 5G 9
Stourport-on-Severn.
Worc 4G 27
Stour Provost. Dors 3F 8
Stour Row. Dors 3G 9
Stourton. Staf 3G 27
Stourton. Warw 8L 27
Stourton. W Yor 4M 41
Stourton. Wilts 2F 8
Stourton Caundle. Dors 4F 8
Stove. Orkn 6F 88
Stove. Shet 5E 90
Stoven. Suff 3L 31
Stow. Linc
nr. Billingborough 6H 37
nr. Gainsborough 1F 36
Stow. Bord 5B 60
Stow Bardolph. Norf 1C 30
Stow Bedon. Norf 2F 30
Stowbridge. Norf 1C 30
Stow cum Quy. Cambs 5B 30
Stowe. Glos 3D 18
Stowe. Shrp 4B 26
Stowe. Staf 8K 35
Stowe-by-Chartley. Staf 7J 35
Stowell. Som 3E 8
Stowey. Bath 8D 18
Stowford. Devn
nr. Colaton Raleigh 7K 7
nr. Combe Martin 1F 6
nr. Tavistock 7D 6
Stowlangtoft. Suff 5F 30
Stow Longa. Cambs 4J 29
Stow Maries. Essx 4E 22
Stowmarket. Suff 6G 31
Stow-on-the-Wold. Glos 1K 19
Stowting. Kent 1H 13
Stowupland. Suff 6G 31
Straad. Arg 3K 57
Strabane. Derr 4C 92
Strachan. Abers 6F 72
Stradbroke. Suff 4J 31
Stradishall. Suff 6D 30
Stradsett. Norf 1C 30
Stragglethorpe. Linc 4G 37
Stragglethorpe. Notts 6D 36
Straid. Ant 4H 93
Straid. ME Ant 4G 93
Straid. S Ayr 2G 51
Straight Soley. Wilts 6M 19
Straiton. Midl 3L 59
Straiton. S Ayr 1J 51
Straloch. Per 1D 66
Stramshall. Staf 6J 35
Strang. IOM 7C 44
Strangford. Here 1D 18
Strangford. New M 6J 93
Stranocum. Caus 2G 93
Stranraer. Dum 5F 50
Strata Florida. Cdgn 6G 25
Stratfield Mortimer. W Ber 7D 20
Stratfield Saye. Hants 7D 20
Stratfield Turgis. Hants 8D 20
Stratford. G Lon 5L 21
Stratford. Worc 8G 27
Stratford St Andrew. Suff 5K 31
Stratford St Mary. Suff 8G 31
Stratford sub Castle. Wilts 2K 9
Stratford Tony. Wilts 3J 9
Stratford-upon-Avon.
Warw 116 (6L 27)
Strath. High
nr. Gairloch 6J 77
nr. Wick 6D 86
Strathan. High
nr. Fort William 6L 69
nr. Lochinver 1A 78
nr. Tongue 5H 85
Strathan Skerray. High 5J 85
Strathaven. S Lan 5F 58
Strathblane. Stir 2D 58
Strathcanaird. High 3B 78
Strathcarron. High 1L 69
Strathcoil. Arg 4A 64
Strathdon. Abers 4C 72
Strathkinness. Fife 6H 67
Strathmashie House. High 6F 70
Strathmiglo. Fife 6F 66
Strathmore Lodge. High 7C 86
Strathpeffer. High 8E 78
Strathrannoch. High 6D 78
Strathtay. Per 2C 66
Strathvaich Lodge. High 6D 78
Strathwhillan. N Ayr 6K 57
Strathy. High
nr. Invergordon 6G 79
nr. Melvich 5L 85
Strathyre. Stir 6K 65
Stratton. Corn 5B 6
Stratton. Dors 6E 8
Stratton. Glos 3J 19
Stratton Audley. Oxon 1D 20
Stratton-on-the-Fosse.
Som 8E 18
Stratton St Margaret. Swin 5K 19
Stratton St Michael. Norf 2J 31
Stratton Strawless. Norf 7J 39
Stravithie. Fife 6J 67
Straw. M Ulst 4E 92
Stream. Som 2K 7
Streat. E Sus 4L 11
Streatham. G Lon 6L 21
Streatley. C Beds 1H 21
Streatley. W Ber 5C 20
Street. Corn 6B 6
Street. Lanc 2D 40
Street. N Yor 5E 48
Street. Som
nr. Chard 5B 8
Street. Som
nr. Glastonbury 2C 8
Street Ash. Som 4A 8
Street Dinas. Shrp 6B 34
Street End. Kent 8H 23
Street End. W Sus 6F 10
Streetgate. Tyne 6F 54
Streethay. Staf 8K 35
Streethouse. W Yor 5A 42
Streetlam. N Yor 6M 47
Street Lane. Derbs 5A 36
Streetly. W Mid 2J 27
Streetly End. Cambs 7C 30
Street on the Fosse. Som 2E 8
Strefford. Shrp 3C 26
Strelley. Notts 5C 36
Strensall. York 1D 42
Strensall Camp. York 2D 42
Stretcholt. Som 1A 8
Strete. Devn 7L 5
Stretford. G Man 8G 41
Stretford. Here 6D 26
Strethall. Essx 8A 30
Stretham. Cambs 4B 30
Stretton. Ches W 4C 34
Stretton. Derbs 3A 36
Stretton. Rut 8G 37
Stretton. Staf
nr. Brewood 8G 35
nr. Burton upon Trent 7L 35
Stretton. Warr 1E 34
Stretton en le Field. Leics 8M 35
Stretton Grandison. Here 7E 26
Stretton Heath. Shrp 8B 34
Stretton-on-Dunsmore.
Warw 4B 28
Stretton-on-Fosse. Warw 8L 27
Stretton Sugwas. Here 7C 26
Stretton under Fosse.
Warw 3B 28
Stretton Westwood. Shrp 2D 26
Strichen. Abers 8J 81
Strines. G Man 1H 35
Stringston. Som 1L 7
Strixton. Nptn 5G 29
Stroanfreggan. Dum 2M 51
Stroat. Glos 4D 18
Stromeferry. High 2K 69
Stromemore. High 2K 69
Stromness. Orkn 1D 86
Stronachie. Per 7D 66
Stronachlachar. Stir 6J 65
Stronchreggan. High 8A 70
Strone. Arg 1L 57
Strone. High
nr. Drumnadrochit 3F 70
nr. Kingussie 5H 71
Stronenaba. High 7C 70
Stronganess. Shet 3K 91
Stronmilchan. Arg 5F 64
Stronsay Airport. Orkn 7F 88
Strontian. High 1C 64
Strood. Kent 2E 12
Strood. Medw 7D 22
Strood Green. Surr 1K 11
Strood Green. W Sus
nr. Billingshurst 3H 11
nr. Horsham 2J 11
Strothers Dale. Nmbd 6C 54
Stroud. Glos 3G 19
Stroud. Hants 3E 10
Stroud Green. Essx 4E 22
Stroxton. Linc 6G 37
Struan. High 2E 68
Struan. Per 1B 66
Struanmore. High 2E 68
Strubby. Linc 1A 38
Strugg's Hill. Linc 6K 37
Strumpshaw. Norf 1K 31
Strutherhill. S Lan 4F 58
Struy. High 2E 70
Stryd. IOA 2B 32
Stryt-issa. Wrex 5A 34
Stuartfield. Abers 1J 73
Stubbington. Hants 5C 10
Stubbins. Lanc 6F 40
Stubble Green. Cumb 5K 45
Stubb's Cross. Kent 2F 12
Stubbs Green. Norf 2K 31
Stubhampton. Dors 4H 9
Stubton. Linc 5F 36
Stubwood. Staf 6J 35
Stuckton. Hants 4K 9
Studham. C Beds 2H 21
Studland. Dors 7J 9
Studley. Warw 5J 27
Studley. Wilts 6H 19
Studley Roger. N Yor 8L 47
Stuntney. Cambs 4B 30
Stunts Green. E Sus 4C 12
Sturbridge. Staf 6G 35
Sturgate. Linc 1F 36
Sturmer. Essx 7C 30
Sturminster Marshall. Dors 5H 9
Sturminster Newton. Dors 4F 8
Sturry. Kent 7H 23
Sturton. N Lin 7G 43
Sturton by Stow. Linc 1F 36
Sturton le Steeple. Notts 1E 36
Stuston. Suff 4H 31
Stutton. N Yor 3B 42
Stutton. Suff 8H 31
Styal. Ches E 1G 35
Stydd. Lanc 4E 40
Styrrup. Notts 8D 42
Suainebost. W Isl 5J 83
Suardail. W Isl 8H 83
Succoth. Abers 2D 72
Succoth. Arg 7G 65
Suckley. Worc 6F 26
Suckley Knowl. Worc 6F 26
Sudborough. Nptn 3G 29
Sudbourne. Suff 6L 31
Sudbrook. Linc 5G 37
Sudbrook. Mon 5D 18

Sudbrooke. Linc 2H 37
Sudbury. Derbs 6K 35
Sudbury. Suff 7E 30
Sudgrove. Glos 3H 19
Suffield. Norf 6J 39
Suffield. N Yor 6G 49
Sugnall. Staf 6F 34
Sugwas Pool. Here 7C 26
Suisnish. High 2G 69
Sulaisiadar. W Isl 8J 83
Sùlaisiadar Mòr. High 1F 68
Sulby. IOM 5C 44
Sulgrave. Nptn 7C 28
Sulham. W Ber 6D 20
Sulhamstead. W Ber 7D 20
Sullington. W Sus 4H 11
Sullom. Shet 6H 91
Sully. V Glam 8L 17
Sumburgh. Shet 7E 90
Sumburgh Airport. Shet 6D 90
Summer Bridge. N Yor 1L 41
Summercourt. Corn 6A 4
Summergangs. Hull 4J 43
Summer Hill. W Mid 2H 27
Summerhill. Aber 5J 73
Summerhill. Pemb 6H 15
Summerhouse. Darl 4L 47
Summersdale. W Sus 5F 10
Summerseat. G Man 6F 40
Summit. G Man 6H 41
Sunbury. Surr 7J 21
Sunderland. Cumb 8F 52
Sunderland. Lanc 2C 40
Sunderland. Tyne 116 (6G 55)
Sunderland Bridge. Dur 8F 54
Sundon Park. Lutn 1H 21
Sundridge. Kent 8A 22
Sunk Island. E Yor 6K 43
Sunningdale. Wind 7G 21
Sunninghill. Wind 7G 21
Sunningwell. Oxon 3B 20
Sunniside. Dur 8E 54
Sunniside. Tyne 6F 54
Sunny Bank. Cumb 6A 46
Sunny Hill. Derb 6M 35
Sunnyhurst. Bkbn 5E 40
Sunnylaw. Stir 8A 66
Sunnymead. Oxon 3C 20
Sunnyside. S Yor 8B 42
Sunnyside. W Sus 2L 11
Sunton. Wilts 8L 19
Surbiton. G Lon 7J 21
Surby. IOM 7B 44
Surfleet. Linc 7K 37
Surfleet Seas End. Linc 7K 37
Surlingham. Norf 1K 31
Surrex. Essx 1E 22
Sustead. Norf 6H 39
Susworth. Linc 7F 42
Sutcombe. Devn 4C 6
Suton. Norf 2G 31
Sutors of Cromarty. High 7J 79
Sutterby. Linc 2L 37
Sutterton. Linc 6K 37
Sutterton Dowdyke. Linc 6K 37
Sutton. Buck 6H 21
Sutton. Cambs 4M 29
Sutton. C Beds 7K 29
Sutton. E Sus 6A 12
Sutton. G Lon 7K 21
Sutton. Kent 1K 13
Sutton. Norf 7K 39
Sutton. Notts 6E 36
Sutton. Oxon 3B 20
Sutton. Pemb 5F 14
Sutton. Pet 2H 29
Sutton. Shrp
  nr. Bridgnorth 3F 26
  nr. Market Drayton 6E 34
  nr. Oswestry 7B 34
  nr. Shrewsbury 8D 34
Sutton. Som 2E 8
Sutton. S Yor 6C 42
Sutton. Staf 7F 34
Sutton. Suff 7K 31
Sutton. W Sus 4G 11
Sutton. Worc 5E 26
Sutton Abinger. Surr 1J 11
Sutton at Hone. Kent 6B 22
Sutton Bassett. Nptn 2E 28
Sutton Benger. Wilts 6H 19
Sutton Bingham. Som 4D 8
Sutton Bonington. Notts 7C 36
Sutton Bridge. Linc 7A 38
Sutton Cheney. Leics 1B 28
Sutton Coldfield, Royal. W Mid 2K 27
Sutton Corner. Linc 7M 37
Sutton Courtenay. Oxon 4C 20
Sutton Crosses. Linc 7M 37
Sutton cum Lound. Notts 1D 36
Sutton Gault. Cambs 4M 29
Sutton Grange. N Yor 8L 47
Sutton Green. Surr 8H 21
Sutton Howgrave. N Yor 8M 47
Sutton in Ashfield. Notts 4B 36
Sutton-in-Craven. N Yor 3J 41
Sutton Ings. Hull 4J 43
Sutton in the Elms. Leics 2C 28
Sutton Lane Ends. Ches E 2H 35
Sutton Leach. Mers 8D 40
Sutton Maddock. Shrp 1F 26
Sutton Mallet. Som 2B 8
Sutton Mandeville. Wilts 3H 9
Sutton Montis. Som 3E 8
Sutton on Hull. Hull 4J 43
Sutton on Sea. Linc 1B 38
Sutton-on-the-Forest. N Yor 1C 42
Sutton on the Hill. Derbs 6L 35
Sutton on Trent. Notts 3E 36
Sutton Poyntz. Dors 7F 8
Sutton St Edmund. Linc 8L 37
Sutton St Edmund's Common. Linc 1L 29
Sutton St James. Linc 8L 37
Sutton St Michael. Here 7D 26
Sutton St Nicholas. Here 7D 26
Sutton Scarsdale. Derbs 3B 36
Sutton Scotney. Hants 2B 10
Sutton-under-Brailes. Warw 8M 27
Sutton-under-Whitestonecliffe. N Yor 7B 48
Sutton upon Derwent. E Yor 3E 42
Sutton Valence. Kent 1E 12
Sutton Veny. Wilts 1H 9
Sutton Waldron. Dors 4G 9
Sutton Weaver. Ches W 2D 34
Swaby. Linc 2L 37
Swadlincote. Derbs 8L 35
Swaffham. Norf 1E 30
Swaffham Bulbeck. Cambs 5B 30
Swaffham Prior. Cambs 5B 30
Swafield. Norf 6J 39
Swainby. N Yor 5B 48
Swainshill. Here 7C 26
Swainsthorpe. Norf 1J 31
Swainswick. Bath 7F 18
Swalcliffe. Oxon 8A 28
Swalecliffe. Kent 7H 23
Swallow. Linc 7J 43
Swallow Beck. Linc 3G 37
Swallowcliffe. Wilts 3H 9
Swallowfield. Wok 7E 20
Swallownest. S Yor 1B 36
Swampton. Hants 8B 20
Swanage. Dors 8J 9
Swanbister. Orkn 1E 86
Swanbourne. Buck 1F 20
Swanbridge. V Glam 8L 17
Swan Green. Ches W 2F 34
Swanland. E Yor 5G 43
Swanley. Kent 7B 22
Swanmore. Hants 4C 10
Swannington. Leics 8B 36
Swannington. Norf 8H 39
Swanpool. Linc 3G 37
Swanscombe. Kent 6C 22
Swansea. Swan 117 (5F 16)
Swan Street. Essx 1E 22
Swanton Abbott. Norf 7J 39
Swanton Morley. Norf 8G 39
Swanton Novers. Norf 6G 39
Swanton Street. Kent 8E 22
Swanwick. Derbs 4B 36
Swanwick. Hants 5C 10
Swanwick Green. Ches E 5D 34
Swarby. Linc 5H 37
Swardeston. Norf 1J 31
Swarister. Shet 5K 91
Swarkestone. Derbs 7A 36
Swarland. Nmbd 1E 54
Swarraton. Hants 2C 10
Swartha. W Yor 3J 41
Swarthmoor. Cumb 8A 46
Swaton. Linc 6J 37
Swatragh. M Ulst 3F 93
Swavesey. Cambs 5L 29
Sway. Hants 6L 9
Swayfield. Linc 7G 37
Swaythling. Sotn 4B 10
Sweet Green. Worc 5E 26
Sweetham. Devn 6H 7
Sweetholme. Cumb 4D 46
Sweets. Corn 6A 6
Sweetshouse. Corn 5C 4
Swefling. Suff 5K 31
Swell. Som 3B 8
Swepstone. Leics 8A 36
Swerford. Oxon 8A 28
Swettenham. Ches E 3G 35
Swetton. N Yor 8K 47
Swffryd. Blae 5M 17
Swiftsden. E Sus 3D 12
Swilland. Suff 6H 31
Swillington. W Yor 4A 42
Swimbridge. Devn 3F 6
Swimbridge Newland. Devn 2F 6
Swinbrook. Oxon 2L 19
Swincliffe. N Yor 2L 41
Swincliffe. W Yor 5L 41
Swinderby. Linc 3F 36
Swindon. Glos 1H 19
Swindon. Nmbd 2C 54
Swindon. Staf 2G 27
Swindon. Swin 117 (5K 19)
Swine. E Yor 4J 43
Swinefleet. E Yor 5E 42
Swineford. S Glo 7E 18
Swineshead. Bed 5H 29
Swineshead. Linc 5K 37
Swineshead Bridge. Linc 5K 37
Swiney. High 8D 86
Swinford. Leics 4C 28
Swinford. Oxon 3B 20
Swingate. Notts 5C 36
Swingbrow. Cambs 3L 29
Swingfield Minnis. Kent 1J 13
Swingfield Street. Kent 1J 13
Swingleton Green. Suff 7F 30
Swinhill. S Lan 5F 58
Swinhoe. Nmbd 7K 61
Swinhope. Linc 8K 43
Swinister. Shet 5H 91
Swinithwaite. N Yor 7J 47
Swinmore Common. Here 7E 26
Swinscoe. Staf 5K 35
Swinside Hall. Bord 8E 60
Swinstead. Linc 7H 37
Swinton. G Man 7F 40
Swinton. N Yor
  nr. Malton 8E 48
  nr. Masham 8L 47
Swinton. Bord 5F 60
Swinton. S Yor 8B 42
Swithland. Leics 8C 36
Swordale. High 7F 78
Swordly. High 5K 85
Sworton Heath. Ches E 1E 34
Swyddffynnon. Cdgn 6F 24
Swynnerton. Staf 6G 35
Swyre. Dors 7D 8
Sycharth. Powy 8M 33
Sychdyn. Flin 4M 33
Sychnant. Powy 5J 25
Sychtyn. Powy 2J 25
Syde. Glos 2H 19
Sydenham. G Lon 6L 21
Sydenham. Oxon 3E 20
Sydenham. Som 2B 8
Sydenham Damerel. Devn 8D 6
Syderstone. Norf 6E 38
Sydling St Nicholas. Dors 6E 8
Sydmonton. Hants 8B 20
Sydney. Ches E 4F 34
Syerston. Notts 5E 36
Syke. G Man 6G 41
Sykehouse. S Yor 6D 42
Sykes. Lanc 2E 40
Syleham. Suff 4J 31
Sylen. Carm 6M 15
Sylfaen. Powy 2L 25
Symbister. Shet 1F 90
Symington. S Ayr 6B 58
Symington. S Lan 6H 59
Symondsbury. Dors 6C 8
Symonds Yat. Here 2D 18
Synod Inn. Cdgn 1L 15
Syre. High 7J 85
Syreford. Glos 1J 19
Syresham. Nptn 7D 28
Syston. Leics 8D 36
Syston. Linc 5G 37
Sytchampton. Worc 5G 27
Sywell. Nptn 5F 28

T

Tabost. W Isl
  nr. Cearsiadar 2E 76
  nr. Suainebost 5J 83
Tachbrook Mallory. Warw 5M 27
Tackley. Oxon 1B 20
Tacleit. W Isl 8E 82
Tacolneston. Norf 2H 31
Tadcaster. N Yor 3B 42
Taddington. Derbs 2K 35
Taddington. Glos 8J 27
Taddiport. Devn 4D 6
Tadley. Hants 7D 20
Tadlow. Cambs 7K 29
Tadmarton. Oxon 8A 28
Tadwick. Bath 6F 18
Tadworth. Surr 8K 21
Tafarnaubach. Blae 3L 17
Tafarn-y-bwlch. Pemb 3G 15
Tafarn-y-Gelyn. Den 4L 33
Taff's Well. Rhon 6L 17
Tafolwern. Powy 2H 25
Tai-bach. Powy 8L 33
Taibach. Neat 6G 17
Taigh a Ghearraidh. W Isl 6J 75
Taigh Bhuirgh. W Isl 4B 76
Tain. High
  nr. Invergordon 5H 79
  nr. Thurso 5D 86
Tai-Nant. Wrex 5A 34
Tai'n Lon. Gwyn 5D 32
Tairbeart. W Isl 4C 76
Tairgwaith. Neat 3G 17
Takeley. Essx 1B 22
Takeley Street. Essx 1B 22
Talachddu. Powy 1K 17
Talacre. Flin 2L 33
Talardd. Gwyn 8H 33
Talaton. Devn 6K 7
Talbenny. Pemb 5E 14
Talbot Green. Rhon 6K 17
Taleford. Devn 6K 7
Talerddig. Powy 2J 25
Talgarreg. Cdgn 1L 15
Talgarth. Powy 1L 17
Talisker. High 2E 68
Talke. Staf 4G 35
Talkin. Cumb 6K 53
Talladale. High 6L 77
Talla Linnfoots. Bord 7K 59
Tallaminnock. S Ayr 2J 51
Tallarn Green. Wrex 5C 34
Tallentire. Cumb 8F 52
Talley. Carm 1F 16
Tallington. Linc 1H 29
Talmine. High 5H 85
Talog. Carm 4K 15
Talsarn. Carm 2G 17
Talsarn. Cdgn 1M 15
Talsarnau. Gwyn 7F 32
Talskiddy. Corn 5B 4
Talwrn. IOA 3D 32
Talwrn. Wrex 5A 34
Tal-y-Bont. Cnwy 4G 33
Tal-y-bont. Cdgn 4F 24
Tal-y-bont. Gwyn
  nr. Bangor 3F 32
  nr. Barmouth 8E 32
Talybont-on-Usk. Powy 2L 17
Tal-y-cafn. Cnwy 3G 33
Tal-y-coed. Mon 2C 18
Tal-y-llyn. Gwyn 2G 25
Talyllyn. Powy 2L 17
Talysarn. Gwyn 5D 32
Tal-y-waenydd. Gwyn 6F 32
Talywain. Torf 3A 18
Tal-y-Wern. Powy 2H 25
Tamerton Foliot. Plym 5G 5
Tamlaght. Ferm 6C 92
Tamlaght O'Crilly. M Ulst 3F 93
Tamnamore. M Ulst 5F 93
Tamworth. Staf 1L 27
Tamworth Green. Linc 5L 37
Tandlehill. Ren 3C 58
Tandragee. Arm 6G 93
Tandridge. Surr 8L 21
Tanerdy. Carm 4L 15
Tanfield. Dur 6E 54
Tanfield Lea. Dur 6E 54
Tangasdal. W Isl 5C 74
Tang Hall. York 2D 42
Tangiers. Pemb 5F 14
Tangley. Hants 8M 19
Tangmere. W Sus 5G 11
Tangwick. Shet 6G 91
Tankerness. Orkn 1G 87
Tankersley. S Yor 8M 41
Tankerton. Kent 7H 23
Tan-lan. Cnwy 4G 33
Tan-lan. Gwyn 6F 32
Tannach. High 7E 86
Tannadice. Ang 2H 67
Tanner's Green. Worc 4J 27
Tannington. Suff 5J 31
Tannochside. N Lan 3F 58
Tan Office Green. Suff 6D 30
Tansley. Derbs 4M 35
Tansley Knoll. Derbs 3M 35
Tansor. Nptn 2H 29
Tantobie. Dur 6E 54
Tanton. N Yor 4C 48
Tanvats. Linc 3J 37
Tanworth-in-Arden. Warw 4K 27
Tan-y-bwlch. Gwyn 6F 32
Tan-y-fron. Cnwy 4J 33
Tanyfron. Wrex 4A 34
Tanygrisiau. Gwyn 6F 32
Tan-y-groes. Cdgn 2J 15
Tan-y-pistyll. Powy 8K 33
Tan-yr-allt. Den 2K 33
Taobh a Chaolais. W Isl 4D 74
Taobh a Deas Loch Aineort. W Isl 3D 74
Taobh a Ghlinne. W Isl 2E 76
Taobh a Tuath Loch Aineort. W Isl 3D 74
Taplow. Buck 5G 21
Tapton. Derbs 2A 36
Tarbert. Arg
  on Jura 1F 56
  on Kintyre 3H 57
Tarbert. W Isl 4C 76
Tarbet. Arg 7H 65
Tarbet. High
  nr. Mallaig 6J 69
  nr. Scourie 7D 84
Tarbock Green. Mers 1C 34
Tarbolton. S Ayr 7C 58
Tarbrax. S Lan 4J 59
Tardebigge. Worc 5H 27
Tarfside. Ang 8D 72
Tarland. Abers 5D 72
Tarleton. Lanc 5C 40
Tarlogie. High 5H 79
Tarlscough. Lanc 6C 40
Tarlton. Glos 4H 19
Tarnbrook. Lanc 2D 40
Tarnock. Som 8B 18
Tarns. Cumb 7F 52
Tarporley. Ches W 3D 34
Tarpots. Essx 5D 22
Tarr. Som 2L 7
Tarrant Crawford. Dors 5H 9
Tarrant Gunville. Dors 4H 9
Tarrant Hinton. Dors 4H 9
Tarrant Keyneston. Dors 5H 9
Tarrant Launceston. Dors 5H 9
Tarrant Monkton. Dors 5H 9
Tarrant Rawston. Dors 5H 9
Tarrant Rushton. Dors 5H 9
Tarrel. High 5J 79
Tarring Neville. E Sus 5M 11
Tarrington. Here 7E 26
Tarsappie. Per 5E 66
Tarscabhaig. High 5G 69
Tarskavaig. High 5G 69
Tarves. Abers 2H 73
Tarvie. High 8E 78
Tarvin. Ches W 3C 34
Tasburgh. Norf 2J 31
Tasley. Shrp 2E 26
Tassagh. Arm 7F 93
Taston. Oxon 1A 20
Tatenhill. Staf 7L 35
Tathall End. Mil 7F 28
Tatham. Lanc 1E 40
Tathwell. Linc 1L 37
Tatling End. Buck 5H 21
Tatsfield. Surr 8M 21
Tattenhall. Ches W 4C 34
Tatterford. Norf 7E 38
Tattersett. Norf 6E 38
Tattershall. Linc 4K 37
Tattershall Bridge. Linc 4J 37
Tattershall Thorpe. Linc 4K 37
Tattingstone. Suff 8H 31
Tattingstone White Horse. Suff 8H 31
Tattle Bank. Warw 5K 27
Tatworth. Som 5B 8
Taunton. Som 117 (3M 7)
Taverham. Norf 8H 39
Taverners Green. Essx 2B 22
Tavernspite. Pemb 5H 15
Tavistock. Devn 8D 6
Tavool House. Arg 5K 63
Taw Green. Devn 6F 6
Tawstock. Devn 3E 6
Taxal. Derbs 1J 35
Tayinloan. Arg 5F 56
Taynish. Arg 1G 57
Taynton. Glos 1F 18
Taynton. Oxon 2L 19
Taynuilt. Arg 4E 64
Tayport. Fife 5H 67
Tay Road Bridge. D'dee 5H 67
Tayvallich. Arg 1G 57
Tealby. Linc 8J 43
Tealing. Ang 4H 67
Teams. Tyne 5F 54
Teangue. High 5H 69
Teanna Mhachair. W Isl 7J 75
Tebay. Cumb 5E 46
Tebworth. C Beds 1G 21
Tedburn St Mary. Devn 6H 7
Teddington. Glos 8H 27
Teddington. G Lon 6J 21
Tedsmore. Shrp 7B 34
Tedstone Delamere. Here 6E 26
Tedstone Wafer. Here 6E 26
Teemore. Ferm 7C 92
Teesport. Red C 3C 48
Teesside. Stoc T 3C 48
Teeton. Nptn 4D 28
Teffont Evias. Wilts 2H 9
Teffont Magna. Wilts 2H 9
Tegryn. Pemb 3J 15
Teigh. Rut 8F 36
Teigncombe. Devn 7F 6
Teigngrace. Devn 8H 7
Teignmouth. Devn 8J 7
Telford. Telf 8E 34
Telham. E Sus 4D 12
Tellisford. Som 8G 19
Telscombe. E Sus 5M 11
Telscombe Cliffs. E Sus 5L 11
Tempar. Per 2L 65
Templand. Dum 3E 52
Temple. Corn 4D 4
Temple. Glas 3D 58
Temple. Midl 4M 59
Temple Balsall. W Mid 4L 27
Temple Bar. Carm 3E 16
Temple Bar. Cdgn 1M 15
Temple Cloud. Bath 8E 18
Templecombe. Som 3F 8
Temple Ewell. Kent 1J 13
Temple Grafton. Warw 6K 27
Temple Guiting. Glos 1J 19
Templehall. Fife 8F 66
Temple Hirst. N Yor 5D 42
Temple Normanton. Derbs 3B 36
Templepatrick. Ant 4H 93
Temple Sowerby. Cumb 3E 46
Templeton. Devn 4H 7
Templeton. Pemb 5H 15
Templeton. W Ber 7A 20
Templetown. Dur 7E 54
Tempo. Ferm 6C 92
Tempsford. C Beds 6J 29
Tenandry. Per 1C 66
Tenbury Wells. Worc 5D 26
Tenby. Pemb 6H 15
Tendring. Essx 1H 23
Tendring Green. Essx 1H 23
Tenga. Arg 3L 63
Ten Mile Bank. Norf 2C 30
Tenterden. Kent 2E 12
Terfyn. Cnwy 3J 33
Terhill. Som 2L 7
Terling. Essx 2D 22
Termon Rock. Ferm 5E 92
Ternhill. Shrp 6E 34
Terregles. Dum 4D 52
Terrick. Buck 3F 20
Terrington. N Yor 8D 48
Terrington St Clement. Norf 7B 38
Terrington St John. Norf 8B 38
Terry's Green. Warw 4K 27
Teston. Kent 8D 22
Testwood. Hants 4M 9
Tetbury. Glos 4G 19
Tetbury Upton. Glos 4G 19
Tetchill. Shrp 6B 34
Tetcott. Devn 6C 6
Tetford. Linc 2L 37
Tetney. Linc 7L 43
Tetney Lock. Linc 7L 43
Tetsworth. Oxon 3D 20
Tettenhall. W Mid 1G 27
Teversal. Notts 3B 36
Teversham. Cambs 6A 30
Teviothead. Bord 1J 53
Tewel. Abers 7H 73
Tewin. Herts 2K 21
Tewkesbury. Glos 8G 27
Teynham. Kent 7F 22
Teynham Street. Kent 7F 22
Thackthwaite. Cumb 3C 46
Thakeham. W Sus 4J 11
Thame. Oxon 3E 20
Thames Ditton. Surr 7J 21
Thames Haven. Thur 5D 22
Thamesmead. G Lon 5A 22
Thamesport. Medw 6E 22
Thanington Without. Kent 8H 23
Thankerton. S Lan 6H 59
Tharston. Norf 2H 31
Thatcham. W Ber 7C 20
Thatto Heath. Mers 8D 40
Thaxted. Essx 8C 30
Theakston. N Yor 7M 47
Thealby. N Lin 6F 42
Theale. Som 1C 8
Theale. W Ber 6D 20
Thearne. E Yor 4H 43
Theberton. Suff 5L 31
Theddingworth. Leics 3D 28
Theddlethorpe All Saints. Linc 1A 38
Theddlethorpe St Helen. Linc 1A 38
Thelbridge Barton. Devn 4G 7
Thelnetham. Suff 4G 31
Thelveton. Norf 3H 31
Thelwall. Warr 1E 34
Themelthorpe. Norf 7G 39
Thenford. Nptn 7C 28
Therfield. Herts 8L 29
Thetford. Linc 8J 37
Thetford. Norf 3E 30
Thethwaite. Cumb 7H 53
Theydon Bois. Essx 4M 21
Thick Hollins. W Yor 6K 41
Thickwood. Wilts 6G 19
Thimbleby. Linc 3K 37
Thimbleby. N Yor 6B 48
Thingwall. Mers 1A 34
Thirlby. N Yor 7B 48
Thirlestane. Bord 5C 60
Thirn. N Yor 7L 47
Thirsk. N Yor 7B 48
Thirtleby. E Yor 4J 43
Thistleton. Lanc 4C 40
Thistleton. Rut 8G 37
Thistley Green. Suff 4C 30
Thixendale. N Yor 1F 42
Thockrington. Nmbd 4C 54
Tholomas Drove. Cambs 1M 29
Tholthorpe. N Yor 1B 42
Thomas Chapel. Pemb 6H 15
Thomas Close. Cumb 7J 53
Thomastown. Abers 1G 73
Thomastown. Rhon 6K 17
Thompson. Norf 2F 30
Thomshill. Mor 8B 80
Thong. Kent 6C 22
Thongsbridge. W Yor 7K 41
Thoralby. N Yor 7J 47
Thoresby. Notts 2D 36
Thoresway. Linc 8J 43
Thorganby. Linc 8K 43
Thorganby. N Yor 3D 42
Thorgill. N Yor 6E 48
Thorington. Suff 4L 31
Thorington Street. Suff 8G 31
Thorlby. N Yor 2H 41
Thorley. Herts 2A 22
Thorley Street. Herts 2A 22
Thorley Street. IOW 7A 10
Thormanby. N Yor 8B 48
Thorn. Powy 5A 26
Thornaby-on-Tees. Stoc T 4B 48
Thornage. Norf 6G 39
Thornborough. Buck 8E 28
Thornborough. N Yor 8L 47
Thornbury. Devn 5D 6
Thornbury. Here 6E 26
Thornbury. S Glo 4E 18
Thornby. Cumb 6G 53
Thornby. Nptn 4D 28
Thorncliffe. Staf 4J 35
Thorncombe. Dors 5B 8
Thorncombe Street. Surr 1G 11
Thorncote Green. C Beds 7J 29
Thorndon. Suff 5H 31
Thorndon Cross. Devn 6E 6
Thorne. S Yor 6D 42
Thornehillhead. Devn 4D 6
Thorner. W Yor 3A 42
Thorne St Margaret. Som 3K 7
Thorney. Notts 2F 36
Thorney. Pet 1K 29
Thorney. Som 3C 8
Thorney Hill. Hants 6K 9
Thorney Toll. Cambs 1L 29
Thornfalcon. Som 3A 8
Thornford. Dors 4E 8
Thorngrafton. Nmbd 5A 54
Thorngrove. Som 2B 8
Thorngumbald. E Yor 5K 43
Thornham. Norf 5D 38
Thornham Magna. Suff 4H 31
Thornham Parva. Suff 4H 31
Thornhaugh. Pet 1H 29
Thornhill. Cphy 6L 17
Thornhill. Cumb 4K 45
Thornhill. Derbs 1K 35
Thornhill. Dum 2C 52
Thornhill. Sotn 4B 10
Thornhill. Stir 8L 65
Thornhill. W Yor 6L 41
Thornhill Lees. W Yor 6L 41
Thornhills. W Yor 5K 41
Thornholme. E Yor 1J 43
Thornicombe. Dors 5G 9
Thornington. Nmbd 6F 60
Thornley. Dur
  nr. Durham 8G 55
  nr. Tow Law 8E 54
Thornley Gate. Nmbd 6B 54
Thornliebank. E Ren 3D 58
Thornroan. Abers 2H 73
Thorns. Suff 6D 30
Thornsett. Derbs 1J 35
Thornthwaite. Cumb 2M 45
Thornthwaite. N Yor 2K 41
Thornton. Ang 3G 67
Thornton. Buck 8E 28
Thornton. E Yor 3E 42
Thornton. Fife 8F 66
Thornton. Lanc 3B 40
Thornton. Leics 1B 28
Thornton. Linc 3K 37
Thornton. Mers 7B 40
Thornton. Midd 4B 48
Thornton. Nmbd 5G 61
Thornton. Pemb 6F 14
Thornton. W Yor 4J 41
Thornton Curtis. N Lin 6H 43
Thorntonhall. S Lan 4D 58
Thornton Heath. G Lon 7L 21
Thornton Hough. Mers 1B 34
Thornton-in-Craven. N Yor 3H 41
Thornton in Lonsdale. N Yor 8E 46
Thornton-le-Beans. N Yor 6A 48
Thornton-le-Clay. N Yor 1D 42
Thornton-le-Dale. N Yor 7F 48
Thornton le Moor. Linc 8H 43
Thornton-le-Moor. N Yor 7A 48
Thornton-le-Moors. Ches W 2C 34
Thornton-le-Street. N Yor 7B 48
Thorntonloch. E Lot 2E 60
Thornton Rust. N Yor 7H 47
Thornton Steward. N Yor 7K 47
Thornton Watlass. N Yor 7L 47
Thornwood Common. Essx 3A 22
Thornythwaite. Cumb 3B 46
Thoroton. Notts 5E 36
Thorp Arch. W Yor 3B 42
Thorpe. Derbs 4K 35
Thorpe. E Yor 3G 43
Thorpe. Linc 1A 38
Thorpe. Norf 2L 31
Thorpe. N Yor 1J 41
Thorpe. Notts 5E 36
Thorpe. Surr 7H 21
Thorpe Abbotts. Norf 4H 31
Thorpe Acre. Leics 7C 36
Thorpe Arnold. Leics 7E 36
Thorpe Audlin. W Yor 6B 42
Thorpe Bassett. N Yor 8F 48
Thorpe Bay. S'end 5F 22
Thorpe by Water. Rut 2F 28
Thorpe Common. S Yor 8A 42
Thorpe Common. Suff 8J 31
Thorpe Constantine. Staf 1L 27
Thorpe End. Norf 8J 39
Thorpe Fendike. Linc 3A 38
Thorpe Green. Essx 1H 23
Thorpe Green. Suff 6F 30
Thorpe Hall. N Yor 8C 48
Thorpe Hamlet. Norf 1J 31
Thorpe Hesley. S Yor 8A 42
Thorpe in Balne. S Yor 6C 42
Thorpe in the Fallows. Linc 1G 37
Thorpe Langton. Leics 2E 28
Thorpe Larches. Dur 3A 48
Thorpe Latimer. Linc 5J 37
Thorpe-le-Soken. Essx 1H 23
Thorpe le Street. E Yor 3F 42
Thorpe Malsor. Nptn 4F 28
Thorpe Mandeville. Nptn 7C 28
Thorpe Market. Norf 6J 39
Thorpe Marriott. Norf 8H 39
Thorpe Morieux. Suff 6F 30
Thorpeness. Suff 6L 31
Thorpe on the Hill. Linc 3G 37
Thorpe on the Hill. W Yor 5M 41
Thorpe St Andrew. Norf 1J 31
Thorpe St Peter. Linc 3A 38
Thorpe Salvin. S Yor 1C 36
Thorpe Satchville. Leics 8E 36
Thorpe Thewles. Stoc T 3A 48
Thorpe Tilney. Linc 4J 37
Thorpe Underwood. N Yor 2B 42
Thorpe Waterville. Nptn 3H 29
Thorpe Willoughby. N Yor 4C 42
Thorpland. Norf 1C 30
Thorrington. Essx 1G 23
Thorverton. Devn 5J 7
Thrandeston. Suff 4H 31
Thrapston. Nptn 4G 29
Thrashbush. N Lan 3F 58
Threapland. Cumb 8F 52
Threapland. N Yor 1H 41
Threapwood. Ches W 5C 34
Threapwood. Staf 5J 35
Three Ashes. Here 1D 18
Three Bridges. Linc 1M 37
Three Bridges. W Sus 2K 11
Three Burrows. Corn 4L 3
Three Chimneys. Kent 2E 12
Three Cocks. Powy 1L 17
Three Crosses. Swan 5E 16
Three Cups Corner. E Sus 3C 12
Threehammer Common. Norf 7K 39
Three Holes. Norf 1B 30
Threekingham. Linc 6H 37
Three Leg Cross. E Sus 2C 12
Three Legged Cross. Dors 5J 9
Three Mile Cross. Wok 7E 20
Threemilestone. Corn 4L 3
Three Oaks. E Sus 4E 12
Threlkeld. Cumb 3B 46
Threshfield. N Yor 1H 41
Thrigby. Norf 8L 39
Thringarth. Dur 3H 47
Thringstone. Leics 8B 36
Thrintoft. N Yor 6M 47
Thriplow. Cambs 7M 29
Throckenholt. Linc 1L 29
Throcking. Herts 8L 29
Throckley. Tyne 5E 54
Throckmorton. Worc 7H 27
Throop. Bour 6K 9
Throphill. Nmbd 3E 54
Thropton. Nmbd 1D 54
Throsk. Stir 8B 66
Througham. Glos 3H 19
Throughgate. Dum 3C 52
Throwleigh. Devn 6F 6
Throwley. Kent 8F 22
Throwley Forstal. Kent 8F 22
Throxenby. N Yor 7H 49
Thrumpton. Notts 6C 36
Thrumster. High 7E 86
Thrunton. Nmbd 8H 61
Thrupp. Glos 3G 19
Thrupp. Oxon 2B 20
Thrushelton. Devn 7D 6
Thrushgill. Lanc 1E 40
Thrussington. Leics 8D 36
Thruxton. Hants 1L 9
Thruxton. Here 8C 26
Thrybergh. S Yor 8B 42
Thulston. Derbs 6B 36
Thundergay. N Ayr 5H 57
Thundersley. Essx 5D 22
Thundridge. Herts 2L 21
Thurcaston. Leics 8C 36
Thurcroft. S Yor 1B 36
Thurdon. Corn 4B 6
Thurgarton. Norf 6H 39
Thurgarton. Notts 5D 36
Thurgoland. S Yor 7L 41
Thurlaston. Leics 2C 28
Thurlaston. Warw 4B 28
Thurlbear. Som 3A 8
Thurlby. Linc
  nr. Alford 2A 38
  nr. Baston 8J 37
  nr. Lincoln 3G 37
Thurleigh. Bed 6H 29
Thurlestone. Devn 7J 5
Thurloxton. Som 2A 8
Thurlstone. S Yor 7L 41
Thurlton. Norf 2L 31
Thurmaston. Leics 1D 28
Thurnby. Leics 1D 28
Thurne. Norf 8L 39
Thurnham. Kent 8E 22
Thurning. Norf 7G 39
Thurning. Nptn 3H 29
Thurnscoe. S Yor 7B 42
Thursby. Cumb 6H 53
Thursford. Norf 6F 38
Thursford Green. Norf 6F 38
Thursley. Surr 2G 11
Thurso. High 5C 86
Thurso East. High 5C 86
Thurstaston. Mers 2M 33
Thurston. Suff 5F 30
Thurston End. Suff 6D 30
Thurstonfield. Cumb 6H 53
Thurstonland. W Yor 6K 41
Thurton. Norf 1K 31
Thurvaston. Derbs
  nr. Ashbourne 6K 35
  nr. Derby 6L 35
Thuxton. Norf 1G 31
Thwaite. Dur 4J 47
Thwaite. N Yor 6G 47
Thwaite. Suff 5H 31
Thwaite Head. Cumb 6B 46
Thwaites. W Yor 3J 41
Thwaite St Mary. Norf 2K 31
Thwing. E Yor 8H 49
Tibbermore. Per 5D 66
Tibberton. Glos 1F 18
Tibberton. Telf 7E 34
Tibberton. Worc 6H 27
Tibenham. Norf 3H 31
Tibshelf. Derbs 3B 36
Tibthorpe. E Yor 2G 43
Ticehurst. E Sus 2C 12
Tichborne. Hants 2C 10
Tickencote. Rut 1G 29
Tickenham. N Som 6C 18
Tickhill. S Yor 8C 42
Ticklerton. Shrp 2C 26
Ticknall. Derbs 7A 36
Tickton. E Yor 3H 43
Tidbury Green. W Mid 4K 27
Tidcombe. Wilts 8L 19
Tiddington. Oxon 3D 20
Tiddington. Warw 6L 27
Tiddleywink. Wilts 6G 19
Tidebrook. E Sus 3C 12
Tideford. Corn 6F 4
Tideford Cross. Corn 5F 4
Tidenham. Glos 4D 18
Tideswell. Derbs 2K 35
Tidmarsh. W Ber 6D 20
Tidmington. Warw 8L 27
Tidpit. Hants 4J 9
Tidworth. Wilts 1L 9
Tidworth Camp. Wilts 1L 9
Tiers Cross. Pemb 5F 14
Tiffield. Nptn 6D 28
Tifty. Abers 1G 73
Tigerton. Ang 1J 67
Tighnabruaich. Arg 2J 57
Tigley. Devn 5K 5
Tilbrook. Cambs 5H 29
Tilbury. Thur 6C 22
Tilbury Green. Essx 7D 30
Tilbury Juxta Clare. Essx 7D 30
Tile Hill. W Mid 4L 27
Tilehurst. Read 6D 20
Tilford. Surr 1F 10
Tilgate Forest Row. W Sus 2K 11
Tillathrowie. Abers 2D 72
Tillers Green. Glos 8E 26
Tillery. Abers 3J 73
Tilley. Shrp 7D 34
Tillicoultry. Clac 8C 66
Tillingham. Essx 3F 22
Tillington. Here 7C 26
Tillington. W Sus 3G 11
Tillington Common. Here 7C 26
Tillybirloch. Abers 5F 72
Tillyfourie. Abers 4F 72
Tilmanstone. Kent 8K 23
Tilney All Saints. Norf 8B 38
Tilney Fen End. Norf 8B 38
Tilney High End. Norf 8B 38
Tilney St Lawrence. Norf 8B 38
Tilshead. Wilts 1J 9
Tilstock. Shrp 6D 34
Tilston. Ches W 4C 34
Tilstone Fearnall. Ches W 3D 34
Tilsworth. C Beds 1G 21
Tilton on the Hill. Leics 1E 28
Tiltups End. Glos 4G 19
Timberland. Linc 4J 37
Timbersbrook. Ches E 3G 35
Timberscombe. Som 1J 7
Timble. N Yor 2K 41
Timperley. G Man 1F 34
Timsbury. Bath 8E 18
Timsbury. Hants 3M 9
Timsgearraidh. W Isl 8D 82
Timworth Green. Suff 5E 30
Tincleton. Dors 6F 8
Tindale. Cumb 6L 53
Tindale Crescent. Dur 3L 47
Tingewick. Buck 8D 28
Tingrith. C Beds 8H 29
Tingwall. Orkn 7D 88
Tinhay. Devn 7C 6
Tinshill. W Yor 4L 41
Tinsley. S Yor 8B 42
Tinsley Green. W Sus 2K 11
Tintagel. Corn 3C 4
Tintern. Mon 3D 18
Tintinhull. Som 4C 8
Tintwistle. Derbs 8J 41
Tinwald. Dum 3E 52
Tinwell. Rut 1H 29
Tippacott. Devn 1G 7
Tipperty. Abers 3J 73
Tipps End. Cambs 2B 30
Tiptoe. Hants 6L 9
Tipton. W Mid 2H 27
Tipton St John. Devn 6K 7
Tiptree. Essx 2E 22
Tiptree Heath. Essx 2E 22
Tirabad. Powy 8H 25
Tircoed Forest Village. Swan 4F 16
Tiree Airport. Arg 3F 62
Tirinie. Per 1B 66
Tirley. Glos 1G 19
Tiroran. Arg 5K 63
Tir-Phil. Cphy 4L 17
Tirril. Cumb 3D 46
Tirryside. High 2F 78
Tir-y-dail. Carm 3F 16
Tisbury. Wilts 3H 9
Tisman's Common. W Sus 2H 11
Tissington. Derbs 4K 35
Titchberry. Devn 3B 6
Titchfield. Hants 5C 10
Titchmarsh. Nptn 4H 29
Titchwell. Norf 5D 38
Tithby. Notts 6D 36
Titley. Here 6B 26
Titlington. Nmbd 8H 61
Titsey. Surr 8M 21
Titson. Corn 5B 6
Tittensor. Staf 6G 35
Tittleshall. Norf 7E 38
Titton. Worc 5G 27
Tiverton. Ches W 3D 34
Tiverton. Devn 4J 7
Tivetshall St Margaret. Norf 3H 31
Tivetshall St Mary. Norf 3H 31
Tivington. Som 1J 7
Tixall. Staf 7H 35
Tixover. Rut 1G 29
Toab. Orkn 1G 87
Toab. Shet 6D 90
Toadmoor. Derbs 4A 36
Tobermore. M Ulst 4F 93
Tobermory. Arg 2L 63
Toberonochy. Arg 7B 64
Tobha Beag. W Isl 2D 74
Tobha-Beag. W Isl 6A 76
Tobha Mor. W Isl 2D 74
Tobhtarol. W Isl 8E 82
Tobson. W Isl 8E 82
Tocabhaig. High 4H 69
Tocher. Abers 2F 72
Tockenham. Wilts 6J 19
Tockenham Wick. Wilts 5J 19
Tockholes. Bkbn 5E 40
Tockington. S Glo 5E 18
Tockwith. N Yor 2B 42
Todber. Dors 3G 9
Todding. Here 4C 26
Toddington. C Beds 1H 21
Toddington. Glos 8J 27
Todenham. Glos 8L 27
Todhills. Cumb 5H 53
Todmorden. W Yor 5H 41
Todwick. S Yor 1B 36
Toft. Cambs 6L 29
Toft. Linc 8H 37
Toft Hill. Dur 3K 47
Toft Monks. Norf 2L 31
Toft next Newton. Linc 1H 37
Toftrees. Norf 7E 38
Tofts. High 5E 86
Toftwood. Norf 8F 38
Togston. Nmbd 1F 54
Tokavaig. High 4H 69
Tokers Green. Oxon 6E 20
Tolastadh a Chaolais. W Isl 8E 82
Tolladine. Worc 6G 27
Tolland. Som 2L 7
Tollard Farnham. Dors 4H 9
Tollard Royal. Wilts 4H 9
Toll Bar. S Yor 7C 42
Toller Fratrum. Dors 6D 8
Toller Porcorum. Dors 6D 8
Tollerton. N Yor 1C 42
Tollerton. Notts 6D 36
Toller Whelme. Dors 5D 8
Tollesbury. Essx 2F 22
Tolleshunt D'Arcy. Essx 2F 22
Tolleshunt Knights. Essx 2F 22
Tolleshunt Major. Essx 2F 22
Tollie. High 8F 78
Tollie Farm. High 6K 77
Tolm. W Isl 8H 83
Tolpuddle. Dors 6F 8
Tolstadh bho Thuath. W Isl 7J 83
Tolworth. G Lon 7J 21
Tomachlaggan. Mor 3A 72
Tomaknock. Per 5B 66
Tomatin. High 3J 71
Tombuidhe. Arg 7E 64
Tomdoun. High 5B 70
Tomich. High
  nr. Cannich 3D 70
  nr. Invergordon 6H 79
  nr. Lairg 3G 79
Tomintoul. Mor 4A 72
Tomnavoulin. Mor 3B 72
Tomsléibhe. Arg 4M 63
Ton. Mon 4B 18
Tonbridge. Kent 1B 12
Tondu. B'end 6H 17
Tonedale. Som 3L 7
Tonfanau. Gwyn 2E 24
Tong. Shrp 1F 26
Tonge. Leics 7B 36
Tong Forge. Shrp 1F 26
Tongham. Surr 1F 10
Tongland. Dum 6A 52
Tong Norton. Shrp 1F 26
Tongue. High 6H 85
Tongue End. Linc 8J 37
Tongwynlais. Card 6L 17
Tonmawr. Neat 5H 17
Tonna. Neat 5G 17
Tonnau. Neat 5G 17
Ton Pentre. Rhon 5J 17
Ton-Teg. Rhon 6K 17
Tonwell. Herts 2L 21
Tonypandy. Rhon 5J 17
Tonyrefail. Rhon 6K 17
Toome. Ant 4F 93
Toot Baldon. Oxon 3C 20
Toot Hill. Essx 3B 22
Toothill. Hants 4A 10
Topcliffe. N Yor 8B 48
Topcliffe. W Yor 5L 41
Topcroft. Norf 2J 31
Topcroft Street. Norf 2J 31
Toppesfield. Essx 8D 30
Toppings. G Man 6F 40
Toprow. Norf 2H 31
Topsham. Devn 7J 7
Torbay. Torb 5M 5
Torbeg. N Ayr 7H 57
Torbothie. N Lan 4G 59
Torbryan. Devn 5L 5
Torcross. Devn 7L 5
Tore. High 8G 79
Torgyle. High 4D 70
Torinturk. Arg 3H 57
Torksey. Linc 2F 36
Torlum. W Isl 8J 75
Torlundy. High 8B 70
Tormarton. S Glo 6F 18
Tormitchell. S Ayr 2H 51
Tormore. High 5H 69
Tormore. N Ayr 6H 57
Tornagrain. High 1H 71
Tornaveen. Abers 5F 72
Torness. High 3F 70
Toronto. Dur 8E 54
Torpenhow. Cumb 8G 53
Torphichen. W Lot 2H 59
Torphins. Abers 5F 72
Torpoint. Corn 6G 5
Torquay. Torb 5M 5
Torr. Devn 6H 5
Torra. Arg 4C 56
Torran. High 1G 69
Torrance. E Dun 2E 58
Torrans. Arg 5K 63
Torranyard. N Ayr 5B 58
Torre. Som 2K 7
Torre. Torb 5M 5
Torridon. High 8L 77
Torrin. High 3G 69
Torrisdale. Arg 6G 57
Torrisdale. High 5J 85
Torrish. High 2K 79
Torrisholme. Lanc 1C 40
Torroble. High 3F 78
Torroy. High 4F 78
Torry. Aber 5J 73
Torryburn. Fife 1J 59
Torthorwald. Dum 4E 52
Tortington. W Sus 5H 11
Tortworth. S Glo 4F 18
Torvaig. High 1F 68
Torver. Cumb 6A 46
Torwood. Falk 1G 59
Torworth. Notts 1D 36
Toscaig. High 2J 69
Toseland. Cambs 5K 29
Tosside. N Yor 2F 40
Tostock. Suff 5F 30
Totaig. High 8C 76
Totardor. High 2E 68
Tote. High 1F 68
Totegan. High 5L 85
Tothill. Linc 1M 37
Totland. IOW 7M 9
Totley. S Yor 2M 35
Totnell. Dors 5E 8
Totnes. Devn 5L 5
Toton. Notts 6B 36
Totronald. Arg 2G 63
Totscore. High 7E 76
Tottenham. G Lon 4L 21
Tottenhill. Norf 8C 38
Tottenhill Row. Norf 8C 38
Totteridge. G Lon 4K 21
Totternhoe. C Beds 1G 21
Tottington. G Man 6F 40
Totton. Hants 4A 10
Touchen-end. Wind 6F 20
Toulvaddie. High 5J 79
The Towans. Corn 5J 3
Toward. Arg 3L 57
Towcester. Nptn 7D 28
Towednack. Corn 5H 3
Tower End. Norf 8C 38
Tower Hill. Mers 7C 40
Tower Hill. W Sus 3J 11
Towersey. Oxon 3E 20
Towie. Abers 4D 72
Towiemore. Mor 1C 72
Tow Law. Dur 8E 54
The Town. IOS 1G 3
Town End. Cambs 2M 29
Town End. Cumb
  nr. Ambleside 5C 46
  nr. Kirkby Thore 3E 46
  nr. Lindale 7C 46
  nr. Newby Bridge 7B 46
Town End. Mers 1C 34
Townend. W Dun 2C 58
Townfield. Dur 7C 54
Towngate. Cumb 7K 53
Towngate. Linc 8J 37
Town Green. Lanc 7C 40
Town Head. Cumb
  nr. Grasmere 5B 46
  nr. Great Asby 4E 46
Townhead. Cumb
  nr. Lazonby 8K 53
  nr. Maryport 8E 52
  nr. Ousby 8L 53
Townhead. Dum 7A 52
Townhead of Greenlaw. Dum 5B 52
Townhill. Fife 1K 59
Townhill. Swan 5F 16
Townjoy. M Ulst 5F 93
Town Kelloe. Dur 8G 55
Town Littleworth. E Sus 4M 11
Town Row. E Sus 2B 12
Towns End. Hants 8C 20
Townsend. Herts 3J 21
Townshend. Corn 5J 3
Town Street. Suff 3D 30
Town Yetholm. Bord 7F 60
Towthorpe. E Yor 1G 43
Towthorpe. York 2D 42
Towton. N Yor 4B 42
Towyn. Cnwy 3J 33
Toxteth. Mers 1B 34
Toynton All Saints. Linc 3L 37
Toynton Fen Side. Linc 3L 37
Toynton St Peter. Linc 3M 37
Toy's Hill. Kent 8A 22
Trabboch. E Ayr 7C 58
Traboe. Corn 6L 3
Tradespark. High 8J 79
Tradespark. Orkn 1F 86
Trafford Park. G Man 8F 40
Trallong. Powy 2J 17
Y Trallwng. Powy 2M 25
Tranent. E Lot 2B 60
Tranmere. Mers 1B 34
Trantlebeg. High 6L 85
Trantlemore. High 6L 85
Tranwell. Nmbd 3E 54
Trapp. Carm 3F 16
Traquair. Bord 6M 59
Trash Green. W Ber 7D 20
Trawden. Lanc 4H 41
Trawscoed. Powy 1K 17
Trawsfynydd. Gwyn 7G 33
Trawsgoed. Cdgn 5F 24
Treaddow. Here 1D 18
Trealaw. Rhon 5K 17
Treales. Lanc 4C 40
Trearddur. IOA 3B 32
Treaslane. High 8E 76
Treator. Corn 4B 4
Trebanog. Rhon 5K 17
Trebanos. Neat 4G 17
Trebarber. Corn 5A 4
Trebartha. Corn 8B 6
Trebarwith. Corn 3C 4
Trebetherick. Corn 4B 4
Treborough. Som 2K 7
Trebudannon. Corn 5A 4
Trebullett. Corn 8C 6
Treburley. Corn 8C 6
Treburrick. Corn 4A 4
Trebyan. Corn 5C 4
Trecastle. Powy 2H 17
Trecenydd. Cphy 6L 17
Trecott. Devn 5F 6
Trecwn. Pemb 3F 14
Trecynon. Rhon 4J 17
Tredaule. Corn 7B 6
Tredavoe. Corn 6H 3
Tredegar. Blae 4L 17
Trederwen. Powy 8A 34
Tredington. Glos 1H 19
Tredington. Warw 7L 27
Tredinnick. Corn
  nr. Bodmin 5D 4
  nr. Looe 6E 4
  nr. Padstow 4B 4
Tredogan. V Glam 8K 17
Tredomen. Powy 1L 17
Tredunnock. Mon 4B 18
Tredustan. Powy 1L 17
Treen. Corn
  nr. Land's End 6G 3
  nr. St Ives 5H 3
Treeton. S Yor 1B 36
Trefaldwyn. Powy 3M 25
Trefasser. Pemb 3E 14
Trefdraeth. IOA 3D 32
Trefdraeth. Pemb 3G 15
Trefecca. Powy 1L 17
Trefechan. Mer T 4K 17
Trefeglwys. Powy 3J 25
Trefenter. Cdgn 6F 24
Treffgarne. Pemb 4F 14
Treffynnon. Flin 3L 33
Treffynnon. Pemb 4E 14
Trefil. Blae 3L 17
Trefilan. Cdgn 1M 15
Trefin. Pemb 3E 14
Treflach. Shrp 7A 34
Trefnant. Den 3K 33
Trefonen. Shrp 7A 34
Trefor. Gwyn 6C 32
Trefor. IOA 2C 32
Treforest. Rhon 6K 17
Trefrew. Corn 3D 4
Trefriw. Cnwy 4G 33
Tref-y-Clawdd. Powy 4A 26
Trefynwy. Mon 2D 18
Tregada. Corn 7C 6
Tregadillett. Corn 7B 6
Tregare. Mon 2C 18
Tregarne. Corn 6L 3
Tregaron. Cdgn 7F 24
Tregarth. Gwyn 4F 32
Tregear. Corn 6A 4
Tregeare. Corn 7B 6
Tregeiriog. Wrex 7L 33
Tregele. IOA 1C 32
Tregeseal. Corn 5G 3
Tregiskey. Corn 7C 4
Tregole. Corn 6A 6
Tregolwyn. V Glam 7J 17
Tregonetha. Corn 5B 4
Tregonhawke. Corn 6G 5
Tregony. Corn 7B 4
Tregoodwell. Corn 3D 4
Tregorrick. Corn 6C 4
Tregoss. Corn 5B 4
Tregowris. Corn 6L 3
Tregoyd. Powy 1L 17
Tregrehan Mills. Corn 6C 4

Tre-groes—Welford-on-Avon

Tre-groes. *Cdgn* 2L 15
Tregullon. *Corn* 5C 4
Tregurrian. *Corn* 5A 4
Tregynon. *Powy* 3K 25
Trehafod. *Rhon* 5K 17
Trehan. *Corn* 6G 5
Treharris. *Mer T* 5K 17
Treherbert. *Rhon* 5J 17
Trehunist. *Corn* 5F 4
Trekenner. *Corn* 8C 6
Trekenning. *Corn* 5B 4
Treknow. *Corn* 3C 4
Trelales. *B'end* 6H 17
Trelan. *Corn* 7L 3
Trelash. *Corn* 6A 6
Trelassick. *Corn* 6A 4
Trelawnyd. *Flin* 3K 33
Trelech. *Carm* 3J 15
Treleddyd-fawr. *Pemb* 4D 14
Trelewis. *Mer T* 5L 17
Treligga. *Corn* 3C 4
Trelights. *Corn* 4B 4
Trelill. *Corn* 4C 4
Trelissick. *Corn* 5M 3
Trellech. *Mon* 3D 18
Trelleck Grange. *Mon* 3C 18
Trelogan. *Flin* 2L 33
Trelystan. *Powy* 1A 26
Tremadog. *Gwyn* 6E 32
Tremail. *Corn* 7A 6
Tremain. *Cdgn* 2J 15
Tremaine. *Corn* 7B 6
Tremar. *Corn* 5E 4
Trematon. *Corn* 6F 4
Tremeirchion. *Den* 3K 33
Tremore. *Corn* 5C 4
Tremorfa. *Card* 7M 17
Trenance. *Corn*
nr. Newquay 5A 4
nr. Padstow 4B 4
Trenarren. *Corn* 7C 4
Trench. *Telf* 8E 34
Trencreek. *Corn* 2M 3
Trendeal. *Corn* 6A 4
Trenear. *Corn* 5K 3
Treneglos. *Corn* 7B 6
Trenewan. *Corn* 6D 4
Trengune. *Corn* 6A 6
Trent. *Dors* 4D 8
Trentham. *Stoke* 5G 35
Trentishoe. *Devn* 1F 6
Trentlock. *Derbs* 6B 36
Treoes. *V Glam* 7J 17
Treorchy. *Rhon* 5J 17
Treorci. *Rhon* 5J 17
Tre'r-ddol. *Cdgn* 3F 24
Tre'r llai. *Powy* 2M 25
Trerulefoot. *Corn* 6F 4
Tresaith. *Cdgn* 1J 15
Trescott. *Staf* 2G 27
Trescowe. *Corn* 5J 3
Tresham. *Glos* 4F 18
Tresigin. *V Glam* 7J 17
Tresillian. *Corn* 7A 4
Tresimwn. *V Glam* 7K 17
Tresinney. *Corn* 3D 4
Treskillard. *Corn* 5K 3
Treskinnick Cross. *Corn* 6B 6
Tresmeer. *Corn* 7B 6
Tresparrett. *Corn* 2D 4
Tresparrett Posts. *Corn* 6A 6
Tressady. *High* 3G 79
Tressait. *Per* 1B 66
Tresta. *Shet*
on Fetlar 4L 91
on Mainland 2D 90
Treswell. *Notts* 2E 36
Treswithian. *Corn* 5K 3
Tre Taliesin. *Cdgn* 3F 24
Trethomas. *Cphy* 6L 17
Trethosa. *Corn* 6B 4
Trethurgy. *Corn* 6C 4
Tretio. *Pemb* 4D 14
Tretire. *Here* 1D 18
Tretower. *Powy* 2L 17
Treuddyn. *Flin* 4A 34
Trevadlock. *Corn* 8B 6
Trevalga. *Corn* 3C 4
Trevalyn. *Wrex* 4B 34
Trevance. *Corn* 4B 4
Trevanger. *Corn* 4B 4
Trevanson. *Corn* 4B 4
Trevarrack. *Corn* 5H 3
Trevarren. *Corn* 5B 4
Trevarrian. *Corn* 5A 4
Trevarrick. *Corn* 7B 4
Trevaughan. *Carm*
nr. Carmarthen 4L 15
nr. Whitland 5H 15
Treveighan. *Corn* 4C 4
Trevellas. *Corn* 3L 3
Trevelmond. *Corn* 5E 4
Treverva. *Corn* 5L 3
Trevescan. *Corn* 6G 3
Trevethin. *Torf* 3A 18
Trevia. *Corn* 3C 4
Trevigro. *Corn* 5F 4
Trevilley. *Corn* 6G 3
Treviscoe. *Corn* 6B 4
Trevivian. *Corn* 7A 6
Trevone. *Corn* 4A 4
Trevor. *Wrex* 5A 34
Trevor Uchaf. *Den* 6M 33
Trew. *Corn* 6K 3
Trewalder. *Corn* 3C 4
Trewarlett. *Corn* 7C 6
Trewarmett. *Corn* 3C 4
Trewassa. *Corn* 3D 4
Treween. *Corn* 7B 6
Trewellard. *Corn* 5G 3
Trewen. *Corn* 7B 6
Trewennack. *Corn* 6K 3
Trewern. *Powy* 8A 34
Trewetha. *Corn* 4C 4
Trewidland. *Corn* 6E 4
Trewint. *Corn* 6A 6
Trewithian. *Corn* 8A 4
Trewoofe. *Corn* 6H 3
Trewoon. *Corn* 6B 4
Treworthal. *Corn* 8A 4
Trewyddel. *Pemb* 2H 15
Treyarnon. *Corn* 4A 4
Treyford. *W Sus* 4F 10
Triangle. *Staf* 1J 27
Triangle. *W Yor* 5J 41
Trickett's Cross. *Dors* 5J 9
Trillick. *Ferm* 6C 92
Trimdon. *Dur* 8G 55
Trimdon Colliery. *Dur* 8G 55
Trimdon Grange. *Dur* 8G 55
Trimingham. *Norf* 6J 39
Trimley Lower Street. *Suff* 8J 31
Trimley St Martin. *Suff* 8J 31
Trimley St Mary. *Suff* 8J 31
Trimpley. *Worc* 4F 26
Trimsaran. *Carm* 6L 15
Trimstone. *Devn* 1E 6
Trinafour. *Per* 1M 65
Trinant. *Cphy* 5M 17
Tring. *Herts* 2G 21
Trinity. *Ang* 1K 67
Trinity. *Edin* 2L 59
Trisant. *Cdgn* 5G 25
Triscombe. *Som* 2L 7
Trislaig. *High* 8A 70
Trispen. *Corn* 3M 3
Tritlington. *Nmbd* 2F 54
Trochry. *Per* 3C 66
Troedrhiwdalar. *Powy* 7J 25
Troedrhiwfuwch. *Cphy* 4L 17
Troedrhiw-gwair. *Blae* 4L 17
Troedyraur. *Cdgn* 2K 15
Troedyrhiw. *Mer T* 4K 17
Trondavoe. *Shet* 6H 91
Troon. *Corn* 5K 3
Troon. *S Ayr* 6B 58
Troqueer. *Dum* 4D 52
Troston. *Suff* 4E 30
Trottiscliffe. *Kent* 7C 22
Trotton. *W Sus* 3F 10
Troutbeck. *Cumb*
nr. Ambleside 5C 46
nr. Penrith 3B 46
Troutbeck Bridge. *Cumb* 5C 46
Troway. *Derbs* 2A 36
Trowbridge. *Wilts* 8G 19
Trowell. *Notts* 6B 36
Trowle Common. *Wilts* 8G 19
Trowley Bottom. *Herts* 2H 21
Trowse Newton. *Norf* 1J 31
Trudoxhill. *Som* 1F 8
Trull. *Som* 3M 7
Trumaisgearraidh. *W Isl* 6K 75
Trumpan. *High* 7D 76
Trumpet. *Here* 8E 26
Trumpington. *Cambs* 6M 29
Trumps Green. *Surr* 7G 21
Trunch. *Norf* 6J 39
Trunnah. *Lanc* 3B 40
Truro. *Corn* 4M 3
Trusham. *Devn* 7H 7
Trusley. *Derbs* 6L 35
Trusthorpe. *Linc* 1B 38
Tryfil. *IOA* 2D 32
Trysull. *Staf* 2G 27
Tubney. *Oxon* 4B 20
Tuckenhay. *Devn* 6L 5
Tuckhill. *Shrp* 3F 26
Tuckingmill. *Corn* 4K 3
Tuckton. *Bour* 6K 9
Tuddenham. *Suff* 4D 30
Tuddenham St Martin.
Suff 7H 31
Tudeley. *Kent* 1C 12
Tudhoe. *Dur* 8F 54
Tudhoe Grange. *Dur* 8F 54
Tudorville. *Here* 1D 18
Tudweiliog. *Gwyn* 7B 32
Tuesley. *Surr* 1G 11
Tufton. *Hants* 1B 10
Tufton. *Pemb* 4G 15
Tugby. *Leics* 1E 28
Tugford. *Shrp* 3D 26
Tughall. *Nmbd* 7K 61
Tulchan. *Per* 5C 66
Tullibardine. *Per* 6C 66
Tullibody. *Clac* 8B 66
Tullich. *Arg* 6E 64
Tullich. *High*
nr. Lochcarron 1L 69
nr. Tain 6J 79
Tullich. *Mor* 1C 72
Tullich Muir. *High* 6H 79
Tulliemet. *Per* 2C 66
Tulloch. *Abers* 2H 73
Tulloch. *High*
nr. Bonar Bridge 4G 79
nr. Fort William 7D 70
nr. Grantown-on-Spey 4K 71
Tulloch. *Per* 5D 66
Tullochgorm. *Arg* 8D 64
Tullybeagles Lodge. *Per* 4D 66
Tullyhogue. *M Ulst* 5F 93
Tullymurdoch. *Per* 2F 66
Tullynessle. *Abers* 4E 72
Tumble. *Carm* 5M 15
Tumbler's Green. *Essx* 1E 22
Tumby. *Linc* 3K 37
Tumby Woodside. *Linc* 4K 37
Tummel Bridge. *Per* 2A 66
Tunbridge Wells, Royal.
Kent 2B 12
Tunga. *W Isl* 8H 83
Tungate. *Norf* 7J 39
Tunley. *Bath* 8E 18
Tunstall. *E Yor* 4L 43
Tunstall. *Kent* 7E 22
Tunstall. *Lanc* 8E 46
Tunstall. *Norf* 1L 31
Tunstall. *N Yor* 6L 47
Tunstall. *Staf* 7F 34
Tunstall. *Stoke* 4G 35
Tunstall. *Suff* 6K 31
Tunstall. *Tyne* 6G 55
Tunstead. *Derbs* 2K 35
Tunstead. *Norf* 7J 39
Tunstead Milton. *Derbs* 1J 35
Tunworth. *Hants* 1D 10
Tupsley. *Here* 7D 26
Tupton. *Derbs* 3A 36
Turfholm. *S Lan* 6G 59
Turfmoor. *Devn* 5A 8
Turgis Green. *Hants* 8D 20
Turkdean. *Glos* 2K 19
Turkey Island. *Hants* 4C 10
Tur Langton. *Leics* 2E 28
Turleigh. *Wilts* 7G 19
Turlin Moor. *Pool* 6H 9
Turnastone. *Here* 8B 26
Turnberry. *S Ayr* 1H 51
Turnchapel. *Plym* 6G 5
Turnditch. *Derbs* 5L 35
Turners Hill. *W Sus* 2L 11
Turners Puddle. *Dors* 6G 9
Turnford. *Herts* 3L 21
Turnhouse. *Edin* 2K 59
Turnworth. *Dors* 5G 9
Turriff. *Abers* 1G 73
Tursdale. *Dur* 8G 55
Turton Bottoms. *Bkbn* 6F 40
Turtory. *Mor* 1E 72
Turves Green. *W Mid* 4J 27
Turvey. *Bed* 6G 29
Turville. *Buck* 4E 20
Turville Heath. *Buck* 4E 20
Turweston. *Buck* 8D 28
Tushielaw. *Bord* 8M 59
Tutbury. *Staf* 7L 35
Tutnall. *Worc* 4H 27
Tutshill. *Glos* 4D 18
Tuttington. *Norf* 7J 39
Tutts Clump. *W Ber* 6C 20
Tutwell. *Corn* 8C 6
Tuxford. *Notts* 2E 36
Twatt. *Orkn* 7B 88
Twatt. *Shet* 2D 90
Twechar. *E Dun* 2E 58
Tweedale. *Telf* 1F 26
Tweedbank. *Bord* 6C 60
Tweedmouth. *Nmbd* 4G 61
Tweedsmuir. *Bord* 7J 59
Twelveheads. *Corn* 4L 3
Twemlow Green. *Ches E* 3F 34
Twenty. *Linc* 7J 37
Twerton. *Bath* 7F 18
Twickenham. *G Lon* 6J 21
Twigworth. *Glos* 1G 19
Twineham. *W Sus* 4K 11
Twinhoe. *Bath* 8F 18
Twinstead. *Essx* 8E 30
Twinstead Green. *Essx* 8E 30
Twiss Green. *Warr* 8E 40
Twiston. *Lanc* 3G 41
Twitchen. *Devn* 2G 7
Twitchen. *Shrp* 4B 26
Two Bridges. *Devn* 8F 6
Two Bridges. *Glos* 3E 18
Two Dales. *Derbs* 3L 35
Two Gates. *Staf* 1L 27
Two Mile Oak. *Devn* 5L 5
Twycross. *Leics* 1M 27
Twyford. *Buck* 1D 20
Twyford. *Derbs* 7M 35
Twyford. *Dors* 4G 9
Twyford. *Hants* 3B 10
Twyford. *Leics* 8E 36
Twyford. *Norf* 7G 39
Twyford. *Wok* 6E 20
Twyford Common. *Here* 8D 26
Twynholm. *Dum* 6A 52
Twyning. *Glos* 8G 27
Twyning Green. *Glos* 8H 27
Twynllanan. *Carm* 2G 17
Twyn-y-Sheriff. *Mon* 3C 18
Twywell. *Nptn* 4G 29
Tyberton. *Here* 8B 26
Tyburn. *W Mid* 2K 27
Tyby. *Norf* 7G 39
Tycroes. *Carm* 3F 16
Tycrwyn. *Powy* 1L 25
Tyddewi. *Pemb* 4D 14
Tydd Gote. *Linc* 8A 38
Tydd St Giles. *Cambs* 8M 37
Tydd St Mary. *Linc* 8M 37
Tye. *Hants* 5E 10
Tye Green. *Essx*
nr. Bishop's Stortford 1B 22
nr. Braintree 1D 22
nr. Saffron Walden 8B 30
Tyersal. *W Yor* 4K 41
Ty Issa. *Powy* 7L 33
Tyldesley. *G Man* 7E 40
Tyler Hill. *Kent* 7H 23
Tyler's Green. *Essx* 3B 22
Tylers Green. *Buck* 4F 20
Tylorstown. *Rhon* 5K 17
Tylwch. *Powy* 4J 25
Y Tymbl. *Carm* 5M 15
Tynan. *Arm* 6E 92
Ty-nant. *Cnwy* 6J 33
Tyndrum. *Stir* 4H 65
Tyneham. *Dors* 7G 9
Tynehead. *Midl* 4A 60
Tynemouth. *Tyne* 5G 55
Tyneside. *Tyne* 5F 54
Tyne Tunnel. *Tyne* 5G 55
Tynewydd. *Rhon* 5J 17
Tyninghame. *E Lot* 2D 60
Tynron. *Dum* 2C 52
Ty'n-y-bryn. *Rhon* 6K 17
Tyn-y-celyn. *Wrex* 7L 33
Tyn-y-cwm. *Swan* 4F 16
Tyn-y-ffridd. *Powy* 7L 33
Tynygongl. *IOA* 2E 32
Tynygraig. *Cdgn* 6F 24
Ty'n-y-groes. *Cnwy* 3G 33
Ty'n-yr-eithin. *Cdgn* 6F 24
Tyn-y-rhyd. *Powy* 1K 25
Tyn-y-wern. *Powy* 8K 33
Tyrie. *Abers* 7J 81
Tyringham. *Mil* 7F 28
Tythecott. *Devn* 4D 6
Tythegston. *B'end* 7H 17
Tytherington. *Ches E* 2H 35
Tytherington. *S Glo* 5E 18
Tytherington. *Som* 1F 8
Tytherington. *Wilts* 1H 9
Tytherleigh. *Devn* 5B 8
Tywardreath. *Corn* 6C 4
Tywardreath Highway. *Corn* 6C 4
Tywyn. *Cnwy* 3G 33
Tywyn. *Gwyn* 2E 24

U

Uachdar. *W Isl* 8K 75
Uags. *High* 2J 69
Ubbeston Green. *Suff* 4K 31
Ubley. *Bath* 8D 18
Uckerby. *N Yor* 5L 47
Uckfield. *E Sus* 3A 12
Uckinghall. *Worc* 8G 27
Uckington. *Glos* 1H 19
Uckington. *Shrp* 1D 26
Uddingston. *S Lan* 3E 58
Uddington. *S Lan* 6G 59
Udimore. *E Sus* 4E 12
Udny Green. *Abers* 3H 73
Udny Station. *Abers* 3J 73
Udston. *S Lan* 4E 58
Udstonhead. *S Lan* 5F 58
Uffcott. *Wilts* 6K 19
Uffculme. *Devn* 4K 7
Uffington. *Linc* 1H 29
Uffington. *Oxon* 5M 19
Uffington. *Shrp* 8D 34
Ufford. *Pet* 1H 29
Ufford. *Suff* 6J 31
Ufton. *Warw* 5A 28
Ufton Nervet. *W Ber* 7D 20
Ugadale. *Arg* 7G 57
Ugborough. *Devn* 6J 5
Ugford. *Wilts* 2J 9
Uggeshall. *Suff* 3L 31
Ugglebarnby. *N Yor* 5F 48
Ugley. *Essx* 1B 22
Ugley Green. *Essx* 1B 22
Ugthorpe. *N Yor* 4E 48
Uidh. *W Isl* 6C 74
Uig. *Arg* 2G 63
Uig. *High*
nr. Balgown 7E 76
nr. Dunvegan 8C 76
Uigshader. *High* 1F 68
Uisken. *Arg* 6J 63
Ulbster. *High* 7E 86
Ulcat Row. *Cumb* 3C 46
Ulceby. *Linc* 2M 37
Ulceby. *N Lin* 6J 43
Ulceby Skitter. *N Lin* 6J 43
Ulcombe. *Kent* 1E 12
Uldale. *Cumb* 8G 53
Uley. *Glos* 4F 18
Ulgham. *Nmbd* 2F 54
Ullapool. *High* 4B 78
Ullenhall. *Warw* 5K 27
Ulleskelf. *N Yor* 4C 42
Ullesthorpe. *Leics* 3C 28
Ulley. *S Yor* 1B 36
Ullingswick. *Here* 6D 26
Ullinish. *High* 2E 68
Ullock. *Cumb* 2K 45
Ulpha. *Cumb* 5L 45
Ulrome. *E Yor* 2J 43
Ulsta. *Shet* 5J 91
Ulting. *Essx* 3E 22
Ulva House. *Arg* 4K 63
Ulverston. *Cumb* 8A 46
Ulwell. *Dors* 7J 9
Umberleigh. *Devn* 3F 6
Unapool. *High* 8E 84
Underbarrow. *Cumb* 6C 46
Undercliffe. *W Yor* 4K 41
Underdale. *Shrp* 8D 34
Underhoull. *Shet* 3K 91
Underriver. *Kent* 8B 22
Under Tofts. *S Yor* 1M 35
Underton. *Shrp* 2E 26
Underwood. *Newp* 5B 18
Underwood. *Notts* 4B 36
Underwood. *Plym* 6H 5
Undley. *Suff* 3C 30
Undy. *Mon* 5C 18
Union Mills. *IOM* 7C 44
Union Street. *E Sus* 2D 12
Unstone. *Derbs* 2A 36
Unstone Green. *Derbs* 2A 36
Unthank. *Cumb*
nr. Carlisle 7H 53
nr. Gamblesby 7L 53
nr. Penrith 8J 53
Unthank End. *Cumb* 8J 53
Upavon. *Wilts* 8K 19
Up Cerne. *Dors* 5E 8
Upchurch. *Kent* 7E 22
Upcott. *Devn* 5E 6
Upcott. *Here* 6B 26
Upend. *Cambs* 6C 30
Up Exe. *Devn* 5J 7
Upgate. *Norf* 8H 39
Upgate Street. *Norf* 2G 31
Uphall. *Dors* 5D 8
Uphall. *W Lot* 2J 59
Uphall Station. *W Lot* 2J 59
Upham. *Devn* 5H 7
Upham. *Hants* 3C 10
Uphampton. *Here* 5B 26
Uphampton. *Worc* 5G 27
Up Hatherley. *Glos* 1H 19
Uphill. *N Som* 8B 18
Up Holland. *Lanc* 7D 40
Uplawmoor. *E Ren* 4C 58
Upleadon. *Glos* 1F 18
Upleatham. *Red C* 4D 48
Uplees. *Kent* 7F 22
Uploders. *Dors* 6D 8
Uplowman. *Devn* 4K 7
Uplyme. *Devn* 6B 8
Up Marden. *W Sus* 4E 10
Upminster. *G Lon* 5B 22
Up Nately. *Hants* 8D 20
Upottery. *Devn* 5M 7
Uppat. *High* 3J 79
Upper Affcot. *Shrp* 3C 26
Upper Arley. *Worc* 3F 26
Upper Armley. *W Yor* 4L 41
Upper Arncott. *Oxon* 2D 20
Upper Astrop. *Nptn* 8C 28
Upper Badcall. *High* 7D 84
Upper Ballinderry. *Lis* 5G 93
Upper Bangor. *Gwyn* 3E 32
Upper Basildon. *W Ber* 6C 20
Upper Batley. *W Yor* 5L 41
Upper Beeding. *W Sus* 4J 11
Upper Benefield. *Nptn* 3G 29
Upper Bentley. *Worc* 5H 27
Upper Bighouse. *High* 6L 85
Upper Boddam. *Abers* 2F 72
Upper Boddington. *Nptn* 6B 28
Upper Bogside. *Mor* 8B 80
Upper Booth. *Derbs* 1K 35
Upper Borth. *Cdgn* 4F 24
Upper Boyndlie. *Abers* 7J 81
Upper Brailes. *Warw* 7M 27
Upper Breinton. *Here* 7C 26
Upper Broughton. *Notts* 7D 36
Upper Brynamman. *Carm* 3G 17
Upper Bucklebury. *W Ber* 7C 20
Upper Bullington. *Hants* 1B 10
Upper Burgate. *Hants* 4K 9
Upper Caldecote. *C Beds* 7J 29
Upper Canterton. *Hants* 4L 9
Upper Catesby. *Nptn* 6C 28
Upper Chapel. *Powy* 8K 25
Upper Cheddon. *Som* 3M 7
Upper Chicksgrove. *Wilts* 3H 9
Upper Church Village.
Rhon 6K 17
Upper Chute. *Wilts* 8L 19
Upper Clatford. *Hants* 1A 10
Upper Coberley. *Glos* 2H 19
Upper Coedcae. *Torf* 3A 18
Upper Cound. *Shrp* 1D 26
Upper Cudworth. *S Yor* 7A 42
Upper Cumberworth.
W Yor 7L 41
Upper Cuttlehill. *Abers* 1D 72
Upper Cwmbran. *Torf* 4A 18
Upper Dallachy. *Mor* 7C 80
Upper Dean. *Bed* 5H 29
Upper Denby. *W Yor* 7L 41
Upper Derraid. *High* 2L 71
Upper Diabaig. *High* 7K 77
Upper Dicker. *E Sus* 5B 12
Upper Dinchope. *Shrp* 3C 26
Upper Dochcarty. *High* 7F 78
Upper Dounreay. *High* 5A 86
Upper Dovercourt. *Essx* 8J 31
Upper Dunsforth. *N Yor* 1B 42
Upper Dunsley. *Herts* 2G 21
Upper Eastern Green.
W Mid 3L 27
Upper Elkstone. *Staf* 4J 35
Upper Ellastone. *Staf* 5K 35
Upper End. *Derbs* 2J 35
Upper Enham. *Hants* 1A 10
Upper Farmcote. *Shrp* 2F 26
Upper Farringdon. *Hants* 2E 10
Upper Framilode. *Glos* 2F 18
Upper Froyle. *Hants* 1E 10
Upper Gills. *High* 4E 86
Upper Glenfintaig. *High* 7C 70
Upper Godney. *Som* 1C 8
Upper Gravenhurst. *C Beds* 8J 29
Upper Green. *Essx* 8M 29
Upper Green. *W Ber* 7A 20
Upper Green. *W Yor* 5L 41
Upper Grove Common.
Here 1D 18
Upper Hackney. *Derbs* 3L 35
Upper Hale. *Surr* 1F 10
Upper Halliford. *Surr* 7H 21
Upper Halling. *Medw* 7C 22
Upper Hambleton. *Rut* 1G 29
Upper Hardres Court.
Kent 8H 23
Upper Hardwick. *Here* 6C 26
Upper Hartfield. *E Sus* 2A 12
Upper Haugh. *S Yor* 8B 42
Upper Hayton. *Shrp* 3D 26
Upper Heath. *Shrp* 3D 26
Upper Hellesdon. *Norf* 8J 39
Upper Helmsley. *N Yor* 2D 42
Upper Hengoed. *Shrp* 6A 34
Upper Hergest. *Here* 6A 26
Upper Heyford. *Nptn* 6D 28
Upper Heyford. *Oxon* 1B 20
Upper Hill. *Here* 6C 26
Upper Hindhope. *Bord* 1A 54
Upper Hopton. *W Yor* 6K 41
Upper Howsell. *Worc* 7F 26
Upper Hulme. *Staf* 3J 35
Upper Inglesham. *Swin* 4L 19
Upper Kilcott. *S Glo* 5F 18
Upper Killay. *Swan* 5E 16
Upper Kirkton. *Abers* 2G 73
Upper Kirkton. *N Ayr* 4L 57
Upper Knockando. *Mor* 1A 72
Upper Knockchoilum.
High 4E 70
Upper Lambourn. *W Ber* 5M 19
Upperlands. *M Ulst* 3F 93
Upper Langford. *N Som* 8C 18
Upper Langwith. *Derbs* 3C 36
Upper Largo. *Fife* 7H 67
Upper Latheron. *High* 8C 86
Upper Layham. *Suff* 7G 31
Upper Leigh. *Staf* 6J 35
Upper Lenie. *High* 3F 70
Upper Lochton. *Abers* 6F 72
Upper Longdon. *Staf* 8J 35
Upper Longwood. *Shrp* 1E 26
Upper Lybster. *High* 8D 86
Upper Lydbrook. *Glos* 2E 18
Upper Lye. *Here* 5B 26
Upper Maes-coed. *Here* 8B 26
Upper Midway. *Derbs* 7L 35
Uppermill. *G Man* 7H 41
Upper Millichope. *Shrp* 3D 26
Upper Milovaig. *High* 1C 68
Upper Minety. *Wilts* 4J 19
Upper Mitton. *Worc* 4G 27
Upper Nash. *Pemb* 6G 15
Upper Neepaback. *Shet* 5K 91
Upper Netchwood. *Shrp* 2E 26
Upper Nobut. *Staf* 6J 35
Upper North Dean. *Buck* 4F 20
Upper Norwood. *W Sus* 4G 11
Upper Nyland. *Dors* 3F 8
Upper Oddington. *Glos* 1L 19
Upper Ollach. *High* 2G 69
Upper Outwoods. *Staf* 7L 35
Upper Padley. *Derbs* 2L 35
Upper Pennington. *Hants* 6M 9
Upper Poppleton. *York* 2C 42
Upper Quinton. *Warw* 7K 27
Upper Rissington. *Glos* 2L 19
Upper Rochford. *Worc* 5E 26
Upper Rusko. *Dum* 5L 51
Upper Sandaig. *High* 4J 69
Upper Sanday. *Orkn* 1G 87
Upper Sapey. *Here* 5E 26
Upper Seagry. *Wilts* 5H 19
Upper Shelton. *C Beds* 7G 29
Upper Sheringham. *Norf* 5H 39
Upper Skelmorlie. *N Ayr* 3L 57
Upper Slaughter. *Glos* 1K 19
Upper Sonachan. *Arg* 5E 64
Upper Soudley. *Glos* 2E 18
Upper Staploe. *Bed* 6J 29
Upper Stoke. *Norf* 1J 31
Upper Stondon. *C Beds* 8J 29
Upper Stowe. *Nptn* 6D 28
Upper Street. *Hants* 4K 9
Upper Street. *Norf*
nr. Horning 8K 39
nr. Hoveton 8K 39
Upper Street. *Suff* 8H 31
Upper Strensham. *Worc* 8H 27
Upper Studley. *Wilts* 8G 19
Upper Sundon. *C Beds* 1H 21
Upper Swell. *Glos* 1K 19
Upper Tankersley. *S Yor* 8M 41
Upper Tean. *Staf* 6J 35
Upperthong. *W Yor* 7K 41
Upperthorpe. *N Lin* 7E 42
Upper Thurnham. *Lanc* 2C 40
Upper Tillyrie. *Per* 7E 66
Upperton. *W Sus* 3G 11
Upper Tooting. *G Lon* 6K 21
Upper Town. *Derbs*
nr. Bonsall 4L 35
nr. Hognaston 4L 35
Upper Town. *Here* 7D 26
Upper Town. *N Som* 7D 18
Uppertown. *Derbs* 3M 35
Uppertown. *High* 4E 86
Uppertown. *Nmbd* 4B 54
Uppertown. *Orkn* 2F 86
Upper Tysoe. *Warw* 7M 27
Upper Upham. *Wilts* 6L 19
Upper Upnor. *Medw* 6D 22
Upper Urquhart. *Fife* 7E 66
Upper Wardington. *Oxon* 7B 28
Upper Weald. *Mil* 8E 28
Upper Weedon. *Nptn* 6D 28
Upper Wellingham. *E Sus* 4M 11
Upper Whiston. *S Yor* 1B 36
Upper Wield. *Hants* 2D 10
Upper Winchendon.
Buck 2E 20
Upperwood. *Derbs* 4L 35
Upper Woodford. *Wilts* 2K 9
Upper Wootton. *Hants* 8C 20
Upper Wraxall. *Wilts* 6G 19
Upper Wyche. *Worc* 7F 26
Uppincott. *Devn* 5H 7
Uppingham. *Rut* 2F 28
Uppington. *Shrp* 1E 26
Upsall. *N Yor* 7B 48
Upsettlington. *Bord* 5F 60
Upshire. *Essx* 3M 21
Up Somborne. *Hants* 2A 10
Upstreet. *Kent* 7J 23
Up Sydling. *Dors* 5E 8
Upthorpe. *Suff* 4F 30
Upton. *Buck* 2E 20
Upton. *Cambs* 4J 29
Upton. *Ches W* 3C 34
Upton. *Corn*
nr. Bude 5B 6
nr. Liskeard 8B 6
Upton. *Cumb* 8H 53
Upton. *Devn*
nr. Honiton 5K 7
nr. Kingsbridge 7K 5
Upton. *Dors*
nr. Poole 6H 9
nr. Weymouth 7F 8
Upton. *E Yor* 2J 43
Upton. *Hants*
nr. Andover 8A 20
nr. Southampton 4A 10
Upton. *IOW* 6C 10
Upton. *Leics* 2A 28
Upton. *Linc* 1F 36
Upton. *Mers* 1A 34
Upton. *Norf* 8K 39
Upton. *Nptn* 5E 28
Upton. *Notts*
nr. Retford 2E 36
nr. Southwell 4E 36
Upton. *Oxon* 5C 20
Upton. *Pemb* 6G 15
Upton. *Pet* 1J 29
Upton. *Slo* 6G 21
Upton. *Som*
nr. Somerton 3C 8
nr. Wiveliscombe 3J 7
Upton. *Warw* 6K 27
Upton. *W Yor* 6B 42
Upton. *Wilts* 2G 9
Upton Bishop. *Here* 1E 18
Upton Cheyney. *S Glo* 7E 18
Upton Cressett. *Shrp* 2E 26
Upton Crews. *Here* 1E 18
Upton Cross. *Corn* 8B 6
Upton End. *C Beds* 8J 29
Upton Grey. *Hants* 1D 10
Upton Heath. *Ches W* 3C 34
Upton Hellions. *Devn* 5H 7
Upton Lovell. *Wilts* 1H 9
Upton Magna. *Shrp* 8D 34
Upton Noble. *Som* 2F 8
Upton Pyne. *Devn* 6J 7
Upton St Leonards. *Glos* 2G 19
Upton Scudamore. *Wilts* 1G 9
Upton Snodsbury. *Worc* 6H 27
Upton upon Severn. *Worc* 7G 27
Upton Warren. *Worc* 5H 27
Upwaltham. *W Sus* 4G 11
Upware. *Cambs* 4B 30
Upwell. *Norf* 1B 30
Upwey. *Dors* 7E 8
Upwick Green. *Herts* 1A 22
Upwood. *Cambs* 3K 29
Urafirth. *Shet* 6H 91
Uragaig. *Arg* 8J 63
Urchany. *High* 1J 71
Urchfont. *Wilts* 8J 19
Urdimarsh. *Here* 7D 26
Ure. *Shet* 6G 91
Ure Bank. *N Yor* 8M 47
Urgha. *W Isl* 4C 76
Urlay Nook. *Stoc T* 4B 48
Urmston. *G Man* 8F 40
Urquhart. *Mor* 7B 80
Urra. *N Yor* 5C 48
Urray. *High* 8F 78
Usan. *Ang* 2L 67
Ushaw Moor. *Dur* 7F 54
Usk. *Mon* 3B 18
Usselby. *Linc* 8H 43
Usworth. *Tyne* 6G 55
Utkinton. *Ches W* 3D 34
Uton. *Devn* 6H 7
Utterby. *Linc* 8L 43
Uttoxeter. *Staf* 6J 35
Uwchmynydd. *Gwyn* 8A 32
Uxbridge. *G Lon* 5H 21
Uyeasound. *Shet* 3K 91
Uzmaston. *Pemb* 5F 14

V

Valley. *IOA* 3B 32
Valley End. *Surr* 7G 21
Valley Truckle. *Corn* 3D 4
Valsgarth. *Shet* 2L 91
Valtos. *High* 7G 77
Van. *Powy* 4J 25
Vange. *Essx* 5D 22
Varteg. *Torf* 3A 18
Vatsetter. *Shet* 5K 91
Vatten. *High* 1D 68
Vaul. *Arg* 3F 62
The Vauld. *Here* 7D 26
Vaynor. *Mer T* 3K 17
Veensgarth. *Shet* 3E 90
Velindre. *Powy* 1L 17
Vellow. *Som* 2K 7
Velly. *Devn* 3B 6
Veness. *Orkn* 7E 88
Venhay. *Devn* 4G 7
Venn. *Devn* 7K 5
Venngreen. *Devn* 4C 6
Vennington. *Shrp* 1B 26
Venn Ottery. *Devn* 6K 7
Venn's Green. *Here* 7D 26
Venny Tedburn. *Devn* 6H 7
Venterdon. *Corn* 8C 6
Ventnor. *IOW* 8C 10
Vernham Dean. *Hants* 8M 19
Vernham Street. *Hants* 8M 19
Vernolds Common. *Shrp* 3C 26
Verwood. *Dors* 5J 9
Veryan. *Corn* 8B 4
Veryan Green. *Corn* 8B 4
Vicarage. *Devn* 7M 7
Vickerstown. *Cumb* 8L 45
Victoria. *Corn* 5B 4
Victoria Bridge. *Derr* 4C 92
Vidlin. *Shet* 1E 90
Viewpark. *N Lan* 3F 58
Vigo. *W Mid* 1J 27
Vigo Village. *Kent* 7C 22
Vinehall Street. *E Sus* 3D 12
Vine's Cross. *E Sus* 4B 12
Viney Hill. *Glos* 3E 18
Virginia Water. *Surr* 7G 21
Virginstow. *Devn* 6C 6
Vobster. *Som* 1F 8
Voe. *Shet*
nr. Hillside 1E 90
nr. Swinister 5H 91
Vole. *Som* 1B 8
Vowchurch. *Here* 8B 26
Voxter. *Shet* 6H 91
Voy. *Orkn* 8B 88
Vulcan Village. *Mers* 8D 40

W

Waberthwaite. *Cumb* 5L 45
Wackerfield. *Dur* 3K 47
Wacton. *Norf* 2H 31
Wadbister. *Shet* 3E 90
Wadborough. *Worc* 7H 27
Wadbrook. *Devn* 5B 8
Waddesdon. *Buck* 2E 20
Waddeton. *Devn* 6L 5
Waddicar. *Mers* 8B 40
Waddingham. *Linc* 8G 43
Waddington. *Lanc* 3F 40
Waddington. *Linc* 3G 37
Waddon. *Devn* 8H 7
Wadebridge. *Corn* 4B 4
Wadeford. *Som* 4B 8
Wadenhoe. *Nptn* 3H 29
Wadesmill. *Herts* 2L 21
Wadhurst. *E Sus* 2C 12
Wadshelf. *Derbs* 2M 35
Wadsley. *S Yor* 8M 41
Wadsley Bridge. *S Yor* 8M 41
Wadswick. *Wilts* 7G 19
Wadwick. *Hants* 8B 20
Wadworth. *S Yor* 8C 42
Waen. *Den*
nr. Llandymog 4L 33
nr. Nantglyn 4J 33
Waen. *Powy* 3J 25
Waen Fach. *Powy* 1M 25
Waen Goleugoed. *Den* 3K 33
Wag. *High* 1L 79
Wainfleet All Saints. *Linc* 4A 38
Wainfleet Bank. *Linc* 4A 38
Wainfleet St Mary. *Linc* 4A 38
Wainhouse Corner. *Corn* 6A 6
Wainscott. *Medw* 6D 22
Wainstalls. *W Yor* 5J 41
Waitby. *Cumb* 5F 46
Waithe. *Linc* 7K 43
Wakefield. *W Yor* 5M 41
Wakerley. *Nptn* 2G 29
Wakes Colne. *Essx* 1E 22
Walberswick. *Suff* 4L 31
Walberton. *W Sus* 5G 11
Walbottle. *Tyne* 5E 54
Walby. *Cumb* 5J 53
Walcombe. *Som* 1D 8
Walcot. *Linc* 6H 37
Walcot. *N Lin* 5F 42
Walcot. *Swin* 5K 19
Walcot. *Telf* 8D 34
Walcot. *Warw* 6K 27
Walcote. *Leics* 3C 28
Walcot Green. *Norf* 3H 31
Walcott. *Linc* 4J 37
Walcott. *Norf* 6K 39
Walden. *N Yor* 7J 47
Walden Head. *N Yor* 7H 47
Walden Stubbs. *N Yor* 6C 42
Walderslade. *Medw* 7D 22
Walderton. *W Sus* 4E 10
Walditch. *Dors* 6C 8
Waldley. *Derbs* 6K 35
Waldridge. *Dur* 6F 54
Waldringfield. *Suff* 7J 31
Waldron. *E Sus* 4B 12
Wales. *S Yor* 1B 36
Walesby. *Linc* 8J 43
Walesby. *Notts* 2D 36
Walford. *Here*
nr. Leintwardine 4B 26
nr. Ross-on-Wye 1D 18
Walford. *Shrp* 7C 34
Walford. *Staf* 6G 35
Walford Heath. *Shrp* 8C 34
Walgherton. *Ches E* 5E 34
Walgrave. *Nptn* 4F 28
Walhampton. *Hants* 6M 9
Walkden. *G Man* 7F 40
Walker. *Tyne* 5F 54
Walkerburn. *Bord* 6A 60
Walker Fold. *Lanc* 3E 40
Walkeringham. *Notts* 8E 42
Walkerith. *Linc* 8E 42
Walkern. *Herts* 1K 21
Walker's Green. *Here* 7D 26
Walkerton. *Fife* 7F 66
Walkerville. *N Yor* 6L 47
Walkford. *Dors* 6L 9
Walkhampton. *Devn* 5H 5
Walkington. *E Yor* 4G 43
Walkley. *S Yor* 1M 35
Walk Mill. *Lanc* 4G 41
Wall. *Corn* 5K 3
Wall. *Nmbd* 5C 54
Wall. *Staf* 1K 27
Wallaceton. *Dum* 3C 52
Wallacetown. *Shet* 2D 90
Wallacetown. *S Ayr*
nr. Ayr 7B 58
nr. Dailly 1H 51
Wallands Park. *E Sus* 4M 11
Wallasey. *Mers* 8A 40
Wallaston Green. *Pemb* 6F 14
Wallbrook. *W Mid* 2H 27
Wallcrouch. *E Sus* 2C 12
Wall End. *Cumb* 6M 45
Wallend. *Medw* 6E 22
Wall Heath. *W Mid* 3G 27
Wallingford. *Oxon* 5D 20
Wallington. *G Lon* 7K 21
Wallington. *Hants* 5C 10
Wallington. *Herts* 8K 29
Wallis. *Pemb* 4G 15
Wallisdown. *Bour* 6J 9
Walliswood. *Surr* 2J 11
Wall Nook. *Dur* 7F 54
Walls. *Shet* 3C 90
Wallsend. *Tyne* 5G 55
Wallsworth. *Glos* 1G 19
Wall under Heywood. *Shrp* 2D 26
Wallyford. *E Lot* 2A 60
Walmer. *Kent* 8K 23
Walmer Bridge. *Lanc* 5C 40
Walmersley. *G Man* 6G 41
Walmley. *W Mid* 2K 27
Walnut Grove. *Per* 5E 66
Walpole. *Suff* 4K 31
Walpole Cross Keys. *Norf* 8B 38
Walpole Gate. *Norf* 8B 38
Walpole Highway. *Norf* 8B 38
Walpole Marsh. *Norf* 8A 38
Walpole St Andrew. *Norf* 8B 38
Walpole St Peter. *Norf* 8B 38
Walsall. *W Mid* 2J 27
Walsall Wood. *W Mid* 1J 27
Walsden. *W Yor* 5H 41
Walsgrave on Sowe.
W Mid 3A 28
Walsham le Willows. *Suff* 4G 31
Walshaw. *G Man* 6F 40
Walshford. *N Yor* 2B 42
Walsoken. *Norf* 8A 38
Walston. *S Lan* 5J 59
Walsworth. *Herts* 8J 29
Walter's Ash. *Buck* 4F 20
Walterston. *V Glam* 7K 17
Walterstone. *Here* 1B 18
Waltham. *Kent* 1H 13
Waltham. *NE Lin* 7K 43
Waltham Abbey. *Essx* 3L 21
Waltham Chase. *Hants* 4C 10
Waltham Cross. *Herts* 3L 21
Waltham on the Wolds.
Leics 7F 36
Waltham St Lawrence.
Wind 6F 20
Waltham's Cross. *Essx* 8C 30
Walthamstow. *G Lon* 5L 21
Walton. *Cumb* 5K 53
Walton. *Derbs* 3A 36
Walton. *Leics* 3C 28
Walton. *Mers* 8B 40
Walton. *Mil* 8F 28
Walton. *Pet* 1J 29
Walton. *Powy* 6A 26
Walton. *Som* 2C 8
Walton. *Staf*
nr. Eccleshall 7G 35
nr. Stone 6G 35
Walton. *Suff* 8J 31
Walton. *Telf* 8D 34
Walton. *Warw* 6L 27
Walton. *W Yor*
nr. Wakefield 6A 42
nr. Wetherby 3B 42
Walton Cardiff. *Glos* 8H 27
Walton East. *Pemb* 4G 15
Walton Elm. *Dors* 4F 8
Walton Highway. *Norf* 8A 38
Walton in Gordano. *N Som* 6C 18
Walton-le-Dale. *Lanc* 5D 40
Walton-on-Thames. *Surr* 7J 21
Walton on the Hill. *Surr* 8K 21
Walton-on-the-Hill. *Staf* 7H 35
Walton-on-the-Naze. *Essx* 1J 23
Walton on the Wolds. *Leics* 8C 36
Walton-on-Trent. *Derbs* 8L 35
Walton West. *Pemb* 5E 14
Walwick. *Nmbd* 4C 54
Walworth. *Darl* 4L 47
Walworth Gate. *Darl* 3L 47
Walwyn's Castle. *Pemb* 5E 14
Wambrook. *Som* 5A 8
Wampool. *Cumb* 6G 53
Wanborough. *Surr* 1G 11
Wanborough. *Swin* 5L 19
Wandel. *S Lan* 7H 59
Wandsworth. *G Lon* 6K 21
Wangford. *Suff*
nr. Lakenheath 3D 30
nr. Southwold 4L 31
Wanlip. *Leics* 8C 36
Wanlockhead. *Dum* 8G 59
Wannock. *E Sus* 5B 12
Wansford. *E Yor* 2H 43
Wansford. *Pet* 2H 29
Wanshurst Green. *Kent* 1D 12
Wanstead. *G Lon* 5M 21
Wanstrow. *Som* 1F 8
Wanswell. *Glos* 3E 18
Wantage. *Oxon* 5B 20
Wapley. *S Glo* 6F 18
Wappenbury. *Warw* 5A 28
Wappenham. *Nptn* 7D 28
Warbleton. *E Sus* 4C 12
Warblington. *Hants* 5E 10
Warborough. *Oxon* 4C 20
Warboys. *Cambs* 3L 29
Warbreck. *Bkpl* 4B 40
Warbstow. *Corn* 6B 6
Warburton. *G Man* 1F 34
Warcop. *Cumb* 4F 46
Warden. *Kent* 6G 23
Warden. *Nmbd* 5C 54
Ward End. *W Mid* 3K 27
Ward Green. *Suff* 5G 31
Ward Green Cross. *Lanc* 4E 40
Wardhedges. *C Beds* 8H 29
Wardhouse. *Abers* 2E 72
Wardington. *Oxon* 7B 28
Wardle. *Ches E* 4E 34
Wardle. *G Man* 6H 41
Wardley. *Rut* 1F 28
Wardley. *W Sus* 3F 10
Wardlow. *Derbs* 2K 35
Wardsend. *Ches E* 1H 35
Wardy Hill. *Cambs* 3A 30
Ware. *Herts* 2L 21
Ware. *Kent* 7J 23
Wareham. *Dors* 7H 9
Warehorne. *Kent* 2F 12
Warenford. *Nmbd* 7J 61
Waren Mill. *Nmbd* 6J 61
Warenton. *Nmbd* 6J 61
Wareside. *Herts* 2L 21
Waresley. *Cambs* 6K 29
Waresley. *Worc* 5G 27
Warfield. *Brac* 6F 20
Warfleet. *Devn* 6L 5
Wargate. *Linc* 6K 37
Wargrave. *Wok* 6E 20
Warham. *Norf* 5F 38
Waringsford. *Arm* 6H 93
Waringstown. *Arm* 6G 93
Wark. *Nmbd*
nr. Coldstream 6F 60
nr. Hexham 4B 54
Warkleigh. *Devn* 3F 6
Warkton. *Nptn* 4F 28
Warkworth. *Nptn* 7B 28
Warkworth. *Nmbd* 1F 54
Warlaby. *N Yor* 6M 47
Warland. *W Yor* 5H 41
Warleggan. *Corn* 5D 4
Warlingham. *Surr* 8L 21
Warmanbie. *Dum* 5F 52
Warmfield. *W Yor* 5A 42
Warmingham. *Ches E* 3F 34
Warminghurst. *W Sus* 4J 11
Warmington. *Nptn* 2H 29
Warmington. *Warw* 7B 28
Warminster. *Wilts* 1G 9
Warmley. *S Glo* 6E 18
Warmsworth. *S Yor* 7C 42
Warmwell. *Dors* 7F 8
Warndon. *Worc* 6G 27
Warners End. *Herts* 3H 21
Warnford. *Hants* 3D 10
Warnham. *W Sus* 2J 11
Warningcamp. *W Sus* 5H 11
Warninglid. *W Sus* 3K 11
Warren. *Ches E* 2G 35
Warren. *Pemb* 7F 14
Warrenby. *Red C* 3C 48
Warren Corner. *Hants*
nr. Aldershot 1F 10
nr. Petersfield 3E 10
Warrenpoint. *New M* 7G 93
Warren Row. *Wind* 5F 20
Warren Street. *Kent* 8F 22
Warrington. *Mil* 6F 28
Warrington. *Warr* 1E 34
Warsash. *Hants* 5B 10
Warse. *High* 4E 86
Warslow. *Staf* 4J 35
Warsop. *Notts* 3C 36
Warsop Vale. *Notts* 3C 36
Warter. *E Yor* 2F 42
Warthermarske. *N Yor* 8L 47
Warthill. *N Yor* 2D 42
Wartling. *E Sus* 5C 12
Wartnaby. *Leics* 7E 36
Warton. *Lanc*
nr. Carnforth 8C 46
nr. Freckleton 5C 40
Warton. *Nmbd* 1D 54
Warton. *Warw* 1L 27
Warwick. *Warw* 5L 27
Warwick Bridge. *Cumb* 6J 53
Warwick-on-Eden. *Cumb* 6J 53
Warwick Wold. *Surr* 8L 21
Wasbister. *Orkn* 6C 88
Wasdale Head. *Cumb* 4L 45
Wash. *Derbs* 1J 35
Washaway. *Corn* 5C 4
Washbourne. *Devn* 6L 5
Washbrook. *Suff* 7H 31
Wash Common. *W Ber* 7B 20
Washerwall. *Staf* 5H 35
Washfield. *Devn* 4J 7
Washfold. *N Yor* 5J 47
Washford. *Som* 1K 7
Washford Pyne. *Devn* 4H 7
Washingborough. *Linc* 2H 37
Washington. *Tyne* 6G 55
Washington. *W Sus* 4J 11
Washington Village. *Tyne* 6G 55
Waskerley. *Dur* 7D 54
Wasperton. *Warw* 6L 27
Wasp Green. *Surr* 1L 11
Wasps Nest. *Linc* 3H 37
Wass. *N Yor* 8C 48
Watchet. *Som* 1K 7
Watchfield. *Oxon* 4L 19
Watchgate. *Cumb* 6D 46
Watchhill. *Cumb* 7F 52
Watcombe. *Torb* 5M 5
Watendlath. *Cumb* 4A 46
Water. *Devn* 7G 7
Water. *Lanc* 5G 41
Waterbeach. *Cambs* 5A 30
Waterbeach. *W Sus* 5F 10
Waterbeck. *Dum* 4G 53
Waterditch. *Hants* 6K 9
Water End. *C Beds* 8H 29
Water End. *E Yor* 4E 42
Water End. *Essx* 7B 30
Water End. *Herts*
nr. Hatfield 3K 21
nr. Hemel Hempstead 2H 21
Waterfall. *Staf* 4J 35
Waterfoot. *Caus* 2H 93
Waterfoot. *E Ren* 4D 58
Waterfoot. *Lanc* 5G 41
Waterford. *Herts* 2L 21
Water Fryston. *W Yor* 5B 42
Waterhead. *Cumb* 5B 46
Waterhead. *E Ayr* 8D 58
Waterhead. *S Ayr* 2J 51
Waterheads. *Bord* 4L 59
Waterhouses. *Dur* 7E 54
Waterhouses. *Staf* 4J 35
Wateringbury. *Kent* 8C 22
Waterlane. *Glos* 3H 19
Waterlip. *Som* 1E 8
Waterloo. *Cphy* 6L 17
Waterloo. *Corn* 4D 4
Waterloo. *Here* 7B 26
Waterloo. *High* 3H 69
Waterloo. *Mers* 8B 40
Waterloo. *Norf* 8J 39
Waterloo. *N Lan* 4G 59
Waterloo. *Pemb* 6F 14
Waterloo. *Per* 4D 66
Waterloo. *Pool* 6J 9
Waterloo. *Shrp* 6C 34
Waterlooville. *Hants* 5D 10
Watermead. *Buck* 2F 20
Watermillock. *Cumb* 3C 46
Water Newton. *Cambs* 2J 29
Water Orton. *Warw* 2K 27
Waterperry. *Oxon* 3D 20
Waterrow. *Som* 3K 7
Watersfield. *W Sus* 4H 11
Waterside. *Buck* 3G 21
Waterside. *Cambs* 4C 30
Waterside. *Cumb* 7G 53
Waterside. *E Ayr*
nr. Ayr 1K 51
nr. Kilmarnock 5C 58
Waterside. *E Dun* 2E 58
Waterstein. *High* 1C 68
Waterstock. *Oxon* 3D 20
Waterston. *Pemb* 6F 14
Water Stratford. *Buck* 8D 28
Waters Upton. *Telf* 8E 34
Water Yeat. *Cumb* 7A 46
Watford. *Herts* 4J 21
Watford. *Nptn* 5D 28
Wath. *Cumb* 5E 46
Wath. *N Yor*
nr. Pateley Bridge 1K 41
nr. Ripon 8M 47
Wath Brow. *Cumb* 3K 45
Wath upon Dearne. *S Yor* 7B 42
Watlington. *Norf* 8C 38
Watlington. *Oxon* 4D 20
Watten. *High* 6D 86
Wattisfield. *Suff* 4G 31
Wattisham. *Suff* 6G 31
Wattlesborough Heath.
Shrp 8B 34
Watton. *Dors* 6C 8
Watton. *E Yor* 2H 43
Watton. *Norf* 1F 30
Watton at Stone. *Herts* 2K 21
Wattston. *N Lan* 2F 58
Wattstown. *Rhon* 5K 17
Wattsville. *Cphy* 5M 17
Wauldby. *E Yor* 5G 43
Waulkmill. *Abers* 6F 72
Waun. *Powy* 1M 25
Y Waun. *Wrex* 6A 34
Waunarlwydd. *Swan* 5F 16
Waun Fawr. *Cdgn* 4F 24
Waunfawr. *Gwyn* 5E 32
Waungilwen. *Carm* 3K 15
Waun-Lwyd. *Blae* 4L 17
Waun y Clyn. *Carm* 6L 15
Wavendon. *Mil* 8G 29
Waverbridge. *Cumb* 7G 53
Waverley. *Surr* 1F 10
Waverton. *Ches W* 3C 34
Waverton. *Cumb* 7G 53
Wavertree. *Mers* 1B 34
Wawne. *E Yor* 4H 43
Waxham. *Norf* 7L 39
Waxholme. *E Yor* 5L 43
Wayford. *Som* 5C 8
Way Head. *Cambs* 3A 30
Waytown. *Dors* 6C 8
Way Village. *Devn* 4H 7
Wdig. *Pemb* 3F 14
Wealdstone. *G Lon* 5J 21
Weardley. *W Yor* 3L 41
Weare. *Som* 8C 18
Weare Giffard. *Devn* 3D 6
Wearhead. *Dur* 8B 54
Wearne. *Som* 3C 8
Weasdale. *Cumb* 5E 46
Weasenham All Saints.
Norf 7E 38
Weasenham St Peter. *Norf* 7E 38
Weaverham. *Ches W* 2E 34
Weaverthorpe. *N Yor* 8G 49
Webheath. *Worc* 5J 27
Webton. *Here* 8C 26
Wedderlairs. *Abers* 2H 73
Weddington. *Warw* 2A 28
Wedhampton. *Wilts* 8J 19
Wedmore. *Som* 1C 8
Wednesbury. *W Mid* 2H 27
Wednesfield. *W Mid* 1H 27
Weecar. *Notts* 3F 36
Weedon. *Buck* 2F 20
Weedon Bec. *Nptn* 6D 28
Weedon Lois. *Nptn* 7D 28
Weeford. *Staf* 1K 27
Week. *Devn*
nr. Barnstaple 3E 6
nr. Okehampton 5F 6
nr. South Molton 4G 7
nr. Totnes 5K 5
Week. *Som* 2J 7
Weeke. *Devn* 5G 7
Weeke. *Hants* 2B 10
Week Green. *Corn* 6B 6
Weekley. *Nptn* 3F 28
Week St Mary. *Corn* 6B 6
Weel. *E Yor* 4H 43
Weeley. *Essx* 1H 23
Weeley Heath. *Essx* 1H 23
Weem. *Per* 3B 66
Weeping Cross. *Staf* 7H 35
Weethly. *Warw* 6J 27
Weeting. *Norf* 3D 30
Weeton. *E Yor* 5L 43
Weeton. *Lanc* 4B 40
Weeton. *N Yor* 3L 41
Weetwood Hall. *Nmbd* 7H 61
Weir. *Lanc* 5G 41
Welborne. *Norf* 8G 39
Welbourn. *Linc* 4G 37
Welburn. *N Yor*
nr. Kirkbymoorside 7D 48
nr. Malton 1E 42
Welbury. *N Yor* 5A 48
Welby. *Linc* 6G 37
Welches Dam. *Cambs* 3A 30
Welcombe. *Devn* 4B 6
Weld Bank. *Lanc* 6D 40
Weldon. *Nptn* 3G 29
Weldon. *Nmbd* 2E 54
Welford. *Nptn* 3D 28
Welford. *W Ber* 6B 20
Welford-on-Avon. *Warw* 6K 27

Woodall—Zouch

Woodall. *S Yor* 1B 36
Woodbank. *Ches W* 2B 34
Woodbastwick. *Norf* 8K 39
Woodbeck. *Notts* 2E 36
Woodborough. *Notts* 5D 36
Woodborough. *Wilts* 8K 19
Woodbridge. *Devn* 6L 7
Woodbridge. *Dors* 4F 8
Woodbridge. *Suff* 7J 31
Wood Burcote. *Nptn* 7D 28
Woodbury. *Devn* 7K 7
Woodbury Salterton. *Devn* 7K 7
Woodchester. *Glos* 3G 19
Woodchurch. *Kent* 2F 12
Woodchurch. *Mers* 1A 34
Woodcock Heath. *Staf* 7J 35
Woodcombe. *Som* 1J 7
Woodcote. *Oxon* 5D 20
Woodcote Green. *Worc* 4H 27
Woodcott. *Hants* 8B 20
Woodcroft. *Glos* 4D 18
Woodcutts. *Dors* 4H 9
Wood Dalling. *Norf* 7G 39
Woodditton. *Cambs* 6C 30
Wood Eaton. *Staf* 8G 35
Woodeaton. *Oxon* 2C 20
Wood End. *Bed* 5H 29
Wood End. *Herts* 1L 21
Wood End. *Warw*
nr. Bedworth 3L 27
nr. Dordon 2L 27
nr. Tanworth-in-Arden 4K 27
Woodend. *Cumb* 5L 45
Woodend. *Nptn* 7D 28
Woodend. *Staf* 7K 35
Woodend. *W Sus* 5F 10
Wood Enderby. *Linc* 3K 37
Woodend Green. *Essx* 1B 22
Woodfalls. *Wilts* 3K 9
Woodfield. *Oxon* 1C 20
Woodfields. *Lanc* 4E 40
Woodford. *Corn* 4B 6
Woodford. *Devn* 6K 5
Woodford. *Glos* 4E 18
Woodford. *G Lon* 4L 21
Woodford. *G Man* 1G 35
Woodford. *Nptn* 4G 29
Woodford. *Plym* 6H 5
Woodford Green. *G Lon* 4M 21
Woodford Halse. *Nptn* 6C 28
Woodgate. *Norf* 8G 39
Woodgate. *W Mid* 3H 27
Woodgate. *W Sus* 5G 11
Woodgate. *Worc* 5H 27
Wood Green. *G Lon* 4K 21
Woodgreen. *Hants* 4K 9
Woodgreen. *Oxon* 2A 20
Woodhall. *Inv* 2B 58
Woodhall. *Linc* 3K 37
Woodhall. *N Yor* 6H 47
Woodhall Spa. *Linc* 3J 37
Woodham. *Surr* 7H 21
Woodham Ferrers. *Essx* 4D 22
Woodham Mortimer. *Essx* 3E 22
Woodham Walter. *Essx* 3E 22
Woodhaven. *Fife* 5H 67
Wood Hayes. *W Mid* 1H 27
Woodhead. *Abers*
nr. Fraserburgh 7J 81
nr. Fyvie 2G 73
Woodhill. *N Som* 6C 18
Woodhill. *Shrp* 3F 26
Woodhill. *Som* 3B 8
Woodhorn. *Nmbd* 3F 54
Woodhouse. *Leics* 8C 36
Woodhouse. *S Yor* 1B 36
Woodhouse. *W Yor*
nr. Leeds 4L 41
nr. Normanton 5A 42
Woodhouse Eaves. *Leics* 8C 36
Woodhouses. *Ches W* 2D 34
Woodhouses. *G Man*
nr. Failsworth 7H 41
nr. Sale 8F 40
Woodhouses. *Staf* 8K 35
Woodhuish. *Devn* 6M 5
Woodhurst. *Cambs* 4L 29
Woodingdean. *Brig* 5L 11
Woodland. *Devn* 5K 5
Woodland. *Dur* 3J 47
Woodland Head. *Devn* 6G 7
Woodlands. *Abers* 6G 73
Woodlands. *Dors* 5J 9
Woodlands. *Hants* 4M 9
Woodlands. *Kent* 7B 22
Woodlands. *N Yor* 2M 41
Woodlands. *S Yor* 7C 42
Woodlands Park. *Wind* 6F 20
Woodlands St Mary. *W Ber* 6M 19
Woodlane. *Shrp* 7E 34
Woodlane. *Staf* 7K 35
Woodleigh. *Devn* 7K 5
Woodlesford. *W Yor* 5A 42
Woodley. *G Man* 8H 41
Woodley. *Wok* 6E 20
Woodmancote. *Glos*
nr. Cheltenham 1H 19
nr. Cirencester 3J 19
Woodmancote. *W Sus*
nr. Chichester 5E 10
nr. Henfield 4K 11
Woodmancote. *Worc* 7H 27
Woodmancott. *Hants* 1C 10
Woodmansey. *E Yor* 4H 43
Woodmansgreen. *W Sus* 3F 10
Woodmansterne. *Surr* 8K 21
Woodmanton. *Devn* 7K 7
Woodmill. *Staf* 7K 35
Woodminton. *Wilts* 3J 9
Woodnesborough. *Kent* 8K 23
Woodnewton. *Nptn* 2H 29
Woodnook. *Linc* 6G 37
Wood Norton. *Norf* 7G 39
Woodplumpton. *Lanc* 4D 40
Woodrising. *Norf* 1F 30
Wood Row. *W Yor* 5A 42
Woodrow. *Cumb* 7G 53
Woodrow. *Dors*
nr. Fifehead Neville 4F 8
nr. Hazelbury Bryan 5F 8
Woods Eaves. *Here* 7A 26
Woodseaves. *Shrp* 6E 34
Woodseaves. *Staf* 7G 35
Woodsend. *Wilts* 6L 19
Woodsetts. *S Yor* 1C 36
Woodsford. *Dors* 6F 8
Wood's Green. *E Sus* 2C 12
Woodshaw. *Wilts* 5J 19
Woodside. *Aber* 5J 73
Woodside. *Brac* 6G 21
Woodside. *Derbs* 5A 36
Woodside. *Dum* 4E 52
Woodside. *Dur* 3K 47
Woodside. *Fife* 7H 67
Woodside. *Herts* 3K 21
Woodside. *Per* 4F 66
Wood Stanway. *Glos* 8J 27
Woodstock. *Oxon* 2B 20
Woodstock Slop. *Pemb* 4G 15
Woodston. *Pet* 2J 29
Wood Street. *Norf* 7K 39
Wood Street Village. *Surr* 8G 21
Woodthorpe. *Derbs* 2B 36
Woodthorpe. *Leics* 8C 36
Woodthorpe. *Linc* 1M 37
Woodthorpe. *Notts* 5C 36
Woodthorpe. *York* 3C 42
Woodton. *Norf* 2J 31
Woodtown. *Devn*
nr. Bideford 3D 6
nr. Littleham 3D 6
Woodvale. *Mers* 6B 40
Woodville. *Derbs* 8M 35
Woodwalton. *Cambs* 3K 29
Woodwick. *Orkn* 7C 88
Woodyates. *Dors* 4J 9
Woody Bay. *Devn* 1F 6
Woofferton. *Shrp* 5D 26
Wookey. *Som* 1D 8
Wookey Hole. *Som* 1D 8
Wool. *Dors* 7G 9
Woolacombe. *Devn* 1D 6
Woolage Green. *Kent* 1J 13
Woolage Village. *Kent* 8J 23
Woolaston. *Glos* 4D 18
Woolavington. *Som* 1B 8
Woolbeding. *W Sus* 3F 10
Woolcotts. *Som* 2J 7
Wooldale. *W Yor* 7K 41
Wooler. *Nmbd* 7G 61
Woolfardisworthy. *Devn*
nr. Bideford 3C 6
nr. Crediton 5H 7
Woolfords. *S Lan* 4J 59
Woolgarston. *Dors* 7H 9
Woolhampton. *W Ber* 7C 20
Woolhope. *Here* 8E 26
Woolland. *Dors* 5F 8
Woollard. *Bath* 7E 18
Woolley. *Bath* 7F 18
Woolley. *Cambs* 4J 29
Woolley. *Corn* 4B 6
Woolley. *Derbs* 3A 36
Woolley. *W Yor* 6M 41
Woolley Green. *Wilts* 7G 19
Woolmere Green. *Worc* 5H 27
Woolmer Green. *Herts* 2K 21
Woolminstone. *Som* 5C 8
Woolpit. *Suff* 5F 30
Woolridge. *Glos* 1G 19
Woolscott. *Warw* 5B 28
Woolsery. *Devn* 3C 6
Woolsington. *Tyne* 5E 54
Woolstaston. *Shrp* 2C 26
Woolsthorpe By Belvoir. *Linc* 6F 36
Woolsthorpe-by-Colsterworth. *Linc* 7G 37
Woolston. *Devn* 7K 5
Woolston. *Shrp*
nr. Church Stretton 3C 26
nr. Oswestry 7B 34
Woolston. *Som* 3E 8
Woolston. *Sotn* 4B 10
Woolston. *Warr* 1E 34
Woolstone. *Glos* 8H 27
Woolstone. *Oxon* 5L 19
Woolston Green. *Devn* 5K 5
Woolton. *Mers* 1C 34
Woolton Hill. *Hants* 7B 20
Woolverstone. *Suff* 8H 31
Woolverton. *Som* 8F 18
Woolwell. *Devn* 5H 5
Woolwich. *G Lon* 6M 21
Woonton. *Here*
nr. Kington 6B 26
nr. Leominster 5D 26
Wooperton. *Nmbd* 7H 61
Woore. *Shrp* 5F 34
Wooth. *Dors* 6C 8
Wooton. *Shrp* 3F 26
Wootton. *Bed* 7H 29
Wootton. *Hants* 6L 9
Wootton. *IOW* 6C 10
Wootton. *Kent* 1J 13
Wootton. *Nptn* 6E 28
Wootton. *N Lin* 6H 43
Wootton. *Oxon*
nr. Abingdon 3B 20
nr. Woodstock 2B 20
Wootton. *Shrp*
nr. Ludlow 4C 26
nr. Oswestry 7B 34
Wootton. *Staf*
nr. Eccleshall 7G 35
nr. Ellastone 5K 35
Wootton Bassett, Royal. *Wilts* 5J 19
Wootton Bridge. *IOW* 6C 10
Wootton Common. *IOW* 6C 10
Wootton Courtenay. *Som* 1J 7
Wootton Fitzpaine. *Dors* 6B 8
Wootton Rivers. *Wilts* 7K 19
Wootton St Lawrence. *Hants* 8C 20
Wootton Wawen. *Warw* 5K 27
Worcester. *Worc* 117 (6G 27)
Worcester Park. *G Lon* 7K 21
Wordsley. *W Mid* 3G 27
Worfield. *Shrp* 2F 26
Work. *Orkn* 8D 88
Workhouse Green. *Suff* 8F 30
Workington. *Cumb* 2J 45
Worksop. *Notts* 2C 36
Worlaby. *N Lin* 6H 43
World's End. *W Ber* 6B 20
World's End. *W Sus* 4L 11
Worlds End. *Hants* 4D 10
Worlds End. *W Mid* 3K 27
Worldsend. *Shrp* 2C 26
Worle. *N Som* 7B 18
Worleston. *Ches E* 4E 34
Worlingham. *Suff* 3L 31
Worlington. *Suff* 4C 30
Worlingworth. *Suff* 5J 31
Wormbridge. *Here* 8C 26
Wormegay. *Norf* 8C 38
Wormelow Tump. *Here* 8C 26
Wormhill. *Derbs* 2K 35
Wormingford. *Essx* 8F 30
Worminghall. *Buck* 3D 20
Wormington. *Glos* 8J 27
Worminster. *Som* 1D 8
Wormit. *Fife* 5G 67
Wormleighton. *Warw* 6B 28
Wormley. *Herts* 3L 21
Wormley. *Surr* 2G 11
Wormshill. *Kent* 8E 22
Wormsley. *Here* 7C 26
Worplesdon. *Surr* 8G 21
Worrall. *S Yor* 8M 41
Worsbrough. *S Yor* 7A 42
Worsley. *G Man* 7F 40
Worstead. *Norf* 7K 39
Worsthorne. *Lanc* 4G 41
Worston. *Lanc* 3F 40
Worth. *Kent* 8K 23
Worth. *W Sus* 2K 11
Wortham. *Suff* 4G 31
Worthen. *Shrp* 1B 26
Worthenbury. *Wrex* 5C 34
Worthing. *Norf* 8F 38
Worthing. *W Sus* 5J 11
Worthington. *Leics* 7B 36
Worth Matravers. *Dors* 8H 9
Worting. *Hants* 8D 20
Wortley. *Glos* 4F 18
Wortley. *S Yor* 8M 41
Wortley. *W Yor* 4L 41
Worton. *N Yor* 7H 47
Worton. *Wilts* 8H 19
Wortwell. *Norf* 3J 31
Wotherton. *Shrp* 1A 26
Wothorpe. *Pet* 1H 29
Wotter. *Devn* 5H 5
Wotton. *Glos* 2G 19
Wotton. *Surr* 1J 11
Wotton-under-Edge. *Glos* 4F 18
Wotton Underwood. *Buck* 2D 20
Wouldham. *Kent* 7D 22
Wrabness. *Essx* 8H 31
Wrafton. *Devn* 2D 6
Wragby. *Linc* 2J 37
Wragby. *W Yor* 6B 42
Wramplingham. *Norf* 1H 31
Wrangbrook. *W Yor* 6B 42
Wrangle. *Linc* 4M 37
Wrangle Lowgate. *Linc* 4M 37
Wrangway. *Som* 4L 7
Wrantage. *Som* 3B 8
Wrawby. *N Lin* 7H 43
Wraxall. *N Som* 6C 18
Wraxall. *Som* 2E 8
Wray. *Lanc* 1E 40
Wraysbury. *Wind* 6H 21
Wrayton. *Lanc* 8E 46
Wrea Green. *Lanc* 4B 40
Wreay. *Cumb*
nr. Carlisle 7J 53
nr. Penrith 3C 46
Wrecclesham. *Surr* 1F 10
Wrecsam. *Wrex* 4B 34
Wrekenton. *Tyne* 6F 54
Wrelton. *N Yor* 7E 48
Wrenbury. *Ches E* 5D 34
Wreningham. *Norf* 2H 31
Wrentham. *Suff* 3L 31
Wrenthorpe. *W Yor* 5M 41
Wrentnall. *Shrp* 1C 26
Wressle. *E Yor* 4E 42
Wressle. *N Lin* 7G 43
Wrestlingworth. *C Beds* 7K 29
Wretton. *Norf* 2C 30
Wrexham. *Wrex* 4B 34
Wreyland. *Devn* 7G 7
Wrickton. *Shrp* 3E 26
Wrightington Bar. *Lanc* 6D 40
Wright's Green. *Essx* 2B 22
Wrinehill. *Staf* 5F 34
Wrington. *N Som* 7C 18
Writtle. *Essx* 3C 22
Wrockwardine. *Telf* 8E 34
Wroot. *N Lin* 7E 42
Wrotham. *Kent* 8C 22
Wrotham Heath. *Kent* 8C 22
Wroughton. *Swin* 5K 19
Wroxall. *IOW* 7C 10
Wroxall. *Warw* 4L 27
Wroxeter. *Shrp* 1D 26
Wroxham. *Norf* 8K 39
Wroxton. *Oxon* 7B 28
Wyaston. *Derbs* 5K 35
Wyatt's Green. *Essx* 4B 22
Wybers Wood. *NE Lin* 7K 43
Wyberton. *Linc* 5L 37
Wyboston. *Bed* 6J 29
Wybunbury. *Ches E* 5E 34
Wychbold. *Worc* 5H 27
Wych Cross. *E Sus* 2M 11
Wychnor. *Staf* 8K 35
Wychnor Bridges. *Staf* 8K 35
Wyck. *Hants* 2E 10
Wyck Hill. *Glos* 1K 19
Wyck Rissington. *Glos* 1K 19
Wycliffe. *Dur* 4K 47
Wycombe Marsh. *Buck* 4F 20
Yr Wyddgrug. *Flin* 4M 33
Wyddial. *Herts* 8L 29
Wye. *Kent* 1G 13
Wyesham. *Mon* 2D 18
Wyfold. *Oxon* 5D 20
Wyfordby. *Leics* 8E 36
The Wyke. *Shrp* 1F 26
Wyke. *Devn* 6H 7
Wyke. *Dors* 3F 8
Wyke. *Shrp* 1E 26
Wyke. *Surr* 8G 21
Wyke. *W Yor* 5K 41
Wyke Champflower. *Som* 2E 8
Wykeham. *Linc* 7K 37
Wykeham. *N Yor*
nr. Malton 8F 48
nr. Scarborough 7G 49
Wyken. *Shrp* 2F 26
Wyken. *W Mid* 3A 28
Wyke Regis. *Dors* 8E 8
Wykey. *Shrp* 7B 34
Wykin. *Leics* 2B 28
Wylam. *Nmbd* 5E 54
Wylde Green. *W Mid* 2K 27
Wylye. *Wilts* 2J 9
Wymering. *Port* 5D 10
Wymeswold. *Leics* 7D 36
Wymington. *Bed* 5G 29
Wymondham. *Leics* 8F 36
Wymondham. *Norf* 1H 31
Wyndham. *B'end* 5J 17
Wynford Eagle. *Dors* 6D 8
Wyng. *Orkn* 2E 86
Wynyard Village. *Stoc T* 3B 48
Wyre Piddle. *Worc* 7H 27
Wysall. *Notts* 7D 36
Wyson. *Here* 5D 26
Wythall. *Worc* 4J 27
Wytham. *Oxon* 3B 20
Wythenshawe. *G Man* 1G 35
Wythop Mill. *Cumb* 2L 45
Wyton. *Cambs* 4K 29
Wyton. *E Yor* 4J 43
Wyverstone. *Suff* 5G 31
Wyverstone Street. *Suff* 5G 31
Wyville. *Linc* 7F 36
Wyvis Lodge. *High* 6E 78

Y

Yaddlethorpe. *N Lin* 7F 42
Yafford. *IOW* 7B 10
Yafforth. *N Yor* 6M 47
Yalding. *Kent* 8C 22
Yanley. *N Som* 7D 18
Yanwath. *Cumb* 3D 46
Yanworth. *Glos* 2J 19
Yapham. *E Yor* 2E 42
Yapton. *W Sus* 5G 11
Yarburgh. *Linc* 8L 43
Yarcombe. *Devn* 5M 7
Yarde. *Som* 2K 7
Yardley. *W Mid* 3K 27
Yardley Gobion. *Nptn* 7E 28
Yardley Hastings. *Nptn* 6F 28
Yardley Wood. *W Mid* 3K 27
Yardro. *Powy* 7M 25
Yarhampton. *Worc* 5F 26
Yarkhill. *Here* 7E 26
Yarlet. *Staf* 7H 35
Yarley. *Som* 1D 8
Yarlington. *Som* 3E 8
Yarm. *Stoc T* 4B 48
Yarmouth. *IOW* 7A 10
Yarnbrook. *Wilts* 8G 19
Yarnfield. *Staf* 6G 35
Yarnscombe. *Devn* 3E 6
Yarnton. *Oxon* 2B 20
Yarpole. *Here* 5C 26
Yarrow. *Nmbd* 3M 53
Yarrow. *Bord* 7A 60
Yarrow. *Som* 1B 8
Yarrow Feus. *Bord* 7M 59
Yarrow Ford. *Bord* 6B 60
Yarsop. *Here* 7C 26
Yarwell. *Nptn* 2H 29
Yate. *S Glo* 5F 18
Yateley. *Hants* 7F 20
Yatesbury. *Wilts* 6J 19
Yattendon. *W Ber* 6C 20
Yatton. *Here*
nr. Leominster 5C 26
nr. Ross-on-Wye 8E 26
Yatton. *N Som* 7C 18
Yatton Keynell. *Wilts* 6G 19
Yaverland. *IOW* 7D 10
Yawl. *Devn* 6B 8
Yaxham. *Norf* 8G 39
Yaxley. *Cambs* 2J 29
Yaxley. *Suff* 4H 31
Yazor. *Here* 7C 26
Yeading. *G Lon* 5J 21
Yeadon. *W Yor* 3L 41
Yealand Conyers. *Lanc* 8D 46
Yealand Redmayne. *Lanc* 8D 46
Yealand Storrs. *Lanc* 8C 46
Yealmpton. *Devn* 6H 5
Yearby. *Red C* 3D 48
Yearngill. *Cumb* 7F 52
Yearsett. *Here* 6F 26
Yearsley. *N Yor* 8C 48
Yeaton. *Shrp* 8C 34
Yeaveley. *Derbs* 5K 35
Yeavering. *Nmbd* 6G 61
Yedingham. *N Yor* 8F 48
Yeldersley Hollies. *Derbs* 5L 35
Yelford. *Oxon* 3A 20
Yelland. *Devn* 2D 6
Yelling. *Cambs* 5K 29
Yelsted. *Kent* 7E 22
Yelvertoft. *Nptn* 4C 28
Yelverton. *Devn* 5H 5
Yelverton. *Norf* 1J 31
Yenston. *Som* 3F 8
Yeoford. *Devn* 6G 7
Yeolmbridge. *Corn* 7C 6
Yeo Mill. *Devn* 3H 7
Yeovil. *Som* 4D 8
Yeovil Marsh. *Som* 4D 8
Yeovilton. *Som* 3D 8
Yerbeston. *Pemb* 6G 15
Yesnaby. *Orkn* 8B 88
Yetlington. *Nmbd* 1D 54
Yetminster. *Dors* 4D 8
Yett. *N Lan* 4F 58
Yett. *S Ayr* 7C 58
Yettington. *Devn* 7K 7
Yetts o' Muckhart. *Clac* 7D 66
Yielden. *Bed* 5H 29
Yieldshields. *S Lan* 4G 59
Yiewsley. *G Lon* 5H 21
Yinstay. *Orkn* 8E 88
Ynysboeth. *Rhon* 5K 17
Ynysddu. *Cphy* 5L 17
Ynysforgan. *Swan* 5F 16
Ynyshir. *Rhon* 5K 17
Ynyslas. *Cdgn* 3F 24
Ynysmaerdy. *Rhon* 6K 17
Ynysmeudwy. *Neat* 4G 17
Ynystawe. *Swan* 4F 16
Ynys-wen. *Rhon* 5J 17
Ynyswen. *Powy* 3H 17
Ynys y Barri. *V Glam* 8L 17
Ynysybwl. *Rhon* 5K 17
Ynysymaerdy. *Neat* 5G 17
Yockenthwaite. *N Yor* 8H 47
Yockleton. *Shrp* 8C 34
Yokefleet. *E Yor* 5F 42
Yoker. *Glas* 3D 58
Yonder Bognie. *Abers* 1E 72
Yonderton. *Abers* 2J 73
York. *York* 117 (2D 42)
Yorkletts. *Kent* 7G 23
Yorkley. *Glos* 3E 18
Yorton. *Shrp* 7D 34
Yorton Heath. *Shrp* 7D 34
Youlgreave. *Derbs* 3L 35
Youlthorpe. *E Yor* 2E 42
Youlton. *N Yor* 1B 42
Young's End. *Essx* 2D 22
Young Wood. *Linc* 2J 37
Yoxall. *Staf* 8K 35
Yoxford. *Suff* 5K 31
Ysbyty Cynfyn. *Cdgn* 5G 25
Ysbyty Ifan. *Cnwy* 6H 33
Ysbyty Ystwyth. *Cdgn* 5G 25
Ysceifiog. *Flin* 3L 33
Yspitty. *Carm* 5E 16
Ystalyfera. *Neat* 4G 17
Ystrad. *Rhon* 5J 17
Ystrad Aeron. *Cdgn* 1M 15
Ystradfellte. *Powy* 3J 17
Ystradffin. *Carm* 8G 25
Ystradgynlais. *Powy* 3G 17
Ystradmeurig. *Cdgn* 6G 25
Ystrad Mynach. *Cphy* 5L 17
Ystradowen. *Carm* 3G 17
Ystradowen. *V Glam* 7K 17
Ystumtuen. *Cdgn* 5G 25
Ythanbank. *Abers* 2J 73
Ythanwells. *Abers* 2F 72

Z

Zeal Monachorum. *Devn* 5G 7
Zeals. *Wilts* 2F 8
Zelah. *Corn* 3M 3
Zennor. *Corn* 5H 3
Zouch. *Notts* 7C 36

INDEX TO SELECTED PLACES OF INTEREST

(1) A strict alphabetical order is used e.g. Benmore Botanic Gdn. follows Ben Macdui but precedes Ben Nevis.

(2) Places of Interest which fall on City and Town Centre maps are referenced first to the detailed map page, followed by the main map page if appropriate. The name of the map is included if it is not clear from the index entry.
e.g. Ashmolean Mus. of Art & Archaeology (OX1 2PH) . . . . **Oxford 114** (3C **20**)

(3) Entries in italics are not named on the map but are shown with a symbol only.
*e.g. Aberdour Castle (KY3 0XA) 1K **59***

SAT NAV POSTCODES

Postcodes are shown to assist Sat Nav users and are included on this basis.
It should be noted that postcodes have been selected by their proximity to the Place of Interest and that they may not form part of the actual postal address. Drivers should follow the Tourist Brown Signs when available.

ABBREVIATIONS USED IN THIS INDEX

Centre : Cen. Garden : Gdn. Gardens : Gdns. Museum : Mus. National : Nat. Park : Pk.

A

Abbeydale Industrial Hamlet (S7 2QW) 1M 35
Abbey House Mus. (LS5 3EH) 4L 41
Abbot Hall Art Gallery. (LA9 5AL) 6D 46
Abbotsbury Subtropical Gdns. (DT3 4LA) 7D 8
Abbotsbury Swannery (DT3 4JG) 7D 8
Abbotsford (TD6 9BQ) 6C 60
Aberdeen Maritime Mus. (AB11 5BY) 106 (5J 73)
Aberdour Castle. (KY3 0XA) 1K 59
Aberdulais Falls (SA10 8EU) 4G 17
Aberglasney Gdns. (SA32 8QH) 2E 16
Abernethy Round Tower (PH2 9RT) 6E 66
Aberystwyth Castle. (SY23 1DZ) 4E 24
Acorn Bank Gdn. & Watermill (CA10 1SP) 3E 46
Acton Burnell Castle. (SY5 7PF) 1D 26
Acton Scott Historic Working Farm (SY6 6QN) 3C 26
Adlington Hall (SK10 4LF) 1H 35
Africa Alive! (NR33 7TF) 3M 31
Aintree Racecourse (L9 5AS) 8B 40
Aira Force (CA11 0JX) 3C 46
A la Ronde (EX8 5BD) 7K 7
Alby Gdns. (NR11 7QE) 6J 39
Aldeburgh Mus. (IP15 5DS) 6L 31
Alfred Corry Mus. (IP18 6NB) 4M 31
Alfriston Clergy House (BN26 5TL) 5B 12
Alloa Tower (FK10 1PP) 8B 66
Alnwick Castle. (NE66 1NQ) 8J 61
Alnwick Gdn. (NE66 1YU) 8J 61
Althorp (NN7 4HQ) 5D 28
Alton Towers (ST10 4DB) 5J 35
Amberley Mus. & Heritage Cen. (BN18 9LT) 4H 11
The American Mus. in Britain (BA2 7BD) 7F 18
Angel of the North (NE9 6PG) 6F 54
Anglesey Abbey & Lode Mill (CB25 9EJ) 5B 30
Anne Hathaway's Cottage (CV37 9HH) 6K 27
Antonine Wall, Rough Castle (FK4 2AA) 2G 59
Antony (PL11 2QA) 6G 5
Appuldurcombe House (PO38 3EW) 7C 10
Arbeia Roman Fort & Mus. (NE33 2BB) 5G 55
Arbroath Abbey. (DD11 1JQ) 3K 67
Arbury Hall (CV10 7PT) 3M 27
Arbuthnott House Gdn. (AB30 1PA) 8G 73
Ardkinglas Woodland Gdns. (PA26 8BG) 6F 64
Ardnamurchan Point (PH36 4LN) 1J 63
Ardress House (BT62 1SQ) 6F 93
Arduaine Gdn. (PA34 4XQ) 6B 64
Ardwell Gdns. (DG9 9LY) 7G 51
The Argory (BT71 6NA) 6F 93
Argyll's Lodging (FK8 1EG) Stirling 116 (8A 66)
Arley Hall & Gdns. (CW9 6NA) 1E 34
Arlington Court (EX31 4LP) 2F 6
Arlington Row (GL7 5NJ) 3K 19
Armadale Castle Gdns. (IV45 8RS) 5H 69
Armagh County Mus. (BT61 9BE) 6F 93
Armagh Planetarium (BT61 9DB) 6F 93
Arniston House (EH23 4RY) 4M 59
Arundel Castle. (BN18 9AB) 5H 11
Arundel Wetland Cen. (BN18 9PB) 5H 11
Ascot Racecourse (SL5 7JX) 7G 21
Ascott (LU7 0PT) 1F 20
Ashby-de-la-Zouch Castle. (LE65 1BR) 8A 36
Ashdown Forest (TN7 4EU) 2A 12
Ashdown House (RG17 8RE) 5L 19
Ashmolean Mus. of Art & Archaeology (OX1 2PH) Oxford 114 (3C 20)
Astley Hall Mus. & Art Gallery. (PR7 1NP) 6D 40
Athelhampton House & Gdns. (DT2 7LG) 6F 8
Attingham Pk. (SY4 4TP) 1D 26
Auchingarrich Wildlife Cen. (PH6 2JE) 6A 66
Auckland Castle. (DL14 7NP) 8F 54
Audley End House & Gdns. (CB11 4JF) 8B 30
Avebury (SN8 1RE) 6K 19
Avoncroft Mus. of Historic Buildings (B60 4JR) 5H 27
Avon Valley Adventure & Wildlife Pk. (BS31 1TP) 7E 18
Avon Valley Railway (BS30 6HD) 6E 18
Aydon Castle (NE45 5PJ) 5C 54
Ayr Racecourse (KA8 0JE) 7B 58
Ayscoughfee Hall Mus. & Gdns. (PE11 2RA) 7K 37
Aysgarth Falls (DL8 3SR) 7J 47
Ayton Castle (Eyemouth). (TD14 5RD) 3G 61

B

Bachelors' Club (KA5 5RB) 7C 58
Baconsthorpe Castle. (NR25 6PS) 6H 39
Baddesley Clinton (B93 0DQ) 4K 27
Bala Lake Railway (LL23 7DD) 7H 33
Ballindalloch Castle (AB37 9AX) 2A 72
Balmoral Castle (AB35 5TB) 6B 72
Balvaird Castle (PH2 9PY) 6E 66
Balvenie Castle (AB55 4DH) 1C 72
Bamburgh Castle. (NE69 7DF) 6J 61
Bangor Cathedral. (LL57 1DN) 3E 32
Banham Zoo (NR16 2HE) 3G 31
Bannockburn Battle Site (FK7 0PL) 8A 66
Barbara Hepworth Mus. & Sculpture Gdn. (TR26 1AD) 4J 3
Barnard Castle. (DL12 8PR) 4J 47
Barnsdale Gdns. (LE15 8AH) 8G 37
Barrington Court (TA19 0NQ) 4B 8
Basildon Pk. (RG8 9NR) 6D 20
Basing House (RG24 8AE) 8D 20
Basingwerk Abbey (CH8 7GH) 3L 33
Bateman's (TN19 7DS) 3C 12
Bath Abbey (BA1 1LT) 106 (7F 18)
Bath Assembly Rooms (BA1 2QH) 106
Battle Abbey (TN33 0AD) 4D 12
The Battlefield Line Railway (CV13 0BS) 1A 28
The Battle of Britain Memorial (CT18 7JJ) 2J 13
Battle of Britain Memorial Flight Visitors Cen. (LN4 4SY) 4K 37
Battle of Hastings Site (TN33 0AD) 4D 12
Bayham Abbey (TN3 8BG) 2C 12
Beachy Head (BN20 7YA) 6B 12
Beamish (DH9 0RG) 6F 54
The Beatles Story (L3 4AD) Liverpool 111
Beaulieu Abbey (SO42 7ZN) 5A 10
Beauly Priory (IV4 7BL) 1F 70
Beaumaris Castle. (LL58 8AP) 3F 32
Beck Isle Mus. (YO18 8DU) 7E 48
Bedgebury National Pinetum (TN17 2SL) 2D 12
Bedruthan Steps (PL27 7UW) 5A 4
Beeston Castle & Woodland Pk. (CW6 9TX) 4D 34
Bekonscot Model Village & Railway (HP9 2PL) 4G 21
Belfast Castle (BT15 5GR) 5H 93
Belfast Zoological Gdns. (BT36 7PN) 4H 93
Belgrave Hall Mus. & Gdns. (LE4 5PE) 1C 28
Belleek Pottery (BT93 3FY) 6A 92
Belmont House & Gdns. (ME13 0HH) 8F 22
Belsay Hall, Castle & Gdns. (NE20 0DX) 4D 54
Belton House (NG32 2LS) 6G 37
Belvoir Castle (NG32 1PD) 6F 36
Beningbrough Hall & Gdns. (YO30 1DD) 2C 42
Benington Lordship Gdns. (SG2 7BS) 1K 21
Ben Lawers (PH15 2PA) 3L 65
Ben Lomond (FK8 3TR) 7H 65
Ben Macdui (PH22 1RB) 6K 71
Benmore Botanic Gdn. (PA23 8QU) 1L 57
Ben Nevis (PH33 6SY) 8B 70
Benthall Hall (TF12 5RX) 1E 26
Bentley Wildfowl & Motor Mus. (BN8 5AF) 4A 12
Berkeley Castle (GL13 9BQ) 4E 18
Berkhamsted Castle (HP4 1LJ) 3G 21
Berney Arms Windmill (NR31 9HU) 1L 31
Berrington Hall (HR6 0DW) 5D 26
Berry Pomeroy Castle (TQ9 6LJ) 5L 5
Bessie Surtees House (NE1 3JF) Newcastle upon Tyne 111
Beverley Minster (HU17 0DP) 4H 43
Bicton Gdns. (EX9 7BJ) 7K 7
Biddulph Grange Gdn. (ST8 7SD) 4G 35
Big Ben (SW1A 2PW) London 113
Bignor Roman Villa (RH20 1PH) 4G 11
Big Pit National Coal Mus. (NP4 9XP) 4M 17
Binham Priory (NR21 0DJ) 5F 38
Birmingham Mus. & Art Gallery (B3 3DH) 106
Bishop's Waltham Palace (SO32 1DP) 4C 10
Black Country Living Mus. (DY1 4SQ) 2H 27
Blackgang Chine (PO38 2HN) 8B 10
Blackhouse (HS2 9DB) 7G 83
Blackness Castle (EH49 7NH) 1J 59
Blackpool Pleasure Beach (FY4 1EZ) 4B 40
Blackpool Zoo (FY3 8PP) 4B 40
The Blackwell Arts & Crafts House (LA23 3JR) 6C 46
Blaenavon Ironworks (NP4 9RJ) 4M 17
Blaenavon World Heritage Cen. (NP4 9AS) 4M 17
Blair Castle (PH18 5TL) 1B 66
Blair Drummond Safari & Adventure Pk. (FK9 4UR) 8M 65
Blakeney Point (NR25 7SA) 5G 39
Blakesley Hall (B25 8RN) 3K 27
Blenheim Palace (OX20 1PX) 2B 20
Bletchley Pk. (MK3 6EB) 8F 28
Blickling Estate (NR11 6NF) 7H 39
Blists Hill Victorian Town (TF7 5DS) 1E 26
Bluebell Railway (TN22 3QL) 3L 11
Blue John Cavern (S33 8WP) 1K 35
Blue Reef Aquarium
Newquay (TR7 1DU) 2M 3
Hastings (TN34 3DW) 5E 12
Portsmouth (PO5 3PB) 115 (6D 10)
Tynemouth (NE30 4JF) 4G 55
Boath Doocot (IV12 5TD) 8K 79
Bodelwyddan Castle (LL18 5YA) 3J 33
Bodiam Castle. (TN32 5UA) 3D 12
Bodleian Library (OX1 3BG) Oxford 114
Bodmin & Wenford Railway (PL31 1AQ) 5C 4
Bodmin Moor (PL15 7TN) 8A 6
Bodnant Gdn. (LL28 5RE) 3H 33
Bodrhyddan Hall (LL18 5SB) 3K 33
Bolingbroke Castle (PE23 4HH) 3L 37
Bolsover Castle. (S44 6PR) 2B 36
Bolton Castle (DL8 4ET) 6J 47
Bolton Priory (BD23 6AL) 2J 41
Bonawe Historic Iron Furnace (PA35 1JQ) 4E 64
Bo'ness & Kinneil Railway (EH51 9AQ) 1H 59
Booth Mus. of Natural History (BN1 5AA) Brighton & Hove 106 (5K 11)
Borde Hill Gdn. (RH16 1XP) 3L 11
Borth Wild Animal Kingdom (SY24 5NA) 4F 24
Boscobel House (ST19 9AR) 1G 27
Boston Stump. (PE21 6NQ) 5L 37
Bosworth Field Battle Site (CV13 0AB) 1A 28
Bothwell Castle (G71 8BL) 4E 58
Boughton House (NN14 1BJ) 3G 29
Bowes Castle. (DL12 9LE) 4H 47
Bowes Mus. (DL12 8NP) 4J 47
Bowhill House & Country Estate (TD7 5ET) 7B 60
Bowood House & Gdns. (SN11 0LZ) 7H 19
Box Hill (KT20 7LF) 8J 21
Braemar Castle (AB35 5XR) 6A 72
Bramall Hall (SK7 3NX) 1G 35
Bramber Castle. (BN44 3FJ) 4J 11
Bramham Pk. (LS23 6ND) 3B 42
Brands Hatch (DA3 8NG) 7B 22
Brantwood (LA21 8AD) 6B 46
Breamore House (SP6 2DF) 4K 9
Brean Down (TA8 2RS) 8A 18
Brecon Beacons Nat. Pk. (CF44 9JG) 2J 17
Brecon Mountain Railway (CF48 2UP) 3K 17
Bressingham Steam & Gdns. (IP22 2AB) 3G 31
Brimham Rocks (HG3 4DW) 1L 41
Brindley Mill & The James Brindley Mus. (ST13 8FA) 4H 35
Brinkburn Priory (NE65 8AR) 2E 54
Bristol Aquarium (BS1 5TT) 107
Bristol Cathedral (BS1 5TJ) 107 (6D 18)
Bristol Zoo Gdns. (BS8 3HA) 107 (6D 18)
Britannia Bridge (LL61 5YH) 3E 32
British Airways i360 (BN1 2LN) Brighton & Hove 106 (5L 11)
British Golf Mus. (KY16 9AB) 6J 67
British in India Mus. (BB9 8AD) 4G 41
British Library (NW1 2DB) London 113
British Motor Mus. (CV35 0BJ) 6A 28
British Mus. (WC1B 3DG) London 113
Broadlands (SO51 9ZD) 3A 10
Broads Nat. Pk. (NR3 1BJ) 1L 31
Broadway Tower (WR12 7LB) 8K 27
Brobury House Gdns. (HR3 6BS) 7B 26
Brockhampton Estate (WR6 5TB) 6E 26
Brockhole, Lake District Visitor Cen. (LA23 1LJ) 5B 46
Brodick Castle & Gdn. (KA27 8HY) 6K 57
Brodie Castle (IV36 2TE) 8K 79
Brodsworth Hall & Gdns. (DN5 7XJ) 7C 42
Brogdale (ME13 8XU) 8G 23
Bronllys Castle (LD3 0HL) 1L 17
Brontë Parsonage Mus. (BD22 8DR) 4J 41
Broseley Pipeworks. (TF12 5LX) 1E 26
Brougham Castle. (CA10 2AA) 3D 46
Brough Castle. (CA17 4EJ) 4F 46
Broughton Castle (OX15 5EB) 8B 28
Broughton House & Gdn. (DG6 4JX) 6A 52
Brownsea Island (BH13 7EE) 7J 9
Bruce's Stone (DG7 3SQ) 4L 51
Brunel's SS Great Britain (BS1 6TY) Bristol 107
Bubblecar Mus. (PE22 7AW) 5K 37
Buckfast Abbey (TQ11 0EE) 5K 5
Buckingham Palace (SW1A 1AA) London 113
Buckland Abbey (PL20 6EY) 5G 5
Buckler's Hard Maritime Mus. (SO42 7XB) 6B 10
Buildwas Abbey (TF8 7BW) 1E 26
Bungay Castle. (NR35 1DD) 3K 31
Bure Valley Railway (NR11 6BW) 7J 39
Burford House Gdns. (WR15 8HQ) 5D 26
Burghley (PE9 3JY) 1H 29
Burleigh Castle (KY13 9TD) 7E 66
Burnby Hall Gdns. & Mus. (YO42 2QF) 3F 42
Burns House Mus. (KA5 5BZ) 7C 58
Burton Agnes Hall (YO25 4ND) 1J 43
Burton Constable Hall (HU11 4LN) 4J 43
Buscot Pk. (SN7 8BU) 4L 19
Butser Ancient Farm (PO8 0QF) 4E 10
The Buttertubs (DL11 6DR) 6G 47
Buxton Pavilion Gdns. (SK17 6XN) 2J 35
Byland Abbey (YO61 4BD) 8C 48

C

Cadair Idris (LL40 1TN) 1F 24
Cadbury World (B30 1JR) 3J 27
Caerlaverock Castle (DG1 4RU) 5E 52
Caerleon Roman Fortress (NP18 1AY) 4B 18
Caernarfon Castle. (LL55 2AY) 4D 32
Caerphilly Castle. (CF83 1JD) 6L 17
Cairngorms Nat. Pk. (PH26 3HG) 5K 71
Cairnpapple Hill (EH48 4NW) 2H 59
Caister Castle (NR30 5SN) 8M 39
Calanais Standing Stones (HS2 9DY) 8F 82
Caldey Island (SA70 7UH) 7H 15
Caldicot Castle. (NP26 5JB) 5C 18
Caledonian Railway (DD9 7AF) 2K 67
Calke Abbey (DE73 7LE) 7A 36
Calshot Castle. (SO45 1BR) 5B 10
Camber Castle (TN31 7TB) 4F 12
Cambo Gdns. (KY16 8QD) 6K 67
Cambridge University Botanic Gdn. (CB2 1JE) 107 (6A 30)
Camperdown Wildlife Cen. (DD2 4TF) 4G 67
Canal Mus. (NN12 7SE) 6E 28
Cannock Chase (WS12 4PW) 8H 35
Cannon Hall Mus. (S75 4AT) 7L 41
Canons Ashby House (NN11 3SD) 6C 28
Canterbury Cathedral (CT1 2EH) 107 (8H 23)
Capesthorne Hall (SK11 9JY) 2G 35
Cape Wrath (IV27 4QQ) 4E 84
Captain Cook Schoolroom Mus. (TS9 6NB) 4C 48
Cardiff Castle (CF10 3RB) 107 (7L 17)
Cardoness Castle (DG7 2EH) 6L 51
Carew Castle. (SA70 8SL) 6G 15
Carisbrooke Castle & Mus. (PO30 1XY) 7B 10
Carlisle Castle (CA3 8UR) 107 (6H 53)
Carlisle Cathedral (CA3 8TZ) 107 (6H 53)
Carlyle's Birthplace (DG11 3DG) 4F 52
Carnasserie Castle (PA31 8RQ) 7C 64
Carn Euny Ancient Village (TR20 8RB) 6H 3
Carnfunnock Country Pk. (BT40 2QG) 3H 93
Carreg Cennen Castle & Farm (SA19 6UA) 3F 16
Carrick-a-Rede Rope Bridge (BT54 6LS) 1G 93
Carrickfergus Castle (BT38 7BG) 4J 93
Carsluith Castle (DG8 7DY) 6K 51
Cartmel Priory (LA11 6QQ) 8B 46
Castell Coch. (CF15 7JQ) 6L 17
Castell Dinas Bran (LL20 8DY) 6M 33
Castell y Bere (LL36 9TP) 2F 24
Castle Acre Castle. (PE32 2XB) 8E 38
Castle Acre Priory (PE32 2AA) 8E 38
Castle & Gdns. of Mey (KW14 8XH) 4D 86
Castle Campbell & Gdn. (FK14 7PP) 8C 66
Castle Coole (BT74 6JY) 6C 92
Castle Drogo (EX6 6PB) 6G 7
Castle Fraser (AB51 7LD) 4G 73
Castle Howard (YO60 7DA) 8E 48
Castle Kennedy Gdns. (DG9 8SJ) 5G 51
Castle Leod (IV14 9AA) 8E 78
Castle Menzies (PH15 2JD) 3B 66
Castlerigg Stone Circle (CA12 4RN) 3A 46
Castle Rising Castle. (PE31 6AH) 7C 38
Castle Ward (BT30 7LS) 6J 93
Catalyst Science Discovery Cen. (WA8 0DF) 1D 34
Cawdor Castle. (IV12 5RD) 1J 71
Cerne Giant (DT2 7TS) 5E 8
Chanonry Point (IV10 8SD) 8H 79
Charlecote Pk. (CV35 9ER) 6L 27
Charleston (BN8 6LL) 5A 12
Chartwell (TN16 1PS) 8A 22
Chastleton House (GL56 0SU) 1L 19
Chatsworth House (DE45 1PP) 2L 35
Chavenage House (GL8 8XP) 4G 19
Cheddar Gorge (BS40 7XT) 8C 18
Chedworth Roman Villa (GL54 3LJ) 2J 19
Cheltenham Racecourse (GL50 4SH) 1H 19
Chenies Manor House & Gdns. (WD3 6ER) 4H 21
Chepstow Castle (NP16 5EZ) 4D 18
Chepstow Racecourse (NP16 6EG) 4D 18
Chesil Beach (DT3 4ED) 7E 8
Chessington World of Adventures (KT9 2NE) 7J 21
Chester Cathedral (CH1 2HU) 108 (3C 34)
Chester Roman Amphitheatre (CH1 1RF) 108
Chesters Roman Fort & Mus. (NE46 4EU) 4C 54
Chester Zoo (CH2 1LH) 2C 34
Chichester Cathedral. (PO19 1PX) 5F 10
Chiddingstone Castle (TN8 7AD) 1A 12
Chillingham Castle. (NE66 5NJ) 7H 61
Chillingham Wild Cattle (NE66 5NJ) 7H 61
Chillington Hall (WV8 1RE) 1G 27
Chiltern Hills (RG9 6DR) 5D 20
Chiltern Open Air Mus. (HP8 4AB) 4H 21
Chirk Castle (LL14 5AF) 6A 34
Cholmondeley Castle Gdns. (SY14 8AH) 4D 34
Christchurch Castle & Norman House (BH23 1BW) 6K 9
Churnet Valley Railway (ST13 7EE) 4H 35
Chysauster Ancient Village (TR20 8XA) 5H 3
Cilgerran Castle. (SA43 2SF) 2H 15
Cissbury Ring (BN14 0SQ) 5J 11
Clandon Pk. (GU4 7RQ) 8H 21
Claremont Landscape Gdn. (KT10 9JG) 7J 21
Claydon (MK18 2EY) 1E 20
Clearwell Caves (GL16 8JR) 3D 18
Cleeve Abbey (TA23 0PS) 1K 7
Clevedon Court (BS21 6QU) 6C 18
Clifford's Tower (YO1 9SA) York 117 (2D 42)
Clifton Suspension Bridge (BS8 3PA) Bristol 107
Cliveden (SL6 0JA) 5G 21
Clouds Hill (BH20 7NQ) 6G 9
Clumber Pk. (S80 3BX) 2D 36
Clun Castle. (SY7 8JR) 3A 26
Clyde Muirshiel Regional Pk. (PA10 2PZ) 3A 58
Coalbrookdale Mus. of Iron (TF8 7DQ) 1E 26
Coalport China Mus. (TF8 7HT) 1E 26
Coed y Brenin Visitor Cen. (LL40 2HZ) 8G 33
Coggeshall Grange Barn (CO6 1RE) 1E 22
Coity Castle. (CF35 6AU) 6J 17
Colby Woodland Gdn. (SA67 8PP) 6H 15
Colchester Castle Mus. (CO1 1TJ) 1G 23
Colchester Zoo (CO3 0SL) 1F 22
Coleridge Cottage (TA5 1NQ) 2L 7
Coleton Fishacre (TQ6 0EQ) 6M 5
Colour Experience (BD1 2PW) Bradford 106
Colzium Walled Gdn. (G65 0PY) 2F 58
Combe Martin Wildlife & Dinosaur Pk. (EX34 0NG) 1E 6
Compton Acres (BH13 7ES) 7J 9
Compton Castle. (TQ3 1TA) 5L 5
Compton Verney (CV35 9HZ) 6M 27
Conisbrough Castle. (DN12 3BU) 8C 42
Conishead Priory (LA12 9QQ) 8B 46
Conkers (DE12 6GA) 8M 35
Constable Burton Hall Gdns. (DL8 5LJ) 6K 47
Conwy Castle. (LL32 8LD) 3G 33
Coombes & Churnet Nature Reserve. (ST13 7NN) 4J 35
Corbridge Roman Town (NE45 5NT) 5C 54
Corfe Castle (BH20 5EZ) 7H 9
Corgarff Castle (AB36 8YP) 5B 72
Corinium Mus. (GL7 2BX) 3J 19
Cornish Seal Sanctuary (TR12 6UG) 6L 3
Corrieshalloch Gorge (IV23 2PJ) 6C 78
Corsham Court (SN13 0BZ) 6G 19
Cotehele (PL12 6TA) 5G 5
Coton Manor Gdn. (NN6 8RQ) 4D 28
Cotswold Farm Pk. (GL54 5UG) 1K 19
Cotswold Hills (GL8 8NU) 4H 19
Cotswold Water Pk. (GL7 5TL) 4J 19
Cottesbrooke Hall & Gdns. (NN6 8PF) 4E 28
Cotton Mechanical Music Mus. (IP14 4QN) 5G 31
Coughton Court (B49 5JA) 5J 27
The Courts Gdn. (BA14 6RR) 7G 19
Coventry Cathedral (CV1 5AB) 108 (4M 27)
Coventry Transport Mus. (CV1 1JD) 108 (4M 27)
Cowdray House (GU29 9AL) 3F 10
Cragside (NE65 7PX) 1D 54
Craigievar Castle (AB33 8JF) 5E 72
Craigmillar Castle. (EH16 4SY) 2L 59
Craignethan Castle (ML11 9PL) 5G 59
Craigston Castle (AB53 5PX) 8G 81
Cranborne Manor Gdns. (BH21 5PS) 4J 9
Cranwell Aviation Heritage Cen. (NG34 8QR) 5H 37
Crarae Gdn. (PA32 8YA) 8D 64
Crathes Castle, Gdn. & Estate (AB31 5QJ) 6G 73
Creswell Crags (S80 3LH) 2C 36
Crewe Heritage Cen. (CW1 2DD) 4F 34
Criccieth Castle. (LL52 0DP) 7D 32
Crichton Castle (EH37 5XA) 3A 60
Crich Tramway Village (DE4 5DP) 4M 35
Croft Castle (HR6 9PW) 5C 26
Croft Circuit (DL2 2PL) 5L 47
Crom (BT92 8AP) 7C 92
Cromford Mill (DE4 3RQ) 4L 35
Cromwell Mus. (PE29 3LF) 4K 29
Crookston Castle (G53 5RR) 3D 58
Croome (WR8 9JS) 7G 27
Crossraguel Abbey (KA19 8HQ) 1H 51
Croxden Abbey (ST14 5JG) 6J 35
Croxteth Hall (L12 0HB) 8C 40
Cruachan Power Station (PA33 1AN) 5E 64
Culloden Battlefield Visitor Cen. (IV2 5EU) 1H 71
Culloden Battle Site (IV2 5EU) 1H 71
Culross Palace (KY12 8JH) 1H 59
Culzean Castle (KA19 8LE) 8M 57
Curraghs Wildlife Pk. (IM7 5EA) 5C 44
Cusworth Hall. (DN5 7TU) 7C 42
Cymer Abbey (LL40 2HE) 1G 25

D

Dalemain (CA11 0HB) 3C 46
Dales Countryside Mus. (DL8 3NT) 6G 47
Dallas Dhu Historic Distillery (IV36 2RR) 8L 79
Dalmeny House (EH30 9TQ) 2K 59
Darby Houses (TF8 7DQ) 1E 26
Dartington Crystal (EX38 7AN) 4D 6
Dartington Hall Gdns. (TQ9 6EL) 5L 5
Dartmoor Nat. Pk. (TQ13 9JQ) 7E 6
Dartmoor Zoo (PL7 5DG) 6H 5
Dartmouth Castle (TQ6 0JN) 6L 5
Dartmouth Steam Railway (TQ4 6AF) 6L 5
Dawyck Botanic Gdn. (EH45 9JU) 6K 59
Deal Castle. (CT14 7BA) 8K 23
Dean Castle (KA3 1XB) 6C 58
Dean Forest Railway (GL15 4ET) 3E 18
Deene Pk. (NN17 3EW) 2G 29
The Deep (HU1 4DP) Kingston upon Hull 110 (5J 43)
Deep Sea World (KY11 1JR) 1K 59
Delamere Forest Pk. (CW8 2JD) 2D 34
Delgatie Castle (AB53 5TD) 8G 81
The Den & The Glen (AB12 5FT) 6H 73
Denbigh Castle. (LL16 3NB) 4K 33
Derrymore House. (BT35 7EF) 7G 93
Devil's Dyke (BN45 7DE) 4K 11
Devil's Punch Bowl (GU26 6AB) 2F 10
Dewa Roman Experience (CH1 1NL) Chester 108
DH Lawrence Birthplace Mus. (NG16 3AW) 5B 36
Dickens House Mus. (CT10 1QS) 7K 23
Didcot Railway Cen. (OX11 7NJ) 4C 20
Dinefwr Castle (SA19 6PF) 2F 16
Dinefwr Pk. (SA19 6RT) 2F 16
Dinorwig Power Station (LL55 4UR) 5E 32
Dinosaur Adventure (NR9 5JW) 8H 39
The Dinosaur Mus. (DT1 1EW) 6E 8
Dirleton Castle & Gdn. (EH39 5ER) 1C 60
Discovery Mus. (NE1 4JA) Newcastle upon Tyne 111 (5F 54)
Discovery Point, Dundee (DD1 4XA) 108
Dock Mus. (LA14 2PW) 8L 45
Doddington Hall & Gdns. (LN6 4RU) 2F 36
Doddington Place Gdns. (ME9 0BB) 8F 22
Dolaucothi Gold Mines (SA19 8RR) 1F 16
Dolbadarn Castle (LL55 4SU) 5E 32
Dolforwyn Castle (SY15 6JH) 3L 25
Dolwyddelan Castle. (LL25 0JD) 5G 33
Doncaster Racecourse (DN2 6BB) 7D 42
Donington Pk. (DE74 2RP) 7B 36
Donnington Castle. (RG14 2LE) 7B 20
Dorfold Hall (CW5 8LD) 4E 34
Dorothy Clive Gdn. (TF9 4EU) 6F 34
Doune Castle. (FK16 6EA) 7M 65
Dove Cottage (LA22 9SH) 5B 46
Dovedale (DE6 1NL) 4K 35
Dover Castle (CT16 1HU) 108 (1K 13)
Downhill Demesne (BT51 4RP) 2E 92
Down House (BR6 7JT) 7M 21
Dozmary Pool (PL15 7TP) 8A 6
Drayton Manor Theme Pk. (B78 3TW) 1K 27
Drum Castle & Gdn. (AB31 5EY) 5G 73
Drumlanrig Castle (DG3 4AQ) 2C 52
Drummond Gdns. (PH5 2AA) 6B 66
Drusillas (BN26 5QS) 5B 12
Dryburgh Abbey (TD6 0RQ) 6C 60
Dryslwyn Castle. (SA32 8JQ) 2E 16
Duart Castle (PA64 6AP) 4B 64
Dudmaston Estate (WV15 6QN) 3F 26
Duff House Country Gallery (AB45 3SX) 7F 80
Duffus Castle (IV30 5RH) 7A 80
The Dukeries (S80 3BT) 2D 36
Dumbarton Castle (G82 1JJ) 2C 58
Dunblane Cathedral. (FK15 0AQ) 7A 66
Dun Carloway (HS2 9AZ) 7E 82
Duncombe Pk. (YO62 5EB) 7D 48
Dundonald Castle. (KA2 9HD) 6B 58
Dundrennan Abbey (DG6 4QH) 7B 52
Dunfermline Abbey. (KY12 7PE) 1J 59
Dungeon Ghyll Force (LA22 9JY) 5A 46
Dunge Valley Rhododendron Gdns. (SK23 7RF) 2H 35
Dunham Massey (WA14 4SJ) 1F 34
Dunkeld Cathedral. (PH8 0AW) 3D 66
Dunkery Beacon (TA24 7AT) 1H 7
Dunnet Head (KW14 8XS) 4D 86
Dunninald (DD10 9TD) 2L 67
Dunnottar Castle (AB39 2TL) 7H 73
Dunrobin Castle (KW10 6SF) 3J 79
Dunstaffnage Castle (PA37 1PZ) 4C 64
Dunstanburgh Castle (NE66 3TG) 7K 61
Dunster Castle. (TA24 6SL) 1J 7
Dunvegan Castle (IV55 8WF) 1D 68
Durdle Door (BH20 5PU) 7G 9
Durham Cathedral (DH1 3EH) 108 (7F 54)
Dyffryn Gdns. (CF5 6SU) 7K 17
Dylan Thomas Boathouse (SA33 4SD) 5K 15
Dynamic Earth (EH8 8AS) Edinburgh 109
Dyrham Pk., Gloucestershire (SN14 8ER) 6F 18

E

Eagle Heights Wildlife Pk. (DA4 0JB) 7B 22
Easby Abbey (DL10 7JU) 5K 47
East Anglian Railway Mus. (CO6 2DS) 1E 22
East Bergholt Place Gdn. (CO7 6UP) 8G 31
East Kent Railway (CT15 7PD) 1J 13
East Lambrook Manor Gdns. (TA13 5HH) 4C 8
East Lancashire Railway (BB4 6AG) 5G 41
Eastnor Castle (HR8 1RD) 8F 26
East Pool Mine (TR15 3NP) 4K 3
East Riddlesden Hall (BD20 5EL) 3J 41
East Somerset Railway (BA4 4QP) 1E 8
Eden Project (PL24 2SG) 6C 4
Edinburgh Castle (EH1 2NG) 109 (2L 59)
Edinburgh St Giles' Cathedral (EH1 1RE) 109 (2L 59)
Edinburgh Zoo. (EH12 6TS) 2L 59
Edzell Castle & Gdn. (DD9 7UE) 1J 67
Egglestone Abbey (DL12 9TN) 4J 47
Eilean Donan Castle (IV40 8DX) 3K 69
Elcho Castle. (PH2 8QQ) 5E 66
Electric Mountain (LL55 4UR) 4E 32
Elgar's Birthplace (WR2 6RH) 6G 27
Elgin Cathedral. (IV30 1EL) 7B 80
Eltham Palace & Gdns. (SE9 5QE) 6M 21
Elton Hall House & Gdns. (PE8 6SH) 2H 29
Ely Cathedral. (CB7 4DL) 3B 30
Embsay & Bolton Abbey Steam Railway (BD23 6AF) 2J 41
Emmetts Gdn. (TN14 6BA) 8A 22
Enginuity (TF8 7DQ) 1E 26
Epping Ongar Railway (CM5 9BN) 3B 22
Epsom Downs Racecourse (KT18 5LQ) 8K 21
Erddig (LL13 0YT) 5B 34
Etal Castle. (TD12 4TN) 6G 61
Eureka! The National Children's Mus. (HX1 2NE) 5J 41
Euston Hall (IP24 2QW) 4E 30
Ewloe Castle. (CH5 3BZ) 3A 34
Exbury Gdns. (SO45 1AZ) 5B 10
Exeter Cathedral (EX1 1HS) 109 (6J 7)
Exmoor Nat. Pk. (TA22 9HL) 2H 7
Exploris Aquarium (BT22 1NZ) 6J 93
Eyam Hall (S32 5QW) 2L 35
Eye Castle. (IP23 7AP) 4H 31
Eynsford Castle. (DA4 0AA) 7B 22

F

Fairbourne Steam Railway (LL38 2PZ) 1F 24
Fairhaven Woodland & Water Gdn. (NR13 6DZ) 8K 39
Falkirk Wheel (FK1 4RS) 1G 59
Falkland Palace (KY15 7BU) 7F 66
Falls of Glomach (IV40 8DS) 3M 69
Farleigh Hungerford Castle. (BA2 7RS) 8F 18
Farmland Mus. & Denny Abbey (CB25 9PQ) 5A 30
Farnborough Hall (OX17 1DU) 7B 28
Farne Islands (NE68 7SY) 6K 61
Farnham Castle Keep. (GU9 0AE) 1F 10
Felbrigg Hall (NR11 8PR) 6H 39
Fell Foot Pk. (LA12 8NN) 7B 46
Ferniehirst Castle (TD8 6NX) 8D 60
Ffestiniog Railway (LL49 9NF) 6F 32
Fiddleford Manor (DT10 2BU) 4G 9
Finchale Priory (DH1 5SH) 7F 54
Finch Foundry (EX20 2NW) 6F 6
Fingal's Cave (PA73 6NA) 4J 63
Finlaystone Country Estate (PA14 6TJ) 2B 58
Firle Place (BN8 6LP) 5A 12
The Firs (WR2 6RH) 6G 27
Fishbourne Roman Palace & Gdns. (PO19 3QR) 5F 10
Fitzwilliam Mus. (CB2 1RB) Cambridge 107 (6M 29)
Five Sisters of Kintail (IV40 8HQ) 4L 69
Flambards (TR13 0QA) 6K 3
Flamingo Land (YO17 6UX) 8E 48
Fleet Air Arm Mus. (BA22 8HT) 3D 8
Flint Castle. (CH6 5PE) 3M 33
Floors Castle & Gdns. (TD5 7SF) 6E 60
Florence Court (BT92 1DB) 7B 92
Fonmon Castle. (CF62 3ZN) 8K 17
Forde Abbey & Gdns. (TA20 4LU) 5B 8
Ford Green Hall. (ST6 1NG) 4G 35
Forest of Dean (GL15 4SL) 3E 18
Fort George (IV2 7TD) 8H 79
Forth Bridge (EH30 9TB) 1K 59
Fort Nelson (Royal Armouries) (PO17 6AN) 5D 10
Fountains Abbey & Studley Royal Water Gdn. (HG4 3DY) 1L 41
Foxfield Steam Railway (ST11 9BG) 5H 35
Foxton Locks (LE16 7RA) 3D 28
Framlingham Castle. (IP13 9BP) 5J 31
Froghall Wharf (ST10 2HH) 5J 35
Furness Abbey (LA13 0PG) 7M 45
Furzey Gdns. (SO43 7GL) 4L 9
Fyne Court (TA5 2EQ) 2M 7
Fyvie Castle. (AB53 8JS) 2G 73

G

Gainsborough Old Hall (DN21 2NB) 8F 42
Gainsborough's House (CO10 2EU) 7E 30
Gallery of Modern Art, Glasgow (G1 3AH) 109
Galloway Forest Pk. (DG8 6TA) 3K 51
Galloway House Gdns. (DG8 8HF) 7K 51

144 A-Z Great Britain Road Atlas